RUNNING
LINUX

Related titles from O'Reilly

Building Secure Servers with Linux

Learning Red Hat Linux

Linux Device Drivers

Linux in a Nutshell

Linux Network Administrator's Guide

LPI Linux Certification in a Nutshell

Managing RAID on Linux

Running Linux

Understanding the Linux Kernel

Also available

The Linux Web Server CD Bookshelf

RUNNING LINUX

FOURTH EDITION

Matt Welsh,
Matthias Kalle Dalheimer,
Terry Dawson, and Lar Kaufman

O'REILLY®

Beijing · Cambridge · Farnham · Köln · Paris · Sebastopol · Taipei · Tokyo

Running Linux, Fourth Edition

by Matt Welsh, Matthias Kalle Dalheimer, Terry Dawson, and Lar Kaufman

Published by O'Reilly & Associates, Inc., 1005 Gravenstein Highway North, Sebastopol, CA 95472.

O'Reilly & Associates books may be purchased for educational, business, or sales promotional use. Online editions are also available for most titles (*safari.oreilly.com*). For more information, contact our corporate/institutional sales department: (800) 998-9938 or *corporate@oreilly.com*.

Editor:	Andy Oram
Production Editor:	Sarah Sherman
Cover Designer:	Edie Freedman
Interior Designer:	David Futato

Printing History:

May 1995:	First Edition.
August 1996:	Second Edition.
August 1999:	Third Edition.
December 2002:	Fourth Edition.

ISBN: 0-596-00272-6

[M]

Table of Contents

Preface

"Technical knowledge is not enough. One must transcend techniques so that the art becomes an artless art, growing out of the unconscious."
—Daisetsu Suzuki (1870-1966)

This is a book about Linux, a free, open source operating system that's changing the world of computing. In this book, we show how you can completely change the way you work with computers by exploring a powerful and free operating system. Linux goes against the traditional computing mainstream, being developed by a loosely organized group of thousands of volunteers across the Internet. Linux started as a real underground movement—guerrilla hacking, if you will—and brings a lot of excitement, discovery, and self-empowerment back into today's corporate-dominated computing culture. We invite you to dive in, enjoy yourself, and join the throng of people who know what it means to tweak your dot clocks and *rdev* your kernel image.

The Zen quote at the beginning of this preface summarizes our philosophy in this book. We're targeting readers who are inquisitive and creative enough to delve full-tilt into the world of Linux, and who want to get at the heart of the system. Linux represents a rebellion against commercial operating systems, and many of its users like living on the edge of the latest technological trends. Of course, the casual reader can set up and run a Linux system (or hundreds of them!) without much trouble, but the purpose of this book is to dig more deeply into the system—to bring you completely into the Linux mentality, to reach Linux "enlightenment." Rather than gloss over messy details, we explain the concepts by which the system actually works so that you can troubleshoot problems on your own. By sharing the accumulated expertise of several Linux experts, we hope to give you enough confidence to call yourself a true Linux Guru. (Your first koan: what is the sound of one user hacking?)

You have in your hands the fourth edition of *Running Linux*, and by most accounts this book is considered the classic text on installing, maintaining, and learning to use a Linux system. The first edition was published way back in 1996, and had its roots in a free book called *Linux Installation and Getting Started*, which is still floating around the Internet. Since then, *Running Linux* has gone through many improvements and changes to keep the text up-to-date with the latest developments in the Linux world. Kalle Dalheimer joined Matt Welsh and Lar Kaufman for the third edition, and has done most of the updates for this edition as well. Terry Dawson has contributed some material on security.

In this edition, we have completely updated the installation, configuration, and tutorial information to be up-to-date with the latest Linux software distributions (including Red Hat and its derivatives, SuSE, and Debian) and many application packages. The core of the book, however, has not changed much. This was intentional: in the first three editions we made a great effort to make the book as robust as possible, even though Linux itself is under constant development. No book can adequately capture *everything* there is to know about Linux. (You won't find chapters here on using Linux on the Space Shuttle, or on finding weaknesses in data encryption algorithms, although it's been done!) Our approach has worked remarkably well and has been preserved in this new, updated edition. We think this book will be of use to you for a long time to come.

The world of Linux has changed a lot since the last edition of *Running Linux*. Apart from increased performance and robustness, Linux sports an increasing range of applications, from personal productivity tools to high-end databases. Linux is used to running mission-critical services, and drives many popular Internet sites, search engines, and content delivery networks. Linux is also being increasingly adopted on the desktop, and desktop systems such as KDE and GNOME are making it easier than ever before to get the most out of Linux.

In the preface to the first edition, we said that "Linux has the potential to completely change the face of the PC operating system world." Looking back, it's clear that our prediction was right! Linux has erupted into the computing mainstream with an amazing force: it has been covered by every major media channel, has helped usher in the so-called "Open Source Revolution," and is widely claimed as the most viable competitor to Microsoft's dominance in the operating systems market. Today, most estimates place the number of Linux users worldwide at well over 200 million. Linux has matured to the point where many people can dive in and start using Linux without knowing most of the hairy details behind device drivers, XFree86 configuration files, and bootloaders. Still, we think it's best to give you some of the behind-the-scenes views, so you have an understanding of the workings of the system, even if it's not strictly necessary for casual Linux use.

Why People Like Linux

There are many reasons why people are finding that Linux is the right operating system for them. It might have to do with cost, performance, flexibility, size, or features. Or it might have something to do with that intangible thrill that you get from running your own system, rather than simply installing a bunch of software that comes out of a box. Windows XP and Mac OS X are good operating systems, but they are focused on the needs of home users. As such, they have some limitations and are a lot less flexible than Linux. Here are a few reasons why people are switching to Linux:

It's free. That is, Linux is a freely redistributable clone of the Unix operating system. You can get Linux free from someone who has it or from the World Wide Web, or you can buy it at a reasonable cost on CD-ROM from a vendor who has packaged it (probably with added value), possibly with support services. Linux is also "free as in speech" (not just "free as in beer"): anyone can modify and distribute modifications and improvements to the system. (We'll get into all of this later, when we talk about open source and free software.)

It's popular. It runs on a wide range of hardware platforms, including popular Pentium (Pentium II, III, and 4), AMD, and Cyrix chips, and even older 386/486 machines. Linux also runs on higher-end systems based on the Itanium, SPARC, or Alpha architectures, as well as on PowerPC and 68k-based Macs. Linux even runs on IBM 390 mainframes, and stripped-down versions run on personal digital assistants (PDAs) like the Palm Pilot and Compaq iPAQ. Linux supports a broad range of hardware, including video cards, sound cards, CD-ROMs, disk drives, printers, scanners, and many other devices.

Linux has an enormous user community presence on the World Wide Web, with many web sites devoted to providing information and discussion about the system. A growing number of commercial software vendors are developing applications for Linux, including Corel WordPerfect Office 2000 Suite, the StarOffice suite from Sun Microsystems, and a number of database products from big names such as Oracle, Informix, and IBM.

It's powerful. Linux is efficient and fast, and makes excellent use of hardware. Many users switching to Linux from Windows are surprised at how fast and responsive the system is, even with many processes running and with multiple windows open. A Linux machine with a reasonably fast processor and a sufficient amount of memory can perform as well, or better, than Unix workstations costing tens of thousands of dollars. Linux is a multiuser, multitasking operating system that can run many applications (and even have many users logged into the same system) at once. Linux also supports multiprocessor systems, and Linux is commonly used in high-end server environments where this kind of hardware is the norm. Linux is used for building large "clusters" consisting of hundreds of machines connected with a fast network, used for massive scientific calculations or for driving large web sites.

It's under your control. Whereas most GUI-heavy proprietary systems embody a policy of keeping the user as ignorant of system processes as possible, Linux is very open and makes it easy for you to know what is happening under the hood. At the same time, if you like, you can relinquish some control and rely on easy-to-use tools like SuSE's *yast*.

It's robust. Linux is being developed in the open by thousands of programmers, as well as numerous companies and universities, all contributing new features, performance enhancements, and bug fixes. It incorporates the work of these many developers in the form of advanced compilers, editors, and utilities. As a result, Linux is extremely robust; many users have Linux systems that stay up for *months* at a time (say goodbye to the "blue screen of death!"). Linux has an enormous base of freely available applications, ranging from desktop publishing and office suites to scientific tools to multimedia applications to games.

It's full-featured. Linux supports of the features of modern Unix-based operating systems, including virtual memory, threads, multiprocessors, and advanced networking (including IPv6, DHCP, firewalling, network address translation, and more). Linux supports a vast array of software packages, programming languages, and hardware devices. Linux uses the X Window System graphical user interface (GUI) and supports several advanced desktop environments, including KDE and GNOME (all covered later in this book).

It's highly compatible with Windows. Linux will happily coexist on the same machine as any flavor of Windows (including Windows 95/98/NT, Windows 2000, or Windows XP), or other operating systems such as OS X and FreeBSD. Linux can directly access Windows files, either across the network, or on the Windows portions of your hard drive on the same system. Using the popular Samba tool, Linux can also act as a Windows file and print server. Note that Linux does not run under Windows; it is completely independent of it, but features have been added to allow the separate systems to work together.

It's small. The core operating system can run on just 8 MB of system memory, including a desktop GUI and several applications. A basic Linux system can fit into 20 MB or so of disk storage, and many people run a basic Linux "rescue system" from a single 1.44 MB floppy! Linux has even been tuned to run on low-memory embedded systems (such as those used in network routers or robots), and in hand-held PDAs.

It's big. Some of the larger distributions can fill several gigabytes of disk space with applications, source code, and datafiles. The number of powerful utilities and applications ported to Linux grows constantly. Most Linux users can run a complete system in 300 MB or so of disk space. This includes all the basics, as well as nice extras such as programming libraries, compilers, text-processing tools, and more. But if you're a real power user, much more is available.

It's supported. The most important line of support is the many web sites devoted to Linux, as well as the many newsgroups and mailing lists online. You can also contract for support from an independent company or buy a supported version of Linux from one of its distributors.

It's well-documented. There is this book (a good start, we commend you on that!), which is also available in Spanish, German, French, Italian, Portuguese, Czech, Polish, Chinese, Taiwanese, and Japanese. The Linux development community established the Linux Documentation Project (LDP) early on, which maintains a large amount of online documentation about the system. The many books, FAQ lists, and "how-to" documents from the LDP can guide you through almost any task that needs to be done under Linux. Once you get over a few installation humps, Linux is more or less like any other Unix system, so the many general books about Unix use and administration will give you all the help you need. Finally, there is the popular press, which has written hundreds of books on Linux—both introductory and advanced—which have been translated into most major languages around the world.

It's sexy. Let's face it: there's nothing particularly daring or edgy about running the latest shrink-wrapped release from the world's largest software company (need we name names?). Linux has an attitude, a philosophy, and a *joie de vivre* that you're not going to find in any other operating system. There's much, much more to Linux than a bunch of bits on a CD-ROM…can you dig it?

Organization of This Book

Each chapter of this book contains a big chunk of information. It takes you into a world of material that could easily take up several books. But we move quickly through the topics you need to know.

Chapter 1 tries to draw together many different threads. It explains why Linux came to be and what makes it different from other versions of Unix as well as other operating systems for personal computers.

Chapter 2 describes preliminary tasks that you may have to do before installation, such as partitioning your disk (in case you want to run another operating system as well as Linux).

Chapter 3 is a comprehensive tutorial on installing and configuring Linux on your system.

Chapter 4 offers a system administrator's introduction to Unix, for people who need one. It is intended to give you enough tools to perform the basic tasks you'll need to do throughout the book. Basic commands are covered, along with some tips for administrators and some concepts you should know.

Chapter 5, Chapter 6, Chapter 7, and Chapter 8 cover system administration and maintenance. These are perhaps the most important and useful chapters of the book; they cover user account management, backups, software upgrading, building a new kernel, audio configuration, and more.

Chapter 9 introduces you to the most popular and commonly used text tools and editors on Linux—*vi* and Emacs—and shows you how to print a document and how to use various graphics programs.

Chapter 10 shows you how to install and configure the X Window System, a powerful GUI for Linux and Unix systems. We show you how to overcome problems you might encounter when your distribution installs the software and how to configure it for the best performance on your video hardware.

Chapter 11 shows you how to set up your own visual environment under the X Window System, covering a wide range of the powerful customizations the system makes available, the KDE and GNOME desktops, and a few useful programs that run under X.

Chapter 12 presents various tools for interfacing with DOS and Windows systems, particularly the Samba server that integrates Linux with other users running PCs.

Chapter 13 and Chapter 14 are for programmers. Compilers, interpreters, debuggers, and many other tools for programming under Linux are presented.

Chapter 15 tells you how to set up your all-important connection to the outside world. It shows you how to configure your system so that it can work on a local area network or communicate with an Internet service provider using Point-to-Point Protocol (PPP).

Chapter 16 goes beyond basic network configuration and shows you how to configure electronic mail, set up the Elm and Netscape mail readers, and even run your own World Wide Web server.

Chapter 17 offers the most basic, critical rules for securing an Internet-connected system. It will not guarantee by any means that you are safe from break-ins, but it will help you eliminate the obvious and trivial weaknesses in your system.

Chapter 18 introduces the most popular set of tools that web site administrators use to serve up content. This collection is called LAMP, which stands for Linux, Apache, MySQL, and PHP.

Appendix A tells you about other useful documentation for Linux and other sources of help.

Appendix B shows you how to install Linux on the first non-Intel system that supported it, the 64-bit Digital Alpha machine.

The Bibliography lists a number of books, HOWTOs, and Internet RFCs of interest to Linux users and administrators.

Conventions Used in This Book

The following is a list of the typographical conventions used in this book:

Italic

Is used for file and directory names, program and command names, command-line options, email addresses and path names, site names, and all new terms.

`Constant Width`

Is used in examples to show the contents of files or the output from commands, to indicate environment variables and keywords that appear in code, and for machine names, hostnames, usernames, IDs, and Emacs commands.

`Constant Width Bold`

Is used in examples to show commands or other text that should be typed literally by the user.

`Constant Width Italic`

Is used to indicate variable options, keywords, or text that the user is to replace with an actual value.

 This icon designates a note, which is an important aside to the nearby text.

 This icon designates a warning relating to the nearby text.

How to Contact Us

We have tested and verified the information in this book to the best of our ability, but you may find that features have changed (or even that we have made mistakes!). Please let us know about any errors you find, as well as your suggestions for future editions, by writing to:

O'Reilly & Associates, Inc.
1005 Gravenstein Highway North
Sebastopol, CA 95472
1-800-998-9938 (in the U.S. or Canada)
1-707-829-0515 (international or local)
1-707-829-0104 (fax)

You can send us messages electronically. To be put on the mailing list or to request a catalog, send email to:

info@oreilly.com

To ask technical questions or to comment on the book, send email to:

bookquestions@oreilly.com

We have a web site for the book, where we'll list examples, errata, and any plans for future editions. You can access this page at:

http://www.oreilly.com/catalog/runux4/

For more information about this book and others, see the O'Reilly web site:

http://www.oreilly.com

Acknowledgments

This book is the result of many people's efforts, and as expected, it would be impossible to list them all here. First of all, we would like to thank Andy Oram, who did an excellent job of editing, writing, and whip-cracking to get this book into shape. Apart from being the overall editor, Andy contributed the Unix tutorial chapter as well as material for the X and Perl sections. It was Andy who approached us about writing for O'Reilly in the first place, and he has demonstrated the patience of a saint when waiting for our updates to trickle in.

Those of you who are already familiar with Linux may notice that some portions of this book, such as the introductory and installation chapters, have been released as part of *Linux Installation and Getting Started*, a free book available via the Internet. O'Reilly allowed us to release those portions (originally written for this book) to the I&GS, so they could benefit the Internet-based Linux community and we would get feedback and corrections from its readership. Thanks to everyone who contributed edits to those sections.

We would also like to thank the following people for their work on the Linux operating system—without all of them, there wouldn't be anything to write a book about: Linus Torvalds, Richard Stallman, Donald Becker, Alan Cox, Remy Card, Eric Raymond, Ted T'so, H.J. Lu, Miguel de Icaza, Ross Biro, Drew Eckhardt, Ed Carp, Eric Youngdale, Fred van Kempen, Steven Tweedie, Patrick Volkerding, Dirk Hohndel, Matthias Ettrichand, and all of the other hackers, from the kernel grunts to the lowly docos, too numerous to mention here.

Special thanks to the following people for their contributions to the Linux Documentation Project, technical review of this book, or general friendliness and support: Phil Hughes, Melinda McBride, Bill Hahn, Dan Irving, Michael Johnston, Joel Goldberger, Michael K. Johnson, Adam Richter, Roman Yanovsky, Jon Magid, Erik Troan, Lars Wirzenius, Olaf Kirch, Greg Hankins, Alan Sondheim, Jon David, Anna Clark, Adam Goodman, Lee Gomes, Rob Walker, Rob Malda, Jeff Bates, and Volker Lendecke. We are grateful to Shawn Wallace and Umberto Crenca for the gorgeous shot in Chapter 9 of The Gimp in use.

For the third edition, we thank Phil Hughes, Robert J. Chassell, Tony Cappellini, Craig Small, Nat Makarevitch, Chris Davis, Chuck Toporek, Frederic HongFeng, and David Pranata for wide-ranging comments and corrections. Particularly impressive were the efforts put in by an entire team of Debian developers and users, organized for us by Ossama Othman and Julian T. J. Midgley. Julian set up a CVS repository for comments and the book was examined collectively by him, Chris Lawrence, Robert J. Chassell, Kirk Hilliard, and Stephen Zander.

For the fourth edition, we thank David Collier-Brown, Oliver Flimm, Phil Hughes, Chris Lawrence, Rich Payne, Craig Small, Jeff Tranter, and Aaron Weber for their reviews. Matt Welsh would especially like to thank his fiancée, Amy Bauer, for her love and support, as well as for paying for half of the DSL line at home.

Kalle would like to thank Valerica Vatafu from Buzau, Romania, for lots of help with the chapter about LAMP. He would also like to thank his colleagues in his company Klarälvdalens Datakonsult AB—Michael Boyer de la Giroday, Tanja Dalheimer, Steffen Hansen, Jesper Pedersen, Lutz Rogowski, Bo Thorsen, and Karl-Heinz Zimmer—for their constructive comments on drafts of the book as well as for being general "Linux thought amplifiers."

This edition benefited from the contributions of experts in various subject areas. In particular, we'd like to thank Jeff Tranter, for the audio configuration information in Chapter 9 and for updating online sources of Linux information in Appendix A and in the Bibliography; Aaron Weber of Ximian, for the material on the GNOME desktop in Chapter 11; Kyle Dent, for the material on the Postfix mail transfer agent in Chapter 16; Jay Ts, for rewriting the section on Samba in Chapter 12; Chris Lawrence, for the material on upgrading packages on Debian in Chapter 7; and Barrett G. Lyon and Richard Payne, for the material on installing Linux on Compaq/Digital Alpha systems in Appendix B (updated by Richard Payne for the fourth edition).

If you have questions, comments, or corrections for this book, please feel free to get in touch with the authors. Matt Welsh can be reached on the Internet at *mdw@cs. berkeley.edu*. Lar Kaufman can be reached at *lark@conserve.org*. Kalle Dalheimer can be reached at *kalle@dalheimer.de*.

## CHAPTER 1

Introduction to Linux

This is a book about Linux, a free, open source operating system that supports full multitasking, the X Window System, TCP/IP networking, and much more. Hang tight and read on: in the pages that follow, we describe the system in meticulous detail.

Linux has generated more excitement in the computer field than any other development of the past several years. It has spread surprisingly fast, and the loyalty it inspires recalls the excitement of do-it-yourself computing that used to characterize earlier advances in computer technology. Ironically, it succeeds by rejuvenating one of the oldest operating systems still in widespread use: Unix. Linux is both a new technology and an old one.

In narrow technical terms, Linux is just the operating system kernel, offering the basic services of process scheduling, virtual memory, file management, and device I/O. In other words, Linux itself is the lowest-level part of the operating system.

However, most people use the term "Linux" to refer to the complete system—the kernel along with the many applications that it runs: a complete development and work environment including compilers, editors, graphical interfaces, text processors, games, and more.

This book will be your guide to Linux's shifting and many-faceted world. Linux has developed into an operating system for businesses, education, and personal productivity, and this book will help you get the most out of it.

Linux can transform any personal computer into a high-end workstation and server. Corporations are installing Linux on entire networks of machines, using the operating system to manage financial and hospital records, distributed-user computing environments, telecommunications, and more. Universities worldwide are using Linux for teaching courses on operating system programming and design. And, of course, computing enthusiasts everywhere are using Linux at home, for programming, document production, and all-around hacking. People use Linux on high-end desktop machines, handheld PDAs, mobile laptops, and even old clunkers sitting in the closet doing nothing more than spooling print jobs.

Apart from workstation and personal use, Linux is also being used to drive big servers. Increasingly, people are discovering that Linux is powerful, stable, and flexible enough to run the largest disk arrays and multiprocessor systems—with applications ranging from World Wide Web servers to corporate databases. Linux drives many mission-critical business applications, Internet sites, search engines, and content delivery networks. Scientists are connecting arrays of Linux machines into enormous "clusters" to solve the most computationally intensive problems in physics and engineering. With the Samba software suite, Linux can even act as a Windows file and print server—with better performance than Windows!

What makes Linux so different is that it's a *free* implementation of Unix. It was and still is developed by a group of volunteers, primarily on the Internet, who exchange code, report bugs, and fix problems in an open environment. Anyone is welcome to join in the Linux development effort: all it takes is interest in hacking a free Unix clone and some kind of programming know-how.

In this book, we assume you're comfortable with a personal computer (running any operating system, such as Windows 98, or some other version of Unix). We also assume that you're willing to do some experimentation to get everything working correctly—after all, this is half of the fun of getting into Linux. Linux has evolved into a system that is amazingly easy to install and configure, but because it is so powerful, some details are more complex than you'll find in the Windows world. With this book as your guide, we hope you'll find that setting up and running your own Linux system is quite easy and a great deal of fun.

About This Book

This book is an overview and entry-level guide to the Linux system. We attempt to present enough general and interesting information on a number of topics to satisfy Unix novices and wizards alike. This book should provide sufficient material for almost anyone to install and use Linux and get the most out of it. Instead of covering many of the volatile technical details—those things that tend to change with rapid development—we give you enough background to find out more on your own.

This book is geared for those people who really want to exploit the power that Linux provides. Rather than gloss over all the tricky details, we give you enough background to truly understand how the various parts of the system work, so you can customize, configure, and troubleshoot the system on your own. Linux is not difficult to install and use. However, as with any implementation of Unix, there is often some black magic involved to get everything working correctly.

In this book, we cover the following topics:

- What is Linux? The design and philosophy of this unique operating system, and what it can do for you.
- Information on what you need to run Linux, including suggestions on what kind of hardware configuration is recommended for a complete system.
- How to obtain and install Linux. We cover the Red Hat, SuSE, and Debian distributions in more detail than others, but the background here should be adequate to cover any release of the system.
- For new users, an introduction to the Unix system, including an overview of the most important commands and concepts.
- The care and feeding of the Linux system, including system administration and maintenance, upgrading the system, and how to fix things when they don't work.
- Getting the most out of your Linux system, with "power tools" such as TEX, Emacs, KDE, GNOME, and more.
- The Linux programming environment. The tools of the trade for programming and developing software on the Linux system. We introduce compilation and debugging of C and C++ programs, Java, Perl, and shell scripts.
- Using Linux for telecommunications and networking, including the basics of TCP/IP configuration, PPP for Internet connectivity over a modem, ISDN configuration, email, news, and web access—we even show how to configure your Linux system as a web server.

There are a million things we'd love to show you how to do with Linux. Unfortunately, in order to cover them all, this book would be the size of the unabridged *Oxford English Dictionary* and would be impossible for anyone (let alone the poor authors) to maintain. Instead we've tried to include the most salient and interesting aspects of the system and show you how to find out more.

While much of the discussion in this book is not overly technical, it helps to have previous experience with another Unix system. For those who don't have Unix experience, we have included a short tutorial in Chapter 4, for new users. Chapter 5 is a complete chapter on systems administration that should help even seasoned Unix users run a Linux system.

If you are new to Unix, you'll want to pick up a more complete guide to Unix basics. We don't dwell for long on the fundamentals, instead preferring to skip to the fun parts of the system. At any rate, while this book should be enough to get you running, more information on using Unix and its many tools will be essential for most readers. See Appendix A, for a list of sources of information.

A Brief History of Linux

Unix is one of the most popular operating systems worldwide because of its large support base and distribution. It was originally developed as a multitasking system for minicomputers and mainframes in the mid-1970s. It has since grown to become one of the most widely used operating systems anywhere, despite its sometimes confusing interface and lack of central standardization. There is no single implementation of Unix. Originally developed by Bell Labs, Unix eventually forked into several versions, including a popular distribution from the University of California at Berkeley, called BSD. Over the years, many vendors have developed their own implementations of Unix, either from scratch or starting with another version. Linux was built from the ground up, although earlier versions included some code from BSD as well.

While Unix underwent a dip in market strength during the early 1990s, under the onslaught of the new Windows NT system, it came back strong and has become the mainstay of large computers.

Unix has quite a cult following in the operating systems community. Many hackers feel that Unix is the Right Thing—the One True Operating System. Hence, the development of Linux by an expanding group of Unix hackers who want to get their hands dirty with their own system. Moreover, Linux is not a "product" that ties you to a particular vendor or software developer. Because Linux is free, and all the source code is available (more on that later), anyone can modify the system to fit their own needs. Rather than waiting for some large company to release the latest features and service packs, the Linux user community is empowered to improve, adapt, and fix the system themselves. It's this empowerment that has helped Linux become so powerful.

Linux is a freely distributable version of Unix, originally developed by Linus Torvalds, who began work on Linux in 1991 as a student at the University of Helsinki in Finland. Linus now works for Transmeta Corporation, a company in Santa Clara, California, and continues to maintain the Linux *kernel*, that is, the lowest-level core component of the operating system.

Linus released the initial version of Linux for free on the Internet, inadvertently spawning one of the largest software development phenomena of all time. Today, Linux is authored and maintained by thousands of developers loosely collaborating across the Internet. Companies have sprung up to provide Linux support, to package it into easy-to-install distributions, and to sell workstations preinstalled with the Linux software. In March 1999, the first Linux World Expo trade show was held in San Jose, California, with reportedly well over 12,000 people in attendance. These days, most estimates place the number of Linux users in the millions.

Inspired by Andrew Tanenbaum's Minix operating system (one of the original Unix systems for PCs, intended for teaching operating system design), Linux began as a class project in which Linus wanted to build a simple Unix system that could run on a '386-based PC. The first discussions about Linux were on the Usenet newsgroup, *comp.os.minix*. These discussions were concerned mostly with the development of a small, academic Unix system for Minix users who wanted more.

The very early development of Linux dealt mostly with the task-switching features of the 80386 protected-mode interface, all written in assembly code. Linus writes:

> After that it was plain sailing: hairy coding still, but I had some devices, and debugging was easier. I started using C at this stage, and it certainly speeds up development. This is also when I start to get serious about my megalomaniac ideas to make "a better Minix than Minix." I was hoping I'd be able to recompile *gcc* under Linux some day ...

> Two months for basic setup, but then only slightly longer until I had a disk driver (seriously buggy, but it happened to work on my machine) and a small filesystem. That was about when I made 0.01 available [around late August of 1991]: it wasn't pretty, it had no floppy driver, and it couldn't do much anything. I don't think anybody ever compiled that version. But by then I was hooked, and didn't want to stop until I could chuck out Minix.

No announcement was ever made for Linux Version 0.01. The 0.01 release wasn't even executable: it contained only the bare rudiments of the kernel source and assumed that you had access to a Minix machine to compile and play with them.

On October 5, 1991, Linus announced the first "official" version of Linux, Version 0.02. At this point, Linus was able to run *bash* (the GNU Bourne Again Shell) and *gcc* (the GNU C compiler), but not much else was working. Again, this was intended as a hacker's system. The primary focus was kernel development; none of the issues of user support, documentation, distribution, and so on had even been addressed. Today, the situation is quite different—the real excitement in the Linux world deals with graphical user environments, easy-to-install distribution packages, and high-level applications such as graphics utilities and productivity suites.

Linus wrote in *comp.os.minix*:

> Do you pine for the nice days of Minix-1.1, when men were men and wrote their own device drivers? Are you without a nice project and just dying to cut your teeth on an OS you can try to modify for your needs? Are you finding it frustrating when everything works on Minix? No more all-nighters to get a nifty program working? Then this post might be just for you.

> As I mentioned a month ago, I'm working on a free version of a Minix-lookalike for AT-386 computers. It has finally reached the stage where it's even usable (though may not be depending on what you want), and I am willing to put out the sources for wider distribution. It's just version 0.02 ... but I've successfully run *bash*, *gcc*, GNU *make*, GNU *sed*, *compress*, etc. under it.

After Version 0.03, Linus bumped the version number up to 0.10, as more people started to work on the system. After several further revisions, Linus increased the version number to 0.95, to reflect his expectation that the system was ready for an "official" release very soon. (Generally, software is not assigned the version number 1.0 until it's theoretically complete or bug-free.) This was in March 1992. It wasn't until two years later, in March 1994, that Version 1.0 finally appeared. As of the time of this writing (September 2002), the current kernel version is 2.4.19, while the 2.5

kernel versions are being concurrently developed. (We'll explain the Linux versioning conventions in detail later.)

Linux could not have come into being without the GNU tools created by the Free Software Foundation. The Free Software Foundation is a group formed in 1984 by Richard Stallman to promote the development of software that can be developed, redistributed, and modified by anyone—here, "free" refers to freedom, not just cost. Underlying the Free Software Foundation's philosophy is a deep-rooted moral conviction that all software should be free (again, in the sense of freedom); this philosophy is shared by many in the Linux community. This ideal is embodied in the GNU General Public License (or GPL), the copyright license under which Linux is released. We'll discuss this in more detail later in the chapter.

The GNU Project, which is the main result of the Free Software Foundation's efforts, has produced many invaluable tools and applications that Linux has depended upon, including the Emacs text editor, *gcc* compiler suite, and many others. GNU tools have been intertwined with the development of Linux from the beginning. Because of the critical contributions of the GNU Project, the Free Software Foundation even requests that distributions of Linux with accompanying utilities be called GNU/Linux.

Berkeley Unix (BSD) has also played an important role in Linux—not so much in its creation, but in providing the tools that make it popular. The so-called Berkeley Software Distribution was developed at the University of California, Berkeley in the late 1970s by a group of developers working from the original AT&T Unix sources. The BSD group made a number of enhancements to the core Unix design, and soon, BSD took on a life of its own. These days, many variants of the BSD system are available for a range of hardware platforms, and the BSD community rivals that of Linux in terms of popularity. The Mac OS X operating system is even based on a variant of BSD! Some of the networking utilities and daemons used by Linux are derived from original BSD sources.

Today, Linux is a full-featured, complete implementation of Unix, with a vast array of applications, programming languages, tools, and hardware support. Linux supports the X Window System GUI, TCP/IP networking, multiprocessor machines, advanced hardware and software for scientific and parallel computing, and much more. Nearly every major free software package has been ported to Linux, and a great deal of commercial software is available. In fact, many developers start by writing applications for Linux, and port them to other Unix systems later. More hardware is supported than in original versions of the kernel. Many people have executed benchmarks on Linux systems and found them to be faster than expensive workstations, and Linux performs better than or as well as Windows NT/2000/XP on a wide range of benchmarks. Who would have ever guessed that this "little" Unix clone would have grown up to take on the entire world of personal and server computing?

Who's Using Linux?

Application developers, system administrators, network providers, kernel hackers, students, and multimedia authors are just a few of the categories of people who find that Linux has a particular charm.

Unix programmers are increasingly using Linux because of its cost—they can pick up a complete programming environment for a few dollars and run it on cheap PC hardware—and because Linux offers a great basis for portable programs. It's a modern operating system that is POSIX-compliant and looks a lot like System V, so code that works on Linux should work on other contemporary Unix systems.

Networking is one of Linux's strengths. It has been adopted with gusto by people who run large networks, due to its simplicity of management, performance, and low cost. Many Internet sites are making use of Linux to drive large web servers, e-commerce applications, search engines, and more. Linux supports common networking standards, such as Network File System (NFS) and Network Information Service (NIS), making it easy to merge a Linux machine into a corporate or academic network with other Unix machines. It's easy to share files, support remote logins, and run applications on other systems. Linux also supports the Samba software suite, which allows a Linux machine to act as a Windows file and print server. Many people are discovering that the combination of Linux and Samba for this purpose is faster (and cheaper) than running Windows 2000.

One of the most popular uses of Linux is in driving large enterprise applications, including web servers, databases, business-to-business systems, and e-commerce sites. A large number of businesses are discovering that Linux is an inexpensive, efficient, and robust system capable of driving the most mission-critical applications. The fact that Linux can be readily customized—even down to the guts of the kernel—makes the system very attractive for companies that need to exercise control over the inner workings of the system. Linux supports RAID, a mechanism which allows an array of disks to be treated as a single logical storage device, greatly increasing reliability. The combination of Linux, the Apache web server, the MySQL database engine, and the PHP scripting language is so common that it has its own acronym—LAMP. We'll cover LAMP in more detail in Chapter 18.

Kernel hackers were the first to come to Linux—in fact, the developers who helped Linus Torvalds create Linux are still a formidable community. The Linux kernel mailing lists see a great deal of activity, and it's the place to be if you want to stay on the bleeding edge of operating system design. If you're into tuning page replacement algorithms, twiddling network protocols, or optimizing buffer caches, Linux is a great choice. Linux is also good for learning about the internals of operating system design, and many universities are making use of Linux systems in advanced operating system courses.

Finally, Linux is becoming an exciting forum for multimedia. This is because it's compatible with an enormous variety of hardware, including the majority of modern sound and video cards. Several programming environments, including the MESA 3D toolkit (a free OpenGL implementation), have been ported to Linux. The GIMP (a free Adobe Photoshop work-alike) was originally developed under Linux, and is becoming the graphics manipulation and design tool of choice for many artists. Many movie production companies regularly use Linux as the workhorse for advanced special-effects rendering—the popular movies *Titanic* and *The Matrix* used "render farms" of Linux machines to do much of the heavy lifting.

Linux also has some real-world applications. Linux systems have traveled the high seas of the North Pacific, managing telecommunications and data analysis for an oceanographic research vessel. Linux systems are being used at research stations in Antarctica, and large "clusters" of Linux machines are used at many research facilities for complex scientific simulations ranging from star formation to earthquakes. On a more basic level, several hospitals are using Linux to maintain patient records. One of the reviewers of this book uses Linux in the U.S. Marine Corps. Linux is proving to be as reliable and useful as other implementations of Unix.

So Linux is spreading out in many directions. Even naive end users can enjoy it if they get the support universities and corporations typically provide their computer users. Configuration and maintenance require some dedication. But Linux proves to be cost-effective, powerful, and empowering for people who like having that extra control over their environments.

System Features

Linux supports most of the features found in other implementations of Unix, plus quite a few not found elsewhere. This section provides a nickel tour of the Linux kernel features.

A Note on Linux Version Numbers

One potentially confusing aspect of Linux for newcomers is the way in which different pieces of software are assigned a version number. When you first approach Linux, chances are you'll be looking at a CD-ROM distribution, such as "Red Hat Version 7. 1" or "SuSE Linux Version 6.0." It's important to understand that these version numbers only relate to the particular distribution (which is a prepackaged version of Linux along with tons of free application packages, usually sold on CD-ROM). Therefore, the version number assigned by Red Hat, SuSE, or Debian might not have anything to do with the individual version numbers of the software in that distribution.

The Linux kernel, as well as each application, component, library, or software package in a Linux distribution, generally has its *own* version number. For example, you might be using *gcc* Version 2.96, as well as the XFree86 GUI Version 4.0.3. As you can guess, the higher the version number, the newer the software is. If you install Linux in the form of a distribution (such as Red Hat and SuSE), all of this is simplified for you since the latest versions of each package are usually included in the distribution, and the distribution vendors make sure that the software on a particular distribution works together.

The Linux kernel has a peculiar version numbering scheme with which you should be familiar. As mentioned before, the kernel is the core operating system itself, responsible for managing all the hardware resources in your machine—such as disks, network interfaces, memory, and so on. Unlike Windows systems, the Linux kernel doesn't include any application-level libraries or GUIs. In some sense, as a user you will never interact with the kernel directly, but rather through interfaces, such as the shell or the GUI (more on this later).

However, many people still consider the Linux kernel version to be the version of the "entire system," which is somewhat misleading. Someone might say, "I'm running kernel Version 2.5.12," but this doesn't mean much if everything else on the system is years out of date.

The Linux kernel versioning system works as follows. At any given time, there are *two* "latest" versions of the kernel out there (meaning available for download from the Internet)—the "stable" and "development" releases. The *stable release* is meant for most Linux users who aren't interested in hacking on bleeding-edge experimental features, but who need a stable, working system that isn't changing underneath them from day to day. The *development release*, on the other hand, changes very rapidly as new features are added and tested by developers across the Internet. Changes to the stable release consist mostly of bug fixes and security patches, while changes to the development release can be anything from major new kernel subsystems to minor tweaks in a device driver for added performance. The Linux developers don't guarantee that the development kernel version will work for everyone, but they do maintain the stable version with the intention of making it run well everywhere.

The stable kernel release has an even minor version number (such as 2.4), while the development release has an odd minor version number (such as 2.5). Note that the current development kernel always has a minor version number exactly one greater than the current stable kernel. So, when the current stable kernel is 2.6, the current development kernel will be 2.7. (Unless, of course, Linus decides to bump the kernel version to 3.0—in which case the development version will be 3.1, naturally).

Each kernel version has a third "patch-level" version number associated with it, such as 2.4.19 or 2.5.12. The patch level specifies the particular revision of that kernel version, with higher numbers specifying newer revisions. As of the time of this writing in November 2002, the latest stable kernel is 2.4.19 and the current development kernel is 2.5.45.

A Bag of Features

Linux is a complete multitasking, multiuser operating system (as are all other versions of Unix). This means that many users can be logged onto the same machine at once, running multiple programs simultaneously. Linux also supports multiprocessor systems (such as dual-Pentium motherboards), with support for up to 32 processors in a system, which is great for high-performance servers and scientific applications.

The Linux system is mostly compatible with a number of Unix standards (inasmuch as Unix has standards) on the source level, including IEEE POSIX.1, System V, and BSD features. Linux was developed with source portability in mind: therefore, you will probably find features in the Linux system that are shared across multiple Unix implementations. A great deal of free Unix software available on the Internet and elsewhere compiles on Linux out of the box.

If you have some Unix background, you may be interested in some other specific internal features of Linux, including POSIX job control (used by shells such as the C shell, *csh*, and *bash*), pseudoterminals (*pty* devices), and support for national or customized keyboards using dynamically loadable keyboard drivers. Linux also supports *virtual consoles*, which allow you to switch between multiple login sessions from the system console in text mode. Users of the *screen* program will find the Linux virtual console implementation familiar (although nearly all users make use of a GUI desktop instead).

Linux can quite happily coexist on a system that has other operating systems installed, such as Windows 95/98, Windows NT/2000/XP, Mac OS, or other versions of Unix. The Linux bootloader (LILO) and the GRand Unified Bootloader (GRUB) allow you to select which operating system to start at boot time, and Linux is compatible with other bootloaders as well (such as the one found in Windows 2000).

Linux can run on a wide range of CPU architectures, including the Intel x86 (the whole Pentium line including the '386/'486), Itanium, SPARC/UltraSPARC, ARM, PA-RISC, Alpha, PowerPC, MIPS, m68k, and IBM 370/390 mainframes. Linux has also been ported to a number of embedded processors, and stripped-down versions have been built for various PDAs, including the PalmPilot and Compaq iPaq. In the other direction, Linux is being considered for top-of-the-line computers as well. In April 2002, Hewlett-Packard announced that it was going to release a supercomputer with Linux as the operating system. A large number of scalable clusters—supercomputers built out of arrays of PCs—run Linux as well.

Linux supports various filesystem types for storing data. Some filesystems, such as the Second Extended Filesystem (*ext2fs*), have been developed specifically for Linux. Other Unix filesystem types, such as the Minix-1 and Xenix filesystems, are also supported. The Windows NTFS (Windows 2000 and NT), VFAT (Windows 95/98), and FAT (MS-DOS) filesystems have been implemented as well, allowing you to access Windows files directly. Support is included for Macintosh, OS/2, and Amiga filesystems as well. The ISO 9660 CD-ROM filesystem type, which reads all standard formats of CD-ROMs, is also supported. We'll talk more about filesystems in Chapter 3 and Chapter 5.

Networking support is one of the greatest strengths of Linux, both in terms of functionality and performance. Linux provides a complete implementation of TCP/IP networking. This includes device drivers for many popular Ethernet cards, PPP and SLIP (allowing you to access a TCP/IP network via a serial connection or modem), Parallel Line Internet Protocol (PLIP), and the NFS. Linux also supports the modern IPv6 protocol suite, and many other protocols including DHCP, Appletalk, IRDA, DECnet, and even AX.25 for packet radio networks. The complete range of TCP/IP clients and services is supported, such as FTP, Telnet, NNTP, and Simple Mail Transfer Protocol (SMTP). The Linux kernel includes complete network firewall support, allowing you to configure any Linux machine as a firewall (which screens network packets, preventing unauthorized access to an intranet, for example). It is widely held that networking performance under Linux is superior to other operating systems. We'll talk more about networking in Chapter 15.

Kernel

The *kernel* is the guts of the operating system itself; it's the code that controls the interface between user programs and hardware devices, the scheduling of processes to achieve multitasking, and many other aspects of the system. The kernel is not a separate process running on the system. Instead, you can think of the kernel as a set of routines, constantly in memory, to which every process has access. Kernel routines can be called in a number of ways. One direct method to utilize the kernel is for a process to execute a *system call*, which is a function that causes the kernel to execute some code on behalf of the process. For example, the *read* system call will read data from a file descriptor. To the programmer, this looks like any other C function, but in actuality the code for *read* is contained within the kernel.

Kernel code is also executed in other situations. For example, when a hardware device issues an interrupt, the interrupt handler is found within the kernel. When a process takes an action that requires it to wait for results, the kernel steps in and puts the process to sleep, scheduling another process in its place. Similarly, the kernel switches control between processes rapidly, using the clock interrupt (and other means) to trigger a switch from one process to another. This is basically how multitasking is accomplished.

The Linux kernel is known as a *monolithic* kernel, in that all core functions and device drivers are part of the kernel proper. Some operating systems employ a *microkernel* architecture whereby device drivers and other components (such as filesystems and memory management code) are *not* part of the kernel—rather, they are treated as independent services or regular user applications. There are advantages and disadvantages to both designs: the monolithic architecture is more common among Unix implementations and is the design employed by classic kernel designs, such as System V and BSD. Linux does support loadable device drivers (which can be loaded and unloaded from memory through user commands); this is the subject of the section "Loadable Device Drivers" in Chapter 7.

The Linux kernel on Intel platforms is developed to use the special protected-mode features of the Intel x86 processors (starting with the 80386 and moving on up to the current Pentium 4). In particular, Linux makes use of the protected-mode descriptor-based memory management paradigm and many of the other advanced features of these processors. Anyone familiar with x86 protected-mode programming knows that this chip was designed for a multitasking system such as Unix (the x86 was actually inspired by Multics). Linux exploits this functionality.

Like most modern operating systems, Linux is a multiprocessor operating system: it supports systems with more than one CPU on the motherboard. This feature allows different programs to run on different CPUs at the same time (or "in parallel"). Linux also supports *threads*, a common programming technique that allows a single program to create multiple "threads of control" that share data in memory. Linux supports several kernel-level and user-level thread packages, and Linux's kernel threads run on multiple CPUs, taking advantage of true hardware parallelism. The Linux kernel threads package is compliant with the POSIX 1003.1c standard.

The Linux kernel supports demand-paged loaded executables. That is, only those segments of a program that are actually used are read into memory from disk. Also, if multiple instances of a program are running at once, only one copy of the program code will be in memory. Executables use dynamically linked shared libraries, meaning that executables share common library code in a single library file found on disk. This allows executable files to occupy much less space on disk. This also means that a single copy of the library code is held in memory at one time, thus reducing overall memory usage. There are also statically linked libraries for those who wish to maintain "complete" executables without the need for shared libraries to be in place. Because Linux shared libraries are dynamically linked at runtime, programmers can replace modules of the libraries with their own routines.

In order to make the best use of the system's memory, Linux implements so-called *virtual memory* with disk paging. That is, a certain amount of *swap space** can be allocated on disk. When applications require more physical memory than is actually installed in the machine, it will swap inactive pages of memory out to disk. (A *page* is simply the unit of memory allocation used by the operating system; on most architectures, it's equivalent to 4 KB.) When those pages are accessed again, they will be

---

* If you are a real OS geek, you will note that swap space is inappropriately named: entire processes are not swapped, but rather individual pages of memory are paged out. While in some cases entire processes will be swapped out, this is not generally the case. The term "swap space" originates from the early days of Linux and should technically be called "paging space."

read from disk back into main memory. This feature allows the system to run larger applications and support more users at once. Of course, swap is no substitute for physical RAM; it's much slower to read pages from disk than from memory.

The Linux kernel keeps portions of recently accessed files in memory, to avoid accessing the (relatively slow) disk any more than necessary. The kernel uses all the free memory in the system for caching disk accesses, so when the system is lightly loaded a large number of files can be accessed rapidly from memory. When user applications require a greater amount of physical memory, the size of the disk cache is reduced. In this way physical memory is never left unused.

To facilitate debugging, the Linux kernel generates a *core dump* of a program that performs an illegal operation, such as accessing an invalid memory location. The core dump, which appears as a file called *core* in the directory that the program was running, allows the programmer to determine the cause of the crash. We'll talk about the use of core dumps for debugging in the section "Examining a Core File" in Chapter 14.

Software Features

In this section, we'll introduce you to many of the software applications available for Linux and talk about a number of common computing tasks. After all, the most important part of the system is the wide range of software available for it. What's even more impressive on Linux is that most of this software is freely distributable.

Basic Commands and Utilities

Virtually every utility you would expect to find on standard implementations of Unix has been ported to Linux. This includes basic commands such as *ls*, *awk*, *tr*, *sed*, *bc*, *more*, and so on. There are Linux ports of many popular software packages including Perl, Python, the Java Development Kit, and more. You name it, Linux has it. Therefore, you can expect your familiar working environment on other Unix systems to be duplicated on Linux. All the standard commands and utilities are there.

Many text editors are available, including *vi* (as well as "modern" versions, such as *vim*), *ex*, *pico*, and *jove*, as well as GNU Emacs and variants, such as XEmacs (which incorporates extensions for use under the X Window System) and *joe*. Whatever text editor you're accustomed to using has more than likely been ported to Linux.

The choice of a text editor is an interesting one. Many Unix users still use "simple" editors such as *vi* (in fact, the first edition of this book was written using *vi* under Linux). However, *vi* has many limitations due to its age, and more modern (and complex) editors, such as Emacs, are gaining popularity. Emacs supports a complete LISP-based macro language and interpreter, a powerful command syntax, and other fun-filled extensions. Emacs macro packages exist to allow you to read electronic mail and news, edit the contents of directories, and even engage in an artificially intelligent psychotherapy session (indispensable for stressed-out Linux hackers). In Chapter 9, we include a complete *vi* tutorial and describe Emacs in detail.

One interesting note is that most of the basic Linux utilities are GNU software. These GNU utilities support advanced features not found in the standard versions from BSD or AT&T. For example, GNU's version of the *vi* editor, *elvis*, includes a structured macro language. However, the GNU utilities strive to remain compatible with their BSD and System V counterparts. Many people consider the GNU versions of these programs superior to the originals. Examples of this are the GNU *gzip* and *bzip2* file-compression utilities, which compress data much more efficiently than the original Unix *compress* utility. (Of course, if you want to be "old school," you can still use programs like *ex* and *compress*. This is a good way to impress your friends who are probably used to using a cushy point-and-click GUI for everything.)

The most important utility to many users is the *shell*. The shell is a program that reads and executes commands from the user. In addition, many shells provide features such as *job control* (allowing the user to manage several running processes at once—not as Orwellian as it sounds), input and output redirection, and a command language for writing *shell scripts*. A shell script is a file containing a program in the shell command language, analogous to a "batch file" under MS-DOS.

Many types of shells are available for Linux. The most important difference between shells is the command language. For example, the C shell (*csh*) uses a command language somewhat like the C programming language. The classic Bourne shell uses a different command language. One's choice of a shell is often based on the command language it provides. The shell that you use defines, to some extent, your working environment under Linux.

No matter what Unix shell you're accustomed to, some version of it has probably been ported to Linux. The most popular shell is the GNU Bourne Again Shell (*bash*), a Bourne shell variant. *bash* includes many advanced features, such as job control, command history, command and filename completion, an Emacs-like (or optionally, a *vi*-like) interface for editing the command line, and powerful extensions to the standard Bourne shell language. Another popular shell is *tcsh*, a version of the C shell with advanced functionality similar to that found in *bash*. Other shells include the Korn shell (*ksh*), BSD's *ash*, *zsh*, a small Bourne-like shell, and *rc*, the Plan 9 shell.

What's so important about these basic utilities? Linux gives you the unique opportunity to tailor a custom system to your needs. For example, if you're the only person who uses your system, and you prefer to use the *vi* editor and the *bash* shell exclusively, there's no reason to install other editors or shells. The "do it yourself" attitude is prevalent among Linux hackers and users.

Text Processing and Word Processing

Almost every computer user has a need for some kind of document preparation system. (In fact, one of the authors has almost entirely forgotten how to write with pen and paper.) In the PC world, *word processing* is the norm: it involves editing and manipulating text (often in a "What-You-See-Is-What-You-Get" [WYSIWYG] environment) and producing printed copies of the text, complete with figures, tables, and other garnishes.

In the Unix world, *text processing* is much more common, which is quite different from the concept of word processing. With a text processing system, the author enters text using a "typesetting language" that describes how the text should be formatted. Instead of entering the text within a special word processing environment, the author may modify the source with any text editor, such as *vi* or Emacs. Once the source text (in the typesetting language) is complete, the user formats the text with a separate program, which converts the source to a format suitable for printing. This is somewhat analogous to programming in a language such as C, and "compiling" the document into a printable form.

Many text-processing systems are available for Linux. One is *groff*, the GNU version of the classic *troff* text formatter originally developed by Bell Labs and still used on many Unix systems worldwide. Another modern text processing system is TeX, developed by Donald Knuth of computer science fame. Dialects of TeX, such as LaTeX, are also available, as are numerous extensions and packages. One example is PDF&LATEX, a package that Adobe generates PDF files directly from LaTeX documents.

Text processors such as TeX and *groff* differ mostly in the syntax of their formatting languages. The choice of one formatting system over another is also based upon what utilities are available to satisfy your needs, as well as personal taste.

For example, some people consider the *groff* formatting language to be a bit obscure, so they use TeX, which is more readable by humans. However, *groff* is capable of producing plain ASCII output, viewable on a terminal, while TeX is intended primarily for output to a printing device. Still, various programs exist to produce plain ASCII from TeX-formatted documents or to convert TeX to *groff*, for example.

Another text processing system is Texinfo, an extension to TeX used for software documentation by the Free Software Foundation. Texinfo is capable of producing a printed document, or an online-browsable hypertext "Info" document from a single source file. Info files are the main format of documentation used by GNU software, such as Emacs.

Text processors are used widely in the computing community for producing papers, theses, magazine articles, and books. (In fact, this book was originally written in the LATEX format, filtered into a home-grown SGML system, and printed from *groff* by the publisher.) The ability to process the source language as a plain-text file opens the door to many extensions to the text processor itself. Because source documents are not stored in an obscure format, readable only by a particular word processor, programmers are able to write parsers and translators for the formatting language, thus extending the system. This approach closely follows the Unix philosophy of building up applications as a set of smaller tools that work together, rather than as large, monolithic "black box" systems.

What does such a formatting language look like? In general, the formatting language source consists mostly of the text itself, along with "control codes" to produce a particular effect, such as changing fonts, setting margins, creating lists, and so on.

The most famous text formatting language is HTML, the markup language used by virtually every page on the World Wide Web. Another popular text processing language is Docbook, a kind of industry-standard set of tags for marking up technical documentation, which is also used by the Linux Documentation Project (to be discussed later in this chapter). Here is what one of the earlier paragraphs looks like written in Docbook:

```
<sect2><title>Basic Commands and Utilities</title>

<para>

Virtually every utility you would expect to find on standard
implementations of Unix has been ported to Linux. This
includes basic commands such as <command>ls</command>,
<command>awk</command>, <command>tr</command>,
<command>sed</command>, <command>bc</command>,
<command>more</command>, and so on.  There are Linux ports
of many popular software packages including Perl, Python,
the Java Development Kit, and more. You name it, Linux has it.
Therefore, you can expect your familiar working
environment on other Unix systems to be duplicated on
Linux. All the standard commands and utilities are
there.
</para>
```

At first glance, the typesetting language may appear to be obscure, but it's actually quite easy to learn. Using at processing system enforces typographical standards when writing. For example, all enumerated lists within a document will look the same, unless the author modifies the definition of the enumerated list "environment."

The primary goal of typesetting languages is to allow the author to concentrate on writing the actual text, instead of worrying about typesetting conventions. When the example just shown is printed, the commands in <command> tags will be printed using whatever font, color, or other convention the publisher has chosen, and a command index can easily be generated too. Furthermore, the correct chapter number and title are plugged in where the strange-looking <xref> tag was written, so they are correct even if the authors reorder the chapters after writing the paragraph.

While there are WYSIWYG editors for HTML, getting used to entering tags by hand, like those in the previous example, actually takes only a little practice. The more advanced text editors, such as Emacs and *vim*, have special macros and environments for editing HTML, LaTeX, and other documents, and include nice features such as special fonts and colors to represent different kinds of tags. Tools can then generate output in a standard format, such as PostScript or PDF, and display it on the author's screen or send it to a printer.

WYSIWYG word processors are attractive for many reasons; they provide a powerful, and sometimes complex, visual interface for editing the document. However, this interface is inherently limited to those aspects of text layout that are accessible to the user. For example, many word processors provide a special "format language" for producing complicated expressions such as mathematical formulae. This format language is identical to text processing, albeit on a much smaller scale.

The subtle benefit of text processing is that the system allows you to specify exactly what you mean. Also, text processing systems allow you to edit the source text with any text editor, and the source is easily converted to other formats. The tradeoff for this flexibility and power is the lack of a WYSIWYG interface. Many users of word processors are used to seeing the formatted text as they edit it. On the other hand, when writing with a text processor, one generally doesn't worry about how the text will appear once it's formatted. The writer learns to expect how the text should look from the formatting commands used in the source.

There are programs that allow you to view the formatted document on a graphics display before printing. One example is the *xdvi* program, which displays a "device-independent" file generated by the system under the X Window System. Other software applications, such as *xfig*, provide a WYSIWYG graphics interface for drawing figures and diagrams, which are subsequently converted to the text processing language for inclusion in your document.

Many other text processing utilities are available. The powerful METAFONT system, used to design fonts for TeX, is included with the Linux port of TeX. Other programs include *ispell*, an interactive spell checker; *makeindex*, an index generator for LaTeX documents; and many *groff* and TeX-based macro packages for formatting various types of documents and mathematical texts. Conversion programs are available to translate between TeX or *groff* source and many other formats.

Commercial Applications

There has been a groundswell of support by commercial application developers for Linux. These products include office productivity suites, word processors, scientific applications, network administration utilities, and large-scale database engines. Linux has become a major force in the commercial software market, so you may be surprised to find how many popular commercial applications are available for Linux. We can't possibly discuss all of them here, so we'll only touch on the most popular applications and briefly mention some of the others.

StarOffice is a complete office productivity suite for Linux, released by Sun Microsystems (originally developed by a smaller company called Star Division, which was bought by Sun). This suite, which is also available for Windows and Solaris, is more or less a clone of Microsoft Office, including a word processor, spreadsheet, HTML editor, presentation manager, and other tools. It is capable of reading file formats from a wide range of similar applications (including Microsoft Office) and is available for free download for noncommercial use.

Corel has released WordPerfect Office 2000 for Linux, another office suite which includes a word processor, spreadsheet, presentation software, personal information manager, and other applications. It is free for personal use and commercial licenses are also available. Corel has also released the CorelDRAW professional graphics suite for Linux.

Oracle, IBM, Informix, Sybase, and Interbase have released commercial database engines for Linux. Many of the Linux database products have demonstrated better performance than their counterparts running on Windows 2000 systems.

One very popular database for Linux is MySQL, a free and easy-to-use database engine available from *http://www.mysql.com*. Because MySQL is easy to install, configure, and use, it has rapidly become the database engine of choice for many applications that can forego the complexity of the various proprietary engines. Furthermore, even though it's free software, MySQL is supported professionally by the company that developed it, MySQL AB. We describe the basic use of MySQL in Chapter 18.

MySQL does not include some of the more advanced features of the proprietary databases, however. Some database users prefer the open source database PostgresSQL, and Red Hat features it in some of its products.

A wide range of enterprise applications are available for Linux in addition to databases. Linux is one of the most popular platforms for Internet service hosting, so it is appropriate that high-end platforms for scalable web sites, including BEA WebLogic and IBM WebSphere, have been released for Linux. Commercial, high-performance Java Virtual Machines and other software are available from Sun, IBM, and other vendors. IBM has released the popular Lotus Domino messaging and web application server, as well as the WebSphere MQ (formerly MQSeries) messaging platform.

Scientists, engineers, and mathematicians will find that a range of popular commercial products are available for Linux, such as Maple, Mathematica, MATLAB, and Simulink. Other commercial applications for Linux include high-end CAD systems, network management tools, firewalls, and software development environments.

Programming Languages and Utilities

Linux provides a complete Unix programming environment, including all the standard libraries, programming tools, compilers, and debuggers that you would expect to find on other Unix systems. The most commonly used compiler on Linux is the GNU's Compiler Collection, or *gcc*. *gcc* is capable of compiling C, C++, Objective C (another object-oriented dialect of C), Chill (a programming language mainly used for telecommunications), FORTRAN, and Java. Within the Unix software development world, applications and systems programming is usually done in C or C++, and *gcc* is one of the best C/C++ compilers around, supporting many advanced features and optimizations.

Java, a relative newcomer on the programming-language scene, is fully supported under Linux. Several vendors and independent projects have released ports of the Java Development Kit for Linux, including Sun, IBM, and the Blackdown Project (which did one of the first ports of Java for Linux). Java is an object-oriented programming language and runtime environment that supports a diverse range of applications like web page applets, Internet-based distributed systems, database connectivity, and more. Programs written for Java can be run on any system (regardless of CPU architecture or operating system) that supports the Java Virtual Machine. A number of Java "just-in-time" (or JIT) compilers are available, and the IBM and Sun Java Development Kits (JDKs) for Linux come bundled with high-performance JIT compilers that perform as well as those found on Windows or other Unix systems. IBM has released VisualAge for Java, a complete Java integrated development environment. *gcc* is also capable of compiling Java programs directly to executables, and includes limited support for the standard JDK libraries.

Besides C, C++, and Java, many other compiled and interpreted programming languages have been ported to Linux, such as Smalltalk, FORTRAN, Pascal, LISP, Scheme, and Ada. In addition, various assemblers for writing machine code are available. A network of open source developers is developing a project called Mono with the goal of duplicating the building blocks of Microsoft's .NET project on Unix and Linux systems. Perhaps the most important class of programming languages for Linux are the many scripting languages, including Perl (the script language to end all script languages), Python (the first scripting language to be designed as object-oriented from the ground up), and Tcl/Tk (a shell-like command-processing system that includes support for developing simple X Window System applications).

Linux systems make use of the advanced *gdb* debugger, which allows you to step through a program to find bugs or examine the cause for a crash using a core dump. *gprof*, a profiling utility, will give you performance statistics for your program, letting you know where your program is spending most of its time. The Emacs and *vim* text editors provide interactive editing and compilation environments for various programming languages. Other tools that are available for Linux include the GNU *make* build utility, used to manage compilation of large applications, as well as source-code control systems such as CVS and Revision Control System.

Linux is an ideal system for developing Unix applications. It provides a modern programming environment with all the bells and whistles, and many professional Unix programmers claim that Linux is their favorite operating system for development and debugging. Computer science students can use Linux to learn Unix programming and to explore other aspects of the system, such as kernel architecture. With Linux, not only do you have access to the complete set of libraries and programming utilities, but you also have the complete kernel and library source code at your fingertips. Chapter 13, and Chapter 14 are devoted to the programming languages and tools available for Linux.

The X Window System

The X Window System is the standard GUI for Unix systems. It was originally developed at MIT in the 1980s with the goal of allowing applications to run across a range of Unix workstations from different vendors. X is a powerful graphical environment supporting many applications. Many X-specific applications have been written, such as games, graphics utilities, programming and documentation tools, and so on.

Unlike Microsoft Windows, the X Window System has built-in support for networked applications: for example, you can run an X application on a server machine and have its windows display on your desktop, over the network. Also, X is extremely customizable: you can easily tailor just about any aspect of the system to your liking. You can adjust the fonts, colors, window decorations, and icons for your personal taste. You can go so far as to configure keyboard macros to run new applications at a keystroke. It's even possible for X to emulate the Windows and Macintosh desktop environments, if you want to keep a familiar interface.

The X Window System is freely distributable. However, many commercial vendors have distributed proprietary enhancements to the original X software. The version of X available for Linux is known as XFree86, which is a port of X11R6 (X Window System Version 11, Release 6) made freely distributable for PC-based Unix systems, such as Linux. XFree86 supports a wide range of video hardware, including standard VGA and many accelerated video adapters. XFree86 is a complete distribution of the X software, containing the X server itself, many applications and utilities, programming libraries, and documentation. It comes bundled with nearly every Linux distribution.

Standard X applications include *xterm* (a terminal emulator used for most text-based applications within an X window), *xdm* (the X Session Manager, which handles logins), *xclock* (a simple clock display), *xman* (an X-based manual page reader), and more. The many X applications available for Linux are too numerous to mention here, but the base XFree86 distribution includes the "standard" applications found in the original MIT release. Many others are available separately, and theoretically any application written for X should compile cleanly under Linux.

The look and feel of the X interface are controlled to a large extent by the *window manager*. This friendly program is in charge of the placement of windows, the user interface for resizing, iconifying, and moving windows, the appearance of window frames, and so on. The standard XFree86 distribution includes several window managers, including the popular *fvwm2*. *fvwm2* provides a number of advanced features, including a virtual desktop: if the user moves the mouse to the edge of the screen, the entire desktop is shifted as if the display were much larger than it actually is. *fvwm2* is greatly customizable and allows all functions to be accessed from the keyboard as well as from the mouse.

The XFree86 distribution contains programming libraries and includes files for those wily programmers who wish to develop X applications. Various widget sets, such as Athena, Open Look, and Xaw3D, are supported. All the standard fonts, bitmaps, manual pages, and documentation are included. PEX (a programming interface for 3D graphics) is also supported, as is Mesa, a free implementation of the OpenGL 3D graphics primitives.

In Chapter 10 and Chapter 11, we'll discuss how to install and use the X Window System on your Linux machine.

KDE and GNOME

While the X Window System provides a flexible windowing system, many users want a complete desktop environment, with a customizable look and feel for all windows and widgets (such as buttons and scrollbars), a simplified user interface, and advanced features such as the ability to "drag and drop" data from one application to another. The KDE and GNOME projects are separate efforts that are striving to provide such an advanced desktop environment for Linux. By building up a powerful suite of development tools, libraries, and applications that are integrated into the desktop environment, KDE and GNOME aim to usher in the next era of Linux desktop computing. Both systems provide a rich GUI, window manager, utilities, and applications that rival or exceed the features of systems such as the Windows 2000 desktop.

With KDE and GNOME, even casual users and beginners will feel right at home with Linux. Most distributions automatically configure one of these desktop environments during installation, making it unnecessary to ever touch the text-only console interface.

While both KDE and GNOME aim to make the Unix environment more user-friendly, they have different emphases. KDE's main goals are ease of use, stability, and user-interface compatibility with other computing environments (such as

Windows 2000). GNOME, on the other hand, aims more at good looks and maximum configurability. We discuss both of these systems in Chapter 11.

Networking

Linux boasts one of the most powerful and robust networking systems in the world—more and more people are finding that Linux makes an excellent choice as a network server. Linux supports the TCP/IP networking protocol suite that drives the entire Internet, as well as many other protocols, including IPv6 (a new version of the IP protocol for the next-generation Internet), and UUCP (used for communication between Unix machines over serial lines). With Linux, you can communicate with any computer on the Internet, using Ethernet (including Fast and Gigabit Ethernet), Token Ring, dial-up connection, wireless network, packet radio, serial line, ISDN, ATM, IRDA, AppleTalk, IPX (Novell NetWare), and many other network technologies. The full range of Internet-based applications is available, including World Wide Web browsers, web servers, FTP, email, chat, news, *ssh*, *telnet*, and more.

Most Linux users use a dial-up connection through an ISP to connect to the Internet from home. Linux supports the popular PPP and SLIP protocols, used by most ISPs for dial-in access. If you have a broadband connection, such as a T1 line, cable modem, DSL, or other service, Linux supports those technologies as well. You can even configure a Linux machine to act as a router and firewall for an entire network of computers, all connecting to the Internet through a single dial-up or broadband connection.

Linux supports a wide range of web browsers, including Netscape Navigator, Mozilla (the open source spin-off of the Netscape browser), Konquerer (another open source browser packaged with KDE), and the text-based Lynx browser. The Emacs text editor even includes a small text-based web browser.

Linux also hosts a range of web servers, such as the popular and free Apache web server. In fact, it's estimated that Apache running on Linux systems drives more web sites than any other platform in the world. Apache is easy to set up and use; we'll show you how in Chapter 16.

A full range of mail and news readers are available for Linux, such as MH, Elm, Pine, *trn*, as well as the mail/news readers included with the Netscape and Mozilla web browsers. Many of these are compatible with standard mail and news protocols such as IMAP and POP. Whatever your preference, you can configure your Linux system to send and receive electronic mail and news from all over the world.

A variety of other network services are available for Linux. Samba is a package that allows Linux machines to act as a Windows file and print server. NFS allows your system to share files seamlessly with other machines on the network. With NFS, remote files look to you as if they were located on your own system's drives. FTP allows you to transfer files to and from other machines on the network. Other networking features include NNTP-based electronic news systems such as C News and

INN; the *sendmail*, *exim*, and *smail* mail transfer agents; *ssh*, *telnet*, and *rsh*, which allow you to log in and execute commands on other machines on the network; and *finger*, which allows you to get information on other Internet users. There are tons of TCP/IP-based applications and protocols out there.

If you have experience with TCP/IP applications on other Unix systems, Linux will be familiar to you. The system provides a standard socket programming interface, so virtually any program that uses TCP/IP can be ported to Linux. The Linux X server also supports TCP/IP, allowing you to display applications running on other systems on your Linux display. Administration of Linux networking will be familiar to those coming from other Unix systems, as the configuration and monitoring tools are similar to their BSD counterparts.

In Chapter 15, we'll discuss the configuration and setup of TCP/IP, including PPP, for Linux. We'll also discuss configuration of web browsers, web servers, and mail software.

Laptop Support

Linux includes a number of laptop-specific features, such as PCMCIA (or "PC Card") support and APM. The PCMCIA Tools package for Linux includes drivers for many PCMCIA devices, including modems, Ethernet cards, and SCSI adapters. APM allows the kernel to keep track of the laptop's battery power and perform certain actions (such as an automated shutdown) when power is low; it also allows the CPU to go into "low-power" mode when not in use. This is easy to configure as a kernel option. Various tools interact with APM, such as *apm* (which displays information on battery status) and *apmd* (which logs battery status and can be used to trigger power events). These should be included with most Linux distributions.

Interfacing with Windows and MS-DOS

Various utilities exist to interface with the world of Windows and MS-DOS. The most well-known application is a project known as Wine—a Microsoft Windows emulator for the X Window System under Linux. The intent of this project, which is still under development, is to allow Microsoft Windows applications to run directly under Linux and other Intel-based operating systems. This is similar to the proprietary WABI Windows emulator from Sun Microsystems. Wine is in a process of continual development, and now runs a wide variety of Windows software, including many desktop applications and games. See *http://www.winehq.com* for details of the project's progress.

Linux provides a seamless interface for transferring files between Linux and Windows systems. You can mount a Windows partition or floppy under Linux, and directly access Windows files as you would any others. In addition, there is the *mtools* package, which allows direct access to MS-DOS–formatted floppies, as well as *htools*, which does the same for Macintosh floppy disks.

Another application is the Linux MS-DOS Emulator, or DOSEMU, which allows you to run many MS-DOS applications directly from Linux. While MS-DOS–based applications are rapidly becoming a thing of the past, there are still a number of interesting MS-DOS tools and games that you might want to run under Linux. It's even possible to run the old Microsoft Windows 3.1 under DOSEMU.

Although Linux does not have complete support for emulating Windows and MS-DOS environments, you can easily run these other operating systems on the same machine with Linux, and choose which operating system to run when you boot the machine. We'll show you how to set up the LILO bootloader, which allows you to select between Linux, Windows, and other operating systems at boot time.

Another popular option is to run a system-level "virtual machine," which literally allows you to run Linux and Windows *at the same time*. A *virtual machine* is a software application that emulates many of the hardware features of your system, tricking the operating system into believing that it is running on a physical computer. Using a virtual machine, you can boot Linux and then run Windows at the same time—with both Linux and Windows applications on your desktop at once. Alternately, you can boot Windows and run Linux under the virtual machine. While there is some performance loss when using virtual machines, many people are very happy employing them for casual use, such as running a Windows-based word processor within a Linux desktop. The most popular virtual machines are VMWare (*http://www.vmware.com/*), which is a commercial product, and Plex86 (*http://www.plex86.org/*), which is an open source project.

Other Applications

A host of miscellaneous applications are available for Linux, as one would expect from an operating system with such a diverse set of users. Linux's primary focus is currently for personal Unix computing, but this is rapidly changing. Business and scientific software are expanding, and commercial software vendors have contributed a growing pool of applications.

The scientific community has wholly embraced Linux as the platform of choice for inexpensive numerical computing. A large number of scientific applications have been developed for Linux, including the popular technical tools MATLAB and Mathematica. A wide range of free packages are also available, including FELT (a finite-element analysis tool), Spice (a circuit design and analysis tool), and Khoros (an image/digital signal processing and visualization system). Many popular numerical computing libraries have been ported to Linux, including the LAPACK linear algebra library. There is also a Linux-optimized version of the BLAS code upon which LAPACK depends.

Linux is one of the most popular platforms for parallel computing using *clusters*, which are collections of inexpensive machines usually connected with a fast (gigabit-per-second or faster) network. The NASA Beowulf project first popularized the idea of tying a large number of Linux-based PCs into a massive supercomputer for scientific and numerical computing. Today, Linux-based clusters are the rule, rather than the exception, for many scientific applications. In fact, Linux clusters are finding their way into increasingly diverse applications—for example, the Google search engine uses a cluster of 4,000 Linux machines!

As with any operating system, Linux has its share of games. A number of popular commercial games have been released for Linux, including Quake, Quake II, Quake III Arena, Doom, SimCity 3000, Descent, and more. Most of the popular games support play over the Internet or a local network, and clones of other commercial games are popping up for Linux. There are also classic text-based dungeon games such as Nethack and Moria; MUDs (multiuser dungeons, which allow many users to interact in a text-based adventure) such as DikuMUD and TinyMUD; and a slew of free graphical games, such as *xtetris*, *netrek*, and *Xboard* (the X11 frontend to *gnuchess*).

For audiophiles, Linux has support for a wide range of sound hardware and related software, such as CDplayer (a program that can control a CD-ROM drive as a conventional CD player, surprisingly enough), MIDI sequencers and editors (allowing you to compose music for playback through a synthesizer or other MIDI-controlled instrument), and sound editors for digitized sounds.

Can't find the application you're looking for? A number of web sites provide comprehensive directories of Linux applications. A few of the most popular Linux software directories are Freshmeat (*http://www.freshmeat.net*), Icewalkers (*http://www.icewalkers.com*), and Linux on Dave Central (*http://linux.davecentral.com/*). While these directories are far from complete, they contain a great deal of software, all categorized and rated by users. Take a look at these sites just to see the enormous amount of code that has been developed for Linux.

If you absolutely can't find what you need, you can always attempt to port the application from another platform to Linux. Or, if all else fails, you can write the application yourself. That's the spirit of Free Software—if you want something to be done right, do it yourself! While it's sometimes daunting to start a major software project on your own, many people find that if they can release an early version of the software to the public, many helpers pop up in the free software community to carry on the project.

About Linux's Copyright

Linux is covered by what is known as the GNU GPL. The GPL, which is sometimes referred to as a "copyleft" license, was developed for the GNU project by the Free Software Foundation. It makes a number of provisions for the distribution and modification of "free software." "Free," in this sense, refers to freedom, not just cost. The GPL has always been subject to misinterpretation, and we hope that this summary will help you to understand the extent and goals of the GPL and its effect on Linux. A complete copy of the GPL is available at *http://www.gnu.org/copyleft/gpl.html*.

Originally, Linus Torvalds released Linux under a license more restrictive than the GPL, which allowed the software to be freely distributed and modified, but prevented any money changing hands for its distribution and use. The GPL allows people to sell and make profit from free software, but doesn't allow them to restrict the right for others to distribute the software in any way.

First, we should explain that "free software" covered by the GPL is *not* in the public domain. Public domain software is software that is not copyrighted and is literally owned by the public. Software covered by the GPL, on the other hand, is copyrighted to the author or authors. This means that the software is protected by standard international copyright laws and that the author of the software is legally defined. Just because the software may be freely distributed doesn't mean it is in the public domain.

GPL-licensed software is also not "shareware." Generally, shareware software is owned and copyrighted by the author, but the author requires users to send in money for its use after distribution. On the other hand, software covered by the GPL may be distributed and used free of charge.

The GPL also allows people to take and modify free software, and distribute their own versions of the software. However, any derived works from GPL software must also be covered by the GPL. In other words, a company could not take Linux, modify it, and sell it under a restrictive license. If any software is derived from Linux, that software must be covered by the GPL as well.

People and organizations can distribute GPL software for a fee and can even make a profit from its sale and distribution. However, in selling GPL software, the distributor can't take those rights away from the purchaser; that is, if you purchase GPL software from some source, you may distribute the software for free or sell it yourself as well.

This might sound like a contradiction at first. Why sell software for profit when the GPL allows anyone to obtain it for free? When a company bundles a large amount of free software on a CD-ROM and distributes it, it needs to charge for the overhead of producing and distributing the CD-ROM, and it may even decide to make profit from the sale of the software. This is allowed by the GPL.

Organizations that sell free software must follow certain restrictions set forth in the GPL. First, they can't restrict the rights of users who purchase the software. This means that if you buy a CD-ROM of GPL software, you can copy and distribute that CD-ROM free of charge, or you can resell it yourself. Second, distributors must make it obvious to users that the software is indeed covered by the GPL. Third, distributors must provide, free of charge, the complete source code for the software being distributed, or they must point their customers on demand to where the software can be downloaded. This will allow anyone who purchases GPL software to make modifications to that software.

Allowing a company to distribute and sell free software is a very good thing. Not everyone has access to the Internet to download software, such as Linux, for free. The GPL allows companies to sell and distribute software to those people who do not have free (cost-wise) access to the software. For example, many organizations sell Linux on floppy, tape, or CD-ROM via mail order, and make profit from these sales. The developers of Linux may never see any of this profit; that is the understanding that is reached between the developer and the distributor when software is licensed by the GPL. In other words, Linus knew that companies may wish to sell Linux and that he may not see a penny of the profits from those sales. (If Linus isn't rich, at least he's famous!)

In the free-software world, the important issue is not money. The goal of free software is always to develop and distribute fantastic software and to allow anyone to obtain and use it. In the next section, we'll discuss how this applies to the development of Linux.

Open Source and the Philosophy of Linux

When new users encounter Linux, they often have a few misconceptions and false expectations of the system. Linux is a unique operating system, and it's important to understand its philosophy and design in order to use it effectively. At the center of the Linux philosophy is a concept that we now call open source software.

Open source is a term that applies to software for which the source code—the inner workings of the program—is freely available for anyone to download, modify, and redistribute. Software covered under the GNU GPL, described in the previous section, fits into the category of open source. Not surprisingly, though, so does software that uses copyright licenses that are similar, but not identical, to the GPL. For example, software that can be freely modified but that does not have the same strict requirements for redistribution as the GPL is also considered open source. Various licenses fit this category, including the BSD License and the Apache Software License.

The so-called "open source" and "free software" development models started with the Free Software Foundation and were popularized with Linux. They represent a totally different way of producing software that opens up every aspect of development, debugging, testing, and study to anyone with enough interest in doing so. Rather than relying upon a single corporation to develop and maintain a piece of software, open source allows the code to evolve, openly, in a community of developers and users who are motivated by desire to *create good software*, rather than simply make a profit.

O'Reilly & Associates, Inc. has published a book, *Open Sources*, which serves as a good introduction to the open source development model. It's a collection of essays about the open source process by leading developers (including Linus Torvalds and Richard Stallman) and was edited by Chris DiBona, Sam Ockman, and Mark Stone.

Open source has received a lot of media attention, and some are calling the phenomenon the "next wave" in software development, which will sweep the old way of doing things under the carpet. It still remains to be seen whether that will happen, but there have been some encouraging events that make this outcome seem likely. For example, Netscape Corporation has released the code for its web browser as an open source project called Mozilla, and companies such as Sun Microsystems, IBM, and Apple have released certain products as open source in the hopes that they will flourish in a community-driven software development effort.

Open source has received a lot of media attention, and Linux is at the center of all of it. In order to understand where the Linux development mentality is coming from, however, it might make sense to take a look at how commercial software has traditionally been built.

Commercial software houses tend to base development on a rigorous policy of quality assurance, source and revision control systems, documentation, and bug reporting and resolution. Developers are not allowed to add features or to change key sections of code on a whim: they must validate the change as a response to a bug report and consequently "check in" all changes to the source control system so that the changes can be backed out if necessary. Each developer is assigned one or more parts of the system code, and only that developer may alter those sections of the code while it is "checked out."

Internally, the quality assurance department runs rigorous test suites (so-called "regression tests") on each new pass of the operating system and reports any bugs. It's the responsibility of the developers to fix these bugs as reported. A complicated system of statistical analysis is employed to ensure that a certain percentage of bugs are fixed before the next release, and that the system as a whole passes certain release criteria.

In all, the process used by commercial software developers to maintain and support their code is very complicated, and quite reasonably so. The company must have quantitative proof that the next revision of the software is ready to be shipped. It's a big job to develop a commercial software system, often large enough to employ hundreds (if not thousands) of programmers, testers, documenters, and administrative personnel. Of course, no two commercial software vendors are alike, but you get the general picture. Smaller software houses, such as startups, tend to employ a scaled-down version of this style of development.

On the opposite end of the spectrum sits Linux, which is, and more than likely always will be, a hacker's operating system.* Although many open source projects have adopted elements of commercial software development techniques, such as

---

* Our definition of "hacker" is a feverishly dedicated programmer—a person who enjoys exploiting computers and generally doing interesting things with them. This is in contrast to the common connotation of "hacker" as a computer wrongdoer or an outlaw.

source control and bug tracking systems, the collaborative and distributed nature of Linux's development is a radical departure from the traditional approach.

Linux is primarily developed as a group effort by volunteers on the Internet from all over the world. No single organization is responsible for developing the system. For the most part, the Linux community communicates via various mailing lists and web sites. A number of conventions have sprung up around the development effort: for example, programmers wanting to have their code included in the "official" kernel should mail it to Linus Torvalds. He will test the code and include it in the kernel (as long as it doesn't break things or go against the overall design of the system, he will more than likely include it). As Linux has grown, this job has become too large for Linus to do himself (plus, he has kids now), so other volunteers are responsible for testing and integrating code into certain aspects of the kernel, such as the network subsystem.

The system itself is designed with a very open-ended, feature-rich approach. A new version of the Linux kernel will typically be released about every few weeks (sometimes even more frequently than this). Of course, this is a very rough figure; it depends on several factors, including the number of bugs to be fixed, the amount of feedback from users testing prerelease versions of the code, and the amount of sleep that Linus has had that week.

Suffice it to say that not every single bug has been fixed and not every problem ironed out between releases. (Of course, this is always true of commercial software as well!) As long as the system appears to be free of critical or oft-manifesting bugs, it's considered "stable" and new revisions are released. The thrust behind Linux development is not an effort to release perfect, bug-free code; it's to develop a free implementation of Unix. Linux is for the developers, more than anyone else.

Anyone who has a new feature or software application to add to the system generally makes it available in an "alpha" stage—that is, a stage for testing by those brave users who want to bash out problems with the initial code. Because the Linux community is largely based on the Internet, alpha software is usually uploaded to one or more of the various Linux web sites (see Appendix A), and a message is posted to one of the Linux mailing lists about how to get and test the code. Users who download and test alpha software can then mail results, bug fixes, or questions to the author.

After the initial problems in the alpha code have been fixed, the code enters a "beta" stage, in which it's usually considered stable but not complete (that is, it works, but not all the features may be present). Otherwise, it may go directly to a "final" stage in which the software is considered complete and usable. For kernel code, once it's complete, the developer may ask Linus to include it in the standard kernel, or as an optional add-on feature to the kernel.

Keep in mind these are only conventions, not rules. Some people feel so confident with their software that they don't need to release an alpha or test version. It's always up to the developer to make these decisions.

What happened to regression testing and the rigorous quality process? It's been replaced by the philosophy of "release early and often." Real users are the best testers because they try out the software in a variety of environments and in a host of demanding real-life applications that can't be easily duplicated by any software Quality Assurance group. One of the best features of this development and release model is that bugs (and security flaws) are often found, reported, and fixed within *hours*, not days or weeks.

You might be amazed that such a nonstructured system of volunteers programming and debugging a complete Unix system could get anything done at all. As it turns out, it's one of the most efficient and motivated development efforts ever employed. The entire Linux kernel was written *from scratch*, without employing any code from proprietary sources. A great deal of work was put forth by volunteers to port all the free software under the sun to the Linux system. Libraries were written and ported, filesystems developed, and hardware drivers written for many popular devices.

The Linux software is generally released as a *distribution*, which is a set of prepackaged software making up an entire system. It would be quite difficult for most users to build a complete system from the ground up, starting with the kernel, then adding utilities, and installing all necessary software by hand. Instead, there are a number of software distributions including everything you need to install and run a complete system. Again, there is no standard distribution; there are many, each with their own advantages and disadvantages. In this book, we describe how to install the Red Hat, SuSE, and Debian distributions, but this book can help you with any distribution you choose.

Despite the completeness of the Linux software, you still need a bit of Unix know-how to install and run a complete system. No distribution of Linux is completely bug-free, so you may be required to fix small problems by hand after installation. While some readers might consider this a pain, a better way to think about it is as the "joy of Linux"—that of having fun tinkering with, learning about, and fixing up your own system. It's this very attitude that distinguishes Linux enthusiasts from mere users. Linux can be either a hobby, an adventure sport, or a lifestyle. (Just like snowboarding and mountain biking, Linux geeks have their own lingo and style of dress—if you don't believe us, hang out at any Linux trade show!) Many new Linux users report having a great time learning about this new system, and find that Linux rekindles the fascination they had when first starting to experiment with computers.

Hints for Unix Novices

Installing and using your own Linux system doesn't require a great deal of background in Unix. In fact, many Unix novices successfully install Linux on their systems. This is a worthwhile learning experience, but keep in mind that it can be very frustrating to some. If you're lucky, you will be able to install and start using your Linux system without any Unix background. However, once you are ready to delve into the more complex tasks of running Linux—installing new software, recompiling the kernel, and so forth—having background knowledge in Unix is going to be a necessity. (Note, however, that many distributions of Linux are as easy to install and configure as Windows 98 and certainly easier than Windows 2000.)

Fortunately, by running your own Linux system, you will be able to learn the essentials of Unix necessary to perform these tasks. This book contains a good deal of information to help you get started. Chapter 4 is a tutorial covering Unix basics, and Chapter 5 contains information on Linux system administration. You may wish to read these chapters before you attempt to install Linux at all; the information contained therein will prove to be invaluable should you run into problems.

Just remember that nobody can expect to go from being a Unix novice to a Unix system administrator overnight. No implementation of Unix is expected to run trouble- and maintenance-free, and you will undoubtedly encounter hang-ups along the way. Treat this as an opportunity to learn more about Linux and Unix, and try not to get discouraged when things don't always go as expected!

Hints for Unix Gurus

Even those people with years of Unix programming and system administration experience may need assistance before they are able to pick up and install Linux. There are still aspects of the system Unix wizards need to be familiar with before diving in. For one thing, Linux is not a commercial Unix system. It doesn't attempt to uphold the same standards as other Unix systems you may have come across. But in some sense, Linux is *redefining* the Unix world by giving all other systems a run for their money. To be more specific, while stability is an important factor in the development of Linux, it's not the *only* factor.

More important, perhaps, is functionality. In many cases, new code will make it into the standard kernel even though it's still buggy and not functionally complete. The assumption is that it's more important to release code that users can test and use than delay a release until it's "complete." Nearly all open source software projects have an alpha release before they are completely tested. In this way, the open source community at large has a chance to work with the code, test it, and develop it further, while those who find the alpha code "good enough" for their needs can use it. Commercial Unix vendors rarely, if ever, release software in this manner.

Even if you're a Unix ultra-wizard who can disassemble Solaris kernels in your sleep and recode an AIX superblock with one hand tied behind your back, Linux might take some getting used to. The system is very modern and dynamic, with a new kernel release approximately every few months and new utilities constantly being released. One day your system may be completely up to date with the current trend, and the next day the same system is considered to be in the Stone Age.

With all of this dynamic activity, how can you expect to keep up with the ever-changing Linux world? For the most part, it's best to upgrade incrementally; that is, upgrade only those parts of the system that *need* upgrading, and then only when you think an upgrade is necessary. For example, if you never use Emacs, there is little reason to continuously install every new release of Emacs on your system. Furthermore, even if you are an avid Emacs user, there is usually no reason to upgrade it unless you find that a missing feature is in the next release. There is little or no reason to always be on top of the newest version of software.

Keep in mind that Linux was developed by its users. This means, for the most part, that the hardware supported by Linux is that which users and developers actually have access to. As it turns out, most of the popular hardware and peripherals for 80x86 systems are supported (in fact, Linux probably supports more hardware than any commercial implementation of Unix). However, some of the more obscure and esoteric devices, as well as those with proprietary drivers for which the manufacturers do not easily make the specifications available, aren't supported yet. As time goes on, a wider range of hardware will be supported, so if your favorite devices aren't listed here, chances are that support for them is forthcoming.

Another drawback for hardware support under Linux is that many companies have decided to keep the hardware interface proprietary. The upshot of this is that volunteer Linux developers simply can't write drivers for those devices (if they could, those drivers would be owned by the company that owned the interface, which would violate the GPL). The companies that maintain proprietary interfaces write their own drivers for operating systems, such as Microsoft Windows; the end user (that's you) never needs to know about the interface. Unfortunately, this does not allow Linux developers to write drivers for those devices.

Little can be done about the situation. In some cases, programmers have attempted to write hackish drivers based on assumptions about the interface. In other cases, developers work with the company in question and attempt to obtain information about the device interface, with varying degrees ofsuccess.

Sources of Linux Information

As you have probably guessed, many sources of information about Linux are available, apart from this book.

Online Documents

If you have access to the Internet, you can get many Linux documents via web and anonymous FTP sites all over the world. If you do not have direct Internet access, these documents may still be available to you; many Linux distributions on CD-ROM contain all the documents mentioned here and are often available off the retail shelf. Also, they are distributed on many other networks, such as Fidonet and CompuServe.

A great number of web and FTP archive sites carry Linux software and related documents. Appendix A contains a listing of some of the Linux documents available via the Internet.

Examples of available online documents are the Linux FAQ, a collection of frequently asked questions about Linux; the Linux HOWTO documents, each describing a specific aspect of the system—including the Installation HOWTO, the Printing HOWTO, and the Ethernet HOWTO; and the Linux META-FAQ, a list of other sources of Linux information on the Internet.

Most of these documents are also posted regularly to one or more Linux-related Usenet newsgroups; see the section "Usenet Newsgroups" later in this chapter.

The Linux Documentation home page is available to web users at *http://www.tlpd. org*. This page contains many HOWTOs and other documents, as well as pointers to other sites of interest to Linux users, including the Linux Documentation Project manuals (see the following section).

Books and Other Published Works

The bibliography at the end of this book points you to a wealth of sources that will help you use your system. There are a number of published works specifically about Linux. In addition, a number of free books are distributed on the Internet by the Linux Documentation Project (LDP), a project carried out over the Internet to write and distribute a bona fide set of "manuals" for Linux. These manuals are analogs to the documentation sets available with commercial versions of Unix: they cover everything from installing Linux to using and running the system, programming, networking, kernel development, and more.

The LDP manuals are available via the Web, as well as via mail order from several sources. The lists the manuals that are available and covers the means of obtaining them in detail. O'Reilly & Associates, Inc. has published the *Linux Network Administrator's Guide* from the LDP.

Aside from the growing number of Linux books, there are a large number of books about Unix in general that are certainly applicable to Linux—as far as using and programming the system is concerned, Linux doesn't differ greatly from other implementations of Unix in most respects. In fact, this book is meant to be complemented by the large library of Unix books currently available; here, we present the most important Linux-specific details and hope you will look to other sources for more in-depth information.

Armed with a number of good books about using Unix, as well as the book you hold in your hands, you should be able to tackle just about anything. The

Bibliography includes a list of highly recommended Unix books, for Unix newcomers and wizards alike.

There are at least two monthly magazines about Linux: *Linux Journal* and *Linux Magazine*. These are an excellent way to keep in touch with the many goings-on in the Linux community.

Usenet Newsgroups

Usenet is a worldwide electronic news and discussion forum with a heavy contingent of so-called "newsgroups," or discussion areas devoted to a particular topic. Much of the development of Linux has been done over the waves of the Internet and Usenet, and not surprisingly, a number of Usenet newsgroups are available for discussions about Linux.

There are far too many newsgroups devoted to Linux to list here. The ones dealing directly with Linux are under the *comp.os.linux* hierarchy, and you'll find others on related topics like *comp.windows.x*.

Internet Mailing Lists

If you have access to Internet electronic mail, you can participate in a number of mailing lists devoted to Linux. These run the gamut from kernel hacking to basic user questions. Many of the popular Linux mailing lists have associated web sites with searchable archives, allowing you to easily find answers to common questions. We list some of these resources in Appendix A.

Getting Help

You will undoubtedly require some degree of assistance during your adventures in the Linux world. Even the most wizardly of Unix wizards is occasionally stumped by some quirk or feature of Linux, and it's important to know how and where to find help when you need it.

The primary means of getting help in the Linux world are Internet mailing lists and Usenet newsgroups, as described earlier. A number of businesses also provide commercial support for Linux. A "subscription fee" allows you to call consultants for help with your Linux problems. Several Linux distribution vendors provide online and telephone-based technical support, which can often be very helpful. However, if you have access to Usenet and Internet mail, you may find the free support found there just as good.

Keeping the following suggestions in mind should improve your experiences with Linux and guarantee you more success in finding help to your problems:

Consult all available documentation first. The first thing to do when encountering a problem is consult the various sources of information listed in the previous section and Appendix A. These documents were laboriously written for people like you—people who need help with the Linux system. Even books written for Unix in general are applicable to Linux, and you should take advantage of them. Impossible as it might seem, more than likely you will find the answer to your problems somewhere in this documentation.

If you have access to the Web, Usenet news, or any of the Linux-related mailing lists, be sure to actually read the information there before posting for help with your problem. Many times, solutions to common problems are not easy to find in documentation and are instead well-covered in the newsgroups and mailing lists devoted to Linux. If you only post to these groups and don't actually read them, you are asking for trouble.

Use the search engines! It's amazing how much Linux-specific information you can turn up simply by using popular web search engines. In fact, Google even has an entire search engine devoted just to Linux, at *http://www.google.com/linux*. The Google usenet newsgroup archive (*http://groups.google.com/*) is also a good place to start. Instead of hunting for information by surfing the many Linux web sites, HOWTO guides, and mailing list archives, a few pointed queries to your favorite search engine can usually turn up results much more quickly.

Of course, you should learn how to use search engines effectively: a generic query like "Linux help" isn't likely to turn up exactly what you're looking for. On the other hand, "Linux Sony Vaio CD-ROM" is a much better way to go (assuming, of course, you're looking for help on your Vaio CD-ROM!).

Learn to appreciate self-maintenance. In most cases, it's preferable to do as much independent research and investigation into the problem as possible before seeking outside help. Remember that Linux is about hacking and fixing problems yourself. It's not a commercial operating system, nor does it try to look like one. Hacking won't kill you. In fact, it will teach you a great deal about the system to investigate and solve problems yourself—maybe even enough to one day call yourself a Linux guru. Learn to appreciate the value of hacking the system and fixing problems yourself. You can't expect to run a complete, home-brew Linux system without some degree of handiwork.

Remain calm. It's vital to refrain from getting frustrated with the system. Nothing is earned by taking an axe—or worse, a powerful electromagnet—to your Linux system in a fit of anger. The authors have found that a large punching bag or similar inanimate object is a wonderful way to relieve the occasional stress attack. As Linux matures and distributions become more reliable, we hope that this problem will go away. However, even commercial Unix implementations can be tricky at times. When all else fails, sit back, take a few deep breaths, and go after the problem again when you feel relaxed. Your mind will be clearer, and your system will thank you. Remember our Zen advice from the preface!

Refrain from posting spuriously. Many people make the mistake of posting to Usenet or mailing messages pleading for help prematurely. When encountering a problem, do not—we repeat, do *not*—rush immediately to your nearest terminal and post a message to one of the Linux Usenet newsgroups. Often, you will catch your own mistake five minutes later and find yourself in the curious situation of defending your own sanity in a public forum. Before posting anything to any of the Linux mailing lists or newsgroups, first attempt to resolve the problem yourself and be absolutely certain what the problem is. Does your system not respond when you turn it on? Perhaps the machine is unplugged.

If you do post for help, make it worthwhile. If all else fails, you may wish to post a message for help in any of the number of electronic forums dedicated to Linux, such as Usenet newsgroups and mailing lists. When posting, remember that the people reading your post are not there to help you. The network is not your personal consulting service. Therefore, it's important to remain as polite, terse, and informative as possible.

How can one accomplish this? First, you should include as much (relevant) information about your system and your problem as possible. Posting the simple request "I can't seem to get email to work" will probably get you nowhere unless you include information on your system, what software you are using, what you have attempted to do so far, and what the results were. When including technical information, it's usually a good idea to include general information on the version(s) of your software (Linux kernel version, for example), as well as a brief summary of your hardware configuration. However, don't overdo it—including information on the brand and type of monitor that you have is probably irrelevant if you're trying to configure networking software.

Second, remember that you need to make some attempt—however feeble—at solving your problem before you go to the Net. If you have never attempted to set up electronic mail, for instance, and first decide to ask folks on the Net how to go about doing it, you are making a big mistake. A number of documents are available (see the previous section "Sources of Linux Information") on how to get started with many common tasks under Linux. The idea is to get as far along as possible on your own and *then* ask for help if and when you get stuck.

Also remember that the people reading your message, however helpful, may occasionally get frustrated by seeing the same problem over and over again. Be sure to actually read the Linux HOWTOs, FAQs, newsgroups, and mailing lists before posting your problems. Many times, the solution to your problem has been discussed repeatedly, and all that's required to find it is to browse the current messages.

Third, when posting to electronic newsgroups and mailing lists, try to be as polite as possible. It's much more effective and worthwhile to be polite, direct, and informative—more people will be willing to help you if you master a humble tone. To be sure, the flame war is an art form across many forms of electronic communication, but don't allow that to preoccupy your and other people's time. The network is an excellent way to get help with your Linux problems—but it's important to know how to use the network *effectively*.

## CHAPTER 2

Preparing to Install Linux

This chapter represents your first step in installing Linux. We'll describe how to obtain the Linux software, in the form of one of the various prepackaged distributions, and how to prepare your system. We'll include ways to partition disks so that Linux can coexist with Windows, or another operating system.

As we have mentioned, there is no single "official" distribution of the Linux software; there are, in fact, many distributions, each serving a particular purpose and set of goals. These distributions are available via anonymous FTP from the Internet and via mail on CD-ROM and DVD, as well as in retail stores.

Distributions of Linux

Because Linux is free software, no single organization or entity is responsible for releasing and distributing the software. Therefore, anyone is free to put together and distribute the Linux software, as long as the restrictions in the GPL are observed. The upshot of this is that there are many distributions of Linux, available via anonymous FTP or mail order.

You are now faced with the task of deciding on a particular distribution of Linux that suits your needs. Not all distributions are alike. Many of them come with just about all the software you'd need to run a complete system—and then some. Other Linux distributions are "small" distributions intended for users without copious amounts of disk space.

You might also want to consider that distributions have different target groups. Some are meant more for businesses, others more for the home user. Some put more emphasis on server use, others on desktop use.

The Linux Distribution HOWTO contains a list of Linux distributions available via the Internet as well as mail order.

How can you decide among all these distributions? If you have access to Usenet news, or another computer conferencing system, you might want to ask there for opinions from people who have installed Linux. Even better, if you know someone who has installed Linux, ask him for help and advice. In actuality, most of the popular Linux distributions contain roughly the same set of software, so the distribution you select is more or less arbitrary.

Getting Linux via Mail Order or Other Hard Media

If you don't have Internet access, you can get many Linux distributions via mail order CD-ROM or DVD. Many distributors accept credit cards as well as international orders, so no matter where you live, you should be able to obtain Linux in this way.

Linux is free software, but distributors are allowed by the GPL to charge a fee for it. Therefore, ordering Linux via mail order might cost you between U.S. $5 and U.S. $150, depending on the distribution. However, if you know people who have already purchased or downloaded a release of Linux, you are free to borrow or copy their software for your own use. Linux distributors are not allowed to restrict the license or redistribution of the software in any way. If you are thinking about installing an entire lab of machines with Linux, for example, you need to purchase only a single copy of one of the distributions, which can be used to install all the machines. There is one exception to this rule, though: in order to add value to their distribution, some vendors include commercial packages that you might not be allowed to install on several machines. If this is the case, it should be explicitly stated on the package.

Many Linux user groups offer their own distributions; see if there's a user group near you. For special platforms like Alpha, a user group may be an excellent place to get Linux.

Getting Linux from the Internet

If you have access to the Internet, the easiest way to obtain Linux is via anonymous FTP.* One major FTP site is *ftp://ftp.ibiblio.org*, and the various Linux distributions can be found there in the directory */pub/Linux/distributions*.

When downloading the Linux software, be sure to use binary mode for all file transfers (with most FTP clients, the command *binary* enables this mode).

You might run into a minor problem when trying to download files for one system (like Linux) with another system (like Windows), because the systems are not always prepared to handle each other's files sensibly. However, with the hints given in this chapter, you should be able to complete the installation process nevertheless.

Some distributions are released via anonymous FTP as a set of disk images. That is, the distribution consists of a set of files, and each file contains the binary image of a

---

* If you do not have direct Internet access, you can obtain Linux via the FTPMAIL service, provided that you have the ability to exchange email with the Internet.

floppy. In order to copy the contents of the image file onto the floppy, you can use the *RAWRITE.EXE* program under Windows. This program copies, block for block, the contents of a file to a floppy, without regard for disk format. *RAWRITE.EXE* is available on the various Linux FTP sites, including *ftp://ftp.ibiblio.org* in the directory */pub/Linux/system/Install/rawwrite*.

Be forewarned that this is a labor-intensive way of installing Linux: the distribution can easily come to more than 50 floppies.

To proceed, download the set of floppy images and use *RAWRITE.EXE* with each image in turn to create a set of floppies. Boot from the so-called "boot floppy," and you're ready to roll. The software is usually installed directly from the floppies, although some distributions allow you to install from a Windows partition on your hard drive, while others allow you to install over a TCP/IP network. The documentation for each distribution should describe these installation methods if they are available.

Other Linux distributions are installed from a set of MS-DOS–formatted floppies. For example, the Slackware distribution of Linux requires *RAWRITE.EXE* only for the boot and root floppies. The rest of the floppies are copied to MS-DOS–formatted floppies using the MS-DOS COPY command. The system installs the software directly from the MS-DOS floppies. This saves you the trouble of having to use *RAWRITE.EXE* for many image files, although it requires you to have access to an MS-DOS system to create the floppies.

If you have access to a Unix workstation with a floppy drive, you can also use the *dd* command to copy the file image directly to the floppy. A command such as `dd of=/dev/rfd0 if=foo bs=18k` will "raw write" the contents of the file *foo* to the floppy device on a Sun workstation. Consult your local Unix gurus for more information on your system's floppy devices and the use of *dd*.

Each distribution of Linux available via anonymous FTP should include a *README* file describing how to download and prepare the floppies for installation. Be sure to read all available documentation for the release you are using.

Today, some of the bigger Linux distributions are also distributed as one or a few ISO images that you can burn on a CD-ROM or DVD. Downloading these is feasible only for people with big hard-disks and a broadband connection to the Internet, due to the enormous amounts of data involved.

Preparing to Install Linux

After you have obtained a distribution of Linux, you're ready to prepare your system for installation. This takes a certain degree of planning, especially if you're already running other operating systems. In the following sections, we'll describe how to plan for the Linux installation.

Installation Overview

While each release of Linux is different, in general the method used to install the software is as follows:

1. *Repartition your hard drive(s).* If you have other operating systems already installed, you will need to repartition the drives in order to allocate space for Linux. This is discussed in the section "Repartitioning Your Drives" later in this chapter. In some distributions, this step is integrated into the installation procedure. Check the documentation of your distribution to see whether this is the case. Still, it won't hurt you to follow the steps given here and repartition your hard drive in advance.

2. *Boot the Linux installation media.* Each distribution of Linux has some kind of installation media—usually a "boot floppy" or a bootable CD-ROM—that is used to install the software. Booting this media will either present you with some kind of installation program, which will step you through the Linux installation, or allow you to install the software by hand.

3. *Create Linux partitions.* After repartitioning to allocate space for Linux, you create Linux partitions on that empty space. This is accomplished with the Linux *fdisk* program, covered in the section "Creating Linux Partitions" in Chapter 3, or with some other distribution-specific program, such as the Disk Druid, that comes with Red Hat Linux.

4. *Create filesystems and swap space.* At this point, you will create one or more filesystems, used to store files, on the newly created partitions. In addition, if you plan to use swap space (which you should, unless you have really huge amounts of physical memory, or RAM), you will create the swap space on one of your Linux partitions. This is covered in the sections "Creating Swap Space" and "Creating Linux Partitions," both in Chapter 3.

5. *Install the software on the new filesystems.* Finally, you will install the Linux software on your newly created filesystems. After this, if all goes well, it's smooth sailing. This is covered in the section "Installing the Software" in Chapter 3. Later, in the section "Running into Trouble," also in Chapter 3, we describe what to do if anything goes wrong.

People who want to switch back and forth between different operating systems sometimes wonder which to install first: Linux or the other system? We can testify that some people have had trouble installing Windows 95/98/ME after Linux. Windows 95/98/ME tends to wipe out existing boot information when it's installed, so you're safer installing it first and then installing Linux afterward using the information in this chapter. Windows NT/2000 seems to be more tolerant of existing boot information. We would assume that this is the same for Windows XP, being an evolution of Windows 2000, but we don't have any personal experiences (no pun intended) with this yet.

Many distributions of Linux provide an installation program that will step you through the installation process and automate one or more of the previous steps for you. Keep in mind throughout this chapter and the next that any number of the previous steps may be automated for you, depending on the distribution.

 While preparing to install Linux, the best advice we can give is to take notes during the entire procedure. Write down everything you do, everything you type, and everything you see that might be out of the ordinary. The idea here is simple: if (or when!) you run into trouble, you want to be able to retrace your steps and find out what went wrong. Installing Linux isn't difficult, but there are many details to remember. You want to have a record of all these details so that you can experiment with other methods if something goes wrong. Also, keeping a notebook of your Linux installation experience is useful when you want to ask other people for help—for example, when posting a message to one of the Linux-related Usenet groups. Your notebook is also something you'll want to show to your grandchildren someday.[*]

Repartitioning Concepts

In general, hard drives are divided into *partitions*, with one or more partitions devoted to an operating system. For example, on one hard drive you may have several separate partitions—one devoted to, say, Windows, another to OS/2, and another two to Linux.

If you already have other software installed on your system, you may need to resize those partitions in order to free up space for Linux. You will then create one or more Linux partitions on the resulting free space for storing the Linux software and swap space. We call this process *repartitioning*.

Many Windows systems utilize a single partition inhabiting the entire drive. To Windows, this partition is known as C:. If you have more than one partition, Windows names them D:, E:, and so on. In a way, each partition acts like a separate hard drive.

On the first sector of the disk is a *master boot record* along with a *partition table*. The boot record (as the name implies) is used to boot the system. The partition table contains information about the locations and sizes of your partitions.

There are three kinds of partitions: *primary*, *extended*, and *logical*. Of these, primary partitions are used most often. However, because of a limit on the size of the partition table, you can have only four primary partitions on any given drive. This is due to the poor design of MS-DOS and Windows; even other operating systems that originated in the same era do not have such limits.

---

[*] Matt shamefully admits that he kept a notebook of all his tribulations with Linux for the first few months of working with the system. It is now gathering dust on his bookshelf.

The way around this four-partition limit is to use an extended partition. An extended partition doesn't hold any data by itself; instead, it acts as a "container" for logical partitions. Therefore, you could create one extended partition, covering the entire drive, and within it create many logical partitions. However, you are limited to only one extended partition per drive.

Linux Partition Requirements

Before we explain how to repartition your drives, you need an idea of how much space you will be allocating for Linux. We will be discussing how to create these partitions later, in the section "Creating Linux Partitions" in Chapter 3.

On Unix systems, files are stored on a *filesystem*, which is essentially a section of the hard drive (or other medium, such as CD-ROM or floppy) formatted to hold files. Each filesystem is associated with a specific part of the directory tree; for example, on many systems, there is a filesystem for all the files in the directory */usr*, another for */tmp*, and so on. The *root filesystem* is the primary filesystem, which corresponds to the topmost directory, */*.

Under Linux, each filesystem lives on a separate partition on the hard drive. For instance, if you have a filesystem for */* and another for */usr*, you will need two partitions to hold the two filesystems.

Before you install Linux, you will need to prepare filesystems for storing the Linux software. You must have at least one filesystem (the root filesystem), and therefore one partition, allocated to Linux. Many Linux users opt to store all their files on the root filesystem, which, in most cases, is easier to manage than several filesystems and partitions.

However, you may create multiple filesystems for Linux if you wish—for example, you may want to use separate filesystems for */usr* and */home*. Those readers with Unix system administration experience will know how to use multiple filesystems creatively. In the section "Creating Filesystems" in Chapter 6, we discuss the use of multiple partitions and filesystems.

Why use more than one filesystem? The most commonly stated reason is safety; if, for some reason, one of your filesystems is damaged, the others will (usually) be unharmed. On the other hand, if you store all your files on the root filesystem, and for some reason the filesystem is damaged, you may lose all your files in one fell swoop. This is, however, rather uncommon; if you back up the system regularly, you should be quite safe.

On the other hand, using several filesystems has the advantage that you can easily upgrade your system without endangering your own precious data. You might have a partition for the users' home directories, and when upgrading the system, you leave this partition alone, wipe out the others, and reinstall Linux from scratch. Of course, nowadays distributions all have quite elaborate update procedures, but from time to time, you might want a "fresh start."

Another reason to use multiple filesystems is to divvy up storage among multiple hard drives. If you have, say, 100 MB free on one hard drive, and 2 GB free on another, you might want to create a 100-MB root filesystem on the first drive and a 2-GB /usr filesystem on the other. It is possible to have a single filesystem span multiple drives by using a tool called *Logical Volume Manager* (LVM), but setting this up requires considerable knowledge, unless your distribution's installation program automates it for you.

In summary, Linux requires at least one partition, for the root filesystem. If you wish to create multiple filesystems, you need a separate partition for each additional filesystem. Some distributions of Linux automatically create partitions and filesystems for you, so you may not need to worry about these issues at all.

Another issue to consider when planning your partitions is swap space. *Swap space* is a portion of the disk used by an operating system to temporarily store parts of programs that were loaded by the user but aren't currently in use. You are not required to use swap space with Linux, but if you have less than 64 MB of physical RAM, it is strongly suggested that you do.

You have two options. The first is to use a *swap file* that exists on one of your Linux filesystems. You will create the swap file for use as virtual RAM after you install the software. The second option is to create a *swap partition*, an individual partition to be used only as swap space. Most people use a swap partition instead of a swap file.

A single swap file or partition may be up to 2 GB.[*] If you wish to use more than 2 GB of swap (hardly ever necessary), you can create multiple swap partitions or files—up to eight in all.

Setting up a swap partition is covered in the section "Creating Swap Space" in Chapter 3, and setting up a swap file in the section "Managing Swap Space" in Chapter 6.

Therefore, in general, you will create at least two partitions for Linux: one for use as the root filesystem, and the other for use as swap space. There are, of course, many variations on partitioning, but this is the minimal setup.

Of course, you need to know how much *space* these partitions will require. The size of your Linux filesystems (containing the software itself) depends greatly on how much software you're installing and what distribution of Linux you are using. Hopefully, the documentation that came with your distribution will give you an approximation of the space requirements. A small Linux system can use 60 MB or less; a larger system anywhere from 500 MB to 2 GB, perhaps even more. Keep in mind that in addition to the space required by the software itself, you need to allocate extra space for user directories, room for future expansion, and so forth.

---

[*] This value applies to machines with Intel processors. On other architectures it can be both higher and lower.

If you use several partitions, you can use a rather small partition for the root directory. A partition of 128 MB should suffice. Use at least 30 to 50 MB more if you keep /var on the same partition, as most people do. On the other hand, you will probably want to have a largish /usr partition.

The size of your swap partition (should you elect to use one) depends on how much virtual RAM you require. A rule of thumb is to use a swap partition that measures twice the space of your physical RAM; for example, if you have 64 MB of physical RAM, a 128-MB swap partition should suffice. Of course, this is mere speculation; the actual amount of swap space you require depends on the software you will be running. If you have a great deal of physical RAM (say, 256 MB or more), you may not wish to use swap space at all.

Because of BIOS limitations, it is sometimes impossible to boot from partitions using cylinders numbered over 1023. Therefore, when setting aside space for Linux, keep in mind you may not want to use a partition in the over-1023 cylinder range for your Linux root filesystem. Linux can still *use* partitions with cylinders numbered over 1023, but you may not be able to *boot* Linux from such a partition. This advice may seem premature, but it is important to know when planning your drive layout, and today, many people have large disks with more than 1023 cylinders. There are also some newer tools that let you get around this restriction, but we would still advise against using these unless absolutely necessary.

If you must use a partition with cylinders numbered over 1023 for your Linux root filesystem, and other options do not work, you can always boot Linux from a floppy. This is not so bad, actually; it takes only a few seconds longer to boot from a floppy than from the hard drive.

Repartitioning Your Drives

In this section, we'll describe how to resize your current partitions (if any) to make space for Linux. If you are installing Linux on a "clean" hard drive, skip this section and proceed to Chapter 3.

The usual way to resize an existing partition is to delete it (thus destroying all data on that partition) and re-create it. Before repartitioning your drives, *back up your system*. After resizing the partitions, you can reinstall your original software from the backup. However, several programs are available for Windows that resize partitions nondestructively. One of these is known as FIPS and can be found on many Linux FTP sites.

Also, keep in mind that because you'll be shrinking your original partitions, you may not have space to reinstall everything. In this case, you need to delete enough unwanted software to allow the rest to fit on the smaller partitions.

The program used to create and assign partitions is known as *fdisk*. Each operating system has its own analog of this program; for example, under Windows, it is invoked with the FDISK command. You should consult your documentation for whatever operating systems you are currently running for information on repartitioning. Here, we'll discuss how to resize partitions for Windows using *fdisk*, but this information should be easily extrapolated to other operating systems.

The *fdisk* program (on any operating system) is responsible for reading the partition table on a given drive and manipulating it to add or delete partitions. However, some versions of *fdisk* do more than this, such as adding information to the beginning of a new partition to make it usable by a certain operating system. For this reason, you should usually only create partitions for an operating system with the version of *fdisk* that comes with it. You can't create Windows partitions with Linux *fdisk*; partitions created in this way can't be used correctly by Windows. (Actually, if you really know what you are doing, you might be lucky in creating Windows partitions from Linux, but we would not advise doing so.) Similarly, Windows *fdisk* may not be able to recognize Linux partitions. As long as you have a version of *fdisk* for each operating system you use, you should be fine. (Note that not all systems name this program *fdisk*; some refer to it as a "disk manager" or "volume manager.")

Later, in the section "Creating Linux Partitions" in Chapter 3, we describe how to create new Linux partitions, but for now we are concerned with resizing your current ones.

 Consult the documentation for your current operating systems before repartitioning your drive. This section is meant to be a general overview of the process; there are many subtleties we do not cover here. You can lose all the software on your system if you do not repartition the drive correctly.

Let's say that you have a single hard drive on your system, currently devoted entirely to Windows. Hence, your drive consists of a single Windows partition, commonly known as C:. Because this repartitioning method will destroy the data on that partition, you need to create a bootable Windows "system disk," which contains everything necessary to run *fdisk* and restore the software from backup after the repartitioning is complete.

In many cases, you can use the Windows installation disks for this purpose. However, if you need to create your own system disk, format a floppy with the command:

    FORMAT /s A:

Copy onto this floppy all necessary Windows utilities (usually most of the software in the directory \DOS on your drive), as well as the programs *FORMAT.COM* and *FDISK.EXE*. You should now be able to boot this floppy and run the command:

    FDISK C:

to start up *fdisk*.

Use of *fdisk* should be self-explanatory, but consult the Windows documentation for details. When you start *fdisk*, use the menu option to display the partition table, and write down the information displayed there. It is important to keep a record of your original setup in case you want to back out of the Linux installation.

To delete an existing partition, choose the FDISK menu option "Delete an MS-DOS Partition or Logical DOS Drive." Specify the type of partition you wish to delete (primary, extended, or logical) and the number of the partition. Verify all the warnings. Poof!

To create a new (smaller) partition for Windows, choose the FDISK option "Create an MS-DOS Partition or Logical DOS Drive." Specify the type of partition (primary, extended, or logical) and the size of the partition to create (specified in megabytes). *fdisk* should create the partition, and you're ready to roll.

After you're done using *fdisk*, exit the program and reformat any new partitions. For example, if you resized the first DOS partition on your drive (C:), you should run the command:

```
FORMAT /s C:
```

You may now reinstall your original software from backup.

## CHAPTER 3

Installation and Initial Configuration

At this point, you should have your Linux distribution and have disk space set aside for Linux. In this chapter, we present a general overview of the installation process. Each distribution has its own installation instructions, but armed with the concepts presented here, you should be able to feel your way through any installation. Appendix A, lists sources of information for installation instructions and other help, if you're at a total loss.

Different Linux distributions store files in different locations, which can make it hard to describe how to administer Linux. For instance, the same files may be found on Red Hat, SuSE, and Debian systems, but they may be under the */etc* directory on one system and the */sbin* directory on another. Gradually, the vendors are standardizing the set of locations listed in a document called the Filesystem Hierarchy Standard, but in this book we'll just try to deal with lagging discrepancies by listing the locations of the most important files in the version of each major distribution that we checked.

Installing the Linux Software

After resizing your existing partitions to make space for Linux, you are ready to install the software. Here is a brief overview of the procedure:

1. Boot the Linux installation medium.
2. Run *fdisk* under Linux to create Linux partitions.
3. Run *mke2fs* and *mkswap* to create Linux filesystems and swap space. (You may need to use a different command than *mke2fs* if you want to install a different filesystem; available filesystems are listed in "Filesystem Types" in Chapter 6.)
4. Install the Linux software and configure it.
5. Finally, either install the LILO bootloader on your hard drive, or create a boot floppy in order to boot your new Linux system.

As we have said, most of these steps are likely to be automated for you by the installation procedure (or at least integrated into it), depending on the distribution of Linux you are using. Please consult your distribution's documentation for specific instructions.

Booting Linux

The first step is to boot the Linux installation medium. In most cases, this is either a boot floppy, which contains a small Linux system, or a bootable CD-ROM. Upon booting the floppy or the CD-ROM, you are presented with an installation menu of some kind that leads you through the steps of installing the software. On other distributions, you are presented with a login prompt when booting this floppy. Here, you usually log in as root or install to begin the installation process.

The documentation that comes with your particular distribution will explain what is necessary to boot Linux from the installation medium.

Most distributions of Linux use a boot floppy that allows you to enter hardware parameters at a boot prompt to force hardware detection of various devices. For example, if your SCSI controller is not detected when booting the floppy, you will need to reboot and specify the hardware parameters (such as I/O address and IRQ) at the boot prompt. Likewise, IBM PS/1, older ThinkPad, and ValuePoint machines do not store drive geometry in the CMOS (the battery-backed up memory that stores vital information while your computer is turned off), so you must specify it at boot time.

The boot prompt is often displayed automatically when booting the boot floppy or CD-ROM. This is the case for the Red Hat distribution. With distributions that do not show the prompt by default, you need to hold down the Shift or Control key or press the Scroll Lock key while booting the floppy or CD-ROM if you want to enter something at the boot prompt. If successful, you should see the prompt:

    boot:

and possibly other messages. What you are seeing here is a boot prompt presented by LILO (the LInux LOader), a program used to boot the Linux operating system and specify hardware-detection parameters at boot time. After you have installed Linux, you may wish to install LILO on your hard drive, which allows you to select between Linux and other operating systems (such as Windows) when the system is booted.

At this point you have several options. You can press the Enter key to simply boot Linux from the floppy with no special parameters. (You should try this first, and if installation seems to go well, you're all set. If all you have in terms of storage media is an IDE hard drive and CD-ROM, chances are high that you won't have to specify anything.) You can also wait until the installation proceeds. Because today's distributions set a timeout, the installation will only wait for a fixed time for you to enter something and then just continue booting. Thus, if you are unsure what to type, just type any key (like the space key), which will cancel the timeout and give you all the time you want.

If you cannot boot Linux properly without specifying parameters, you may have to specify hardware-detection parameters at this boot prompt, to force the system to properly identify the hardware installed in your system. But in general, the rule is: use the defaults first and see whether that works. Only if it doesn't, should you start to fiddle with the settings. Chances are you will never have to do this, however.

If you don't want to try any hardware-detection parameters now, just press Enter at the boot prompt. Watch the messages as the system boots. If you have an SCSI controller, for example, you should see a listing of the SCSI hosts detected. If you see the message:

```
SCSI: 0 hosts
```

your SCSI controller was not detected, and you will have to use the hardware detection procedure we'll describe in a moment.

Most new distributions often follow a different path of choosing hardware. They come with a minimal kernel on the boot disk and then load so-called *kernel modules* from either a second floppy disk or a CD-ROM. In this case, you will probably be dropped into some menu where you can select additional modules to be probed. Even specifying modules is largely automated: you just ask the installation program to probe for SCSI adapters and see whether yours is found. The same goes for Ethernet cards and other devices that are needed for the installation process. Devices that are not needed during the installation, such as sound boards, are unlikely to be detected at this point of the installation. You will probably be given the option to configure them later. Again, try to swim with the stream and just accept the defaults and see whether this works.

If the automated hardware detection procedures do not work for you (which normally is the case only if you have very old, very new, or very unusual hardware), you will have to help Linux a bit by forcing hardware detection.

To force hardware detection, you must enter the appropriate parameters at the boot prompt, using the following syntax:

```
linux parameters
```

There are many such parameters, some of which are listed later in this section. We don't expect you to understand what all these parameters mean or are used for; rather, you should be able to determine which of these hardware options corresponds to your own system. We are presenting a more comprehensive list here, in one place, as you may find them useful later on.

For example, if you have an AHA152x-based SCSI controller, and you know that under Windows you must configure the board for a particular I/O address and

IRQ, you can use the corresponding option (aha152x=) here. In fact, many of these boot options are simply unnecessary for initial installation.

One other piece of advice: write down and remember the boot options you use to get your system running. After you have installed Linux, you'll need to use the same boot options in order for your hardware to be properly detected each time you boot. If you install the LILO loader on your hard drive, you can configure it to automatically use a certain set of boot options so that you won't have to type them each time.

nosmp
> Tells a kernel configured for symmetric multiprocessing (multiple CPUs) to work like a single-processor kernel.

root=*device*
> Specifies the device to use as the root filesystem when booting the system. For initial installation this should not be used; after installation of the system you can use this to override the default location of your Linux root filesystem.

ro
> Mounts the root filesystem in a read-only state; used for system maintenance.

lock
> Saves the boot parameters for the future so that you do not have to enter them each time you boot the system.

rw
> Mounts the root filesystem in a read-write state; used for system maintenance.

debug
> Forces the kernel to print verbose debugging messages to the console as the system runs.

ramdisk=*kilobytes*
> Tells the system to reserve the given number of kilobytes for a ramdisk. This is often used by installation boot floppies that load an entire filesystem image into memory. You don't want to use this option for initial installation, but if you want to experiment with ramdisks at a later date, this is the option to use.

mem=*size*
> The system BIOS in most PCs only reports up to 64 MB of installed RAM; Linux uses this information to determine the amount of installed memory. If you have more than 64 MB and use an older (pre-2.2) kernel, you may need to use this parameter to allow the rest of your system memory to be used. The *size* parameter can be a number with k or M appended; for example, mem=96M would specify a system with 96 MB of RAM installed. Note that if you tell the system it has more memory than is actually installed, Bad Things will eventually happen.

hd=*cylinders,heads,sectors*
> Specifies the hard drive geometry for IDE and standard ST-506 drives (not SCSI drives). Required for systems such as the IBM PS/1, ValuePoint, and older

ThinkPads. For example, if your drive has 683 cylinders, 16 heads, and 32 sectors per track, use:

```
hd=683,16,32
```

This option can also be used as hda=, hdb=, hdc=, or hdd= to specify the geometry for a particular IDE drive. Note that use of the hd= option may be necessary on some older systems if you are using a large IDE drive (over 1024 cylinders). If Linux has problems recognizing the geometry of your drive (you'll find out when you try to partition the disk for Linux), try using this option.

max_scsi_luns=*num*

If *num* is 1, the system won't probe for SCSI devices that have a Logical Unit Number (LUN) other than zero. This parameter is required for some poorly designed SCSI devices that lock up when probed at non-zero LUNs. Note that this has nothing to do with the SCSI device ID; LUNs allow the addressing of multiple logical units or subdevices within a single SCSI device, such as a disk drive.

aha152x=*iobase,irq,scsi-id,reconnect,parity*

Specifies parameters for Adaptec AHA151x, AHA152x, AIC6260, AIC6230, and SB16-SCSI interfaces. *iobase* must be specified in hexadecimal, as in 0x340. All arguments except *iobase* are optional.

aha1542=*iobase*

Specifies the I/O base (in hex) for Adaptec AHA154x SCSI interfaces.

aic7xxx=*extended,no-reset*

Specifies parameters for Adaptec AHA274x, AHA284x, and AIC7xxx SCSI interfaces. A non-zero value for *extended* indicates that extended translation for large disks is enabled. If *no-reset* is non-zero, the driver will not reset the SCSI bus when configuring the adapter at boot time.

buslogic=*iobase*

Specifies the I/O base (in hex) for Buslogic SCSI interfaces.

tmc8xx=*mem-base,irq*

Specifies the base of the memory-mapped I/O region (in hex) and IRQ for Future Domain TMC-8xx and TMC-950 SCSI interfaces.

pas16=*iobase,irq*

Specifies the I/O base (in hex) and IRQ for Pro Audio Spectrum SCSI interfaces.

st0x=*mem-base,irq*

Specifies the base of the memory-mapped I/O region (in hex) and IRQ for Seagate ST-0x SCSI interfaces.

t128=*mem-base,irq*

Specifies the base of the memory-mapped I/O region (in hex) and IRQ for Trantor T128 SCSI interfaces.

aztcd=*iobase*

Specifies the I/O base (in hex) for Aztech CD-ROM interfaces.

`cdu31a=`*iobase,irq,pas*

Specifies the I/O base (in hex) and IRQ for CDU-31A and CDU-33A Sony CD-ROM interfaces. These options are used on some Pro Audio Spectrum sound cards, as well as boards from Sony. The *irq* and *pas* parameters are optional. If the board does not support interrupts, *irq* is 0 (as is the case with some boards). The only valid value for the *pas* option is `PAS`, indicating that a Pro Audio Spectrum card is being used.

`soncd535=`*iobase,irq*

Specifies the I/O base (in hex) and IRQ (optional) for Sony CDU-535 interfaces.

`gscd=`*iobase*

Specifies I/O base (in hex) for GoldStar CD-ROM interfaces.

`mcd=`*iobase,irq*

Specifies the I/O base (in hex) and IRQ (optional) for Mitsumi standard CD-ROM interfaces.

`optcd=`*iobase*

Specifies the I/O base (in hex) for Optics Storage Interface CD-ROM interfaces.

`cm206=`*iobase,irq*

Specifies the I/O base (in hex) and IRQ for Philips CM206 CD-ROM interfaces.

`sjcd=`*iobase,irq,dma*

Specifies the I/O base (in hex), IRQ, and Direct Memory Access (DMA) channel for Sanyo CD-ROM interfaces. The *irq* and *dma* parameters are optional.

`sbpcd=`*iobase,type*

Specifies the I/O base (in hex) for SoundBlaster Pro and compatible CD-ROM interfaces. The *type* parameter must be `SoundBlaster`, `LaserMate`, or `SPEA`, based on what type of board you have. Note that this option specifies parameters *only* for the CD-ROM interface, not for the sound hardware on the board. This applies to very old, pre-ATAPI CD-ROM drives, but most users do not need to be concerned about this.

`ether=`*irq,iobase,parameters…*

Specifies the IRQ and I/O base for Ethernet cards. If you are having problems detecting your Ethernet card and wish to use it for installation (e.g., via FTP or NFS), check out the Linux Ethernet HOWTO that describes the various boot options for Ethernet cards in much detail. There are too many to detail here.

`floppy=thinkpad`

Tells the floppy driver that you have an older ThinkPad; necessary for floppy access on older ThinkPad systems.

`floppy=0,thinkpad`

Tells the floppy driver that you do not have a ThinkPad, in case it's confused.

`bmouse=`*`irq`*

Specifies IRQ for busmouse[*] interface.

`msmouse=`*`irq`*

Specifies IRQ for Microsoft busmouse interface.

Quite a few other options are available; the previous options are generally necessary for normal use of your system. (For example, we have left out the many parameters available for sound card drivers; we urge you to read the appropriate HOWTO documents if you have a life-threatening situation involving use of your sound card.)

For each of these, you must enter *linux* followed by the parameters you wish to use.

If you have questions about these boot-time options, read the Linux Bootprompt HOWTO, Linux SCSI HOWTO, and Linux CD-ROM HOWTO. These three documents should be available on any Linux FTP site (as well as most Linux CD-ROMs) and describe the LILO boot arguments in more detail.

Drives and Partitions Under Linux

Many distributions require you to create Linux partitions by hand using the *fdisk* program. Others may automatically create partitions for you. Either way, you should know the following information about Linux partitions and device names. (This information applies only to Intel and Alpha systems booted from AlphaBIOS; other systems, such PowerPC, SPARC, and m68k, do not have logical and extended partitions.)

Drives and partitions under Linux are given different names from their counterparts under other operating systems. Under Windows, floppy drives are referred to as A: and B:, while hard-drive partitions are named C:, D:, and so on. Under Linux, the naming convention is quite different.

Device drivers, found in the directory */dev*, are used to communicate with devices on your system (such as hard drives, mice, and so on). For example, if you have a mouse on your system, you might access it through the driver */dev/mouse*. Floppy drives, hard drives, and individual partitions are all given individual device drivers of their own. Don't worry about the device-driver interface for now; it is important only to understand how the various devices are named in order to use them. The section "Device Files" in Chapter 6 talks more about devices.

Table 3-1 lists the names of these various device drivers where multiple names can be created with increasing numbers (0, 1, etc.). One or two are shown in the table as examples.

---

[*] A busmouse is a mouse attached to the system bus, instead of a serial port or a PS/2-style mouse port.

Table 3-1. Linux partition names

Device	Name
First floppy (A:)	/dev/fd0
Second floppy (B:)	/dev/fd1
First hard drive (entire drive) or CD-ROM	/dev/hda
First hard drive, primary partition 1	/dev/hda1
First hard drive, primary partition 2	/dev/hda2
First hard drive, primary partition 3	/dev/hda3
First hard drive, primary partition 4	/dev/hda4
First hard drive, logical partition 1	/dev/hda5
First hard drive, logical partition 2 ⋮	/dev/hda6
Second hard drive (entire drive) or CD-ROM	/dev/hdb
Second hard drive, primary partition 1 ⋮	/dev/hdb1
First SCSI hard drive (entire drive)	/dev/sda
First SCSI hard drive, primary partition 1 ⋮	/dev/sda1
Second SCSI hard drive (entire drive)	/dev/sdb
Second SCSI hard drive, primary partition 1 ⋮	/dev/sdb1
First SCSI CD-ROM drive	/dev/scd0
Second SCSI CD-ROM drive ⋮	/dev/scd1
First generic SCSI device (such as scanners, CDR writers, etc.). Note that newer systems use numbers instead of letters (i.e., /dev/sg0 instead of /dev/sga).	/dev/sga
Second generic SCSI device ⋮	/dev/sgb

A few notes about this table: */dev/fd0* corresponds to the first floppy drive (A: under Windows), and */dev/fd1* corresponds to the second floppy (B:).

Also, SCSI hard drives are named differently from other drives. IDE, MFM, and RLL drives are accessed through the devices */dev/hda*, */dev/hdb*, and so on. The individual partitions on the drive */dev/hda* are */dev/hda1*, */dev/hda2*, and so on. This also applies to ATAPI and IDE CD-ROM drives. However, SCSI drives are named */dev/sda*, */dev/sdb*, and so on, with partition names such as */dev/sda1* and */dev/sda2*.

Most systems, of course, do not have four primary partitions. But the names */dev/hda1* through */dev/hda4* are still reserved for these partitions; they cannot be used to name logical partitions.

Here's an example. Let's say you have a single IDE hard drive, with three primary partitions. The first two are set aside for Windows, and the third is an extended partition that contains two logical partitions, both for use by Linux. The devices referring to these partitions would be:

Device	Name
First Windows partition (C:)	*/dev/hda1*
Second Windows partition (D:)	*/dev/hda2*
Extended partition	*/dev/hda3*
First Linux logical partition	*/dev/hda5*
Second Linux logical partition	*/dev/hda6*

Note that */dev/hda4* is skipped; it corresponds to the fourth primary partition, which we don't have in this example. Logical partitions are named consecutively starting with */dev/hda5*.

Creating Linux Partitions

Now you are ready to create Linux partitions with the *fdisk* command. In general, you need to create at least one partition for the Linux software itself and another partition for swap space.

Here we are describing the basic text-mode usage of *fdisk,* which should be available with all distributions. Many distributions nowadays provide a more user-friendly interface to *fdisk*. While those are usually not as flexible as plain *fdisk*, they can help you make the right choices more easily. Whatever tool you use, this section is helpful for understanding the underlying concepts. The tools all do more or less the same things in the end; some simply have more sugar-coating than others. You can also make use of the information presented here for fixing or checking something that you suspect didn't go right with the graphical tool.

After booting the installation medium, run *fdisk* by typing:

    fdisk *drive*

where *drive* is the Linux device name of the drive to which you plan to add partitions (see Table 3-1). For instance, if you want to run *fdisk* on the first SCSI disk in your system, use the command:

    # fdisk /dev/sda

/dev/hda (the first IDE drive) is the default if you don't specify one.

If you are creating Linux partitions on more than one drive, run *fdisk* once for each drive:

```
# fdisk /dev/hda

Command (m for help):
```

Here *fdisk* is waiting for a command; you can type m to get a list of options:

```
Command (m for help): m
Command action
   a   toggle a bootable flag
   d   delete a partition
   l   list known partition types
   m   print this menu
   n   add a new partition
   p   print the partition table
   q   quit without saving changes
   t   change a partition's system id
   u   change display/entry units
   v   verify the partition table
   w   write table to disk and exit
   x   extra functionality (experts only)

Command (m for help):
```

The n command is used to create a new partition. Most other options you won't need to worry about. To quit *fdisk* without saving any changes, use the q command. To quit *fdisk* and write the changes to the partition table to disk, use the w command. This is worth repeating: so long as you quit with q without writing, you can mess around as much as you want with *fdisk* without risking harm to your data. Only when you type w can you cause potential disaster to your data if you do something wrong.

The first thing you should do is display your current partition table and write the information down for later reference. Use the p command to see the information. It is a good idea to copy the information to your notebook after each change you have made to the partition table. If, for some reason, your partition table is damaged, you will not access any data on your hard disk any longer, even though the data itself is still there. But by using your notes, you might be able to restore the partition table and get your data back in many cases by running *fdisk* again and deleting and re-creating the partitions with the parameters you previously wrote down. Don't forget to save the restored partition table when you are done.

Here is an example of a printed partition table, where blocks, sectors, and cylinders are units into which a hard disk is organized:

```
Command (m for help): p

Disk /dev/hda: 16 heads, 38 sectors, 683 cylinders
```

```
Units = cylinders of 608 * 512 bytes
   Device Boot  Begin  Start    End  Blocks   Id  System
/dev/hda1    *      1      1    203  61693     6  DOS 16-bit >=32M

Command (m for help):
```

In this example, we have a single Windows partition on */dev/hda1*, which is 61693 blocks (about 60 MB).* This partition starts at cylinder number 1 and ends on cylinder 203. We have a total of 683 cylinders in this disk; so there are 480 cylinders left on which to create Linux partitions.

To create a new partition, use the n command. In this example, we'll create two primary partitions (*/dev/hda2* and */dev/hda3*) for Linux:

```
Command (m for help): n
Command action
   e   extended
   p   primary partition (1-4)
   p
```

Here, *fdisk* is asking which type of the partition to create: extended or primary. In our example, we're creating only primary partitions, so we choose p:

```
Partition number (1-4):
```

fdisk will then ask for the number of the partition to create; because partition 1 is already used, our first Linux partition will be number 2:

```
Partition number (1-4): 2
First cylinder (204-683):
```

Now, we enter the starting cylinder number of the partition. Because cylinders 204 through 683 are unused, we'll use the first available one (numbered 204). There's no reason to leave empty space between partitions:

```
First cylinder (204-683): 204
Last cylinder or +size or +sizeM or +sizeK (204-683):
```

fdisk is asking for the size of the partition we want to create. We can either specify an ending cylinder number, or a size in bytes, kilobytes, or megabytes. Because we want our partition to be 80 MB in size, we specify +80M. When specifying a partition size in this way, *fdisk* will round the actual partition size to the nearest number of cylinders:

```
Last cylinder or +size or +sizeM or +sizeK (204-683): +80M
```

If you see a warning message such as this, it can be ignored. *fdisk* prints the warning because it's an older program and dates back before the time that Linux partitions were allowed to be larger than 64 MB.

---

* A block, under Linux, is 1024 bytes.

Now we're ready to create our second Linux partition. For sake of demonstration, we'll create it with a size of 10 MB:

```
Command (m for help): n
Command action
   e   extended
   p   primary partition (1-4)
p
Partition number (1-4): 3
First cylinder (474-683): 474
Last cylinder or +size or +sizeM or +sizeK (474-683): +10M
```

At last, we'll display the partition table. Again, write down all this information—especially the block sizes of your new partitions. You'll need to know the sizes of the partitions when creating filesystems. Also, verify that none of your partitions overlaps:

```
Command (m for help): p

Disk /dev/hda: 16 heads, 38 sectors, 683 cylinders
Units = cylinders of 608 * 512 bytes
   Device Boot   Begin   Start    End  Blocks   Id  System
/dev/hda1    *       1       1    203   61693    6  DOS 16-bit >=32M
/dev/hda2          204     204    473   82080   83  Linux native
/dev/hda3          474     474    507   10336   83  Linux native
```

As you can see, */dev/hda2* is now a partition of size 82080 blocks (which corresponds to about 80 MB), and */dev/hda3* is 10336 blocks (about 10 MB).

Note that most distributions require you to use the t command in *fdisk* to change the type of the swap partition to "Linux swap," which is numbered 82. You can use the L command to print a list of known partition type codes, and then use the t command to set the type of the swap partition to that which corresponds to "Linux swap."

This way the installation software will be able to automatically find your swap partitions based on type. If the installation software doesn't seem to recognize your swap partition, you might want to rerun *fdisk* and use the t command on the partition in question.

In the previous example, the remaining cylinders on the disk (numbered 508 to 683) are unused. You may wish to leave unused space on the disk, in case you want to create additional partitions later.

Finally, we use the w command to write the changes to disk and exit *fdisk*:

```
Command (m for help): w
#
```

Keep in mind that none of the changes you make while running *fdisk* takes effect until you give the w command, so you can toy with different configurations and save them when you're done. Also, if you want to quit *fdisk* at any time without saving the changes, use the q command. Remember that you shouldn't modify partitions for operating systems other than Linux with the Linux *fdisk* program.

You may not be able to boot Linux from a partition using cylinders numbered over 1023. Therefore, you should try to create your Linux root partition within the sub-1024 cylinder range, which is almost always possible (e.g., by creating a small root partition in the sub-1024 cylinder range). If, for some reason, you cannot or do not want to do this, you can simply boot Linux from floppy.

Some Linux distributions require you to reboot the system after running *fdisk* to allow the changes to the partition table to take effect before installing the software. Newer versions of *fdisk* automatically update the partition information in the kernel, so rebooting isn't necessary. To be on the safe side, after running *fdisk* you should reboot from the installation medium before proceeding.

Creating Swap Space

If you are planning to use a swap partition for virtual RAM, you're ready to prepare it.[*] In the section "Managing Swap Space" in Chapter 6, we discuss the preparation of a swap file, in case you don't want to use an individual partition.

Many distributions require you to create and activate swap space before installing the software. If you have a small amount of physical RAM, the installation procedure may not be successful unless you have some amount of swap space enabled.

The command used to prepare a swap partition is *mkswap*, and it takes the following form:

```
mkswap -c partition
```

where *partition* is the name of the swap partition. For example, if your swap partition is */dev/hda3*, use the command:

```
# mkswap -c /dev/hda3
```

With older versions of *mkswap*, you had to specify the size of the partition, which was dangerous, as one typo could destroy your disk logically.

The -c option tells *mkswap* to check for bad blocks on the partition when creating the swap space. Bad blocks are spots on the magnetic medium that do not hold the data correctly. This occurs only rarely with today's hard disks, but if it does occur, and you do not know about it, it can cause you endless trouble. Always use the -c option to have *mkswap* check for bad blocks. It will exclude them from being used automatically.

---

[*] Again, some distributions of Linux prepare the swap space for you automatically, or via an installation menu option.

If you are using multiple swap partitions, you need to execute the appropriate *mkswap* command for each partition.

After formatting the swap space, you need to enable it for use by the system. Usually, the system automatically enables swap space at boot time. However, because you have not yet installed the Linux software, you need to enable it by hand.

The command to enable swap space is *swapon*, and it takes the following form:

```
swapon partition
```

After the *mkswap* command shown, we use the following command to enable the swap space on */dev/hda3*:

```
# swapon /dev/hda3
```

Creating the Filesystems

Before you can use your Linux partitions to store files, you must create filesystems on them. Creating a filesystem is analogous to formatting a partition under Windows or other operating systems. We discussed filesystems briefly in the section "Linux Partition Requirements" in Chapter 2.

Several types of filesystems are available for Linux. Each filesystem type has its own format and set of characteristics (such as filename length, maximum file size, and so on). Linux also supports several "third-party" filesystem types, such as the Windows filesystem.

The most commonly used filesystem type is the *Second Extended Filesystem*, or *ext2fs*. The *ext2fs* is one of the most efficient and flexible filesystems; it allows filenames of up to 256 characters and filesystem sizes of up to 32 terabytes. In the section "Filesystem Types" in Chapter 6, we discuss the various filesystem types available for Linux. Initially, however, we suggest you use the *ext2fs* filesystem.

To create an *ext2fs* filesystem, use the command:

```
mke2fs -c partition
```

where *partition* is the name of the partition. For example, to create a filesystem on */dev/hda2*, use the command:

```
# mke2fs -c /dev/hda2
```

If you're using multiple filesystems for Linux, you need to use the appropriate *mke2fs* command for each filesystem.

If you have encountered any problems at this point, see the section "Running into Trouble" later in this chapter.

Installing the Software

Finally, you are ready to install the software on your system. Every distribution has a different mechanism for doing this. Many distributions have a self-contained program that steps you through the installation. On other distributions, you have to *mount* your filesystems in a certain subdirectory (such as */mnt*) and copy the software to them by hand. On CD-ROM distributions, you may be given the option to install a portion of the software on your hard drive and leave most of the software on the CD-ROM. This is often called a "live filesystem." Such a live filesystem is convenient for trying out Linux before you make a commitment to install everything on your disk.

Some distributions offer several different ways to install the software. For example, you may be able to install the software directly from a Windows partition on your hard drive instead of from floppies. Or you may be able to install over a TCP/IP network via FTP or NFS. See your distribution's documentation for details.

For example, the Slackware distribution requires you to do the following:

1. Create partitions with *fdisk*.
2. Optionally create swap space with *mkswap* and *swapon* (if you have 16 MB or less of RAM).
3. Run the *setup* program to install the software. *setup* leads you through a self-explanatory menu system.

The exact method used to install the Linux software differs greatly with each distribution.

You might be overwhelmed by the choice of software to install. Modern Linux distributions can easily contain a thousand or more packages spread over several CD-ROMs. There are basically three methods for selecting the software package:

Selection by task
> This is the easiest means of selection for beginners. You don't have to think about whether you need a certain package. You just pick whether your Linux computer should act as a workstation, a development machine, or a network router, and the installation program will pick the appropriate packages for you. In all cases, you can then either refine the selection by hand or come back to the installation program later.

Selection of individual packages by series
> With this selection mechanism, all the packages are grouped into series like "Networking," "Development," or "Graphics." You can go through all the series and pick the individual packages there. This requires more decisions than if you choose selection by task, because you have to decide whether you need each package; however, you can skip an entire series when you are sure that you are not interested in the functions it offers.

Selection of individual packages sorted alphabetically

This method is useful only when you already know which packages you want to install; otherwise you won't see the forest for the trees.

Choosing one selection method does not exclude the use of the others. Most distributions offer two or more of the aforementioned selection mechanisms.

It might still be difficult to decide which package to pick. Good distributions show a short description of each package on screen to make it easier for you to select the correct ones, but if you are still unsure, our advice is this: when in doubt, leave it out! You can always go back and add packages later.

Modern distributions have a very nifty feature, called *dependency tracking*. Some packages work only when some other packages are installed (e.g., a graphics viewer might need special graphics libraries to import files). With dependency tracking, the installation program can inform you about those dependencies and will let you automatically select the package you want along with all the ones it depends on. Unless you are very sure about what you are doing, you should always accept this offer, or the package might not work afterward.

Installation programs can help you make your selection and avoid mistakes in other ways. For example, the installation program might refuse to start the installation when you deselect a package that is absolutely crucial for even the most minimal system to boot (like the basic directory structure). Or, it might check for mutual exclusions, such as cases in which you can only have one package or the other, but not both.

Some distributions, such as SuSE, come with a large book that, among other things, lists all the packages together with short descriptions. It might be a good idea to at least skim those descriptions to see what's in store for you, or you might be surprised when you select the packages and are offered the 25th text editor.

Creating the Boot Floppy or Installing LILO

Every distribution provides some means of booting your new Linux system after you have installed the software. In many cases, the installation procedure suggests you create a boot floppy, which contains a Linux kernel configured to use your newly created root filesystem. In order to boot Linux, you could boot from this floppy; control is transferred to your hard drive after you boot. On other distributions, this boot floppy is the installation floppy itself.

Many distributions give you the option of installing LILO on your hard drive. LILO is a program that resides on your drive's master boot record. It boots a number of operating systems, including Windows and Linux, and allows you to select to which boot at startup time.

In order for LILO to be installed successfully, it needs to know a good deal of information about your drive configuration: for example, which partitions contain which operating systems, how to boot each operating system, and so on. Many distributions, when installing LILO, attempt to "guess" at the appropriate parameters for your configuration. Occasionally, the automated LILO installation provided by some distributions can fail and leave your master boot record in shambles (however it's very doubtful that any damage to the actual data on your hard drive will take place). In particular, if you use OS/2's Boot Manager, you should *not* install LILO using the automated procedure; there are special instructions for using LILO with the Boot Manager, which will be covered in Chapter 5.

In many cases, it is best to use a boot floppy until you have a chance to configure LILO yourself, by hand. If you're exceptionally trusting, though, you can go ahead with the automated LILO installation if it is provided with your distribution.

In the section "Using LILO" in Chapter 5, we'll cover in detail how to configure and install LILO for your particular setup.

 There are also other boot loaders besides LILO, including the Grand Unified BootLoader (GRUB). Most distributions use LILO, though.

If everything goes well, congratulations! You have just installed Linux on your system. Go have a cup of tea or something; you deserve it.

In case you ran into trouble, the section "Running into Trouble," later in this chapter, describes the most common sticking points for Linux installations, and how to get around them.

Additional Installation Procedures

Some distributions of Linux provide a number of additional installation procedures, allowing you to configure various software packages, such as TCP/IP networking, the X Window System, and so on. If you are provided with these configuration options during installation, you may wish to read ahead in this book for more information on how to configure this software. Otherwise, you should put off these installation procedures until you have a complete understanding of how to configure the software.

It's up to you; if all else fails, just go with the flow and see what happens. It's doubtful that anything you do incorrectly now cannot be undone in the future (knock on wood).

Post-Installation Procedures

After you have completed installing the Linux software, you should be able to reboot the system, log in as root, and begin exploring the system. (Each distribution has a different method for doing this; follow the instructions given by the distribution.)

Before you strike out on your own, however, there are some tasks you should do now that may save you a lot of grief later. Some of these tasks are trivial if you have the right hardware and Linux distribution; others may involve a little research on your part, and you may decide to postpone them.

Creating a User Account

In order to start using your system, you need to create a user account for yourself. Eventually, if you plan to have other users on your system, you'll create user accounts for them as well. But before you begin to explore you need at least one account.

Why is this? Every Linux system has several preinstalled accounts, such as root. The root account, however, is intended exclusively for administrative purposes. As root you have all kinds of privileges and can access all files on your system.

However, using root can be dangerous, especially if you're new to Linux. Because there are no restrictions on what root can do, it's all too easy to mistype a command, inadvertently delete files, damage your filesystem, and so on. You should log in as root only when you need to perform system administration tasks, such as fixing configuration files, installing new software, and so on. See the section "Maintaining the System" in Chapter 5 for details.*

For normal usage, you should create a standard user account. Unix systems have built-in security that prevents users from deleting other users' files and corrupting important resources, such as system configuration files. As a regular user, you'll be protecting yourself from your own mistakes. This is especially true for users who don't have Unix system administration experience.

Many Linux distributions provide tools for creating new accounts. These programs are usually called *useradd* or *adduser*. As root, invoking one of these commands should present you with a usage summary for the command, and creating a new account should be fairly self-explanatory.

Most modern distributions provide a generic system administration tool for various tasks, one of which is creating a new user account.

---

* A side note: on a Windows 95/98/ME system, the user is always the equivalent to a root user, whether that power is needed or not.

Again, other distributions, such as SuSE Linux, Red Hat Linux, or Caldera Open Linux, integrate system installation and system administration in one tool—e.g., *yast* or *yast2* on SuSE Linux, and *lisa* on Caldera Open Linux.

If all else fails, you can create an account by hand. Usually, all that is required to create an account is:

1. Edit the file */etc/passwd* to add the new user. (Doing this with *vipw*—instead of editing the file directly—will protect you against concurrent changes of the password file, but *vipw* is not available on all distributions.)

2. Optionally edit the file */etc/shadow* to specify "shadow password" attributes for the new user.

3. Create the user's home directory.

4. Copy skeleton configuration files (such as *.bashrc*) to the new user's home directory. These can sometimes be found in the directory */etc/skel*.

We don't want to go into great detail here: the particulars of creating a new user account can be found in virtually every book on Unix system administration (see the Bibliography for suggested reading). We also talk about creating users in the section "Managing User Accounts" in Chapter 5. You should be able to find a tool that takes care of these details for you.

Keep in mind that to set or change the password on the new account, you use the *passwd* command. For example, to change the password for the user duck, issue the following command:

```
# passwd duck
```

This will prompt you to set or change the password for duck. If you execute the *passwd* command as root, it will not prompt you for the original password. In this way, if you have forgotten your old password, but can still log in as root, you can reset it.

Getting Online Help

Linux provides online help in the form of manual pages. Throughout this book, we'll be directing you to look at the manual pages for particular commands to get more information. Manual pages describe programs and applications on the system in detail, and it's important for you to learn how to access this online documentation in case you get into a bind.

To get online help for a particular command, use the *man* command. For example, to get information on the *passwd* command, type the following command:

```
$ man passwd
```

This should present you with the manual page for *passwd*.

Usually, manual pages are provided as an optional package with most distributions, so they won't be available unless you have opted to install them. However, we very strongly advise you to install the manual pages. You will feel lost many times without them.

In addition, certain manual pages may be missing or incomplete on your system. It depends on how complete your distribution is and how up-to-date the manual pages are.

Linux manual pages also document system calls, library functions, configuration file formats, and kernel internals. In the section "Manual Pages" in Chapter 4, we'll describe their use in more detail.

Besides traditional manual pages, there are also so-called Info pages. These can be read with the text editor Emacs, the command *info,* or one of many graphical info readers available.

Many distributions also provide documentation in HTML format that you can read with any web browser, such as Konqueror, as well as with Emacs.

Finally, there are documentation files that are simply plain text. You can read these with any text editor or simply with the command *more.*

If you cannot find documentation for a certain command, you can also try running it with either the *-h* or *--help* option. Most commands then provide a brief summary of their usage.

Editing /etc/fstab

In order to ensure that all your Linux filesystems will be available when you reboot the system, you may need to edit the file */etc/fstab*, which describes your filesystems. Many distributions automatically generate the */etc/fstab* file for you during installation, so all may be well. However, if you have additional filesystems that were not used during the installation process, you may need to add them to */etc/fstab* in order to make them available. Swap partitions should be included in */etc/fstab* as well.

In order to access a filesystem, it must be *mounted* on your system. Mounting a filesystem associates that filesystem with a particular directory. For example, the root filesystem is mounted on /, the */usr* filesystem on */usr*, and so on. (If you did not create a separate filesystem for */usr*, all files under */usr* will be stored on the root filesystem.)

We don't want to smother you with technical details here, but it is important to understand how to make your filesystems available before exploring the system. For more details on mounting filesystems, see the section "Mounting Filesystems" in Chapter 6, or any book on Unix system administration.

The root filesystem is automatically mounted on / when you boot Linux. However, your other filesystems must be mounted individually. Usually, this is accomplished with the command:

```
# mount -av
```

in one of the system startup files in */etc/rc.d* or wherever your distribution stores its configuration files. This tells the *mount* command to mount any filesystems listed in the file */etc/fstab*. Therefore, in order to have your filesystems mounted automatically at boot time, you need to include them in */etc/fstab*. (Of course, you could always mount the filesystems by hand, using the *mount* command after booting, but this is unnecessary work.)

Here is a sample */etc/fstab* file, shortened by omitting the last two parameters in each line, which are optional and not relevant to the discussion here. In this example, the root filesystem is on */dev/hda1*, the */home* filesystem is on */dev/hdb2*, and the swap partition is on */dev/hdb1*:

```
# /etc/fstab
# device        directory   type    options
#
/dev/hda1       /           ext2    defaults
/dev/hdb2       /home       ext2    defaults
/dev/hdb1       none        swap    sw
/proc           /proc       proc    defaults
```

The lines beginning with the "#" character are comments. Also, you'll notice an additional entry for */proc*. */proc* is a "virtual filesystem" used to gather process information by commands such as *ps*.

As you can see, */etc/fstab* consists of a series of lines. The first field of each line is the device name of the partition, such as */dev/hda1*. The second field is the *mount point*—the directory where the filesystem is mounted. The third field is the type; Linux *ext2fs* filesystems should use ext2 for this field. swap should be used for swap partitions. The fourth field is for mounting options. You should use defaults in this field for filesystems and sw for swap partitions.

Using this example as a model, you should be able to add entries for any filesystems not already listed in the */etc/fstab* file.

How do we add entries to the file? The easiest way is to edit the file, as root, using an editor such as *vi* or Emacs. We won't get into the use of text editors here. *vi* and Emacs are both covered at the beginning of Chapter 9.

After editing the file, you'll need to issue the command:

```
# /bin/mount -a
```

or reboot for the changes to take effect.

If you're stuck at this point, don't be alarmed. We suggest that Unix novices do some reading on basic Unix usage and system administration. We offer a lot of introductory material in upcoming chapters, and most of the remainder of this book is going to assume familiarity with these basics, so don't say we didn't warn you.

Shutting Down the System

You should never reboot or shut down your Linux system by pressing the reset switch or simply turning off the power. As with most Unix systems, Linux caches disk writes in memory. Therefore, if you suddenly reboot the system without shutting down "cleanly," you can corrupt the data on your drives. Note, however, that the "Vulcan nerve pinch" (pressing Ctrl-Alt-Delete in unison) is generally safe: the kernel traps the key sequence and passes it to the *init* process, which, in turn, initiates a clean shutdown of the system (or whatever it is configured to do in this case; see the section "init, inittab, and rc Files" in Chapter 5). Your system configuration might reserve the Ctrl-Alt-Delete for the system administrator so that normal users cannot shut down the network server that the whole department depends upon. To set permissions for this keystroke combination, create a file called */etc/shutdown.allow* that lists the names of all the users who are allowed to shut down the machine.

The easiest way to shut down the system is with the *shutdown* command. As an example, to shut down and reboot the system immediately, use the following command as root:

```
# shutdown -r now
```

This will cleanly reboot your system. The manual page for *shutdown* describes the other available command-line arguments. Instead of *now*, you can also specify when the system should be shut down. Most distributions also provide *halt*, which calls *shutdown now*. Some distributions also provide *poweroff,* which actually shuts down the computer and turns it off. Whether it works depends on the hardware (which must support APM), not on Linux.

Running into Trouble

Almost everyone runs into some kind of snag or hang-up when attempting to install Linux the first time. Most of the time, the problem is caused by a simple misunderstanding. Sometimes, however, it can be something more serious, such as an oversight by one of the developers or a bug.

This section will describe some of the most common installation problems and how to solve them. It also describes unexpected error messages that can pop up during installations that appear to be successful.

In general, the proper boot sequence is:

1. After booting from the LILO prompt, the system must load the kernel image from floppy. This may take several seconds; you know things are going well if the floppy drive light is still on.

2. While the kernel boots, SCSI devices must be probed for. If you have no SCSI devices installed, the system will "hang" for up to 15 seconds while the SCSI probe continues; this usually occurs after the line:

   ```
   lp_init: lp1 exists (0), using polling driver
   ```

   appears on your screen.

3. After the kernel is finished booting, control is transferred to the system bootup files on the floppy. Finally, you will be presented with a login prompt, or be dropped into an installation program. If you are presented with a login prompt such as:

   ```
   Linux login:
   ```

   you should then log in (usually as root or install—this varies with each distribution). After you enter the username, the system may pause for 20 seconds or more while the installation program or shell is being loaded from floppy. Again, the floppy drive light should be on. Don't assume the system is hung.

Problems with Booting the Installation Medium

When attempting to boot the installation medium for the first time, you may encounter a number of problems. Note that the following problems are *not* related to booting your newly installed Linux system. See the section "Problems after Installing Linux" for information on these kinds of pitfalls.

Floppy or medium error occurs when attempting to boot. The most popular cause for this kind of problem is a corrupt boot floppy. Either the floppy is physically damaged, in which case you should re-create the disk with a brand-new floppy, or the data on the floppy is bad, in which case you should verify that you downloaded and transferred the data to the floppy correctly. In many cases, simply re-creating the boot floppy will solve your problems. Retrace your steps and try again.

If you received your boot floppy from a mail-order vendor or some other distributor, instead of downloading and creating it yourself, contact the distributor and ask for a new boot floppy—but only after verifying that this is indeed the problem. This can, of course, be difficult, but if you get funny noises from your floppy drive or messages like *cannot read sector* or similar, chances are that your medium is damaged.

System "hangs" during boot or after booting. After the installation medium boots, you see a number of messages from the kernel itself, indicating which devices were detected and configured. After this, you are usually presented with a login prompt, allowing you to proceed with installation (some distributions instead drop you right into an installation program of some kind). The system may appear to "hang" during several of these steps. Be patient; loading software from floppy is very slow. In many cases, the system has not hung at all, but is merely taking a long time. Verify that there is no drive or system activity for at least several minutes before assuming that the system is hung.

Each activity listed at the beginning of this section may cause a delay that makes you think the system has stopped. However, it is possible that the system actually may "hang" while booting, which can be due to several causes. First of all, you may not have enough available RAM to boot the installation medium. (See the following item for information on disabling the ramdisk to free up memory.)

Hardware incompatibility causes many system hangs. Even if your hardware is supported, you may run into problems with incompatible hardware configurations that are causing the system to hang. See the next section, "Hardware Problems," for a discussion of hardware incompatibilities. The section "Hardware Requirements" in Chapter 10 lists the currently supported video chipsets, which are a major issue in running graphics on Linux.

System reports out-of-memory errors while attempting to boot or install the software.   This problem relates to the amount of RAM you have available. Keep in mind that Linux itself requires at least 4 MB of RAM to run at all; almost all current distributions of Linux require 8 MB or more. On systems with 8 MB of RAM or less, you may run into trouble booting the installation medium or installing the software itself. This is because many distributions use a *ramdisk*, which is a filesystem loaded directly into RAM, for operations while using the installation medium. The entire image of the installation boot floppy, for example, may be loaded into a ramdisk, which may require more than 1 MB of RAM.

The solution to this problem is to disable the ramdisk option when booting the install medium. Each distribution has a different procedure for doing this. Please see your distribution documentation for more information.

You may not see an out-of-memory error when attempting to boot or install the software; instead, the system may unexpectedly hang or fail to boot. If your system hangs, and none of the explanations in the previous section seems to be the cause, try disabling the ramdisk.

The system reports an error, such as "Permission denied" or "File not found," while booting.   This is an indication that your installation boot medium is corrupt. If you attempt to boot from the installation medium (and you're sure you're doing everything correctly), you should not see any such errors. Contact the distributor of your Linux software and find out about the problem, and perhaps obtain another copy of the boot medium if necessary. If you downloaded the boot disk yourself, try re-creating the boot disk, and see if this solves your problem.

The system reports the error "VFS: Unable to mount root" when booting.

This error message means that the root filesystem (found on the boot medium itself) could not be found. This means that either your boot medium is corrupt or you are not booting the system correctly.

For example, many CD-ROM distributions require you to have the CD-ROM in the drive when booting. Also be sure that the CD-ROM drive is on, and check for any activity. It's also possible the system is not locating your CD-ROM drive at boot time; see the next section, "Hardware Problems," for more information.

If you're sure you are booting the system correctly, your boot medium may indeed be corrupt. This is an uncommon problem, so try other solutions before attempting to use another boot floppy or tape. One handy feature here is RedHat's new mediacheck option on the CD-ROM. This will check if the CD is OK.

Hardware Problems

The most common problem encountered when attempting to install or use Linux is an incompatibility with hardware. Even if all your hardware is supported by Linux, a misconfiguration or hardware conflict can sometimes cause strange results: your devices may not be detected at boot time, or the system may hang.

It is important to isolate these hardware problems if you suspect they may be the source of your trouble. In the following sections, we describe some common hardware problems and how to resolve them.

Isolating hardware problems

If you experience a problem you believe is hardware-related, the first thing to do is attempt to isolate the problem. This means eliminating all possible variables and (usually) taking the system apart, piece by piece, until the offending piece of hardware is isolated.

This is not as frightening as it may sound. Basically, you should remove all nonessential hardware from your system (after turning the power off), and then determine which device is actually causing the trouble—possibly by reinserting each device, one at a time. This means you should remove all hardware other than the floppy and video controllers, and, of course, the keyboard. Even innocent-looking devices, such as mouse controllers, can wreak unknown havoc on your peace of mind unless you consider them nonessential. So, to be sure, really remove everything that you don't absolutely need for booting when experimenting, and add the devices one by one later when reassembling the system.

For example, let's say the system hangs during the Ethernet board detection sequence at boot time. You might hypothesize that there is a conflict or problem with the Ethernet board in your machine. The quick and easy way to find out is to pull the Ethernet board and try booting again. If everything goes well when you reboot, you know that either the Ethernet board is not supported by Linux, or there is an address or IRQ conflict with the board. In addition, some badly designed network boards (mostly ISA-based NE2000 clones, which are luckily dying out by now) can hang the entire system when they are auto-probed. If this appears to be the case for you, your best bet is to remove the network board from the system during the installation and put it back in later, or pass the appropriate kernel parameters during boot-up so that auto-probing of the network board can be avoided. The most permanent fix is to dump that card and get a new one from another vendor that designs its hardware more carefully.

What does "Address or IRQ conflict?" mean, you may ask. All devices in your machine use an *interrupt request line*, or IRQ, to tell the system they need something done on their behalf. You can think of the IRQ as a cord the device tugs when it needs the system to take care of some pending request. If more than one device is tugging on the same cord, the kernel won't be able to determine which device it needs to service. Instant mayhem.

Therefore, be sure all your installed non-PCI devices are using unique IRQ lines. In general, the IRQ for a device can be set by jumpers on the card; see the documentation for the particular device for details. Some devices do not require an IRQ at all, but it is suggested you configure them to use one if possible (the Seagate ST01 and ST02 SCSI controllers are good examples). The PCI bus is more cleverly designed, and PCI devices can and do quite happily share interrupt lines.

In some cases, the kernel provided on your installation medium is configured to use a certain IRQ for certain devices. For example, on some distributions of Linux, the kernel is preconfigured to use IRQ 5 for the TMC-950 SCSI controller, the Mitsumi CD-ROM controller, and the busmouse driver. If you want to use two or more of these devices, you'll need first to install Linux with only one of these devices enabled, then recompile the kernel in order to change the default IRQ for one of them. (See the section "Building a New Kernel" in Chapter 7 for information on recompiling the kernel.)

Another area where hardware conflicts can arise is with DMA channels, I/O addresses, and shared memory addresses. All these terms describe mechanisms through which the system interfaces with hardware devices. Some Ethernet boards, for example, use a shared memory address as well as an IRQ to interface with the system. If any of these are in conflict with other devices, the system may behave unexpectedly. You should be able to change the DMA channel, I/O, or shared memory addresses for your various devices with jumper settings. (Unfortunately, some devices don't allow you to change these settings.)

The documentation for your various hardware devices should specify the IRQ, DMA channel, I/O address, or shared memory address the devices use, and how to configure them. Of course, a problem here is that some of these settings are not known before the system is assembled and may thus be undocumented. Again, the simple way to get around these problems is to temporarily disable the conflicting devices until you have time to determine the cause of the problem.

Table 3-2 is a list of IRQ and DMA channels used by various "standard" devices found on most systems. Almost all systems have some of these devices, so you should avoid setting the IRQ or DMA of other devices to these values.

Table 3-2. Common device settings

Device	I/O address	IRQ	DMA
ttyS0 (COM1)	3f8	4	n/a
ttyS1 (COM2)	2f8	3	n/a
ttyS2 (COM3)	3e8	4	n/a
ttyS3 (COM4)	2e8	3	n/a
lp0 (LPT1)	378 – 37f	7	n/a
lp1 (LPT2)	278 – 27f	5	n/a
fd0, fd1 (floppies 1 and 2)	3f0 – 3f7	6	2
fd2, fd3 (floppies 3 and 4)	370 – 377	10	3

Problems recognizing hard drive or controller

When Linux boots, you see a series of messages on your screen, such as the following:

```
Console: colour VGA+ 80x25
Floppy drive(s): fd0 is 1.44M
ttyS00 at 0x03f8 (irq = 4) is a 16550A
…
```

Here, the kernel is detecting the various hardware devices present on your system. At some point, you should see the line:

```
Partition check:
```

followed by a list of recognized partitions, for example:

```
Partition check:
  hda: hda1 hda2
  hdb: hdb1 hdb2 hdb3
```

If, for some reason, your drives or partitions are not recognized, you will not be able to access them in any way.

Several conditions can cause this to happen:

Hard drive or controller not supported
> If you are using a hard drive or controller (IDE, SCSI, or otherwise) not supported by Linux, the kernel will not recognize your partitions at boot time.

Drive or controller improperly configured

Even if your controller is supported by Linux, it may not be configured correctly. (This is a problem particularly for SCSI controllers; most non-SCSI controllers should work fine without additional configuration.)

Refer to the documentation for your hard drive and controller for information on solving these kinds of problems. In particular, many hard drives will need to have a jumper set if they are to be used as a "slave" drive (e.g., as the second hard drive). The acid test for this kind of condition is to boot up Windows or some other operating system known to work with your drive and controller. If you can access the drive and controller from another operating system, the problem is not with your hardware configuration.

See the previous section, "Isolating hardware problems," for information on resolving possible device conflicts and the following section, "Problems with SCSI controllers and devices," for information on configuring SCSI devices.

Controller properly configured, but not detected

Some BIOS-less SCSI controllers require the user to specify information about the controller at boot time. The following section, "Problems with SCSI controllers and devices," describes how to force hardware detection for these controllers.

Hard-drive geometry not recognized

Some older systems, such as the IBM PS/ValuePoint, do not store hard-drive geometry information in the CMOS memory where Linux expects to find it. Also, certain SCSI controllers need to be told where to find drive geometry in order for Linux to recognize the layout of your drive.

Most distributions provide a boot option to specify the drive geometry. In general, when booting the installation medium, you can specify the drive geometry at the LILO boot prompt with a command such as:

```
boot: linux hd=cylinders,heads,sectors
```

where *cylinders*, *heads*, and *sectors* correspond to the number of cylinders, heads, and sectors per track for your hard drive.

After installing the Linux software, you can install LILO, allowing you to boot from the hard drive. At that time, you can specify the drive geometry to the LILO installation procedure, making it unnecessary to enter the drive geometry each time you boot. See the section "Using LILO" in Chapter 5 for more about LILO.

Problems with SCSI controllers and devices

Presented here are some of the most common problems with SCSI controllers and devices, such as CD-ROMs, hard drives, and tape drives. If you are having problems getting Linux to recognize your drive or controller, read on. Let us again emphasize that most distributions use a modularized kernel and that you might have to load a module supporting your hardware during an early phase of the installation process. This might also be done automatically for you.

The Linux SCSI HOWTO contains much useful information on SCSI devices in addition to that listed here. SCSIs can be particularly tricky to configure at times.

It might be a false economy, for example, to use cheap cables, especially if you use wide SCSI. Cheap cables are a major source of problems and can cause all kinds of failures, as well as major headaches. If you use SCSI, use proper cabling.

Here are common problems and possible solutions:

An SCSI device is detected at all possible IDs. This problem occurs when the system straps the device to the same address as the controller. You need to change the jumper settings so that the drive uses a different address from the controller itself.

Linux reports sense errors, even if the devices are known to be error-free. This can be caused by bad cables or by bad termination. If your SCSI bus is not terminated at both ends, you may have errors accessing SCSI devices. When in doubt, always check your cables. In addition to disconnected cables, bad-quality cables are a common source of troubles.

SCSI devices report timeout errors. This is usually caused by a conflict with IRQ, DMA, or device addresses. Also, check that interrupts are enabled correctly on your controller.

SCSI controllers using BIOS are not detected. Detection of controllers using BIOS will fail if the BIOS is disabled, or if your controller's "signature" is not recognized by the kernel. See the Linux SCSI HOWTO for more information about this.

Controllers using memory-mapped I/O do not work. This happens when the memory-mapped I/O ports are incorrectly cached. Either mark the board's address space as uncacheable in the XCMOS settings, or disable cache altogether.

When partitioning, you get a warning "cylinders > 1024," or you are unable to boot from a partition using cylinders numbered above 1023. BIOS limits the number of cylinders to 1024, and any partition using cylinders numbered above this won't be accessible from the BIOS. As far as Linux is concerned, this affects only booting; once the system has booted, you should be able to access the partition. Your options are to either boot Linux from a boot floppy, or boot from a partition using cylinders numbered below 1024. See the section "Creating the Boot Floppy or Installing LILO" earlier in this chapter.

CD-ROM drive or other removable media devices are not recognized at boot time.
Try booting with a CD-ROM (or disk) in the drive. This is necessary for some devices.

If your SCSI controller is not recognized, you may need to force hardware detection at boot time. This is particularly important for SCSI controllers without BIOS. Most distributions allow you to specify the controller IRQ and shared memory address when booting the installation medium. For example, if you are using a TMC-8xx controller, you may be able to enter:

```
boot: linux tmx8xx=interrupt,memory-address
```

at the LILO boot prompt, where *interrupt* is the controller IRQ, and *memory-address* is the shared memory address. Whether you can do this depends on the distribution of Linux you are using; consult your documentation for details.

Problems Installing the Software

Installing the Linux software should be trouble-free if you're lucky. The only problems you might experience would be related to corrupt installation media or lack of space on your Linux filesystems. Here is a list of common problems:

System reports "Read error, file not found" or other errors while attempting to install the software. This is indicative of a problem with your installation medium. If you are installing from floppy, keep in mind that floppies are quite susceptible to media errors of this type. Be sure to use brand-new, newly formatted floppies. If you have a Windows partition on your drive, many Linux distributions allow you to install the software from the hard drive. This may be faster and more reliable than using floppies.

If you are using a CD-ROM, be sure to check the disk for scratches, dust, or other problems that might cause media errors.

The cause of the problem may also be that the medium is in the incorrect format. For example, many Linux distributions require floppies to be formatted in high-density Windows format. (The boot floppy is the exception; it is not in Windows format in most cases.) If all else fails, either obtain a new set of floppies, or re-create the floppies (using new ones) if you downloaded the software yourself.

System reports errors such as "tar: read error" or "gzip: not in gzip format". This problem is usually caused by corrupt files on the installation medium itself. In other words, your floppy may be error-free, but the data on the floppy is in some way corrupted. For example, if you downloaded the Linux software using text mode, rather than binary mode, your files will be corrupt and unreadable by the installation software. When using FTP, just issue the *binary* command to set that mode before you request a file transfer.

System reports errors such as "device full" while installing. This is a clear-cut sign that you have run out of space when installing the software. If the disk fills up, not all distributions can clearly recover, so aborting the installation won't give you a working system.

The solution is usually to re-create your filesystems with the *mke2fs* command, which will delete the partially installed software. You can then attempt to reinstall the software, this time selecting a smaller amount of software to install. If you can't do without that software, you may need to start completely from scratch, and rethink your partition and filesystem sizes.

System reports errors such as "read_intr: 0x10" while accessing the hard drive.

This is usually an indication of bad blocks on your drive. However, if you receive these errors while using `mkswap` or `mke2fs`, the system may be having trouble accessing your drive. This can either be a hardware problem (see the section "Hardware Problems" earlier in this chapter), or it might be a case of poorly specified geometry. If you used the option:

```
hd=cylinders,heads,sectors
```

at boot time to force detection of your drive geometry and incorrectly specified the geometry, you could receive this error. This can also happen if your drive geometry is incorrectly specified in the system CMOS.

System reports errors such as "file not found" or "permission denied". This problem can occur if the necessary files are not present on the installation medium or if there is a permissions problem with the installation software. For example, some distributions of Linux have been known to have bugs in the installation software itself; these are usually fixed rapidly and are quite infrequent. If you suspect that the distribution software contains bugs, and you're sure that you have done nothing wrong, contact the maintainer of the distribution to report the bug.

If you have other strange errors when installing Linux (especially if you downloaded the software yourself), be sure you actually obtained all the necessary files when downloading.

For example, some people use the FTP command:

```
mget *.*
```

when downloading the Linux software via FTP. This will download only those files that contain a "." in their filenames; files without the "." will not be downloaded. The correct command to use in this case is:

```
mget *
```

The best advice is to retrace your steps when something goes wrong. You may think that you have done everything correctly, when in fact you forgot a small but important step somewhere along the way. In many cases, just attempting to redownload or reinstall the Linux software can solve the problem. Don't beat your head against the wall any longer than you have to!

Also, if Linux unexpectedly hangs during installation, there may be a hardware problem of some kind. See the section "Hardware Problems" for hints.

Problems after Installing Linux

You've spent an entire afternoon installing Linux. In order to make space for it, you wiped your Windows and OS/2 partitions and tearfully deleted your copies of

SimCity 2000 and Railroad Tycoon 2. You reboot the system and nothing happens. Or, even worse, *something* happens, but it's not what should happen. What do you do?

In the section "Problems with Booting the Installation Medium," earlier in this chapter, we covered the most common problems that can occur when booting the Linux installation medium; many of those problems may apply here. In addition, you may be victim to one of the following maladies.

Problems booting Linux from floppy

If you are using a floppy to boot Linux, you may need to specify the location of your Linux root partition at boot time. This is especially true if you are using the original installation floppy itself and not a custom boot floppy created during installation.

While booting the floppy, hold down the Shift or Ctrl key. This should present you with a boot menu; press Tab to see a list of available options. For example, many distributions allow you to boot from a floppy by entering:

```
boot: linux root=partition
```

at the boot menu, where *partition* is the name of the Linux root partition, such as */dev/hda2*. SuSE Linux offers a menu entry early in the installation program that boots your newly created Linux system from the installation boot floppy. Consult the documentation for your distribution for details.

Problems booting Linux from the hard drive

If you opted to install LILO instead of creating a boot floppy, you should be able to boot Linux from the hard drive. However, the automated LILO installation procedure used by many distributions is not always perfect. It may make incorrect assumptions about your partition layout, in which case you need to reinstall LILO to get everything right. Installing LILO is covered in the section "Using LILO" in Chapter 5.

Here are some common problems:

System reports "Drive not bootable—Please insert system disk". You will get this error message if the hard drive's master boot record is corrupt in some way. In most cases, it's harmless, and everything else on your drive is still intact. There are several ways around this:

- While partitioning your drive using *fdisk*, you may have deleted the partition that was marked as "active." Windows and other operating systems attempt to boot the "active" partition at boot time (Linux, in general, pays no attention to whether the partition is "active," but the Master Boot Records installed by some distributions like Debian do). You may be able to boot MS-DOS from floppy and run *fdisk* to set the active flag on your MS-DOS partition, and all will be well.

Another command to try (with MS-DOS 5.0 and higher, including all Windows versions since Windows 95) is:

```
FDISK /MBR
```

This command will attempt to rebuild the hard drive master boot record for booting Windows, overwriting LILO. If you no longer have Windows on your hard drive, you'll need to boot Linux from floppy and attempt to install LILO later.

- If you created a Windows partition using Linux's version of *fdisk*, or vice versa, you may get this error. You should create Windows partitions only by using Windows' version of *fdisk*. (The same applies to operating systems other than Windows.) The best solution here is either to start from scratch and repartition the drive correctly, or to merely delete and re-create the offending partitions using the correct version of *fdisk*.

- The LILO installation procedure may have failed. In this case, you should boot either from your Linux boot floppy (if you have one), or from the original installation medium. Either of these should provide options for specifying the Linux root partition to use when booting. At boot time, hold down the Shift or Ctrl key and press Tab from the boot menu for a list of options.

When you boot the system from the hard drive, Windows (or another operating system) starts instead of Linux. First of all, be sure you actually installed LILO when installing the Linux software. If not, the system will still boot Windows (or whatever other operating system you may have) when you attempt to boot from the hard drive. In order to boot Linux from the hard drive, you need to install LILO (see the section "Using LILO" in Chapter 5).

On the other hand, if you *did* install LILO, and another operating system boots instead of Linux, you have LILO configured to boot that other operating system by default. While the system is booting, hold down the Shift or Ctrl key and press Tab at the boot prompt. This should present you with a list of possible operating systems to boot; select the appropriate option (usually just linux) to boot Linux.

If you wish to select Linux as the default operating system to boot, you will need to reinstall LILO.

It also may be possible that you attempted to install LILO, but the installation procedure failed in some way. See the previous item on installation.

Problems logging in

After booting Linux, you should be presented with a login prompt:

```
Linux login:
```

At this point, either the distribution's documentation or the system itself will tell you what to do. For many distributions, you simply log in as root, with no password. Other possible usernames to try are guest or test.

Most Linux distributions ask you for an initial root password. Hopefully, you have remembered what you typed in during installation; you will need it again now. If your distribution does not ask you for a root password during installation, you can try using an empty password.

If you simply can't log in, consult your distribution's documentation; the username and password to use may be buried in there somewhere. The username and password may have been given to you during the installation procedure, or they may be printed on the login banner.

One possible cause of this password impasse may be a problem with installing the Linux login and initialization files. If this is the case, you may need to reinstall (at least parts of) the Linux software, or boot your installation medium and attempt to fix the problem by hand.

Problems using the system

If login is successful, you should be presented with a shell prompt (such as # or $) and can happily roam around your system. The next step in this case is to try the procedures in Chapter 4. However, some initial problems with using the system sometimes creep up.

The most common initial configuration problem is incorrect file or directory permissions. This can cause the error message:

```
Shell-init: permission denied
```

to be printed after logging in. (In fact, anytime you see the message permission denied, you can be fairly certain it is a problem with file permissions.)

In many cases, it's a simple matter of using the *chmod* command to fix the permissions of the appropriate files or directories. For example, some distributions of Linux once used the incorrect file mode 0644 for the root directory (/). The fix was to issue the command:

```
# chmod 755 /
```

as root. (File permissions are covered in the section "File Ownership and Permissions" in Chapter 4.) However, in order to issue this command, you needed to boot from the installation medium and mount your Linux root filesystem by hand—a hairy task for most newcomers.

As you use the system, you may run into places where file and directory permissions are incorrect, or software does not work as configured. Welcome to the world of Linux! While most distributions are quite trouble-free, you can't expect them to be perfect. We don't want to cover all those problems here. Instead, throughout the book we help you to solve many of these configuration problems by teaching you how to find them and fix them yourself. In Chapter 1, we discussed this philosophy in some detail. In Chapter 5, we give hints for fixing many of these common configuration problems.

## CHAPTER 4

Basic Unix Commands
and Concepts

If you've come to Linux from Windows or another non-Unix operating system, you have a steep learning curve ahead of you. We might as well be candid on this point. Unix is a world all its own.

In this chapter, we're going to introduce the rudiments of Unix for those readers who have never had exposure to this operating system. If you are coming from Microsoft Windows or other environments, the information in this chapter will be absolutely vital to you. Unlike other operating systems, Unix is not at all intuitive. Many of the commands have seemingly odd names or syntax, the reasons for which usually date back many years to the early days of this system. And, although many of the commands may appear to be similar to their counterparts in the Windows command-line interpreter, there are important differences.

Dozens of other books cover basic Unix usage. You should be able to go to the computer section of any chain bookstore and find at least several of them on the shelf. (A few we like are listed in the Bibliography.) However, most of these books cover Unix from the point of view of someone sitting down at a workstation or terminal connected to a large mainframe, not someone who is running his own Unix system on a personal computer. A popular introduction to Unix usage that also covers Linux is *Learning the Unix Operating System* by Grace Todino, John Strang, and Jerry Peek, published by O'Reilly.

Also, these books often dwell upon the more mundane aspects of Unix: boring text-manipulation commands, such as *awk*, *tr*, and *sed*, most of which you will never need unless you start doing some serious Unix trickery. In fact, many Unix books talk about the original *ed* line editor, which has long been made obsolete by *vi* and Emacs. Therefore, although many of the Unix books available today contain a great deal of useful information, many of them contain pages upon pages of humdrum material you couldn't probably care less about at this point.

Instead of getting into the dark mesh of text processing, shell syntax, and other issues, in this chapter we strive to cover the basic commands needed to get you up to speed with the system if you're coming from a non-Unix environment. This chapter is far from complete; a real beginner's Unix tutorial would take an entire book. It's our hope that this chapter will give you enough to keep you going in your adventures with Linux, and that you'll invest in a good Unix book once you have a need to do so. We'll give you enough Unix background to make your terminal usable, keep track of jobs, and enter essential commands.

Chapter 5 contains material on system administration and maintenance. This is by far the most important chapter for anyone running his own Linux system. If you are completely new to Unix, the material found in Chapter 5 should be easy to follow once you've completed the tutorial here.

One big job we don't cover in this chapter is how to edit files. It's one of the first things you need to learn on any operating system. The two most popular editors for Linux, *vi* and Emacs, are discussed at the beginning of Chapter 9.

Logging In

Let's assume that your installation went completely smoothly, and you are facing the following prompt on your screen:

```
Linux login:
```

Many Linux users are not so lucky; they have to perform some heavy tinkering when the system is still in a raw state or in single-user mode. But for now, we'll talk about logging into a functioning Linux system.

Logging in, of course, distinguishes one user from another. It lets several people work on the same system at once and makes sure that you are the only person to have access to your files.

You may have installed Linux at home and are thinking right now, "Big deal. No one else shares this system with me, and I'd just as soon not have to log in." But logging in under your personal account also provides a certain degree of protection: your account won't have the ability to destroy or remove important system files. The system administration account (covered in the next chapter) is used for such touchy matters.

If you connect your computer to the Internet, even via a modem, make sure you set nontrivial passwords on all your accounts. Use punctuation and strings that don't represent real words or names.

Note that some distributions install a so-called graphical login manager right away, so you might not be greeted by the somewhat arcane login: prompt in white letters on black background, but with a fancy graphical login screen, possibly even presenting you with the user accounts available on your system as well as different modes to log into. The basic login procedure is the same as described here, however; you still type your username and password.

You were probably asked to set up a login account for yourself when you installed Linux. If you have such an account, type the name you chose at the Linux login: prompt. If you don't have an account yet, type root because that account is certain to exist. Some distributions may also set up an account called install or some other name for fooling around when you first install the system.

After you choose your account, you see:

```
Password:
```

and you need to enter the correct password. The terminal turns off the normal echoing of characters you enter for this operation so that people looking at the screen cannot read your password. If the prompt does not appear, you should add a password to protect yourself from other people's tampering; we'll go into this later.

By the way, both the name and the password are case-sensitive. Make sure the Caps Lock key is not set because typing ROOT instead of root will not work.

When you have successfully logged in, you will see a prompt. If you're root, this may be a simple:

```
#
```

For other users, the prompt is usually a dollar sign ($). The prompt may also contain the name you assigned to your system or the directory you're in currently. Whatever appears here, you are now ready to enter commands. We say that you are at the "shell level" here and that the prompt you see is the "shell prompt." This is because you are running a program called the shell that handles your commands. Right now we can ignore the shell, but later in this chapter we'll find that it does a number of useful things for us.

As we show commands in this chapter, we'll show the prompt simply as $. So if you see:

```
$ pwd
```

it means that the shell prints $ and that pwd is what you're supposed to enter.

Setting a Password

If you don't already have a password, we recommend you set one. Just enter the command *passwd*. The command will prompt you for a password and then ask you to enter it a second time to make sure you enter it without typos.

There are standard guidelines for choosing passwords so that they're hard for other people to guess. Some systems even check your password and reject any that don't meet the minimal criteria. For instance, it is often said that you should have at least six characters in the password. Furthermore, you should mix uppercase and lower-case characters or include characters other than letters and digits.

To change your password, just enter the *passwd* command again. It prompts you for your old password (to make sure you're you) and then lets you change it.

Virtual Consoles

As a multiprocessing system, Linux gives you a number of interesting ways to do several things at once. You can start a long software installation and then switch to reading mail or compiling a program simultaneously.

Most Linux users, when they want this asynchronous access, will employ the X Window System. But before you get X running, you can do something similar through virtual consoles. This feature appears on a few other versions of Unix, but is not universally available.

To try out virtual consoles, hold down the left Alt key and press one of the function keys, F1 through F8. As you press each function key, you see a totally new screen complete with a login prompt. You can log in to different virtual consoles just as if you were two different people, and you can switch between them to carry out different activities. You can even run a complete X session in each console. The X Window System will use the virtual console 7 by default. So if you start X and then switch to one of the text-based virtual consoles, you can go back again to X by typing Alt-F7. If you discover that the Alt-+ function key combination brings up an X menu or some other function instead of switching virtual consoles, use Ctrl + Alt + function key.

Popular Commands

The number of commands on a typical Unix system is enough to fill a few hundred reference pages. And you can add new commands too. The commands we'll tell you about here are just enough to navigate and to see what you have on the system.

Directories

As with Windows, and virtually every modern computer system, Unix files are organized into a hierarchical directory structure. Unix imposes no rules about where files have to be, but conventions have grown up over the years. Thus, on Linux you'll find a directory called */home* where each user's files are placed. Each user has a subdirectory under */home*. So if your login name is mdw, your personal files are located in */home/mdw*. This is called your home directory. You can, of course, create more subdirectories under it.

If you come from a Windows system, the slash (/) as a path separator may look odd to you because you are used to the backslash (\). There is nothing tricky about the slash. Slashes were actually used as path separators long before people even started to think about MS-DOS or Windows. The backslash has a different meaning on Unix (turning off the special meaning of the next character, if any).

As you can see, the components of a directory are separated by slashes. The term *pathname* is often used to refer to this slash-separated list.

What directory is */home* in? The directory named */,* of course. This is called the root directory. We have already mentioned it when setting up filesystems.

When you log in, the system puts you in your home directory. To verify this, use the "print working directory" or *pwd* command:

```
$ pwd
/home/mdw
```

The system confirms that you're in */home/mdw*.

You certainly won't have much fun if you have to stay in one directory all the time. Now try using another command, *cd*, to move to another directory:

```
$ cd /usr/bin
$ pwd
/usr/bin
$ cd
```

Where are we now? A *cd* with no arguments returns us to our home directory. By the way, the home directory is often represented by a tilde (~). So the string *~/programs* means that *programs* is located right under your home directory.

While we're thinking about it, let's make a directory called *~/programs*. From your home directory, you can enter either:

```
$ mkdir programs
```

or the full pathname:

```
$ mkdir /home/mdw/programs
```

Now change to that directory:

```
$ cd programs
$ pwd
/home/mdw/programs
```

The special character sequence .. refers to "the directory just above the current one." So you can move back up to your home directory by typing the following:

```
$ cd ..
```

The opposite of *mkdir* is *rmdir*, which removes directories:

```
$ rmdir programs
```

Similarly, the *rm* command deletes files. We won't show it here because we haven't yet shown how to create a file. You generally use the *vi* or Emacs editor for that (see Chapter 9, but some of the commands later in this chapter will create files too. With the *-r* (recursive) option, *rm* deletes a whole directory and all its contents. (Use with care!)

Listing Files

Enter *ls* to see what is in a directory. Issued without an argument, the *ls* command shows the contents of the current directory. You can include an argument to see a different directory:

```
$ ls /home
```

Some systems have a fancy *ls* that displays special files—such as directories and executable files—in bold, or even in different colors. If you want to change the default colors, edit the file */etc/DIR_COLORS*, or create a copy of it in your home directory named *.dir_colors* and edit that.

Like most Unix commands, *ls* can be controlled with options that start with a hyphen (-). Make sure you type a space before the hyphen. One useful option for *ls* is *-a* for "all," which will reveal to you riches that you never imagined in your home directory:

```
$ cd
$ ls -a
.                    .bashrc              .fvwmrc
..                   .emacs               .xinitrc
.bash_history        .exrc
```

The single dot refers to the current directory, and the double dot refers to the directory right above it. But what are those other files beginning with a dot? They are called hidden files. Putting a dot in front of their names keeps them from being shown during a normal *ls* command. Many programs employ hidden files for user options—things about their default behavior that you want to change. For instance, you can put commands in the file *.Xdefaults* to alter how programs using the X Window System operate. So most of the time you can forget these files exist, but when you're configuring your system you'll find them very important. We'll list some of them later.

Another useful *ls* option is *-1* for "long." It shows extra information about the files. Figure 4-1 shows typical output and what each field means. Adding the -h ("human option") shows the filesizes rounded to something more easily readable.

We'll discuss the permissions, owner, and group fields later in this chapter, in the section "File Ownership and Permissions." The *ls* command also shows the size of each file and when it was last modified.

Viewing Files, More or Less

One way to look at a file is to invoke an editor, such as:

```
$ emacs .bashrc
```

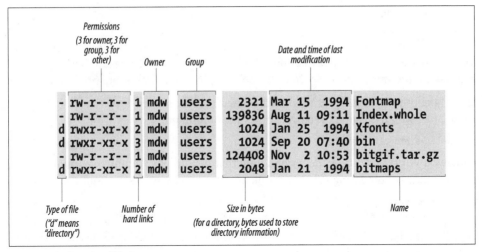

Figure 4-1. Output of ls –l

But if you just want to scan a file quickly, rather than edit it, other commands are quicker. The simplest is the strangely named *cat* command (named after the verb *concatenate* because you can also use it to concatenate several files into one):

```
$ cat .bashrc
```

But a long file will scroll by too fast for you to see it, so most people use the *more* command instead:

```
$ more .bashrc
```

This prints a screenfull at a time and waits for you to press the spacebar before printing more. *more* has a lot of powerful options. For instance, you can search for a string in the file: press the slash key (/), type the string, and press Return.

A popular variation on the *more* command is called *less*. It has even more powerful features; for instance, you can mark a particular place in a file and return there later.

Symbolic Links

Sometimes you want to keep a file in one place and pretend it is in another. This is done most often by a system administrator, not a user. For instance, you might keep several versions of a program around, called *prog.0.9*, *prog.1.1*, and so on, but use the name *prog* to refer to the version you're currently using. Or you may have a file installed in one partition because you have disk space for it there, but the program that uses the file needs it to be in a different partition because the pathname is hard-coded into the program.

Unix provides *links* to handle these situations. In this section, we'll examine the *symbolic link*, which is the most flexible and popular type. A symbolic link is a kind of dummy file that just points to another file. If you edit or read or execute the symbolic link, the system is smart enough to give you the real file instead. Symbolic links work a lot like shortcuts under Windows 95/98, but are much more powerful.

Let's take the *prog* example. You want to create a link named *prog* that points to the actual file, which is named *prog.1.1*. Enter the command:

```
$ ln -s prog.1.1 prog
```

Now you've created a new file named *prog* that is kind of a dummy file; if you run it, you're really running *prog.1.1*. Let's look at what *ls -l* has to say about the file:

```
$ ls -l prog
lrwxrwxrwx    2 mdw        users          8 Nov 17 14:35 prog -> prog.1.1
```

The l at the beginning of the line shows that the file is a link, and the little -> indicates the real file to which the link points.

Symbolic links are really simple, once you get used to the idea of one file pointing to another. You'll encounter links all the time when installing software packages.

Shells

As we said before, logging into the system in console mode puts you into a shell. If your system is configured with a graphical login, logging in brings you to the graphical interface where you can open an *xterm* (or similar) window in order to get a shell. The shell interprets and executes all your commands. Let's look a bit at different shells before we keep going, because they're going to affect some of the material coming up.

If it seems confusing that Unix offers many different shells, just accept it as an effect of evolution. Believe us, you wouldn't want to be stuck using the very first shell developed for Unix, the Bourne shell. While it was a very powerful user interface for its day (the mid-1970s), it lacked a lot of useful features for interactive use—including the ones shown in this section. So other shells have been developed over time, and you can now choose the one that best suits your way of working.

Some of the shells available on Linux are:

bash

> Bourne Again shell. The most commonly used (and most powerful) shell on Linux. POSIX-compliant, compatible with Bourne shell, created and distributed by the GNU project (Free Software Foundation). Offers command-line editing, history substitution, and Bourne shell compatibility.

csh

> C shell. Developed at Berkeley. Mostly compatible with the Bourne shell for interactive use, but has a very different interface for programming. Does not offer command-line editing, although it does have a sophisticated alternative called history substitution. On Linux, *csh* is just another name for the newer *tcsh*.

ksh

> Korn shell. Perhaps the most popular on Unix systems generally, and the first to introduce modern shell techniques (including some borrowed from the C shell) into the Bourne shell. Compatible with Bourne shell. Offers command-line editing.

sh

> Bourne shell. The original shell. Does not offer command-line editing.

tcsh

> Enhanced C shell. Offers command-line editing.

zsh

> Z shell. The newest of the shells. Compatible with Bourne shell. Offers command-line editing.

Try the following command to find out what your shell is. It prints out the full pathname where the shell is located. Don't forget to type the dollar sign:

```
$ echo $SHELL
```

You are probably running *bash*, the Bourne Again shell. If you're running something else, this might be a good time to change to *bash*. It's powerful, POSIX-compliant, well-supported, and very popular on Linux. Use the *chsh* command to change your shell:

```
$ chsh
Enter password: Type your password here—this is for security's sake
Changing the login shell for mdw
Enter the new value, or press return for the default

        Login Shell [/bin/sh]:/bin/bash
```

Before a user can choose a particular shell as a login shell, that shell must be installed and the system administrator must make it available by entering it in */etc/shells*.

There are a couple of ways to conceptualize the differences between shells. One is to distinguish Bourne-compatible shells from *csh*-compatible shells. This will be of interest to you when you start to program with the shell, also known as writing shell scripts. The Bourne shell and C shell have different programming constructs. Most people now agree that Bourne-compatible shells are better, and there are many Unix utilities that recognize only the Bourne shell.

Another way to categorize shells is to identify those that offer command-line editing (all the newer ones) versus those that do not. *sh* and *csh* lack this useful feature.

When you combine the two criteria—being compatible with the Bourne shell and offering command-line editing—your best choice comes down to *bash*, *ksh*, or *zsh*. Try out several shells before you make your choice; it helps to know more than one, in case someday you find yourself on a system that limits your choice of shells.

Useful Keys and How to Get Them to Work

When you type a command, pressing the Backspace key should remove the last character. Ctrl-U should delete the line from the cursor to the beginning of the line, thus this key combination will delete the whole line if the cursor is at the end of the line.* When you have finished entering a command, and it is executing, Ctrl-C should abort it, and Ctrl-Z should suspend it. (When you want to resume the suspended program, enter *fg* for "foreground.")

Ctrl-S stops the terminal output until you turn it off again with Ctrl-Q. This is probably less useful today, as most terminal emulations provide scrolling facilities anyway, but it's important to know if you have hit Ctrl-S by accident and the terminal all of a sudden "becomes unresponsive." Just hit Ctrl-Q to make it respond again; it was just waiting for you.

If any of these keys fail to work, your terminal is not configured correctly for some reason. You can fix it through the *stty* command. Use the syntax:

```
stty function key
```

where *function* is what you want to do, and *key* is the key that you press. Specify a control key by putting a circumflex (^) in front of the key.

Here is a set of sample commands to set up the functions described earlier:

```
$ stty erase ^H
$ stty kill ^U
$ stty intr ^C
$ stty susp ^Z
```

The first control key shown, ^H, represents the ASCII code generated by the Backspace key.

By the way, you can generate a listing of your current terminal settings by entering *stty -a*. But that doesn't mean you can understand the output: *stty* is a complicated command with many uses, some of which require a lot of knowledge about terminals.

---

* Ctrl-U means hold down the Control key and press u.

Typing Shortcuts

If you've been following along with this tutorial at your terminal, you may be tired of typing the same things over and over again. It can be particularly annoying when you make a mistake and have to start over again. Here is where the shell really makes life easier. It doesn't make Unix as simple as a point-and-click interface, but it can help you work really fast in a command environment.

This section discusses command-line editing. The tips here work if your shell is *bash*, *ksh*, *tcsh*, or *zsh*. Command-line editing treats the last 50 or so lines you typed as a buffer in an editor. You can move around within these lines and change them the way you'd edit a document. Every time you press the Return key, the shell executes the current line.

Word Completion

First, let's try something simple that can save you a lot of time. Type the following, without pressing the Return key:

    $ cd /usr/inc

Now press the Tab key. The shell will add `lude` to complete the name of the directory */usr/include*. Now you can press the Return key, and the command will execute.

The criterion for specifying a filename is "minimal completion." Type just enough characters to distinguish a name from all the others in that directory. The shell can find the name and complete it—up to and including a slash, if the name is a directory.

You can use completion on commands too. For instance, if you type:

    $ ema

and press the Tab key, the shell will add the `cs` to make `emacs` (unless some other command in your path begins with ema).

What if multiple files match what you've typed? If they all start with the same characters, the shell completes the word up to the point where names differ. Beyond that, most shells do nothing. *bash* has a neat enhancement: if you press the Tab key twice, it displays all the possible completions. For instance, if you enter:

    $ cd /usr/l

and press the Tab key twice, *bash* prints something like:

    lib   local

Moving Around Among Commands

Press the up arrow, and the command you typed previously appears. The up arrow takes you back through the command history, while the down arrow takes you forward. If you want to change a character on the current line, use the left or right arrow keys.

As an example, suppose you tried to execute:

```
$ mroe .bashrc
bash: mroe: command not found
```

Of course, you typed mroe instead of more. To correct the command, call it back by pressing the up arrow. Then press the left arrow until the cursor lies over the o in mroe. You could use the Backspace key to remove the o and r and retype them correctly. But here's an even neater shortcut: just press Ctrl-T. It will reverse o and r, and you can then press the Return key to execute the command.

Many other key combinations exist for command-line editing. But the basics shown here will help you quite a bit. If you learn the Emacs editor, you will find that most keys work the same way in the shell. And if you're a *vi* fan, you can set up your shell so that it uses *vi* key bindings instead of Emacs bindings. To do this in *bash*, *ksh*, or *zsh*, enter the command:

```
$ export VISUAL=vi
```

In *tcsh* enter:

```
$ setenv VISUAL vi
```

Filename Expansion

Another way to save time in your commands is to use special characters to abbreviate filenames. You can specify many files at once by using these characters. This feature of the shell is sometimes called "globbing."

The Windows command-line interpreter offers a few crude features of this type. You can use a question mark to mean "any character" and an asterisk to mean "any string of characters." Unix provides these wildcards too, but in a more robust and rigorous way.

Let's say you have a directory containing the following C source files:

```
$ ls
inv1jig.c   inv2jig.c   inv3jig.c   invinitjig.c   invpar.c
```

To list the three files containing digits in their names, you could enter:

```
$ ls inv?jig.c
inv1jig.c   inv2jig.c   inv3jig.c
```

The shell looks for a single character to replace the question mark. Thus, it displays *inv1jig.c*, *inv2jig.c*, and *inv3jig.c*, but not *invinitjig.c* because that name contains too many characters.

If you're not interested in the second file, you can specify the ones you want using brackets:

```
$ ls inv[13]jig.c
inv1jig.c   inv3jig.c
```

If any single character within the brackets matches a file, that file is displayed. You can also put a range of characters in the brackets:

```
$ ls inv[1-3]jig.c
inv1jig.c   inv2jig.c   inv3jig.c
```

Now we're back to displaying all three files. The hyphen means "match any character from 1 through 3, inclusive." You could ask for any numeric character by specifying 0-9, and any alphabetic character by specifying [a-zA-Z]. In the latter case, two ranges are required because the shell is case-sensitive. The order used, by the way, is that of the ASCII character set.

Suppose you want to see the *init* file, too. Now you can use an asterisk because you want to match any number of characters between the inv and the jig:

```
$ ls inv*jig.c
inv1jig.c   inv2jig.c   inv3jig.c   invinitjig.c
```

The asterisk actually means "zero or more characters," so if a file named *invjig.c* existed, it would be shown too.

Unlike the Windows command-line interpreter, the Unix shells let you combine special characters and normal characters any way you want. Let's say you want to look for any source (*.c*) or object (*.o*) file that contains a digit. The resulting pattern combines all the expansions we've studied in this section:

```
$ ls *[0-9]*.[co]
```

Filename expansion is very useful in shell scripts (programs), where you don't always know exactly how many files exist. For instance, you might want to process multiple log files named *log001*, *log002*, and so on. No matter how many there are, the expression *log** will match them all.

 Filename expansions are not the same as regular expressions, which are used by many utilities to specify groups of strings. Regular expressions are beyond the scope of this book, but are described by many books that explain Unix utilities. A taste of regular expressions appears in Chapter 9.

Saving Your Output

System administrators (and other human beings too) see a lot of critical messages fly by on the computer screen. It's often important to save these messages so that you can scrutinize them later, or (all too often) send them to a friend who can figure out what went wrong. So, in this section, we'll explain a little bit about redirection, a powerful feature provided by Unix shells. If you come from Windows, you have probably seen a similar, but more limited, type of redirection in the command-line interpreter there.

If you put a greater-than sign (>) and a filename after any command, the output of the command will be sent to that file. For instance, to capture the output of *ls*, you can enter:

```
$ ls /usr/bin > ~/Binaries
```

A listing of */usr/bin* will be stored in your home directory in a file named *Binaries*. If *Binaries* had already existed, the > would wipe out what was there and replace it with the output of the *ls* command. Overwriting a current file is a common user error. If your shell is *csh* or *tcsh*, you can prevent overwriting with the command:

```
$ set noclobber
```

And in *bash* you can achieve the same effect by entering:

```
$ noclobber=1
```
It doesn't have to be 1; any value will have the same effect.

Another (and perhaps more useful) way to prevent overwriting is to append new output. For instance, having saved a listing of */usr/bin*, suppose we now want to add the contents of */bin* to that file. We can append it to the end of the *Binaries* file by specifying two greater-than signs:

```
$ ls /bin >> ~/Binaries
```

You will find the technique of output redirection very useful when you are running a utility many times and saving the output for troubleshooting.

Most Unix programs have two output streams. One is called the standard output, and the other is the standard error. If you're a C programmer you'll recognize these: the standard error is the file pointer named *stderr* to which you print messages.

The > character does not redirect the standard error. It's useful when you want to save legitimate output without mucking up a file with error messages. But what if the error messages are what you want to save? This is quite common during troubleshooting. The solution is to use a greater-than sign followed by an ampersand. (This construct works in almost every modern Unix shell.) It redirects both the standard output and the standard error. For instance:

```
$ gcc invinitjig.c >& error-msg
```

This command saves all the messages from the *gcc* compiler in a file named *error-msg*. On the Bourne shell and *bash* you can also say it slightly differently:

```
$ gcc invinitjig.c &> error-msg
```

Now let's get really fancy. Suppose you want to save the error messages but not the regular output—the standard error but not the standard output. In the Bourne-compatible shells you can do this by entering the following:

```
$ gcc invinitjig.c 2> error-msg
```

The shell arbitrarily assigns the number 1 to the standard output and the number 2 to the standard error. So the preceding command saves only the standard error.

Finally, suppose you want to throw away the standard output—keep it from appearing on your screen. The solution is to redirect it to a special file called /dev/null. (Have you heard people say things like "Send your criticisms to /dev/null"? Well, this is where the phrase came from.) The /dev directory is where Unix systems store special files that refer to terminals, tape drives, and other devices. But /dev/null is unique; it's a place you can send things so that they disappear into a black hole. For example, the following command saves the standard error and throws away the standard output:

```
$ gcc invinitjig.c 2>error-msg >/dev/null
```

So now you should be able to isolate exactly the output you want.

In case you've wondered whether the less-than sign (<) means anything to the shell: yes, it does. It causes commands to take their input from a file. But most commands allow you to specify input files on their command lines anyway, so this "input redirection" is rarely necessary.

Sometimes you want one utility to operate on the output of another utility. For instance, you can use the *sort* command to put the output of other commands into a more useful order. A crude way to do this would be to save output from one command in a file, and then run *sort* on it. For instance:

```
$ du > du_output
$ sort -nr du_output
```

Unix provides a much more succinct and efficient way to do this using a *pipe*. Just place a vertical bar between the first and second commands:

```
$ du | sort -nr
```

The shell sends all the input from the *du* program to the *sort* program.

In the previous example, *du* stands for "disk usage" and shows how many blocks each file occupies under the current directory. Normally, its output is in a somewhat random order:

```
$ du
10          ./zoneinfo/Australia
13          ./zoneinfo/US
9           ./zoneinfo/Canada
4           ./zoneinfo/Mexico
5           ./zoneinfo/Brazil
3           ./zoneinfo/Chile
20          ./zoneinfo/SystemV
118         ./zoneinfo
298         ./ghostscript/doc
183         ./ghostscript/examples
3289        ./ghostscript/fonts
    .
    .
    .
```

So we have decided to run it through *sort* with the *-n* and *-r* options. The *-n* option means "sort in numerical order" instead of the default ASCII sort, and the *-r* option means "reverse the usual order" so that the highest number appears first. The result is output that quickly shows you which directories and files hog the most space:

```
$ du | sort -rn
34368    .
16005    ./emacs
16003    ./emacs/20.4
13326    ./emacs/20.4/lisp
4039     ./ghostscript
3289     ./ghostscript/fonts
  .
  .
  .
```

Because there are so many files, we had better use a second pipe to send output through the *more* command (one of the more common uses of pipes):

```
$ du | sort -rn | more
34368    .
16005    ./emacs
16003    ./emacs/20.4
13326    ./emacs/20.4/lisp
4039     ./ghostscript
3289     ./ghostscript/fonts
  .
  .
  .
```

An alternative to *more* could be using the *head* command here, which only shows the first few lines (10 by default). Of course, if there is a *head* command, there also needs to be a *tail* command which just shows the last few lines.

What Is a Command?

We've said that Unix offers a huge number of commands and that you can add new ones. This makes it radically different from most operating systems, which contain a strictly limited table of commands. So what are Unix commands, and how are they stored? On Unix, a command is simply a file. For instance, the *ls* command is a binary file located in the directory *bin*. So, instead of *ls*, you could enter the full pathname, also known as the *absolute pathname*:

```
$ /bin/ls
```

This makes Unix very flexible and powerful. To provide a new utility, a system administrator can simply install it in a standard directory where commands are located. There can also be different versions of a command—for instance, you can offer a new version of a utility for testing in one place while leaving the old version in another place, and users can choose the one they want.

Here's a common problem: sometimes you enter a command that you expect to be on the system, but you receive a message such as "Not found." The problem may be that the command is located in a directory that your shell is not searching. The list of directories where your shell looks for commands is called your *path*. Enter the following to see what your path is (remember the dollar sign, otherwise you won't see the contents of the environment variable, but only its name, which you know anyway!):

```
$ echo $PATH
/usr/local/bin:/usr/bin:/usr/X11R6/bin:/bin:/usr/lib/java/bin:\
/usr/games:/usr/bin/TeX:.
```

This takes a little careful eyeballing. The output is a series of pathnames separated by colons. The first pathname, for this particular user, is */usr/local/bin*. The second is */usr/bin*, and so on. So if two versions of a command exist, one in */usr/local/bin* and the other in */usr/bin*, the one in */usr/local/bin* will execute. The last pathname in this example is simply a dot; it refers to the current directory. Unlike the Windows command-line interpreter, Unix does not look automatically in your current directory. You have to tell it to explicitly, as shown here. Some people think it's a bad idea to look in the current directory, for security reasons. (An intruder who gets into your account might copy a malicious program to one of your working directories.) However, this mostly applies to root, so normal users generally do not need to worry about this.

If a command is not found, you have to figure out where it is on the system and add that directory to your path. The manual page should tell you where it is. Let's say you find it in */usr/sbin*, where a number of system administration commands are installed. You realize you need access to these system administration commands, so you enter the following (note that the first PATH doesn't have a dollar sign, but the second one does):

```
$ export PATH=$PATH:/usr/sbin
```

This command adds */usr/sbin*, but makes it the last directory that is searched. The command is saying, "Make my path equal to the old path plus */usr/sbin*."

The previous command works for some shells but not others. It's fine for most Linux users who are working in a Bourne-compatible shell like *bash*. But if you use *csh* or *tcsh*, you need to issue the following command instead:

```
set path = ( $PATH /usr/sbin )
```

Finally, there are a few commands that are not files; *cd* is one. Most of these commands affect the shell itself and therefore have to be understood and executed by the shell. Because they are part of the shell, they are called built-in commands.

Putting a Command in the Background

Before the X Window System, which made it easy to run multiple programs at once, Unix users took advantage of Unix's multitasking features by simply putting an ampersand at the end of commands, as shown in this example:

```
$ gcc invinitjig.c &
[1] 21457
```

The ampersand puts the command into the background, meaning that the shell prompt comes back, and you can continue to execute other commands while the *gcc* command is compiling your program. The [1] is a job number that is assigned to your command. The 21457 is a process ID, which we'll discuss later. Job numbers are assigned to background commands in order and therefore are easier to remember and type than process IDs.

Of course, multitasking does not come for free. The more commands you put into the background, the slower your system runs as it tries to interleave their execution.

You wouldn't want to put a command in the background if it requires user input. If you do so, you see an error message, such as:

```
Stopped (tty input)
```

You can solve this problem by bringing the job back into the foreground through the *fg* command. If you have many commands in the background, you can choose one of them by its job number or its process ID. For our long-lived *gcc* command, the following commands are equivalent:

```
$ fg %1
$ fg 21457
```

Don't forget the percent sign on the job number; that's what distinguishes job numbers from process IDs.

To get rid of a command in the background, issue a *kill* command:

```
$ kill %1
```

Manual Pages

The most empowering information you can get is how to conduct your own research. Following this precept, we'll now tell you about the online help system that comes built into Unix systems. It is called manual pages, or manpages for short.

Actually, manual pages are not quite the boon they ought to be. This is because they are short and take a lot of Unix background for granted. Each one focuses on a particular command and rarely helps you decide why you should use that command. Still, they are critical. Commands can vary slightly on different Unix systems, and the manual pages are the most reliable way to find out what your system does. (LDP deserves a lot of credit for the incredible number of hours they have put into creating manual pages.) To find out about a command, enter a command, such as:

```
$ man ls
```

Manual pages are divided into different sections depending on their purpose. User commands are in section 1, Unix system calls in section 2, and so on. The sections that will interest you most are 1, 5 (file formats), and 8 (system administration commands). When you view manpages online, the section numbers are conceptual; you can optionally specify them when searching for a command:

```
$ man 1 ls
```

But if you consult a hardcopy manual, you'll find it divided into actual sections according to the numbering scheme. Sometimes an entry in two different sections can have the same name. (For instance, *chmod* is both a command and a system call.) So you will sometimes see the name of a manual page followed by the section number in parentheses, as in *ls(1)*.

There is one situation in which you will need the section number on the command line: when there are several manual pages for the same keyword (e.g., one for a command with that name and one for a system function with the same name). Suppose you want to look up a library call, but the *man* shows you the command because its default search order looks for the command first. In order to see the manual page for the library call, you need to give its section number.

Look near the top of a manual page. The first heading is NAME. Under it is a brief one-line description of the item. These descriptions can be valuable if you're not quite sure what you're looking for. Think of a word related to what you want, and specify it in an *apropos* command:

```
$ apropos edit
```

The previous command shows all the manual pages that have something to do with editing. It's a very simple algorithm: *apropos* simply prints out all the NAME lines that contain the string you request.

Many other utilities, particularly those offered by the desktops discussed in Chapter 11, present manual pages attractively.

Like commands, manual pages are sometimes installed in strange places. For instance, you may install some site-specific programs in the directory */usr/local*, and put their manual pages in */usr/local/man*. The *man* command will not automatically look in */usr/local/man*, so when you ask for a manual page you may get the message "No manual entry." Fix this by specifying all the top *man* directories in a variable called MANPATH. For example (you have to put in the actual directories where the manual pages are on your system):

```
$ export MANPATH=/usr/man:/usr/local/man
```

The syntax is like PATH, described earlier in this chapter. Each pair of directories are separated by a colon. If your shell is *csh* or *tcsh*, you need to say:

```
$ setenv MANPATH /usr/man:/usr/local/man
```

Another environment variable that you may want to set is MANSECT. It determines the order in which the sections of the manual pages are searched for an entry. For example:

```
$ export MANSECT="2:3:1:5:4:6:7:8:n:9"
```

searches in section 2 first.

Have you read some manual pages and still found yourself confused? They're not meant to be introductions to new topics. Get yourself a good beginner's book about Unix, and come back to manual pages gradually as you become more comfortable on the system; then they'll be irreplaceable.

Manual pages are not the only source of information on Unix systems. Programs from the GNU project often have Info pages that you read with the program *info*. For example, to read the Info pages for the command *find*, you would enter:

```
info find
```

The *info* program is arcane and has lots of navigation features; to learn it, your best bet will be to type Ctrl-H in the *info* program and read through the Help screen. Fortunately, there are also programs that let you read Info pages more easily, notably *tkinfo* and *kdehelp*. These commands use the X Window System to present a graphical interface. You can also read Info pages from Emacs (see the section "The Emacs Editor" in Chapter 9) or use the command *pinfo* available on some Linux distributions that works more like the Lynx web browser.

In recent times, more and more documentation is provided in the form of HTML pages. You can read those with any web browser (see Chapter 16). For example, in the Konqueror web browser, you select Open Location... from the Location menu and press the button with the folder symbol, which opens an ordinary file selection dialog where you can select your documentation file.

File Ownership and Permissions

Ownership and permissions are central to security. It's important to get them right, even when you're the only user, because odd things can happen if you don't. For the files that users create and use daily, these things usually work without much thought (although it's still useful to know the concepts). For system administration, matters are not so easy. Assign the wrong ownership or permission, and you might get into a frustrating bind like being unable to read your mail. In general, the message:

```
Permission denied
```

means that someone has assigned an ownership or permission that restricts access more than you want.

What Permissions Mean

Permissions refer to the ways in which someone can use a file. There are three such permissions under Unix:

- *Read* permission means you can look at the file's contents.
- *Write* permission means you can change or delete the file.
- *Execute* permission means you can run the file as a program.

When each file is created, the system assigns some default permissions that work most of the time. For instance, it gives you both read and write permission, but most of the world has only read permission. If you have a reason to be paranoid, you can set things up so that other people have no permissions at all.

Additionally, most utilities know how to assign permissions. For instance, when the compiler creates an executable program, it automatically assigns executable permission.

There are times when defaults don't work, though. For instance, if you create a shell script or Perl program, you'll have to assign executable permission yourself so that you can run it. We'll show how to do that later in this section, after we get through the basic concepts.

Permissions have different meanings for a directory:

- Read permission means you can list the contents of that directory.
- Write permission means you can add or remove files in that directory.
- Execute permission means you can list information about the files in that directory.

Don't worry about the difference between read and execute permission for directories; basically, they go together. Assign both or neither.

Note that, if you allow people to add files to a directory, you are also letting them remove files. The two privileges go together when you assign write permission. However, there is a way you can let users share a directory and keep them from deleting each other's files. See the section "Upgrading Other Software" in Chapter 7.

There are more files on Unix systems than the plain files and directories we've talked about so far. These are special files (devices), sockets, symbolic links, and so forth—each type observing its own rules regarding permissions. But you don't need to know the details on each type.

Owners and Groups

Now, who gets these permissions? To allow people to work together, Unix has three levels of permission: owner, group, and other. The "other" level covers everybody who has access to the system and who isn't the owner or a member of the group.

The idea behind having groups is to give a set of users, like a team of programmers, access to a file. For instance, a programmer creating source code may reserve write permission to herself, but allow members of her group to have read access through a group permission. As for "other," it might have no permission at all so that people outside the team can't snoop around. (You think your source code is *that* good?)

Each file has an owner and a group. The owner is generally the user who created the file. Each user also belongs to a default group, and that group is assigned to every file the user creates. You can create many groups, though, and assign each user to multiple groups. By changing the group assigned to a file, you can give access to any collection of people you want. We'll discuss groups more when we get to the section "The Group File" in Chapter 5.

Now we have all the elements of our security system: three permissions (read, write, execute) and three levels (user, group, other). Let's look at some typical files and see what permissions are assigned.

Figure 4-2 shows a typical executable program. We generated this output by executing *ls* with the *-l* option.

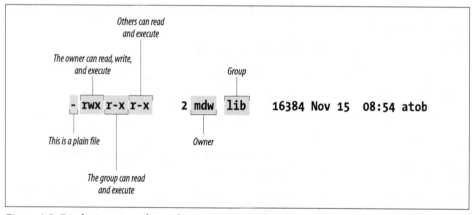

Figure 4-2. Displaying ownership and permissions

Two useful facts stand right out: the owner of the file is an author of this book and your faithful guide, mdw, while the group is lib (perhaps a group created for programmers working on libraries). But the key information about permissions is encrypted in the set of letters on the left side of the display.

The first character is a hyphen, indicating a plain file. The next three bits apply to the owner; as we would expect, mdw has all three permissions. The next three bits apply to members of the group: they can read the file (not too useful for a binary file) and execute it, but they can't write to it because the field that should contain a w contains a hyphen instead. And the last three bits apply to "other"; they have the same permissions in this case as the group.

Here is another example: if you ask for a long listing of a C source file, it would look something like this:

```
$ ls -l
-rw-rw-r--   1 kalle    kalle      12577 Apr 30 13:13 simc.c
```

The listing shows that the owner has read and write (rw) privileges, and so does the group. Everyone else on the system has only read privileges.

Now suppose we compile the file to create an executable program. The file *simc* is created by the *gcc* compiler:

```
$ gcc -osimc simc.c
$ ls -l
total 36
-rwxrwxr-x   1 kalle    kalle      19365 Apr 30 13:14 simc
-rw-rw-r--   1 kalle    kalle      12577 Apr 30 13:13 simc.c
```

In addition to the read and write bits, *gcc* has set the executable (x) bit for owner, group, and other on the executable file. This is the appropriate thing to do so that the file can be run:

```
$ ./simc
(output here)
```

One more example—a typical directory:

```
drwxr-xr-x   2 mdw      lib          512 Jul 17 18:23 perl
```

The leftmost bit is now a d to show that this is a directory. The executable bits are back because you want people to see the contents of the directory.

Files can be in some obscure states that aren't covered here; see the *ls* manual page for gory details. But now it's time to see how you can change ownership and permissions.

Changing the Owner, Group, and Permissions

As we said, most of the time you can get by with the default security the system gives you. But there are always exceptions, particularly for system administrators. To take a simple example, suppose you are creating a directory under */home* for a new user. You have to create everything as root, but when you're done you have to change the ownership to the user; otherwise, that user won't be able to use the files! (Fortunately, if you use the *adduser* command discussed in the section "Creating Accounts" in Chapter 5, it takes care of ownership for you.)

Similarly, certain utilities such as UUCP and News have their own users. No one ever logs in as UUCP or News, but those users and groups must exist so that the utilities can do their job in a secure manner. In general, the last step when installing software is usually to change the owner, group, and permissions as the documentation tells you to do.

The *chown* command changes the owner of a file, and the *chgrp* command changes the group. On Linux, only root can use *chown* for changing ownership of a file, but any user can change the group to another group to which he belongs.

So after installing some software named *sampsoft*, you might change both the owner and the group to bin by executing:

```
# chown bin sampsoft
# chgrp bin sampsoft
```

You could also do this in one step by using the dot notation:

```
# chown bin.bin sampsoft
```

The syntax for changing permissions is more complicated. The permissions can also be called the file's "mode," and the command that changes permissions is *chmod*. Let's start our exploration of this command through a simple example; say you've written a neat program in Perl or Tcl named *header*, and you want to be able to execute it. You would type the following command:

```
$ chmod +x header
```

The plus sign means "add a permission," and the x indicates which permission to add.

If you want to remove execute permission, use a minus sign in place of a plus:

```
$ chmod -x header
```

This command assigns permissions to all levels—user, group, and other. Let's say that you are secretly into software hoarding and don't want anybody to use the command but yourself. No, that's too cruel; let's say instead that you think the script is buggy and want to protect other people from hurting themselves until you've exercised it. You can assign execute permission just to yourself through the command:

```
$ chmod u+x header
```

Whatever goes before the plus sign is the level of permission, and whatever goes after is the type of permission. User permission (for yourself) is u, group permission is g, and other is o. So to assign permission to both yourself and the file's group, enter:

```
$ chmod ug+x header
```

You can also assign multiple types of permissions:

```
$ chmod ug+rwx header
```

You can learn a few more shortcuts from the *chmod* manual page in order to impress someone looking over your shoulder, but they don't offer any functionality besides what we've shown you.

As arcane as the syntax of the mode argument may seem, there's another syntax that is even more complicated. We have to describe it, though, for several reasons. First of all, there are several situations that cannot be covered by the syntax, called *symbolic mode*, that we've just shown. Second, people often use the other syntax, called

---

absolute mode, in their documentation. Third, there are times you may actually find the absolute mode more convenient.

To understand absolute mode, you have to think in terms of bits and octal notation. Don't worry, it's not too hard. A typical mode contains three characters, corresponding to the three levels of permission (user, group, and other). These levels are illustrated in Figure 4-3. Within each level, there are three bits corresponding to read, write, and execute permission.

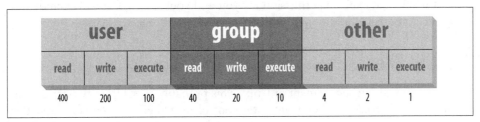

Figure 4-3. Bits in absolute mode

Let's say you want to give yourself read permission and no permission to anybody else. You want to specify just the bit represented by the number 400. So the *chmod* command would be:

```
$ chmod 400 header
```

To give read permission to everybody, choose the correct bit from each level: 400 for yourself, 40 for your group, and 4 for other. The full command is:

```
$ chmod 444 header
```

This is like using a mode +r, except that it simultaneously removes any write or execute permission. (To be precise, it's just like a mode of =r, which we didn't mention earlier. The equal sign means "assign these rights and no others.")

To give read and execute permission to everybody, you have to add up the read and execute bits: 400 plus 100 is 500, for instance.

So the corresponding command is:

```
$ chmod 555 header
```

which is the same as =rx. To give someone full access, you would specify that digit as a 7—the sum of 4, 2, and 1.

One final trick: how to set the default mode that is assigned to each file you create (with a text editor, the > redirection operator, and so on). You do so by executing an *umask* command, or putting one in your shell's startup file. This file could be called *.bashrc*, *.cshrc*, or something else depending on the shell you use (we'll discuss startup files in the next section).

The *umask* command takes an argument like the absolute mode in *chmod*, but the meaning of the bits is inverted. You have to determine the access you want to grant for user, group, and other, and subtract each digit from 7. That gives you a three-digit mask.

For instance, say you want yourself to have all permissions (7), your group to have read and execute permissions (5), and others to have no permissions (0). Subtract each bit from 7 and you get 0 for yourself, 2 for your group, and 7 for other. So the command to put in your startup file is:

```
umask 027
```

A strange technique, but it works. The *chmod* command looks at the mask when it interprets your mode; for instance, if you assign execute mode to a file at creation time, it will assign execute permission for you and your group, but will exclude others because the mask doesn't permit them to have any access.

Startup Files

Configuration is a strong element of Unix. This probably stems from two traits commonly found in hackers: they want total control over their environment, and they strive to minimize the number of keystrokes and other hand movements they have to perform. So all the major utilities on Unix—editors, mailers, debuggers, X Window System clients—provide files that let you override their default behaviors in a bewildering number of ways. Many of these files have names ending in *rc*, which means *resource configuration*.

Startup files are usually in your home directory. Their names begin with a period, which keeps the *ls* command from displaying them under normal circumstances. None of the files is required; all the affected programs are smart enough to use defaults when the file does not exist. But everyone finds it useful to have the startup files. Here are some common ones:

.bashrc

> For the *bash* shell. The file is a shell script, which means it can contain commands and other programming constructs. Here's a very short startup file that might have been placed in your home directory by the tool that created your account:
>
> ```
> PS1='\u$'          # The prompt contains the user's login name.
>
> HISTSIZE=50          # Save 50 commands for when the user presses the up arrow.
>
> # All the directories to search for commands.
> PATH=/usr/local/bin:/usr/bin:/bin:/usr/bin/X11
>
> # To prevent the user from accidentally ending a login session,
> # disable Ctrl-D as a way to exit.
> IGNOREEOF=1
>
> stty erase "^H"          # Make sure the backspace key erases.
> ```

.bash_profile

For the *bash* shell. Another shell script. The difference between this script and *.bashrc* is that *.bash_profile* runs only when you log in. It was originally designed so that you could separate interactive shells from those run by background processors like *cron* (discussed in Chapter 8). But it is not very useful on modern computers with the X Window System because when you open a new terminal window, only *.bashrc* runs. If you start up a window with the command *xterm -ls*, it will run *.bash_profile* too.

.cshrc

For the C shell or *tcsh*. The file is a shell script using C shell constructs.

.login

For the C shell or *tcsh*. The file is a shell script using C shell constructs. Like *.bash_profile* in the *bash* shell, this runs only when you log in. Here are some commands you might find in *.cshrc* or *.login*:

```
set prompt='% '        # Simple % for prompt.

set history=50         # Save 50 commands for when the user presses the up arrow.

# All the directories to search for commands.
set path=(/usr/local/bin /usr/bin /bin /usr/bin/X11)

# To prevent the user from accidentally ending a login session,
# disable Ctrl-D as a way to exit.
set ignoreeof

stty erase "^H"        # Make sure the backspace key erases.
```

.emacs

For the Emacs editor. Consists of LISP functions. See the section "The X Resource Database" **in** Chapter 11.

.exrc

For the *vi* editor (also known as *ex*). Each line is an editor command. See the section "Basics of X Customization **in** Chapter 11.

.newsrc

For news readers. Contains a list of all newsgroups offered at the site.

.Xdefaults

For programs using the X Window System. Each line specifies a resource (usually the name of a program and some property of that program) along with the value that resource should take. This file is described in the section "The X Resource Database" in Chapter 11.

.xinitrc

> For the X Window System. Consists of shell commands that run whenever you log into an X session. See the section "Basics of X Customization" in Chapter 11 for details on using this file.

.kde/share/config

> This is actually a whole directory with configuration files for the K Desktop Environment (KDE). You will find a lot of files here, all starting with the name of the program they configure and ending in *rc*. Note that you should normally not need to edit these files manually; the respective programs all come with their own configuration dialogs. Depending on the KDE version, this path might start with *.kde2* or *.kde3*.

.gnome

> Like the previous entry a whole directory of configuration files, this time for the GNOME graphical desktop.

Important Directories

You already know about */home*, where user files are stored. As a system administrator and programmer, several other directories will be important to you. Here are a few, along with their contents:

/bin

> The most essential Unix commands, such as *ls*.

/usr/bin

> Other commands. The distinction between */bin* and */usr/bin* is arbitrary; it was a convenient way to split up commands on early Unix systems that had small disks.

/usr/sbin

> Commands used by the superuser for system administration.

/boot

> Location where the kernel and other files used during booting are sometimes stored.

/etc

> Files used by subsystems such as networking, NFS, and mail. Typically, these contain tables of network services, disks to mount, and so on. Many of the files here are used for booting the system or individual services of it and will be discussed elsewhere in this book.

/var

> Administrative files, such as log files, used by various utilities.

/var/spool

> Temporary storage for files being printed, sent by UUCP, and so on.

/usr/lib

Standard libraries, such as *libc.a*. When you link a program, the linker always searches here for the libraries specified in *-l* options.

/usr/lib/X11

The X Window System distribution. Contains the libraries used by X clients, as well as fonts, sample resources files, and other important parts of the X package. This directory is usually a symbolic link to */usr/X11R6/lib/X11*.

/usr/include

Standard location of include files used in C programs, such as *<stdio.h>*.

/usr/src

Location of sources to programs built on the system.

/usr/local

Programs and datafiles that have been added locally by the system administrator.

/etc/skel

Sample startup files you can place in home directories for new users.

/dev

This directory contains the so-called device files, the interface between the filesystem and the hardware (e.g., */dev/modem* represents your modem in the system).

/proc

Just as */dev* is the interface between the filesystem and the hardware devices, */proc* is the interface between the filesystem and the running processes, the CPU and memory. The files here (which are not real files, but rather virtual files generated on-the-fly when you view them) can give you information about the environment of a certain process, the state and configuration of the CPU, how your I/O ports are configured, etc.

Programs That Serve You

We're including this section because you should start to be interested in what's running on your system behind your back.

Many modern computer activities are too complex for the system simply to look at a file or some other static resource. Sometimes these activities need to interact with another running process.

For instance, take FTP, which you may have used to download some Linux-related documents or software. When you FTP to another system, another program has to be running on that system to accept your connection and interpret your commands. So there's a program running on that system called *ftpd*. The *d* in the name stands for *daemon*, which is a quaint Unix term for a server that runs in the background all the time. Most daemons handle network activities.

You've probably heard of the buzzword *client/server* enough to make you sick, but here it is in action—it has been in action for decades on Unix.

Daemons start up when the system is booted. To see how they get started, look in the */etc/inittab* and */etc/inetd.conf* files, as well as distribution-specific configuration files. We won't go into their formats here. But each line in these files lists a program that runs when the system starts. You can find the distribution-specific files either by checking the documentation that came with your system or by looking for pathnames that occur frequently in */etc/inittab*. Those normally indicate the directory tree where your distribution stores its system startup files.

To give an example of how your system uses */etc/inittab*, look at one or more lines with the string getty or agetty. This is the program that listens at a terminal (tty) waiting for a user to log in. It's the program that displays the login : prompt we talked about at the beginning of this chapter.

The */etc/inetd.conf* file represents a more complicated way of running programs—another level of indirection. The idea behind */etc/inetd.conf* is that it would waste a lot of system resources if a dozen or more daemons were spinning idly, waiting for a request to come over the network. So, instead, the system starts up a single daemon named *inetd*. This daemon listens for connections from clients on other machines, and when an incoming connection is made, it starts up the appropriate daemon to handle it. For example, when an incoming FTP connection is made, *inetd* starts up the FTP daemon (*ftpd*) to manage the connection. In this way, the only network daemons running are those actually in use.

In the next section, we'll show you how to see which daemons are running on your system. There's a daemon for every service offered by the system to other systems on a network: *fingerd* to handle remote *finger* requests, *rwhod* to handle *rwho* requests, and so on. A few daemons also handle non-networking services, such as *kerneld*, which handles the automatic loading of modules into the kernel. (In Versions 2.4 and up, this is called *kmod* instead and is no longer a process, but rather a kernel thread.)

Processes

At the heart of Unix lies the concept of a process. Understanding this concept will help you keep control of your login session as a user. If you are also a system administrator, the concept is even more important.

A process is an independently running program that has its own set of resources. For instance, we showed in an earlier section how you could direct the output of a program to a file while your shell continued to direct output to your screen. The reason that the shell and the other program can send output to different places is that they are separate processes.

On Unix, the finite resources of the system, like the memory and the disks, are managed by one all-powerful program called the kernel. Everything else on the system is a process.

Thus, before you log in, your terminal is monitored by a *getty* process. After you log in, the *getty* process dies (a new one is started by the kernel when you log out) and your terminal is managed by your shell, which is a different process. The shell then creates a new process each time you enter a command. The creation of a new process is called *forking* because one process splits into two.

If you are using the X Window System, each process starts up one or more windows. Thus, the window in which you are typing commands is owned by an *xterm* process. That process forks a shell to run within the window. And that shell forks yet more processes as you enter commands.

To see the processes you are running, enter the command *ps*. Figure 4-4 shows some typical output and what each field means. You may be surprised how many processes you are running, especially if you are using X. One of the processes is the *ps* command itself, which of course dies as soon as the output is displayed.

```
$    ps
     PID     TTY     STAT     TIME     COMMAND
     1663    pp3     S        0:01     -bash
     1672    pp3     T        0:07     emacs
     1676    pp3     R        0:00     ps
```

PID - *Process ID (used to kill a process)*   TIME - *CPU time used so far*
TTY - *Controlling terminal*   COMMAND - *Command running*
STAT - *State*

Figure 4-4. Output of ps command

The first field in the *ps* output is a unique identifier for the process. If you have a runaway process that you can't get rid of through Ctrl-C or other means, you can kill it by going to a different virtual console or X window and entering:

```
$ kill process-id
```

The TTY field shows which terminal the process is running on, if any. (Everything run from a shell uses a terminal, of course, but background daemons don't have a terminal.)

The STAT field shows what state the process is in. The shell is currently suspended, so this field shows an S. An Emacs editing session is running, but it's suspended using Ctrl-Z. This is shown by the T in its STAT field. The last process shown is the *ps* that is generating all this input; its state, of course, is R because it is running.

The TIME field shows how much CPU time the processes have used. Because both *bash* and Emacs are interactive, they actually don't use much of the CPU.

You aren't restricted to seeing your own processes. Look for a minute at all the processes on the system. The *a* option stands for all processes, while the *x* option includes processes that have no controlling terminal (such as daemons started at runtime):

```
$ ps ax | more
```

Now you can see the daemons that we mentioned in the previous section.

Recent versions of the *ps* command have a nice additional option. If you are looking for a certain process of which you know the name or at least parts of it, you can use the option -*C*, followed by the name to see only the processes whose names match the name you specify:

```
$ ps -C httpd
```

And here, with a breathtaking view of the entire Unix system at work, we end this chapter (the lines are cut off at column 76; if you want to see the command lines in their full glory, add the option -*w* to the *ps* command):

```
kalle@owl:~ > ps aux
USER       PID %CPU %MEM   VSZ  RSS TTY       STAT START   TIME COMMAND
root         1  0.0  0.0   416   64 ?         S    Mar23   0:57 init [3]
root         2  0.0  0.0     0    0 ?         SW   Mar23  30:05 [kflushd]
root         3  0.0  0.0     0    0 ?         SW   Mar23  13:26 [kupdate]
root         4  0.0  0.0     0    0 ?         SW   Mar23  11:39 [kswapd]
root         5  0.0  0.0     0    0 ?         SW<  Mar23   0:00 [mdrecoveryd]
root         9  0.0  0.0     0    0 ?         SW   Mar23   0:00 [khubd]
bin       1512  0.0  0.0  1272    0 ?         SW   Mar23   0:00 [portmap]
root      1530  0.0  0.0  1328  216 ?         S    Mar23   0:17 /sbin/syslogd
root      1534  0.0  0.0  1728  180 ?         S    Mar23   0:03 /sbin/klogd -c 1
root      1560  0.0  0.0  1236    0 ?         SW   Mar23   0:00 [usbmgr]
root      1570  0.0  0.0  1728    0 ?         SW   Mar23   0:00 [nlservd]
at        1578  0.0  0.0  1388  108 ?         S    Mar23   0:00 /usr/sbin/atd
nobody    1585  0.0  0.0  5592   24 ?         S    Mar23   0:00 [in.identd]
nobody    1586  0.0  0.0  5592   24 ?         S    Mar23   0:49 [in.identd]
nobody    1587  0.0  0.0  5592   24 ?         S    Mar23   0:00 [in.identd]
nobody    1588  0.0  0.0  5592   24 ?         S    Mar23   0:00 [in.identd]
root      1618  0.0  0.0  1676   96 ?         S    Mar23   0:42 /usr/sbin/rpc.mou
root      1621  0.0  0.0  1696   92 ?         S    Mar23   0:41 /usr/sbin/rpc.nfs
root      1649  0.0  0.1  2352  340 ?         S    Mar23   0:23 sendmail: accepti
root      1657  0.0  0.1  2156  404 ?         S    Mar23   0:47 /usr/sbin/nmbd -D
root      1664  0.0  0.0  2652  196 ?         S    Mar23   0:00 [smbd]
root      1681  0.0  0.0  1408  164 ?         S    Mar23   0:15 /usr/sbin/cron
root      1689  0.0  0.0  1328   32 ?         S    Mar23   0:00 /usr/sbin/lpd
root      1713  0.0  0.1 11724  352 ?         S    Mar23   0:03 /usr/sbin/nscd
root      1731  0.0  0.0  1280  168 ?         S    Mar23   0:00 /usr/sbin/inetd
root      1795  0.0  0.0  1996    0 tty1      SW   Mar23   0:00 [login]
root      1796  0.0  0.0  1996    0 tty2      SW   Mar23   0:00 [login]
```

```
root       1798  0.0  0.0  1228     0 tty4    SW  Mar23   0:00 [mingetty]
root       1799  0.0  0.0  1228     0 tty5    SW  Mar23   0:00 [mingetty]
root       1800  0.0  0.0  1228     0 tty6    SW  Mar23   0:00 [mingetty]
kalle      2302  0.0  0.0  2584     0 tty1    SW  Mar23   0:00 [bash]
root       2309  0.0  0.0  2428     0 tty2    SW  Mar23   0:00 [bash]
root       2356  0.0  0.0  1292    56 ?       S   Mar23  19:32 /usr/sbin/gpm -t
root       5860  0.0  0.0  2108    88 ?       S   Mar23   0:01 [sshd]
root      21391  0.0  0.0  2004     0 tty3    SW  Mar30   0:00 [login]
kdeuser   21394  0.0  0.0  2548     0 tty3    SW  Mar30   0:00 [bash]
kalle     17613  0.0  0.0  1660     0 ?       SW  Mar31   0:00 [ssh-agent]
kalle     20007  0.0  0.1  2628   512 tty1    S   Apr03   0:00 /bin/bash
kalle     27278  0.0  0.4  2384  1140 tty1    S   Apr22   0:00 sh /usr/X11R6/bin
kalle     27279  0.0  0.2  1552   636 tty1    S   Apr22   0:00 tee /home/kalle/.
kalle     27291  0.0  0.3  2728   824 tty1    S   Apr22   0:00 xinit /home/kalle
root      27292 25.2  7.2 45724 19080 ?       S   Apr22 2531:10 X :0 -auth /home
kalle     27308  0.0  0.4  2376  1124 tty1    S   Apr22   0:00 bash /home/kalle/
kalle     27316  0.0  0.4  2500  1296 tty1    S   Apr22   0:00 bash --login /opt
kalle     27374  0.0  0.4 14048  1212 ?       S   Apr22   0:08 kdeinit: dcopserv
kalle     27376  0.0  0.6 14540  1812 ?       S   Apr22   0:01 kdeinit: klaunche
kalle     27378  0.0  0.7 13964  1852 ?       S   Apr22   5:36 kdeinit: kded
kalle     27381  0.1  2.3 18564  6252 ?       S   Apr22  12:03 kdeinit: kdesktop
kalle     27388  0.0  0.6 14164  1716 ?       S   Apr22   0:00 kdeinit: kxmlrpcd
kalle     27399  0.1  2.0 15324  5468 ?       S   Apr22  13:10 kdeinit: klipper
kalle     27401  0.0  1.4 14316  3920 ?       S   Apr22   0:02 kdeinit: khotkeys
kalle     27403  0.0  0.1 13608   296 ?       S   Apr22   0:00 kdeinit: Running.
kalle     27404  0.0  1.6 14516  4204 ?       S   Apr22   0:01 kdeinit: kwrited
kalle     27406  0.0  0.1  1440   520 pts/0   S   Apr22   0:00 /bin/cat
kalle     27409  0.0  2.1 13680  5664 tty1    S   Apr22   0:06 knotify
kalle     27413  0.0  1.8 10476  4844 tty1    S   Apr22   0:03 ksmserver --resto
kalle     27415  0.3  1.0 15032  2728 ?       S   Apr22  30:35 kdeinit: kwin -se
kalle     27426  0.0  0.9 15496  2436 ?       S   Apr22   0:29 kdeinit: konsole
kalle     27429  0.0  0.9 15456  2424 ?       S   Apr22   0:03 kdeinit: konsole
kalle     27430  0.0  0.5  2672  1568 pts/2   S   Apr22   0:00 /bin/bash
kalle     27431  0.0  0.6  2908  1776 pts/1   S   Apr22   0:01 /bin/bash
kalle     27489  0.0  2.1 15616  5648 ?       S   Apr22   0:06 kdeinit: kio_uise
kalle     27492  0.0  1.9 14636  5092 ?       S   Apr22   0:03 kdeinit: kcookiej
kalle     27494  0.0  0.7  9896  1916 ?       S   Apr22   0:05 kdesud
kalle     30812  0.0  1.1 17620  2900 pts/1   S   Apr23   6:01 kicker
kalle     30893  0.0  0.6 15556  1784 ?       S   Apr23   0:22 kdeinit: konsole
kalle     30894  0.0  0.6  2680  1580 pts/3   S   Apr23   0:00 /bin/bash
kalle     30902  0.0  2.7 13912  7132 pts/3   S   Apr23   0:26 xemacs
kalle     30924  0.0  7.7 36564 20152 ?       S   Apr23   1:29 konqueror -mimety
root       1573  0.0  1.2  4740  3320 ?       S   Apr23   1:07 /usr/sbin/smbd -D
kalle      5812  0.0  0.9 15600  2408 ?       S   Apr24   1:35 kdeinit: konsole
kalle      5813  0.0  0.6  2836  1720 pts/4   S   Apr24   0:00 /bin/bash
kalle      5820  0.1  5.3 18904 13908 pts/4   S   Apr24  12:13 xemacs
kalle      6100  0.0  0.1  1660   400 ?       S   Apr24   0:00 ssh-agent
kalle     11670  0.0  6.2 26836 16376 ?       S   Apr25   0:16 konqueror -mimety
kalle     13390  0.0  0.6 15596  1812 ?       S   Apr25   0:20 kdeinit: konsole
kalle     13391  0.0  0.6  2684  1592 pts/5   S   Apr25   0:00 /bin/bash
kalle     15039  0.0  0.1  1656   396 ?       S   Apr25   0:00 ssh-agent
kalle     15337  0.0  0.9 15836  2560 ?       S   Apr25   0:03 designer
```

```
kalle    18660  0.0  6.4 24592 16976 pts/5  S   Apr26   4:29 xemacs
kalle    22903  0.2 13.2 42784 34756 ?      S   Apr26  11:59 kmail -caption KM
kalle     8744  0.0  3.3 15336 8712  ?      S   10:09   0:22 ksnapshot
kalle    12077  4.3  4.4 14796 11756 ?      R   20:42   0:34 xemacs
kalle    12130  0.0  1.2 13692 3204  ?      S   20:50   0:00 kdeinit: kio_file
kalle    12132  0.0  1.2 13692 3204  ?      S   20:50   0:00 kdeinit: kio_file
kalle    12152  1.2  0.5  2560 1340  pts/6  S   20:55   0:00 /bin/bash -i
kalle    12162  0.0  0.3  2688  988  pts/6  R   20:56   0:00 ps aux
kalle@owl:~ >
```

Essential System Management

If you're running your own Linux system, one of the first tasks at hand is to learn the ropes of system administration. You won't be able to get by for long without having to perform some kind of system maintenance, software upgrade, or mere tweaking to keep things in running order.

Running a Linux system is not unlike riding and taking care of a motorcycle.[*] Many motorcycle hobbyists prefer caring for their own equipment—routinely cleaning the points, replacing worn-out parts, and so forth. Linux gives you the opportunity to experience the same kind of "hands-on" maintenance with a complex operating system.

While a passionate administrator can spend any amount of time tuning it for performance, you really have to perform administration only when a major change occurs: you install a new disk, a new user comes on the system, or a power failure causes the system to go down unexpectedly. We discuss all these situations over the next four chapters.

Linux is surprisingly accessible, in all respects—from the more mundane tasks of upgrading shared libraries to the more esoteric, such as mucking about with the kernel. Because all the source code is available, and the body of Linux developers and users has traditionally been of the hackish breed, system maintenance is not only a part of daily life but also a great learning experience. Trust us: there's nothing like telling your friends how you upgraded from XFree86 3.3.6 to XFree86 4.0.3 in less than half an hour, and all the while you were recompiling the kernel to support the ISO 9660 filesystem. (They may have no idea what you're talking about, in which case you can give them a copy of this book.)

In the next few chapters, we explore your Linux system from the mechanic's point of view—showing you what's under the hood, as it were—and explain how to take care

---

[*] At least one author attests a strong correspondence between Linux system administration and Robert Pirsig's *Zen and the Art of Motorcycle Maintenance*. Does Linux have the Buddha nature?

of it all, including software upgrades, managing users, filesystems, and other resources, performing backups, and what to do in emergencies.

Once you put the right entries in startup files, your Linux system will, for the most part, run itself. As long as you're happy with the system configuration and the software that's running on it, very little work will be necessary on your part. However, we'd like to encourage Linux users to experiment with their system and customize it to taste. Very little about Linux is carved in stone, and if something doesn't work the way that you'd like it to, you should be able to change that. For instance, if you'd prefer to read blinking green text on a cyan background rather than the traditional white-on-black, we'll show you how to configure that. (As long as you promise not to let anyone know who told you.) But we'll also show you something even more important: after installing a Linux distribution, you usually have lots of services running that you may not need (like a web server). Any of these services could be a potential security hole, so you might want to fiddle with the startup files to get only the services you absolutely need.

It should be noted that many Linux systems include fancy tools to simplify many system administration tasks. These include YaST on SuSE systems, COAS on Caldera systems, and a number of utilities on Red Hat systems. These tools can do everything from managing user accounts to creating filesystems to doing your laundry. These utilities can make your life either easier or more difficult, depending on how you look at them. In these chapters, we present the "guts" of system administration, demonstrating the tools that should be available on any Linux system and indeed nearly all Unix systems. These are the core of the system administrator's toolbox: the metaphorical hammer, screwdriver, and socket wrench that you can rely on to get the job done. If you'd rather use the 40-hp circular saw, feel free, but it's always nice to know how to use the hand tools in case the power goes out. Good follow-up books, should you wish to investigate more topics in Unix system administration, include the *Unix System Administration Handbook*, by Evi Nemeth et. al. (Prentice Hall) and *Essential System Administration*, by Æleen Frisch (O'Reilly).

Maintaining the System

Being the system administrator for any Unix system requires a certain degree of responsibility and care. This is equally true for Linux, even if you're the only user on your system.

Many of the system administrator's tasks are done by logging into the root account. This account has special properties on Unix systems; specifically, the usual file permissions and other security mechanisms simply don't apply to root. That is, root can access and modify any file on the system, no matter to whom it belongs. Whereas normal users can't damage the system (say, by corrupting filesystems or touching other users' files), root has no such restrictions.

Why does the Unix system have security in the first place? The most obvious reason for this is to allow users to choose how they wish their own files to be accessed. By changing file-permission bits (with the *chmod* command), users can specify that certain files should be readable, writable, or executable only by certain groups of other users, or by no other users at all. Permissions help ensure privacy and integrity of data; you wouldn't want other users to read your personal mailbox, for example, or to edit the source code for an important program behind your back.

The Unix security mechanisms also prevent users from damaging the system. The system restricts access to many of the raw device files (accessed via */dev*—more on this in the section "Device Files" in Chapter 6) corresponding to hardware, such as your hard drives. If normal users could read and write directly to the disk-drive device, they could wreak all kinds of havoc: say, completely overwriting the contents of the drive. Instead, the system requires normal users to access the drives via the filesystem—where security is enforced via the file permission bits described previously.

It is important to note that not all kinds of "damage" that can be caused are necessarily malevolent. System security is more a means to protect users from their own natural mistakes and misunderstandings rather than to enforce a police state on the system. And, in fact, on many systems security is rather lax; Unix security is designed to foster the sharing of data between groups of users who may be, say, cooperating on a project. The system allows users to be assigned to groups, and file permissions may be set for an entire group. For instance, one development project might have free read and write permission to a series of files, while at the same time other users are prevented from modifying those files. With your own personal files, you get to decide how public or private the access permissions should be.

The Unix security mechanism also prevents normal users from performing certain actions, such as calling certain system calls within a program. For example, there is a system call that causes the system to halt, called by programs such as *shutdown* (more on this later in the chapter) to reboot the system. If normal users could call this function within their programs, they could accidentally (or purposefully) halt the system at any time.

In many cases, you have to bypass Unix security mechanisms in order to perform system maintenance or upgrades. This is what the root account is for. Because no such restrictions apply to root, it is easy for a knowledgeable system administrator to get work done without worrying about the usual file permissions or other limitations. The usual way to log in as root is with the *su* command. *su* allows you to assume the identification of another user. For example:

    su andy

will prompt you for the password for andy, and if it is correct it will set your user ID to that of andy. A superuser often wants to temporarily assume a regular user's identity to correct a problem with that user's files or some similar reason. Without a username argument, *su* will prompt you for the root password, validating your user ID as root. Once you are finished using the root account, you log out in the usual way and return to your own mortal identity.

Why not simply log in as root from the usual login prompt? As we'll see, this is desirable in some instances, but most of the time it's best to use *su* after logging in as yourself. On a system with many users, use of *su* records a message, such as:

```
Nov  1 19:28:50 loomer su: mdw on /dev/ttyp1
```

in the system logs, such as */var/log/messages* (we'll talk more about these files later). This message indicates that the user mdw successfully issued an *su* command, in this case for root. If you were to log in directly as root, no such message would appear in the logs; you wouldn't be able to tell which user was mucking about with the root account. This is important if multiple administrators are on the machine: it is often desirable to find out who used *su* and when.

There is an additional little twist to the *su* command. Just running it as described previously while only change your user ID, but not give you the settings made for this ID. You might have special configuration files for each user (we'll show you later how to create these), but these are not executed when using *su* this way. In order to emulate a real login with all the configuration files being executed, you need to add a -, like this:

```
su - andy
```

or

```
su -
```

for becoming root and executing root's configuration files.

The root account can be considered a magic wand—both a useful and potentially dangerous tool. Fumbling the magic words you invoke while holding this wand can wreak unspeakable damage on your system. For example, the simple eight-character sequence rm -rf / will delete every file on your system, if executed as root, and if you're not paying attention. Does this problem seem far-fetched? Not at all. You might be trying to delete an old directory, such as */usr/src/oldp*, and accidentally slip in a space after the first slash, producing the following:

```
rm -rf / usr/src/oldp
```

Also problematic are directory names with spaces in them. Let's say you have directory names *Dir\ 1* and *Dir\ 2*, where the backslash indicates that *Dir\ 1* is really one filename containing a space character. Now you want to delete both directories, but by mistake add an extra space again:

```
rm -rf Dir\  *
```

Now there are two spaces between the backslash and the asterisk. The first one is protected by the backslash, but not the second one, so it separates the arguments and makes the asterisk a new argument. Oops, your current directory and everything below it are gone.

Another common mistake is to confuse the arguments for commands such as *dd*, a command often used to copy large chunks of data from one place to another. For instance, in order to save the first 1024 bytes of data from the device */dev/hda* (which contains the boot record and partition table for that drive), one might use the command:

```
dd if=/dev/hda of=/tmp/stuff bs=1k count=1
```

However, if we reverse if and of in this command, something quite different happens: the contents of */tmp/stuff* are written to the top of */dev/hda*. More likely than not, you've just succeeded in hosing your partition table and possibly a filesystem superblock. Welcome to the wonderful world of system administration!

The point here is that you should sit on your hands before executing any command as root. Stare at the command for a minute before pressing Enter and make sure it makes sense. If you're not sure of the arguments and syntax of the command, quickly check the manual pages or try the command in a safe environment before firing it off. Otherwise you'll learn these lessons the hard way; mistakes made as root can be disastrous.

A nice tip is to use the *alias* command to make some of the commands less dangerous for root. For example, you could use:

```
alias rm="rm -i"
```

The -i option stands for *interactively* and means that the rm command will ask you before deleting each file. Of course, this does not protect you against the horrible mistake shown above; the -f option (which stands for *force*) simply overrides the -i because it comes later.

In many cases, the prompt for the root account differs from that for normal users. Classically, the root prompt contains a hash mark (#), while normal user prompts contain $ or %. (Of course, use of this convention is up to you; it is utilized on many Unix systems, however.) Although the prompt may remind you that you are wielding the root magic wand, it is not uncommon for users to forget this or accidentally enter a command in the wrong window or virtual console.

Like any powerful tool, the root account can also be abused. It is important, as the system administrator, to protect the root password, and if you give it out at all, to give it only to those users whom you trust (or who can be held responsible for their actions on the system). If you're the only user of your Linux system, this certainly doesn't apply—unless, of course, your system is connected to a network or allows dial-in login access.

The primary benefit of not sharing the root account with other users is not so much that the potential for abuse is diminished, although this is certainly the case. Even more important is that if you're the one person with the ability to use the root account, you have complete knowledge of how the system is configured. If anyone were able to, say, modify important system files (as we'll talk about in this chapter), the system configuration could be changed behind your back, and your assumptions about how things work would be incorrect. Having one system administrator act as the arbiter for the system configuration means that one person always knows what's going on.

Also, allowing other people to have the root password means that it's more likely someone will eventually make a mistake using the root account. Although each person with knowledge of the root password may be trusted, anybody can make mistakes. If you're the only system administrator, you have only yourself to blame for making the inevitable human mistakes as root.

That being said, let's dive into the actual tasks of system administration under Linux. Buckle your seatbelt.

Booting the System

There are several ways of booting Linux on your system. The most common methods involve booting from the hard drive or using a boot floppy. In many cases, the installation procedure will have configured one or both of these for you; in any case, it's important to understand how to configure booting for yourself.

Using a Boot Floppy

Traditionally, a Linux boot floppy simply contains a kernel image, which is loaded into memory when you insert the floppy and start the system.*

Many Linux distributions create a boot floppy for you in this way when installing the system. Using a boot floppy is an easy way to boot Linux if you don't want to bother booting from the hard drive. (For example, Windows NT/2000's boot manager is somewhat difficult to configure for booting Linux. We'll talk about this in the next section.) Once the kernel has booted from the floppy, you are free to use the floppy drive for other purposes.

We'll include some technical information here in order to explain the boot process, but rest assured that in most cases, you can just insert the floppy disk, and booting works. Reading the following paragraphs will help you understanding your system, though.

The kernel image is usually compressed, using the same algorithm as the *gzip* or the *bzip2* compression programs (more on this in the section "Building the Kernel" in

---

* A Linux boot floppy may instead contain a LILO boot record, which causes the system to boot a kernel from the hard drive. We'll discuss this in the next section, when we talk more about LILO.

Chapter 7). Compression allows the kernel, which may be a megabyte or more in size, to require only a few hundred kilobytes of disk space. Part of the kernel code is not compressed: this part contains the routines necessary to uncompress the kernel from the disk image and load it into memory. Therefore, the kernel actually "bootstraps" itself at boot time by uncompressing into memory.

A number of parameters are stored in the kernel image. Among these parameters is the name of the device to use as the root filesystem once the kernel boots. Another parameter is the text mode to use for the system console. All these parameters may be modified using the *rdev* command, which we'll discuss later in this section.

After the kernel has started, it attempts to mount a filesystem on the root device hardcoded in the kernel image itself. This will serve as the root filesystem—that is, the filesystem on /. The section "Managing Filesystems" in Chapter 6 discusses filesystems in more detail; all that you need to know for now is that the kernel image must contain the name of your root filesystem device. If the kernel can't mount a filesystem on this device, it gives up, issuing a kernel "panic" message. (Essentially, a *kernel panic* is a fatal error signaled by the kernel itself. A panic will occur whenever the kernel is terminally confused and can't continue with execution. For example, if there is a bug in the kernel itself, a panic might occur when it attempts to access memory that doesn't exist. We'll talk about kernel panics more in the section "What to Do in an Emergency" in Chapter 8.)

The root device stored in the kernel image is that of your root filesystem on the hard drive. This means that once the kernel boots, it mounts a hard-drive partition as the root filesystem, and all control transfers to the hard drive. Once the kernel is loaded into memory, it stays there—the boot floppy need not be accessed again (until you reboot the system, of course).

Given a kernel image, you can create your own boot floppy. On many Linux systems, the kernel itself is stored in the file */boot/vmlinuz.*[*] This is not a universal convention, however; other Linux systems store the kernel in */vmlinuz* or */vmlinux*, and still others in a file such as */Image*. (If you have multiple kernel images, you can use LILO to select which one to boot. See the next section.) Note that newly installed Linux systems may not have a kernel image on the hard drive if a boot floppy was created for you. In any case, you can build your own kernel. It's often a good idea to do this anyway; you can "customize" the kernel to include only those drivers for your particular hardware. See the section "Building the Kernel" in Chapter 7 for details.

---

[*] Why the silly filename? On many Unix systems, the kernel is stored in a file named */vmunix* where *vm* stands for "virtual memory." Naturally, Linux has to be different and names its kernel images *vmlinux*, and places them in the directory */boot* to get them out of the root directory. The name *vmlinuz* was adopted to differentiate compressed kernel images from uncompressed images. Actually, the name and location of the kernel don't matter a bit, as long as you have either a boot floppy containing a kernel, or LILO knows how to find the kernel image.

All right. Let's say that you have a kernel image in the file */boot/vmlinuz*. To create a boot floppy, the first step is to use *rdev* to set the root device to that of your Linux root filesystem. (If you built the kernel yourself, this should be already set to the correct value, but it can't hurt to check with *rdev*.) We discussed how to create the root device in the sections "Drives and Partitions Under Linux" and "Creating Linux Partitions" in Chapter 3.

As root, use *rdev -h* to print a usage message. As you will see, there are many supported options, allowing you to specify the root device (our task here), the swap device, ramdisk size, and so on. For the most part, you needn't concern yourself with these options now.

If we use the command *rdev /boot/vmlinuz*, the root device encoded in the kernel found in */boot/vmlinuz* will be printed:

```
courgette:/# rdev /boot/vmlinuz
Root device /dev/hda1
```

If this is incorrect, and the Linux root filesystem is actually on */dev/hda3*, we should use the following command:

```
courgette:/# rdev /boot/vmlinuz /dev/hda3
courgette:/#
```

rdev is the strong, silent type; nothing is printed when you set the root device, so run *rdev /boot/vmlinuz* again to check that it is set correctly.

Now you're ready to create the boot floppy. For best results, use a brand-new, formatted floppy. You can format the floppy under Windows or using *fdformat* under Linux;* this will lay down the sector and track information so that the system can auto-detect the size of the floppy. (See the section "Managing Filesystems" in Chapter 6 for more on using floppies.)

To create the boot floppy, use *dd* to copy the kernel image to it, as in:

```
courgette:/# dd if=/boot/vmlinuz of=/dev/fd0 bs=8192
```

If you're interested in *dd*, the manual page will be illustrative; in brief, this copies the input file (*if* option) named */boot/vmlinuz* to the output file (*of* option) named */dev/fd0* (the first floppy device), using a block size (*bs*) of 8192 bytes. Of course, the plebian *cp* can be used as well, but we Unix sysadmins love to use cryptic commands to complete relatively simple tasks. That's what separates us from mortal users.

Your boot floppy should now be ready to go. You can shut down the system (see the section "Shutting Down the System" later in this chapter) and boot with the floppy, and if all goes well, your Linux system should boot as it usually does. It might be a good idea to make an extra boot floppy as a spare, and in the section "What to Do in

---

* Some versions of the Debian distribution don't have an *fdformat* command; use the aptly named *superformat* instead.

an Emergency" in Chapter 8, we describe methods by which boot floppies can be used to recover from disaster.

Using LILO

LILO is a general-purpose boot manager that can boot whatever operating systems you have installed on your machine, including Linux. There are dozens of ways to configure LILO. Here, we're going to discuss the two most common methods: installing LILO on the master boot record of your hard drive and installing LILO as a secondary boot loader for Linux only.

LILO is the most common way to boot Linux from the hard drive. (By the expression "boot from the hard drive," we mean that the kernel itself is stored on the hard drive and no boot floppy is required, but remember that even when you use a boot floppy, control is transferred to the hard drive once the kernel is loaded into memory.) If LILO is installed on your drive's master boot record, or MBR, it is the first code to run when the hard drive is booted. LILO can then boot other operating systems—such as Linux or Windows—and allow you to select between them at boot time.

 It should be mentioned here that LILO is not the only boot manager available for booting Linux. There are alternatives like *grub* (Grand Unified Bootloader) that work just as well. However, because most distributions use LILO, this is also what we will cover here.

However, Windows NT and later versions of Windows have boot managers of their own that occupy the MBR. If you are using one of these systems, in order to boot Linux from the hard drive, you may have to install LILO as the "secondary" boot loader for Linux only. In this case, LILO is installed on the boot record for just your Linux root partition, and the boot manager software (for Windows NT/2000) takes care of executing LILO from there when you wish to boot Linux.

As we'll see, however, the Windows NT/2000 boot managers are somewhat uncooperative when it comes to booting LILO. This is a poor design decision, and if you must absolutely use one of these boot managers, it might be easier to boot Linux from floppy instead. Read on. Or, if you really want to go with Linux all the way, you can use LILO to boot Windows NT/2000 and dump the Windows boot managers completely.

Use of LILO with Windows 95/98/ME/2000 is quite simple. You just configure LILO to boot Windows 95/98/ME/2000 (see the next section). However, if you install Windows 95/98/ME/2000 after installing LILO, you need to reinstall LILO (as the Windows 95/98/ME/2000 installation procedure overwrites the MBR of your primary hard drive). Just be sure you have a Linux boot floppy on hand so that you can boot Linux and rerun LILO.

Before proceeding you should note that a number of Linux distributions are capable of configuring and installing LILO when you first install the Linux software. However, it's often best to configure LILO yourself, just to ensure that everything is done correctly.

The /etc/lilo.conf file

The first step in configuring LILO is to set up the LILO configuration file, which is often stored in */etc/lilo.conf*. (On other systems, the file may be found in */boot/lilo.conf* or */etc/lilo/config*.)

We are going to walk through a sample *lilo.conf* file. You can use this file as a base for your own *lilo.conf* and edit it for your own system.

The first section of this file sets up some basic parameters:

```
boot = /dev/hda
compact
install = /boot/boot.b
map = /boot/map
```

The boot line sets the name of the device where LILO should install itself in the boot record. In this case, we want to install LILO in the master boot record of */dev/hda*, the first non-SCSI hard drive. If you're booting from a SCSI hard drive, use a device name such as */dev/sda* instead. If you give a partition device name (such as */dev/hda2*), instead of a drive device, LILO will be installed as a secondary boot loader on the named partition. We'll talk about this in more detail later.

The compact line tells LILO to perform some optimization; always use this unless you are seriously hacking on your LILO configuration.* Likewise, always use the install and map lines as shown. install names the file containing the boot sector to use on the MBR, and map specifies the "map file" that LILO creates when installed. On many distributions (like SuSE), these files should be in the directory */boot*, although on other systems they may be found in */etc/lilo*. */boot/map* won't be created until you install LILO for the first time.

Now, for each operating system you wish LILO to boot, add a stanza to */etc/lilo.conf*. For example, a Linux stanza might look like this:

```
# Stanza for Linux with root partition on /dev/hda2.
   image = /boot/vmlinuz    # Location of kernel
   label = linux            # Name of OS (for the LILO boot menu)
   root = /dev/hda2         # Location of root partition
   vga = ask                # Ask for VGA text mode at boot time
```

---

* In some cases, you will need the linear option, which should not be used together with compact. See the LILO documentation for more information.

The image line specifies the name of the kernel image. Subfields include label, which gives this stanza a name to use with the LILO boot menu (more on this later); root, which specifies the Linux root partition; and vga, which specifies the VGA text mode to use for the system console.

Valid modes for vga are normal (for standard 80x25 display), extended (for extended text mode, usually 132x44 or 132x60), ask (to be prompted for a mode at boot time), or an integer (such as 1, 2, or 3). The integer corresponds to the number of the mode you select when using ask. The exact text modes available depend on your video card; use vga = ask to get a list.

If you wish to boot multiple Linux kernels—for example, if you're doing some kernel debugging—you can add an image stanza for each one. The only required subfield of the image stanza is label. If you don't specify root or vga, the defaults coded into the kernel image itself using *rdev* will be used. If you do specify root or vga, these override the values you may have set using *rdev*. Therefore, if you are booting Linux using LILO, there's no need to use *rdev*; the LILO configuration file sets these boot parameters for you.

A stanza for booting Windows 95/98/ME/2000 would look like the following:

```
# Stanza for Win 95/Win 98/Win ME/Win 2000 partition on /dev/hda1.
    other = /dev/hda1    # Location of partition
    table = /dev/hda     # Location of partition table for /dev/hda2
    label = windows       # Name of OS (for boot menu)
```

If you wish to boot a Windows 95/98/ME/2000 partition located on the second drive, you should add the line:

```
    loader = /boot/any_d.b
```

to the Windows other stanza.

Many more options are available for LILO configuration. The LILO distribution itself (found on most Linux FTP sites and distributions) includes an extensive manual describing them all. The previous examples should suffice for most systems, however.

Once you have your */etc/lilo.conf* ready, you can run the command:

```
    /sbin/lilo
```

as root. This should display information, such as the following:

```
courgette:/# /sbin/lilo
Added linux
Added windows
courgette:/#
```

Using the -v option with *lilo* prints more diagnostic information should something go wrong; also, using the -C option allows you to specify a configuration file other than */etc/lilo.conf*.

Once this is done, you're ready to shut down your system (again, see the section "Shutting Down the System" later in this chapter for details), reboot, and try it out. The first operating system stanza listed in *etc/lilo.conf* will be booted by default. To select one of the other kernels or operating systems listed in *etc/lilo.conf*, hold down the Shift or Ctrl key or simply press the Scroll Lock key while the system boots. This should present you with a LILO boot prompt:

```
boot:
```

Here, you can press Tab to get a list of available boot options:

```
boot: tab-key
linux windows
```

These are the names given with `label` lines in *etc/lilo.conf*. Enter the appropriate label, and that operating system will boot. In this case, entering `windows` causes Windows to boot from *dev/hda1*, as we specified in the *lilo.conf* file.

It should be noted here that some distributions add a fancy GUI to LILO (typically, this involves a Tux, the Linux penguin, in the background). However, configuring these should be no different from configuring the plain, old text-mode LILO.

Using LILO as a secondary bootloader

If you're using the Windows NT/2000 boot manager, installing the Debian distribution of Linux, or don't want LILO to inhabit the master boot record of your drive, you can configure LILO as a secondary bootloader, which will live on the boot record of just your Linux root partition.

To do this, simply change the `boot = ...` line of *etc/lilo.conf* to the name of the Linux root partition. For example:

```
boot = /dev/hda2
```

will install LILO on the boot record of *dev/hda2*, to boot Linux only. Note that this works only for primary partitions on the hard drive (not for extended or logical partitions). This restriction does not apply to the Debian distribution, however, where the MBR can boot an operating system from a boot sector in an extended (but not logical) partition. In order to boot Linux in this way, the Linux root partition should be marked as "active" in the partition table. This can be done using *fdisk* under Linux or Windows. When booting the system, the BIOS will read the boot record of the first "active" partition to start Linux.

If you are using Windows NT/2000's boot manager, you should install LILO in this way, and then tell the boot manager to boot another operating system from that partition on your hard drive. The method for doing this depends on the boot manager in question; see your documentation for details.

Specifying boot time options

When you first installed Linux, more than likely you booted either from a floppy or a CD-ROM, which gave you the now-familiar LILO boot prompt. At this prompt you can enter several boot time options, such as:

    hd=cylinders,heads,sectors

to specify the hard-drive geometry. Each time you boot Linux, it may be necessary to specify these parameters in order for your hardware to be detected correctly, as described in the section "Booting Linux" in Chapter 3. If you are using LILO to boot Linux from the hard drive, you can specify these parameters in *lilo.conf* instead of entering them at the boot prompt each time. To the Linux stanza of the *lilo.conf* file, just add a line, such as:

    append = "hd=683,16,38"

This causes the system to behave as though hd=683,16,38 were entered at the LILO boot prompt. If you wish to specify multiple boot options, you can do so with a single append line, as in:

    append = "hd=683,16,38 hd=64,32,202"

In this case, we specify the geometry for the first and second hard drives, respectively.

Note that you need to use such boot options only if the kernel doesn't detect your hardware at boot time, which is unlikely unless you have very old or very uncommon hardware. You should already know if this is necessary, based on your experiences with installing Linux; in general, you should have to use an append line in *lilo.conf* only if you had to specify these boot options when first booting the Linux installation media.

There are a number of other boottime options. Most of them deal with hardware detection, which has already been discussed in Chapter 3. However, the following additional options may also be useful to you:

single
> Boot the system in single-user mode; skip all the system configuration and start a root shell on the console. See the section "What to Do in an Emergency" in Chapter 8 for hints on using this.

root=*partition*
> Mounts the named *partition* as the Linux root filesystem. This overrides any value given in *lilo.conf*.

ro
> Mounts the root filesystem as read-only. This is usually done in order to run *fsck*; see the section "Checking and Repairing Filesystems" in Chapter 6.

`ramdisk=size`

> Specifies a size, in bytes, for the ramdisk device. This overrides any value in */etc/lilo.conf*. Most users need not worry about using the ramdisk; it's useful primarily for installation.

`vga=mode`

> Sets the VGA display mode. This overrides any value in */etc/lilo.conf*. Valid modes are `normal`, `extended`, `ask`, or an integer. This option is equivalent to the `vga =` values used in *lilo.conf*; see the section "The /etc/lilo.conf file" earlier in this chapter.

`mem=size`

> Tells the kernel how much RAM you have. If you have 64 MB or less, the kernel can get this information from the BIOS, but if you use an older kernel and you have more, you will have to tell the kernel the exact amount, or it will use only the first 64 MB. For example, if you have 128 MB, specify `mem=128m`. Fortunately, this is no longer necessary with newer kernels.

Any of these options can be entered by hand at the LILO boot prompt or specified with the append option in */etc/lilo.conf*.

LILO includes complete documentation that describes all the configuration options available. On many Linux systems this documentation can be found in */usr/src/lilo*; on Debian systems, it is in */usr/share/doc/lilo/Manual.txt.gz*. If you can't seem to find anything, grab the LILO distribution from one of the Linux archive sites, or ask your Linux vendor to provide the sources and documentation for LILO. This documentation includes a manual that describes all the concepts of booting and using LILO in detail, as well as a *README* file that contains excerpts from this manual, formatted as plain text.

Removing LILO

If you have LILO installed on your MBR, the easiest way to remove it is to use Windows *fdisk*. The command:

```
FDISK /MBR
```

runs *fdisk* and overwrites the MBR with a valid Windows boot record.

LILO saves backup copies of your original boot record in the files */boot/boot.0300* (for IDE drives) and */boot/boot.0800* (for SCSI drives). These files contain the MBR of the drive before LILO was installed. You can use the *dd* command to replace the boot record on the drive with this backup copy. For example:

```
dd if=/boot/boot.0300 of=/dev/hda bs=446 count=1
```

copies the first 446 bytes of the file */boot/boot.0300* to */dev/hda*. Even though the files are 512 bytes in size, only the first 446 bytes should be copied back to the MBR.

Be very careful when using this command! This is one of those cases where blindly executing commands you find in a book can cause real trouble if you're not sure what you're doing. Use this method only as a last resort and only if you're certain that the files */boot/boot.0300* or */boot/boot.0800* contain the boot record you want. Many distributions of Linux come installed with bogus versions of these two files; you might need to delete them before you install LILO.

The LILO documentation contains further hints for removing LILO and debugging your LILO configuration.

System Startup and Initialization

In this section, we're going to talk about exactly what happens when the system boots. Understanding this process and the files involved is important for performing various kinds of system configuration.

Kernel Boot Messages

The first step is booting the kernel. As described in the previous section, this can be done from floppy or hard drive. As the kernel loads into memory, it will print messages to the system console, but usually also saves them in the system log files as well. As root, you can always check the file */var/log/messages* (which contains kernel messages emitted during runtime as well). The command *dmesg* prints out the last lines of the kernel message ring buffer; directly after booting, naturally, you will get the boot messages.

In the following few paragraphs, we'll go through a couple of the more interesting messages and explain what they mean. These messages are all printed by the kernel itself, as each device driver is initialized. The exact messages printed depend on what drivers are compiled into your kernel and what hardware you have on your system. You are likely to have more, fewer or different messages; we'll concentrate here on the messages that are quite common.

The line:

```
Linux version 2.4.10-64GB-SMP (root@SMP_X86.suse.de) \
(gcc version 2.95.3 20010315) #1 SMP Fri Sep 28 17:26:36 GMT 2001
```

tells you the version number of the kernel, on which machine, when, and with which compiler it was built.

Next, the kernel reports which processors it has found and, because this output is from a system with two processors, how the processors will work together:

```
Intel MultiProcessor Specification v1.1
    Virtual Wire compatibility mode.
OEM ID: OEM00000 Product ID: PROD00000000 APIC at: 0xFEE00000
Processor #0 Pentium(tm) Pro APIC version 17
```

```
    Floating point unit present.
    Machine Exception supported.
    64 bit compare & exchange supported.
    Internal APIC present.
    Bootup CPU
Processor #1 Pentium(tm) Pro APIC version 17
    Floating point unit present.
    Machine Exception supported.
    64 bit compare & exchange supported.
    Internal APIC present.
...
I/O APIC #2 Version 17 at 0xFEC00000.
Processors: 2
mapped APIC to ffffe000 (fee00000)
mapped IOAPIC to ffffd000 (fec00000)
Detected 498673 kHz processor.
```

Then, it tells us which console font it has picked and which console type it has detected:

```
Console: color VGA+ 80x25
```

Note that this involves only the text mode being used by the kernel, not the capabilities of your video card. (An SVGA video card is reported as VGA+ as far as the console text mode is concerned.)

The kernel gathers information about the PCI bus and checks for any PCI cards present in the system:

```
PCI: PCI BIOS revision 2.10 entry at 0xfb140, last bus=1
PCI: Using configuration type 1
PCI: Probing PCI hardware
PCI: Using IRQ router PIIX [8086/7110] at 00:07.0
PCI: Found IRQ 14 for device 00:07.2
PCI: Sharing IRQ 14 with 00:0b.0
Limiting direct PCI/PCI transfers.
```

You'll then see the "BogoMIPS" calculation for your processor:

```
Calibrating delay loop... 996.14 BogoMIPS
Calibrating delay loop... 996.14 BogoMIPS
Total of 2 processors activated (1992.29 BogoMIPS).
```

This is an utterly bogus (hence the name) measurement of processor speed, which is used to obtain optimal performance in delay loops for several device drivers. The kernel also prints information on the system memory:

```
Memory: 770672k/786368k available (1390k kernel code, 15308k reserved, 392k data,
128k init, 0k highmem)
```

Here, we see that 770672 KB of RAM are available for the system to use; the kernel itself is using 1390 KB.

Various memory structures and properties of the CPU are then determined. For example, the line:

```
CPU serial number disabled.
```

---

tells you that the Linux kernel has simply turned off the infamous serial number feature of the Pentium III CPU.

Linux then sets up networking, the mouse port, and the serial driver. A line such as:

```
ttyS00 at 0x03f8 (irq = 4) is a 16550A
```

means that the first serial device (*/dev/ttyS00*, or COM1) was detected at address 0x03f8, IRQ 4, using 16550A UART functions. Next comes some more hardware detection like the real-time clock and the floppy drive:

```
Real Time Clock Driver v1.10e
...
Floppy drive(s): fd0 is 1.44M
FDC 0 is a post-1991 82077
loop: loaded (max 8 devices)
ide-floppy driver 0.97.sv
...
```

A bit later, the system is checking for a SCSI host adapter. The kernel prints out information about all SCSI devices found; this is verbose and not really worth reproducing here. The line:

```
Adding Swap: 120480k swap-space (priority 42)
```

tells you how much swap space the kernel has found. Among the further tasks performed during a typical boot are finding and configuring a parallel port (lp1), detecting and configuring the network card, and finally setting up the USB subsystem.

init, inittab, and rc Files

Once the device drivers are initialized, the kernel executes the program *init*, which is found in */etc*, */bin*, or */sbin* (it's */sbin/init* on most systems). *init* is a general-purpose program that spawns new processes and restarts certain programs when they exit. For example, each virtual console has a *getty* process running on it, started by *init*. Upon login, the *getty* process is replaced with another. After logging out, *init* starts a new *getty* process, allowing you to log in again.

init is also responsible for running a number of programs and scripts when the system boots. Everything *init* does is controlled by the file */etc/inittab*. In order to understand this file, you need to understand the concept of *runlevels* first.

A runlevel is a number or letter that specifies the current system state, as far as *init* is concerned. For example, when the system runlevel is changed to 3, all entries in */etc/inittab* containing 3 in the column specifying the runlevels will be executed. Runlevels are a useful way to group entries in */etc/inittab* together. For example, you might want to say that runlevel 1 executes only the bare minimum of configuration scripts, runlevel 2 executes everything in runlevel 1 plus networking configuration, runlevel 3 executes everything in levels 1 and 2 plus dial-in login access, and so on. Today, the Red Hat distribution is set up so that runlevel 5 automatically starts the X

Window System graphical interface. The SuSE distribution does it at runlevel 3, and the Debian distribution does so at runlevel 2—provided you have installed X.

For the most part, you don't need to concern yourself with runlevels. When the system boots, it enters the default runlevel (set in /etc/inittab, as we will soon show). On most systems, this default is runlevel 2 or 3. After we discuss normal booting, we'll show you how to enter another runlevel that you will sometimes need to use—runlevel 1, or single-user mode.

Let's take a look at a sample /etc/inittab file:

```
# Set the default runlevel to three
id:3:initdefault:

# Execute /etc/rc.d/rc.sysinit when the system boots
si:S:sysinit:/etc/rc.d/rc.sysinit

# Run /etc/rc.d/rc with the runlevel as an argument
l0:0:wait:/etc/rc.d/rc 0
l1:1:wait:/etc/rc.d/rc 1
l2:2:wait:/etc/rc.d/rc 2
l3:3:wait:/etc/rc.d/rc 3
l4:4:wait:/etc/rc.d/rc 4
l5:5:wait:/etc/rc.d/rc 5
l6:6:wait:/etc/rc.d/rc 6

# Executed when we press ctrl-alt-delete
ca::ctrlaltdel:/sbin/shutdown -t3 -rf now

# Start agetty for virtual consoles 1 through 6
c1:12345:respawn:/sbin/agetty 38400 tty1
c2:12345:respawn:/sbin/agetty 38400 tty2
c3:45:respawn:/sbin/agetty 38400 tty3
c4:45:respawn:/sbin/agetty 38400 tty4
c5:45:respawn:/sbin/agetty 38400 tty5
c6:45:respawn:/sbin/agetty 38400 tty6
```

Fields are separated by colons. The last field is the most recognizable: it is the command that init executes for this entry. The first field is an arbitrary identifier (it doesn't matter what it is so long as it's unique in the file) while the second indicates what runlevels cause the command to be invoked. The third field tells init how to handle this entry; for example, whether to execute the given command once or to respawn the command whenever it exits.

The exact contents of /etc/inittab depend on your system and the distribution of Linux you have installed.

In our sample file, we see first that the default runlevel is set to 3. The action field for this entry is initdefault, which causes the given runlevel to be set to the default. That's the runlevel normally used whenever the system boots. You can override the default with any level you want by running init manually (which you might do when debugging your configuration) and passing in the desired runlevel as an argument. For instance, the following command shuts down all current processes and starts runlevel 5 (warn all your users to log off before doing this!):

```
tigger# init 5
```

LILO can also boot in single-user mode (usually runlevel 1)—see the section "Specifying boot time options" earlier in this chapter.

The next entry tells *init* to execute the script */etc/rc.d/rc.sysinit* when the system boots. (The *action* field is sysinit, which specifies that this entry should be executed when *init* is first started at system boot.) This file is simply a shell script containing commands to handle basic system initialization; for example, swapping is enabled, filesystems are checked and mounted, and the system clock is synchronized with the CMOS clock. You can take a look at this file on your system; we'll be talking more about the commands contained therein in Chapter 6; see the sections "Managing Filesystems" and "Managing Swap Space." On other distributions, this file might be elsewhere. For example, on SuSE it is */etc/init.d/boot*, which is also where it should be according to the Linux Filesystem Hierarchy Standard (FHS).

Next, we see that the system executes the script */etc/rc.d/rc* when it enters any of the runlevels 0 through 6, with the appropriate runlevel as an argument. *rc* is a generic startup script that executes other scripts as appropriate for that runlevel. The *action* field here is wait, which tells *init* to execute the given *command*, and to wait for it to complete execution before doing anything else.

rc Files

Linux stores startup commands in files with *rc* in the name, using an old Unix convention. The commands do all the things necessary to have a fully functioning system, like starting the servers or daemons mentioned in Chapter 4. Thanks to these commands, the system comes up ready with logging facilities, mail, a web server, or whatever you installed and asked it to run. As explained in the previous section, the files are invoked from */etc/inittab*. The commands are standard shell commands, and you can simply read the various *rc* files to see what they do.

In this section, we describe the structure of the *rc* files so that you can understand where everything starts, and so that you can start or stop servers manually in the rare case that they don't do what you want them to do. We'll use Red Hat as our model, but once you get the idea of what to look for, you can find the corresponding files on any Linux distribution. Red Hat is both a good and a bad example because it violates the FHS. The Linux FHS is a distribution-neutral initiative to define standard directory names and filenames for important system files. Any Linux distribution that wants to be a good Linux citizen should follow this standard. Red Hat has decided—not for the first time—not to be a good citizen, so the path- and file-names given here for Red Hat give you an example of the variety that you may encounter when looking for system files. Examples for distributions following the FHS are SuSE and Debian.

On Red Hat, the top-level *rc* script is */etc/rc.d/rc*. The path is slightly different in other distributions (*/etc/init.d/rc* on SuSE, for instance), but the contents are similar. In the previous section, you saw how the */etc/inittab* invokes the script under a variety of circumstances with different numbers from 0 to 6 as arguments. The numbers correspond to runlevels, and each one causes the *rc* files to invoke a different set of scripts. So our next step is to find the scripts corresponding to each runlevel.

On Red Hat, scripts for each runlevel are stored in the directory */etc/rc.d/rcN.d* where *N* is the runlevel being started. Thus, for runlevel 3, scripts in */etc/rc.d/rc3.d* would be used. Again, slightly different conventions are the rule in other distributions. On Debian, for instance, the directory for each runlevel is */etc/rcN.d/*.

Take a look in one of those directories; you will see a number of filenames of the form *Snnxxxx* or *Knnxxxx* where *nn* is a number from 00 to 99, and *xxxx* is the name of some system service. The scripts whose names begin with K are executed by */etc/rc.d/rc* first to kill any existing services, and then the scripts whose names begin with S are executed to start new services.

The numbers *nn* in the names are used to enforce an ordering on the scripts as they are executed: scripts with lower numbers are executed before those with higher numbers. The name *xxxx* is simply used to help you identify to which system service the script corresponds. This naming convention might seem odd, but it makes it easy to add or remove scripts from these directories and have them automatically executed at the appropriate time by */etc/rc.d/rc*. For customizing startup scripts, you'll find it convenient to use a graphical runlevel editor, such as *ksysv* in KDE.

For example, the script to initialize networking might be called *S10network*, while the script to stop the system logging daemon might be called *K70syslog*. If these files are placed in the appropriate */etc/rc.d/rcN.d* directories, */etc/rc.d/rc* will run them, in numerical order, at system startup or shutdown time. If the default runlevel of your system is 3, look in */etc/rc.d/rc3.d* to see which scripts are executed when the system boots normally.

Because the same services are started or stopped at different runlevels, the Red Hat distribution uses symbolic links instead of repeating the same script in multiple places. Thus, each S or K file is a symbolic link that points to a central directory that stores startup or shutdown scripts for all services. On Red Hat, this central directory is */etc/rc.d/init.d*, while on SuSE and Debian, it is */etc/init.d*. On Debian and SuSE, the directory contains a script called *skeleton* that you can adapt to start and stop any new daemons you might write.

Knowing the location of a startup or shutdown script is useful in case you don't want to completely reboot or enter a different runlevel, but need to start or stop a particular service. Look in the *init.d* directory for a script of the appropriate name and execute it, passing the parameter start or stop. For example, on SuSE, if you want the

Apache web server to be running but your system is in a runlevel that does not include Apache, just enter the following:

```
tigger# /sbin/init.d/apache start
```

Another important system configuration script is */etc/rc.d/rc.local*, which is executed after the other system initialization scripts are run. (How is this accomplished? Generally, a symbolic link to *rc.local* is made in each */etc/rc.d/rcN.d* directory with the name *S99local*. Because 99 is the largest numerical order any of the S scripts can have, it is executed last. *Voilà!*) You can edit *rc.local* to accomplish any peculiar or otherwise out-of-place system commands at boot time, or if you're not sure where else they should be executed. Debian doesn't have an equivalent of the *rc.local* script, but nothing stops you from adding it and invoking it from *rc* if you're used to having it.

The next entry, labeled ca, is executed when the key combination Ctrl-Alt-Delete is pressed on the console. This key combination produces an interrupt that usually reboots the system. Under Linux, this interrupt is caught and sent to *init*, which executes the entry with the *action* field of ctrlaltdel. The command shown here, */sbin/shutdown -t3 -rf now*, will do a "safe" reboot of the system. (See the section "Shutting Down the System" later in this chapter.) This way we protect the system from sudden reboot when Ctrl-Alt-Delete is pressed.

Finally, the *inittab* file includes entries that execute */sbin/agetty* for the first six virtual consoles. *agetty* is one of the several *getty* variants available for Linux. These programs permit logins on terminals; without them the terminal would be effectively dead and would not respond when a user walked up and pressed a key or mouse button. The various *getty* commands open a terminal device (such as a virtual console or a serial line), set various parameters for the terminal driver, and execute */bin/login* to initiate a login session on that terminal. Therefore, to allow logins on a given virtual console, you must be running *getty* or *agetty* on it. *agetty* is the version used on a number of Linux systems, but others use *getty*, which has a slightly different syntax. See the manual pages for *getty* and *agetty* on your system.

agetty takes two arguments: a baud rate and a device name. The port names for Linux virtual consoles are */dev/tty1*, */dev/tty2*, and so forth. *agetty* assumes the given device name is relative to */dev*. The baud rate for virtual consoles should generally be 38400.

Note that the *action* field for each *agetty* entry is respawn. This means that *init* should restart the command given in the entry when the *agetty* process dies, which is every time a user logs out.

Now you should be familiar with *init*, but the various files and commands in */etc/rc.d*, which do all the work, remain a mystery. We can't delve into these files without more background on other system administration tasks, such as managing filesystems. We'll lead you through these tasks in the next few chapters, and eventually all should be clear.

Single-User Mode

Most of the time, you operate the system in multiuser mode so that users can log in. But there is a special state called *single-user mode* in which Unix is running but there is no login prompt. When you're in single-user mode, you're basically the superuser (root). You may have to enter this mode during installation if something goes wrong. Single-user mode is important for certain routine system administration tasks, such as checking corrupted filesystems. (This is not fun; try not to corrupt your filesystem. For instance, always shut down the system through a *shutdown* command before you turn off the power. This is described in the next section.)

Under single-user mode, the system is nearly useless; very little configuration is done, filesystems are unmounted, and so on. This is necessary for recovering from certain kinds of system problems; see the section "What to Do in an Emergency" in Chapter 8 for details.

Note that Unix is still a multiprocessing system, even in single-user mode. You can run multiple programs at once. Servers can run in the background so that special functions, such as the network, can operate. But if your system supports more than one terminal, only the console can be used. And the X Window System cannot run.

Shutting Down the System

Fortunately, shutting down the Linux system is much simpler than booting and startup. However, it's not just a matter of hitting the reset switch. Linux, like all Unix systems, buffers disk reads and writes in memory. This means disk writes are delayed until absolutely necessary, and multiple reads on the same disk block are served directly from RAM. This greatly increases performance as disks are extremely slow relative to the CPU.

The problem is that if the system were to be suddenly powered down or rebooted, the buffers in memory would not be written to disk, and data could be lost or corrupted. */sbin/update* is a program started from */etc/rc.d/boot* on most systems; it flushes dirty buffers (ones that have been changed since they were read from the disk) back to disk every five seconds to prevent serious damage from occurring should the system crash. However, to be completely safe, the system needs to undergo a "safe" shutdown before rebooting. This will not only ensure that disk buffers are properly synchronized, but also allow all running processes to exit cleanly.

shutdown is the general, all-purpose command used to halt or reboot the system. As root, you can issue the command:

```
/sbin/shutdown -r +10
```

to cause the system to reboot in 10 minutes. The -r switch indicates the system should be rebooted after shutdown, and +10 is the amount of time to wait (in minutes) until shutting down. The system will print a warning message to all active terminals, counting down until the shutdown time. You can add your own warning message by including it on the command line, as in:

```
/sbin/shutdown -r +10 "Rebooting to try new kernel"
```

You can also specify an absolute time to shutdown, as in:

```
/sbin/shutdown -r 13:00
```

to reboot at 1:00 pm. Likewise, you can say:

```
/sbin/shutdown -r now
```

to reboot immediately (after the safe shutdown process).

Using the *-h* switch instead of *-r* will cause the system to simply be halted after shutdown; you can then turn off the system power without fear of losing data. If you specify neither *-h* nor *-r*, the system will go into single-user mode.

As we saw in the section "init, inittab, and rc Files," you can have *init* catch the Ctrl-Alt-Delete key sequence and execute a *shutdown* command in response to it. If you're used to rebooting your system in this way it might be a good idea to check that your */etc/inittab* contains a ctrlaltdel entry. Note that you should never reboot your Linux system by pressing the system power switch or the reboot switch on the front panel of your machine. Unless the system is flat-out hung (a rare occurrence), you should always use *shutdown*. The great thing about a multi-processing system is that one program may hang, but you can almost always switch to another window or virtual console to recover.

shutdown provides a number of other options. The *-c* switch will cancel a currently running shutdown. (Of course, you can kill the process by hand using *kill*, but *shutdown* *-c* might be easier.) The *-k* switch will print the warning messages but not actually shut down the system. See the manual page for *shutdown*(8) if you're interested in the gory details.

The /proc Filesystem

Unix systems have come a long way with respect to providing uniform interfaces to different parts of the system; as you will learn in the next chapter, hardware is represented in Linux in the form of a special type of file. There is, however, a special filesystem called the */proc* filesystem that goes even one step further: it unifies files and processes.

From the user's or the system administrator's point of view, the */proc* filesystem looks just like any other filesystem; you can navigate around it with the *cd* command, list directory contents with the *ls* command, and view file contents with the *cat* command. However, none of these files and directories occupies any space on your hard disk. The kernel traps accesses to the */proc* filesystem and generates directory and file contents on the fly. In other words, whenever you list a directory or view file contents in the /proc filesystem, the kernel dynamically generates the contents you want to see.

To make this less abstract, let's see some examples. The following example displays the list of files in the top-level directory of the /proc filesystem:

```
owl # ls /proc
1      1618   17613   27191   27317   2859   8929          kcore_elf   rtc
11120  1621   1795    27192   27320   2860   9             kmsg        scsi
11121  1649   1796    27204   27324   28746  bus           ksyms       self
11153  1657   1798    27205   27326   28747  cmdline       loadavg     slabinfo
15039  1664   1799    27221   27374   28754  config.gz     locks       stat
1512   1681   1800    27229   27377   29877  cpuinfo       lvm         swaps
1530   1689   2       27287   27379   29878  devices       mdstat      sys
1534   1703   20007   27289   27380   29944  dma           meminfo     tty
1560   1708   21391   27292   27381   3      fb            misc        uptime
1570   1709   21394   27297   27397   4      filesystems   modules     version
1578   1710   2302    27308   27515   5      fs            mounts
1585   1711   2309    27310   27518   5841   ide           mtrr
1586   1712   2356    27312   27521   5842   interrupts    net
1587   1713   27182   27314   2786    5860   ioports       partitions
1588   1731   27183   27315   28536   6100   kcore         pci
```

The numbers will be different on your system, but the general organization will be the same. All those numbers are directories that represent each of the processes running on your system. For example, let's look at the information about the process with the ID 1534:

```
tigger # ls /proc/1534
cmdline  environ  fd     mem   stat    status
cwd      exe      maps   root  statm
```

You see a number of files that each contain information about this process. For example, the *cmdline* file shows the command line with which this process was started. *status* gives information about the internal state of the process and *cwd* links to the current working directory of this process.

Probably you'll find the hardware information even more interesting than the process information. All the information that the kernel has gathered about your hardware is collected in the /proc filesystem, even though it can be difficult to find the information you are looking for.

Let's start by checking your machine's memory. This is represented by the file /proc/meminfo:

```
owl # cat /proc/meminfo
         total:      used:      free:  shared:  buffers:  cached:
Mem:   267919360  255311872  12607488        0  40587264  77791232
Swap:  123371520    5861376  117510144
MemTotal:     261640 kB
```

```
MemFree:       12312 kB
MemShared:         0 kB
Buffers:       39636 kB
Cached:        75968 kB
BigTotal:          0 kB
BigFree:           0 kB
SwapTotal:    120480 kB
SwapFree:     114756 kB
```

If you then try the command *free*, you can see that you get exactly the same information, only the numbers are reformatted a bit. *free* does nothing more than read */proc/meminfo* and rearrange the output a bit.

Most tools on your system that report information about your hardware do it this way. The */proc* filesystem is a portable and easy way to get at this information. The information is especially useful if you want to add new hardware to your system. For example, most hardware boards need a few I/O addresses to communicate with the CPU and the operating system. If you configured two boards to use the same I/O addresses, disaster is about to happen. You can avoid this by checking which I/O addresses the kernel has already detected as being in use:

```
tiger # more /proc/ioports
0000-001f : dma1
0020-003f : pic1
0040-005f : timer
0060-006f : keyboard
0080-009f : dma page reg
00a0-00bf : pic2
00c0-00df : dma2
00f0-00ff : npu
01f0-01f7 : ide0
0220-022f : soundblaster
02e8-02ef : serial(auto)
0388-038b : OPL3/OPL2
03c0-03df : vga+
03f0-03f5 : floppy
03f6-03f6 : ide0
03f7-03f7 : floppy DIR
03f8-03ff : serial(auto)
0530-0533 : WSS config
0534-0537 : MSS audio codec
e000-e0be : aic7xxx
e400-e41f : eth0
```

Now you can look for I/O addresses that are free. Of course, the kernel can show I/O addresses only for boards that it has detected and recognized, but in a correctly configured system, this should be the case for all boards.

You can use the */proc* filesystem for the other information you might need when configuring new hardware as well: */proc/interrupts* lists the occupied interrupt lines (IRQs) and */proc/dma* lists the DMA channels in use.

Managing User Accounts

Even if you're the only actual human being who uses your Linux system, understanding how to manage user accounts is important—even more so if your system hosts multiple users.

User accounts serve a number of purposes on Unix systems. Most prominently, they give the system a way to distinguish between different people who use the system for reasons of identification and security. Each user has a personal account with a separate username and password. As discussed in the section "File Ownership and Permissions" in Chapter 4, users may set permissions on their files, allowing or restricting access to them by other users. Each file on the system is "owned" by a particular user, who may set the permissions for that file. User accounts are used to authenticate access to the system; only those people with accounts may access the machine. Also, accounts are used to identify users, keep system logs, tag electronic mail messages with the name of the sender, and so forth.

Apart from personal accounts, there are users on the system who provide administrative functions. As we've seen, the system administrator uses the root account to perform maintenance—but usually not for personal system use. Such accounts are accessed using the *su* command, allowing another account to be accessed after logging in through a personal account.

Other accounts on the system may not involve human interaction at all. These accounts are generally used by system daemons, which must access files on the system through a specific user ID other than root or one of the personal user accounts. For example, if you configure your system to receive a newsfeed from another site, the news daemon must store news articles in a spool directory that anyone can access but only one user (the news daemon) can write to. No human being is associated with the news account; it is an "imaginary" user set aside for the news daemon only.

One of the permission bits that can be set on executables is the *setuid* bit, which causes the program to be executed with the permissions of the owner of that file. For example, if the news daemon were owned by the user news, and the *setuid* bit were set on the executable, it would run as if by the user news. news would have write access to the news spool directory, and all other users would have read access to the articles stored there. This is a security feature. News programs can give users just the right amount of access to the news spool directory, but no one can just play around there.

As the system administrator, it is your job to create and manage accounts for all users (real and virtual) on your machine. This is actually a painless, hands-off task in most cases, but it's important to understand how it works.

The passwd File

Every account on the system has an entry in the file *letc/passwd*. This file contains entries, one line per user, that specify several attributes for each account, such as the username, real name, and so forth.

Each entry in this file is of the format:

```
username:password:uid:gid:gecos:homedir:shell
```

The following list explains each field:

username

A unique character string, identifying the account. For personal accounts, this is the name the user logs in with. On most systems it is limited to eight alphanumeric characters—for example, `larry` or `kirsten`.

password

An encrypted representation of the user's password. This field is set using the *passwd* program to set the account's password; it uses a one-way encryption scheme that is difficult (but not impossible) to break. You don't set this by hand; the *passwd* program does it for you. Note, however, that if the first character of the *passwd* field is * (an asterisk), the account is "disabled"; the system will not allow logins as this user. See the section "Creating Accounts" later in this chapter.

uid

The user ID, a unique integer the system uses to identify the account. The system uses the *uid* field internally when dealing with process and file permissions; it's easier and more compact to deal with integers than byte strings. Therefore, both the *uid* and the *username* identify a particular account: the *uid* is more important to the system, while *username* is more convenient for humans.

gid

The group ID, an integer referring to the user's default group, found in the file *letc/group*. See the section "The Group File," later in this chapter.

gecos

Miscellaneous information about the user, such as the user's real name, and optional "location information" such as the user's office address or phone number. Such programs as *mail* and *finger* use this information to identify users on the system; we'll talk more about it later. By the way, *gecos* is a historical name dating back to the 1970s; it stands for *General Electric Comprehensive Operating System*. GECOS has nothing to do with Unix, except that this field was originally added to *letc/passwd* to provide compatibility with some of its services.

homedir

> The user's home directory, for his personal use; more on this later. When the user first logs in, her shell finds its current working directory in the named *homedir*.

shell

> The name of the program to run when the user logs in; in most cases, this is the full pathname of a shell, such as */bin/bash* or */bin/tcsh*.

Many of these fields are optional; the only required fields are *username*, *uid*, *gid*, and *homedir*. Most user accounts have all fields filled in, but "imaginary" or administrative accounts may use only a few.

Here are two sample entries you might find in */etc/passwd*:

```
root:ZxPsI9ZjiVd9Y:0:0:The root of all evil:/root:/bin/bash
aclark:BjDf5hBysDsii:104:50:Anna Clark:/home/aclark:/bin/bash
```

The first entry is for the root account. First of all, notice that the uid of root is 0. This is what makes root root: the system knows that uid 0 is "special" and that it does not have the usual security restrictions. The gid of root is also 0, which is mostly a convention. Many of the files on the system are owned by root and the root group, which have a uid and gid of 0, respectively. More on groups in a minute.

On many systems, root uses the home directory */root*, or just /. This is not usually relevant because you most often use *su* to access root from your own account. Also, it is tradition to use a Bourne-shell variant (in this case */bin/bash*) for the root account, although you can use the C shell if you like. (Shells are discussed in the section "Shells" in Chapter 4.) Be careful, though: Bourne shells and C shells have differing syntax, and switching between them when using root can be confusing and lead to mistakes.

The second entry is for an actual human being, username aclark. In this case, the *uid* is 104. The *uid* field can technically be any unique integer; on many systems, it's customary to have user accounts numbered 100 and above and administrative accounts in the sub-100 range. The gid is 50, which just means that aclark is in whatever group is numbered 50 in the */etc/group* file. Hang on to your horses; groups are covered in section "The Group File" later in this chapter.

Home directories are often found in */home*, and named for the username of their owner. This is, for the most part, a useful convention that avoids confusion when finding a particular user's home directory, but you can technically place a home directory anywhere. You should, however, observe the directory layout used on your system.

Note that as the system administrator, it's not usually necessary to modify the */etc/ passwd* file directly. Several programs are available that can help you create and maintain user accounts; see the section "Creating Accounts," which follows.

Shadow Passwords

To some extent, it is a security risk to let everybody with access to the system view the encrypted passwords in */etc/passwd*. Special crack programs are available that try a huge number of possible passwords and check whether the encrypted version of those passwords is equal to a specified one.

To overcome this potential security risk, *shadow passwords* have been invented. When shadow passwords are used, the password field in */etc/passwd* contains only an x or a *, which can never occur in the encrypted version of a password. Instead, a second file called */etc/shadow* is used. This file contains entries that look very similar to those in */etc/passwd*, but contain the real encrypted password in the password field. */etc/shadow* is readable only by root, so normal users do not have access to the encrypted passwords. The other fields in */etc/shadow*, except the username and the password, are present as well, but normally contain bogus values or are empty.

Note that in order to use shadow passwords, you need special versions of the programs that access or modify user information, such as *passwd* or *login*. Nowadays, most distributions come with shadow passwords already set up so that this should not be a problem for you. Debian users should use "shadowconfig on" instead to ensure that shadow passwords are enabled on their systems.

There are two tools for converting "normal" user entries to shadow entries and back. *pwconv* takes the */etc/passwd* file, looks for entries that are not yet present in */etc/shadow*, generates shadow entries for those, and merges them with the entries already present in */etc/shadow*.

pwunconv is rarely used because it gives you less security instead of more. It works like *pwconv*, but generates traditional */etc/passwd* entries that work without */etc/shadow* counterparts.

PAM and Other Authentication Methods

You might think that having two means of user authentication, */etc/passwd* and */etc/shadow*, is already enough choice, but you are wrong in this case. There are a number of other authentication methods with strange names, such as Kerberos authentication (so named after the dog from Greek mythology that guards the entrance to Hell). While we think that shadow passwords provide enough security for almost all cases, it all depends on how much security you really need and how paranoid you want to be.

The problem with all those authentication methods is that you cannot simply switch from one to another because you always need a set of programs, such as *login* and *passwd,* that go with those tools. To overcome this problem, the *Pluggable Authentication Methods (PAM)* system has been invented. Once you have a PAM-enabled set of tools, you can change the authentication method of your system by reconfiguring

PAM. The tools will automatically get the code necessary to perform the required authentication procedures from dynamically loaded shared libraries.

Setting up and using PAM is beyond the scope of this book, but you can get all the information you need from *http://www.kernel.org/pub/linux/libs/pam/*. Most modern distributions will set up PAM for you as well.

The Group File

User groups are a convenient way to logically organize sets of user accounts and allow users to share files within their group or groups. Each file on the system has both a user and a group owner associated with it. Using *ls -1*, you can see the owner and group for a particular file, as in:

```
rutabaga% ls -l boiler.tex
-rwxrw-r--  1 mdw      megabozo    10316 Oct  6 20:19 boiler.tex
rutabaga%
```

This file is owned by the user mdw and belongs to the megabozo group. We can see from the file permissions that mdw has read, write, and execute access to the file; that anyone in the megabozo group has read and write access; and that all other users have read access only.

This doesn't mean that mdw is in the megabozo group; it simply means the file may be accessed, as shown by the permission bits, by anyone in the megabozo group (which may or may not include mdw).

This way files can be shared among groups of users, and permissions can be specified separately for the owner of the file, the group to which the file belongs, and everyone else. An introduction to permissions appears in the section "File Ownership and Permissions" in Chapter 4.

Every user is assigned to at least one group, which you specify in the *gid* field of the */etc/passwd* file. However, a user can be a member of multiple groups. The file */etc/group* contains a one-line entry for each group on the system, very similar in nature to */etc/passwd*. The format of this file is:

```
groupname:password:gid:members
```

Here, *groupname* is a character string identifying the group; it is the group name printed when using commands such as *ls -1*.

password is an optional encrypted password associated with the group, which allows users not in this group to access the group with the *newgrp* command. Read on for information on this.

gid is the group ID used by the system to refer to the group; it is the number used in the *gid* field of */etc/passwd* to specify a user's default group.

members is a comma-separated list of usernames (with no whitespace in between), identifying those users who are members of this group, but who have a different *gid* in */etc/passwd*. That is, this list need not contain those users who have this group set as their "default" group in */etc/passwd*; it's only for users who are additional members of the group.

For example, */etc/group* might contain the following entries:

```
root:*:0:
bin:*:1:root,daemon
users:*:50:
bozo:*:51:linus,mdw
megabozo:*:52:kibo
```

The first entries, for the groups root and bin, are administrative groups, similar in nature to the "imaginary" accounts used on the system. Many files are owned by groups, such as root and bin. The other groups are for user accounts. Like user IDs, the group ID values for user groups are often placed in ranges above 50 or 100.

The *password* field of the *group* file is something of a curiosity. It isn't used much, but in conjunction with the *newgrp* program it allows users who aren't members of a particular group to assume that group ID if they have the password. For example, using the command:

```
rutabaga% newgrp bozo
Password: password for group bozo
rutabaga%
```

starts a new shell with the group ID of bozo. If the *password* field is blank, or the first character is an asterisk, you receive a permission denied error if you attempt to *newgrp* to that group.

However, the *password* field of the *group* file is seldom used and is really not necessary. (In fact, most systems don't provide tools to set the password for a group; you could use *passwd* to set the password for a dummy user with the same name as the group in */etc/passwd* and copy the encrypted *password* field to */etc/group*.) Instead, you can make a user a member of multiple groups simply by including the username in the *members* field for each additional group. In the previous example, the users linus and mdw are members of the bozo group, as well as whatever group they are assigned to in the */etc/passwd* file. If we wanted to add linus to the megabozo group as well, we'd change the last line of the previous example to:

```
megabozo:*:52:kibo,linus
```

The command *groups* tells you which groups you belong to, as in:

```
rutabaga% groups
users bozo
```

Giving a list of usernames to *groups* lists the groups to which each user in the list belongs.

When you log in, you are automatically assigned to the group ID given in */etc/ passwd*, as well as any additional groups for which you're listed in */etc/group*. This means you have "group access" to any files on the system with a group ID contained in your list of groups. In this case, the group permission bits (set with *chmod g+...*) for those files apply to you (unless you're the owner, in which case the owner permission bits apply instead).

Now that you know the ins and outs of groups, how should you assign groups on your system? This is really a matter of style and depends on how your system will be used. For systems with just one or a handful of users, it's easiest to have a single group (called, say, users) to which all personal user accounts belong. Note that all the system groups—those groups contained within */etc/group* when the system is first installed—should probably be left alone. Various daemons and programs may depend upon them.

If you have a number of users on your machine, there are several ways to organize groups. For example, an educational institution may have separate groups for students, faculty, and staff. A software company might have different groups for each design team. On other systems, each user is placed into a separate group, named identically to the username. This keeps each pigeon in its own hole, so to speak. Files can also be assigned to special groups; many users create new groups and place files into them for sharing the files between users. However, this requires adding users to the additional groups, a task that usually requires the system administrator to intervene (by editing */etc/group* or using utilities, such as *gpasswd* on Debian systems). It's really up to you.

Another situation in which groups are often used is special hardware groups. Let's say that you have a scanner that is accessed via */dev/scanner*. If you do not want to give everybody access to the scanner, you could create a special group called scanner, assign */dev/scanner* to this group, make this special file readable for the group and nonreadable for everybody else, and add everybody who is allowed to use the scanner to the scanner group in the */etc/groups* file.

Creating Accounts

Creating a user account requires several steps: adding an entry to */etc/passwd*, creating the user's home directory, and setting up the user's default configuration files (such as *.bashrc*) in her home directory. Luckily, you don't have to perform these steps manually; nearly all Linux systems include a program called *adduser* to do this for you.*

Running *adduser* as root should work as follows. Just enter the requested information at the prompts; many of the prompts have reasonable defaults you can select by pressing Enter:

```
Adding a new user. The username should not exceed 8 characters
in length, or you many run into problems later.
```

```
Enter login name for new account (^C to quit): norbert

Editing information for new user [norbert]

Full Name: Norbert Ebersol
GID [100]: 117

Checking for an available UID after 500
First unused uid is 501

UID [501]: (enter)
Home Directory [/home/norbert]: (enter)
Shell [/bin/bash]: (enter)
Password [norbert]: (norbert's password)

Information for new user [norbert]:
Home directory: [/home/norbert] Shell: [/bin/bash]
Password: [(norbert's password)] uid: [501] gid: [117]

Is this correct? [y/N]: y

Adding login [norbert] and making directory [/home/norbert]
Adding the files from the /etc/skel directory:
./.emacs -> /home/norbert/./.emacs
./.kermrc -> /home/norbert/./.kermrc
./.bashrc -> /home/norbert/./.bashrc
... more files ...
```

There should be no surprises here; just enter the information as requested or choose the defaults. Note that *adduser* uses 100 as the default group ID, and looks for the first unused user ID after 500 (500 is used as the minimum on SuSE and Red Hat, Debian uses 1000). It should be safe to go along with these defaults; in the previous example we used a group ID of 117 because we designated that to be the group for the user, as well as the default user ID of 501.

After the account is created, the files from */etc/skel* are copied to the user's home directory. */etc/skel* contains the "skeleton" files for a new account; they are the default configuration files (such as *.emacs* and *.bashrc*) for the new user. Feel free to place other files here if your new user accounts should have them.

After this is done, the new account is ready to roll; norbert can log in, using the password set using *adduser*. To guarantee security, new users should always change their own passwords, using *passwd*, immediately after logging in for the first time.

---

* Note that some Linux systems, such as Red Hat or SuSE, use a different set of tools for account creation and deletion. If the sequence of inputs in this section does not work for you, check the documentation for your distribution. (Red Hat allows accounts to be managed through the `control-panel` tool, and SuSE does it via *YaST*; Debian includes a noninteractive "adduser" script that automatically sets up users based on the configuration file */etc/adduser.conf*). In addition, there are graphical user management programs like *kuser* from KDE (see Chapter 11).

root can set the password for any user on the system. For example, the command:

```
passwd norbert
```

prompts for a new password for norbert, without asking for the original password. Note, however, that you must know the root password in order to change it. If you forget the root password entirely, you can boot Linux from an "emergency floppy," and clear the *password* field of the */etc/passwd* entry for root. See the section "What to Do in an Emergency" in Chapter 8.

Some Linux systems provide the command-line–driven *useradd* instead of *adduser*. This program requires you to provide all relevant information as command-line arguments. If you can't locate *adduser* and are stuck with *useradd*, see the manual pages, which should help you out.

Deleting and Disabling Accounts

Deleting a user account is much easier than creating one; this is the well-known concept of entropy at work. To delete an account, you must remove the user's entry in */etc/passwd*, remove any references to the user in */etc/group*, and delete the user's home directory, as well as any additional files created or owned by the user. For example, if the user has an incoming mailbox in */var/spool/mail*, it must be deleted as well.

The command *userdel* (the yin to *useradd*'s yang) deletes an account and the account's home directory. For example:

```
userdel -r norbert
```

will remove the recently created account for norbert. The *-r* option forces the home directory to be removed as well. Other files associated with the user—for example, the incoming mailbox, *crontab* files, and so forth—must be removed by hand. Usually these are quite insignificant and can be left around. By the end of this chapter, you should know where these files are, if they exist. A simple way to find the files associated with a particular user is through the command:

```
find / -user username -ls
```

This will give an *ls -l* listing of each file owned by *username*. Of course, to use this, the account associated with *username* must still have an entry in */etc/passwd*. If you deleted the account, use the *-uid num* argument instead, where *num* is the numeric user ID of the dearly departed user.

Temporarily (or not-so-temporarily) disabling a user account, for whatever reason, is even simpler. You can either remove the user's entry in */etc/passwd* (leaving the home directory and other files intact), or add an asterisk to the first character of the *password* field of the */etc/passwd* entry, as so:

```
aclark:*BjDf5hBysDsii:104:50:Anna Clark:/home/aclark:/bin/bash
```

This will disallow logins to the account in question. Note that if you use shadow password, you need to do the same thing in *etc/shadow*.

Modifying User Accounts

Modifying attributes of user accounts and groups is usually a simple matter of editing *etc/passwd* and *etc/group*. Many systems provide commands such as *usermod* and *groupmod* to do just this; it's often easier to edit the files by hand.

To change a user's password, use the *passwd* command, which will prompt for a password, encrypt it, and store the encrypted password in the *etc/passwd* file.

If you need to change the user ID of an existing account, you can do this by editing the uid field of *etc/passwd* directly. However, you should also *chown* the files owned by the user to that of the new uid. For example:

```
chown -R aclark /home/aclark
```

will set the ownership for all files in the home directory used by aclark back to aclark, if you changed the uid for this account. If *ls -l* prints a numeric user ID, instead of a username, this means there is no username associated with the uid owning the files. Use *chown* to fix this.

## CHAPTER 6

Managing Filesystems, Swap Space, and Devices

You probably created filesystems and swap space when you first installed Linux (most distributions help you do the basics). Here is a chance to fine-tune these resources. Most of the time, you do these things shortly after installing your operating system, before you start loading up your disks with fun stuff. But occasionally you will want to change a running system, in order to add a new device or perhaps upgrade the swap space when you upgrade your RAM.

Managing Filesystems

To Unix systems, a filesystem is some device (such as a hard drive, floppy, or CD-ROM) that is formatted to store files. Filesystems can be found on hard drives, floppies, CD-ROMs, and other storage media that permit random access. (A tape allows only sequential access, and therefore can't contain a filesystem per se.)

The exact format and means by which files are stored is not important; the system provides a common interface for all *filesystem types* it recognizes. Under Linux, filesystem types include the Second Extended filesystem, or *ext2fs*, which you probably use to store Linux files (also *ext3* is slowly taking over); the VFAT filesystem, which allows files on Windows 95/98/ME partitions and floppies to be accessed under Linux; and several others, including the ISO 9660 filesystem used by CD-ROM.

Each filesystem type has a very different underlying format for storing data. However, when you access any filesystem under Linux, the system presents the data as files arranged into a hierarchy of directories, along with owner and group IDs, permission bits, and the other characteristics with which you're familiar.

In fact, information on file ownership, permissions, and so forth is provided only by filesystem types that are meant to be used for storing Linux files. For filesystem types that don't store this information, the kernel drivers used to access these filesystems "fake" the information. For example, the MS-DOS filesystem has no concept of file ownership; therefore, all files are presented as if they were owned by root. This way, above a certain level, all filesystem types look alike, and each file has certain attributes associated with it. Whether this data is actually used in the underlying filesystem is another matter altogether.

As the system administrator, you need to know how to create filesystems should you want to store Linux files on a floppy or add additional filesystems to your hard drives. You also need to know how to use the various tools to check and maintain filesystems should data corruption occur. Also, you must know the commands and files used to access filesystems—for example, those on floppy or CD-ROM.

Filesystem Types

Table 6-1 lists the filesystem types supported by the Linux kernel as of Version 2.4.10. New filesystem types are always being added to the system, and experimental drivers for several filesystems not listed here are available. To find out what filesystem types your kernel supports, look at the file */proc/filesystems*. You can select which filesystem types to support when building your kernel; see the section "Building the Kernel" in Chapter 7.

Table 6-1. Linux filesystem types

Filesystem	Type	Description
Second Extended filesystem	ext2	Most common Linux filesystem
Reiser filesystem	reiserfs	A journaling filesystem for Linux
Third Extended filesystem	ext3	Another journaling filesystem for Linux that is downward-compatible with *ext2*
Minix filesystem	minix	Original Minix filesystem; rarely used
ROM filesystem	romfs	A tiny read-only filesystem, mainly used for ramdisks
CRAM filesystem	cramfs	A compressed read-only filesystem, often used on PDAs
Network File System (NFS)	NFS	Allows access to remote files on network
UMSDOS filesystem	umsdos	Installs Linux on an MS-DOS partition
DOS-FAT filesystem	msdos	Accesses MS-DOS files
VFAT filesystem	vfat	Accesses Windows 95/98 files
NT filesystem	ntfs	Accesses Windows NT files
HPFS filesystem	hpfs	OS/2 filesystem
/proc filesystem	proc	Provides process information for *ps*
Device filesystem	devfs	An alternate way of representing the files in the */dev* directory
ISO 9660 filesystem	iso9660	Used by most CD-ROMs
Joliet filesystem	iso9660	An extension to the ISO 9660 filesystem that can handle Unicode filenames
UDF filesystem	udf	The most modern CD-ROM filesystem

Table 6-1. Linux filesystem types (continued)

Filesystem	Type	Description
System V filesystem	*sysv*	Accesses files from System V variants
Coherent filesystem	*coherent*	Accesses files from Coherent
UFS filesystem	*ufs*	Accesses files from UFS filesystems, like those on SunOS, BSD, or Tru64 Unix.
BFS filesystem	*bfs*	Accesses files on SCO Unixware
EFS filesystem	*efs*	Accesses files on older Irix versions
ADFS filesystem	*adfs*	Accesses files from Acorn partitions
AFFS filesystem	*affs*	Accesses files from standard AmigaOS filesystem partitions
Apple Mac filesystem	*hfs*	Accesses files from Apple Macintosh
QNX4 filesystem	*qnx4*	Accesses files from QNX4 partitions
JFFS filesystem	*jffs*	A filesystem for Flash-based devices
Novell filesystem	*ncpfs*	Accesses files from a Novell server over the network
SMB filesystem	*smbfs*	Accesses files from a Windows server over the network
Coda filesystem	*coda*	An advanced network file system, similar to NFS
RAM filesystem	*ramfs*	A filesystem for RAM disks
Temporary filesystem	*tmpfs*	Another filesystem that is kept entirely in RAM

Each filesystem type has its own attributes and limitations; for example, the MS-DOS filesystem restricts filenames to eight characters plus a three-character extension and should be used only to access existing MS-DOS floppies or partitions. For most of your work with Linux, you'll use the Second Extended (*ext2*) filesystem, which was developed primarily for Linux and supports 256-character filenames, a 32-terabyte maximum filesystem size, and a slew of other goodies, or you will use the Reiser (*reiserfs*) or the Third Extended (*ext3*) filesystem. Earlier Linux systems used the Extended filesystem (no longer supported) and the Minix filesystem. (The Minix filesystem was originally used for several reasons. First of all, Linux was originally cross-compiled under Minix. Also, Linus was quite familiar with the Minix filesystem, and it was straightforward to implement in the original kernels.) The Xia and Xenix filesystems available in older Linux kernels are no longer supported.

The main difference between the Second Extended filesystem and the Reiser filesystem is the fact that the latter is *journalled*. Journalling is an advanced technique that keeps track of the changes made to a filesystem, making it much easier (and faster!) to restore a corrupted filesystem (e.g., after a system crash or a power failure). Another journalled filesystem is the Third Extended filesystem, the successor to the Second Extended filesystem. This has the advantage of being downward-compatible with the Second Extended filesystem, but because it hasn't been around for long, it is not used as much as the Second Extended and Reiser filesystems.

You will rarely need the ROM filesystem, which is very small, does not support write operations, and is meant to be used in ramdisks at system configuration, startup time, or even in EPROMS. Also in this group fits the Cram filesystem, which is used for ROMs as well and compresses its contents. This is primarily meant for embedded devices where space is at a premium.

The UMSDOS filesystem is used to install Linux under a private directory of an existing MS-DOS partition. This is a good way for new users to try out Linux without repartitioning, at the expense of poorer performance. The DOS-FAT filesystem, on the other hand, is used to access MS-DOS files directly. Files on partitions created with Windows 95 or 98 can be accessed via the VFAT filesystem, while the NTFS filesystem lets you access Windows NT filesystems. The HPFS filesystem is used to access the OS/2 filesystem.

With the CVF-FAT extension to the DOS-FAT filesystem, it is possible to access partitions that have been compressed with DoubleSpace/DriveSpace from Microsoft or Stacker from Stac. See the file *Documentation/filesystems/fat_cvf.txt* in the Linux kernel sources for further details.

/proc is a virtual filesystem; that is, no actual disk space is associated with it. See "The /proc Filesystem" in Chapter 5.*

Like */proc*, *devfs* is a virtual filesystem. It is meant as a replacement for the current */dev* directory (see the section "Device Files" later in this chapter) and has the advantage that the special files there do not have to be created manually by the system administrator, but are rather created automatically and on demand by the kernel.

The ISO 9660 filesystem (previously known as the High Sierra Filesystem and abbreviated *hsfs* on other Unix systems) is used by most CD-ROMs. Like MS-DOS, this filesystem type restricts filename length and stores only limited information about each file. However, most CD-ROMs provide the Rock Ridge Extensions to ISO 9660, which allow the kernel filesystem driver to assign long filenames, ownerships, and permissions to each file. The net result is that accessing an ISO 9660 CD-ROM under MS-DOS gives you 8.3-format filenames, but under Linux gives you the "true," complete filenames.

In addition, Linux now supports the Microsoft Joliet extensions to ISO 9660, which can handle long filenames made up of Unicode characters. This is not widely used now but may become valuable in the future because Unicode has been accepted internationally as the standard for encoding characters of scripts worldwide.

---

* Note that the */proc* filesystem under Linux is not the same format as the */proc* filesystem under SVR4 (say, Solaris 2.x). Under SVR4, each running process has a single "file" entry in */proc*, which can be opened and treated with certain *ioctl()* calls to obtain process information. On the contrary, Linux provides most of its information in */proc* through *read()* and *write()* requests.

Recently, Linux also received support for UDF, a filesystem that is meant for use with CD-RWs and DVDs.

Next, we have six filesystem types for other platforms. Linux supports the formats that are popular on those platforms in order to allow dual-booting and other interoperation. The systems in question are UFS, EFS, BFS, System V, and Coherent. (The latter two are actually handled by the same kernel driver, with slightly different parameters for each.) If you have filesystems created in one of these formats under a foreign operating system, you'll be able to access the files from Linux.

Finally, there is a slew of filesystems for accessing data on partitions; these are created by operating systems other than the DOS and Unix families. Those filesystems support the Acorn Disk Filing System (ADFS), the AmigaOS filesystems (no floppy disk support except on Amigas), the Apple Mac HFS, and the QNX4 filesystem. Most of the specialized filesystems are useful only on certain hardware architectures; for instance, you won't have hard disks formatted with the Amiga FFS filesystem in an Intel machine. If you need one of those drivers, please read the information that comes with them; some are only in an experimental state.

Besides these filesystems that are used to access local hard disks, there are also network filesystems for accessing remote resources. Covering these is beyond the scope of this book; we have to point you to the *Linux Network Administrator's Guide* by Olaf Kirch and Terry Dawson (O'Reilly) instead.

Mounting Filesystems

In order to access any filesystem under Linux, you must mount it on a certain directory. This makes the files on the filesystem appear as though they reside in the given directory, allowing you to access them.

Before we tell you how to mount filesystems, we should also mention that some distributions come with automounting setups that require you to simply load a diskette or CD into the respective drive and access it like you would on other platforms. For everybody, there are times, however, when you need to know how to mount and unmount media directly. We'll cover how to set up automounting yourself later.

The *mount* command is used to do this and usually must be executed as root. (As we'll see later, ordinary users can use *mount* if the device is listed in the */etc/fstab* file.) The format of this command is:

```
mount -t type device mount-point
```

where *type* is the type name of the filesystem as given in Table 6-1, *device* is the physical device where the filesystem resides (the device file in */dev*), and *mount-point* is the directory on which to mount the filesystem. You have to create the directory before issuing *mount*.

For example, if you have a Second Extended filesystem on the partition */dev/hda2* and wish to mount it on the directory */mnt*, use the command:

```
mount -t ext2 /dev/hda2 /mnt
```

If all goes well you should be able to access the filesystem under */mnt*. Likewise, to mount a floppy that was created on a Windows system and therefore is in DOS format, you use the command:

```
mount -t msdos /dev/fd0 /mnt
```

This makes the files available on an MS-DOS–format floppy under */mnt*. Note that using msdos means that you use the old DOS format that is limited to filenames of 8 plus 3 characters. If you use vfat instead, you get the newer format that was introduced with Windows 95. Of course, the floppy or hard disk needs to be written with that format as well.

There are many options to the *mount* command, which can be specified with the *-o* switch. For example, the MS-DOS and ISO 9660 filesystems support "autoconversion" of text files from MS-DOS format (which contain CR-LF at the end of each line), to Unix format (which contain merely a newline at the end of each line). Using a command, such as:

```
mount -o conv=auto -t msdos /dev/fd0 /mnt
```

turns on this conversion for files that don't have a filename extension that could be associated with a binary file (such as *.exe*, *.bin*, and so forth).

One common option to mount is *-o ro* (or, equivalently, *-r*), which mounts the filesystem as read-only. All write access to such a filesystem is met with a "permission denied" error. Mounting a filesystem as read-only is necessary for media like CD-ROMs that are nonwritable. You can successfully mount a CD-ROM without the *-r* option, but you'll get the annoying warning message:

```
mount: block device /dev/cdrom is write-protected, mounting read-only
```

Use a command, such as:

```
mount -t iso9660 -r /dev/cdrom /mnt
```

instead. This is also necessary if you are trying to mount a floppy that has the write-protect tab in place.

The *mount* manual page lists all available mounting options. Not all are of immediate interest, but you might have a need for some of them, someday. A useful variant of using *mount* is *mount -a*, which mounts all filesystems listed in */etc/fstab* except those marked with the noauto option.

The inverse of mounting a filesystem is, naturally, unmounting it. Unmounting a filesystem has two effects: it synchronizes the system's buffers with the actual contents of the filesystem on disk, and it makes the filesystem no longer available from its mount point. You are then free to mount another filesystem on that mount point.

Unmounting is done with the *umount* command (note that the first "n" is missing from the word "unmount"), as in:

```
umount /dev/fd0
```

to unmount the filesystem on *dev/fd0*. Similarly, to unmount whatever filesystem is currently mounted on a particular directory, use a command, such as:

```
umount /mnt
```

It is important to note that removable media, including floppies and CD-ROMs, should not be removed from the drive or swapped for another disk while mounted. This causes the system's information on the device to be out of sync with what's actually there and could lead to no end of trouble. Whenever you want to switch a floppy or CD-ROM, unmount it first, using the *umount* command, insert the new disk, and then remount the device. Of course, with a CD-ROM or a write-protected floppy, there is no way the device itself can get out of sync, but you could run into other problems. For example, some CD-ROM drives won't let you eject the disk until it is unmounted.

Reads and writes to filesystems on floppies are buffered in memory as they are for hard drives. This means that when you read or write data to a floppy, there may not be any immediate drive activity. The system handles I/O on the floppy asynchronously and reads or writes data only when absolutely necessary. So if you copy a small file to a floppy, but the drive light doesn't come on, don't panic; the data will be written eventually. You can use the *sync* command to force the system to write all filesystem buffers to disk, causing a physical write of any buffered data. Unmounting a filesystem makes this happen as well.

If you wish to allow mortal users to mount and unmount certain devices, you have two options. The first option is to include the user option for the device in */etc/fstab* (described later in this section). This allows any user to use the *mount* and *umount* command for a given device. Another option is to use one of the mount frontends available for Linux. These programs run setuid root and allow ordinary users to mount certain devices. In general, you wouldn't want normal users mounting and unmounting a hard-drive partition, but you could be more lenient about the use of CD-ROM and floppy drives on your system.

Quite a few things can go wrong when attempting to mount a filesystem. Unfortunately, the *mount* command will give you the same error message in response to a number of problems:

```
mount: wrong fs type, /dev/cdrom already mounted, /mnt busy, or other error
```

wrong fs type is simple enough: this means that you may have specified the wrong type to *mount*. If you don't specify a type, *mount* tries to guess the filesystem type from the superblock (this works only for *minix*, *ext2*, and *iso9660*). If *mount* still cannot determine the type of the filesystem, it tries all the types for which drivers are included in the kernel (as listed in */proc/filesystems*). If this still does not lead to success, *mount* fails. *device* already mounted means just that: the device is already mounted on another directory. You can find out what devices are mounted, and where, using the *mount* command with no arguments:

```
rutabaga# mount
/dev/hda2 on / type ext2 (rw)
/dev/hda3 on /windows type vfat (rw)
/dev/cdrom on /cdrom type iso9660 (ro)
/proc on /proc type proc (rw,none)
```

Here, we see two hard-drive partitions, one of type *ext2* and the other of type *vfat*, a CD-ROM mounted on */cdrom*, and the */proc* filesystem. The last field of each line (for example, (rw)) lists the options under which the filesystem is mounted. More on these soon. Note that the CD-ROM device is mounted in */cdrom*. If you use your CD-ROM often, it's convenient to create a special directory such as */cdrom* and mount the device there. */mnt* is generally used to temporarily mount filesystems such as floppies.

The error *mount-point* busy is rather odd. Essentially, it means some activity is taking place under *mount-point* that prevents you from mounting a filesystem there. Usually, this means that an open file is under this directory, or some process has its current working directory beneath *mount-point*. When using *mount*, be sure your root shell is not within *mount-point*; do a *cd* / to get to the top-level directory. Or, another filesystem could be mounted with the same *mount-point*. Use *mount* with no arguments to find out.

Of course, other error isn't very helpful. There are several other cases in which *mount* could fail. If the filesystem in question has data or media errors of some kind, *mount* may report it is unable to read the filesystem's *superblock*, which is (under Unix-like filesystems) the portion of the filesystem that stores information on the files and attributes for the filesystem as a whole. If you attempt to mount a CD-ROM or floppy drive, and there's no CD-ROM or floppy in the drive, you will receive an error message, such as:

```
mount: /dev/cdrom is not a valid block device
```

Floppies are especially prone to physical defects (more so than you might initially think), and CD-ROMs suffer from dust, scratches, and fingerprints, as well as being inserted upside-down. (If you attempt to mount your Stan Rogers CD as ISO 9660 format, you will likely run into similar problems.)

Also, be sure the mount point you're trying to use (such as */mnt*) exists. If not, you can simply create it with the *mkdir* command.

If you have problems mounting or accessing a filesystem, data on the filesystem may be corrupt. Several tools help repair certain filesystem types under Linux; see "Checking and Repairing Filesystems" later in this chapter.

The system automatically mounts several filesystems when the system boots. This is handled by the file *etc/fstab*, which includes an entry for each filesystem that should be mounted at boot time. Each line in this file is of the format:

```
device mount-point type options
```

Here, *device*, *mount-point*, and *type* are equivalent to their meanings in the *mount* command, and *options* is a comma-separated list of options to use with the *-o* switch to *mount*.

A sample *etc/fstab* is shown here:

```
# device        directory      type      options
/dev/hda2       /              ext2      defaults
/dev/hda3       /windows       vfat      defaults
/dev/cdrom      /cdrom         iso9660   ro
/proc           /proc          proc      none

/dev/hda1       none           swap      sw
```

The last line of this file specifies a swap partition. This is described in the section "Managing Swap Space" later in this chapter.

The *mount*(8) manual page lists the possible values for *options*; if you wish to specify more than one option, you can list them with separating commas and no whitespace, as in:

```
/dev/cdrom      /cdrom         iso9660   ro,user
```

The user option allows users other than root to mount the filesystem. If this option is present, a user can execute a command, such as:

```
mount /cdrom
```

to mount the device. Note that if you specify only a device or mount point (not both) to *mount*, it looks up the device or mount point in *etc/fstab* and mounts the device with the parameters given there. This allows you to mount devices listed in *etc/fstab* with ease.

The option defaults should be used for most filesystems; it enables a number of other options, such as rw (read-write access), async (buffer I/O to the filesystem in memory asynchronously), and so forth. Unless you have a specific need to modify one of these parameters, use defaults for most filesystems and ro for read-only devices such as CD-ROMs. Another potentially useful option is umask, which lets you set the default mask for the permission bits, something that is especially useful with some foreign filesystems.

The command *mount -a* will mount all filesystems listed in *etc/fstab*. This command is executed at boot time by one of the scripts found in *etc/rc.d*, such as *rc.sysinit* (or wherever your distribution stores its configuration files). This way, all filesystems listed in *etc/fstab* will be available when the system starts up; your hard-drive partitions, CD-ROM drive, and so on will all be mounted.

There is an exception to this: the *root filesystem*. The root filesystem, mounted on /, usually contains the file */etc/fstab* as well as the scripts in */etc/rc.d*. In order for these to be available, the kernel itself must mount the root filesystem directly at boot time. The device containing the root filesystem is coded into the kernel image and can be altered using the *rdev* command (see "Using a Boot Floppy" in Chapter 5). While the system boots, the kernel attempts to mount this device as the root filesystem, trying several filesystem types in succession. If at boot time the kernel prints an error message, such as:

```
VFS: Unable to mount root fs
```

one of the following has happened:

- The root device coded into the kernel is incorrect.
- The kernel does not have support compiled in for the filesystem type of the root device. (See "Building the Kernel" in Chapter 7 for more details. This is usually relevant only if you build your own kernel.)
- The root device is corrupt in some way.

In any of these cases, the kernel can't proceed and panics. See "What to Do in an Emergency" in Chapter 8 for clues on what to do in this situation. If filesystem corruption is the problem, this can usually be repaired; see "Checking and Repairing Filesystems" later in this chapter.

A filesystem does not need to be listed in */etc/fstab* in order to be mounted, but it does need to be listed there in order to be mounted "automatically" by *mount -a*, or to use the user mount option.

Automounting Devices

If you need to access a lot of different filesystems, especially networked ones, you might be interested in a special feature in the Linux kernel: the *automounter*. This is a combination of kernel functionality, a daemon, and some configuration files that automatically detect when somebody wants to access a certain filesystem and mounts the filesystem transparently. When the filesystem is not used for some time, the automounter automatically unmounts it in order to save resources like memory and network throughput.

If you want to use the automounter, you first need to turn this feature on when building your kernel. (See "Building the Kernel" in Chapter 7 for more details.) You will also need to enable the NFS option.

Next, you need to start the *automount* daemon. Because this feature is quite new, your distribution might not yet have it. Look for the directory */usr/lib/autofs*. If it is not there, you will need to get the *autofs* package from your friendly Linux archive and compile and install it according to the instructions.

Note that there are two versions of automount support: Version 3 and Version 4. Version 3 is the one still contained in most distributions, so that's what we describe here.

You can automount filesystems wherever you like, but for simplicity's sake, we will assume here that you want to automount all filesystems below one directory that we will call *automount* here. If you want your automount points to be scattered over your filesystem, you will need to use multiple *automount* daemons.

If you have compiled the *autofs* package yourself, it might be a good idea to start by copying the sample configuration files that you can find in *sample* directory, and adapt them to your needs. To do this, copy the files *sample/auto.master* and *sample/auto.misc* into the */etc* directory, and the file *sample/rc.autofs* under the name *autofs* wherever your distribution stores its boot scripts. We'll assume here that you use */etc/init.d*.

The first configuration file to edit is */etc/auto.master*. This lists all the directories (the so-called *mount points*) below which the automounter should mount partitions. Because we have decided to use only one partition in this chapter's example, we will need to make only one entry here. The file could look like this:

```
/automount       /etc/auto.misc
```

This file consists of lines with two entries each, separated by whitespace. The first entry specifies the mount point, and the second entry names a so-called *map file* that specifies how and where to mount the devices or partitions to be automounted. You need one such map file for each mount point.

In our case, the file */etc/auto.misc* looks like the following:

```
cd              -fstype=iso9660,ro      :/dev/scd0
floppy           -fstype=auto             :/dev/fd0
```

Again, this file consists of one-line entries that each specify one particular device or partition to be automounted. The lines have two mandatory and one optional field, separated by whitespaces. The first value is mandatory and specifies the directory onto which the device or partition of this entry is automounted. This value is appended to the mount point so that the CD-ROM will be automounted onto */automount/cd*.

The second value is optional and specifies flags to be used for the *mount* operation. These are equivalent to those for the *mount* command itself, with the exception that the type is specified with the option *-fstype=* instead of *-t*.

Finally, the third value specifies the partition or device to be mounted. In our case, we specify the first SCSI CD-ROM drive and the first floppy drive, respectively. The colon in front of the entry is mandatory; it separates the host part from the device/ directory part, just as with *mount*. Because those two devices are on a local machine, there is nothing to the left of the colon. If we wanted to automount the directory *sources* from the NFS server sourcemaster, we would specify something, such as:

```
sources    -fstype=nfs,soft    sourcemaster:/sources
```

After editing the configuration files to reflect your system, you can start the automount daemon by issuing (replace the path with the path that suits your system):

```
tigger# /etc/init.d/autofs start
```

Because this command is very taciturn, you should check whether the automounter has really started. One way to do this is to issue:

```
tigger# /etc/init.d/autofs status
```

but it is difficult to determine from the output whether the automounter is really running. Your best bet, therefore, is to check whether the *automount* process exists:

```
tigger# ps aux | grep automount
```

If this command shows the automount process, everything should be all right. If it doesn't, you need to check your configuration files again. It could also be the case that the necessary kernel support is not available: either the automount support is not in your kernel, or you have compiled it as a module but not installed this module. If the latter is the case, you can fix the problem by issuing:

```
tigger# modprobe autofs
```

If that doesn't work, you need to use:

```
tigger# modprobe autofs4
```

instead.* When your automounter works to your satisfaction, you might want to put the *modprobe* call as well as the *autofs* call in one of your system's startup configuration files like */etc/rc.local*, */etc/init.d/boot.local*, or whatever your distribution uses.

If everything is set up correctly, all you need to do is access some directory below the mount point, and the automounter will mount the appropriate device or partition for you. For example, if you type:

```
tigger$ ls /automount/cd
```

the automounter will automatically mount the CD-ROM so that *ls* can list its contents. The only difference between normal and automounting is that with automounting you will notice a slight delay before the output comes.

In order to conserve resources, the automounter unmounts a partition or device if it has not been accessed for a certain amount of time (the default is five minutes).

The automounter supports a number of advanced options; for example, you do not need to read the map table from a file but can also access system databases or even have the automounter run a program and use this program's output as the mapping data. See the manpages for *autofs*(5) and *automount*(8) for further details.

---

* We'll cover the *modprobe* command in the next chapter.

Creating Filesystems

You can create a filesystem using the *mkfs* command. Creating a filesystem is analo-gous to "formatting" a partition or floppy, allowing it to store files.

Each filesystem type has its own *mkfs* command associated with it—for example, MS-DOS filesystems may be created using *mkfs.msdos*, Second Extended filesystems using *mkfs.ext2*, and so on. The program *mkfs* itself is a frontend that creates a file-system of any type by executing the appropriate version of *mkfs* for that type.*

When you installed Linux, you may have created filesystems by hand using a com-mand such as *mke2fs*. (If not, the installation software created the filesystems for you.) In fact, *mke2fs* is equivalent to *mkfs.ext2*. The programs are the same (and on many systems, one is a symbolic link to the other), but the *mkfs.fs-type* filename makes it easier for *mkfs* to execute the appropriate filesystem-type–specific program. If you don't have the *mkfs* frontend, you can use *mke2fs* or *mkfs.ext2* directly.

Assuming that you're using the *mkfs* frontend, you can create a filesystem using this command:

```
mkfs -t type device
```

where *type* is the type of filesystem to create, given in Table 6-1, and *device* is the device on which to create the filesystem (such as */dev/fd0* for a floppy).

For example, to create an *ext2* filesystem on a floppy, you use this command:

```
mkfs -t ext2 /dev/fd0
```

You could create an MS-DOS floppy using *-t msdos* instead.

We can now mount the floppy, as described in the previous section, copy files to it, and so forth. Remember to unmount the floppy before removing it from the drive.

Creating a filesystem deletes all data on the corresponding physical device (floppy, hard-drive partition, whatever). *mkfs* usually does not prompt you before creating a filesystem, so be absolutely sure you know what you're doing.

Creating a filesystem on a hard-drive partition is done exactly as shown earlier, except that you would use the partition name, such as */dev/hda2*, as the *device*. Don't try to create a filesystem on a device, such as */dev/hda*. This refers to the entire drive, not just a single partition on the drive. You can create partitions using *fdisk*, as described in the section "Creating Linux Partitions" in Chapter 3.

You should be especially careful when creating filesystems on hard-drive partitions. Be absolutely sure that the *device* and *size* arguments are correct. If you enter the wrong *device*, you could end up destroying the data on your current filesystems, and

---

* Under Linux the *mkfs* command historically created a Minix filesystem. On newer Linux systems, *mkfs* is a frontend for any filesystem type, and Minix filesystems are created using *mkfs.minix*.

if you specify the wrong *size*, you could overwrite data on other partitions. Be sure that *size* corresponds to the partition size as reported by Linux *fdisk*.

When creating filesystems on floppies, it's usually best to do a low-level format first. This lays down the sector and track information on the floppy so that its size can be automatically detected using the devices */dev/fd0* or */dev/fd1*. One way to do a low-level format is with the MS-DOS FORMAT command; another way is with the Linux program *fdformat.* For example, to format the floppy in the first floppy drive, use the command:

```
rutabaga# fdformat /dev/fd0
Double-sided, 80 tracks, 18 sec/track. Total capacity 1440 kB.
Formatting ... done
Verifying ... done
```

Using the *-n* option with *fdformat* will skip the verification step.

Each filesystem-specific version of *mkfs* supports several options you might find useful. Most types support the *-c* option, which causes the physical media to be checked for bad blocks while creating the filesystem. If bad blocks are found, they are marked and avoided when writing data to the filesystem. In order to use these type-specific options, include them after the *-t type* option to *mkfs*, as follows:

```
mkfs -t type -c device blocks
```

To determine what options are available, see the manual page for the type-specific version of *mkfs*. (For example, for the Second Extended filesystem, see *mke2fs*.)

You may not have all available type-specific versions of *mkfs* installed. If this is the case, *mkfs* will fail when you try to create a filesystem of a type for which you have no *mkfs.type*. Many filesystem types supported by Linux have a corresponding *mkfs.type* available, somewhere.

If you run into trouble using *mkfs*, it's possible that Linux is having problems accessing the physical device. In the case of a floppy, this might just mean a bad floppy. In the case of a hard drive, it could be more serious; for example, the disk device driver in the kernel might be having problems reading your drive. This could be a hardware problem or a simple matter of your drive geometry being specified incorrectly. See the manual pages for the various versions of *mkfs*, and read the sections in Chapter 3 on troubleshooting installation problems. They apply equally here.[†]

---

* Debian users should use *superformat* instead.

† Also, the procedure for making an ISO 9660 filesystem for a CD-ROM is more complicated than simply formatting a filesystem and copying files. See the CD-Writing HOWTO for more details.

Checking and Repairing Filesystems

It is sometimes necessary to check your Linux filesystems for consistency and repair them if there are any errors or if you lose data. Such errors commonly result from a system crash or loss of power, making the kernel unable to sync the filesystem buffer cache with the contents of the disk. In most cases, such errors are relatively minor. However, if the system were to crash while writing a large file, that file may be lost and the blocks associated with it marked as "in use," when in fact no file entry is corresponding to them. In other cases, errors can be caused by accidentally writing data directly to the hard-drive device (such as */dev/hda*), or to one of the partitions.

The program *fsck* is used to check filesystems and correct any problems. Like *mkfs*, *fsck* is a frontend for a filesystem-type–specific *fsck.type*, such as *fsck.ext2* for Second Extended filesystems. (As with *mkfs.ext2*, *fsck.ext2* is a symbolic link to *e2fsck*, either of which you can execute directly if the *fsck* frontend is not installed.)

Use of *fsck* is quite simple; the format of the command is:

```
fsck -t type device
```

where *type* is the type of filesystem to repair, as given in Table 6-1, and *device* is the device (drive partition or floppy) on which the filesystem resides.

For example, to check an *ext2* filesystem on */dev/hda2*, you use:

```
rutabaga# fsck -t ext2 /dev/hda2
Parallelizing fsck version 1.06 (7-Oct-96)
e2fsck 1.06, 7-Oct-96 for EXT2 FS 0.5b, 95/08/09
/dev/hda2 is mounted.  Do you really want to continue (y/n)? y

/dev/hda2 was not cleanly unmounted, check forced.
Pass 1: Checking inodes, blocks, and sizes
Pass 2: Checking directory structure
Pass 3: Checking directory connectivity
Pass 4: Checking reference counts.
Pass 5: Checking group summary information.

Free blocks count wrong for group 3 (3331, counted=3396).  FIXED
Free blocks count wrong for group 4 (1983, counted=2597).  FIXED
Free blocks count wrong (29643, counted=30341).  FIXED
Inode bitmap differences: -8280.  FIXED
Free inodes count wrong for group #4 (1405, counted=1406).  FIXED
Free inodes count wrong (34522, counted=34523).  FIXED

/dev/hda2: ***** FILE SYSTEM WAS MODIFIED *****
/dev/hda2: ***** REBOOT LINUX *****
/dev/hda2: 13285/47808 files, 160875/191216 blocks
```

First of all, note that the system asks for confirmation before checking a mounted filesystem. If any errors are found and corrected while using *fsck*, you'll have to reboot the system if the filesystem is mounted. This is because the changes made by *fsck* may not be propagated back to the system's internal knowledge of the filesystem layout. In general, it's not a good idea to check mounted filesystems.

As we can see, several problems were found and corrected, and because this filesystem was mounted, the system informed us that the machine should be rebooted.

How can you check filesystems without mounting them? With the exception of the root filesystem, you can simply *umount* any filesystems before running *fsck* on them. The root filesystem, however, can't be unmounted while running the system. One way to check your root filesystem while it's unmounted is to use a boot/root floppy combination, such as the installation floppies used by your Linux distribution. This way, the root filesystem is contained on a floppy, the root filesystem (on your hard drive) remains unmounted, and you can check the hard-drive root filesystem from there. See "What to Do in an Emergency" in Chapter 8 for more details about this.

Another way to check the root filesystem is to mount it as read-only. This can be done using the option ro from the LILO boot prompt (see the section "Specifying boot time options" in Chapter 5). However, other parts of your system configuration (for example, the programs executed by */etc/init* at boot time) may require write access to the root filesystem, so you can't boot the system normally or these programs will fail. To boot the system with the root filesystem mounted as read-only you might want to boot the system into single-user mode as well (using the boot option single). This prevents additional system configuration at boot time; you can then check the root filesystem and reboot the system normally.

To cause the root filesystem to be mounted as read-only, you can use either the ro boot option, or *rdev* to set the read-only flag in the kernel image itself.

Many Linux systems automatically check the filesystems at boot time. This is usually done by executing *fsck* from */etc/rc.d/rc.sysinit*. When this is done, the system usually mounts the root filesystem initially as read-only, runs *fsck* to check it, and then runs the command:

```
mount -w -o remount /
```

The *-o remount* option causes the given filesystem to be remounted with the new parameters; the -w option (equivalent to -o rw) causes the filesystem to be mounted as read-write. The net result is that the root filesystem is remounted with read-write access.

When *fsck* is executed at boot time, it checks all filesystems other than root before they are mounted. Once *fsck* completes, the other filesystems are mounted using *mount*. Check out the files in */etc/rc.d*, especially *rc.sysinit* (if present on your system), to see how this is done. If you want to disable this feature on your system, comment out the lines in the appropriate */etc/rc.d* file that executes *fsck*.

You can pass options to the type-specific *fsck*. Most types support the option -a, which automatically confirms any prompts that *fsck.type* may display; -c, which does bad-block checking, as with *mkfs*; and -v, which prints verbose information during the check operation. These options should be given after the -t *type* argument to *fsck*, as in:

```
fsck -t type -v device
```

to run *fsck* with verbose output.

See the manual pages for *fsck* and *e2fsck* for more information.

Not all filesystem types supported by Linux have a *fsck* variant available. To check and repair MS-DOS filesystems, you should use a tool under MS-DOS, such as the Norton Utilities, to accomplish this task. You should be able to find versions of *fsck* for the Second Extended filesystem, Minix filesystem, and Xia filesystem at least.

In the section "What to Do in an Emergency" in Chapter 8, we provide additional information on checking filesystems and recovering from disaster. *fsck* will by no means catch and repair every error to your filesystems, but most common problems should be handled. If you delete an important file, there is currently no easy way to recover it—*fsck* can't do that for you. There is work underway to provide an "undelete" utility in the Second Extended filesystem. Be sure to keep backups, or use *rm -i*, which always prompts you before deleting a file.

Managing Swap Space

Swap space is a generic term for disk storage used to increase the amount of apparent memory available on the system. Under Linux, swap space is used to implement *paging*, a process whereby memory pages are written out to disk when physical memory is low and read back into physical memory when needed (a page is 4096 bytes on Intel x86 systems; this value can differ on other architectures). The process by which paging works is rather involved, but it is optimized for certain cases. The virtual memory subsystem under Linux allows memory pages to be shared between running programs. For example, if you have multiple copies of Emacs running simultaneously, only one copy of the Emacs code is actually in memory. Also, text pages (those pages containing program code, not data) are usually read-only, and therefore not written to disk when swapped out. Those pages are instead freed directly from main memory and read from the original executable file when they are accessed again.

Of course, swap space cannot completely make up for a lack of physical RAM. Disk access is much slower than RAM access, by several orders of magnitude. Therefore, swap is useful primarily as a means to run a number of programs simultaneously that would not otherwise fit into physical RAM; if you are switching between these programs rapidly you'll notice a lag as pages are swapped to and from disk.

At any rate, Linux supports swap space in two forms: as a separate disk partition or a file somewhere on your existing Linux filesystems. You can have up to eight swap areas, with each swap area being a disk file or partition up to 2 GB in size (again, these values can differ on non-Intel systems). You math whizzes out there will realize that this allows up to 16 GB of swap space. (If anyone has actually attempted to use this much swap, the authors would love to hear about it, whether you're a math whiz or not.)

Note that using a swap partition can yield better performance because the disk blocks are guaranteed to be contiguous. In the case of a swap file, however, the disk blocks may be scattered around the filesystem, which can be a serious performance hit in some cases. Many people use a swap file when they must add additional swap space temporarily—for example, if the system is thrashing because of lack of physical RAM and swap. Swap files are a good way to add swap on demand.

Nearly all Linux systems utilize swap space of some kind—usually a single swap partition. In Chapter 3, we explained how to create a swap partition on your system during the Linux installation procedure. In this section we describe how to add and remove swap files and partitions. If you already have swap space and are happy with it, this section may not be of interest to you.

How much swap space do you have? The *free* command reports information on system-memory usage:

```
rutabaga% free
             total        used      free     shared    buffers     cached
Mem:         127888      126744      1144      27640       1884      51988
-/+          buffers/cache:  72872    55016
Swap:        130748       23916    106832
```

All the numbers here are reported in 1024-byte blocks. Here, we see a system with 127,888 blocks (about 127 MB) of physical RAM, with 126,744 (about 126 MB) currently in use. Note that your system actually has more physical RAM than that given in the "total" column; this number does not include the memory used by the kernel for its own sundry needs.

The "shared" column lists the amount of physical memory shared between multiple processes. Here, we see that about 27 MB of pages are being shared, which means that memory is being utilized well. The "buffers" column shows the amount of memory being used by the kernel buffer cache. The buffer cache (described briefly in the previous section) is used to speed up disk operations by allowing disk reads and writes to be serviced directly from memory. The buffer cache size will increase or decrease as memory usage on the system changes; this memory is reclaimed if applications need it. Therefore, although we see that 126 MB of system memory is in use, not all (but most) of it is being used by application programs. The "cache" column indicates how many memory pages the kernel has cached for faster access later.

Because the memory used for buffers and cache can easily be reclaimed for use by applications, the second line (-/+ buffers/cache) provides an indication of the memory actually used by applications (the "used" column) or available to applications (the "free" column). The sum of the memory used by buffers and cache reported in the first line is subtracted from the total used memory and added to the total free memory to give the two figures on the second line.

In the third line, we see the total amount of swap, 130,748 blocks (about 128 MB). In this case, only very little of the swap is being used; there is plenty of physical RAM available. If additional applications were started, larger parts of the buffer cache memory would be used to host them. Swap space is generally used as a last resort when the system can't reclaim physical memory in other ways.

Note that the amount of swap reported by *free* is somewhat less than the total size of your swap partitions and files. This is because several blocks of each swap area must be used to store a map of how each page in the swap area is being utilized. This overhead should be rather small; only a few kilobytes per swap area.

If you're considering creating a swap file, the *df* command gives you information on the amount of space remaining on your various filesystems. This command prints a list of filesystems, showing each one's size and what percentage is currently occupied.

Creating Swap Space

The first step in adding additional swap is to create a file or partition to host the swap area. If you wish to create an additional swap partition, you can create the partition using the *fdisk* utility, as described in the section "Creating Linux Partitions" in Chapter 3.

To create a swap file, you'll need to open a file and write bytes to it equaling the amount of swap you wish to add. One easy way to do this is with the *dd* command. For example, to create a 32-MB swap file, you can use the command:

```
dd if=/dev/zero of=/swap bs=1024 count=32768
```

This will write 32768 blocks (32 MB) of data from */dev/zero* to the file */swap*. (*/dev/zero* is a special device in which read operations always return null bytes. It's something like the inverse of */dev/null*.) After creating a file of this size, it's a good idea to use the *sync* command to sync the filesystems in case of a system crash.

Once you have created the swap file or partition, you can use the *mkswap* command to "format" the swap area. As described in the section "Creating Swap Space" in Chapter 3, the format of the *mkswap* command is:

```
mkswap -c device size
```

where *device* is the name of the swap partition or file, and *size* is the size of the swap area in blocks (again, one block is equal to one kilobyte). You normally do not need to specify this when creating a swap area because *mkswap* can detect the partition size on its own. The *-c* switch is optional and causes the swap area to be checked for bad blocks as it is formatted.

For example, for the swap file created in the previous example, you would use the command:

```
mkswap -c /swap 8192
```

If the swap area is a partition, you would substitute the name of the partition (such as */dev/hda3*) and the size of the partition, also in blocks.

If you are using a swap file (and not a swap partition), you need to change its permissions first, like this:

```
chmod 0600 /swap
```

After running *mkswap* on a swap file, use the *sync* command to ensure the format information has been physically written to the new swap file. Running *sync* is not necessary when formatting a swap partition.

Enabling the Swap Space

In order for the new swap space to be utilized, you must enable it with the *swapon* command. For example, after creating the previous swap file and running *mkswap* and *sync*, we could use the command:

```
swapon /swap
```

This adds the new swap area to the total amount of available swap; use the *free* command to verify that this is indeed the case. If you are using a new swap partition, you can enable it with a command, such as:

```
swapon /dev/hda3
```

if */dev/hda3* is the name of the swap partition.

Like filesystems, swap areas are automatically enabled at boot time using the *swapon -a* command from one of the system startup files (usually in */etc/rc.d/rc.sysinit*). This command looks in the file */etc/fstab*, which, as you'll remember from the section "Mounting Filesystems" earlier in this chapter, includes information on filesystems and swap areas. All entries in */etc/fstab* with the *options* field set to sw are enabled by *swapon -a*.

Therefore, if */etc/fstab* contains the entries:

```
# device     directory    type    options
/dev/hda3    none         swap    sw
/swap        none         swap    sw
```

the two swap areas */dev/hda3* and */swap* will be enabled at boot time. For each new swap area, you should add an entry to */etc/fstab*.

Disabling Swap Space

As is usually the case, undoing a task is easier than doing it. To disable swap space, simply use the command:

```
swapoff device
```

where *device* is the name of the swap partition or file that you wish to disable. For example, to disable swapping on the device */dev/hda3*, use the command:

```
swapoff /dev/hda3
```

If you wish to disable a swap file, you can simply remove the file, using *rm*, *after* using *swapoff*. Don't remove a swap file before disabling it; this can cause disaster.

If you have disabled a swap partition using *swapoff*, you are free to reuse that partition as you see fit: remove it using *fdisk* or your preferred repartitioning tool.

Also, if there is a corresponding entry for the swap area in */etc/fstab*, remove it. Otherwise, you'll get errors when you next reboot the system and the swap area can't be found.

Device Files

Device files allow user programs to access hardware devices on the system through the kernel. They are not "files" per se, but look like files from the program's point of view: you can read from them, write to them, *mmap()* onto them, and so forth. When you access such a device "file," the kernel recognizes the I/O request and passes it a device driver, which performs some operation, such as reading data from a serial port or sending data to a sound card.

Device files (although they are inappropriately named, we will continue to use this term) provide a convenient way to access system resources without requiring the applications programmer to know how the underlying device works. Under Linux, as with most Unix systems, device drivers themselves are part of the kernel. In the section "Building the Kernel" in Chapter 7, we show you how to build your own kernel, including only those device drivers for the hardware on your system.

Device files are located in the directory */dev* on nearly all Unix-like systems. Each device on the system should have a corresponding entry in */dev*. For example, */dev/ttyS0* corresponds to the first serial port, known as COM1 under MS-DOS; */dev/hda2* corresponds to the second partition on the first IDE drive. In fact, there should be entries in */dev* for devices you do not have. The device files are generally created during system installation and include every possible device driver. They don't necessarily correspond to the actual hardware on your system.

A number of pseudo-devices in */dev* don't correspond to any actual peripheral. For example, */dev/null* acts as a byte sink; any write request to */dev/null* will succeed, but the data written will be ignored. Similarly, we've already demonstrated the use of */dev/zero* to create a swap file; any read request on */dev/zero* simply returns null bytes.

When using *ls -l* to list device files in */dev*, you'll see something like the following:

```
brw-rw----   1 root     disk      3,   0 May 19 1994 /dev/hda
```

This is */dev/hda*, which corresponds to the first IDE drive. First of all, note that the first letter of the permissions field is b, which means this is a block device file. (Recall that normal files have an – in this first column, directories a d, and so on.) Device files are denoted either by b, for block devices, or c, for character devices. A block device is usually a peripheral such as a hard drive: data is read and written to the device as entire blocks (where the block size is determined by the device; it may not be 1024 bytes as we usually call "blocks" under Linux), and the device may be accessed randomly. In contrast, character devices are usually read or written sequentially, and I/O may be done as single bytes. An example of a character device is a serial port.

Also, note that the size field in the *ls -1* listing is replaced by two numbers, separated by a comma. The first value is the *major device number* and the second is the *minor device number*. When a device file is accessed by a program, the kernel receives the I/O request in terms of the major and minor numbers of the device. The major number generally specifies a particular driver within the kernel, and the minor number specifies a particular device handled by that driver. For example, all serial port devices have the same major number, but different minor numbers. The kernel uses the major number to redirect an I/O request to the appropriate driver, and the driver uses the minor number to figure out which specific device to access. In some cases, minor numbers can also be used for accessing specific functions of a device.

The naming convention used by files in */dev* is, to put it bluntly, a complete mess. Because the kernel itself doesn't care what filenames are used in */dev* (it cares only about the major and minor numbers), the distribution maintainers, applications programmers, and device driver writers are free to choose names for a device file. Often, the person writing a device driver will suggest a name for the device, and later the name will be changed to accommodate other, similar devices. This can cause confusion and inconsistency as the system develops; hopefully, you won't encounter this problem unless you're working with newer device drivers—those that are under testing.

At any rate, the device files included in your original distribution should be accurate for the kernel version and for device drivers included with that distribution. When you upgrade your kernel or add additional device drivers (see the section "Building a New Kernel" in Chapter 7), you may need to add a device file using the *mknod* command. The format of this command is:

```
mknod -m permissions name type major minor
```

where:

- *name* is the full pathname of the device to create, such as */dev/rft0*
- *type* is either c for a character device or b for a block device
- *major* is the major number of the device
- *minor* is the minor number of the device
- *-m permissions* is an optional argument that sets the permission bits of the new device file to *permissions*

For example, let's say you're adding a new device driver to the kernel, and the documentation says that you need to create the block device */dev/bogus*, major number 42, minor number 0. You would use the command:

```
mknod /dev/bogus b 42 0
```

Making devices is even easier with the shell script */dev/MAKEDEV* that comes with many distributions—you specify only the kind of device you want, and MAKEDEV finds out the major and minor numbers for you.

If you don't specify the *-m permissions* argument, the new device is given the permissions for a newly created file, modified by your current umask—usually 0644. To set the permissions for */dev/bogus* to 0660 instead, we use:

```
mknod -m 660 /dev/bogus b 42 0
```

You can also use *chmod* to set the permissions for a device file after creation.

Why are device permissions important? Like any file, the permissions for a device file control who may access the raw device, and how. As we saw in the previous example, the device file for */dev/hda* has permissions 0660, which means that only the owner and users in the file's group (here, the group disk is used) may read and write directly to this device. (Permissions are introduced in "File Ownership and Permissions" in Chapter 4.)

In general, you don't want to give any user direct read and write access to certain devices—especially those devices corresponding to disk drives and partitions. Otherwise, anyone could, say, run *mkfs* on a drive partition and completely destroy all data on the system.

In the case of drives and partitions, write access is required to corrupt data in this way, but read access is also a breach of security; given read access to a raw device file corresponding to a disk partition, a user could peek in on other users' files. Likewise, the device file */dev/mem* corresponds to the system's physical memory (it's generally used only for extreme debugging purposes). Given read access, clever users could spy on other users' passwords, including the one belonging to root, as they are entered at login time.

Be sure that the permissions for any device you add to the system correspond to how the device can and should be accessed by users. Devices such as serial ports, sound cards, and virtual consoles are generally safe for mortals to have access to, but most other devices on the system should be limited to use by root (and to programs running setuid as root).

Many files found in */dev* are actually symbolic links (created using *ln -s*, in the usual way) to another device file. These links make it easier to access certain devices by using a more common name. For example, if you have a serial mouse, that mouse might be accessed through one of the device files */dev/ttyS0*, */dev/ttyS1*, */dev/ttyS2*, or */dev/ttyS3*, depending on which serial port the mouse is attached to. Many people create a link named */dev/mouse* to the appropriate serial device, as in:

```
ln -s /dev/ttyS2 /dev/mouse
```

In this way, users can access the mouse from */dev/mouse*, instead of having to remember which serial port it is on. This convention is also used for devices such as */dev/cdrom* and */dev/modem*. These files are usually symbolic links to a device file in */dev* corresponding to the actual CD-ROM or modem device.

To remove a device file, just use *rm*, as in:

```
rm /dev/bogus
```

Removing a device file does not remove the corresponding device driver from memory or from the kernel; it simply leaves you with no means to talk to a particular device driver. Similarly, adding a device file does not add a device driver to the system; in fact, you can add device files for drivers that don't even exist. Device files simply provide a "hook" into a particular device driver should such a driver exist in the kernel.

CHAPTER 7
Upgrading Software
and the Kernel

In this chapter, we'll show you how to upgrade software on your system, including rebuilding and installing a new operating system kernel. Although most Linux distributions provide some automated means to install, remove, and upgrade specific software packages on your system, it is often necessary to install software by hand.

Non-expert users will find it easiest to install and upgrade software by using a *package* system, which most distributions provide. If you don't use a package system, installations and upgrades are more complicated than with most commercial operating systems. Even though precompiled binaries are available, you may have to uncompress them and unpack them from an archive file. You may also have to create symbolic links or set environment variables so that the binaries know where to look for the resources they use. In other cases, you'll need to compile the software yourself from sources.

Another common Linux activity is building the kernel. This is an important task for several reasons. First of all, you may find yourself in a position where you need to upgrade your current kernel to a newer version, to pick up new features or hardware support. Second, building the kernel yourself allows you to select which features you do (and do not) want included in the compiled kernel.

Why is the ability to select features a win for you? All kernel code and data are "locked down" in memory; that is, it cannot be swapped out to disk. For example, if you use a kernel image with support for hardware you do not have or use, the memory consumed by the support for that hardware cannot be reclaimed for use by user applications. Customizing the kernel allows you to trim it down for your needs.

It should be noted here that most distributions today ship with modularized kernels. This means that the kernel they install by default contains only the minimum functionality needed to bring up the system; everything else is then contained in *modules* that add any additionally needed functionality on demand. We will talk about modules in much greater detail later.

Archive and Compression Utilities

When installing or upgrading software on Unix systems, the first things you need to be familiar with are the tools used for compressing and archiving files. Dozens of such utilities are available. Some of these (such as *tar* and *compress*) date back to the earliest days of Unix; others (such as *gzip* and *bzip2*) are relative newcomers. The main goal of these utilities is to archive files (that is, to pack many files together into a single file for easy transportation or backup) and to compress files (to reduce the amount of disk space required to store a particular file or set of files).

In this section, we're going to discuss the most common file formats and utilities you're likely to run into. For instance, a near-universal convention in the Unix world is to transport files or software as a *tar* archive, compressed using *compress* or *gzip*. In order to create or unpack these files yourself, you'll need to know the tools of the trade. The tools are most often used when installing new software or creating backups—the subject of the following two sections in this chapter.

Using gzip and bzip2

gzip is a fast and efficient compression program distributed by the GNU project. The basic function of *gzip* is to take a file, compress it, save the compressed version as *filename.gz*, and remove the original, uncompressed file. The original file is removed only if *gzip* is successful; it is very difficult to accidentally delete a file in this manner. Of course, being GNU software, *gzip* has more options than you want to think about, and many aspects of its behavior can be modified using command-line options.

First, let's say that we have a large file named *garbage.txt*:

```
rutabaga% ls -l garbage.txt
-rw-r--r--   1 mdw      hack      312996 Nov 17 21:44 garbage.txt
```

To compress this file using *gzip*, we simply use the command:

```
gzip garbage.txt
```

This replaces *garbage.txt* with the compressed file *garbage.txt.gz*. What we end up with is the following:

```
rutabaga% gzip garbage.txt
rutabaga% ls -l garbage.txt.gz
-rw-r--r--   1 mdw      hack      103441 Nov 17 21:44 garbage.txt.gz
```

Note that *garbage.txt* is removed when *gzip* completes.

You can give *gzip* a list of filenames; it compresses each file in the list, storing each with a *.gz* extension. (Unlike the *zip* program for Unix and MS-DOS systems, *gzip* will not, by default, compress several files into a single *.gz* archive. That's what *tar* is for; see the next section.)

How efficiently a file is compressed depends upon its format and contents. For example, many graphics file formats (such as PNG and JPEG) are already well compressed, and *gzip* will have little or no effect upon such files. Files that compress well usually include plain-text files, and binary files, such as executables and libraries. You can get information on a *gzip*ped file using *gzip –l*. For example:

```
rutabaga% gzip -l garbage.txt.gz
compressed  uncompr. ratio uncompressed_name
   103115    312996  67.0% garbage.txt
```

To get our original file back from the compressed version, we use *gunzip*, as in:

```
gunzip garbage.txt.gz
```

After doing this, we get:

```
rutabaga% gunzip garbage.txt.gz
rutabaga% ls -l garbage.txt
-rw-r--r--   1 mdw      hack        312996 Nov 17 21:44 garbage.txt
```

which is identical to the original file. Note that when you *gunzip* a file, the compressed version is removed once the uncompression is complete. Instead of using *gunzip*, you can also use *gzip -d* (e.g., if *gunzip* happens not to be installed).

gzip stores the name of the original, uncompressed file in the compressed version. This way, if the compressed filename (including the *.gz* extension) is too long for the filesystem type (say, you're compressing a file on an MS-DOS filesystem with 8.3 filenames), the original filename can be restored using *gunzip* even if the compressed file had a truncated name. To uncompress a file to its original filename, use the *–N* option with *gunzip*. To see the value of this option, consider the following sequence of commands:

```
rutabaga% gzip garbage.txt
rutabaga% mv garbage.txt.gz rubbish.txt.gz
```

If we were to *gunzip rubbish.txt.gz* at this point, the uncompressed file would be named *rubbish.txt*, after the new (compressed) filename. However, with the *–N* option, we get:

```
rutabaga% gunzip -N rubbish.txt.gz
rutabaga% ls -l garbage.txt
-rw-r--r--   1 mdw      hack        312996 Nov 17 21:44 garbage.txt
```

gzip and *gunzip* can also compress or uncompress data from standard input and output. If *gzip* is given no filenames to compress, it attempts to compress data read from standard input. Likewise, if you use the *–c* option with *gunzip*, it writes uncompressed data to standard output. For example, you could pipe the output of a command to *gzip* to compress the output stream and save it to a file in one step, as in:

```
rutabaga% ls -laR $HOME | gzip > filelist.gz
```

This will produce a recursive directory listing of your home directory and save it in the compressed file *filelist.gz*. You can display the contents of this file with the command:

```
rutabaga% gunzip -c filelist.gz | more
```

This will uncompress *filelist.gz* and pipe the output to the *more* command. When you use *gunzip –c*, the file on disk remains compressed.

The *zcat* command is identical to *gunzip –c*. You can think of this as a version of *cat* for compressed files. Linux even has a version of the pager *less* for compressed files, called *zless*.

When compressing files, you can use one of the options *–1*, *–2*, through *–9* to specify the speed and quality of the compression used. *–1* (also *--fast*) specifies the fastest method, which compresses the files less compactly, while *–9* (also *--best*) uses the slowest, but best compression method. If you don't specify one of these options the default is *–6*. None of these options has any bearing on how you use *gunzip*; *gunzip* will be able to uncompress the file no matter what speed option you use.

gzip is relatively new in the Unix world. The compression programs used on most Unix systems are *compress* and *uncompress*, which were included in the original Berkeley versions of Unix. *compress* and *uncompress* are very much like *gzip* and *gunzip*, respectively; *compress* saves compressed files as *filename.Z* as opposed to *filename.gz*, and uses a slightly less efficient compression algorithm.

However, the free software community has been moving to *gzip* for several reasons. First of all, *gzip* works better. Second, there has been a patent dispute over the compression algorithm used by *compress*—the results of which could prevent third parties from implementing the *compress* algorithm on their own. Because of this, the Free Software Foundation urged a move to *gzip*, which at least the Linux community has embraced. *gzip* has been ported to many architectures, and many others are following suit. Happily, *gunzip* is able to uncompress the .Z format files produced by *compress*.

Another compression/decompression program has also emerged to take the lead from *gzip*. *bzip2* is the new kid on the block and sports even better compression (on the average about 10-20% better than *gzip*), at the expense of longer compression times. You cannot use *bunzip2* to uncompress files compressed with *gzip* and vice versa, and because you cannot expect everybody to have *bunzip2* installed on their machine, you might want to confine yourself to *gzip* for the time being if you want to send the compressed file to somebody else. However, it pays to have *bzip2* installed because more and more FTP servers now provide *bzip2*-compressed packages in order to conserve disk space and bandwidth. You can recognize *bzip2*-compressed files by their *.bz2* filename extension.

While the command-line options of *bzip2* are not exactly the same as those of *gzip*, those that have been described in this section are. For more information, see the *bzip2*(1) manual page.

The bottom line is that you should use *gzip/gunzip* or *bzip2/bunzip2* for your compression needs. If you encounter a file with the extension *.Z*, it was probably produced by *compress*, and *gunzip* can uncompress it for you.

Earlier versions of *gzip* used *.z* (lowercase) instead of *.gz* as the compressed-filename extension. Because of the potential confusion with *.Z*, this was changed. At any rate, *gunzip* retains backwards compatibility with a number of filename extensions and file types.

Using tar

tar is a general-purpose archiving utility capable of packing many files into a single archive file, while retaining information needed to restore the files fully, such as file permissions and ownership. The name *tar* stands for *tape archive* because the tool was originally used to archive files as backups on tape. However, use of *tar* is not at all restricted to making tape backups, as we'll see.

The format of the *tar* command is:

```
tar functionoptions files…
```

where *function* is a single letter indicating the operation to perform, *options* is a list of (single-letter) options to that function, and *files* is the list of files to pack or unpack in an archive. (Note that *function* is not separated from *options* by any space.)

function can be one of the following:

c

    To create a new archive

x

    To extract files from an archive

t

    To list the contents of an archive

r

    To append files to the end of an archive

u

    To update files that are newer than those in the archive

d

    To compare files in the archive to those in the filesystem

You'll rarely use most of these functions; the more commonly used are c, x, and t.

The most common *options* are:

v

> To print verbose information when packing or unpacking archives.

k

> To keep any existing files when extracting—that is, to not overwrite any existing files which are contained within the tar file.

f filename

> To specify that the tar file to be read or written is *filename*.

z

> To specify that the data to be written to the tar file should be compressed or that the data in the tar file is compressed with *gzip*.

j

> Like *z*, but uses *bzip2* instead of *gzip*; works only with newer versions of *tar*. Some intermediate versions of *tar* used *I* instead; older ones don't support *bzip2* at all.

v

> To make *tar* show the files it is archiving or restoring—it is good practice to use this so that you can see what actually happens (unless, of course, you are writing shell scripts).

There are others, which we will cover later in this section.

Although the *tar* syntax might appear complex at first, in practice it's quite simple. For example, say we have a directory named *mt*, containing these files:

```
rutabaga% ls -l mt
total 37
-rw-r--r--  1 root     root            24 Sep 21  1993 Makefile
-rw-r--r--  1 root     root           847 Sep 21  1993 README
-rwxr-xr-x  1 root     root          9220 Nov 16 19:03 mt
-rw-r--r--  1 root     root          2775 Aug  7  1993 mt.1
-rw-r--r--  1 root     root          6421 Aug  7  1993 mt.c
-rw-r--r--  1 root     root          3948 Nov 16 19:02 mt.o
-rw-r--r--  1 root     root         11204 Sep  5  1993 st_info.txt
```

We wish to pack the contents of this directory into a single *tar* archive. To do this, we use the command:

```
tar cf mt.tar mt
```

The first argument to *tar* is the *function* (here, c, for create) followed by any *options*. Here, we use the option *f mt.tar* to specify that the resulting tar archive be named *mt. tar*. The last argument is the name of the file or files to archive; in this case, we give the name of a directory, so *tar* packs all files in that directory into the archive.

Note that the first argument to *tar* must be the function letter and options. Because of this, there's no reason to use a hyphen (-) to precede the options as many Unix commands require. *tar* allows you to use a hyphen, as in:

```
tar -cf mt.tar mt
```

but it's really not necessary. In some versions of *tar*, the first letter must be the *function*, as in c, t, or x. In other versions, the order of letters does not matter.

The function letters as described here follow the so-called "old option style." There is also a newer "short option style" in which you precede the function options with a hyphen, and a "long option style" in which you use long option names with two hyphens. See the Info page for *tar* for more details if you are interested.

Be careful to remember the filename if you use the cf function letters. Otherwise tar will overwrite the first file in your list of files to pack because it will mistake that for the filename!

It is often a good idea to use the v option with *tar*; this lists each file as it is archived. For example:

```
rutabaga% tar cvf mt.tar mt
mt/
mt/st_info.txt
mt/README
mt/mt.1
mt/Makefile
mt/mt.c
mt/mt.o
mt/mt
```

If you use v multiple times, additional information will be printed, as in:

```
rutabaga% tar cvvf mt.tar mt
drwxr-xr-x root/root         0 Nov 16 19:03 1994 mt/
-rw-r--r-- root/root     11204 Sep  5 13:10 1993 mt/st_info.txt
-rw-r--r-- root/root       847 Sep 21 16:37 1993 mt/README
-rw-r--r-- root/root      2775 Aug  7 09:50 1993 mt/mt.1
-rw-r--r-- root/root        24 Sep 21 16:03 1993 mt/Makefile
-rw-r--r-- root/root      6421 Aug  7 09:50 1993 mt/mt.c
-rw-r--r-- root/root      3948 Nov 16 19:02 1994 mt/mt.o
-rwxr-xr-x root/root      9220 Nov 16 19:03 1994 mt/mt
```

This is especially useful as it lets you verify that *tar* is doing the right thing.

In some versions of *tar*, f must be the last letter in the list of options. This is because *tar* expects the f option to be followed by a filename—the name of the tar file to read from or write to. If you don't specify f *filename* at all, *tar* assumes for historical reasons that it should use the device */dev/rmt0* (that is, the first tape drive). In the section "Making Backups," in Chapter 8, we'll talk about using *tar* in conjunction with a tape drive to make backups.

Now, we can give the file *mt.tar* to other people, and they can extract it on their own system. To do this, they would use the command:

```
tar xvf mt.tar
```

This creates the subdirectory *mt* and places all the original files into it, with the same permissions as found on the original system. The new files will be owned by the user running the *tar xvf* (you) unless you are running as root, in which case the original owner is preserved. The x option stands for "extract." The *v* option is used again here to list each file as it is extracted. This produces:

```
courgette% tar xvf mt.tar
mt/
mt/st_info.txt
mt/README
mt/mt.1
mt/Makefile
mt/mt.c
mt/mt.o
mt/mt
```

We can see that *tar* saves the pathname of each file relative to the location where the tar file was originally created. That is, when we created the archive using *tar cf mt.tar mt*, the only input filename we specified was *mt*, the name of the directory containing the files. Therefore, *tar* stores the directory itself and all the files below that directory in the tar file. When we extract the tar file, the directory *mt* is created and the files placed into it, which is the exact inverse of what was done to create the archive.

By default, *tar* extracts all tar files relative to the current directory where you execute *tar*. For example, if you were to pack up the contents of your */bin* directory with the command:

```
tar cvf bin.tar /bin
```

tar would give the warning:

```
tar: Removing leading / from absolute pathnames in the archive.
```

What this means is that the files are stored in the archive within the subdirectory *bin*. When this tar file is extracted, the directory *bin* is created in the working directory of *tar*—not as */bin* on the system where the extraction is being done. This is very important and is meant to prevent terrible mistakes when extracting tar files. Otherwise, extracting a tar file packed as, say, */bin* would trash the contents of your */bin* directory when you extracted it.[*] If you really wanted to extract such a tar file into */bin*, you would extract it from the root directory, /. You can override this behavior using the *P* option when packing tar files, but it's not recommended you do so.

Another way to create the tar file *mt.tar* would have been to *cd* into the *mt* directory itself, and use a command, such as:

```
tar cvf mt.tar *
```

---

[*] Some (older) implementations of Unix (e.g., Sinix and Solaris) do just that.

This way the *mt* subdirectory would not be stored in the tar file; when extracted, the files would be placed directly in your current working directory. One fine point of *tar* etiquette is to always pack tar files so that they have a subdirectory at the top level, as we did in the first example with *tar cvf mt.tar mt*. Therefore, when the archive is extracted, the subdirectory is also created and any files placed there. This way you can ensure that the files won't be placed directly in your current working directory; they will be tucked out of the way and prevent confusion. This also saves the person doing the extraction the trouble of having to create a separate directory (should they wish to do so) to unpack the tar file. Of course, there are plenty of situations where you wouldn't want to do this. So much for etiquette.

When creating archives, you can, of course, give *tar* a list of files or directories to pack into the archive. In the first example, we have given *tar* the single directory *mt*, but in the previous paragraph we used the wildcard *, which the shell expands into the list of filenames in the current directory.

Before extracting a tar file, it's usually a good idea to take a look at its table of contents to determine how it was packed. This way you can determine whether you do need to create a subdirectory yourself where you can unpack the archive. A command, such as:

    tar tvf *tarfile*

lists the table of contents for the named *tarfile*. Note that when using the t function, only one v is required to get the long file listing, as in this example:

```
courgette% tar tvf mt.tar
drwxr-xr-x root/root        0 Nov 16 19:03 1994 mt/
-rw-r--r-- root/root    11204 Sep  5 13:10 1993 mt/st_info.txt
-rw-r--r-- root/root      847 Sep 21 16:37 1993 mt/README
-rw-r--r-- root/root     2775 Aug  7 09:50 1993 mt/mt.1
-rw-r--r-- root/root       24 Sep 21 16:03 1993 mt/Makefile
-rw-r--r-- root/root     6421 Aug  7 09:50 1993 mt/mt.c
-rw-r--r-- root/root     3948 Nov 16 19:02 1994 mt/mt.o
-rwxr-xr-x root/root     9220 Nov 16 19:03 1994 mt/mt
```

No extraction is being done here; we're just displaying the archive's table of contents. We can see from the filenames that this file was packed with all files in the subdirectory *mt* so that when we extract the tar file, the directory *mt* will be created and the files placed there.

You can also extract individual files from a tar archive. To do this, use the command:

    tar xvf *tarfile files*

where *files* is the list of files to extract. As we've seen, if you don't specify any *files*, *tar* extracts the entire archive.

When specifying individual files to extract, you must give the full pathname as it is stored in the tar file. For example, if we wanted to grab just the file *mt.c* from the previous archive *mt.tar*, we'd use the command:

```
tar xvf mt.tar mt/mt.c
```

This would create the subdirectory *mt* and place the file *mt.c* within it.

tar has many more options than those mentioned here. These are the features that you're likely to use most of the time, but GNU *tar*, in particular, has extensions that make it ideal for creating backups and the like. See the *tar* manual page and the following section for more information.

Using tar with gzip and bzip2

tar does not compress the data stored in its archives in any way. If you are creating a tar file from three 200K files, you'll end up with an archive of about 600K. It is common practice to compress tar archives with *gzip* (or the older *compress* program). You could create a *gzip*ped tar file using the commands:

```
tar cvf tarfile files…
gzip -9 tarfile
```

But that's so cumbersome, and requires you to have enough space to store the uncompressed tar file before you *gzip* it.

A much trickier way to accomplish the same task is to use an interesting feature of *tar* that allows you to write an archive to standard output. If you specify - as the tar file to read or write, the data will be read from or written to standard input or output. For example, we can create a *gzip*ped tar file using the command:

```
tar cvf - files… | gzip -9 > tarfile.tar.gz
```

Here, *tar* creates an archive from the named *files* and writes it to standard output; next, *gzip* reads the data from standard input, compresses it, and writes the result to its own standard output; finally, we redirect the *gzip*ped tar file to *tarfile.tar.gz*.

We could extract such a tar file using the command:

```
gunzip -c tarfile.tar.gz | tar xvf -
```

gunzip uncompresses the named archive file and writes the result to standard output, which is read by *tar* on standard input and extracted. Isn't Unix fun?

Of course, both commands are rather cumbersome to type. Luckily, the GNU version of *tar* provides the *z* option which automatically creates or extracts *gzip*ped archives. (We saved the discussion of this option until now, so you'd truly appreciate its convenience.) For example, we could use the commands:

```
tar cvzf tarfile.tar.gz files…
```

and:

```
tar xvzf tarfile.tar.gz
```

to create and extract *gzip*ped tar files. Note that you should name the files created in this way with the *.tar.gz* filename extensions (or the equally often used *.tgz*, which also works on systems with limited filename capabilities) to make their format obvious. The z option works just as well with other tar functions such as t.

Only the GNU version of *tar* supports the z option; if you are using *tar* on another Unix system, you may have to use one of the longer commands to accomplish the same tasks. Nearly all Linux systems use GNU *tar*.

When you want to use *tar* in conjunction with *bzip2*, you need to tell *tar* about your compression program preferences, like this:

```
tar cvf tarfile.tar.bz2 --use-compress-program=bzip2 files...
```

or, shorter:

```
tar cvf tarfile.tar.bz2 --use-compress-program=bzip2 files...
```

or, shorter still:

```
tar cvjf tarfile.tar.bz2 files
```

The last version works only with newer versions of GNU *tar* that support the *j* option.

Keeping this in mind, you could write short shell scripts or aliases to handle cookbook tar file creation and extraction for you. Under *bash*, you could include the following functions in your *.bashrc*:

```
tarc () { tar czvf $1.tar.gz $1 }
tarx () { tar xzvf $1 }
tart () { tar tzvf $1 }
```

With these functions, to create a *gzip*ped tar file from a single directory, you could use the command:

```
tarc directory
```

The resulting archive file would be named *directory.tar.gz*. (Be sure that there's no trailing slash on the directory name; otherwise the archive will be created as *.tar.gz* within the given directory.) To list the table of contents of a *gzip*ped tar file, just use:

```
tart file.tar.gz
```

Or, to extract such an archive, use:

```
tarx file.tar.gz
```

As a final note, we would like to mention that files created with *gzip* and/or *tar* can be unpacked with the well-known *WinZip* utility on Windows systems. *WinZip* doesn't have support for *bzip2* yet, though. If you, on the other hand, get a file in *.zip* format, you can unpack it on your Linux system using the *unzip* command.

tar Tricks

Because *tar* saves the ownership and permissions of files in the archive and retains the full directory structure, as well as symbolic and hard links, using *tar* is an excellent way to copy or move an entire directory tree from one place to another on the same system (or even between different systems, as we'll see). Using the - syntax described earlier, you can write a tar file to standard output, which is read and extracted on standard input elsewhere.

For example, say that we have a directory containing two subdirectories: *from-stuff* and *to-stuff*. *from-stuff* contains an entire tree of files, symbolic links, and so forth— something that is difficult to mirror precisely using a recursive *cp*. In order to mirror the entire tree beneath *from-stuff* to *to-stuff*, we could use the commands:

```
cd from-stuff
tar cf - . | (cd ../to-stuff; tar xvf -)
```

Simple and elegant, right? We start in the directory *from-stuff* and create a tar file of the current directory, which is written to standard output. This archive is read by a subshell (the commands contained within parentheses); the subshell does a *cd* to the target directory, *../to-stuff* (relative to *from-stuff*, that is), and then runs *tar xvf*, reading from standard input. No tar file is ever written to disk; the data is sent entirely via pipe from one *tar* process to another. The second *tar* process has the *v* option that prints each file as it's extracted; in this way, we can verify that the command is working as expected.

In fact, you could transfer directory trees from one machine to another (via the network) using this trick; just include an appropriate *rsh* (or *ssh*) command within the subshell on the right side of the pipe. The remote shell would execute *tar* to read the archive on its standard input. (Actually, GNU *tar* has facilities to read or write tar files automatically from other machines over the network; see the *tar*(1) manual page for details.)

Upgrading Software

Linux is a fast-moving target. Because of the cooperative nature of the project, new software is always becoming available, and programs are constantly being updated with newer versions. This is especially true of the Linux kernel, which has many groups of people working on it. During the development process, it's not uncommon for a new kernel patch to be released on a nightly basis. While other parts of the system may not be as dynamic, the same principles apply.

With this constant development, how can you possibly hope to stay on top of the most recent versions of your system software? The short answer is, you can't. While there are people out there who have a need to stay current with, say, the nightly kernel patch release, for the most part, there's no reason to bother upgrading your software this often. In this section, we're going to talk about why and when to upgrade and show you how to upgrade several important parts of the system.

When should you upgrade? In general, you should consider upgrading a portion of your system only when you have a demonstrated *need* to upgrade. For example, if you hear of a new release of some application that fixes important bugs (that is, those bugs that actually affect your personal use of the application), you might want to consider upgrading that application. If the new version of the program provides new features you might find useful, or has a performance boost over your present version, it's also a good idea to upgrade. When your machine is somehow connected to the Internet, another good reason for upgrading would be plugging a security hole that has been recently reported. However, upgrading just for the sake of having the newest version of a particular program is probably silly.

Upgrading can sometimes be a painful thing to do. For example, you might want to upgrade a program that requires the newest versions of the compiler, libraries, and other software in order to run. Upgrading this program will also require you to upgrade several other parts of the system, which can be a time-consuming process. On the other hand, this can be seen as an argument for keeping your software up to date; if your compiler and libraries are current, upgrading the program in question won't be a problem.

How can you find out about new versions of Linux software? The best way is to watch the Usenet newsgroup *comp.os.linux.announce* (see the section "Usenet Newsgroups" in Chapter 1) where announcements of new software releases and other important information are posted. If you have Internet access, you can then download the software via FTP and install it on your system. Another good source to learn about new Linux software is the web site *http://www.freshmeat.net*.

If you don't have access to Usenet or the Internet, the best way to keep in touch with recent developments is to pay for a CD-ROM subscription. Here you receive an updated copy of the various Linux FTP sites, on CD-ROM, every couple of months. This service is available from a number of Linux vendors. It's a good thing to have, even if you have Internet access.

This brings us to another issue: what's the best upgrade method? Some people feel it's easier to completely upgrade the system by reinstalling everything from scratch whenever a new version of their favorite distribution is released. This way you don't have to worry about various versions of the software working together. For those without Internet access, this may indeed be the easiest method; if you receive a new CD-ROM only once every two months, a great deal of your software may be out of date.

It's our opinion, however, that reinstallation is not a good upgrade plan at all. Most of the current Linux distributions are not meant to be upgraded in this way, and a complete reinstallation may be complex or time-consuming. Also, if you plan to upgrade in this manner, you generally lose all your modifications and customizations to the system, and you'll have to make backups of your user's home directories and any other important files that would be deleted during a reinstallation. Many novices choose this upgrade path because it's the easiest to follow. In actuality, not much changes from release to release, so a complete reinstallation is usually unnecessary and can be avoided with a little upgrading know-how.

In the rest of this section, we'll show you how to upgrade various pieces of your system individually. We'll show you how to upgrade your system libraries and compiler, as well as give you a generic method for installing new software. In the following section, we'll talk about building a new kernel.

Upgrading Libraries

Most of the programs on a Linux system are compiled to use shared libraries. These libraries contain useful functions common to many programs. Instead of storing a copy of these routines in each program that calls them, the libraries are contained in files on the system that are read by all programs at runtime. That is, when a program is executed, the code from the program file itself is read, followed by any routines from the shared library files. This saves a great deal of disk space; only one copy of the library routines is stored on disk.

In some instances, it's necessary to compile a program to have its own copy of the library routines (usually for debugging) instead of using the routines from the shared libraries. We say that programs built in this way are *statically linked*, while programs built to use shared libraries are *dynamically linked*.

Therefore, dynamically linked executables depend upon the presence of the shared libraries on disk. Shared libraries are implemented in such a way that the programs compiled to use them generally don't depend on the version of the available libraries. This means that you can upgrade your shared libraries, and all programs that are built to use those libraries will automatically use the new routines. (There is an exception: if major changes are made to a library, the old programs won't work with the new library. You'll know this is the case because the major version number is different; we'll explain more later. In this case, you keep both the old and new libraries around. All your old executables will continue to use the old libraries, and any new programs that are compiled will use the new libraries.)

When you build a program to use shared libraries, a piece of code is added to the program that causes it to execute *ld.so*, the dynamic linker, when the program is started. *ld.so* is responsible for finding the shared libraries the program needs and loading the routines into memory. Dynamically linked programs are also linked against "stub" routines, which simply take the place of the actual shared library routines in the executable. *ld.so* replaces the stub routine with the code from the libraries when the program is executed.

The *ldd* command can be used to list the shared libraries on which a given executable depends. For example:

```
rutabaga% ldd /usr/bin/X11/xterm
        libXft.so.1 => /usr/X11R6/lib/libXft.so.1 (0x40032000)
        libXrender.so.1 => /usr/X11R6/lib/libXrender.so.1 (0x40088000)
        libXaw.so.7 => /usr/X11R6/lib/libXaw.so.7 (0x4008d000)
        libXmu.so.6 => /usr/X11R6/lib/libXmu.so.6 (0x400e4000)
```

```
libXt.so.6 => /usr/X11R6/lib/libXt.so.6 (0x400fa000)
libSM.so.6 => /usr/X11R6/lib/libSM.so.6 (0x40148000)
libICE.so.6 => /usr/X11R6/lib/libICE.so.6 (0x40152000)
libXpm.so.4 => /usr/X11R6/lib/libXpm.so.4 (0x4016a000)
libXext.so.6 => /usr/X11R6/lib/libXext.so.6 (0x40179000)
libX11.so.6 => /usr/X11R6/lib/libX11.so.6 (0x40188000)
libncurses.so.5 => /lib/libncurses.so.5 (0x4026b000)
libc.so.6 => /lib/libc.so.6 (0x402b5000)
/lib/ld-linux.so.2 => /lib/ld-linux.so.2 (0x40000000)
```

Here, we see that the *xterm* program depends on a number of shared libraries, including *libXaw*, *libXt*, *libX11*, and *libc*. (The libraries starting with *libX* are all related to the X Window System; *libc* is the standard C library.) We also see the version numbers of the libraries for which the program was compiled (that is, the version of the stub routines used), and the name of the file which contains each shared library. This is the file that *ld.so* will find when the program is executed.

In order to use a shared library, the version of the stub routines (in the executable) must be compatible with the version of the shared libraries. Basically, a library is compatible if its major version number matches that of the stub routines. The major version number is the part right after the *.so*. In this case, *libX11* (the most basic library used by the X Window System) is used with the major Version 6. The library file *libX11.so.6* (which usually resides in */usr/X11R6/lib*) might very well just be a symbolic link—e.g., to *libX11.so.6.2*. This means that the library has the major version number 6 and the minor version number 2. Library versions with the same major version number are supposed to be interchangeable. This way, if a program was compiled with Version 6.0 of the stub routines, shared library Versions 6.1, 6.2, and so forth could be used by the executable. If a new version with the major version number 6 and the minor version number 3 were released (and thus had the filename *libX11.so.6.3*), all you would need to do to use this new version is change the symbolic link *libX11.so.6* to point to the new version. The *xterm* executable would then automatically benefit from any bug fixes or similar that are included in the new version. In the section "More Fun with Libraries" in Chapter 13, we describe how to use shared libraries with your own programs.

The file */etc/ld.so.conf* contains a list of directories that *ld.so* searches to find shared library files. An example of such a file is:

```
/usr/lib
/usr/local/lib
/usr/X11R6/lib
```

ld.so always looks in */lib* and */usr/lib*, regardless of the contents of *ld.so.conf*. Usually, there's no reason to modify this file, and the environment variable LD_LIBRARY_PATH can add additional directories to this search path (e.g., if you have your own private shared libraries that shouldn't be used systemwide). However, if you do add entries to */etc/ld.so.conf* or upgrade or install additional libraries on your system, be sure to use the *ldconfig* command which will regenerate the shared library cache in */etc/ld.so.cache* from the *ld.so* search path. This cache is used by *ld.so* to find libraries quickly at runtime without actually having to search the directories on its path. For more information, check the manual pages for *ld.so* and *ldconfig*.

Now that you understand how shared libraries are used, let's move on to upgrading them. The two libraries that are most commonly updated are *libc* (the standard C library) and *libm* (the math library). Because naming is a little bit special for these, we will look at another library here, namely *libncurses*, which "emulates" a graphical windowing system on the text console.

For each shared library, there are two separate files:

library.a
> This is the static version of the library. When a program is statically linked, routines are copied from this file directly into the executable, so the executable contains its own copy of the library routines.*

library.so.version
> This is the shared library image itself. When a program is dynamically linked, the stub routines from this file are copied into the executable, allowing *ld.so* to locate the shared library at runtime. When the program is executed, *ld.so* copies routines from the shared library into memory for use by the program. If a program is dynamically linked, the *library.a* file is not used for this library.

For the *libncurses* library, you'll have files, such as *libncurses.a* and *libncurses.so.5.2*. The *.a* files are generally kept in */usr/lib*, while *.so* files are kept in */lib*. When you compile a program, either the *.a* or the *.so* file is used for linking, and the compiler looks in */lib* and */usr/lib* (as well as a variety of other places) by default. If you have your own libraries, you can keep these files anywhere, and control where the linker looks with the –L option to the compiler. See the section "More Fun with Libraries" in Chapter 13 for details.

The shared library image, *library.so.version*, is kept in */lib* for most systemwide libraries. Shared library images can be found in any of the directories that *ld.so* searches at runtime; these include */lib*, */usr/lib*, and the files listed in *ld.so.conf*. See the *ld.so* manual page for details.

If you look in */lib*, you'll see a collection of files such as the following:

```
lrwxrwxrwx   1 root    root          17 Jul 11 06:45 /lib/libncurses.so.5 \
    -> libncurses.so.5.2
-rwxr-xr-x   1 root    root      319472 Jul 11 06:45 /lib/libncurses.so.5.2
lrwxrwxrwx   1 root    root          13 Jul 11 06:45 libz.so.1 -> libz.so.1.1.3
-rwxr-xr-x   1 root    root       62606 Jul 11 06:45 libz.so.1.1.3
```

Here, we see the shared library images for two libraries—*libncurses* and *libz*. Note that each image has a symbolic link to it, named *library.so.major*, where *major* is the

---

* On some distributions, the static versions of the libraries are moved into a separate package and not necessarily installed by default. If this is the case, you won't find the *.a* files unless you install them.

major version number of the library. The minor number is omitted because *ld.so* searches for a library only by its major version number. When *ld.so* sees a program that has been compiled with the stubs for Version 5.2 of *libncurses*, it looks for a file called *libncurses.so.5* in its search path. Here, */lib/libncurses.so.5* is a symbolic link to */lib/libncurses.so.5.2*, the actual version of the library we have installed.

When you upgrade a library, you must replace the *.a* and *.so.version* files corresponding to the library. Replacing the *.a* file is easy: just copy over it with the new versions. However, you must use some caution when replacing the shared library image, *.so.version*; many of the text-based programs on the system depend on shared library images, so you can't simply delete them or rename them. To put this another way, the symbolic link *library.so.major* must *always* point to a valid library image. To accomplish this, first copy the new image file to */lib*, and then change the symbolic link to point to the new file in one step, using *ln –sf*. This is demonstrated in the following example.

Let's say you're upgrading from Version 5.2 of the *libncurses* library to Version 5.4. You should have the files *libncurses.a* and *libncurses.so.5.4*. First, copy the *.a* file to the appropriate location, overwriting the old version:

```
rutabaga# cp libncurses.a /usr/lib
```

Now, copy the new image file to */lib* (or wherever the library image should be):

```
rutabaga# cp libncurses.so.5.4 /lib
```

Now, if you use the command *ls –l /lib/libncurses*, you should see something like:

```
lrwxrwxrwx    1 root     root             17 Dec 10  1999 /lib/libncurses.so.5 ->
libncurses.so.4.2
-rwxr-xr-x    1 root     root         319472 May 11  2001 /lib/libncurses.so.5.2
-rwxr-xr-x    1 root     root         321042 May 11  2001 /lib/libncurses.so.5.4
```

To update the symbolic link to point to the new library, use the command:

```
rutabaga# ln -sf /lib/libncurses.so.5.4 /lib/libncurses.so.5
```

This gives you:

```
lrwxrwxrwx  1 root  root       14 Oct 23 13:25 libncurses.so.5 ->\
    /lib/libncurses.so.5.4
-rwxr-xr-x  1 root  root   623620 Oct 23 13:24 libncurses.so.5.2
-rwxr-xr-x  1 root  root   720310 Nov 16 11:02 libncurses.so.5.4
```

Now you can safely remove the old image file, *libncurses.so.5.2*. You must use *ln –sf* to replace the symbolic link in one step, especially when updating crucial libraries, such as *libc*. If you were to remove the symbolic link first, and then attempt to use *ln –s* to add it again, more than likely *ln* would not be able to execute because the symbolic link is gone, and as far as *ld.so* is concerned, the *libc* library can't be found. Once the link is gone, nearly all the programs on your system will be unable to execute. Be very careful when updating shared library images. For *libncurses*, things are less critical because you will always have command-line programs left to clean up any mess you have made, but if you are used to using *ncurses*-based programs, such as Midnight Commander, this might still be an inconvenience for you.

Whenever you upgrade or add a library to the system, it's not a bad idea to run *ldconfig* to regenerate the library cache used by *ld.so*. In some cases, a new library may not be recognized by *ld.so* until you run *ldconfig*.

One question remains: where can you obtain the new versions of libraries? Several of the basic system libraries (*libc*, *libm*, and so on) can be downloaded from the directory */pub/Linux/GCC* on *ftp://ftp.ibiblio.org*. It contains the Linux versions of the *gcc* compiler, libraries, include files, and other utilities. Each file there should have a *README* or *release* file that describes what to do and how to install it. Other libraries are maintained and archived separately. At any rate, all libraries you install should include the *.so.version* files and possibly the *.a* files, as well as a set of include files for use with the compiler.

Upgrading the Compiler

One other important part of the system to keep up to date is the C compiler and related utilities. These include *gcc* (the GNU C and C++ compiler itself), the linker, the assembler, the C preprocessor, and various include files and libraries used by the compiler itself. All are included in the Linux *gcc* distribution. Usually, a new version of *gcc* is released along with new versions of the *libc* library and include files, and each requires the other.

You can find the current *gcc* release for Linux on the various FTP archives, including */pub/Linux/GCC* on *ftp://ftp.ibiblio.org*. The release notes there should tell you what to do. Usually, upgrading the compiler is a simple matter of unpacking several tar files as root, and possibly removing some additional files. If you don't have Internet access, you can obtain the newest compiler from CD-ROM archives of the FTP sites, as described earlier.

To find out what version of *gcc* you have, use the command:

```
gcc -v
```

This should tell you something like:

```
Reading specs from /usr/lib/gcc-lib/i486-suse-linux/2.95.3/specs
gcc version 2.95.3 20010315 (SuSE)
```

Note that *gcc* itself is just a frontend to the actual compiler and code-generation tools found under:

```
/usr/lib/gcc-lib/machine/version
```

gcc (usually in */usr/bin*) can be used with multiple versions of the compiler proper, with the –*V* option. In the section "Programming with gcc" in Chapter 13, we describe the use of *gcc* in detail.

We would at this point like to warn you not to try newer compilers without knowing exactly what you are doing. Newer compilers might generate object files that are incompatible with the older ones; this can lead to all kinds of trouble. Version 2.95.3 of *gcc* is, at the time of this writing, considered the standard compiler for Linux that everybody expects to find available. When one distributor (Red Hat) started to ship a newer version instead (and even that newer version was not officially released), users ran into lots of trouble. Of course, by the time you read this, another compiler version might be considered the standard. And if you feel adventurous, by all means try newer versions, just be prepared for some serious tweaking.

General Upgrade Procedure

Of course, you'll have to periodically upgrade other pieces of your system. As discussed in the previous section, it's usually easier and best to upgrade only those applications you need to upgrade. For example, if you never use Emacs on your system, why bother keeping up-to-date with the most recent version of Emacs? For that matter, you may not need to stay completely current with oft-used applications. If something works for you, there's little need to upgrade.

Modern Linux systems provide various ways of upgrading software, some manual (which ultimately are the most flexible, but also the most difficult), others quite automated. In this section, we'll look at three different techniques: using the RPM package system, using the Debian package system, and doing things manually.

We'd like to stress here that using packages and package systems *is* convenient, and even if you are a power-user, you might want to use these techniques because they save you time for other, more fun stuff. Here is a short summary of the advantages:

- You have everything that belongs to a software package in one downloadable file.
- You can remove a software package entirely, without endangering other packages.
- Package systems keep a dependency database and can thus automatically track dependencies. For example, they can tell you if you need to install a newer version of a library in order to run a certain application you are about to install (and will refuse to remove a library package as long as packages are installed that use the libraries this package provides).

Of course, package systems also have a few disadvantages, some of which we discuss when we talk about RPM and the Debian package system. A generic problem is that once you start using a package system (which is almost a requirement if you use the distributions' automated installation interfaces) you ought to really install everything through packages. Otherwise, you can't keep track of the dependencies. For the same reason, mixing different package systems is a bad idea.

Using RPM

RPM, the Red Hat Package Manager, is a tool that automates the installation of software binaries and remembers what files are needed so that you can be assured the software will run properly. Despite the name, RPM is not Red Hat–specific, but is used in many other distributions nowadays, including SuSE and Caldera. Using RPM makes installing and uninstalling software a lot easier.

The basic idea of RPM is that you have a database of packages and the files that belong to a package. When you install a new package, the information about this package is recorded in the database. Then, when you want to uninstall the package for every file of the package, RPM checks whether other installed packages are using this file too. If this is the case, the file in question is not deleted.

In addition, RPM tracks dependencies. Each package can be dependent on one or more other packages. When you install a package, RPM checks whether the packages the new package is dependent on are already installed. If not, it informs you about the dependency and refuses to install the package.

The dependencies are also used for removing packages: when you want to uninstall a package that other packages are still dependent upon, RPM tells you about this, too, and refuses to execute the task.

The increased convenience of using RPM packages comes at a price, however: first, as a developer, it is significantly more difficult to make an RPM package than to simply pack everything in a *tar* archive. And second, it is not possible to retrieve just one file from an RPM package; you have to install everything or nothing.

If you already have an RPM system, installing RPM packages is very easy. Let's say that you have an RPM package called *SuperFrob-4.i386.rpm* (RPM packages always have the extension *.rpm*; the *i386* indicates that this is a binary package compiled for Intel x86 machines). You could then install it with:

```
tigger # rpm -i SuperFrob-4.i386.rpm
```

Instead of *-i*, you can also use the long-named version of this option; choose whatever you like better:

```
tigger # rpm --install SuperFrob-4.i386.rpm
```

If everything goes well, there will be no output. If you want RPM to be more verbose, you can try:

```
tigger # rpm -ivh SuperFrob-4.i386.rpm
```

This prints the name of the package plus a number of hash marks so that you can see how the installation progresses.

If the package you want to install needs another package that is not yet installed, you will get something like the following:

```
tigger # rpm -i SuperFrob-4.i386.rpm
failed dependencies:
```

```
frobnik-2 is needed by SuperFrob-4
```

If you see this, you have to hunt for the package *frobnik-2* and install this first. Of course, this package can itself be dependent on other packages.

If you want to update a package that is already installed, use the *-U* or *--update* option (which is just the *-i* option combined with a few more implied options):

```
tigger # rpm -U SuperFrob-5.i386.rpm
```

Uninstalling a package is done with the *-e* or *--erase* option. In this case, you do not specify the package file (you might not have that around any longer), but rather, the package name and version number:

```
tigger # rpm -e SuperFrob-5
```

Besides the options described so far that alter the state of your system, the *-q* option provides various kinds of information about everything that is recorded in the RPM database as well as package files. Here are some useful things you can do with *-q*:

- Find out the version number of an installed package:

  ```
  tigger# rpm -q SuperFrob
  SuperFrob-5
  ```

- Get a list of all installed packages:

  ```
  tigger# rpm -qa
  SuperFrob-5
  OmniFrob-3
  ...
  glibc-2.2.2-38
  ```

- Find out to which package a file belongs:

  ```
  tigger# rpm -qf /usr/bin/dothefrob
  SuperFrob-5
  tigger# rpm -qf /home/kalle/.xinitrc
  file /home/kalle/.xinitrc is not owned by any package
  ```

- Display information about the specified package:

  ```
  tigger# rpm -qi rpm
  Name        : rpm                       Relocations: (not relocateable)
  Version     : 3.0.6                          Vendor: SuSE GmbH, Nuernberg,
  Germany
  Release     : 78                         Build Date: Fri 11 May 2001 05:18:18
  PM CEST
  Install date: Sun 15 Jul 2001 03:06:14 PM CEST     Build Host: hewitt.suse.de
  Group       : System Environment/Base    Source RPM: rpm-3.0.6-78.src.rpm
  Size        : 7624258                       License: GPL
  Packager    : feedback@suse.de
  Summary     : RPM Package Manager
  Description :
  RPM Package Manager is the main tool for managing software packages
  of the SuSE Linux distribution.
  rpm can be used to install and remove software packages; with rpm it's easy to
  update packages.  rpm keep track of all these manipulations in a central
  database.  This way it is possible to get an overview of all installed
  ```

```
            packages; rpm also supports database queries.

            Authors:
            --------
                Erik Troan <ewt&commat;redhat.com>
                Marc Ewing <marc&commat;redhat.com>

            SuSE series: a
```
- Show the files that will be installed for the specified package file:

```
tigger# rpm -qpl SuperFrob-5.i386.rpm
/usr/bin/dothefrob
/usr/bin/frobhelper
/usr/doc/SuperFrob/Installation
/usr/doc/SuperFrob/README
/usr/man/man1/dothefrob.1
```

What we've just finished showing are the basic modes of operation, which are supplemented by a large number of additional options. You can check those in the manual page for the *rpm*(8) command.

If you are faced with an RPM package that you want to install, but have a system like Slackware or Debian that is not based on RPM, things get a little bit more difficult.

You can either use the fairly self-explanatory command *alien* that can convert between various package formats and comes with most distributions, or you can build the RPM database from scratch.

The first thing you have to do in this latter case is to get the *rpm* program itself. You can download it from *http://www.rpm.org*. Follow the installation instructions to build and install it; if you have the C compiler *gcc* installed on your system, there should be no problems with this.

The next task is to initialize the RPM database. Distributions that come with RPM do the initialization automatically, but on other systems you will have to issue the command:

```
tigger # rpm --initdb
```

This command creates several files in the directory */var/lib/rpm*. The directory */var/lib* should already exist; if it doesn't, create it with the *mkdir* command first.

Now you can install RPM packages the normal way, but because you have not installed the basic parts of the system, such as the C library with RPM, you will get errors like the following:

```
tigger # rpm -i SuperFrob-4.i386.rpm
failed dependencies:
        libm.so.5 is needed by SuperFrob-4
        libdl.so.1 is needed by SuperFrob-4
        libc.so.5 is needed by SuperFrob-4
```

because those files are not recorded in the RPM database. Of course, you really do have those files on your system; otherwise most programs wouldn't run. For RPM to work, you must tell it not to care about any dependencies. You do this by specifying the command-line option *—nodeps*:

```
tigger # rpm -i --nodeps SuperFrob-4.i386.rpm
```

Now, RPM will install the package without complaining. Of course, it will run only if the libraries it needs are installed. The mere fact that you use *--nodeps* doesn't save you when the "dependent" library or software is not installed on your system.

With this information, you should be able to administer your RPM-based system. If you want to know more, read the manual page for the *rpm* command, or check out *http://www.rpm.org*.

Some commercial companies sell automated upgrade services based on RPM. As a subscriber to these services, you can have your system upgraded automatically; the service finds out which new packages are available and installs them for you. If you use the SuSE distribution, SuSE provides such a service for free. Even the Debian distribution (whose package system is described in the next section) has an automated upgrade system (described there). However, some security experts consider these automated upgrades a security risk.

Using dpkg and apt

After *rpm*, the most popular package manager for Linux distributions is *dpkg*, which is used to manage *.deb* archives; as the name implies, the *.deb* format originated with the Debian distribution, but it is also used by Libranet and Xandros, among other vendors. Like the RPM format, the *.deb* format keeps track of dependencies and files to help ensure your system is consistent.

The technical differences between the two formats are actually fairly small; although the RPM and *.deb* formats are incompatible (for example, you can't install a Debian package directly on Red Hat), you can use *alien* to translate *.deb* packages for other distributions (and vice versa). The main difference between the formats is that *.deb* packages are built using tools that help make sure they have a consistent layout and generally conform to policies (most notably, the Debian Policy Manual, provided in the *debian-policy* package) that help developers create high-quality packages.

While *dpkg* is the low-level interface to the Debian package manager, most functions are usually handled through either the *apt* suite of programs or frontends like *dselect*, *aptitude*, *gnome-apt*, *synaptic*, or *kpackage*.

Installing *.deb* packages on a Debian system is quite easy. For example, if you have a package named *superfrob_4-1_i386.deb*, you can install it with:

```
tigger # dpkg -i superfrob_4-1_i386.deb
Selecting previously deselected package superfrob.
(Reading database ... 159540 files and directories currently installed.)
Unpacking superfrob (from superfrob_4-1_i386.deb) ...
Setting up superfrob (4-1) ...
```

If the *superfrob* package is missing a dependency, *dpkg* will issue a warning message:

```
tiger # dpkg -i superfrob_4-1_i386.deb
Selecting previously deselected package superfrob.
(Reading database ... 159540 files and directories currently installed.)
Unpacking superfrob (from superfrob_4-1_i386.deb) ...
dpkg: dependency problems prevent configuration of superfrob:
 superfrob depends on frobnik (>> 2); however:
   Package frobnik is not installed.
dpkg: error processing superfrob (--install):
 dependency problems - leaving unconfigured
Errors were encountered while processing:
 superfrob
```

The output indicates that you would need *frobnik* Version 2 or later for the package to install completely. (The files in the package are installed, but they may not work until *frobnik* is installed too.)

Unlike RPM, *dpkg* doesn't make a distinction between installing a new package and upgrading an existing one; the *-i* (or *--install*) option is used in both cases. For example, if we want to upgrade *superfrob* using a newly downloaded package *superfrob_5-1_i386.deb*, we'd simply type:

```
tiger # dpkg -i superfrob_5-1_i386.deb
(Reading database ... 159546 files and directories currently installed.)
Preparing to replace superfrob 4-1 (using superfrob_5-1_i386.deb) ...
Unpacking replacement superfrob ...
Setting up superfrob (5-1) ...
```

To uninstall a package, you can use either the *-r* (*--remove*) or *-P* (*--purge*) options. The *--remove* option will remove most of the package, but will retain any configuration files, while *--purge* will remove the systemwide configuration files as well. For example, to completely remove *superfrob*:

```
tiger # dpkg -P superfrob
(Reading database ... 159547 files and directories currently installed.)
Removing superfrob ...
```

dpkg can also be used to find out what packages are installed on a system, using the *-l* (*--list*) option:

```
tiger $ dpkg -l
Desired=Unknown/Install/Remove/Purge/Hold
| Status=Not/Installed/Config-files/Unpacked/Failed-config/Half-installed
|/ Err?=(none)/Hold/Reinst-required/X=both-problems (Status,Err: uppercase=bad)
||/ Name           Version        Description
+++-=============-=============-======================================
ii  a2ps           4.13b-15       GNU a2ps 'Anything to PostScript' converter
ii  aalib1         1.4p5-10       ascii art library
ii  abcde          2.0.3-1        A Better CD Encoder
...
ii  zlib1g-dev     1.1.3-19       compression library - development
```

The first three lines of the output are designed to tell you what the first three columns before each package's name mean. Most of the time, they should read *ii*, which means the package is correctly installed. If they don't, you should type *dpkg --audit* for an explanation of what is wrong with your system and how to fix it.

You can also use the *-l* option with a package name or glob-style pattern; for example, you could find out what version of *superfrob* is installed using:

```
tigger $ dpkg -l superfrob
Desired=Unknown/Install/Remove/Purge/Hold
| Status=Not/Installed/Config-files/Unpacked/Failed-config/Half-installed
|/ Err?=(none)/Hold/Reinst-required/X=both-problems (Status,Err: uppercase=bad)
||/ Name           Version       Description
+++-===============-===============-============================================
ii  superfrob      4-1            The superfrobulator
```

dpkg can also be used to find out what package to which a particular file belongs:

```
tigger $ dpkg --search /bin/false
shellutils: /bin/false
tigger $ dpkg --search /home/kalle/.xinitrc
dpkg: /home/kalle/.xinitrc not found.
```

You can also display information about an installed package or *.deb* archive:

```
tigger $ dpkg --status dpkg
Package: dpkg
Essential: yes
Status: install ok installed
Priority: required
Section: base
Installed-Size: 3156
Origin: debian
Maintainer: Dpkg Development <debian-dpkg@lists.debian.org>
Bugs: debbugs://bugs.debian.org
Version: 1.9.19
Replaces: dpkg-doc-ja
Pre-Depends: libc6 (>= 2.2.4-4), libncurses5 (>= 5.2.20020112a-1), libstdc++2.10-
glibc2.2 (>= 1:2.95.4-0.010810)
Conflicts: sysvinit (<< 2.80)
Conffiles:
 /etc/alternatives/README 69c4ba7f08363e998e0f2e244a04f881
 /etc/dpkg/dpkg.cfg 1db461ac9a1d4f4c8b47f5061078f5ee
 /etc/dpkg/dselect.cfg 190f7cf843556324495ef12759b752e3
 /etc/dpkg/origins/debian 24926c0576edec3e316fd9f6072b8118
Description: Package maintenance system for Debian
 This package contains the programs which handle the installation and
 removal of packages on your system.
 .
 The primary interface for the dpkg suite is the 'dselect' program;
 a more low-level and less user-friendly interface is available in
 the form of the 'dpkg' command.
 .
 In order to unpack and build Debian source packages you will need to
 install the developers' package 'dpkg-dev' as well as this one.
```

```
tigger $ dpkg --info reportbug_1.43_all.deb
 new debian package, version 2.0.
 size 66008 bytes: control archive= 1893 bytes.
      40 bytes,     2 lines      conffiles
    1000 bytes,    24 lines      control
     986 bytes,    15 lines      md5sums
    1014 bytes,    41 lines    * postinst            #!/bin/sh
     147 bytes,     5 lines    * postrm              #!/bin/sh
     416 bytes,    19 lines    * prerm               #!/bin/sh
 Package: reportbug
 Version: 1.43
 Section: utils
 Priority: standard
 Architecture: all
 Depends: python
 Recommends: python-newt
 Suggests: postfix | mail-transport-agent, gnupg | pgp, python-ldap (>= 1.8-1)
 Conflicts: python (>> 2.3), python-newt (= 0.50.17-7.1)
 Installed-Size: 195
 Maintainer: Chris Lawrence <lawrencc@debian.org>
 Description: Reports bugs in the Debian distribution.
  reportbug is a tool designed to make the reporting of bugs in Debian
  and derived distributions relatively painless.  Its features include:
  .
   * Integration with the mutt, af, and mh/nmh mail readers.
   * Access to outstanding bug reports to make it easier to identify
     whether problems have already been reported.
   * Support for following-up on outstanding reports.
   * Optional PGP/GnuPG integration.
  .
  reportbug is designed to be used on systems with an installed mail
  transport agent, like exim or sendmail; however, you can edit the
  configuration file and send reports using any available mail server.
```

dpkg can also list the files and directories included in a *.deb* archive:

```
tigger $ dpkg --contents superfrob_4-1_i386.deb
-rwxr-xr-x root/root      44951 2002-02-10 12:16:48 ./usr/bin/dothefrob
-rwxr-xr-x root/root      10262 2002-02-10 12:16:48 ./usr/bin/frobhelper
...
```

dpkg, like *rpm*, has numerous other options; for more details, refer to the manual pages for *dpkg* and *dpkg-deb*.

In addition to *dpkg*, Debian and other Debian-based distributions provide the *apt* suite of programs.* APT is the "Advanced Package Tool," and is designed as an archive-independent system that can handle multiple package formats. Perhaps the most important feature of APT is its ability to resolve dependencies automatically; if, for example, *superfrob* requires Version 2 or later of *frobnik*, APT will try to find

---

* Some RPM-based distributions now include APT as well because APT was designed to work with any packaging format.

frobnik from the sources that are available to it (including CD-ROMs, local mirrors, and the Internet).

The most useful interface to APT is the *apt-get* command. *apt-get* manages the list of available packages (the "package cache") and can be used to resolve dependencies and install packages. A typical session would start with an update of the APT cache:

```
tigger # apt-get update
Get:1 http://http.us.debian.org stable/main Packages [808kB]
Get:2 http://http.us.debian.org stable/main Release [88B]
Hit http://non-us.debian.org stable/non-US/main Packages
Hit http://non-us.debian.org stable/non-US/main Release
Get:3 http://security.debian.org stable/updates/main Packages [62.1kB]
Get:4 http://security.debian.org stable/updates/main Release [93B]
Fetched 870kB in 23s (37kB/s)
Reading Package Lists... Done
Building Dependency Tree... Done
```

The output indicates that there have been updates to the stable distribution, so we may want to upgrade the packages already installed on the system. To do this automatically, we can use *apt-get's upgrade* option:

```
tigger # apt-get upgrade
The following packages have been kept back:
  gnumeric
17 packages upgraded, 0 newly installed, 0 to remove and 1 not upgraded.
Need to get 16.3MB of archives.  After unpacking 5kB will be freed.
Do you want to continue? [Y/n] y
Get:1 http://http.us.debian.org stable/main base-passwd 3.4.6 [17.2kB]
Get:2 http://security.debian.org stable/updates/main ssh 1:3.1.6p4-1 [600kB]
...
(Reading database ... 159546 files and directories currently installed.)
Preparing to replace ssh 1:3.0.3p2-6 (using .../ssh_1%3a3.1.6p4-1_i386.deb) ...
Unpacking replacement ssh ...
...
```

One thing you will notice is that unlike most Linux commands, the actions taken by APT commands are specified *without* dashes. *apt-get* does allow some options, but they are used only to change the behavior of the main action specified.[*]

Note that *gnumeric* was not automatically upgraded, probably because it would have required additional packages to be installed. To upgrade it and resolve dependencies, we can use *apt-get's install* option, with the names of one or more packages: [†]

```
tigger # apt-get install gnumeric
The following extra packages will be installed:
  libgal36 libglade3
```

[*] Some other Linux commands, like *cvs*, also act this way.

[†] Note that *apt-get* does not install packages directly from *.deb* archives; *dpkg*'s *--install* option should be used instead for an archive that you have in a *.deb* archive on disk or have downloaded directly from the Internet. When using *dpkg*, you will need to resolve the dependencies yourself.

```
The following NEW packages will be installed:
  libgal36
2 packages upgraded, 1 newly installed, 0 to remove and 0 not upgraded.
Need to get 8.3MB of archives.  After unpacking 503kB will be used.
Do you want to continue? [Y/n] y
...
```

Another useful feature of APT is its ability to find information about packages in the repository. The *apt-cache* command is used to look up information about packages that are available for installation. One common use of *apt-cache* is to find packages based on keywords in the package's description, by using words, complete phrases (in quotes), or regular expressions. For example, if you want to find a package that allows you to play Ogg Vorbis-encoded music files, you can use the *search* option to find appropriate packages:

```
tigger $ apt-cache search "ogg vorbis"
audacity - A fast, cross-platform audio editor
bitcollider-plugins - bitcollider plugins
cplay - A front-end for various audio players
gqmpeg - a GTK+ front end to mpg321/mpg123 and ogg123
libapache-mod-mp3 - turns Apache into a streaming audio server
libvorbis0 - The Vorbis General Audio Compression Codec
mp3blaster - Full-screen console mp3 and ogg vorbis player
mp3burn - burn audio CDs directly from MP3s or Ogg Vorbis files
oggtst - Read comments in ogg vorbis files
python-pyvorbis - A Python interface to the Ogg Vorbis library
vorbis-tools - Several Ogg Vorbis Tools
xmms - Versatile X audio player that looks like Winamp
xmms-dev - XMMS development static library and header files
mq3 - a mp3/ogg audio player written in Qt.
```

Now, if we are interested in one of these packages, we can find out more about it using the *show* option of *apt-cache*:

```
tigger $ apt-cache show xmms
Package: xmms
Priority: optional
Section: sound
Installed-Size: 4035
Maintainer: Josip Rodin <jrodin@jagor.srce.hr>
...
Description: Versatile X audio player that looks like Winamp
 XMMS (formerly known as X11Amp) is an X/GTK+ based audio player
 for various audio formats.
 .
 It's able to read and play:
  * Audio MPEG layer 1, 2, and 3 (with mpg123 plug-in),
  * WAV, RAW, AU (with internal wav plug-in and MikMod plug-in),
  * MOD, XM, S3M, and other module formats (with MikMod plug-in),
  * CD Audio (with CDAudio plug-in), with CDDB support,
  * .cin files, id Software,
  * Ogg Vorbis files.
 It has eSound, OSS, and disk writer support for outputting sound.
 .
 It looks almost the same as famous Winamp, and includes those neat
```

```
features like general purpose, visualization and effect plug-ins,
several of which come bundled, then spectrum analyzer, oscilloscope,
skins support, and of course, a playlist window.
```

While a full exploration of APT's features was beyond the scope of this chapter, the *apt* manual page (and the manual pages it references) along with the APT HOWTO (available in the *apt-howto-en* package) should answer any questions you may have.

In addition to the command-line tools, a number of easy-to-use text-based and graphical frontends have been developed. One of the most mature frontends is *kpackage*, which is part of the KDE Desktop Environment, but can be used with other desktops such as GNOME. *kpackage* can be run from the command line or found in the System menu of KDE. Figure 7-1 shows a sample screen from *kpackage*.

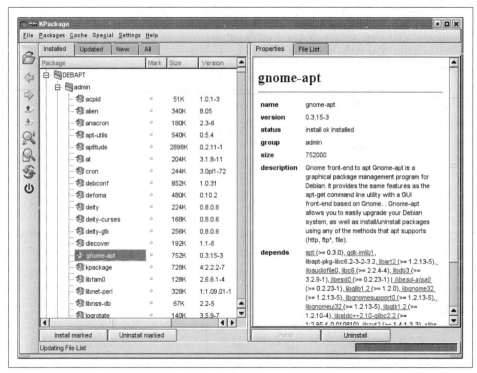

Figure 7-1. kpackage package manager

The main window of *kpackage* displays a list of all the packages available for your system on the left, with a box to the right; when you choose a package in the list, the box to the right includes information about the package you selected. You can install or uninstall packages by selecting them and choosing *Install* or *Uninstall* from the *Packages* menu, or by clicking the column labeled *Mark* to place a checkmark next to them, and then clicking the *Install marked* or *Uninstall marked* buttons. You can also install *.deb* packages directly by clicking the Open button on the toolbar to the left of the screen and selecting the file, or dragging *.deb* icons from KDE file manager windows into *kpackage*'s window. *kpackage* also has tools for finding packages with particular names. Like all KDE applications, *kpackage* has help available by pressing **F1** or using the *Help* menu.

Upgrading Other Software

In order to upgrade other applications, you'll have to obtain the newest release of the software. This is usually available as a *gzipped* or compressed tar file. Such a package could come in several forms. The most common are *binary distributions*, in which the binaries and related files are archived and ready to unpack on your system, and *source distributions*, in which the source code (or portions of the source code) for the software is provided, and you have to issue commands to compile and install it on your system.

Shared libraries make distributing software in binary form easy; as long as you have a version of the libraries installed that is compatible with the library stubs used to build the program, you're set. However, in many cases, it is easier (and a good idea) to release a program as source. Not only does this make the source code available to you for inspection and further development, but it also allows you to build the application specifically for your system, with your own libraries. Many programs allow you to specify certain options at compile time, such as selectively including various features in the program when built. This kind of customization isn't possible if you get prebuilt binaries.

There's also a security issue at play when installing binaries without source code. Although on Unix systems viruses are nearly unheard of,* it's not difficult to write a "Trojan Horse," a program that appears to do something useful but, in actuality, causes damage to the system. For example, someone could write an application that includes the "feature" of deleting all files in the home directory of the user executing the program. Because the program would be running with the permissions of the user executing it, the program itself has the ability to do this kind of damage. (Of course, the Unix security mechanism prevents damage being done to other users' files or to any important system files owned by root.)

While having source won't necessarily prevent this from happening (do you read the source code for every program you compile on your system?), at least it gives you a

---

* A "virus" in the classic sense is a program that attaches to a "host," which runs when the host is executed. On Unix systems, this usually requires root privileges to do any harm, and if programmers could obtain such privileges, they probably wouldn't bother with a virus.

Of course, it is possible to sign packages digitally so that you can check where the package comes from, and you can decide for yourself whether the package source is trusted.

Some companies offer virus scanners for Linux. These are usually meant for mail servers running on Linux systems, however, and do not scan the local hard disks, but the mail spooled on the system before it is delivered to (possibly Windows) clients. These virus scanners thus scan for Windows viruses, not for Linux viruses.

way to verify what the program is really doing. Also, if source code is available, it is likely that some people will peruse it so that using source is a bit safer; but you can't count on that.

At any rate, dealing with source and binary distributions of software is quite simple. If the package is released as a tar file, first use the *tar t* option to determine how the files have been archived. In the case of binary distributions, you may be able to unpack the tar file directly on your system—say, from / or */usr*. When doing this, be sure to delete any old versions of the program and its support files (those that aren't overwritten by the new tar file). If the old executable comes before the new one on your path, you'll continue to run the old version unless you remove it.

Source distributions are a bit trickier. First, you must unpack the sources into a directory of their own. Most systems use */usr/src* for just this. Because you usually don't have to be root to build a software package (although you will usually require root permissions to install the program once compiled!), it might be a good idea to make */usr/src* writable by all users, with the command:

```
chmod 1777 /usr/src
```

This allows any user to create subdirectories in */usr/src* and place files there. The first 1 in the mode is the "sticky" bit, which prevents users from deleting each other's subdirectories.

You can now create a subdirectory under */usr/src* and unpack the tar file there, or you can unpack the tar file directly from */usr/src* if the archive contains a subdirectory of its own.

Once the sources are available, the next step is to read any *README* and *INSTALL* files or installation notes included with the sources. Nearly all packages include such documentation. The basic method used to build most programs is:

1. Check the *Makefile*. This file contains instructions for *make*, which controls the compiler to build programs. Many applications require you to edit minor aspects of the *Makefile* for your own system; this should be self-explanatory. The installation notes will tell you if you have to do this. If there is no *Makefile* in the package, you might have to generate it first. See item 3 for how to do this.

2. Possibly edit other files associated with the program. Some applications require you to edit a file named *config.h*; again, this will be explained in the installation instructions.

3. Possibly run a configuration script. Such a script is used to determine what facilities are available on your system, which is necessary to build more complex applications.

   Specifically, when the sources do not contain a *Makefile* in the top-level directory, but instead a file called *Makefile.in* and a file called *configure*, the package has been built with the Autoconf system. In this (more and more common) case, you run the configuration script like this:

```
./configure
```

The ./ should be used so that the local *configure* is run, and not another *configure* program that might accidentally be in your path. Some packages let you pass options to *configure* that often enable or disable specific features of the package. (You can find out what these options are with *configure --help*.) Once the *configure* script has run, you can proceed with the next step.

4. Run *make*. Generally, this executes the appropriate compilation commands as given in the *Makefile*. In many cases you'll have to give a "target" to *make*, as in *make all* or *make install*. These are two common targets; the former is usually not necessary but can be used to build all targets listed in a *Makefile* (e.g., if the package includes several programs, but only one is compiled by default); the latter is often used to install the executables and support files on the system after compilation. For this reason, *make install* is usually run as root.

Even after the installation, there is often one major difference between programs installed from source or from a binary package. Programs installed from source are often installed below */usr/local* by default, which is rarely the case with binary packages.

You might have problems compiling or installing new software on your system, especially if the program in question hasn't been tested under Linux, or depends on other software you don't have installed. In Chapter 13, we talk about the compiler, *make*, and related tools in detail.

Most software packages include manual pages and other files, in addition to the source and executables. The installation script (if there is one) will place these files in the appropriate location. In the case of manual pages, you'll find files with names such as *foobar.1* or *foobar.man*. These files are usually *nroff* source files, which are formatted to produce the human-readable pages displayed by the *man* command. If the manual page source has a numeric extension, such as *.1*, copy it to the directory */usr/man/man1*, where *1* is the number used in the filename extension. (This corresponds to the manual "section" number; for most user programs, it is 1.) If the file has an extension such as *.man*, it usually suffices to copy the file to */usr/man/man1*, renaming the *.man* extension to *.1*.

Building a New Kernel

Rebuilding the kernel sounds like a pastime for hackers, but it is an important skill for any system administrator. First, you should rebuild the kernel on your system to eliminate the device drivers you don't need. This reduces the amount of memory used by the kernel itself, as described in the section "Managing Swap Space" in Chapter 6. The kernel is always present in memory, and the memory it uses cannot be reclaimed for use by programs if necessary.

You also need to occasionally upgrade your kernel to a newer version. As with any piece of your system, if you know of important bug fixes or new features in a kernel release, you may want to upgrade to pick them up. Those people who are actively developing kernel code will also need to keep their kernel up-to-date in case changes are made to the code they are working on. Sometimes, it is necessary to upgrade your kernel to use a new version of the compiler or libraries. Some applications (such as the X Window System) require a certain kernel version to run.

You can find out what kernel version you are running through the command *uname –a*. This should produce something like:

```
rutabaga% uname -a
Linux owl 2.4.19-64GB-SMP #2 SMP Fri Aug 9 21:46:03 CEST 2002 i686 unknown
```

Here, we see a machine running Version 2.4.19 of the kernel (configured for a machine with more than one processor [SMP] and a maximum of 64 GB RAM), which was last compiled on August 9. We see other information as well, such as the hostname of the machine, the number of times this kernel has been compiled (two), and the fact that the machine is a Pentium Pro or better (as denoted by i686). The manual page for *uname*(1) can tell you more.

The Linux kernel is a many-tentacled beast. Many groups of people work on different pieces of it, and some parts of the code are a patchwork of ideas meeting different design goals. Overall, however, the kernel code is clean and uniform, and those interested in exploring its innards should have little trouble doing so. However, because of the great amount of development going on with the kernel, new releases are made very rapidly—sometimes daily! The chief reason for this is that nearly all device drivers are contained within the kernel code, and every time someone updates a driver, a new release is necessary. As the Linux community moves toward loadable device drivers, the maintainers of those drivers can release them independently of the main kernel, alleviating the necessity of such rapid updates.

Currently, Linus Torvalds maintains the "official" kernel release. Although the GPL allows anyone to modify and rerelease the kernel under the same copyright, Linus's maintenance of an "official" kernel is a helpful convention that keeps version numbers uniform and allows everyone to be on equal footing when talking about kernel revisions. In order for a bug fix or new feature to be included in the kernel, all one must do is send it to Linus (or whoever is in charge for the kernel series in question, Linus himself always maintains the most current kernel), who will usually incorporate the change as long as it doesn't break anything.

Kernel version numbers follow the convention:

```
major.minor.patchlevel
```

major is the major version number, which rarely changes, *minor* is the minor version number, which indicates the current "strain" of the kernel release, and *patchlevel* is the number of the patch to the current kernel version. Some examples of kernel versions are 2.4.4, (patch level 4 of kernel Version 2.4), and 2.5.1 (patch level 1 of kernel Version 2.5).

By convention, even-numbered kernel versions (2.2, 2.4, and so on) are "stable" releases, patches that contain only bug fixes and no new features. Odd-numbered kernel versions (2.3, 2.5, and so on) are "development" releases, patches that contain whatever new code developers wish to add and bug fixes for that code. When a development kernel matures to the point where it is stable enough for wide use, it is renamed with the next highest (even) minor version number, and the development cycle begins again.

For example, kernel Versions 2.2 and 2.3 were worked on concurrently. Patches made to 2.2 were bug fixes—meant only to correct problems in the existing code. Patches to 2.3 included bug fixes as well as a great deal of new code—new device drivers, new features, and so on. When kernel Version 2.3 was stable enough, it was renamed to 2.4; a copy was made and named Version 2.5. Development continued with Versions 2.4 and 2.5. 2.4 is the new "stable" kernel, while 2.5 is a development kernel for new features.*

Note that this version-numbering convention applies only to Linus's official kernel release and only to kernel versions after 1.0. Prior to 1.0 (this is now ancient history), there was only one "current" kernel version and patches were consistently made to it. The kernel development community has found that having two concurrent kernel versions allows those who want to experiment to use the development kernel, and those who need a reliable platform to stick with the stable kernel. In this way, if the development kernel is seriously broken by new code, it shouldn't affect those who are running the newest stable kernel. The general rule is that you should use development kernels if you want to be on the leading edge of new features and are willing to risk problems with your system. Use the development kernels at your own risk.

If you are interested in how the existing kernel versions have evolved, check out *http://www.kernel.org*.

On your system, the kernel sources most probably live in */usr/src/linux* (unless you use the Debian distribution, where you can find the kernel sources in */usr/src/kernel-source-versionsnumber*). If you are going to rebuild your kernel only from the current sources, you don't need to obtain any files or apply any patches. If you wish to upgrade your kernel to a new version, you need to follow the instructions in the following section.

---

* Actually, the first versions of the 2.4 kernel series were not as stable as the number implies, which is why many users stayed with the 2.2 series for a while. By now, the current 2.4 kernel can be considered very stable, though, if you don't use any 2.4 kernels before 2.4.16.

Obtaining Kernel Sources

The official kernel is released as a *gzip*ped tar file, containing the sources along with a series of patch files—one per patch level. The tar file contains the source for the unpatched revision; for example, there is a tar file containing the sources for kernel Version 2.4 with no patches applied. Each subsequent patch level is released as a patch file (produced using *diff*), which can be applied using the *patch* program. In the section "Patching Files" in Chapter 14, we describe the use of *patch* in detail.

Let's say you're upgrading to kernel Version 2.4 patch level 4. You'll need the sources for 2.4 (the file might be named *v2.4.0.tar.gz*) and the patches for patch levels 1 through 4. These files would be named *patch1*, *patch2*, and so forth. (You need *all* the patch files up to the version to which you're upgrading. Usually, these patch files are rather small, and are *gzip*ped on the archive sites.) All these files can be found in the *kernel* directory of the Linux FTP archive sites; for example, on *ftp://ftp.kernel.org*, the directory containing the 2.4 sources and patches is */pub/linux/kernel/v2.4*. You will find the kernel sources here as tar archives, compressed with both *gzip* and *bzip2*.

If you are already at some patch level of the kernel (such as 2.4 patch level 2) and want to upgrade to a newer patch level, you can simply apply the patches from the version you have up to the version to which you'd like to upgrade. If you're upgrading from, say, 2.4 patch level 2 to 2.4 patch level 4, you need the patch files for 2.4.3 and 2.4.4.

Unpacking the sources

First, you need to unpack the source tar file from */usr/src*. You do this with commands such as:

```
rutabaga# cd /usr/src
rutabaga# mv linux linux.old
rutabaga# tar xzf v2.4.0.tar.gz
```

This saves your old kernel source tree as */usr/src/linux.old* and creates */usr/src/linux* containing the new sources. Note that the tar file containing the sources includes the *linux* subdirectory.

You should keep your current kernel sources in the directory */usr/src/linux* because there are two symbolic links—*/usr/include/linux* and */usr/include/asm*—that point into the current kernel source tree to provide certain header files when compiling programs. (You should always have your kernel sources available so that programs using these include files can be compiled.) If you want to keep several kernel source trees around, be sure that */usr/src/linux* points to the most recent one.

Applying patches

If you are applying any patch files, you use the *patch* program. Let's say that you have the files *patch1.gz* through *patch4.gz*, which are *gzip*ped. These patches should be applied from the kernel sources main directory. That doesn't mean the patch files themselves should be located there, but rather that *patch* should be executed from e.g. */usr/src/linux*. For each patch file, use the command:

```
gunzip -c patchfile | patch -p1
```

from */usr/src*. The *–p1* option tells *patch* it shouldn't strip any part of the filenames contained within the patch file except for the first one.

You must apply each patch in numerical order by patch level. This is very important. Note that using a wildcard such as *patch** will not work because the * wildcard uses ASCII order, not numeric order. (Otherwise, if you are applying a larger number of patches, *patch1* might be followed by *patch10* and *patch11*, as opposed to *patch2* and *patch3*.) It is best to run the previous command for each patch file in succession, by hand. This way you can ensure you're doing things in the right order.

You shouldn't encounter problems when patching your source tree in this way unless you try to apply patches out of order or apply a patch more than once. Check the *patch* manual page if you do encounter trouble. If all else fails, remove the new kernel source tree and start over from the original tar file.

To double-check that the patches were applied successfully, use the commands:

```
find /usr/src/linux -follow -name "*.rej" -print
find /usr/src/linux -follow -name "*#" -print
```

This lists any files that are "rejected" portions of the patch process. If any such files exist, they contain sections of the patch file that could not be applied for some reason. Look into these, and if there's any doubt, start over from scratch. You cannot expect your kernel to compile or work correctly if the patch process did not complete successfully and without rejections.

A handy script for patching the kernel is available and can be found in *scripts/patchkernel*. But as always, you should know what you are doing before using automated tools, even more so when it comes to the very core of the operating system, the kernel.

Building the Kernel

There are six steps to building the kernel, and they should be quite painless. All these steps are described in more detail in the following pages.

1. Make sure that all the required tools and utilities are installed and at the appropriate versions. See the file *Documentation/Changes* in the kernel source for the list of requirements.

2. Run *make config*, which asks you various questions about which drivers you wish to include. You could also use the more comfortable variants *make menuconfig* or (only when you are running the X Window System) *make xconfig*.

If you have previously built a kernel and then applied patches to a new version, you can run *make oldconfig* to use your old config but be prompted for any new options that may not have been in the old kernel.

3. Run *make dep* to gather dependencies for each source file and include them in the various makefiles.

4. If you have built a kernel from this source tree before, run *make clean* to clear out old object files and force a complete rebuild.

5. Run *make bzImage* to build the kernel itself.

6. Go have a coffee (or two, depending on the speed of your machine and amount of available memory).

7. Install the new kernel image, either on a boot floppy or via LILO. You can use *make bzDisk* to put the kernel on a boot floppy.

All these commands are executed from */usr/src/linux*, except for Step 5, which you can do anywhere.

A *README* is included in the kernel sources, which should be located at */usr/src/ linux/README* on your system. Read it. It contains up-to-date notes on kernel compilation, which may be more current than the information presented here. Be sure to follow the steps described there, using the descriptions given later in this section as a guide.

The first step is to run *make config*. This executes a script that asks you a set of yes/ no questions about which drivers to include in the kernel. There are defaults for each question, but be careful: the defaults probably don't correspond to what you want. (When several options are available, the default will be shown as a capital letter, as in [Y/n].) Your answers to each question will become the default the next time you build the kernel from this source tree.

Simply answer each question, either by pressing Enter for the default, or pressing y or n (followed by Enter). Some questions don't have a yes/no answer; you may be asked to enter a number or some other value. A number of the configuration questions allow an answer of m in addition to y or n. This option allows the corresponding kernel feature to be compiled as a loadable kernel module, as opposed to building it into the kernel image itself. Loadable modules, covered in the following section, "Loadable Device Drivers," allow portions of the kernel (such as device drivers) to be loaded and unloaded as needed on a running system. If you are unsure about an option, type ? at the prompt; for most options, a message will be shown that tells you more about the option.

Some people say that *make config* has so many options now that it is hardly feasible to run it by hand any longer, as you have to concentrate for a long time to press the right keys in response to the right questions. Therefore, people are moving to the alternatives described next.

An alternative to running *make config* is *make xconfig*, which compiles and runs an X-Window–based kernel configuration program. In order for this to work, you must have the X Window System running, have the appropriate X11 and Tcl/Tk libraries installed, and so forth. Instead of asking a series of questions, the X-based configuration utility allows you to use checkboxes to select which kernel options you want to enable. The system remembers your configuration options each time you run *make config*, so if you're adding or removing only a few features from your kernel, you need not reenter all the options.

Also available is make menuconfig, which uses the text-based *curses* library, providing a similar menu-based kernel configuration if you don't have X installed. *make menuconfig* and *make xconfig* are much more comfortable than *make config*, especially because you can go back to an option and change your mind up to the point where you save your configuration.

The following is part of a session with *make config*. When using *make menuconfig* or *make xconfig*, you will encounter the same options, only presented in a more user-friendly fashion (and we actually recommend the use of these tools if at all possible, as it is very easy to get confused by the myriad of configuration options):

```
rm -f include/asm
( cd include ; ln -sf asm-i386 asm)
/bin/sh scripts/Configure arch/i386/config.in
#
# Using defaults found in .config
#
*
* Code maturity level options
*
Prompt for development and/or incomplete code/drivers (CONFIG_EXPERIMENTAL) [Y/n/?]
*
* Loadable module support
*
Enable loadable module support (CONFIG_MODULES) [Y/n/?]
   Set version information on all module symbols (CONFIG_MODVERSIONS) [N/y/?]
   Kernel module loader (CONFIG_KMOD) [Y/n/?]
*
* Processor type and features
*
Processor family (386, 486, 586/K5/5x86/6x86/6x86MX, Pentium-Classic, ...
   defined CONFIG_MPENTIUMIII
Toshiba Laptop support (CONFIG_TOSHIBA) [N/y/m/?]
/dev/cpu/microcode - Intel IA32 CPU microcode support (CONFIG_MICROCODE) [M/n/y/?]
/dev/cpu/*/msr - Model-specific register support (CONFIG_X86_MSR) [M/n/y/?]
/dev/cpu/*/cpuid - CPU information support (CONFIG_X86_CPUID) [M/n/y/?]
High Memory Support (off, 4GB, 64GB) [4GB]
   defined CONFIG_HIGHMEM4G
Math emulation (CONFIG_MATH_EMULATION) [N/y/?]
MTRR (Memory Type Range Register) support (CONFIG_MTRR) [Y/n/?]
Symmetric multi-processing support (CONFIG_SMP) [Y/n/?]
*
```

```
* General setup
*
Networking support (CONFIG_NET) [Y/n/?]
...and so on...
*** End of Linux kernel configuration.
*** Check the top-level Makefile for additional configuration.
*** Next, you may run 'make bzImage', 'make bzdisk', or 'make
install'.
```

If you have gathered the information about your hardware when installing Linux, that information is probably sufficient to answer the configuration questions, most of which should be straightforward. If you don't recognize some feature, it's a specialized feature that you don't need. The following questions are found in the kernel configuration for Version 2.4.4. If you have applied other patches, additional questions might appear. The same is true for later versions of the kernel. Note that in the following list we don't show all the kernel configuration options; there are simply too many of them, and most are self-explanatory. We have highlighted only those that may require further explanation. Remember that if you're not sure how to answer a particular question, the default answer is often the best choice. When in doubt, it is also a good idea to type ? and check the help message.

It should be noted here that not all Linux device drivers are actually built into the kernel. Instead, some drivers are available only as loadable modules, distributed separately from the kernel sources. (As mentioned earlier, some drivers can be either built into the kernel or compiled as modules.) One notable kernel driver available only as a module is the "floppy tape" driver for QIC-117 tape drives that connect to the floppy controller.

If you can't find support for your favorite hardware device in the list presented by *make config*, it's quite possible that the driver is available as a module or a separate kernel patch. Scour the FTP sites and archive CD-ROMs if you can't find what you're looking for. In the next section, "Loadable Device Drivers," kernel modules are covered in detail.

Prompt for development and/or incomplete code/drivers
> Answer yes for this item if you want to try new features that aren't considered stable enough by the developers. You do not want this option unless you want to help test new features.

Processor family (386, 486, 586/K5/5x86/6x86/6x86MX, Pentium-Classic, Pentium-MMX, Pentium-Pro/Celeron/Pentium-II, Pentium-III/Celeron/Coppermine, Pentium-4, K6/K6-II/K6-III, Athlon/Duron/K7, Crusoe, Winchip-C6, Winchip-2, Winchip-2A/Winchip-3, CyrixIII/C3) [Pentium-III/Celeron/Coppermine]
> Here, you have to specify the CPU type that you have. The kernel will then be compiled with optimizations especially geared toward your machine. Note that if you specify a higher processor here than you actually have, the kernel might not work. Also, the Pentium II MMX is a 686, not a 586 chip.

Math emulation

Answer no if you have a Pentium or better. Answer yes to this item if you do not have a floating-point coprocessor in your machine. This is necessary for the kernel to emulate the presence of a math coprocessor.

Symmetric multi-processing support

This enables kernel support for more than one CPU. If your machine has more than one CPU, say yes here; if not, say no.

Enable loadable module support

This enables the support for dynamically loading additional modules. You definitely want to enable this.

Set version information on all symbols for modules

This is a special option that makes it possible to use a module compiled for one kernel version with another kernel version. A number of problems are attached to this; say no here unless you know exactly what you are doing.

Kernel module loader

If you enable this option, the kernel can automatically load and unload dynamically loadable modules as needed.

Networking support

Answer yes to this option if you want any sort of networking support in your kernel (including TCP/IP, SLIP, PPP, NFS, and so on).

PCI support

Enable this option if your motherboard includes the PCI bus and you have PCI-bus devices installed in your system. The PCI BIOS is used to detect and enable PCI devices; kernel support for it is necessary for use of any PCI devices in your system.

System V IPC

Answering yes to this option includes kernel support for System V interprocess communication (IPC) functions, such as *msgrcv* and *msgsnd*. Some programs ported from System V require this; you should answer yes unless you have a strong aversion to these features.

Sysctl support

This option instructs the kernel to provide a way to change kernel parameters on-the-fly, without rebooting. It is a good idea to enable this unless you have very limited memory and cannot tolerate the extra 8 KB that this option adds to the kernel.

Parallel port support

Enable this option if you have a parallel port in your system and want to access it from Linux. Linux can use the parallel port not only for printers, but also for PLIP (a networking protocol for parallel lines), ZIP drives, scanners, and other things. In most cases, you will need an additional driver to attach a device to the parallel port.

Normal floppy disk support

Answer yes to this option unless you don't want support for floppy drives (this can save some memory on systems where floppy support isn't required).

Enhanced IDE/MFM/RLL disk/cdrom/tape/floppy support

Answer yes to this option unless you don't need IDE/MFM/RLL drive support. After answering yes, you will be prompted for types of devices (hard disks, CD-ROM drives, tape drives, and floppy drives) you want to access over the IDE driver. If you have no IDE hardware (only SCSI), it may be safe to disable this option.

XT harddisk support

Answer yes to this only if you have an older XT disk controller and plan to use it with your Linux system.

Parallel port IDE device support

This option enables support for IDE devices that are attached to the parallel port, such as portable CD-ROM drives.

Networking options

If you previously selected networking support, you will be asked a series of questions about which networking options you want enabled in your kernel. Unless you have special networking needs (in which case you'll know how to answer the questions appropriately), answering the defaults for these questions should suffice. A number of the questions are esoteric in nature (such as IP: Disable Path MTU Discovery) and you should select the defaults for these in almost all cases.

SCSI support

If you have a SCSI controller of any kind, answer yes to this option. You will be asked a series of questions about the specific SCSI devices on your system; be sure you know what type of hardware you have installed. All these questions deal with specific SCSI controller chips and boards; if you aren't sure what sort of SCSI controller you have, check the hardware documentation or consult the Linux HOWTO documents.

You will also be asked if you want support for SCSI disks, tapes, CD-ROMs, and other devices; be sure to enable the options appropriate for your hardware.

If you don't have any SCSI hardware, you should answer no to this option; it greatly reduces the size of your kernel.

Network device support

This is a series of questions about the specific networking controllers Linux supports. If you plan to use an Ethernet card (or some other networking controller), be sure to enable the options for your hardware. As with SCSI devices, you should consult your hardware documentation or the Linux HOWTO documents (such as the Ethernet HOWTO) to determine which driver is appropriate for your network controller.

Amateur Radio support

This option enables basic support for networking over public radio frequencies. If you have the equipment to use the feature, enable this option and read the AX25 and the HAM HOWTO.

ISDN subsystem

If you have ISDN hardware in your system, enable this option and select the ISDN hardware driver suitable for your hardware. You will most probably also want to select Support synchronous PPP (see "PPP over ISDN" in Chapter 15).

Old CD-ROM drivers

This is a series of questions dealing with the specific CD-ROM drivers supported by the kernel, such as the Sony CDU31A/33A, Mitsumi, or SoundBlaster Pro CD-ROM, and so on. If you have a SCSI or IDE CD-ROM controller (and have selected support for it earlier), you need not enable any of these options. Some CD-ROM drives have their own interface boards, and these options enable drivers for them.

Character devices

Linux supports a number of special "character" devices, such as serial and parallel port controllers, QIC-02 tape drives, and mice with their own proprietary interfaces (not mice that connect to the serial port, such as the Microsoft serial mouse). This section also includes the joystick support and the "Video for Linux" drivers that support video and frame-grabbing hardware. Be sure to enable the options corresponding to your hardware.

Filesystems

This is a series of questions for each filesystem type supported by the kernel. As discussed in the section "Managing Filesystems" in Chapter 6, a number of filesystem types are supported by the system, and you can pick and choose which to include in the kernel. Nearly all systems should include support for the Second Extended and /proc filesystems. You should include support for the MS-DOS filesystem if you want to access your MS-DOS files directly from Linux, and the ISO 9660 filesystem to access files on a CD-ROM (most of which are encoded in this way).

Console drivers

Make sure you select at least VGA text console in this section, or you won't be able to use your Linux system from the console.

Sound card support

Answering yes to this option presents you with several questions about your sound card, which drivers you wish to have installed, and other details, such as the IRQ and address of the sound hardware.

Kernel hacking

This section contains options that are useful only if you plan on hacking the Linux kernel yourself. If you do not want to do this, answer no.

After running *make config* or its equivalent, you'll be asked to edit "the top-level Makefile," which means */usr/src/linux/Makefile*. In most cases, it's not necessary to do this. If you wanted to alter some of the compilation options for the kernel, or change the default root device or SVGA mode, you could edit the makefile to accomplish this. Setting the root device and SVGA mode can easily be done by running *rdev* on a compiled kernel image, as we saw in the section "Using a Boot Floppy" in Chapter 5.

If you wish to force a complete recompilation of the kernel, you should issue *make clean* at this point. This removes from this source tree all object files produced from a previous build. If you have never built the kernel from this tree, you're probably safe skipping this step (although it can't hurt to perform it). If you are tweaking minor parts of the kernel, you might want to avoid this step so that only those files that have changed will be recompiled. At any rate, running *make clean* simply ensures the entire kernel will be recompiled "from scratch," and if you're in any doubt, use this command to be on the safe side.

Now you're ready to compile the kernel. This is done with the command *make bzImage*. It is best to build your kernel on a lightly loaded system, with most of your memory free for the compilation. If other users are accessing the system, or if you're trying to run any large applications yourself (such as the X Window System, or another compilation), the build may slow to a crawl. The key here is memory. If a system is low on memory and starts swapping, it will be slow no matter how fast the processor is.

The kernel compilation can take anywhere from a few minutes to many hours, depending on your hardware. There is a great deal of code—well over 10 MB—in the entire kernel, so this should come as no surprise. Slower systems with 4 MB (or less) of RAM can expect to take several hours for a complete rebuild; faster machines with more memory can complete it in less than half an hour. Your mileage will most assuredly vary.

If any errors or warnings occur while compiling, you cannot expect the resulting kernel to work correctly; in most cases, the build will halt if an error occurs. Such errors can be the result of incorrectly applying patches, problems with the *make config* step, or actual bugs in the code. In the "stock" kernels, this latter case is rare, but is more common if you're working with development code or new drivers under testing. If you have any doubt, remove the kernel source tree altogether and start over.

When the compilation is complete, you will be left with the file *bzImage* in the directory */usr/src/linux/arch/i386/boot*. (Of course, if you're attempting to build Linux on a platform other than the Intel x86, the kernel image will be found in the corresponding subdirectory under *arch*.) The kernel is so named because it is the executable image of the kernel, and it has been internally compressed using the *bzip2* algorithm. When the kernel boots, it uncompresses itself into memory: don't attempt to use *bzip2* or *bunzip2* on *bzImage* yourself! The kernel requires much less disk space when compressed in this way, allowing kernel images to fit on a floppy. Earlier kernels supported both the *gzip* and the *bzip2* compression algorithms, the former resulting in a file called *zImage*. Because *bzImage* gives better compression results, however, *gzip* should not be used, as the resulting kernels are usually too big to be installed these days.

If you pick too much kernel functionality, you can get a `kernel too big` error at the end of the kernel compilation. This happens rarely because you need only a very limited amount of hardware support for one machine, but it can happen. In this case, there is one way out: compile some kernel functionality as modules (see the next section, "Loadable Device Drivers").

You should now run *rdev* on the new kernel image to verify that the root filesystem device, console SVGA mode, and other parameters have been set correctly. This is described in the section "Using a Boot Floppy" in Chapter 5.

With your new kernel in hand, you're ready to configure it for booting. This involves either placing the kernel image on a boot floppy, or configuring LILO to boot the kernel from the hard drive. These topics are discussed in the section "Booting the System" in Chapter 5. To use the new kernel, configure it for booting in one of these ways, and reboot the system.

A warning: you should always keep a known good kernel available for booting. Either keep a previous backup kernel selectable from LILO or test new kernels using a floppy first. This will save you if you make a mistake such as omitting a crucial driver in your new kernel, making your system not bootable.

Loadable Device Drivers

Traditionally, device drivers have been included as part of the kernel. There are several reasons for this. First of all, nearly all device drivers require the special hardware access provided by being part of the kernel code. Such hardware access can't be obtained easily through a user program. Also, device drivers are much easier to implement as part of the kernel; such drivers would have complete access to the data structures and other routines in the kernel and could call them freely.

A conglomerate kernel containing all drivers in this manner presents several problems. First of all, it requires the system administrator to rebuild the kernel in order to selectively include device drivers, as we saw in the previous section. Also, this mechanism lends itself to sloppy programming on the part of the driver writers: there's nothing stopping a programmer from writing code that is not completely modular— code which, for example, directly accesses data private to other parts of the kernel. The cooperative nature of the Linux kernel development compounds this problem, and not all parts of the code are as neatly contained as they should be. This can make it more difficult to maintain and debug the code.

In an effort to move away from this paradigm, the Linux kernel supports loadable device drivers—device drivers that are added to or removed from memory at runtime, with a series of commands. Such drivers are still part of the kernel, but they are compiled separately and enabled only when loaded. Loadable device drivers, or *modules*, are generally loaded into memory using commands in one of the boot-time *rc* scripts.

Modules provide a cleaner interface for writing drivers. To some extent, they require the code to be somewhat modular and to follow a certain coding convention. (Note that this doesn't actually prevent a programmer from abusing the convention and writing nonmodular code. Once the module has been loaded, it is just as free to wreak havoc as if it were compiled directly into the kernel.) Using modules makes drivers easier to debug; you can simply unload a module, recompile it, and reload it without having to reboot the system or rebuild the kernel as a whole. Modules can be used for other parts of the kernel, such as filesystem types, in addition to device drivers.

Most device drivers, and a lot of other kernel functionality under Linux, are implemented as modules. One of them is the floppy tape driver (or *ftape* driver), for tape drives that connect to the floppy controller, such as the Colorado Memory Jumbo 120/250 models. If you plan to use this driver on your system, it is good to know how to build, load, and unload modules. While nobody stops you from compiling this module statically into your kernel, a tape drive is something that you need only rarely (normally once a day or so), and its driver shouldn't occupy valuable RAM during the times it is not needed. See the Linux *ftape* HOWTO for more about these devices and supported hardware.

The first thing you'll need is the *modules* package, which contains the commands used to load and unload modules from the kernel. On the FTP archive sites, this is usually found as *modules.tar.gz* in the directory where the kernel sources are kept. This package contains the sources to the commands *insmod*, *modprobe*, *rmmod*, and *lsmod*. Most Linux distributions include these commands (found in *sbin*). If you already have these commands installed, you probably don't need to get the *modules* package. However, it can't hurt to get the package and rebuild these commands, to be sure that you have the most up-to-date version.

To rebuild these commands, unpack *modules.tar.gz* (say, in a subdirectory of */usr/ src*). Follow the installation instructions contained there; usually all you have to do is execute *make* followed by *make install* (as root). The three commands will now be installed in */sbin* and will be ready to use.

A module is simply a single object file containing all the code for the driver. For example, the *ftape* module might be called *ftape.o*. On many systems, the modules themselves are stored in a directory tree below */lib/modules/kernelversion*, where you can find different directories for the various types of modules. For example, the modules compiled for the 2.4.4 kernel would be below */lib/modules/2.4.4*. You might already have a number of modules on your system; check the appropriate directory.

Modules can be either in the kernel sources or external to it. The former is the case for those device drivers, filesystems, and other functionality that are used most often and are maintained as part of the official kernel sources. Using these modules is very easy: during the *make config*, *make menuconfig*, or *make xconfig* step, type m to build a feature as a module. Repeat this for everything you want to compile as a module. Then, after the *make bzImage* step, execute the commands *make modules* and *make modules_install*. This will compile the modules and install them in */lib/modules/ kernelversion*. It is a good idea (for reasons to be explained later in this section) to run the command *depmod -a* afterward to correct module dependencies.

New modules that are not yet integrated into the official kernel sources, or those that are simply too esoteric to be put into the kernel sources (e.g., a device driver for some custom-built hardware that is not publicly available) can be available as stand-alone, external modules. Unpack the archive of this module, compile it according to the instructions that are hopefully included, and copy the resulting module file to the appropriate subdirectory of */lib/modules/kernelversion*. Some modules might have an install script, or allow you to issue the command *make install* to perform the last step.

Once you have a compiled module (either from the kernel sources or external), you can load it using the command:

    insmod *module*

where *module* is the name of the module object file. For example:

    insmod /lib/modules/2.4.4/kernel/drivers/char/ftape/lowlevel/ftape.o

installs the *ftape* driver if it is found in that file.

Once a module is installed, it may display some information to the console (as well as to the system logs), indicating that it is initialized. For example, the *ftape* driver might display the following:

```
ftape v1.14 29/10/94 (c) 1993, 1994 Bas Laarhoven (bas@vimec.nl)
  QIC-117 driver for QIC-40 and QIC-80 tape drives
[000] kernel-interface.c (init_module) - installing QIC-117 ftape\
driver....
[001] kernel-interface.c (init_module) - 3 tape_buffers @ 001B8000.
[002]  calibr.c (time_inb) - inb() duration: 1436 nsec.
[003]  calibr.c (calibrate) - TC for 'udelay()' = 2944 nsec (at 2049\
counts).
[004]  calibr.c (calibrate) - TC for 'fdc_wait()' = 2857 nsec (at 2049\
counts).
```

The exact messages printed depend on the module, of course. Each module should come with ample documentation describing just what it does and how to debug it if there are problems.

It is likely that *insmod* will tell you it could not load the module into the kernel because there were "symbols missing." This means that the module you want to load needs functionality from another part of the kernel that is neither compiled into the kernel nor contained in a module already loaded. You could now try to find out which module contains those functions, load that module first with *insmod*, and try again. You will eventually succeed with this method, but it can be cumbersome, and this would not be Linux if there weren't a better way.

You first need a module database in the file */lib/modules/kernelversion/modules.dep*. You can create this database by calling:

```
depmod -a
```

This goes through all the modules you have and records whether they need any other modules. With this database in place, you can simply replace the *insmod* command with the *modprobe* command, which checks the module database and loads any other modules that might be needed before loading the requested module. For example, our *modules.dep* file contains—among others—the following line:

```
/lib/modules/2.4.4/kernel/drivers/isdn/hisax/hisax.o:        /lib/modules/2.4.4/
kernel/drivers/isdn/isdn.o
```

This means that in order to load the *hisax* module (a device driver for a number of ISDN boards), the *isdn* module must be loaded. If we now load the *hisax* module with *modprobe* (this example is slightly simplified because the *hisax* module needs additional parameters):

```
modprobe hisax
```

modprobe will detect the dependency and load the *isdn* module. If you have compiled a module for the current kernel, you first need to run *depmod -a*, though, so that modprobe can find it.

Some modules need so-called *module parameters*. For example, a device driver might need to be assigned an IRQ. You can pass those parameters in the form *parameter_name=parameter_value* with both the *insmod* and the *modprobe* command. In the following example, several parameters are passed to the *hisax* module:

```
tigger # modprobe hisax type=3 protocol=2 io=0x280 irq=10
```

The documentation for each module should tell you which parameters the module supports. If you are too lazy to read the documentation, a nifty tool you can use is *modinfo* which tells you—among other things—which parameters the module specified as the argument accepts.

One caveat about modules if you use the Debian distribution: Debian uses a file called */etc/modules* that lists the modules that should be loaded at boot time. If a module that you do not want keeps reappearing, check whether it is listed here.

You can list the drivers that are loaded with the command *lsmod*, as in:

```
rutabaga% lsmod
Module:      #pages:                Used by
ftape            40
```

The memory usage of the module is displayed as well; under Linux on an Intel x86 system, a page is 4 KB. The *ftape* driver here is using 160 KB of memory. If any other modules are dependent on this module, they are shown in the third column.

A module can be unloaded from memory using the *rmmod* command, as long as it is not in use. For example:

```
rmmod ftape
```

The argument to *rmmod* is the name of the driver as it appears in the *lsmod* listing.

Once you have modules working to your satisfaction, you can include the appropriate *insmod* commands in one of the *rc* scripts executed at boot time. One of your *rc* scripts might already include a place where *insmod* commands can be added, depending on your distribution.

One feature of the current module support is that you must rebuild a module any time you upgrade your kernel to a new version or patch level. (Rebuilding your kernel while keeping the same kernel version doesn't require you to do this.) This is done to ensure that the module is compatible with the kernel version you're using. If you attempt to load a module with a kernel that is newer or older than that for which it was compiled, *insmod* will complain and not allow the module to be loaded. When rebuilding a module, you must be running the kernel under which it will be used. Therefore, when upgrading your kernel, upgrade and reboot the new kernel first, then rebuild your modules and load them. There is an option that allows you to keep your modules when switching kernels, but a number of problems are associated with it, and we recommend against using it.

Loading Modules Automatically

The automatic loading of modules is an especially useful feature which is implemented by a kernel component called *kmod*. With the help of *kmod*, the kernel can load needed device drivers and other modules automatically and without manual intervention from the system administrator. If the modules are not needed after 60 seconds, they are automatically unloaded as well.

In order to use *kmod*, you need to turn on support for it (Kernel module loader) during kernel configuration in the Loadable module support section.

Modules that need other modules must be correctly listed in */lib/modules/ kernelversion/modules.dep*, and there must be aliases for the major and minor number in */etc/conf.modules*. See the documentation from the *modules* package for further information.

If a module has not been loaded manually with *insmod* or *modprobe*, but was loaded automatically by the kernel, the module is listed with the addition (autoclean) in the *lsmod* output. This tells you that the kernel will remove the module if it has not been used for more than one minute.

We have gone through quite a lot of material now, and you should have all the tools you'll need to build and maintain your own kernels.

## CHAPTER 8

Other Administrative Tasks

After reading the previous three chapters, you now have all the skills you need to start using your system. But eventually you'll want the information in this chapter too. Some of the activities, such as making backup tapes, are important habits to develop. You may also find it useful to have access to files and programs on MS-DOS and Windows. Finally, we'll help you handle events that you hope will never happen, but sometimes do—system panics and corruption.

Making Backups

Making backups of your system is an important way to protect yourself from data corruption or loss in case you have problems with your hardware, or you make a mistake such as deleting important files inadvertently. During your experiences with Linux, you're likely to make quite a few customizations to the system that can't be restored by simply reinstalling from your original installation media. However, if you happen to have your original Linux floppies or CD-ROM handy, it may not be necessary to back up your entire system. Your original installation media already serve as an excellent backup.

Under Linux, as with any Unix-like system, you can make mistakes while logged in as root that would make it impossible to boot the system or log in later. Many newcomers approach such a problem by reinstalling the system entirely from backup, or worse, from scratch. This is seldom, if ever, necessary. In the section "What to Do in an Emergency," later in this chapter, we'll talk about what to do in these cases.

If you do experience data loss, it is sometimes possible to recover that data using the filesystem maintenance tools described in the section "Checking and Repairing Filesystems" in Chapter 6. Unlike some other operating systems, however, it's generally not possible to "undelete" a file that has been removed by *rm* or overwritten by a careless *cp* or *mv* command (for example, copying one file over another destroys the file to which you're copying). In these extreme cases, backups are key to recovering from problems.

Backups are usually made to tape, floppy or CD-R(W). None of these media is 100% reliable, although tape and CD-R(W) are more dependable than floppy in the long term. Many tools are available that help you make backups. In the simplest case, you can use a combination of *gzip* (or *bzip2*) and *tar* to back up files from your hard drive to floppy or tape. This is the best method to use when you make only occasional backups, no more often than, say, once a month.

If you have numerous users on your system or you make frequent changes to the system configuration, it makes more sense to employ an incremental backup scheme. Under such a scheme, you would take a "full backup" of the system only about once a month. Then, every week, you would back up only those files that changed in the last week. Likewise, each night, you could back up just those files that changed over the previous 24 hours. There are several tools to aid you in this type of backup.

The idea behind an incremental backup is that it is more efficient to take backups in small steps; you use fewer floppies, tapes, or CDs, and the weekly and nightly backups are shorter and easier to run. With this method, you have a backup that is at most a day old. If you were to, say, accidentally delete your entire system, you would restore it from backup in the following manner:

1. Restore from the most recent monthly backup. For instance, if you wiped the system on July 17, you would restore the July 1 full backup. Your system now reflects the state of files when the July 1 backup was made.

2. Restore from each weekly backup made so far this month. In our case, we could restore from the two weekly backups from July 7 and 14. Restoring each weekly backup updates all the files that changed during that week.

3. Restore from each daily backup during the last week—that is, since the last weekly backup. In this case, we would restore the daily backups from July 15 and 16. The system now looks as it did when the daily backup was taken on July 16; no more than a day's worth of files have been lost.

Depending on the size of your system, the full monthly backup might require 4 GB or more of backup storage—often not more than one tape using today's tape media, but quite a few ZIP disks. However, the weekly and daily backups would generally require much less storage space. Depending on how your system is used, you might decide to take the weekly backup on Sunday night and not bother with daily backups for the weekend.

One important characteristic that backups should (usually) have is the ability to select individual files from the backup for restoration. This way, if you accidentally delete a single file or group of files, you can simply restore those files without having to do a full system restoration. Depending on how you take backups, however, this task will be either very easy or painfully difficult.

In this section, we're going to talk about the use of *tar*, *gzip*, and a few related tools for making backups to floppy and tape. We'll even cover the use of floppy and tape drives in the bargain. These tools allow you to take backups more or less "by hand"; you can automate the process by writing shell scripts and even schedule your backups to run automatically during the night using *cron*. All you have to do is flip tapes. Other software packages provide a nice menu-driven interface for creating backups, restoring specific files from backup, and so forth. Many of these packages are, in fact, nice frontends to *tar* and *gzip*. You can decide for yourself what kind of backup system suits you best.

Simple Backups

The simplest means of taking a backup is to use *tar* to archive all the files on the system or only those files in a set of specific directories. Before you do this, however, you need to decide what files to back up. Do you need to back up every file on the system? This is rarely necessary, especially if you have your original installation disks or CD-ROM. If you have made important changes to the system, but everything else is just the way it was found on your installation media, you could get by only archiving those files you have made changes to. Over time, however, it is difficult to keep track of such changes.

In general, you will be making changes to the system configuration files in */etc*. There are other configuration files as well, and it can't hurt to archive directories, such as */usr/lib*, and */etc/X11* (which contains the XFree86 configuration files, as we'll see in the section "Installing XFree86" in Chapter 10).

You should also back up your kernel sources (if you have upgraded or built your own kernel); these are found in */usr/src/linux*.

During your Linux adventures it's a good idea to keep notes on what features of the system you've made changes to so that you can make intelligent choices when taking backups. If you're truly paranoid, go ahead and back up the whole system; that can't hurt, but the cost of backup media might.

Of course, you should also back up the home directories for each user on the system; these are generally found in */home*. If you have your system configured to receive electronic mail (see the section "Electronic Mail" in Chapter 16), you might want to back up the incoming mail files for each user. Many people tend to keep old and "important" electronic mail in their incoming mail spool, and it's not difficult to accidentally corrupt one of these files through a mailer error or other mistake. These files are usually found in */var/spool/mail*. Of course, this applies only if you are using the local mail system, not to people who access mail directly via POP3 or IMAP.

Backing up to tape

Assuming you know what files or directories to back up, you're ready to roll. You can use the *tar* command directly, as we saw in the section "Using tar" in Chapter 7, to make a backup. For example, the command:

```
tar cvf /dev/qft0 /usr/src /etc /home
```

archives all the files from */usr/src*, */etc*, and */home* to */dev/qft0*. */dev/qft0* is the first "floppy-tape" device—that is, a tape drive that hangs off of the floppy controller. Many popular tape drives for the PC use this interface. If you have a SCSI tape drive, the device names are */dev/st0*, */dev/st1*, and so on, based on the drive number. Those tape drives with another type of interface have their own device names; you can determine these by looking at the documentation for the device driver in the kernel.

You can then read the archive back from the tape using a command, such as:

```
tar xvf /dev/qft0
```

This is exactly as if you were dealing with a tar file on disk, as seen in the section "Archive and Compression Utilities" in Chapter 7.

When you use the tape drive, the tape is seen as a stream that may be read from or written to in one direction only. Once *tar* is done, the tape device will be closed, and the tape will rewind. You don't create a filesystem on a tape, nor do you mount it or attempt to access the data on it as files. You simply treat the tape device itself as a single "file" from which to create or extract archives.

Be sure your tapes are formatted before you use them. This ensures that the beginning-of-tape marker and bad-blocks information has been written to the tape. For formatting QIC-80 tapes (those used with floppy-tape drivers), you can use a tool called *ftformat* that is either already included with your distribution or can be downloaded from *ftp://sunsite.unc.edu/pub/Linux/kernel/tapes* as part of the *ftape* package.

Creating one tar file per tape might be wasteful if the archive requires but a fraction of the capacity of the tape. In order to place more than one file on a tape, you must first prevent the tape from rewinding after each use, and you must have a way to position the tape to the next "file marker," for both tar file creation and extraction.

The way to do this is to use the nonrewinding tape devices, which are named */dev/nqft0*, */dev/nqft1*, and so on for floppy-tape drivers, and */dev/nst0*, */dev/nst1*, and so on for SCSI tapes. When this device is used for reading or writing, the tape will not be rewound when the device is closed (that is, once *tar* has completed). You can then use *tar* again to add another archive to the tape. The two tar files on the tape won't have anything to do with each other. Of course, if you later overwrite the first tar file, you may overwrite the second file or leave an undesirable gap between the first and second files (which may be interpreted as garbage). In general, don't attempt to replace just one file on a tape that has multiple files on it.

Using the nonrewinding tape device, you can add as many files to the tape as space permits. In order to rewind the tape after use, use the *mt* command. *mt* is a general-purpose command that performs a number of functions with the tape drive.

For example, the command:

```
mt /dev/nqft0 rewind
```

rewinds the tape in the first floppy-tape device. (In this case, you can use the corresponding rewinding tape device as well.)

Similarly, the command:

```
mt /dev/nqft0 reten
```

retensions the tape by winding it to the end and then rewinding it.

When reading files on a multiple-file tape, you must use the nonrewinding tape device with *tar* and the *mt* command to position the tape to the appropriate file.

For example, to skip to the next file on the tape, use the command:

```
mt /dev/nqft0 fsf 1
```

This skips over one file on the tape. Similarly, to skip over two files, use:

```
mt /dev/nqft0 fsf 2
```

Be sure to use the appropriate nonrewinding tape device with *mt*. Note that this command does not move to "file number two" on the tape; it skips over the next two files based on the current tape position. Just use *mt* to rewind the tape if you're not sure where the tape is currently positioned. You can also skip back; see the *mt*(1) manual page for a complete list of options.

You need to use *mt* every time you read a multifile tape. Using *tar* twice in succession to read two archive files usually won't work; this is because *tar* doesn't recognize the file marker placed on the tape between files. Once the first *tar* finishes, the tape is positioned at the beginning of the file marker. Using *tar* immediately will give you an error message because *tar* will attempt to read the file marker. After reading one file from a tape, just use:

```
mt device fsf 1
```

to move to the next file.

Backing up to floppy

Just as we saw in the last section, the command:

```
tar cvf /dev/fd0 /usr/src /etc /home
```

makes a backup of */usr/src*, */etc*, and */home* to */dev/fd0*, the first floppy device. You can then read the backup using a command, such as:

```
tar xvf /dev/fd0
```

Because floppies have a rather limited storage capacity, GNU *tar* allows you to create a "multivolume" archive. (This feature applies to tapes as well, but it is far more useful in the case of floppies.) With this feature, *tar* prompts you to insert a new volume after reading or writing each floppy. To use this feature, simply provide the M option to *tar*, as in:

```
tar cvMf /dev/fd0 /usr/src /etc /home
```

Be sure to label your floppies well, and don't get them out of order when attempting to restore the archive.

One caveat of this feature is that it doesn't support the automatic compression provided by the *z* and *I* options. However, there are various reasons why you may not want to compress your backups created with *tar*, as discussed later. At any rate, you can create your own multivolume backups using *tar* and *gzip* in conjunction with a program that reads and writes data to a sequence of floppies (or tapes), prompting for each in succession. One such program is *backflops*, available on several Linux distributions and on the FTP archive sites. A do-it-yourself way to accomplish the same thing is to write the backup archive to a disk file and use *dd* or a similar command to write the archive as individual chunks to each floppy. If you're brave enough to try this, you can figure it out for yourself.

To compress, or not to compress?

There are good arguments both for and against compression of *tar* archives when making backups. The overall problem is that neither *tar* nor the compression tools *gzip* and *bzip2* are particularly fault-tolerant, no matter how convenient they are. Although compression using *gzip* or *bzip2* can greatly reduce the amount of backup media required to store an archive, compressing entire *tar* files as they are written to floppy or tape makes the backup prone to complete loss if one block of the archive is corrupted, say, through a media error (not uncommon in the case of floppies and tapes). Most compression algorithms, *gzip* and *bzip2* included, depend on the coherency of data across many bytes in order to achieve compression. If any data within a compressed archive is corrupt, *gunzip* may not be able to uncompress the file from that point on, making it completely unreadable to *tar*.

This is much worse than if the tar file were uncompressed on the tape. Although *tar* doesn't provide much protection against data corruption within an archive, if there is minimal corruption within a tar file, you can usually recover most of the archived files with little trouble, or at least those files up until the corruption occurs. Although far from perfect, it's better than losing your entire backup.

A better solution is to use an archiving tool other than *tar* to make backups. Several options are available. *cpio* is an archiving utility that packs files together, similar in fashion to *tar*. However, because of the simpler storage method used by *cpio*, it recovers cleanly from data corruption in an archive. (It still doesn't handle errors well on *gzip*ped files.)

The best solution may be to use a tool such as *afio*. *afio* supports multivolume back-ups and is similar in some respects to *cpio*. However, *afio* includes compression and is more reliable because each individual file is compressed. This means that if data on an archive is corrupted, the damage can be isolated to individual files, instead of to the entire backup.

These tools should be available with your Linux distribution, as well as from all the Internet-based Linux archives. A number of other backup utilities, with varying degrees of popularity and usability, have been developed or ported for Linux. If you're serious about backups, you should look into them.[*] Among those programs are the freely available *taper*, *tob* and *Amanda*, as well as commercial programs like *ARKEIA* (free for use with up to two computers), *BRU*, and *Arcserve*. Lots of free backup tools can also be found at *http://velocom.linux.tucows.com/system/backup.html*.

Incremental Backups

Incremental backups, as described earlier in this chapter, are a good way to keep your system backups up-to-date. For example, you can take nightly backups of only those files that changed in the last 24 hours, weekly backups of all files that changed in the last week, and monthly backups of the entire system.

You can create incremental backups using the tools mentioned previously: *tar, gzip, cpio*, and so on. The first step in creating an incremental backup is to produce a list of files that changed since a certain amount of time ago. You can do this easily with the *find* command.[†] If you use a special backup program, you will most likely not have to do this, but set some option somewhere that you want to do an incremental backup.

For example, to produce a list of all files that were modified in the last 24 hours, we can use the command:

```
find / -mtime -1 \! -type d -print > /tmp/filelist.daily
```

The first argument to *find* is the directory to start from—here, /, the root directory. The *–mtime –1* option tells *find* to locate all files that changed in the last 24 hours.

The *\! –type d* is complicated (and optional), but it cuts some unnecessary stuff from your output. It tells *find* to exclude directories from the resulting file list. The ! is a negation operator (meaning here, "exclude files of type d"), but put a backslash in front of it because otherwise the shell interprets it as a special character.

---

[*] Of course, this section was written after the author took the first backup of his Linux system in nearly four years of use!

[†] If you're not familiar with *find*, become so soon. *find* is a great way to locate files across many directories that have certain filenames, permissions, or modification times. *find* can even execute a program for each file that it locates. In short, *find* is your friend, and all good system administrators know how to use it well.

The *-print* causes all filenames matching the search to be printed to standard output. We redirect standard output to a file for later use. Likewise, to locate all files that changed in the last week, use:

```
find / -mtime -7 -print > /tmp/filelist.weekly
```

Note that if you use *find* in this way, it traverses all mounted filesystems. If you have a CD-ROM mounted, for example, *find* attempts to locate all files on the CD-ROM as well (which you probably do not wish to backup). The *-prune* option can be used to exclude certain directories from the walk that *find* performs across the system; or, you can use *find* multiple times with a first argument other than /. See the manual page for *find*(1) for details.

Now you have produced a list of files to back up. Previously, when using *tar*, we have specified the files to archive on the command line. However, this list of files may be too long for a single command line (which is usually limited to around 2048 characters), and the list itself is contained within a file.

You can use the *-T* option with *tar* to specify a file containing a list of files for *tar* to back up. In order to use this option, you have to use an alternate syntax to *tar* in which all options are specified explicitly with dashes. For example, to back up the files listed in */tmp/filelist.daily* to the device */dev/qft0*, use the command:

```
tar -cv -T /tmp/filelist.daily -f /dev/qft0
```

You can now write a short shell script that automatically produces the list of files and backs them up using *tar*. You can use *cron* to execute the script nightly at a certain time; all you have to do is make sure there's a tape in the drive. You can write similar scripts for your weekly and monthly backups. *cron* is covered in the next section.

Scheduling Jobs Using cron

The original purpose of the computer was to automate routine tasks. If you must back up your disk at 1:00 A.M. every day, why should you have to enter the commands manually each time—particularly if it means getting out of bed? You should be able to tell the computer to do it and then forget about it. On Unix systems, *cron* exists to perform this automating function. Briefly, you use *cron* by running the *crontab* command and entering lines in a special format recognized by *cron*. Each line specifies a command to run and when to run it.

Behind your back, *crontab* saves your commands in a file bearing your username in the */var/spool/cron/crontabs* directory. (For instance, the *crontab* file for user mdw would be called */var/spool/cron/crontabs/mdw*.) A daemon called *crond* reads this file regularly and executes the commands at the proper times. One of the *rc* files on your system starts up *crond* when the system boots. There actually is no command named *cron*, only the *crontab* utility and the *crond* daemon.

On some systems, use of *cron* is limited to the root user. In any case, let's look at a useful command you might want to run as root and show how you'd specify it as a *crontab* entry. Suppose that every day you'd like to clean old files out of the */tmp* directory, which is supposed to serve as temporary storage for files created by lots of utilities.

Notice that *cron* never writes anything to the console. All output and error messages are sent as an email message to the user who owns the corresponding *crontab*. You can override this setting by specifying MAILTO=*address* in the *crontab* file before the jobs themselves.

Most systems remove the contents of */tmp* when the system reboots, but if you keep it up for a long time, you may find it useful to use *cron* to check for old files (say, files that haven't been accessed in the past three days). The command you want to enter is:

```
ls -l filename
```

But how do you know which *filename* to specify? You have to place the command inside a *find* command, which lists all files beneath a directory and performs the operation you specify on each one.

We've already seen the *find* command in the section "Incremental Backups." Here, we'll specify */tmp* as the directory to search, and use the *–atime* option to find files whose last access time is more than three days in the past. The *–exec* option means "execute the following command on every file we find":

```
find /tmp \! -type d -atime +3 -exec ls -l {} \;
```

The command we are asking *find* to execute is *ls –l*, which simply shows details about the files. (Many people use a similar *crontab* entry to remove files, but this is hard to do without leaving a security hole.) The funny string {} is just a way of saying "Do it to each file you find, according to the previous selection material." The string \; tells *find* that the *–exec* option is finished.

Now we have a command that looks for old files on */tmp*. We still have to say how often it runs. The format used by *crontab* consists of six fields:

```
minute   hour   day   month   dayofweek   command
```

Fill the fields as follows:

1. Minute (specify from 0 to 59)
2. Hour (specify from 0 to 23)
3. Day of the month (specify from 1 to 31)
4. Month (specify from 1 to 12, or a name such as jan, feb, and so on)
5. Day of the week (specify from 0 to 6 where 0 is Sunday, or a name such as mon, tue, and so on)
6. Command (can be multiple words)

Figure 8-1 shows a *cron* entry with all the fields filled in. The command is a shell script, run with the Bourne shell *sh*. But the entry is not too realistic: the script runs only when all the conditions in the first five fields are true. That is, it has to run on a Sunday that falls on the 15th day of either January or July—not a common occurrence! So this is not a particularly useful example.

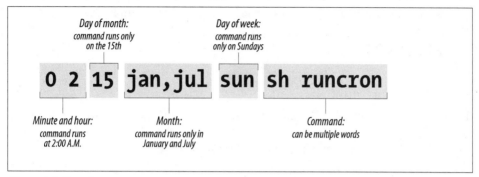

Figure 8-1. Sample cron entry

If you want a command to run every day at 1:00 A.M., specify the minute as 0 and the hour as 1. The other three fields should be asterisks, which mean "every day and month at the given time." The complete line in *crontab* is:

```
0 1 * * * find /tmp -atime 3 -exec ls -l {} \;
```

Because you can do a lot of fancy things with the time fields, let's play with this command a bit more. Suppose you want to run the command just on the first day of each month. You would keep the first two fields, but add a 1 in the third field:

```
0 1 1 * * find /tmp -atime 3 -exec ls -l {} \;
```

To do it once a week on Monday, restore the third field to an asterisk but specify either 1 or mon as the fifth field:

```
0 1 * * mon find /tmp -atime 3 -exec ls -l {} \;
```

To get even more sophisticated, there are ways to specify multiple times in each field. Here, a comma means "run on the 1st and 15th day" of each month:

```
0 1 1,15 * * find /tmp -atime 3 -exec ls -l {} \;
```

while a hyphen means "run every day from the 1st through the 15th, inclusive":

```
0 1 1-15 * * find /tmp -atime 3 -exec ls -l {} \;
```

and a slash followed by a 5 means "run every fifth day" which comes out to the 1st, 6th, 11th, and so on:

```
0 1 */5 * * find /tmp -atime 3 -exec ls -l {} \;
```

Now we're ready to actually put the entry in our *crontab* file. Become root (because this is the kind of thing root should do) and enter the *crontab* command with the *–e* option for "edit":

```
rutabaga# crontab -e
```

By default, this command starts a *vi* edit session. If you'd like to use Emacs instead, you can specify this before you start *crontab*. For a Bourne-compliant shell, enter the command:

```
rutabaga# export VISUAL=emacs
```

For the C shell:

```
rutabaga# setenv VISUAL emacs
```

The environment variable EDITOR also works in place of VISUAL for some versions of *crontab*. Enter a line or two beginning with hash marks (#) to serve as comments explaining what you're doing, then put in your *crontab* entry:

```
# List files on /tmp that are 3 or more days old.  Runs at 1:00 AM
# each morning.
0 1 * * * find /tmp -atime 3 -exec ls -l {} \;
```

When you exit *vi*, the commands are saved. Look at your *crontab* entry by entering:

```
rutabaga# crontab -l
```

We have not yet talked about a critical aspect of our *crontab* entry: where does the output go? By default, *cron* saves up the standard output and standard error and sends them to the user as a mail message. In this example, the mail goes to root, but that should automatically be directed to you as the system administrator. Make sure the following line appears in */usr/lib/aliases* (*/etc/aliases* on SuSE, Debian, and RedHat):

```
root: your-account-name
```

In a moment, we'll show what to do if you want output saved in a file instead of being mailed to you.

Here's another example of a common type of command used in *crontab* files. It performs a tape backup of a directory. We assume that someone has put a tape in the drive before the command runs. First, an *mt* command makes sure the tape in the */dev/qft0* device is rewound to the beginning. Then a *tar* command transfers all the files from the directory */src* to the tape. A semicolon is used to separate the commands; that is standard shell syntax:

```
# back up the /src directory once every two months.
0 2 1 */2 * mt -f /dev/qft0 rewind; tar cf /dev/qft0 /src
```

The first two fields ensure that the command runs at 2:00 A.M., and the third field specifies the first day of the month. The fourth field specifies every two months. We could achieve the same effect, in a possibly more readable manner, by entering:

```
0 2 1 jan,mar,may,jul,sep,nov * mt -f /dev/qft0 rewind; \
       tar cf /dev/qft0 /src
```

The aforementioned section "Making Backups" explains how to perform backups on a regular basis.

The following example uses *mailq* every two days to test whether any mail is stuck in the mail queue, and sends the mail administrator the results by mail. If mail is stuck in the mail queue, the report includes details about addressing and delivery problems, but otherwise the message is empty:

```
0 6 */2 * * mailq -v | \
        mail -s "Tested Mail Queue for Stuck Email" postmaster
```

Probably you don't want to receive a mail message every day when everything is going normally. In the examples we've used so far, the commands do not produce any output unless they encounter errors. But you may want to get into the habit of redirecting the standard output to */dev/null*, or sending it to a log file like this (note the use of two > signs so that we don't wipe out previous output):

```
0 1 * * * find /tmp -atime 3 -exec ls -l {} \; >> /home/mdw/log
```

In this entry, we redirect the standard output, but allow the standard error to be sent as a mail message. This can be a nice feature because we'll get a mail message if anything goes wrong. If you want to make sure you don't receive mail under any circumstances, redirect both the standard output and the standard error to a file:

```
0 1 * * * find /tmp -atime 3 -exec ls -l {} \; >> /home/mdw/log 2>&1
```

When you save output in a log file, you get the problem of a file that grows continuously. You may want another *cron* entry that runs once a week or so, just to remove the file.

Only Bourne shell commands can be used in *crontab* entries. That means you can't use any of the convenient extensions recognized by *bash* and other modern shells, such as aliases or the use of ~ to mean "my home directory." You can use $HOME, however; *cron* recognizes the $USER, $HOME, and $SHELL environment variables. Each command runs with your home directory as its current directory.

Some people like to specify absolute pathnames for commands, like */usr/bin/find* and */bin/rm*, in *crontab* entries. This ensures that the right command is always found, instead of relying on the path being set correctly.

If a command gets too long and complicated to put on a single line, write a shell script and invoke it from *cron*. Make sure the script is executable (use *chmod +x*) or execute it by using a shell, such as:

```
0 1 * * * sh runcron
```

As a system administrator, you often have to create *crontab* files for dummy users, such as news or UUCP. Running all utilities as root would be overkill and possibly dangerous, so these special users exist instead.

The choice of a user also affects file ownership: a *crontab* file for news should run files owned by news, and so on. In general, make sure utilities are owned by the user in whose name you create the *crontab* file.

As root, you can edit other users' *crontab* files by using the *–u* option. For example:

```
tigger # crontab -u news -e
```

This is useful because you can't log in as user news, but you still might want to edit this user's *crontab* entry.

Managing System Logs

The *syslogd* utility logs various kinds of system activity, such as debugging output from *sendmail* and warnings printed by the kernel. *syslogd* runs as a daemon and is usually started in one of the *rc* files at boot time.

The file */etc/syslog.conf* is used to control where *syslogd* records information. Such a file might look like the following (even though they tend to be much more complicated on most systems):

```
*.info;*.notice     /var/log/messages
mail.debug          /var/log/maillog
*.warn              /var/log/syslog
kern.emerg          /dev/console
```

The first field of each line lists the kinds of messages that should be logged, and the second field lists the location where they should be logged. The first field is of the format:

```
facility.level [; facility.level … ]
```

where *facility* is the system application or facility generating the message, and *level* is the severity of the message.

For example, *facility* can be mail (for the mail daemon), kern (for the kernel), user (for user programs), or auth (for authentication programs such as *login* or *su*). An asterisk in this field specifies all facilities.

level can be (in increasing severity): debug, info, notice, warning, err, crit, alert, or emerg.

In the previous */etc/syslog.conf*, we see that all messages of severity info and notice are logged to */var/log/messages*, all debug messages from the mail daemon are logged to */var/log/maillog*, and all warn messages are logged to */var/log/syslog*. Also, any emerg warnings from the kernel are sent to the console (which is the current virtual console, or an *xterm* started with the *–C* option).

The messages logged by *syslogd* usually include the date, an indication of what process or facility delivered the message, and the message itself—all on one line. For example, a kernel error message indicating a problem with data on an *ext2fs* filesystem might appear in the log files, as in:

```
Dec  1 21:03:35 loomer kernel: EXT2-fs error (device 3/2):
  ext2_check_blocks_bit map: Wrong free blocks count in super block,
  stored = 27202, counted = 27853
```

Similarly, if an *su* to the root account succeeds, you might see a log message, such as:

```
Dec 11 15:31:51 loomer su: mdw on /dev/ttyp3
```

Log files can be important in tracking down system problems. If a log file grows too large, you can empty it using *cat /dev/null > logfile*. This clears out the file, but leaves it there for the logging system to write to.

Your system probably comes equipped with a running *syslogd* and an */etc/syslog.conf* that does the right thing. However, it's important to know where your log files are and what programs they represent. If you need to log many messages (say, debugging messages from the kernel, which can be very verbose) you can edit *syslog.conf* and tell *syslogd* to reread its configuration file with the command:

```
kill -HUP `cat /var/run/syslog.pid`
```

Note the use of backquotes to obtain the process ID of *syslogd*, contained in */var/run/syslog.pid*.

Other system logs might be available as well. These include:

/var/log/wtmp

This file contains binary data indicating the login times and duration for each user on the system; it is used by the *last* command to generate a listing of user logins. The output of *last* might look like:

```
mdw       tty3            Sun Dec 11 15:25   still logged in
mdw       tty3            Sun Dec 11 15:24 - 15:25  (00:00)
mdw       tty1            Sun Dec 11 11:46   still logged in
reboot    ~               Sun Dec 11 06:46
```

A record is also logged in */var/log/wtmp* when the system is rebooted.

/var/run/utmp

This is another binary file that contains information on users currently logged into the system. Commands such as *who*, *w*, and *finger* use this file to produce information on who is logged in. For example, the *w* command might print:

```
   3:58pm  up  4:12,  5 users,  load average: 0.01, 0.02, 0.00
User     tty        login@ idle   JCPU   PCPU  what
mdw      ttyp3      11:46am  14                 -
mdw      ttyp2      11:46am          1          w
mdw      ttyp4      11:46am                     kermit
mdw      ttyp0      11:46am  14                 bash
```

We see the login times for each user (in this case, one user logged in many times), as well as the command currently being used. The *w*(1) manual page describes all the fields displayed.

/var/log/lastlog

> This file is similar to *wtmp* but is used by different programs (such as *finger* to determine when a user was last logged in).

Note that the format of the *wtmp* and *utmp* files differs from system to system. Some programs may be compiled to expect one format and others another format. For this reason, commands that use the files may produce confusing or inaccurate information—especially if the files become corrupted by a program that writes information to them in the wrong format.

Log files can get quite large, and if you do not have the necessary hard-disk space, you have to do something about your partitions being filled too fast. Of course, you can delete the log files from time to time, but you may not want to do this, because the log files also contain information that can be valuable in crisis situations.

One option is to copy the log files from time to time to another file and compress this file. The log file itself starts at 0 again. Here is a short shell script that does this for the log file */var/log/messages*:

```
mv /var/log/messages /var/log/messages-backup
cp /dev/null /var/log/messages

CURDATE=`date +"%m%d%y"`

mv /var/log/messages-backup /var/log/messages-$CURDATE
gzip /var/log/messages-$CURDATE
```

First, we move the log file to a different name and then truncate the original file to 0 bytes by copying to it from */dev/null*. We do this so that further logging can be done without problems while the next steps are done. Then, we compute a date string for the current date that is used as a suffix for the filename, rename the backup file, and finally compress it with *gzip*.

You might want to run this small script from *cron*, but as it is presented here, it should not be run more than once a day—otherwise the compressed backup copy will be overwritten because the filename reflects the date but not the time of day (of course, you could change the date format string to include the time). If you want to run this script more often, you must use additional numbers to distinguish between the various copies.

You could make many more improvements here. For example, you might want to check the size of the log file first and copy and compress it only if this size exceeds a certain limit.

Even though this is already an improvement, your partition containing the log files will eventually get filled. You can solve this problem by keeping around only a certain number of compressed log files (say, 10). When you have created as many log files as you want to have, you delete the oldest, and overwrite it with the next one to be copied. This principle is also called *log rotation*. Some distributions have scripts like *savelog* or *logrotate* that can do this automatically.

To finish this discussion, it should be noted that most recent distributions, such as SuSE, Debian, and Red Hat, already have built-in *cron* scripts that manage your log files and are much more sophisticated than the small one presented here.

Managing Print Services

Linux has a fairly complicated printing system, compared to the printing services most PCs use. It allows many users to print documents at the same time, and each user can send documents from one or more applications without waiting for the previous document to finish printing. The printing system processes the files to be printed correctly on different kinds of printers connected to the computer in different ways. If you print on a network, files can be created on one host and printed out on a printer controlled by another host.

Before we go into the inner workings of the Linux printing system, we would like to point you to *www.linuxprinting.org*, a very comprehensive site with information about printing on Linux. If you have problems or questions concerning printing that this chapter cannot answer, this site should be your next stop.

The whole process happens without much fuss, when you press the Print button in an application or issue a command, such as *lpr*, to print a document. That document does not go directly to the printer, though, because it might already be busy. Instead, the document is stored in a temporary file in a directory called the printer spool directory. As the word "spool" suggests, the documents get taken out of the directory one by one as the printer becomes free. Each printer has its own spool directory.

When Linux starts, it sets up a printer daemon (an independently running process) called *lpd*. This process waits around, checking each spool directory for files that should be printed. When the process finds a file, it makes a copy of itself. The new *lpd* takes control of the print spool where the file was placed and queues it for printing. It won't send the next file to that printer until the last file has finished printing. The master *lpd* starts an *lpd* for each spooling directory on the system when a file is sent to it, so there may be as many *lpd* daemons running as the number of active spooling directories, plus the master *lpd*. Each subordinate *lpd* stays around until its spool directory is empty.

Your Linux installation process associates the printer port on your system to a device named in the */dev* directory. You must then link that device name to the convenient printer names you use in your commands; that's the role of the printer capability file called */etc/printcap*.

Another key task in printer management is to make sure you have filters in place for *lpd* to use when formatting documents for printing. These filters are also specified in the */etc/printcap* file, and we'll talk a lot about them in this section.

There are several printer-support packages for Linux. Most distributions use the BSD-derived package that contains the *lpd* printer daemon. These packages include a set of utilities and manpage documents to support traditional Unix-style printing on Linux. The BSD printing system doesn't have as many administrative tools or user controls as, for example, the System V Unix printer-management system (which uses the *lpsched* or *lprng* daemon), but each user controls the files that she sends to the printer. This section describes installation and configuration of the BSD printer-support package. (The various printing utilities are described in the section "Printing" in Chapter 9.)

There is a new system called Common Unix Printer System (CUPS) that is bound to take over the Linux (if not Unix) printing world. At this point, very few distributions come with CUPS preinstalled—the BSD printing system is still ubiquitous—which is why we concentrate on the older system here. We'll look at CUPS in brief later in this chapter, though.

Some Linux distributions provide a printer-management tool that simplifies printer installation and management through a GUI. These tools are documented by the vendor that supplies them. They manage printing by controlling the same tools and files we are about to describe, but with less fine control. They can save you a lot of trouble getting started, but they don't always get things right. If you want to correct an installation set up through these tools or want to improve on their performance, you still should work through the procedures in this section.

Checking Printer Hardware

Before you set up printer services, be sure the printing devices are online. If you also use another operating system, such as Microsoft Windows, you can exercise the hardware to ensure that it is connected properly and working before loading Linux. Successfully printing a document from another operating system immediately eliminates one major source of woe and head scratching. Similarly, if you are going to use printer services on a network, your system should be on the network and all protocols functioning before proceeding.

A word about the so-called GDI printers (or Windows printers) is in order here. GDI printers are really brain-damaged printers in the true sense of the meaning: their "brain," the internal processing unit that builds up a page from the data sent to it, has been removed; this task is performed in the printer driver on the computer itself. The printer itself only consists of the actual printing hardware and a very small amount of software that controls the hardware. Of course, drivers for these printers are typically available only for Microsoft Windows systems (where the graphics subsystem is called GDI, which is where the name comes from), so there is hardly any hope of getting such a printer to work with Linux.

Install printer services as the root user, with superuser privileges. The superuser is the only user besides the *lpd* print daemon able to write directly to a printer by directing output to the corresponding output device. Other users cannot send output directly to the printer and must instead use the printer utilities to handle printing tasks.

Before you get started, you can abuse your root privileges to verify that your system's assigned device files actually have a valid link to the physical device. Just send a brief ASCII test file directly to the printer by redirection. For instance, if you have a printer on your first parallel port, its device name is probably either */dev/lp0* or */dev/lp1*, depending on your installation. The following command outputs some text suited for testing a printer setup, which you can redirect to your printer. (If you have an early PostScript printer, you may need instead to send it a small PostScript test file to prevent it from getting confused. Newer PostScript printers can often perform this conversion themselves.)

```
lptest > /dev/lp1
```

The *lptest* utility (which may not be available on all distributions) is designed to conveniently exercise an ASCII printer or terminal to make sure it is working correctly. It sends a prepend file composed of the 96 ASCII characters in a sequence that creates a "ripple" or "barber-pole" output effect. The default output of *lptest* on Linux is 16,000 characters arrayed in 79-character lines, long enough to require more than one page to print. If you run *lptest* with no arguments, it prints the standard output to your screen, and you can see what should be sent to the printer. The *lptest* command allows you to trim the width of the output column and to limit the number of output lines. For example, to display an output 35 characters wide, limited to six lines, you would enter:

```
lptest 35 6
```

The output should look much like this:

```
!"#$%&'()*+,-./0123456789:;<=>?@ABC
"#$%&'()*+,-./0123456789:;<=>?@ABCD
#$%&'()*+,-./0123456789:;<=>?@ABCDE
$%&'()*+,-./0123456789:;<=>?@ABCDEF
%&'()*+,-./0123456789:;<=>?@ABCDEFG
&'()*+,-./0123456789:;<=>?@ABCDEFGH
```

This output is short enough that you can see the result of redirecting it to your printer without wasting a lot of paper, and it is long enough to identify many obvious problems with printing.

Of course, you can also use the *cat* command to direct a file to the printer. To send a PostScript test file to a PostScript printer, for example, type:

```
cat testfile.ps > /dev/lp1
```

If you have a serial printer, try directing output to the serial port to which it is connected. For the first serial port (COM1 in MS-DOS) try something like:

```
lptest > /dev/ttys0
```

or:

```
lptest > /dev/ttyS0
```

Make sure you send to the correct serial port; don't try to output the file to a serial mouse, for example. If your serial printer is on, say, the second serial port, it is addressed as */dev/ttyS1* or */dev/ttys1*.

If you have a page printer that buffers a partial page, after it stops printing you may need to take the printer offline and press the Form Feed button to get it to print the last partial page. Don't forget to put the printer back online afterward. (A permanent solution is to get Linux to send the formfeed character to the printer, either by forcing it through the */etc/printcap* entry for the printer or by having the printer filter-append it to the end of the file. We'll discuss these options later.)

If your little test resulted in "laddered" text (text that looks something like the following example) and then continued off the page, the printer did not insert a carriage return at the end of each line:

```
!"#$%&'()*+,-./0123456789:;<=>?@ABC
                                   "#$%&'()*+,-./0123456789:;<=>?@ABCD
                                                                      #$
```

You might be able to figure out what went wrong here. Text files in Unix use just a newline (also known as a linefeed, ASCII code 10) to terminate each line. MS-DOS uses both a newline and a carriage return. Your printer was therefore set up to use MS-DOS–style line endings with both newline and carriage-return characters at the end of each line. In order to print a text file from Unix, you can install a printer filter to accommodate the Unix newline, or you can reconfigure your printer to properly return to the start of the line on receipt of a newline character. Often this is simply a matter of setting a dip switch. Check your printer manual. (Be careful about changing your printer characteristics if you use multiple operating systems.)

Laddering won't be an issue if you have a printer using a page-description language, such as PostScript (the universally used page-layout language from Adobe), and you always filter plain text into that output form before printing. Filtering is described later in this chapter.

Gathering Resources

OK, you have your printer hardware set up and connected. You should collect a hardcopy of your resource documents (at least the manpages for the print utilities and files described here, and the Printing HOWTO file). Also, it is useful to have the technical specifications for your printer. Often these are no longer provided when you buy your printer, but you can usually download the information you need from an FTP site or a web site operated by the printer manufacturer. While you are retrieving such information, look around and see if there is documentation (such as a description of printer error messages and their meanings) that can help you trouble-shoot and manage your printer. Most printer manufacturers also offer a technical manual for the printer that you can buy. This may or may not be the same volume as the service manual.

For example, on the Hewlett-Packard web site, *http://www.hp.com/cposupport/software.html*, you can retrieve printer technical data sheets; product specs; port-configuration information; PostScript, PCL, and HP-GL files for testing your printers (and filters); descriptions of printer control sequences you can pass to the printer to control its behavior; and documents telling how you can integrate *lpd*-based printing services with HP's JetAdmin package (and thereby with Netware-networked printers as well).

Now, before starting, take a deep breath; be patient with yourself. Printer services configuration is a skill that takes time to develop. If you have sufficiently standard equipment and successfully use one of the new-fangled printer management utilities to quickly and efficiently install and configure printer services, celebrate! Then note that you can probably fine-tune the installation for better performance by applying the procedures we describe next, and perhaps by using filters and utilities written specifically to support all the features of your printer model. If you decide to revise a successful printer installation, make sure you take notes on the changes you make so that you can find your way back if your changes don't do what you expected.

Choosing Printer Software

In order to print from Linux, you need to install the BSD print system (or an alternative system). This provides basic tools, but it does not support modern printers. Indeed, it was designed to support line printers (hence the name "line printing daemon") and devices common to the computer rooms of the 1960s and 1970s. In order to support modern printers, powerful supplemental packages provide the features most users think of as essential. (The *ftp://ftp.ibiblio.org* FTP site and its mirrors archive the packages we mention here.)

In this section, we discuss some important packages to support modern print services. We assume your system will have at least the *groff* formatter, the Ghostscript page-formatting package, and the *GNU Enscript* filter packages, which are described in Chapter 9. Most Linux distributions already include these as well as other formatting and printing utilities. If yours does not, you can retrieve them from the usual Linux FTP sites or take them from the CD-ROM of another distribution.

It matters where you get formatting and filtering packages. If you receive Ghostscript from a European distribution, for example, it probably defaults to an A4 paper format rather than the 8.5x11-inch paper format kept in U.S. binary archives. In either case, you can easily override the default through an *lpr* option passed to the filter. Alternatively, you can build the tools from source.

The trend in printer technology is away from character-oriented output and toward adoption of a page-description language (PDL) that provides sophisticated graphics and font control. By far the most popular of the PDLs is PostScript, which has been widely adopted in the Unix and Internet communities. A major reason for its acceptance is Ghostscript, a PostScript implementation copyrighted by Aladdin Enterprises. A version is also distributed under the GNU Public License through the Free Software Foundation, along with a large font library that can be used with either version and with other PostScript interpreters. Ghostscript is indispensable if you do any kind of printing besides character-based output, and it is easily extensible.

Ghostscript implements almost all the instructions of the PostScript language and supports viewer utilities, such as Ghostview, that allow PostScript documents to be displayed in an X window. Similarly, excellent filters are readily available that convert PostScript output into other printing languages, such as Hewlett-Packard's PCL, and into forms printable as raster output on inkjet, dot matrix, and laser printers. The Ghostscript package supports Adobe Type 1 and 3 PostScript fonts and provides a number of utilities for graphics format conversion and filtering. It can even generate PDF files—i.e., files that conform to the Adobe Portable Document Format specification.

Ghostscript may be insufficient to use by itself, however, because it doesn't provide printer control to switch between PostScript and text modes. Although Ghostscript does provide a filter that provides this capability (and more), the *nenscript* filter meets the tests of simplicity, flexibility, and reliability for most systems, so we document it here.

A typical Linux formatting and printing system might primarily use *groff* to format documents, creating PostScript output that is then processed by Ghostscript for printing and display.

Checking Print Utilities

You probably also want to install the TeX formatting package. Even if you do not install the full TeX distribution, you should at least install the *xdvi* utility, in order to view TeX output and (processed) Texinfo files in an X window (unless you have installed the KDE Desktop Environment, which contains a more user-friendly replacement called *kdvi*). Other filters can process device independent (DVI) output into forms such as PostScript (*dvips*) or PCL (*dvilj*) if you have an aversion to the Ghostscript package or need to use native printer fonts for efficient data transfer and rapid printing.

The Lout package is also worthy of consideration as an efficient and compact package to format text documents for PostScript output. It supports Level 2 PostScript and the Adobe Structuring Conventions, takes comparatively little memory, and comes with good enough documentation to learn quickly. Lout doesn't create an intermediate output form; it goes directly from markup input to PostScript output.

To support graphics work and X Window System utilities, you probably want to install other tools, some of which probably come with your distribution. A collection of current versions of the most popular print support packages for Linux can be found at the *ftp://ftp.ibiblio.org* Linux archive, in */pub/Linux/system/printing*. The *netpbm* and *pbmplus* packages support a large variety of graphics file format conversions. (Such formats have to be converted to PostScript before you try to print them.) The Ghostview package provides display tools to view PostScript files in an X Window System environment, and also provides PostScript and PDF support for other packages, such as your web browser.

The ImageMagick package, described in Chapter 9, deserves special mention. It lets you display a large number of graphics formats in an X window and convert many file formats to other file formats. (It uses Ghostview and Ghostscript when it needs to display a PostScript image.) Most of the graphics files you can print you can also display using ImageMagick.

A "magic" filter package may also save you much grief in configuring and supporting different document output formats. We will touch on the APSfilter magic filter package, but you may prefer the Magic-Filter package instead. Both are available at the *ftp://ftp.ibiblio.org* FTP archive. For more on magic filters, see the section "Magic Filters: APSfilter and Alternatives" later in this chapter.

If you want to support fax devices, you can use the *tiffg3* utility with Ghostscript to output Group III fax format files. To control a Class 1 or Class 2 fax modem on your Linux host, you can use the efax package, which is provided in many distributions, or you can install and configure the more capable, but more complex, FlexFax or HylaFax packages.

There are additional tools to support double-sided printing on laser printers, and packages that convert PostScript to less common printer-control languages to support Canon and IBM Proprinter devices, for example. There is a package to support printing in Chinese on laser printers and bitmap devices. Most of these packages don't directly affect management of print services, so we don't describe them in detail here, but this is a good time to install them if you wish to use them.

For the benefit of your users, make sure that all the manual pages for the packages you install are prepared properly when you complete your installations. Then run */sbin/mkwhatis* (*/usr/bin/mandb* on Debian) to build the manual page index file that facilitates locating information online. Some packages, such as Ghostscript, also provide additional documenetion that you can print or make available on the system for reference. (Linux distributions tend to omit these documents, but you can FTP them from the sites where the software packages are developed and maintained. The GNU archives of the Free Software Foundation, for example, are accessed by anonymous FTP at *ftp://GNU.ai.mit.edu*.)

Setting Up the Printcap File

The essence of printer configuration is creating correct entries in the printer capabilities file, */etc/printcap*. A simple printcap entry for an HP LaserJet 4MP laser printer attached to the first (bidirectional) parallel port on an ISA bus PC might look something like this:*

```
ljet|lp|ps|PostScript|600dpi 20MB memory|local|LPT1:\
    :lp=/dev/lp0:rw:\
    :sd=/var/spool/lpd/ljet4:mx#0:mc#0:pl#72:pw#85:\
    :lf=/var/log/lpd-errs:if=/usr/local/cap/ljet4:
```

Don't be scared. After reading the following sections, you will find yourself browsing printcap files with ease.

The */etc/printcap* file should accommodate every printer and printer port or address—serial, parallel, SCSI, USB, or networked—your system will use. Make sure it reflects any change in hardware. And as always, be aware that some hardware changes should be performed only when power to your system is shut off.

Printcap file format rules

The printcap file format rules, briefly, are:

- A comment line begins with a pound sign (#).
- Each "line" of the printcap file defines a printer. A line that ends with a backslash character (\) is continued on the next line. Be very careful that no space or tab character follows the backslash character on the line. Traditionally, a continuation line is indented for readability. Multiple printer definitions can use the same actual printer, applying the same or different filters.
- Fields in the line are separated by colon characters (:); fields can be empty. However, a printcap line entry cannot be an empty field.
- Traditionally, the first field in the entry has no preceding colon.
- The first field of the entry line contains names for the printer, each separated by a vertical bar character (|). In the earlier example entry, this portion is the name field:

```
ljet|lp|ps|PostScript|600dpi 20MB memory|local|LPT1
```

---

* In this chapter, we use ljet4 in several examples. Be aware that the HP LaserJet 4 model is available in several versions. Some LaserJet 4 models are PCL5 printers only, and others use PostScript. Unless you are aware that different types exist, you can find it very frustrating trying to debug a printer filter that is expecting, for example, PostScript, when Ghostscript is passing it PCL5 input.

Printer naming is discussed in detail in the next section. You should create a subdirectory of */var/spool/lpd* with the same name as the first printer ID listed in each printcap entry. However, the actual print spool that is used is assigned by the sd variable for the printcap entry; if the sd variable doesn't point to the actual print spool directory, any file sent to that printer definition will vanish.

- There must be at least a default printer entry in printcap. If a printer is named lp, that printer is used as the default system printer. Do not confuse the lp default printer name with the lp local printer variable, which is described next. We recommend you use lp as an alias (one of the names after the | characters) rather than the primary printer name (the first in the list), so you can switch the default printer without difficulty.

- Each local printer must have an lp variable set. In the previous example, the variable was set by this segment of the printcap entry:

    ```
    lp=/dev/lp0
    ```

- For compulsive and sometimes practical reasons, some administrators recommend that the entries of the printcap file be kept in alphabetical order.

Printer names

Most printer entries traditionally begin with a short printer name entry in the first field, at least one fuller printer name, and one longer explanatory entry. Thus, both ljet and PostScript are names for the printer whose nameline is:

```
ljet|lp|ps|PostScript|600dpi 20MB memory|local|LPT1:
```

Documents can be output to any printer named in a nameline in */etc/printcap*.

You might name your printers after the model (HP, Epson), or the type of printer (PS, PCL), or its specific modes. The DeskJet 540, for example, is a printer that should have two definitions in the printcap file, one for black print and another for color. The filters you use to support it are likely to be those for the DeskJet 500 or 550C. For simple administration, you can assign printer names that are the names of a filter or filter parameter used for a specific device. Thus, if you have one LaserJet 4 and will use the ljet4 filter only for it, ljet4 is one logical name for the printer. Similarly, a dot-matrix printer might be named 72dpi when accessed via its low-resolution printer definition line, and have the name 144dpi when accessed in a higher resolution.

If you use a printer administration utility that comes with your Linux distribution, you may have to follow certain arbitrary rules in preparing your printcap entries in order to get the tools working. For example, if you use Red Hat's printer manager utility provided on the administrator's desktop, you may need to make sure that hp is the first name of the first active printer entry in the printcap file. This means that when you need to switch default printers, you need to move the new default printer to the top entry of the list and then remove the hp name from the old default printer and prepare it as the first name of the new default printer. In order to prevent confusion in use of the spool queues, you should just leave the */var/spool/lpd/lp* directory set up and create a new directory with the actual name of the spool directory that corresponds to the name by which you actually will address the printer. Thus, if you want to send your files to print on a printer named moa, you will need to create a directory named */var/spool/lpd/moa*, with appropriate permissions, and specify that directory as the printer spool for that printer. Setting up printer directories is described in the next section.

The rest of the printcap variables

The printcap file provides a number of variables that you can define. Most variables are provided to specify page parameters, files and directories, filters, communications channel settings, and remote access control. Anytime you prepare a printcap file on a new system, read the printcap manual page to make sure you use the correct variable names. Variables set in a printcap entry that are not recognized are passed through to the filter for processing.

The printcap variables described here are listed in roughly their order of importance. Some variables are boolean, and are considered set if they are present. Others are set with the assignment operator (=) or numeric value operator (#) and a value; the variable precedes the operator and the string or number follows the operator. Examples of the variables described in the following list are included in the contrived sample */etc/printcap* file that follows. The printcap manual page has a more complete listing of variables recognized by *lpd*.

sd

> Specifies the spool directory used by the printer. Spool directories should all be in the same directory tree (on a fast hard disk), which is usually */var/spool*. Spool files are defined even for remote printers. Each spool file should have one of the names assigned to the printer it serves.

lp

> Assigns a local printer device, typically connected through a parallel port, serial port, or SCSI interface. The lp variable must be assigned to a device file in the */dev* directory, which may be a link to a physical device. The lp variable must be assigned if there is a local printer. This variable should not be assigned if the rp variable is assigned (that is, the print spool manager is on another host).* If lp assigns a serial device, the baud rate must be specified with the br variable.

---

* A special case arises where the printer to be addressed is a true networked printer (that is, it has its own IP address). In that instance, the lp variable assigns the name of a dummy file that is used for setting a temporary lock on the file when the networked printer is in use. The documentation for the networked printer should describe the procedure for setting up and managing print services to access it.

lf

Specifies the log file for storing error messages. All printers should have this variable set and normally use the same error log file. Error entries include the name of the printer and can reveal problems with the user's printer environment, the host configuration, the communications channel that is used, and sometimes the printer hardware itself.

rw

This variable should be specified if the printer is able to send data back to the host through the specified device file. The rw variable tells *lpd* that the device should be opened for both reading and writing. This can be useful for serial or SCSI PostScript printers, for example, because they may return fairly useful error messages to *lpd*, which stores them in the error log.

mx

Specifies the maximum size of a print job in the spool. A value of zero sets no limit (the default, mx#0), and any other value sets the maximum file size in blocks. Most of the time you don't want to set a limit, but you could, for example, set a value slightly smaller than the expected minimum space available on a disk.

if

Specifies an input filter to use. If you do not specify an input (if) or output (of) filter, the system uses the default */usr/sbin/lpf* filter. For some MS-DOS–style character printers, this is sufficient. Other useful filters are provided in the formatting utilities, and there are some flexible "magic filter" packages that will determine (usually correctly) the filtering to apply from the content of the data file passed to it. See the section "Print Filters" that follows.

of

Specifies an output filter to use. When you assign the of variable and don't assign the if variable, the system uses the filter once when the device is opened. All queued jobs are then sent until the queue is exhausted (and *lpd* removes the lock file from the spool directory). This is not normally useful, but it could serve such purposes as sending faxes to a fax modem for dialed connection over a telephone line.

When you assign both the if and of variables, the if-specified filter normally processes the file, but the of-specified filter prints a banner page before the input filter is applied. Using both input and output filters effectively on the same print queue is notoriously difficult.

br

Specifies the data-transfer rate (baud rate) for a serial port. You must supply this value if the printer is accessed via serial port. A pound sign precedes a numeric value that expresses the data-transfer rate in bits per second (not truly the baud rate, which is an effective rate of flow as opposed to the maximum rate of flow).

The specified rate should not exceed any hardware limits. For example, if your serial port is capable of a 57.6 Kbps rate and the printer can process 28.8 Kbps, the assigned rate should not exceed that lower limit (perhaps br#19200). Supported bps values are the usual multiples for serial communications: 300, 600, 1200, 2400, 4800, 9600, and so on. A number of additional data conditioning values may be set if you do assign a br value, but most of them aren't useful for typical Linux installations. The default behavior is probably acceptable for your printing purposes, but if you intend to print via serial port, study the br, fc, fs, xc, and xs variables in the printcap manual page.

pl

Specifies the page length as the number of lines using the default font characters for character devices (and printers that can use a character mode). An example is pl#66 for an 11-inch page at six lines per inch. This value allows space for cropping and accommodates the limits of some other devices, such as inkjet printers that cannot print to the bottom of the sheet or the edge of the paper. Normally used in conjunction with the pw variable.

pw

Specifies the width of the page supported, in characters, using the default font characters for character devices. pw is set like the pl variable; for example, pw#85 for 10 characters per inch with an 8.5-inch printable page width.

px

Specifies the number of pixels to use on the X axis for a bitmap image file sent to a raster device.

py

Specifies the number of pixels to use on the Y axis for a bitmap image file sent to a raster device.

sh

Suppresses printing of a header or banner page. In most cases, you should set this.

rp

Specifies the name of a remote printer to use. This variable cannot be set if the lp variable is set for the same printer. The printer handling is performed by the remote host assigned in the rm variable, which is required when rp is set. Usually, the only variables set along with these are spooling and error recording. See the example that follows.

rm

Specifies a remote host that controls the remote printer to which you print. The specified host ID assigned by rm should be one that is known to the network services as installed (set up in */etc/hosts* or known through NIS, for example).

rs

Restricts access to local printers to those users with an account on the system.

rg

Specifies a restricted group that can use the printer. For example, to reserve a defined printer for superuser, enter rg=root.

sf

Suppresses the formfeed sent to the printer by default at the end of a print file.

ff

Assigns the formfeed character or string the device should use. The default is Ctrl-L (equivalent to ff='\f'), which is usual for most devices.

fo

Sends a formfeed character to the device before sending the file.

mc

Specifies the maximum number of copies you can print. Values are the same as for the mx variable; usually you want to allow unlimited copies (mc#0), which is the default.

sc

Suppresses multiple copies (equivalent to mc#1).

Example 8-1 contains a sample printcap file that shows off many of the variables discussed in the previous list. It contains an entry for a remote printer; printing to the printer named *hp* (also the default, as it is the first entry) sends the documents to the host spigot.berk.ora.com, where they are printed on the printer queue *lp*.

Example 8-1. Sample /etc/printcap file

```
# Fare well, sweet prints.
hp|bat|west|spigot|berkeley|TI MicroLaser Turbo:\
     :mx#0:rp=lp:\
     :lp=:sd=/var/spool/lpd:rm=spigot.berk.ora.com:\
     :lf=/var/log/lpd-errs:
# To the print room
kiwi|810|rint|Big Apple|Apple 810 via EtherTalk:\
     :lp=/var/spool/lpd/kiwi:sh:\
     :sd=/var/spool/lpd/kiwi:pl#72:pw#85:mx#0:\
     :lf=/var/log/lpd-errs:if=/usr/local/cap/kiwi:


# big bird--agapornis via shielded serial access
samoa|S|PostScript|secure|QMS 1725 by serial adapter:\
     :lp=dev/tty01:br#38400:rw:xc#0:xs#0400040:sh:\
     :sd=/var/spool/lpd/samoa:pl#72:pw#85:mx#0:mc#0:\
     :lf=/var/log/lpd-errs:if=/usr/local/cap/samoa:
# agapornis via printer room subnet (standard access)
moa|ps|QMS 1725 via Ethernet:\
     :lp=/var/spool/lpd/moa/moa:rm=agapornis:rp=samoa:\
     :sd=/var/spool/lpd/moa:mx#0:sh:\
     :lf=/var/log/lpd-errs:if=/usr/local/cap/samoa:
```

Configuring Ghostscript

Ghostscript is included in standard Linux packages; it is an essential utility in an X Window System environment and is useful even if you don't run X. Ghostscript can provide graphics output to a standard VGA display even where no window manager is running and can also process and create PostScript-formatted files without a graphics display. You can examine what devices Ghostscript is configured to recognize and format for on your system by entering Ghostscript in interactive mode. If you enter:

```
$ gs
```

Ghostscript should load in interactive mode and await your instructions:

```
GS>
```

You can then query the devices that Ghostscript is configured to recognize, and Ghostscript will display them:

```
GS> devicenames ==
[/lips3 /ljet3d /djet500 /cdj970 /st800 /iwlo /x11alpha /la75plus
/bjc800 /ljet2p /djet820c /cdj880 /lp8000 /appledmp /la70 /bj200 /stp
/DJ9xxVIP /cdj670 /eps9high /vgalib /dl2100 /lp2563 /pjxl300 /DJ8xx
/cdj500 /epson /x11mono /lex2050 /lj5gray /pjetxl /DJ6xx /cdjcolor
/tek4696 /x11gray2 /lex5700 /ljetplus /paintjet /hpijs /uniprint
/t4693d4 /x11cmyk4 /lxm5700m /ljet4 /djet500c /cdj1600 /stcolor
/iwlq /x11cmyk /ln03 /lbp8 /ljet3 /deskjet /cdj890 /lq850 /iwhi /x11
/la75 /bjc600 /laserjet /AP21xx /cdj850 /epsonc /sxlcrt /la50 /bj10e
/hpdj /DJ9xx /cdj550 /eps9mid /lvga256 /declj250 /cljet5 /pjxl /DJ6xxP
/cdjmono /ap3250 /x11gray4 /lex3200 /lj5mono /pj /DJ630 /cdeskjet
/t4693d8 /x11cmyk8 /lex7000 /lj4dith /dnj650c /chp2200 /hl7x0 /t4693d2
/x11cmyk2 /lj250 /jpeggray /png256 /mgrgray4 /tiffg4 /ppmraw /okiibm
/cif /pnggray /mgrmono /tiffg3 /pnmraw /oki182 /nullpage /cgm8
/pcxcmyk /bitrgb /faxg4 /pgnmraw /necp6 /pxlmono /bmp16m /pcx256
/psrgb /faxg3 /pgmraw /jetp3852 /pswrite /bmp16 /pcxgray /psmono
/dfaxhigh /pbmraw /ibmpro /pdfwrite /bmpmono /mgr8 /tifflzw /plan9bm
/xes /ccr /miff24 /png16m /mgrgray8 /tiff12nc /pkm /r4081 /jpeg /png16
/mgrgray2 /tiffg32d /ppm /oki4w /cgm24 /pngmono /bitcmyk /tiffcrle
/pnm /oce9050 /pxlcolor /cgmmono /pcx24b /bit /faxg32d /pgnm /m8510
/epswrite /bmp256 /pcx16 /psgray /dfaxlow /pgm /imagen /bbox /bmpamono
/pcxmono /tiffpack /inferno /pbm /cp50 /omni /sgirgb /mgr4 /tiff24nc
/pkmraw /sj48]
GS> quit
$
```

If you are not using X, and Ghostscript fails to initialize when you try to invoke it, complaining that it cannot open an X display, the first device Ghostscript loaded in its build file was the X Window System device; Ghostscript uses the first device as its default device. You can work around this problem by specifying some other device that Ghostscript will have installed—for example, gs -sDEVICE=epson. You can guard against the problem in the future by setting a global GS_DEVICE environment variable to some other device on your system that can be opened by Ghostscript.

If you have such an unusual output device that the default Ghostscript installation does not support it, you need to rebuild Ghostscript to support the device, or else process your output files through a filter that converts it to a form usable by your output device. Ghostscript comes with makefiles and is easy to build if you follow the Ghostscript documentation that comes with the distribution.

The more graphics utilities, X window managers, games, and applications you use, the more likely you will need to reinstall Ghostscript to suit your requirements. Read the Ghostscript documentation before running the makefile that comes with the package. (This requires that you have *gcc* installed on your system.)

You can define the GSDIR environment variable to locate the path of the *ghostscript* command and set GS_LIB variables, if you need to build Ghostscript utilities and add them to your installation. For example:

```
export GSDIR=/usr/bin
export GS_LIB=/usr/lib/ghostscript:/usr/local/lib/fonts:/usr/X11R6/fonts
```

Set the GS_LIB_DEFAULTS variable before you make a new build of Ghostscript; see the *gs* manual page.

The Ghostscript package also contains some PostScript programs that provide useful print-support functions, including some sophisticated printing capabilities we do not document here. The *gs_init.ps* file, in particular, affects the general behavior of Ghostscript. Additional scripts (filters, shell scripts, and so on) can be found in */usr/lib/ghostscript* or */usr/local/lib/ghostscript*. You may find it useful to examine the *ps2epsi.ps* utility, which converts PostScript into encapsulated PostScript, and the *ps2ascii.ps* utility, which converts PostScript files into plain text.

Print Filters

Every document passes through a filter before going to the printer, thanks to the `if` variable in the printcap file. A print filter can be found in a Linux distribution, acquired from the printer's vendor, found on the Net, or even made yourself from scratch or by cobbling together existing filters and shell utilities.

An input filter can also be used to restrict use of a printer to a specific user or group, or to users with accounts on a particular host. Typical `if`-assigned filters are executable shell scripts that process the text file, but they can be any program that can take the input data stream and process it for output to a printer.

It is increasingly common for commercial Linux distributions to build a filter interactively. While you can usually improve on such a filter, it can help to use one as a starting point. The Red Hat distribution, for example, created the following shell-script filter (named */var/spool/lpd/ljet4/filter)* on one of our systems from information provided to it in the printer manager window and from default assumptions.

The */etc/printcap* file was modified to specify the use of this filter, which proved to be perfectly functional on our system:

```
#!/bin/sh

DEVICE=ljet4
RESOLUTION=600x600
PAPERSIZE=letter
SENDEOF=

nenscript -TUS -ZB -p- |
if [ "$DEVICE" = "PostScript" ]; then
        cat -
else
        gs -q -sDEVICE=$DEVICE \
                -r$RESOLUTION \
                -sPAPERSIZE=$PAPERSIZE \
                -dNOPAUSE \
                -dSAFER \
                -sOutputFile=- -
fi

if [ "$SENDEOF" != "" ]; then
        printf ""
fi

exit 0
```

There's nothing exotic about this filter. First it sets some variables that appear later as arguments in the Ghostscript command. The script passes output through *nenscript* and passes PostScript files to the *gs* Ghostscript utility. (In this particular case, the automatically generated filter will never invoke *gs* because DEVICE never equals "PostScript" in the if test.) If your printer doesn't eject the final pages of output, you can force it to by setting the SENDEOF variable near the top of the file. For example:

```
SENDEOF='\f'
```

will cause a formfeed to be sent to the printer when it reaches the end of a file.

You might modify such a script and substitute a filter specifically designed for a LaserJet 4 printer, such as the actual ljet4 filter package, for example, and accommodate printing of TeX DVI files by filtering them through *dvips* and feeding them to Ghostscript. There is an elementary discussion of how to create a filter in the Linux Printing HOWTO.

---

* Putting a filter in a printer's spool directory is a convenient technique for a printer-management program to use when setting up your printer system. You may prefer to keep all your print filters and graphics conversion filters in the same directory (following the Unix tradition), such as */usr/sbin* or */var/spool/lpd/filters*. Of course, in that case, each filter you create must be uniquely named.

If you use a character printer that expects a carriage return at the end of each line, it will be unhappy with Linux, which follows Unix fashion in terminating a line with a linefeed, but no carriage return. To force correct treatment of newlines on these printers, the filter has to insert the carriage return. You can do this by writing the processing into the filter, or, alternatively, by using a filter that already has the capability to insert the character.

Some printer vendors provide filters and utilities for their printers, especially where the usual solutions are likely to be inadequate to take advantage of the printer's capabilities. For example, Hewlett-Packard provides a JetAdmin package with filters to use with its TCP/IP network-addressed LaserJet printers.

The default filter that comes with the BSD print-management package is */usr/sbin/lpf*. This filter is undocumented and probably best ignored, unless you wish to retrieve the C source and trace through the program to learn its capabilities. (You can find the full BSD source in the lpr-secure package in the printing directory from *ftp://ftp. ibiblio.org*.)

Most of the print-filtering needs you have were long ago resolved, and there are filters out there to meet your needs. By running:

    apropos filter

you can probably identify several print filters installed on your host.

Changing filters is simple. You need only change the */etc/printcap* input filter specification (if) to specify the filter you want, and then kill and restart *lpd*, which you can do using the *lpc* utility. Enter (as root):

    lpc restart all

The *lpc* utility reports any *lpd* processes it kills, then restarts *lpd*. If files are in a print spool waiting to print, *lpd* also reports that an *lpd* daemon for that printer has been started. The *lpc* printer control utility is described later in this chapter, in the section "Controlling Printer Services with lpc."

Before adopting a strange print filter, study the manual page for that filter and pass some test files through it. We have found that filters don't always perform "as advertised" in their manual page; often the document is obsolete or the filter was compiled by someone using different configuration parameters than the document assumes. There is no substitute for testing all the things you expect the filter to do before adopting it. Two good filtering packages, *nenscript*, a newer version of the traditional Unix filter *enscript*, and APSfilter, are discussed in the next sections.

The nenscript Filter

The *nenscript* filter is a typical modern filter for Linux. You should find it in */usr/ bin/nenscript* if it was provided in your Linux distribution. Otherwise, it may be installed in */usr/local/bin*. *nenscript* controls headers, footers, rotation of text, and so on, and produces PostScript output conforming to the Adobe Structuring Conventions from plain ASCII input (by calling Ghostscript). It sends output to the printer specified by either the user's NENSCRIPT environment variable, if set, or by the user's PRINTER environment variable. If neither variable is set, *nenscript* uses the default printer that *lpr* wants to use.

If *nenscript* is called using the –Z option, it is supposed to pass PostScript files through without altering them. *nenscript* examines the input file, and if the first two characters in the input file are %!, *nenscript* suppresses formatting. Because this output "type-checking" is primitive, it is easily fooled. Obviously if the first two characters happen to be something other than %!, perhaps because a formfeed is the first character, for example, the file will not be recognized as PostScript even if it is. This can easily happen if some filter processing takes place before the file passes through to *nenscript*. Of course, a file can also have %! as the first characters and not be Post-Script (or could be nonconforming PostScript) and therefore may not be handled properly if passed to a PostScript printer. There are smarter filters for this type of checking, including Magic-Filter or APSfilter, but *nenscript* may easily meet your needs, especially if you print only to a PostScript printer.

If you use the *nenscript* filter for a PostScript printer on your system, therefore, you could specify the –Z option in the NENSCRIPT environment variable for all user shells by default, in order to pass through the PostScript received by the filter.

A shell script provided in the *nenscript* package invokes *nenscript* configured to behave as though it were another (similar) traditional Unix filter, *pstext*.

To use *nenscript* to filter your print files, make sure *nenscript* is installed in an appropriate path, and then set the printers for which you want *nenscript* to filter to point to a filter that invokes the *nenscript* filter. You may find that the printcap entry can point directly to the *nenscript* filter if you set a systemwide default NENSCRIPT variable to control its options, or you can create a simple processing filter that calls *nenscript*, much like the sample configuration file shown earlier.

Magic Filters: APSfilter and Alternatives

The most versatile filters are the so-called "magic" filters. A magic filter examines the contents of a file passed to it, and filters the output for printing based on what it learns from the format of the information. If it sees the file is DVI routed to a PostScript printer, for instance, it will apply another filter (perhaps *dvips*) to convert the data into PostScript for printing. This is very convenient, but on occasion, the filter can make a mistake. If that happens, the user can resubmit the file with command-line options that specify which filtering to perform, or the user can preprocess the file by piping it through the needed filtering before passing it to *lpr* for routine print processing. There are some good magic filter packages, including APSfilter (which we have chosen to describe here), Magic-Filter, and the *gslp.ps* filter provided with complete Ghostscript packages.

Some Linux distributions, regrettably, omit Ghostscript's supplemental utilities or documents, but you can always retrieve a complete Ghostscript distribution via FTP from the GNU archive site (*ftp://ftp.gnu.org/gnu/*) or one of its mirrors. You can get the APSfilter and Magic-Filter packages from the *ftp://ftp.ibiblio.org* FTP site in the */pub/Linux/system/printing* directory. The Ghostscript filter, *gslp.ps*, is written in the PostScript language and can be used only with Ghostscript or another interpreter compatible with Adobe PostScript.

The APSfilter package for Linux is a port of a package developed for FreeBSD. For that reason, you should take a few precautions in order to ensure that things configure properly when you install the APSfilter package. On a Linux host, it is probably best to install the APSfilter package in */usr/lib/apsfilter*. The package comes from *ftp://ftp.ibiblio.org* as a *gzip*ped, tarred file. To unpack the package, put it in the */usr/lib* directory and enter:

```
tar xvfz apsfilter*.tar.gz
```

Now the APSfilter package unpacks within subdirectories of the *apsfilter* directory.

Change to the *apsfilter* directory. Before you run the *SETUP* command, make sure you have all the filters you might want to use with APSfilter installed and configured. The */usr/lib/apsfilter/FAQ* file tells you some of the more important and useful packages.

Before you run the installation, read the *INSTALL* document to make sure there aren't any surprises. Then run *./SETUP*. It tests for the presence and location of graphics utilities and other filters APSfilter uses to convert files into a form printable on your printer.

The *SETUP* script lets you know if the filter installed correctly. You can run it again if you wish to install more than one printer or more than one mode for a single printer. For example, if you install a DeskJet 540 printer, you probably will want to use the dj500 definition for the black cartridge and the dj550c definition for the CMYK color cartridge. APSfilter uses very long directory names for its spool directories. If you don't like that, you can rename the spool directories and change the corresponding directory fields in the corresponding */etc/printcap* entry. Be sure not to shorten the name of the filter used; that path is critical. We don't recommend you make things pretty until you are satisfied that things are working.

Before you try your new setup, you need to restart the print daemon:

```
/usr/sbin/lpc restart all
```

APSfilter sets systemwide variables for printer definitions in the */etc/apsfilterrc* file; reading this file can be informative. Common print problems are typically caused by file ownership or permission problems; we show you the proper settings in the upcoming section "File, directory, and utility privileges." Then, read the *FAQ* and *TROUBLESHOOTING* files in the */usr/lib/apsfilter* directory.

If your APSfilter installation didn't work, you can always return to the configuration you had before you installed it by copying back to */etc/printcap* the */etc/printcap.orig* file that APSfilter saved for you.

APSfilter names its printers sequentially, from lp1 up. Don't be confused; that has nothing to do with the actual physical device assigned to the printer. Again, you can change those names.

APSfilter allows you to loosen restrictions so that individual users can set up their own *.apsfilterr* file in their home directories. The default is to not allow it, which is a bit more secure.

The latest version of Magic-Filter (at the time of this writing, Version 1.2) is remarkably easy to install and makes a clean alternative to APSfilter. However, the installation doesn't do any hand-holding. Though there is a useful manual page, there isn't much information to help you set up the alternate processing that the Magic-Filter utility can do for most printing devices. In particular, if you have a versatile printer that outputs in multiple modes (PostScript, PCL5, text, and so on), you may find it worth your while to install and use this package.

BSD Print System Elements: Files, Directories, and Utilities

The print-management system requires you to create directories that match the printcap printer names in order to spool files for printing. It also requires you to create other files for controlling the print process itself. You must set up directories and files with the correct ownership and privileges, and the printer utilities themselves also need correct permissions.

Setting up printer directories

Your Linux installation created a standard spool directory. Ideally, this is on a fast-access disk drive. The basic spool directory (*/var/spool*) is normally used for managing mail, news, and UUCP communications as well as for holding printer files. We recommend you follow this practice, which is a Linux standard. Some utilities or filters you get may expect to find */usr/spool/lpd* as the printer spool path. You will have to make corrections if you find this condition. You can, of course, create */usr/spool* and link it to */var/spool*, but that is a good idea only if */usr* and */var* are on the same disk drive.

You must create your own printer spool directories. The */var/spool/lpd* directory is the standard path containing each printer subdirectory. Each printer subdirectory name must be used as a printer name in the first field in a corresponding */etc/printcap* entry. For example, */var/spool/lpd/moa* is appropriate for a printer with moa in a name field of the printcap entry. In turn, the */etc/printcap* entry for this printer should have

---

an `sd` variable set to point to the spooling directory (`sd=/var/spool/lpd/moa`, for example).

You shouldn't use `lp` as the actual spool directory name unless you never expect to have more than one printer on your system or network because `lp` is the default printer. (If your default printer is somewhere else on the network, your files will still get spooled to */var/spool/lpd/lp* first, before your *lpd* forwards them to the print daemon on the remote host to print.) You may have a printer-management utility that automatically creates an `lp` spool directory, but you can always edit the printcap file to point to any directory you wish.

The spool directory name should be the first name listed in the associated */etc/printcap* entry for the printer to make identification easy. The printcap entry will then be associated with the names under which the *lpq* and *lpc* utilities report print queue status.

File, directory, and utility privileges

The most common problem in establishing print services is with file and directory permissions. Table 8-1 lists the important files, directories, and utilities that comprise BSD print management on Linux. Installed locations may vary according to your Linux distribution. The ownerships and permissions given in the following table are recommended for the files and directories of the printing system. (Additional filters and nonstandard spool paths may be specified in */etc/printcap*.) Different permissions may still work, but if you have permissions problems, this is where you can straighten them out. An asterisk in the first column of the table indicates that many files can exist with the names of different printers. Note that different distributions may have slightly different settings here; some distributions even have different "security modes," which you can select depending on your security requirements and which have an effect on the permissions used.

Table 8-1. BSD's files, directories, and utilities for printing

Directory or file	Permissions	Owner/group	Description
/dev/ttys1	`crwsr-----`	`root/lp`	Typical serial port printing device
/dev/lp1	`crws------`	`root/lp`	Typical parallel port device (not bidirectional)
/usr/bin/lpc	`-rwsrwsr-x`	`root/lp`	Controls print-spooling services
/usr/bin/lpr	`-rwsrwsr-x`	`root/lp`	Receives print file, assigns processing data, and spools both
/usr/bin/lpq	`-rwsrwsr-x`	`root/lp`	Reports on spooled files with user and print queue data
/usr/bin/lprm	`-rwsrwsr--`	`root/lp`	Removes print jobs from spool
/usr/bin/tunelp	`-rwsr-sr--`	`root/lp`	Tests print services to improve them
/usr/bin/lptest	`-rwxr-xr-x`	`root/root`	Outputs an ASCII file for printer and display testing

Table 8-1. BSD's files, directories, and utilities for printing (continued)

Directory or file	Permissions	Owner/group	Description
/usr/sbin/lpd	-rwsr-s---	root/lp	Daemon that manages printing using printcap data and data passed by *lpr*
/usr/sbin/lpf	-rwxr-xr-x	root/lp	Primitive BSD text print filter
/usr/sbin/pac	-rwxr--r--	root/root	BSD utility that reports on printer activity and usage by user ID
/var/spool/	drwxr-sr-x	root/daemon	Basic system location for temporary files
/var/spool/lpd	-rws--s--x	root/lp	Standard path for the print-spooling system
/var/spool/lpd/*	drwxr-sr-x	root/lp	Spooling subdirectories for each defined printer
/var/spool/lpd/*/ filter	-rwxr-xr-x	root/lp	Filters created by Red Hat printer-management utility for each print spool
/var/spool/lpd/lpd. lock	-rw-rw----	root/lp	*lpd* queue control lock
/var/spool/lpd/*/.seq	-rw-rw----	lp/lp	Sequence file that *lpd* uses to order spooled files
/var/spool/lpd/*/lock	-rw-------	root/lp	*lpd* writes this lock file to prevent sending next file until printer is ready
/var/spool/lpd/*/ status	-rw-------	lp/lp	*lpd* stores latest printer status report here
/var/log/lp-acct	-rw-------	root/root	Accounting record file, from which *pac* extracts and formats print data[a]
/var/log/lpd-errs	-rw-rw-r--	root/lp	Standard BSD log file for *lpd* errors

[a] This file remains empty if system accounting is not installed, unless you configure Ghostscript to perform its limited reporting there and make the file writable by all.

The usual Linux printer-management utilities set the print files with root ownership and lp group privilege. Traditionally, BSD distributions have used root ownership and daemon group privilege. You can use either group privilege, but if you use both daemon and lp privileges with different utilities and files, you will have problems. Be particularly careful about this if you add utilities from other packages to your services.

Let's say you (as root) need to create the printer-spooling directory, */var/spool/lpd*. You execute the command:

```
mkdir /var/spool/lpd
```

Assuming your */var/spool* was created with the usual permissions, the new *lpd* directory has permissions of drwxrwxr-x, which is too permissive. If you enter the command:

```
chmod 755 /var/spool/lpd
```

the permissions are changed to drwxr-xr-x. This is close, but not what you want. You need to set the setuid bit, so lp can setuid root:

```
chmod +s /var/spool/lpd
```

This results in drwsr-sr-x, which is what you want. However, the group should be lp, not root, so you need to fix that:

```
chgrp lp /var/spool/lpd
```

Create the spool directories needed for each printer as subdirectories of the */var/ spool/lpd* directory in the same way, and then use *touch* to create a *.seq* file in each print directory:

```
touch .seq
```

Exercising the Printer Daemon

The *lpd* daemon consults */etc/printcap* and then sends files to printers by directing them to a device file in the */dev* directory. Most printers on Linux boxes are serial (usually addressed through devices named */dev/ttys0*, */dev/ttys1*, and so on, or */dev/ ttyS0*, */dev/ttyS1*, and so on) or parallel (*/dev/lp0*, */dev/lp1*, or */dev/lp2*, depending on the physical addresses the ports use). The port assignments are described in the section "Printer System Troubleshooting," later in this chapter. A common mistake when configuring print services is to use the wrong port.

You can link a virtual device—*/dev/fax*, for example—to an actual device you can use by creating a symbolic link. For example:

```
ln -s /dev/ttys1 /dev/fax
```

This allows users to set up scripts and filters that address */dev/fax*, which is much easier to remember than */dev/ttys1*. Also, you can move the physical device (a fax modem, for example) without breaking user setup simply by removing */dev/fax* and then creating it again with a link to the new device.

The BSD printer daemon is notorious for dying or just becoming inert. To be fair, this seems to be less common than it was some years ago, but it still happens. When it does, just kill the old daemon and start a new one. If *lpd* isn't fairly reliable, though, there is a cause somewhere. Something could be wrong with a user's environment, with the specified command-line options used with *lpr*, or with a faulty filter that sends setup data to the printer in a form the printer doesn't like. However, you have every reason to expect to have a "pretty good" printing package installation. If you are having problems, check out "Printer System Troubleshooting," later in this chapter.

OK, let's see if you have a working print system. After making all these changes, you can be sure that *lpd* doesn't know what is going on. So run the *ps* command and find the ID of the *lpd* process. Then enter:

```
kill -9 processid
```

to kill the process you specified.* You should now have no print daemon running. Just enter */usr/sbin/lpd* to start the print daemon.

Now, while watching the activity LEDs on your printer front panel (if there are any), send a file to the printer (still acting with superuser privilege):

```
lptest | lpr
```

The *lptest* ASCII barber pole should begin printing to your default printer, as configured in your */etc/printcap* file. If it doesn't, you have a configuration problem that has nothing to do with privileges.

Did the printer show any activity? Does your default printer have a spool directory? Does the directory have a *.seq* file? Check */var/log/lpd-errs* and see if anything was stored in it. Use the *lpc* command and get a report on the status of the print daemon and the print spool.

If everything else looks good, make sure the printer is using the port you expected by sending a file directly to the port. For example:

```
# lptest > /dev/lp1
```

Or, to test for a serial printer:

```
# lptest > /dev/ttys1
```

and so on. If none of these worked, reexamine your */etc/printcap* file. Is your entry properly formed? Are there no blank spaces or tabs following the continuation character (\) on your entry line? Is the printer queue correctly specified? Does the name lp appear as one of the printer names of the name field? Is the first name in the name field the same name as the spool directory it uses?

Let's assume you got through this first little test unscathed, and you now have several pages of lovely barber-pole printout in your printer tray. Next comes the real challenge. Can you print as a regular user? Log in (or run *su*) to become a normal system user. Now, try the same experiment. If it works, congratulations, you've got a printer! If it doesn't, you have a problem, but it is probably a file or directory ownership or permissions problem. You know what you have to do about that. Become root again, look at the manual pages for *chgrp*, *chmod*, and *chown*, and go down the list of files and directories to find your problem and fix it. Repeat until Joe User can print.

Controlling Printer Services with lpc

The *lpc* utility is provided to manage printer queues and requires root privilege to perform most of its functions. *lpc* reports on all print queues and their attending *lpd*

---

* You may prefer to use *lpc* to perform this task. Also, if your root desktop has a printer-manager tool, you can probably click the lpd button to kill and restart the print daemon.

---

daemons. You can also specify reports on a specific printer or printing system user. To get a status report on all printers and users, type:

```
$ lpc status
ibis:
        queuing is enabled
        printing is enabled
        no entries
        no daemon present
crow:
        queuing is enabled
        printing is enabled
        1 entry in spool area
        crow is ready and printing

ada:
        queuing is disabled
        printing is disabled
        no entries
        no daemon present
```

You can enable queuing within *lpc* through its *enable* command and disable queing using its *disable* command. The *disable* command works by setting a group execute permission on the lock file in the print spool directory.

You can enable printing in *lpc* using its *start* command and disable it using its *stop* command. Jobs held in a print queue when a printer is stopped will remain there until printing is restarted. The *stop* command functions by setting a lock file in the printer spool directory and killing the print daemon for that queue, but it allows the currently printing job to complete. The *abort* command works like *stop*, but also halts any printing job immediately. (Because the job did not complete, *lpr* retains it and starts over again when the queue is restarted.)

The *down* command functions as though both a *disable* and a *stop* command were issued, and the *up* command does the reverse, issuing *enable* and *start* commands.

You could also limit the display to one printer:

```
$ lpc status crow
crow:
        queuing is enabled
        printing is enabled
        1 entry in spool area
        crow is ready and printing
```

The status-reporting feature is useful for anyone, and *lpc* allows all users to use it.

The real work for *lpc* usually involves solving a printing crisis. Sometimes a print daemon dies, and printing jobs back up. Sometimes a printer runs out of ink or paper, or even fails. Jobs in the print spools have to be suspended or moved to another spool where they can be printed. Someone may simply have an urgent printing task that needs to be moved to the top of the queue.

The *lpc* command is a classic Unix command: tight-lipped and forbidding. When you simply enter the *lpc* command, all you get back is a prompt:

```
lpc>
```

The command is interactive and waiting for your instructions. You can get help by entering help or a question mark at the *lpc* prompt. *lpc* responds and gives you a new prompt. For example, entering a question mark displays:

```
# lpc
lpc> ?
Commands may be abbreviated.  Commands are:
abort   enable  disable help    restart status  topq    ?
clean   exit    down    quit    start   stop    up
lpc>
```

You can get additional help by asking for help about a specific command. For example, to learn more about restarting a stalled print queue, type:

```
lpc> help restart
restart         kill (if possible) and restart a spooling daemon
lpc>
```

The *lpc* help message does not offer online help about the secondary arguments you can specify in some places. The manual page will offer you some guidance. Most of the commands accept *all* or a print spool name as a secondary argument.

The *lpc topq* command recognizes a print spool name as the first argument and printer job numbers or user IDs as the following arguments. The arguments are used to reorder the print queue. For example, to move job 237 to the top of the ada print queue, followed by all jobs owned by bckeller in the queue, enter:

```
lpc> topq ada 237 bckeller
```

The *lpd* daemon will start job 237 as soon as the current job is finished and will put any files in the queue owned by bckeller before the rest of the print spool. If you were very impatient, you could use the *abort* and *clean* commands to kill and purge the currently printing job, then use *topq* to put the job you want at the top of the queue, before using *restart* to create a new *lpd* and restart the queue.

When you use the *stop* command to stop a print spool (or all print spools) you can broadcast a message to all system users at the same time. For example:

```
lpc> stop ada "Printer Ada taken down to replace toner cartridge."
```

If you do major surgery on the print spools—stopping queues and moving files around—it is wise to use *lpc*'s *clean* command. This minimizes the risk that some loose end will cause an *lpd* daemon to stall:

```
lpc> clean
```

Then get a new status report and restart or start all stopped print spools before exiting. There is a difference between aborting a process, stopping a process, and bringing a print queue down. If you bring a print queue down (*lpc down ada,* for example) you will find you cannot get *lpd* to serve the print spool again until you restore services with an *lpc up ada* command. Similarly, if you stop a queue, you have to start or restart it.

Follow up after you clear print spool problems using *lpc*. Further status reports will let you know promptly whether the problems were actually solved.

You should not wait for disaster to become familiar with *lpc* commands because printing jobs can pass through a Linux spool very fast, especially when a printer has lots of memory to buffer jobs sent to it. Study the manual page and work with *lpc* enough to be comfortable with the control it gives you over print spools and *lpd* daemons.

You can abbreviate subcommands unless it makes them ambiguous. For instance, in the following command, h stands for *help*:

```
lpc> h topq
```

To exit from *lpc*, enter the command:

```
lpc> quit
```

or:

```
lpc> exit
```

Printer Optimization

For performance improvement, you can first try to maximize the physical tuning of the system. You should try to determine the maximum data flow rates you can sustain to the printers you install. Don't specify a faster rate of communication than can be supported unless your printer is going to return flow control signals to the print daemon. That is, you must have bidirectional communications (and the printer must return the necessary signals) or else you must limit your transmission speeds so that data doesn't get lost en route to the printer. You may have to experiment with this to wring the best possible performance from printers limited by restricted bandwidth.

Old PC serial and parallel cards just don't have the throughput available with later cards. Newer serial cards have faster I/O processors. Newer parallel ports are typically faster and meet the Enhanced Parallel Port (EPP) standard to support bidirectional communications, which may allow *lpd* to control data flow to the printer better. A significant performance improvement may be only a few dollars away.

If your printer is just plain slow and cannot buffer print jobs, there isn't much to be gained from optimizing the data-transfer rate, of course, but it may still be useful for you to use interrupt-driven flow control made possible by bidirectional communications instead of port polling, if your hardware permits, as that will decrease the system load.

You can try out various printer optimizations using the *tunelp* utility. Read the manual page carefully before attempting this. If a tuning procedure fails, you may need to turn the printer off and back on to reset it. Also, don't forget to use *lpc* to restart the *lpd* daemon after each change to the configuration. Back up your working setup before monkeying around with *tunelp*.

An excellent first use for *tunelp* is to cause a print job to abort on receiving a printer error and to notify you. (The default is not to abort.) Setting this up can shorten the test cycle. To cause abort on printer error, enter as root:

```
tunelp -aon
```

If you use a parallel port printer and your parallel port supports interrupt-driven printing, you can use *tunelp* to accelerate printer access:

```
tunelp /dev/lp1 -i7
```

This example switches the port controlled by interrupt 7 to use interrupt-driven printing. If an attempt to print after you made this change fails, you should reset the port and switch back to noninterrupt-driven polling:

```
tunelp /dev/lp1 -r -i0
```

If you don't know the interrupt this device uses, you can query with *tunelp -q on*, and the IRQ setting will be displayed.

You can probably speed up printing a bit by reducing the pause the driver takes when it cannot send a character to the printer after a certain number of tries. For example, a fast laser printer might happily accommodate very brief pauses and not require many attempts to transmit. To try sending a character 10 times before pausing (the default is 250 attempts) and set the pause to .01, type:

```
tunelp /dev/lp1 -c10 -t1
```

The *–t* takes a numeric value that represents a multiple of .01 second. The default pause is .1 second.

Note that the optimal transfer rate for plain-text files is likely to be less efficient for graphics files, which are generally processed more slowly.

When you finish tuning your printing system, you may want to reset the printer abort flag to prevent the process from aborting on receipt of printer error:

```
tunelp -aoff
```

The *tunelp* utility will continue to be developed in subsequent releases of Linux. Check the manual page to see the capabilities of your release.

Printer System Troubleshooting

When you have a printer problem, first resort to *lpc* to generate a status report. The print daemons should be alive and well, and no error should be returned. Restart the daemons if they have stopped. You can also check the contents of the */var/spool/lpd/ printername/status* file and see if an error message from the printer is stored there. Check the */var/log/lpd-errs* file for any errors reported by *lpd*. If you are using Ghostscript and its reporting features are active, use */sbin/pac* on Ghostscript's log file to get a report that may reveal errors Ghostscript generated. (As long as Linux system accounting isn't available, you might as well use */var/log/lp-acct* to store these reports. You'll have to make the file writable by all to do this.)

Look at that *lpc* status report again. Do files get to the print spool? Do they leave the spool? Are the necessary supporting files for *lpd* present (*.seq*, *lock*, and so on)? If *lpc status* reported a printer named " : " there is a malformed */etc/printcap* line; the last character on a continuation line must be the backslash, not a space or tab.

Sometimes the */etc/printcap* file is set up incorrectly, and it makes *lpd* misroute a file. To test for that condition, prepare a file for print but save it to a file instead of spooling it to the printer. Examine the file. Is it in the form you expect? Try a couple of sanity checks:

- If as root you send the file directly to the device (for example, `cat filename.ps > /dev/lp1`), does it print? If so, it means the problem lies in your software configuration, not in the hardware.

- Can you view your PostScript file using Ghostview? If so, you know that the format of the file is correct but the printer or filter is not interpreting it properly.

If you are testing a text file, try preparing it and routing it to a display, passing it through a utility such as *less*, and examine the result. A custom filter can also misroute a file.

Sometimes it is difficult to figure out where a printing problem originates. Printer configuration problems can be masked (or introduced) by having defaults overridden, for example. You may have to start by looking at an individual user's printing habits and then work forward. Individual users can set environment variables in their shell startup files to specify the printer they want to use as a default, and the behavior of formatters and print filters. Default system values are often overridden by environment variables, and they in turn are overridden by option arguments passed to *lpr* on the command line or by another utility.

When a print job terminates abnormally, it may be necessary to clear the lock file for the spool before *lpd* will send another file to print from that spool (*/var/spool/lpd/ printername/lock*). The *lpd* daemon creates the lock file and changes it on completion. You can use *lpc* to stop the print daemon and then clean up the spool before starting it again.

Some problems derive from the data-transfer process. A printer may drop characters or be unable to keep up with the data flow you are attempting to provide, especially if the printer is old and slow or if the cable is unusually long. One possible symptom of data-transfer problems is when the printer can handle plain text readily, but pauses and thrashes when trying to print graphics files. If you suspect some problem of this nature, try increasing the pause the system takes before attempting to resend data and slowing the wait loop. The *tunelp* utility lets you control this conveniently:

```
tunelp -t200 -w5
```

This command tells *lpd* to pause 2 seconds between attempts. The *–w* option sets the number of loops for the busy loop counter to read between strobe signals. Normally *–w* is set to 0. For more information on *tunelp*, see the section "Printer Optimization" earlier in this chapter.

If *lpd* never seems to run on your system, perhaps it isn't started up when the system boots. If this is the case, append a */etc/lpd* line to the end of your */etc/rc.d/rc.local* file. Most Linux distributions start *lpd* these days as part of the default installation.

Some problems may never occur unless you use another package that presents conflicts by attempting to address the same devices. For example, UUCP utilities address a serial port using a */dev/ttyS** device driver. However, UUCP is a daemon with greater privileges than lp, and (although it shouldn't) it can leave the device set with a privilege level to which *lpd* cannot write.

The Linux distribution of the BSD print package is usually installed with lp group permissions. On traditional BSD print-management installations, *lpd* is owned by daemon and has daemon group privileges. (There's no special lp group to support printing.) If you think there are subtle problems relating to device access collisions by processes owned by different daemons, you can change all print utilities, group privileges to daemon and, of course, change directory and file-access privileges as well. That would restore the traditional BSD configuration. A better solution would be to find the problem devices and change their ownership to lp, because UUCP will still be able to use devices lp owns. Be aware that a serial port address can be reached by a number of virtual devices linked to the actual device; you have to correctly set the ownership of the real device.

Occasionally, a user believes his print job is going to the "wrong" printer. This is usually an environment variable problem. Double-check your */etc/printcap*, but also check the user's environment variables. For example, a user may have a GS_DEVICE variable set so that Ghostscript uses that printer as the default printer. If Ghostscript processing precedes *nenscript* processing, for example, the Ghostscript printer assignment could be passed to *nenscript*, overriding a NENSCRIPT or PRINTER device specification. This can also cause strange results if one parameter is overridden while others stay as before so that, for example, a filter performs some special page layout for one printer, but the file goes to another.

Older PostScript printers may simply ignore ASCII files sent to them. If a user complains about disappearing output, maybe the file isn't getting passed through *nenscript* for PostScript encapsulation, or (very rarely) maybe *nenscript* was fooled into thinking it is already PostScript.

A multimode printer that knows when to switch modes (between PCL and plain text, for example) may still fail to eject the page and start the next file on the new page when one file of the same type is queued immediately following another of the same type. If this occurs, you can force the filter to add a formfeed at the end of each document (see the sample filter in the earlier section "Print Filters") at the cost of sometimes printing unnecessary blank pages.

Parallel port printer addressing can be confusing. On an XT bus system, the first parallel port is addressed as */dev/lp0* at 0x3bc, referring to an address in your computer's I/O memory. On the usual ISA bus system, the first parallel port device is */dev/lp1* at 0x378, which is the second parallel port on an XT system (still the */dev/lp1* device). The usual second parallel port on an ISA bus system is */dev/lp2*, as you would expect, at 0x278. However, there are some unusual configurations out there, such as systems with three parallel ports (if installed correctly these will be addressed as */dev/lp0*, */dev/lp1*, and */dev/lp2*). IRQ assignments may also be unusual and present a problem if you are trying to set up interrupt-driven printing.

If all else fails, review the initial installation procedure. Make sure the hardware is actually connected and functional by booting another operating system if possible, testing devices as root user, and so on.

CUPS

CUPS, the *Common Unix Printer System*, is the new kid on the block when it comes to printing subsystems, and probably the one that is going to take over the Linux printing world completely because of its functionality. It supports many features in modern printers like downloadable fonts, color printing, network printer browsing, printer description files (PPD files), etc. Some distributions like Caldera already use CUPS, but at the time of this writing, Red Hat, SuSE, and Debian don't (they still have it on their CDs, though). This does not mean that CUPS does not work on these systems, however. You can always install CUPS yourself.

Currently, CUPS contains printer drivers only for HP and Epson printers, but because most available printers are compatible with these, this is rarely a problem. The authors of CUPS also sell a commercial package that contains drivers for most printers, even the very esoteric ones, and some free third-party drivers are available as well.

If you want to download and install CUPS on your system, you can find both the software and lots of documentation at *http://www.cups.org*.

Setting Terminal Attributes

setterm is a program that sets various characteristics of your terminal (say, each virtual console), such as the keyboard repeat rate, tab stops, and text colors.

Most people use this command to change the colors for each virtual console. In this way, you can tell which virtual console you're currently looking at based on the text color.

For example, to change the color of the current terminal to white text on a blue background, use the command:

```
$ setterm -foreground white -background blue
```

Some programs and actions cause the terminal attributes to be reset to their default values. In order to store the current set of attributes as the default, use:

```
$ setterm -store
```

setterm provides many options (most of which you will probably never use). See the *setterm*(1) manual page or use *setterm –help* for more information.

If your terminal settings get really messed up (as happens, for example, if you try to look at the contents of a binary file with *cat*), you can try typing *setterm -reset* blindly, which should reset your terminal to reasonable settings.

What to Do in an Emergency

It's not difficult to make a simple mistake as root that can cause real problems on your system, such as not being able to log in or losing important files. This is especially true for novice system administrators who are beginning to explore the system. Nearly all new system admins learn their lessons the hard way, by being forced to recover from a real emergency. In this section, we'll give you some hints about what to do when the inevitable happens.

You should always be aware of preventive measures that reduce the impact of such emergencies. For example, take backups of all important system files, if not the entire system. If you happen to have a Linux distribution on CD-ROM, the CD-ROM itself acts as a wonderful backup for most files (as long as you have a way to access the CD-ROM in a tight situation—more on this later). Backups are vital to recovering from many problems; don't let the many weeks of hard work configuring your Linux system go to waste.

Also, be sure to keep notes on your system configuration, such as your partition table entries, partition sizes and types, and filesystems. If you were to trash your partition table somehow, fixing the problem might be a simple matter of rerunning *fdisk*, but this helps only as long as you can remember what your partition table used to look like. (True story: one of the authors once created this problem by booting a blank floppy, and had *no* record of the partition table contents. Needless to say, some guesswork was necessary to restore the partition table to its previous state!)

Of course, for any of these measures to work, you'll need a way to boot the system and access your files, or recover from backups, in an emergency. This is best accomplished with an "emergency disk," or "root disk." Such a disk contains a small root filesystem with the basics required to run a Linux system from floppy—just the essential commands and system files, as well as tools to repair problems. You use such a disk by booting a kernel from another floppy (see the section "Using a Boot Floppy" in Chapter 5) and telling the kernel to use the emergency disk as the root filesystem.

Most distributions of Linux include such a boot/root floppy combination as the original installation floppies. The installation disks usually contain a small Linux system that can be used to install the software as well as perform basic system maintenance. Some systems include both the kernel and root filesystem on one floppy, but this severely limits the number of files that can be stored on the emergency disk. How useful these disks are as a maintenance tool depends on whether they contain the tools (such as *fsck*, *fdisk*, a small editor such as *vi*, and so on) necessary for problem recovery. Some distributions have such an elaborate installation process that the installation floppies don't have room for much else.

At any rate, you can create such a root floppy yourself. Being able to do this from scratch requires an intimate knowledge of what's required to boot and use a Linux system, and exactly what can be trimmed down and cut out. For example, you could dispose of the startup programs *init*, *getty*, and *login*, as long as you know how to rig things so that the kernel starts a shell on the console instead of using a real boot procedure. (One way to do this is to have */etc/init* be a symbolic link to */sbin/bash*, all on the floppy filesystem.)

While we can't cover all the details here, the first step in creating an emergency floppy is to use *mkfs* to create a filesystem on a floppy (see the section "Creating Filesystems" in Chapter 6). You then mount the floppy and place on it whatever files you'll need, including appropriate entries in */dev* (most of which you can copy from */dev* on your hard-drive root filesystem). You'll also need a boot floppy, which merely contains a kernel. The kernel should have its root device set to */dev/fd0*, using *rdev*. This is covered in the section "Using a Boot Floppy" in Chapter 5. You'll also have to decide whether you want the root floppy filesystem loaded into a ramdisk (which you can set using *rdev* as well). If you have more than 4 MB of RAM, this is a good idea because it can free up the floppy drive to be used for, say, mounting another floppy containing additional tools. If you have two floppy drives, you can do this without using a ramdisk.

If you feel that setting up an emergency floppy is too hard for you now after reading all this, you might also want to try some of the scripts available that do it for you (e.g., *tomsrtbt* at *http://www.toms.net/rb/*). But whatever you do, be sure to try the emergency floppy *before* disaster happens!

At any rate, the best place to start is your installation floppies. If those floppies don't contain all the tools you need, create a filesystem on a separate floppy and place the missing programs on it. If you load the root filesystem from floppy into a ramdisk, or have a second floppy drive, you can mount the other floppy to access your maintenance tools.

What tools do you need? In the following sections, we'll talk about common emergencies and how to recover from them; this should guide you as to what programs are required for various situations. It is best if the tools you put on that floppy are statically linked in order to avoid problems with shared libraries not being available at emergency time.

Repairing Filesystems

As discussed in the section "Checking and Repairing Filesystems" in Chapter 6, you can use *fsck* to recover from several kinds of filesystem corruption. Most of these filesystem problems are relatively minor, however, and can be repaired by booting your system in the usual way and running *fsck* from the hard drive. However, it is usually better to check and repair your root filesystem while it is unmounted. In this case, it's easier to run *fsck* from an emergency floppy.

There are no differences between running *fsck* from floppy and from the hard drive; the syntax is exactly the same as described earlier in the chapter. However, remember that *fsck* is usually a frontend to tools such as *fsck.ext2*. On other systems, you'll need to use *e2fsck* (for Second Extended filesystems).

It is possible to corrupt a filesystem so that it cannot be mounted. This is usually the result of damage to the filesystem's *superblock*, which stores information about the filesystem as a whole. If the superblock is corrupted, the system won't be able to access the filesystem at all, and any attempt to mount it will fail (probably with an error to the effect of "can't read superblock").

Because of the importance of the superblock, the filesystem keeps backup copies of it at intervals on the filesystem. Second Extended filesystems are divided into "block groups," where each group has, by default, 8192 blocks. Therefore, there are backup copies of the superblock at block offsets 8193, 16385 (that's $8192 \times 2 + 1$), 24577, and so on. If you use the *ext2* filesystem, check that the filesystem has 8192-block groups with the following command:

```
dumpe2fs device | more
```

(Of course, this works only when the master superblock is intact.) This command will print a great deal of information about the filesystem, and you should see something like:

```
Blocks per group:        8192
```

If another offset is given, use it for computing offsets to the superblock copies, as mentioned earlier.

If you can't mount a filesystem because of superblock problems, chances are that *fsck* (or *e2fsck*) will fail as well. You can tell *e2fsck* to use one of the superblock copies, instead, to repair the filesystem. The command is:

```
e2fsck -f -b offset device
```

where *offset* is the block offset to a superblock copy; usually, this is 8193. The *-f* switch is used to force a check of the filesystem; when using superblock backups, the filesystem may appear "clean," in which case no check is needed. *-f* overrides this. For example, to repair the filesystem on */dev/hda2* with a bad superblock, we can say:

```
e2fsck -f -b 8193 /dev/hda2
```

Superblock copies save the day. The previous commands can be executed from an emergency floppy system and will hopefully allow you to mount your filesystems again.

Recently, so-called journalling filesystems have been introduced in most Linux distributions. Examples of these are the *ext3* filesystem, the Reiser filesystem, and the *jfs* filesystem. These are less prone to filesystem corruption because they keep a log (the "journal") of all changes made. Chances are that with these filesystems, you will never need to use any of the techniques described here.

Accessing Damaged Files

You might need to access the files on your hard-drive filesystems when booting from an emergency floppy. In order to do this, simply use the *mount* command as described in the section "Mounting Filesystems" in Chapter 6, mounting your filesystems under a directory such as */mnt*. (This directory must exist on the root filesystem contained on the floppy.) For example:

```
mount -t ext2 /dev/hda2 /mnt
```

will allow us to access the files on the Second Extended filesystem stored on */dev/hda2* in the directory */mnt*. You can then access the files directly and even execute programs from your hard-drive filesystems. For example, if you wish to execute *vi* from the hard drive, normally found in */usr/bin/vi*, you would use the command:

```
/mnt/usr/bin/vi filename
```

You could even place subdirectories of */mnt* on your path to make this easier.

Be sure to unmount your hard-drive filesystems before rebooting the system. If your emergency disks don't have the ability to do a clean shutdown, unmount your filesystems explicitly with *umount*, to be safe.

Two problems that can arise when doing this are forgetting the root password or trashing the contents of */etc/passwd*. In either case, it might be impossible to log in to the system or *su* to root. To repair this problem, simply boot from your emergency disks, mount your root filesystem under */mnt*, and edit */mnt/etc/passwd*. (It might be a good idea to keep a backup copy of this file somewhere in case you delete it accidentally.) For example, to clear the root password altogether, change the entry for root to:

```
root::0:0:The root of all evil:/:/bin/bash
```

Now root will have no password; you can reboot the system from the hard drive and use the *passwd* command to reset it.

If you are conscientious about system security, you might have shivered by now. You have read correctly: if somebody has physical access to your system, he or she can change your root password by using a boot floppy. Luckily, there are ways to protect your system against possible assaults. Most effective are, of course, the physical ones: if your computer is locked away, nobody can access it and put a boot floppy into it. There are also locks for the floppy drive only, but notice that you need such a protection for the CD-ROM drive as well for floppy-drive locks to be useful. If you don't want to use physical protection, you can also use the BIOS password if your computer supports that: configure the BIOS so that it does not try to boot from CD-ROM or floppy (even if a CD or floppy disk is inserted at boot time) and protect the BIOS settings with a BIOS password. This is not as secure because it is possible to reset the BIOS password with hardware means, but it still protects you against casual would-be intruders. Actually, of course, somebody could steal the whole computer.

Another common problem is corrupt links to shared system libraries. The shared library images in */lib* are generally accessed through symbolic links, such as */lib/libc.so.5*, which point to the actual library, */lib/libc.so.version*. If this link is removed or is pointing to the wrong place, many commands on the system won't run. You can fix this problem by mounting your hard-drive filesystems and relinking the library with a command, such as:

```
cd /mnt/lib; ln -sf libc.so.5.4.47 libc.so.5
```

to force the *libc.so.5* link to point to *libc.so.5.4.47*. Remember that symbolic links use the pathname given on the *ln* command line. For this reason, the command:

```
ln -sf /mnt/lib/libc.so.5.4.47 /mnt/lib/libc.so.5
```

won't do the right thing; *libc.so.5* will point to */mnt/lib/libc.so.5.4.47*. When you boot from the hard drive, */mnt/lib* can't be accessed, and the library won't be located. The first command works because the symbolic link points to a file in the same directory.

Restoring Files from Backup

If you have deleted important system files, it might be necessary to restore backups while booting from an emergency disk. For this reason, it's important to be sure your emergency disk has the tools you need to restore backups; this includes programs such as *tar* and *gzip*, as well as the drivers necessary to access the backup device. For instance, if your backups are made using the floppy tape device driver, be sure that the *ftape* module and *insmod* command are available on your emergency disk. See the section "Loadable Device Drivers" in Chapter 7 for more about this.

All that's required to restore backups to your hard-drive filesystems is to mount those filesystems, as described earlier, and unpack the contents of the archives over those filesystems (using the appropriate *tar* and *gzip* commands, for example; see the section "Making Backups" earlier in this chapter). Remember that every time you restore a backup you will be overwriting other system files; be sure you're doing everything correctly so that you don't make the situation worse. With most archiving programs, you can extract individual files from the archive.

Likewise, if you want to use your original CD-ROM to restore files, be sure the kernel used on your emergency disks has the drivers necessary to access the CD-ROM drive. You can then mount the CD-ROM (remember the *mount* flags *–r –t iso9660*) and copy files from there.

The filesystems on your emergency disks should also contain important system files; if you have deleted one of these from your system, it's easy to copy the lost file from the emergency disk to your hard-drive filesystem.

CHAPTER 9

Editors, Text Tools, Graphics, and Printing

In the next few chapters, we'll introduce a number of popular applications for Linux. We'll start here with text editing, which underlies nearly every activity on the system. (You need an editor to create a file of more than trivial size, whether it is a program to be compiled, a configuration file for your system, or a mail message to send to a friend.) On a related topic, we'll show you some text formatters that can make attractive documents and utilities that manage printing.

Editing Files Using vi

In this section, we're going to cover the use of the *vi* (pronounced "vee-eye") text editor. *vi* was the first real screen-based editor for Unix systems. It is also simple, small, and sleek. If you're a system administrator, learning *vi* can be invaluable; in many cases, larger editors, such as Emacs, won't be available in emergency situations (for instance, when booting Linux from a maintenance disk).

vi is based on the same principles as many other Unix applications: that each program provide a small, specific function and be able to interact with other programs. For example, *vi* doesn't include its own spellchecker or paragraph filler, but those features are provided by other programs that are easy to fire off from within *vi*. Therefore, *vi* itself is a bit limited, but is able to interact with other applications to provide virtually any functionality you might want.

At first, *vi* may appear to be somewhat complex and unwieldy. However, its single-letter commands are fast and powerful once you've learned them. In the next section, we're going to describe Emacs, a more flexible editor (really an integrated work environment) with an easier learning curve. Do keep in mind that knowing *vi* may be essential to you if you are in a situation where Emacs is not available, so we encourage you to learn the basics, as odd as they may seem. It should also be added that a number of *vi* clones are now available that are much more comfortable to use than the original *vi*, the most popular of which is *vim* (*vi* improved). Chances are that your distribution has things set up so that when starting *vi*, you actually start one of those.

We'll stick to the basics here, though, so that you can use the information presented here no matter which version of *vi* you use. You can find coverage of the newer versions in the book *Learning the vi Editor* by Linda Lamb and Arnold Robbins (O'Reilly).

Starting vi

Let's fire up *vi* and edit a file. The syntax for *vi* is:

    vi *filename*

For example:

    eggplant$ **vi test**

will edit the file *test*. Your screen should look like this:

The column of ~ characters indicates that you are at the end of the file.

Inserting Text and Moving Around

While using *vi*, at any one time you are in one of two (or three, depending on how you look at it) modes of operation. These modes are known as *command mode*, *edit mode*, and *ex mode*.

After starting *vi*, you are in command mode. This mode allows you to use a number of (usually single-letter) commands to modify text, as we'll see soon. Text is actually inserted and modified within edit mode. To begin inserting text, press *i* (which will place you into edit mode) and begin typing:

```
Now is the time for all good men to come to the aid of the party.█
~
~
~
~
~
~
~
~
-- INSERT --                                           1,66        All
```

While inserting text, you may type as many lines as you wish (pressing the Enter key after each, of course), and you may correct mistakes using the Backspace key. To end edit mode and return to command mode, press the Escape key.

While in command mode, you can use the arrow keys to move around the file. Alternatively, or when the arrow keys don't work, you may use *h*, *j*, *k*, and *l*, which move the cursor left, down, up, and right, respectively.

There are several ways to insert text other than using the *i* command. The *a* command (for "append") inserts text *after* the current cursor position. For example, use the left arrow key to move the cursor between the words good and men:

```
Now is the time for all good█men to come to the aid of the party.
~
~
~
~
~
~
                                                        1,29        All
```

Press *a*, type *wo*, and then press Escape to return to command mode:

```
Now is the time for all good w█men to come to the aid of the party.
~
~
~
~
~
~
                                                        1,31        All
```

To open a line below the current one and begin inserting text, use the *o* command. Press *o* and type another line or two:

```
Now is the time for all good women to come to the aid of the party.
Afterwards, we'll go out for pizza and beer.█
~
~
~
~
~
-- INSERT --                                            2,45        All
```

Remember that at any time you're either in command mode (where commands such as *i*, *a*, or *o* are valid) or in edit mode (where you're inserting text, followed by Escape to return to command mode). If you're not sure which mode you're in, press Escape.

This takes you out of edit mode, if you are in it, and does nothing except beep if you're already in command mode.

Deleting Text and Undoing Changes

From command mode, the *x* command deletes the character under the cursor. If you press *x* five times, you end up with the following:

```
Now is the time for all good women to come to the aid of the party.
Afterwards, we'll go out for pizza and█
~
~
~
~
~
~
                                                            2,39        All
```

Now press a and insert some text, followed by Escape:

```
Now is the time for all good women to come to the aid of the party.
Afterwards, we'll go out for pizza and Diet Coke.█
~
~
~
~
~
-- INSERT --                                                2,50        All
```

You can delete entire lines using the command *dd* (that is, press d twice in a row). If your cursor is on the second line, *dd* will produce the following:

```
█ow is the time for all good women to come to the aid of the party.
~
~
~
~
~
~
                                                            1,1         All
```

Text that is deleted may be reinserted using the *p* command (for "put"). Pressing *p* now will return the deleted line to the buffer after the current line. Using *P* (uppercase) instead will insert the text before the current line. By default, *p* and *P* insert text from the "undo buffer"; you can also yank and replace text from other buffers, as we'll see later.

The *u* command undoes the latest change (in this case, pressing *u* after *dd* is equivalent to *p*). If you inserted a large amount of text using the *i* command, pressing *u* immediately after returning to command mode would undo it.

To delete the word beneath the cursor, use the *dw* command. Place the cursor on the word Diet and type *dw*:

```
Now is the time for all good women to come to the aid of the party.
Afterwards, we'll go out for pizza and █oke.
~
~
~
~
~
~
~
                                                        2,40        All
```

Changing Text

You can replace text using the *R* command, which overwrites the text beginning at the cursor. Place the cursor on the first letter in pizza, press *R*, and type:

```
Now is the time for all good women to come to the aid of the party.
Afterwards, we'll go out for burgers and fries.█
~
~
~
~
~
~
-- REPLACE --                                           2,48        All
```

The *r* command replaces the single character under the cursor. *r* does not place you in insert mode per se, so there is no reason to use Escape to return to command mode.

The *~* command changes the case of the letter under the cursor from upper- to lowercase, and vice versa. If you place the cursor on the o in Now in the previous example, and repeatedly press *~*, you end up with the following:

```
NOW IS THE TIME FOR ALL GOOD WOMEN TO COME TO THE AID OF THE PARTY█
Afterwards, we'll go out for burgers and fries.
~
~
~
~
~
~
                                                        1,67        All
```

Another useful command for changing words is the *cw* command, which lets you simply type in the new word and—after pressing Escape—removes anything that might be left over from the original word. If the new text is longer than the one being changed, the space is automatically expanded as needed.

Moving Commands

You already know how to use the arrow keys to move around the document. In addition, the w command moves the cursor to the beginning of the next word, and b moves it to the beginning of the current word. The 0 (that's a zero) command moves the cursor to the beginning of the current line, and the $ command moves it to the end of the line.

When editing large files, you'll want to move forward or backward through the file one screen at a time. Pressing Ctrl-F moves the cursor one screen forward, and Ctrl-B moves it one screen backward.

In order to move the cursor to the end of the file, type G. You can also move to an arbitrary line: the command 10G would move the cursor to line 10 in the file. To move to the beginning of the file, use 1G.

Typing / followed by a pattern and the Enter key causes you to jump to the first occurrence of that pattern in the text following the cursor. For example, placing the cursor on the first line of text in our example and typing /burg moves the cursor to the beginning of the word "burgers." Using ? instead of / searches backward through the file.

The pattern following a / or ? command is actually a *regular expression*. Regular expressions are a powerful way to specify patterns for search and replace operations and are used by many Unix utilities. You can find more information about regular expressions in the upcoming section, "Regular Expressions." Using regular expressions, you could, for example, search for the next uppercase letter, using the command:

    /[A-Z]

Therefore, if the pattern you're searching for is not a static string, regular expressions can be used to specify just what you want.

You can couple moving commands with other commands, such as deletion. For example, the command d$ will delete everything from the cursor to the end of the line; dG will delete everything from the cursor to the end of the file.

Saving Files and Quitting vi

Most of the commands dealing with files within *vi* are invoked from *ex* mode. You enter *ex* mode when you press the : key from command mode. This places the cursor on the last line of the display, allowing you to enter various extended commands.

For example, to write the file being edited, use the command :w. Typing : causes you to enter *ex* mode, and typing w followed by the Enter key completes the command. The command :wq writes the file and exits *vi*. (The command ZZ—from command mode, without the ":"—is similar to :wq, but checks first if the file has been changed, and writes it only in this case.)

To quit *vi* without saving changes to the file, use the command :q!. Using :q alone will quit *vi*, but only if modifications to the file have been saved. The ! in :q! means to quit *vi*—and that you really mean it.

Editing Another File

To edit another file, use the :e command. For example, to stop editing *test*, and edit the file *foo* instead, use the command shown at the bottom of the following box:

```
NOW IS THE TIME FOR ALL GOOD WOMEN TO COME TO THE AID OF THE PARTY.
Afterwards, we'll go out for burgers and fries.
~
~
~
~
~
~
~
:e foo
```

If you use :e without writing the file first, you'll get the error message:

```
No write since last change (:edit! overrides)
```

At this point, you can use :w to save the original file, and then use :e, or you can use the command :e! foo, which tells *vi* to edit the new file without saving changes to the original. This can be useful if you edit a file and realize that you have screwed up. You can then use the :e! command; if you don't specify a filename, *vi* discards the changes and re-edits the current file.

Including Other Files

If you use the :r command, you can include the contents of another file in the *vi* buffer. For example, the command:

```
:r foo.txt
```

inserts the contents of the file *foo.txt* after the current line.

Running Shell Commands

The :! command allows you to enter the name of a command, which is executed within *vi*. For example, the command:

```
:!ls -F
```

executes the ls command and displays the results on your screen.

The :r! command is similar to :!, but includes the standard output of the command in the buffer. The command:

```
:r!ls -F
```

produces the following:

```
NOW IS THE TIME FOR ALL GOOD WOMEN TO COME TO THE AID OF THE PARTY.
Afterwards, we'll go out for burgers and fries.
letters/
misc/
papers/
test
~
~
~
~
4 more lines                                              6,1          All
```

If you need to execute a series of shell commands, it's often easier to use the suspend key (usually Ctrl-Z), provided you're using a shell that supports job control, such as *tcsh* or *bash*.

Global Searching and Replacing

There are many more features of *vi* than are documented here; most of these features are implemented through combinations of the simple features we've seen. Here are one or two other tidbits most *vi* users find useful.

The command:

```
:[x,y]s/pattern/replacement/flags
```

searches for pattern between lines x and y in the buffer, and replaces instances of pattern with the replacement text. pattern is a regular expression; replacement is literal text but can contain several special characters to refer to elements in the original pattern. The following command replaces the first occurrence of weeble with wobble on lines 1 through 10, inclusive:

```
:1,10s/weeble/wobble
```

Instead of giving line-number specification, you can use the % symbol to refer to the entire file. Other special symbols can be used in place of x and y. $ refers to the last line of the file. Leave x or y blank to refer to the current line.

Among the *flags* you can use are g to replace all instances of pattern on each line, and c to ask for confirmation for each replacement. In most instances, you will want to use the g flag, unless you want to replace only the first occurrence of pattern on each line.

You can also use *marks* to refer to lines. Marks are just single-letter names that are given to cursor locations within the document. Moving the cursor to a location in the file and typing ma will set the mark a at that point. (Marks may be named any of the letters a–z or A–Z.) You can move the cursor directly to the mark a with the command `a (with a backquote). Using a regular single quote (as in 'a) will move the cursor to the beginning of the line that the mark a is on.

Marks allow you to "remember" cursor locations that denote a region of text. For example, if you want to search and replace a block of text, you can move the cursor to the beginning of the text, set a mark, move the cursor to the end of the text, and use the command:

    :'a,.s/weeble/wobble/

where 'a refers to the line containing mark a, and . refers to the current line.

Moving Text and Using Registers

One way to copy and move text is to delete it (using the d or dd commands) and then replace it with the P command, as described earlier. For example, if you want to delete 10 lines, starting with the line that contains your cursor, and paste them somewhere else, just use the command 10dd (to delete 10 lines), move the cursor to the new location for the text, and type p. You can copy text in this way as well: typing 10dd followed by P (at the same cursor location) deletes the text and immediately replaces it. You can then paste the text elsewhere by moving the cursor and using p multiple times.

Similar to dd is the yy command, which "yanks" text without deleting it. You use p to paste the yanked text as with dd. But note that each yank operation will delete the previously yanked text from the "clipboard."

The deletion and yank commands can be used on more general regions than lines. Recall that the d command deletes text through a move command; for example, d$ deletes text from the cursor to the end of the line. Similarly, y$ yanks text from the cursor to the end of the line.

Let's say you want to yank (or delete) a region of text. This can be done with marks as well. Move the cursor to the beginning of the text to be yanked and set a mark, as in ma. Move the cursor to the end of the text to be yanked and use the command y'a. This yanks text from the cursor position to the mark a. (Remember that the command 'a moves the cursor to the mark a.) Using d instead of y deletes the text from the cursor to the mark.

The most convenient way to cut, copy, and paste portions of text within *vi* is to use *registers*. A register is just a named temporary storage space for text you wish to copy between locations, cut and paste within the document, and so forth.

Registers are given single letter names; any of the characters a–z or A–Z are valid. The " command (a quotation mark) specifies a register; it is followed by the name of the register, as in *"a* for register a. The lowercase letters and their uppercase counterparts refer to the same registers: using the lowercase letter overwrites the previous contents of the register and using the uppercase letter appends to it.

For instance, if we move the cursor to the first line in our example:

```
█OW IS THE TIME FOR ALL GOOD WOMEN TO COME TO THE AID OF THE PARTY.
Afterwards, we'll go out for burgers and fries.
~
~
~
~
~
~
~
~
"test" 2L, 116C                                         1,1          All
```

and use the command "ayy, the current line is yanked into the register a. We can then move the cursor to the second line, and use the command "ap to paste the text from register a after the current line:

```
NOW IS THE TIME FOR ALL GOOD WOMEN TO COME TO THE AID OF THE PARTY.
Afterwards, we'll go out for burgers and fries.
█OW IS THE TIME FOR ALL GOOD WOMEN TO COME TO THE AID OF THE PARTY.
~
~
~
~
~
"test" 2L, 116C                                         3,1          All
```

Similarly, the command "ay'a yanks text from the cursor to mark a into register a. Note that there is no correspondence between mark and register names!

Using registers allows you to copy text between files. Just copy the text to a register, use the :e command to edit a new file, and paste the text from the register.

Extending vi

vi is extensible in many ways. Most of the commands we've introduced can be generalized to arbitrary regions of text. As we've already seen, commands such as d and y operate on the text from the cursor to a move operation, such as $ or G. (dG deletes text from the cursor to the end of the file.) Many other commands operate on text through a move command in the same way. Using marks you can operate on any region of text.

As we mentioned before, *vi* is just a text editor; it doesn't have facilities for spell checking text, compiling programs, and other such features. However, *vi* executes other programs that you can use to extend the editor. The command:

```
:x,y!command
```

executes the named command with the text on lines x through y as standard input, and replaces the lines with the standard output of the command. As with the s (search and replace) command, other specifications, such as % and $, can be used for the line numbers.

For example, let's say you want to prepend a quote character (>) to all the lines in a region of text. One way to do this is to write a short shell or Perl script (see "Programming Languages and Utilities" in Chapter 1) that reads lines of input and outputs those same lines with the quote character prepended. (Or use a *sed* command; there are many alternatives.) You can then send lines of text through this filter, which replaces them with the quoted text within *vi*. If the script is called *quote*, just use a command, such as:

```
:`a,.!quote
```

which quotes the region of text between the cursor location and the mark a.

Be familiar with the various *ex* commands that are available. The :set command allows you to set various options; for example, :set ai turns on auto indentation of text. (:set noai turns it off.)

You can specify *ex* commands (such as :set) to execute when starting up *vi* in the file *.exrc* in your home directory. (The name of this file can be changed with the EXINIT environment variable.) For example, your *.exrc* file might contain:

```
set ai
```

to turn on autoindentation. You don't need the : before *ex* commands in this file.

A number of good tutorials and references for *vi* are available—both online as well as in print. *Learning the vi Editor* is a good place to look for more information. If you have Internet access, the *comp.editors* archives for *vi* contain a number of reference and tutorial documents, as well as interesting *vi* hacks. *ftp://alf.uib.no: /pub/vi* is the archive home site; it is mirrored at *cs.uwp.edu* and elsewhere. The home of *vim* on the Web is *http://www.vim.org*.

The Emacs Editor

Text editors are among the most important applications in the Unix world. They are used so often that many people spend more time within an editor than anywhere else on their Unix system. The same holds true for Linux.

The choice of an editor can be a religious one. Many editors exist, but the Unix community has arranged itself into two major groups: the Emacs camp and the *vi* camp. Because of *vi*'s somewhat nonintuitive user interface, many people (newcomers and seasoned users alike) prefer Emacs over *vi*. However, long-time users of *vi* (and single-finger typists) use it more efficiently than a more complex editor such as Emacs.

If *vi* is one end of the text-editor spectrum, Emacs is the other; they are widely different in their design and philosophy. Emacs is partly the brainchild of Richard Stallman, founder of the Free Software Foundation and author of much of the GNU software.

Emacs is a very large system with more features than any single Unix application to date (some people would even go so far as not to call it an editor but an "integrated environment"). It contains its own LISP language engine that you can use to write extensions for the editor. (Many of the functions within Emacs are written in Emacs LISP.) Emacs includes extensions for everything from compiling and debugging programs to reading and sending electronic mail to X Window System support and more. Emacs also includes its own online tutorial and documentation. The book *Learning GNU Emacs* by Debra Cameron, Bill Rosenblatt, and Eric Raymond (O'Reilly) is a popular guide to the editor.

Most Linux distributions include two variants of Emacs. GNU Emacs is the original version, which is still being developed, but development seems to have slowed down. XEmacs is larger, but much more user-friendly and better integrated with the X Window System (even though you can also use it from the command line, despite its name). If you are not tight on memory and have a reasonably fast computer, we suggest using XEmacs. Another advantage of XEmacs is that many useful packages that you would need to download and install separately with GNU Emacs are already shipped with XEmacs. We will not cover the differences here, though; the discussion in this section applies to both. Whenever we talk about *Emacs* in this section, we mean either version.

Firing It Up

GNU Emacs is simply invoked as:

    $ emacs *options*

Likewise, XEmacs is invoked as:

    $ xemacs *options*

Most of the time, you don't need options. You can specify filenames on the command line, but it's more straightforward to read them in after starting the program.

In Emacs lingo, `C-x` means Ctrl-X, and `M-p` is equivalent to Alt-P. As you might guess, `C-M-p` means Ctrl-Alt-P.

Using these conventions, press `C-x` followed by `C-f` to read in a file or create a new one. The keystrokes display a prompt at the bottom of your screen showing your current working directory. You can create a buffer now to hold what will end up being the content of a new file; let's call the file *wibble.txt*. We now see the following:

The mode line at the bottom indicates the name of the file as well as the type of buffer you're in (which here is Fundamental). Emacs supports many kinds of editing modes; Fundamental is the default for plain-text files, but other modes exist for editing C and TeX source, modifying directories, and so on. Each mode has certain key bindings and commands associated with it, as we'll see soon. Emacs typically determines the mode of the buffer based on the filename extension.

To the right of the buffer type is the word All, which means that you are currently looking at the entire file (which is empty). Typically, you will see a percentage, which represents how far into the file you are.

If you're running Emacs under the X Window System, a new window will be created for the editor with a menu bar at the top, scrollbars, and other goodies. In the section "Emacs and Other Editors," in Chapter 11, we discuss Emacs's special features when used within X.

Simple Editing Commands

Emacs is more straightforward than *vi* when it comes to basic text editing. The arrow keys should move the cursor around the buffer; if they don't (in case Emacs is not configured for your terminal), use the keys C-p (previous line), C-n (next line), C-f (forward character), and C-b (backward character).

If you find using the Alt key uncomfortable, press Escape and then p. Pressing and releasing Escape is equivalent to holding down Alt.

Already we must take the first aside on our tour of Emacs. Literally every command and key within Emacs is customizable. That is, with a "default" Emacs configuration, C-p maps to the internal function *previous-line*, which moves the cursor (also called "point") to the previous line. However, you can easily rebind different keys to these functions, or write new functions and bind keys to them, and so forth. Unless otherwise stated, the keys we introduce here work for the default Emacs configuration. Later we'll show you how to customize the keys for your own use.

Back to editing: using the arrow keys or one of the equivalents moves the cursor around the current buffer. Just start typing text, and it is inserted at the current cursor location. Pressing the Backspace or Delete key should delete text at the cursor. If it doesn't, we'll show how to fix it in the section "Tailoring Emacs" later in this chapter. Now begin to type:

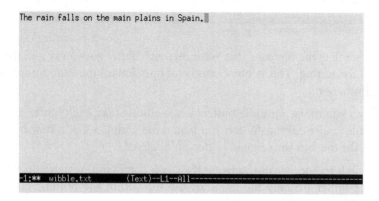

The keys C-a and C-e move the cursor to the beginning and end of the current line, respectively. C-v moves forward a page; M-v moves back a page. There are many more basic editing commands, but we'll allow the Emacs online documentation (discussed shortly) to fill those in.

In order to get out of Emacs, use the command C-x C-c. This is the first of the extended commands we've seen; many Emacs commands require several keys. C-x alone is a "prefix" to other keys. In this case, pressing C-x followed by C-c quits Emacs, first asking for confirmation if you want to quit without saving changes to the buffer.

You can use C-x C-s to save the current file, and C-x C-f to "find" another file to edit. For example, typing C-x C-f presents you with a prompt, such as:

    Find file: /home/loomer/mdw/

where the current directory is displayed. After this, type the name of the file to find. Pressing the Tab key will do filename completion similar to that used in *bash* and *tcsh*. For example, entering:

    Find file: /home/loomer/mdw/**.bash**

and pressing Tab opens another buffer, showing all possible completions, as so:

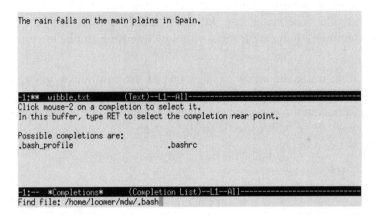

After you complete the filename, the *Completions* buffer goes away and the new file is displayed for editing. This is one example of how Emacs uses temporary buffers to present information.

Emacs allows you to use multiple buffers when editing text; each buffer may contain a different file you're editing. When you load a file with C-x C-f, a new buffer is created to edit the file, but the original buffer isn't deleted.

You can switch to another buffer using the C-x b command, which asks you for the name of the buffer (usually the name of the file within the buffer). For example, pressing C-x b presents the prompt:

```
Switch to buffer: (default wibble.txt)
```

The default buffer is the previous one visited. Press Enter to switch to the default buffer, or type another buffer name. Using C-x C-b will present a buffer list (in a buffer of its own), as so:

```
MR Buffer          Size  Mode            File
-- ------          ----  ----            ----
 % .bashrc         5507  Shell-script    /home/loomer/mdw/.bashrc
   wibble.txt        43  Text            /home/loomer/mdw/wibble.txt
*% *Buffer List*   211   Buffer Menu
   *Completions*   159   Completion List
   *scratch*       182   Text
*  *Messages*      1303  Fundamental






-1:%* *Buffer List*    (Buffer Menu)--L3--All---------------------
```

Popping up the buffer menu splits the Emacs screen into two "windows," which you can switch between using C-x o. More than two concurrent windows are possible as well. In order to view just one window at a time, switch to the appropriate one and press C-x 1. This hides all the other windows, but you can switch to them later using the C-x b command just described. Using C-x k actually deletes a buffer from Emacs's memory.

Tutorial and Online Help

Already Emacs looks a bit complex; that is simply because it's such a flexible system. Before we go any further, it is instructive to introduce Emacs's built-in online help and tutorial. This documentation has also been published in book form as the *GNU Emacs Manual*, by Richard M. Stallman (GNU Press).

Using the C-h command gives you a list of help options on the last line of the display. Pressing C-h again describes what they are. In particular, C-h followed by t drops you into the Emacs tutorial. It should be self-explanatory, and an interactive tutorial about Emacs tells you more about the system than we can hope to cover here.

After going through the Emacs tutorial you should get accustomed to the Info system, where the rest of the Emacs documentation resides. C-h followed by i enters the Info reader. A mythical Info page might look like this:

```
File: intercal.info,  Node: Top,  Next: Instructions,  Up: (dir)

    This file documents the Intercal interpreter for Linux.

  * Menu:

  * Instructions::      How to read this manual.
  * Overview::          Preliminary information.
  * Examples::          Example Intercal programs and bugs.
  * Concept Index::     Index of concepts.
```

As you see, text is presented along with a menu to other "nodes." Pressing m and then entering a node name from the menu will allow you to read that node. You can read nodes sequentially by pressing the spacebar, which jumps to the next node in the document (indicated by the information line at the top of the buffer). Here, the next node is Instructions, which is the first node in the menu.

Each node also has a link to the parent node (Up), which here is (dir), meaning the Info page directory. Pressing u takes you to the parent node. In addition, each node has a link to the previous node, if it exists (in this case, it does not). The p command moves to the previous node. The l command returns you to the node most recently visited.

Within the Info reader, pressing ? gives you a list of commands and pressing h presents you with a short tutorial on using the system. Since you're running Info within Emacs, you can use Emacs commands as well (such as C-x b to switch to another buffer).

If you think that the Info system is arcane and obsolete, please keep in my mind that it was designed to work on all kinds of systems, including those lacking graphics or powerful processing capabilities.

Other online help is available within Emacs. Pressing C-h C-h gives you a list of help options. One of these is C-h k, after which you press a key, and documentation about the function that is bound to that key appears.

Deleting, Copying, and Moving Text

There are various ways to move and duplicate blocks of text within Emacs. These methods involve use of the *mark*, which is simply a "remembered" cursor location you can set using various commands. The block of text between the current cursor location (*point*) and the mark is called the *region*.

You can set the mark using the key C-@ (or C-Space on most systems). Moving the cursor to a location and pressing C-@ sets the mark at that position. You can now move the cursor to another location within the document, and the region is defined as the text between mark and point.

Many Emacs commands operate on the region. The most important of these commands deal with deleting and yanking text. The command C-w deletes the current region and saves it in the *kill ring*. The kill ring is a list of text blocks that have been deleted. You can then paste (*yank*) the text at another location, using the C-y command. (Note that the semantics of the term *yank* differ between *vi* and Emacs. In *vi*, "yanking" text is equivalent to adding it to the undo register without deleting it, while in Emacs, "yank" means to paste text.) Using the kill ring, you can paste not only the most recently deleted block of text, but also blocks of text that were deleted previously.

For example, type the following text into an Emacs buffer:

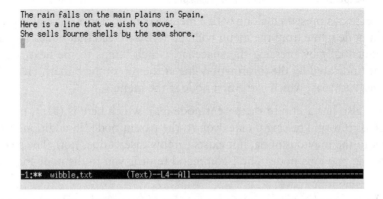

Now, move the cursor to the beginning of the second line ("Here is a line..."), and set the mark with C-@. Move to the end of the line (with C-e), and delete the region using C-w. The buffer should now look like the following:

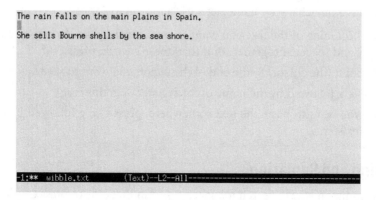

In order to yank the text just deleted, move the cursor to the end of the buffer and press C-y. The line should be pasted at the new location:

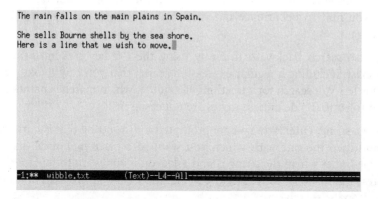

Pressing C-y repeatedly will insert the text multiple times.

You can copy text in a similar fashion. Using M-w instead of C-w will copy the region into the kill ring without deleting it. (Remember that M- means holding down the Alt key or pressing Escape before the w.)

Text that is deleted using other kill commands, such as C-k, is also added to the kill ring. This means that you don't need to set the mark and use C-w to move a block of text; any command that deletes more than one character will do.

In order to recover previously deleted blocks of text (which are saved on the kill ring), use the command M-y after yanking with C-y. M-y replaces the yanked text with the previous block from the kill ring. Pressing M-y repeatedly cycles through the contents of the kill ring. This feature is useful if you wish to move or copy multiple blocks of text.

Emacs also provides a more general *register* mechanism, similar to that found in *vi*. Among other things, you can use this feature to save text you want to paste in later. A register has a one-character name; let's use a for this example:

1. At the beginning of the text you want to save, set the mark by pressing the Control key and spacebar together (or if that doesn't work, press C-@).

2. Move point (the cursor) to the end of the region you want to save.

3. Press C-x x followed by the name of the register (a in this case).

4. When you want to paste the text somewhere, press C-x g followed by the name of the register, a.

Searching and Replacing

The most common way to search for a string within Emacs is to press C-s. This starts what is called an *incremental search*. You then start entering the characters you are looking for. Each time you press a character, Emacs searches forward for a string matching everything you've typed so far. If you make a mistake, just press the Delete key and continue typing the right characters. If the string cannot be found, Emacs beeps. If you find an occurrence but you want to keep searching for another one, press C-s again.

You can also search backward this way using the C-r key. Several other types of searches exist, including a regular expression search that you can invoke by pressing M-C-s. This lets you search for something like jo.*n, which matches names like John, Joan, and Johann. (By default, searches are not case-sensitive.)

To replace a string, enter M-%. You are prompted for the string that is currently in the buffer, and then the one with which you want to replace it. Emacs displays each place in the buffer where the string is and asks you if you want to replace this occurrence. Press the spacebar to replace the string, the Delete key to skip this string, or a period to stop the search.

If you know you want to replace all occurrences of a string that follow your current place in the buffer, without being queried for each one, enter M-x replace-string. (The M-x key allows you to enter the name of an Emacs function and execute it, without use of a key binding. Many Emacs functions are available only via M-x, unless you bind them to keys yourself.) A regular expression can be replaced by entering M-x replace-regexp.

Macros

The name Emacs comes partly from the word "macros." A macro is a simple but powerful feature that makes Emacs a pleasure to use. If you plan on doing anything frequently and repetitively, just press C-x (, perform the operation once, and then press C-x). The two C-x commands with the opening and closing parentheses remember all the keys you pressed. Then you can execute the commands over and over again by pressing C-x e.

Here's a example you can try on any text file; it capitalizes the first word of each line.

1. Press C-x (to begin the macro.

2. Press C-a to put point at the beginning of the current line. It's important to know where you are each time a macro executes. By pressing C-a you are making sure the macro will always go to the beginning of the line, which is where you want to be.

3. Press M-c to make the first letter of the first word a capital letter.

4. Press C-a again to return to the beginning of the line and C-n or the down arrow to go to the beginning of the following line. This ensures that the macro will start execution at the right place next time.

5. Press C-x) to end the macro.

6. Press C-x e repeatedly to capitalize the following lines. Or press C-u several times, followed by C-x e. The repeated uses of C-u are prefix keys, causing the following command to execute many times. If you get to the end of the document while the macro is still executing, no harm is done; Emacs just beeps and stops executing the macro.

Running Commands and Programming within Emacs

Emacs provides interfaces for many programs, which you can run within an Emacs buffer. For example, Emacs modes exist for reading and sending electronic mail, reading Usenet news, compiling programs, and interacting with the shell. In this section, we'll introduce some of these features.

To send electronic mail from within Emacs, press C-x m. This opens up a buffer that allows you to compose and send an email message:

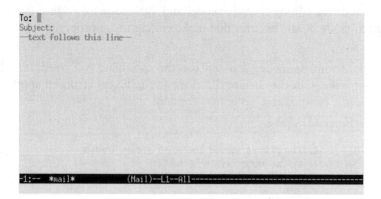

Simply enter your message within this buffer and use C-c C-s to send it. You can also insert text from other buffers, extend the interface with your own Emacs LISP functions, and so on. Furthermore, an Emacs mode called RMAIL lets you read your electronic mail right within Emacs, but we won't discuss it here because most people prefer standalone mailers. (Usually, these mailers let you choose Emacs as your editor for email messages.)

Similar to the RMAIL mail interface is GNUS, the Emacs-based newsreader, which you can start with the M-x gnus command. After startup (and a bit of chewing on your *.newsrc* file), a list of newsgroups will be presented, along with a count of unread articles for each:

```
9:▇comp.os.linux.networking
5:  comp.os.linux.setup
3:  comp.os.linux.x
```

```
--:--   Gnus: *Group* {nntp:news.sonic.net}        (Grou
```

GNUS is an example of the power of using Emacs interfaces to other tools. You get all the convenience of Emacs's navigation, search, and macro capabilities, along with specific key sequences appropriate for the tool you're using.

Using the arrow keys, you can select a newsgroup to read. Press the spacebar to begin reading articles from that group. Two buffers will be displayed, one containing a list of articles and the other displaying the current article.

Using n and p move to the next and previous articles, respectively. Then use f and F to post a follow-up to the current article (either including or excluding the current article), and r and R to reply to the article via electronic mail. There are many other GNUS commands; use C-h m to get a list of them. If you're used to a newsreader, such as *rn*, GNUS will be somewhat familiar.

Emacs provides a number of modes for editing various types of files. For example, there is C mode for editing C source code, and TEX mode for editing (surprise) TEX source. Each mode boasts features that make editing the appropriate type of file easier.

For example, within C mode, you can use the command M-x compile, which, by default, runs *make –k* in the current directory and redirects errors to another buffer. For example, the compilation buffer may contain:

```
cd /home/loomer/mdw/pgmseq/
make -k
gcc -O -O2 -I. -I../include -c stream_load.c -o stream_load.o
stream_load.c:217: syntax error before `struct'
stream_load.c:217: parse error before `struct'
```

You can move the cursor to a line containing an error message and press C-c C-c to make the cursor jump to that line in the corresponding source buffer. Emacs opens a buffer for the appropriate source file if one does not already exist. Now you can edit and compile programs entirely within Emacs.

Emacs also provides a complete interface to the *gdb* debugger, which is described in the section "Using Emacs with gdb" in Chapter 14.

Usually, Emacs selects the appropriate mode for the buffer based on the filename extension. For example, editing a file with the extension *.c* in the filename automatically selects C mode for that buffer.

Shell mode is one of the most popular Emacs extensions. Shell mode allows you to interact with the shell in an Emacs buffer, using the command M-x shell. You can edit, cut, and paste command lines with standard Emacs commands. You can also run single shell commands from Emacs using M-!. If you use M-| instead, the contents of the current region are piped to the given shell command as standard input. This is a general interface for running subprograms from within Emacs.

Tailoring Emacs

The Emacs online documentation should be sufficient to get you on track to learning more about the system and growing accustomed to it. However, sometimes it is hard to locate some of the most helpful hints for getting started. Here we'll present a rundown on certain customization options many Emacs users choose to employ to make life easier.

The Emacs personal customization file is *.emacs*, which should reside in your home directory. This file should contain code, written in Emacs LISP, which runs or defines functions to customize your Emacs environment. (If you've never written LISP before, don't worry; most customizations using it are quite simple.)

One of the most common things users customize are key bindings. For instance, if you use Emacs to edit SGML documents, you can bind the key C-c s to switch to SGML mode. Put this in your *.emacs* file:

```
; C-c followed by s will put buffer into SGML mode."
(global-set-key "\C-cs" 'sgml-mode)
```

Comments in Emacs LISP start with a semicolon. The command that follows runs the command *global-set-key*. Now you don't have to type in the long sequence M-x sgml-mode to start editing in SGML. Just press the two characters C-c s. This works anywhere in Emacs—no matter what mode your buffer is in—because it is global. (Of course, Emacs may also recognize an SGML or XML file by its suffix and put it in SGML mode for you automatically.)

A customization that you might want to use is making the text mode the default mode and turning on the "auto-fill" minor mode (which makes text automatically wrap if it is too long for one line) like this:

```
; Make text mode the default, with auto-fill
(setq default-major-mode 'text-mode)
(add-hook 'text-mode-hook 'turn-on-auto-fill)
```

You don't always want your key mappings to be global. As you use TEX mode, C mode, and other modes defined by Emacs, you'll find useful things you'd like to do only in a single mode. Here, we define a simple LISP function to insert some characters into C code, and then bind the function to a key for our convenience:

```
(defun start-if-block()
  (interactive)
  (insert "if () {\n}\n")
  (backward-char 6)
)
```

We start the function by declaring it "interactive" so that we can invoke it (otherwise, it would be used only internally by other functions). Then we use the *insert* function to put the following characters into our C buffer:

```
if () {
}
```

Strings in Emacs can contain standard C escape characters. Here, we've used \n for a newline.

Now we have a template for an if block. To put on the ribbon and the bow, our function also moves backward six characters so that point is within the parentheses, and we can immediately start typing an expression.

Our whole goal was to make it easy to insert these characters, so now let's bind our function to a key:

```
(define-key c-mode-map "\C-ci" 'start-if-block)
```

The *define-key* function binds a key to a function. By specifying c-mode-map, we indicate that the key works only in C mode. There is also a tex-mode-map for mode, a lisp-mode-map that you will want to know about if you play with your *.emacs* file a lot.

If you'd like to write your own Emacs LISP functions, you should read the Info pages for *elisp*, which should be available on your system. Two good books on writing Emacs LISP functions are *An Introduction to Programming in Emacs Lisp*, by Robert J. Chassell (GNU Press) and *Writing GNU Emacs Extensions*, by Bob Glickstein (O'Reilly).

Now here's an important customization you may need. On many terminals the Backspace key sends the character C-h, which is the Emacs help key. To fix this, you should change the internal table Emacs uses to interpret keys, as follows:

```
(keyboard-translate ?\C-h ?\C-?)
```

Pretty cryptic code. \C-h is recognizable as the Control key pressed with h, which happens to produce the same ASCII code (8) as the Backspace key. \C-? represents the Delete key (ASCII code 127). Don't confuse this question mark with the question marks that precede each backslash. `?\C-h` means "the ASCII code corresponding to `\C-h`." You could just as well specify 8 directly.

So now, both Backspace and `C-h` will delete. You've lost your help key. Therefore, another good customization would be to bind another key to `C-h`. Let's use `C-\`, which isn't used often for anything else. You have to double the backslash when you specify it as a key:

```
(keyboard-translate ?\C-\\ ?\C-h)
```

On the X Window System, there is a way to change the code sent by your Backspace key using the *xmodmap* command, but we'll have to leave it up to you to do your own research. It is not a completely portable solution (so we can't show you an example guaranteed to work), and it may be too sweeping for your taste (it also changes the meaning of the Backspace key in your *xterm* shell and everywhere else).

There are other key bindings you may want to use. For example, you may prefer to use the keys `C-f` and `C-b` to scroll forward (or backward) one page at a time, as in *vi*. In your *.emacs* file you might include the following lines:

```
(global-set-key "\C-f" 'scroll-up)
(global-set-key "\C-b" 'scroll-down)
```

Again, we have to issue a caveat: be careful not to redefine keys that have other important uses. (One way to find out is to use `C-h k` to tell you what a key does in the current mode. You should also consider that the key may have definitions in other modes.) In particular, you'll lose access to a lot of functions if you rebind the *prefix keys* that start commands, such as `C-x` and `C-c`.

You can create your own prefix keys, if you really want to extend your current mode with lots of new commands. Use something like:

```
(global-unset-key "\C-d")
(global-set-key "\C-d\C-f" 'my-function)
```

First, we must unbind the `C-d` key (which simply deletes the character under the cursor) in order to use it as a prefix for other keys. Now, pressing `C-d C-f` will execute *my-function*.

You may also prefer to use another mode besides Fundamental or Text for editing "vanilla" files. Indented Text mode, for example, automatically indents lines of text relative to the previous line so that it starts in the same column (as with the `:set ai` function in *vi*). To turn on this mode by default, use:

```
; Default mode for editing text
(setq default-major-mode 'indented-text-mode)
```

You should also rebind the Enter key to indent the next line of text:

```
(define-key indented-text-mode-map "\C-m" 'newline-and-indent)
```

Emacs also provides "minor" modes, which are modes you use along with major modes. For example, Overwrite mode is a minor mode that causes newly typed characters to overwrite the text in the buffer, instead of inserting it. To bind the key C-r to toggle overwrite mode, use the command:

```
; Toggle overwrite mode.
(global-set-key "\C-r" 'overwrite-mode)
```

Another minor mode is Autofill, which automatically wraps lines as you type them. That is, instead of pressing the Enter key at the end of each line of text, you may continue typing and Emacs automatically breaks the line for you. To enable Autofill mode, use the commands:

```
(setq text-mode-hook 'turn-on-auto-fill)
(setq fill-column 72)
```

This turns on Autofill mode whenever you enter Text mode (through the *text-mode-hook* function). It also sets the point at which to break lines at 72 characters.

Regular Expressions

Even a few regular expression tricks can vastly increase your power to search for text and alter it in bulk. Regular expressions were associated only with Unix tools and languages for a long time; now they are popping up in other environments, such as Microsoft's .NET, but only Unix offers them in a wide variety of places, such as text editors and the *grep* command where ordinary users can exploit them.

Let's suppose you're looking through a file that contains mail messages. You're on a bunch of mailing lists with names, such as gyro-news and gyro-talk, so you're looking for Subject lines with gyro- in them. You can use your text editor or the *grep* command to search for:

```
^Subject:.*gyro-
```

This means "look for lines beginning with Subject:, followed by any number of any kind of character, followed by gyro-." The regular expression is made up of a number of parts, some reproducing the plain text you're looking for and others expressing general concepts like "beginning of line." Figure 9-1 shows what the parts mean and how they fit together.

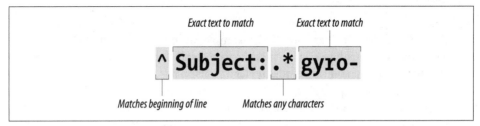

Figure 9-1. Simple regular expression

Just to give a hint of how powerful and sophisticated regular expressions can be, let's refine the one in Figure 9-1 for a narrower search. This time, we know that mailing

---

lists on gyros send out mail with Subject lines that begin with the name of the list in brackets, such as Subject: [gyro-news] or Subject: [gyro-talk]. We can search for precisely such lines, as follows:

```
^Subject: *\[gyro-[a-z]*\]
```

Figure 9-2 shows what the parts of this expression mean. We'll just mention a couple of interesting points here.

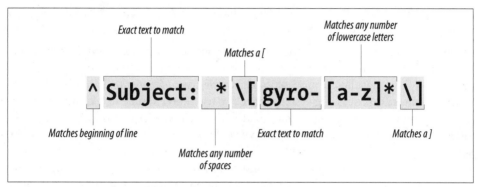

Figure 9-2. Regular expression with more parts

Brackets, like carets and asterisks, are special characters in regular expressions. Brackets are used to mark whole classes of characters you want to search for, such as [a-z] to represent "any lowercase character." We don't want the bracket before gyro to have this special meaning, so we put a backslash in front of it; this is called *escaping* the bracket. (In other words, we let the bracket escape being considered a meta-character in the regular expression.)

The first asterisk in our expression follows a space, so it means "match any number of spaces in succession." The second asterisk follows the [a-z] character class, so it applies to that entire construct. By itself, [a-z] matches one and only one lowercase letter. Together, [a-z]* means "match any number of lowercase letters in succession."

A sophisticated use of regular expressions can take weeks to learn, and readers who want to base applications on regular expressions would do well to read *Mastering Regular Expressions*, by Jeffrey Friedl (O'Reilly).

Text and Document Processing

Now that most of the world uses WYSIWYG word processors, and several good ones are available even for Linux, why use the anachronistic-looking text processors described in this section? Actually, text processing (especially in the form of XML) is the wave of the future. People will desire WYSIWYG interfaces, but they will demand a simple, standard, text format underneath to make their documents portable while allowing an unlimited range of automated tools to manipulate the documents.

Because the tools described here are open source and widely available, you can use one of their formats without guilt and reasonably expect your readers to have access to formatters. You can also use an impressive range of tools developed over the years to handle these formats and do sophisticated processing for you, such as to develop a bibliography in TeX. Finally, filters have been developed (although they don't always work perfectly) to convert documents between each of these formats and other popular formats, including the formats used by commercial word processors. So you're not totally locked in, although you will probably have to exert some manual effort to accomplish an accurate conversion.

In the first chapter, we briefly mentioned various text processing systems available for Linux and how they differ from word processing systems that you may be familiar with. While most word processors allow the user to enter text in a WYSIWYG environment, text processing systems have the user enter source text using a text-formatting language, which can be modified with any text editor. (In fact, Emacs provides special modes for editing various types of text-formatting languages.) Then, the source is processed into a printable (or viewable) document using the text processor itself. Finally, you process the output and send it to a file or to a viewer application for display, or you hand it off to a printer daemon to queue for printing to a local or remote device.

In this section, we'll talk first about WYSIMWYG (what-you-see-is-maybe-what-you-get) word processors like those that predominate on Windows and the Macintosh. After that, we'll discuss some of the most popular text processing systems for Linux: TeX, SGML, *groff*, and Texinfo.

Word Processors

One obvious sign that Linux has come of age is that many popular WYSIWYG word processing systems are available for it today. For some time, it had even been rumored that Microsoft was going to port its office suite to Linux, but this is not likely to happen. A Microsoft suite is not really needed any longer anyway because you can get other quite good word processors.

Another option is to use Anyware Office by VistaSource, Inc. Anyware Office is an office suite that is commercially made but inexpensive for Linux. It includes not only a word processor, but also a spreadsheet, a drawing program, a mail program, and other smaller tools. In some respects, Anyware Office behaves differently from word processors like Microsoft Word or WordPerfect, but once you get used to it, it can be quite useful and handy. Especially noteworthy is its support for importing and exporting FrameMaker documents. The development seems to have stopped somewhat, though, and it is uncertain what will become of this product.

Sun Microsystems provides its office productivity suite StarOffice on a number of platforms, including Linux. It was open sourced a while ago and is now maintained in two branches: the commercial StarOffice one which you can purchase from Sun, and the freely available OpenOffice one which you can download from *http://www.openoffice.org*. Both are supposed to be mostly functionally identical, but OpenOffice may not have all the bells and whistles (like templates, clipart, etc.) that StarOffice has. OpenOffice is released under the GPL, so if you fancy reading through the 3 million lines of source code making up an office productivity suite, this would be an opportunity for you.

OpenOffice is huge, so if you have a slow connection to the Net, check first whether your distribution doesn't already contain it.

In addition, there is KWord, the word processor of the office productivity suite of the KDE desktop environment, KOffice. KWord has made a lot of progress lately. It sports an interesting frame concept that makes it suitable even for some desktop publishing tasks. Of course, you can also write your letter to grandma with it. You can find more information about it at *http://www.kde.org*.

Finally, a good and lightweight alternative is AbiWord, more information about which you can find at *http://www.abiword.org*.

All those programs have one feature in common that many consider a key requirement for doing office-type work on Linux: they can import Microsoft Word documents quite well. While you may well decide, as a new Linux enthusiast, that you won't accept documents sent to you in proprietary formats, sometimes they come from your boss, and you can't refuse to read them just because you are running Linux. In this case, it is good to know that Linux-based solutions are available.

The LyX package (also available as KLyX with a more modern user interface) is another alternative. It provides a decent WYSIWYG X user interface that works with window managers from standard Linux distributions and uses the LATEX and TEX packages in order to format the text for printing. If you can live with the formatting limits of the package (most of us can), you may find that LyX/KLyX is an excellent solution. LyX/KLyX does not know how to display some of the powerful formatting features that TEX provides, so if you are a power TEX user, this isn't for you. LyX/KLyX isn't part of most Linux distributions; to try it you will have to get it from a Linux archive.

TEX and LATEX

TEX is a professional text processing system for all kinds of documents, articles, and books—especially those that contain a great deal of mathematics. It is a somewhat "low-level" text processing language because it describes to the system how to lay out text on the page, how it should be spaced, and so on. TEX doesn't concern itself directly with higher-level elements of text such as chapters, sections, footnotes, and so forth (those things that you, the writer, care about the most). For this reason, TEX is known as a functional text-formatting language (referring to the actual physical layout of text on a page) rather than a logical one (referring to logical elements, such as chapters and sections). TeX was designed by Donald E. Knuth, one of the world's foremost experts in programming. One of Knuth's motives for developing TeX was to produce a typesetting system powerful enough to handle the mathematics formatting needed for his series of computer science textbooks. Knuth ended up taking an eight-year detour to finish TeX; most would agree the result was well worth the wait.

Of course, TeX is very extensible, and it is possible to write macros for TeX that allow writers to concern themselves primarily with the logical, rather than the physical, format of the document. In fact, a number of such macro packages have been developed—the most popular of which is LaTeX, a set of extensions for TeX designed by Leslie Lamport. LaTeX commands are concerned mostly with logical structure, but because LaTeX is just a set of macros on top of TeX, you can use plain commands as well. LaTeX greatly simplifies the use of TeX, hiding most of the low-level functional features from the writer.

In order to write well-structured documents using TeX, you would either have to decide on a prebuilt macro package, such as LaTeX, or develop your own (or use a combination of the two). In *The TeX Book* (Addison Wesley), Knuth presents his own set of macros that he used for production of the book. As you might expect, they include commands for beginning new chapters, sections, and the like—somewhat similar to their LaTeX counterparts. In the rest of this section, we'll concentrate on the use of LaTeX, which provides support for many types of documents: technical articles, manuals, books, letters, and so on. As with plain TeX, LaTeX is extensible as well.

Learning the ropes

If you've never used a text-formatting system before, there are a number of new concepts of which you should be aware. As we said, text processing systems start with a source document, which you enter with a plain-text editor, such as Emacs. The source is written in a text-formatting language, which includes the text you wish to appear in your document, as well as commands that tell the text processor how to format it. In the first chapter we gave a simple example of what the LaTeX language looks like and what kind of output it produces.

So, without further ado, let's dive in and see how to write a simple document and format it, from start to finish. As a demonstration, we'll show how to use LaTeX to write a short business letter. Sit down at your favorite text editor, and enter the following text into a file (without the line numbers, of course). Call it *letter.tex*:

```
1  \documentclass{letter}
2  \address{755 Chmod Way \\ Apt 0x7F \\
3          Pipeline, N.M. 09915}
4  \signature{Boomer Petway}
5
6  \begin{document}
7  \begin{letter}{O'Reilly and Associates, Inc. \\
```

```
 8                    1005 Gravenstein Highway North \\
 9                    Sebastopol, C.A. 95472}
10
11 \opening{Dear Mr. O'Reilly,}
12
13 I would like to comment on the \LaTeX\ example as presented in
14 Chapter~9 of {\em Running Linux}. Although it was a valiant effort,
15 I find that the example falls somewhat short of what
16 one might expect in a discussion of text-formatting systems.
17 In a future edition of the book, I suggest that you replace
18 the example with one that is more instructive.
19
20 \closing{Thank you,}
21
22 \end{letter}
23 \end{document}
```

This is a complete LaTeX document for the business letter that we wish to send. As you can see, it contains the actual text of the letter, with a number of commands (using backslashes and braces) thrown in. Let's walk through it.

Line 1 uses the documentclass command to specify the class of document that we're producing (which is a letter). Commands in LaTeX begin with a backslash and are followed by the actual command name, which in this case is documentclass. Following the command name are any arguments, enclosed in braces. LaTeX supports several document classes, such as article, report, and book, and you can define your own. Specifying the document class defines global macros for use within the TeX document, such as the address and signature commands used on lines 2-4. As you might guess, the address and signature commands specify your own address and name in the letter. The double-backslashes (\\) that appear in the address generate line breaks in the resulting output of the address.

A word about how LaTeX processes input: as with most text-formatting systems, whitespace, line breaks, and other such features in the input source are not passed literally into the output. Therefore, you can break lines more or less wherever you please; when formatting paragraphs, LaTeX will fit the lines back together again. Of course, there are exceptions: blank lines in the input begin new paragraphs, and there are commands to force LaTeX to treat the source text literally.

On line 6, the command \begin{document} signifies the beginning of the document as a whole. Everything enclosed within the \begin{document} and \end{document} on line 22 is considered part of the text to be formatted; anything before \begin{document} is called the *preamble* and defines formatting parameters before the actual body.

On lines 7-9, \begin{letter} begins the actual letter. This is required because you may have many letters within a single source file, and a \begin{letter} is needed for each. This command takes as an argument the address of the intended recipient; as with the address command, double-backslashes signify line breaks in the address.

Line 11 uses the opening command to open the letter. Following on lines 12-18 is the actual body of the letter. As straightforward as it may seem, there are a few tricks hidden in the body as well. On line 13 the LaTeX command generates the logo. You'll notice that a backslash follows as well as precedes the LaTeX command; the trailing backslash is used to force a space after the word "LaTeX" This is because TeX ignores spaces after command invocations; the command must be followed by a backslash and a space. (Otherwise, "LaTeX//" would appear as "LaTeX is fun.")

There are two quirks of note on line 14. First of all, a tilde (~) is present between Chapter and 9, which causes a space to appear between the two words, but prevents a line break between them in the output (that is, to prevent Chapter from being on the end of a line, and 9 from being on the beginning of the next). You need only use the tilde to generate a space between two words that should be stuck together on the same line, as in Chapter~9 and Mr.~Jones. (In retrospect, we could have used the tilde in the \begin{letter} and opening commands, although it's doubtful TeX would break a line anywhere within the address or the opening.)

The second thing to take note of on line 14 is the use of \em to generate *emphasized text* in the output. TeX supports various other fonts, including **boldface** (\bf) and typewriter (\tt).

Line 20 uses the closing command to close off the letter. This also has the effect of appending the signature used on line 4 after the closing in the output. Lines 22–23 use the commands \end{letter} and \end{document} to end the letter and document environments begun on lines 6 and 7.

You'll notice that none of the commands in the LaTeX source has anything to do with setting up margins, line spacing, or other functional issues of text formatting. That's all taken care of by the LaTeX macros on top of the TeX engine. LaTeX provides reasonable defaults for these parameters; if you wanted to change any of these formatting options, you could use other LaTeX commands (or lower-level TeX commands) to modify them.

We don't expect you to understand all the intricacies of using LaTeX from such a limited example, although this should give you an idea of how a living, breathing LaTeX document looks. Now, let's format the document in order to print it out.

Formatting and printing

Believe it or not, the command used to format LaTeX source files into something printable is *latex*. After editing and saving the previous example, *letter.tex*, you should be able to use the command:

```
eggplant$ latex letter
This is TeX, Version 3.14159 (Web2C 7.3.1)
(letter.tex
```

```
LaTeX2e <2000/06/01>
Babel <v3.7h> and hyphenation patterns for american, french, german, ngerman, no
hyphenation, loaded.
(/usr/share/texmf/tex/latex/base/letter.cls
Document Class: letter 1999/04/29 v1.2z Standard LaTeX document class
(/usr/share/texmf/tex/latex/base/size10.clo))
No file letter.aux.
[1] (letter.aux) )
Output written on letter.dvi (1 page, 1128 bytes).
Transcript written on letter.log.
eggplant$
```

latex assumes the extension *.tex* for source files. Here, LaTeX has processed the source *letter.tex* and saved the results in the file *letter.dvi*. This is a "device-independent" file that generates printable output on a variety of printers. Various tools exist for converting *.dvi* files to PostScript, HP LaserJet, and other formats, as we'll see shortly.

Instead of immediately printing your letter, you may wish to preview it to be sure that everything looks right. If you're running the X Window System, you can use the *xdvi* command to preview *.dvi* files on your screen. If you are also using the KDE desktop environment, *kdvi* is a more user-friendly version of *xdvi*. What about printing the letter? First, you need to convert the *.dvi* to something your printer can handle. DVI drivers exist for many printer types. Almost all the program names begin with the three characters *dvi*, as in *dvips*, *dvilj*, and so forth. If your system doesn't have one you need, you have to get the appropriate driver from the archives if you have Internet access. See the FAQ for *comp.text.tex* for details.

If you're lucky enough to have a PostScript printer, you can use *dvips* to generate PostScript from the *.dvi*:

```
eggplant$ dvips -o letter.ps letter.dvi
```

You can then print the PostScript using *lpr*. Or, to do this in one step:

```
eggplant$ dvips letter.dvi | lpr
```

There are printer-specific DVI drivers like *dvilj* for HP LaserJets as well, but most of these are considered obsolete; use *dvips* instead and, if necessary, Ghostscript (see below) instead.

If you can't find a DVI driver for your printer, you might be able to use Ghostscript to convert PostScript (produced by *dvips*) into something you can print. Although some of Ghostscript's fonts are less than optimal, Ghostscript does allow you to use Adobe fonts (which you can obtain for Windows and use with Ghostscript under Linux). Ghostscript also provides an SVGA preview mode you can use if you're not running X. At any rate, after you manage to format and print the example letter, it should end up looking something like that in Figure 9-3.

Finally, it should be mentioned that you can also use TeX to create PDF files, either using the *dvipdf* driver or using a special program called *pdftex*.

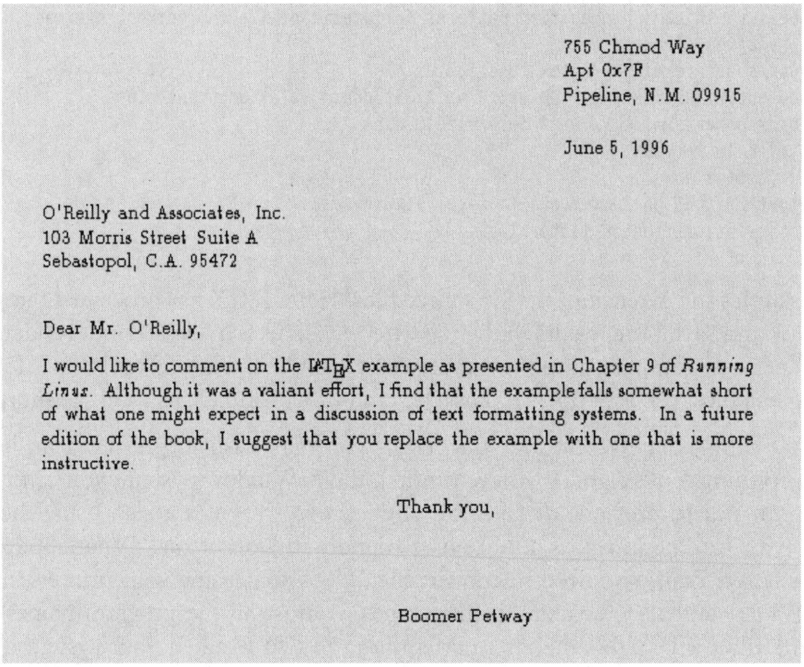

> 755 Chmod Way
> Apt 0x7F
> Pipeline, N.M. 09915
>
> June 5, 1996
>
> O'Reilly and Associates, Inc.
> 103 Morris Street Suite A
> Sebastopol, C.A. 95472
>
> Dear Mr. O'Reilly,
>
> I would like to comment on the LaTeX example as presented in Chapter 9 of *Running
> Linux*. Although it was a valiant effort, I find that the example falls somewhat short
> of what one might expect in a discussion of text formatting systems. In a future
> edition of the book, I suggest that you replace the example with one that is more
> instructive.
>
> Thank you,
>
> Boomer Petway

Figure 9-3. Sample output from a file

Further reading

If LaTeX seems right for your document-processing needs, and you have been able to get at least this initial example working and printed out, we suggest checking into Leslie Lamport's LaTeX *User's Guide and Reference Manual* (Addison Wesley), which includes everything you need to know about LaTeX for formatting letters, articles, books, and more. If you're interested in hacking or want to know more about the underlying workings of TeX (which can be invaluable), Donald Knuth's *The TeX book* (Addison-Wesley) is the definitive guide to the system.

comp.text.tex is the Usenet newsgroup for questions and information about these systems, although information found there assumes you have access to TeX and LaTeX documentation of some kind, such as the manuals mentioned earlier.

SGML, XML, and Docbook

SGML and XML go one step beyond the text markup languages we have discussed so far. They impose a structure on the text that shows the relation of each element to the containing elements. This makes it possible to convert the text to a number of output formats including PostScript and PDF (the Adobe Portable Document Format).

SGML itself is just a framework for defining the structure of a document. A so-called Document Type Description (DTD) or schema then defines what kind of markup you are allowed to use in a document.

While SGML is not widely known, its two descendants—HTML and XML—are famous and even overly hyped. Essentially, HTML is an implementation of SGML with a fixed set of tags that is useful for formatting web pages. XML is a general solution like SGML, but minus some of its difficult features. Both SGML and XML allow people to define any set of tags they like; the exact tags and their relationships are specified in the DTD or schema (which are optional in XML).

For each DTD or schema that you want to use, you need to have processing tools that convert the SGML or XML file to the desired output format. Historically, most free systems did this by means of a system called DSSSL. XSLT is now much more popular for converting XML to other formats. But this is nothing you need to be concerned with unless you want to change the way the output looks.

In the field of computer documentation, the most commonly used DTD is DocBook. Among many other things, most of the freely available Linux documentation is written with DocBook, as well as this book. DocBook users include a huge range of companies and well-known organizations, such as Sun Microsystems, Microsoft, IBM, Hewlett-Packard, Boeing, and the U.S. State Department.

To give you an example of how a DocBook text can look, here is a fragment of an article for a computer magazine:

```
<!DOCTYPE Article  PUBLIC "-//OASIS//DTD DocBook V4.1.2//EN">
<article>
  <artheader>
    <title>Looping the Froz with Foobar</title>
    <author>
      <firstname>Helmer B.</firstname>
      <surname>Technerd</surname>
      <affiliation>
        <orgname>Linux Hackers, Inc.</orgname>
      </affiliation>
    </author>
  </artheader>
  <abstract>
    <para>This article describes a technique that you can employ to
loop the Froz with the Foobar software package.</para>
  </abstract>
  <sect1>
    <title>Motivation</title>
    <para>Blah, blah, blah, ...
    </para>
  </sect1>
</article>
```

The first line specifies the DTD to be used and the root element; in this case we are creating an article using the DocBook DTD. The rest of the source contains the article itself. If you are familiar with HTML, the markup language used for the World Wide Web (see the O'Reilly book *HTML & XHTML: The Definitive Guide*, by Chuck Musciano and Bill Kennedy), this should look a bit familiar. Tags are used to mark up the text logically.

Describing the whole DocBook DTD is well beyond the scope of this book, but if you are interested, check out *DocBook: The Definitive Guide* by Norman Walsh and Leonard Muellner (O'Reilly).

Once you have your article, documentation, or book written, you will want to transform it, of course, into a format that you can print or view on the screen. In order to do this, you need a complete SGML setup, which, unfortunately, is not easy to achieve. In fact, you need so many pieces in place that we cannot describe this here. But there is hope: a number of distributions (including Red Hat, SuSE, and Debian) come with very good SGML setups out of the box; just install their respective SGML packages. If you have a working SGML system, you should be able to transform the above text to HTML (as one example) with a command like this:

```
owl$ db2html myarticle.sgml
input file was called  -- output will be in myarticle
TMPDIR is db2html.GUBPgh
working on ../myarticle.sgml
about to copy cascading stylesheet and admon graphics to temp dir
about to rename temporary directory to "myarticle"
```

The file *myarticle/t1.html* will contain the generated HTML. If you would like to generate PDF instead, use the following command:

```
owl$ db2pdf myarticle.sgml
tex output file name is myarticle.tex
tex file name is myarticle.tex
pdf file name is myarticle.pdf
This is pdfTeX, Version 3.14159-13d (Web2C 7.3.1)
(myarticle.tex[/var/lib/texmf/pdftex/config/pdftex.cfg]
JadeTeX 2001/07/19: 3.11
(/usr/share/texmf/tex/latex/psnfss/t1ptm.fd)
Elements will be labelled
Jade begin document sequence at 20
No file myarticle.aux.
(/usr/share/texmf/tex/latex/cyrillic/t2acmr.fd)
(/usr/share/texmf/tex/latex/base/ts1cmr.fd)
(/usr/share/texmf/tex/latex/hyperref/nameref.sty)
(/usr/share/texmf/tex/latex/psnfss/t1phv.fd) [1.0.31[/var/lib/texmf/dvips/confi
g/pdftex.map]] (myarticle.aux) )<8r.enc>
Output written on myarticle.pdf (1 page, 4446 bytes).
Transcript written on myarticle.log.
```

As you can see, this command uses TEX in the background, or more specifically a special version called Jade which is specifically geared toward documents produced by DSSSL.

SGML opens a whole new world of tools and techniques. A good starting point for getting inspired and reading up on this is the web site of the Linux Documentation Project, which, as mentioned before, uses SGML/DocBook for all its documentation. You'll find the Linux Documentation Project at *http://www.tlpd.org*.

groff

Parallel to and independent to TeX, another major text processing system emerged in the form of *troff* and *nroff*. These were developed at Bell Labs for the original implementation of Unix (in fact, the development of Unix was spurred, in part, to support such a text processing system). The first version of this text processor was called *roff* (for "runoff"); later came *nroff* and *troff*, which generated output for a particular typesetter in use at the time (*nroff* was written for fixed-pitch printers such as dot matrix printers, *troff* for proportional space devices—initially typesetters). Later versions of *nroff* and *troff* became the standard text processor on Unix systems everywhere. *groff* is GNU's implementation of *nroff* and *troff* that is used on Linux systems. It includes several extended features and drivers for a number of printing devices.

groff is capable of producing documents, articles, and books, much in the same vein as TeX. However, *groff* (as well as the original *nroff*) has one intrinsic feature that is absent from TeX and variants: the ability to produce plain-ASCII output. While TeX is great for producing documents to be printed, *groff* is able to produce plain ASCII to be viewed online (or printed directly as plain text on even the simplest of printers). If you're going to be producing documentation to be viewed online as well as in printed form, *groff* may be the way to go (although there are other alternatives as well—Texinfo, which is discussed later, is one).

groff also has the benefit of being much smaller than TeX; it requires fewer support files and executables than even a minimal TeX distribution.

One special application of *groff* is to format Unix manual pages. If you're a Unix programmer, you'll eventually need to write and produce manual pages of some kind. In this section, we'll introduce the use of *groff* through the writing of a short manual page.

As with TeX, *groff* uses a particular text-formatting language to describe how to process the text. This language is slightly more cryptic than TeX but is also less verbose. In addition, *groff* provides several macro packages that are used on top of the basic *groff* formatter; these macro packages are tailored to a particular type of document. For example, the mgs macros are an ideal choice for writing articles and papers, while the man macros are used for manual pages.

Writing a manual page

Writing manual pages with *groff* is actually quite simple. In order for your manual page to look like other manual pages, you need to follow several conventions in the source, which are presented in the following example. In this example, we'll write a manual page for a mythical command *coffee*, which controls your networked coffee machine in various ways.

Enter the following source with your text editor, and save the result as *coffee.man*:

```
1  .TH COFFEE 1 "23 March 94"
2  .SH NAME
3  coffee \- Control remote coffee machine
4  .SH SYNOPSIS
5  \fBcoffee\fP [ -h | -b ] [ -t \fItype\fP ] \fIamount\fP
6  .SH DESCRIPTION
7  \fIcoffee\fP queues a request to the remote coffee machine at the
8  device \fB/dev/cf0\fR. The required \fIamount\fP argument specifies
9  the number of cups, generally between 0 and 15 on ISO standard
10 coffee machines.
11 .SS Options
12 .TP
13 \fB-h\fP
14 Brew hot coffee. Cold is the default.
15 .TP
16 \fB-b\fP
17 Burn coffee. Especially useful when executing \fIcoffee\fP on behalf
18 of your boss.
19 .TP
20 \fB-t \fItype\fR
21 Specify the type of coffee to brew, where \fItype\fP is one of
22 \fBcolombian\fP, \fBregular\fP, or \fBdecaf\fP.
23 .SH FILES
24 .TP
25 \fI/dev/cf0\fR
26 The remote coffee machine device
27 .SH "SEE ALSO"
28 milk(5), sugar(5)
29 .SH BUGS
30 May require human intervention if coffee supply is exhausted.
```

Don't let the amount of obscurity in this source file frighten you. It helps to know that the character sequences \fB, \fI, and \fR are used to change the font to boldface, italics, and roman type, respectively. \fP resets the font to the one previously selected.

Other *groff* requests appear on lines beginning with a dot (.). On line 1, we see that the .TH request sets the title of the manual page to COFFEE and the manual section to 1. (Manual section 1 is used for user commands, section 2 for system calls, and so forth.) The .TH request also sets the date of the last manual page revision.

On line 2, the .SH request starts a section entitled NAME. Note that almost all Unix manual pages use the section progression NAME, SYNOPSIS, DESCRIPTION, FILES, SEE ALSO, NOTES, AUTHOR, and BUGS, with extra optional sections as needed. This is just a convention used when writing manual pages and isn't enforced by the software at all.

Line 3 gives the name of the command and a short description, after a dash (\-). You should use this format for the NAME section so that your manual page can be added to the *whatis* database used by the *man –k* and *apropos* commands.

On lines 4–5, we give the synopsis of the command syntax for *coffee*. Note that italic type \fI...\fP is used to denote parameters on the command line, and that optional arguments are enclosed in square brackets.

Lines 6–10 give a brief description of the command. Italic type generally denotes commands, filenames, and user options. On line 11, a subsection named Options is started with the .SS request. Following this on lines 11-22 is a list of options, presented using a tagged list. Each item in the tagged list is marked with the .TP request; the line *after* .TP is the tag, after which follows the item text itself. For example, the source on lines 12-14:

```
.TP
\fB-h\fP
Brew hot coffee. Cold is the default.
```

will appear as the following in the output:

```
-h      Brew hot coffee. Cold is the default.
```

You should document each command-line option for your program in this way.

Lines 23–26 make up the FILES section of the manual page, which describes any files the command might use to do its work. A tagged list using the .TP request is used for this as well.

On lines 27–28, the SEE ALSO section is given, which provides cross references to other manual pages of note. Notice that the string "SEE ALSO" following the .SH request on line 27 is in quotation marks; this is because .SH uses the first whitespace-delimited argument as the section title. Therefore, any section titles that are composed of more than one word need to be enclosed in quotation marks to make up a single argument. Finally, on lines 29–30, the BUGS section is presented.

Formatting and installing the manual page

In order to format this manual page and view it on your screen, use the command:

```
eggplant$ groff -Tascii -man coffee.man | more
```

The *–Tascii* option tells *groff* to produce plain-ASCII output; *–man* tells *groff* to use the manual-page macro set. If all goes well, the manual page should be displayed as:

```
COFFEE(1)                                              COFFEE(1)


NAME
       coffee - Control remote coffee machine
```

```
SYNOPSIS
       coffee [ -h | -b ] [ -t type ] amount

DESCRIPTION
       coffee  queues  a  request to the remote coffee machine at
       the device /dev/cf0. The required amount  argument  speci-
       fies the number of cups, generally between 0 and 12 on ISO
       standard coffee machines.

   Options
       -h     Brew hot coffee. Cold is the default.

       -b     Burn coffee. Especially useful when executing  cof-
              fee on behalf of your boss.

       -t type
              Specify  the  type of coffee to brew, where type is
              one of colombian, regular, or decaf.

FILES
       /dev/cf0
              The remote coffee machine device

SEE ALSO
       milk(5), sugar(5)

BUGS
       May  require  human  intervention  if  coffee  supply  is
       exhausted.
```

As mentioned before, *groff* is capable of producing other types of output. Using the –*Tps* option in place of –*Tascii* produces PostScript output that you can save to a file, view with Ghostview, or print on a PostScript printer. –*Tdvi* produces device-independent *.dvi* output similar to that produced by TEX.

If you wish to make the manual page available for others to view on your system, you need to install the *groff* source in a directory that is present on the users' MANPATH. The location for standard manual pages is */usr/share/man*, although some systems also use */usr/man* or */usr/local/man*. The source for section 1 manual pages should therefore go in */usr/man/man1*. The command:

```
eggplant$ cp coffee.man /usr/man/man1/coffee.1
```

installs this manual page in */usr/man* for all to use (note the use of the *.1* filename extension, instead of *.man*). When *man coffee* is subsequently invoked, the manual page will be automatically reformatted, and the viewable text saved in */usr/man/cat1/coffee.1.gz*.

If you can't copy manual page sources directly to */usr/man*, you can create your own manual page directory tree and add it to your MANPATH. See the section "Manual Pages" in Chapter 4.

Texinfo

Texinfo is a text-formatting system used by the GNU project to produce both online documentation in the form of hypertext Info pages, and printed manuals through TEX from a single-source file. By providing Texinfo source, users can convert the documentation to Info, HTML, DVI, PostScript, PDF, or plain text files.

Texinfo is documented completely through its own Info pages, which are readable within Emacs (using the C-h i command) or a separate Info reader, such as *info*. If the GNU Info pages are installed in your system, complete Texinfo documentation is contained therein. Just as you'll find yourself using *groff* to write a manual page, you'll use Texinfo to write an Info document.

Writing the Texinfo source

In this section, we're going to present a simple Texinfo source file—chunks at a time—and describe what each chunk does as we go along.

Our Texinfo source file will be called *vacuum.texi*. As usual, you can enter the source using a plain-text editor:

```
\input texinfo @c -*-texinfo-*-
@c %**start of header
@setfilename vacuum.info
@settitle The Empty Info File
@setchapternewpage odd
@c %**end of header
```

This is the header of the Texinfo source. The first line is a TEX command used to input the Texinfo macros when producing printed documentation. Commands in Texinfo begin with the "at" sign, @. The @c command begins a comment; here, the comment -*-texinfo-*- is a tag that tells Emacs this is a Texinfo source file so that Emacs can set the proper major mode. (Major modes were discussed earlier, in the section "Tailoring Emacs.")

The comments @c %**start of header and @c %**end of header are used to denote the Texinfo header. This is required if you wish to format just a portion of the Texinfo file. The @setfilename command specifies the filename to use for the resulting Info file, @settitle sets the title of the document, and @setchapternewpage odd tells Texinfo to start new chapters on an odd-numbered page. These are just cookbook routines that should be used for all Texinfo files.

The next section of the source file sets up the title page, which is used when formatting the document using TEX. These commands should be self-explanatory:

```
@titlepage
@title Vacuum
@subtitle The Empty Info File
@author by Tab U. Larasa
@end titlepage
```

Now we move on to the body of the Texinfo source. The Info file is divided into nodes, where each node is somewhat like a "page" in the document. Each node has links to the next, previous, and parent nodes, and can be linked to other nodes as cross-references. You can think of each node as a chapter or section within the document with a menu to nodes below it. For example, a chapter-level node has a menu that lists the sections within the chapter. Each section node points to the chapter-level node as its parent. Each section also points to the previous and next section, if they exist. This is a little complicated, but will become clear when you see it in action.

Each node is given a short name. The topmost node is called Top. The @node command is used to start a node; it takes as arguments the node name, as well as the names of the next, previous, and parent nodes. As noted earlier, the next and previous nodes should be on the same hierarchical level. The parent node is the node above the current one in the node tree (e.g., the parent of Section 2.1 in a document is Chapter 2). A sample node hierarchy is depicted in Figure 9-4.

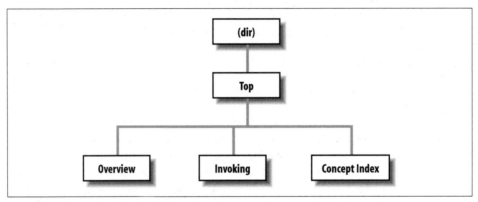

Figure 9-4. Hierarchy of nodes in Texinfo

Here is the source for the Top node:

```
@c     Node, Next, Previous, Up
@node Top ,      ,         , (dir)

@ifinfo
This Info file is a close approximation to a vacuum. It documents
absolutely nothing.
@end ifinfo

@menu
* Overview::           Overview of Vacuum
* Invoking::           How to use the Vacuum
* Concept Index::      Index of concepts
@end menu
```

The @node command is preceded by a comment to remind us of the order of the arguments to @node. Here, Top has no previous or next node, so they are left blank. The parent node for Top is (dir), which denotes the systemwide Info page directory. Supposedly your Info file will be linked into the system's Info page tree, so you want the Top node to have a link back to the overall directory.

Following the @node command is an abstract for the overall document, enclosed in an @ifinfo...@end ifinfo pair. These commands are used because the actual text of the Top node should appear only in the Info file, not the TEX-generated printed document.

The @menu...@end menu commands demarcate the node's menu. Each menu entry includes a node name followed by a short description of the node. In this case, the menu points to the nodes Overview, Invoking, and Concept Index, the source for which appears later in the file. These three nodes are the three "chapters" in our document.

We continue with the Overview node, which is the first "chapter":

```
@c     Node,      Next,      Previous, Up
@node Overview, Invoking,        , Top
@chapter Overview of @code{vacuum}

@cindex Nothingness
@cindex Overview
@cindex Vacuum cleaners

A @code{vacuum} is a space entirely devoid of all matter. That means no
air, no empty beer cans, no dust, no nothing. Vacuums are usually found

in outer space. A vacuum cleaner is a device used to clean a vacuum.
See @xref{Invoking} for information on running @code{vacuum}.
```

The next node for Overview is Invoking, which is the second "chapter" node and also the node to appear after Overview in the menu. Note that you can use just about any structure for your Texinfo documents; however, it is often useful to organize them so that nodes resemble chapters, sections, subsections, and so forth. It's up to you.

The @chapter command begins a chapter, which has an effect only when formatting the source with TEX. Similarly, the @section and @subsection commands begin (you guessed it) sections and subsections in the resulting TEX document. The chapter (or section or subsection) name can be more descriptive than the brief name used for the node itself.

You'll notice that the @code... command is used in the chapter name. This is just one way to specify text to be emphasized in some way. @code should be used for the names of commands, as well as source code that appears in a program. This causes the text within the @code... to be printed in constant-width type in the TEX output, and enclosed in single quotes (like 'this') in the Info file.

Following this are three @cindex commands, which produce entries in the concept index at the end of the document. Next is the actual text of the node. Again, @code marks the name of the vacuum "command."

The @xref command produces a cross-reference to another node, which the reader can follow with the f command in the Info reader. @xref can also make cross-references between other Texinfo documents. See the Texinfo documentation for a complete discussion.

Our next node is Invoking:

```
@node Invoking, Concept Index, Overview, Top
@chapter Running @code{vacuum}

@cindex Running @code{vacuum}
@code{vacuum} is executed as follows:

@example
vacuum @var{options} @dots{ }
@end example
```

Here, @example...@end example sets off an example. Within the example, @var denotes a metavariable, a placeholder for a string provided by the user (in this case, the options given to the *vacuum* command). @dots{ } produces ellipsis points. The example will appear as:

```
vacuum options ...
```

in the TeX-formatted document, and as:

```
vacuum OPTIONS ...
```

in the Info file. Commands, such as @code and @var, provide emphasis that can be represented in different ways in the TeX and Info outputs.

Continuing the Invoking node, we have:

```
@cindex Options
@cindex Arguments
The following options are supported:

@cindex Getting help
@table @samp
@item -help
Print a summary of options.

@item -version
Print the version number for @code{vacuum}.

@cindex Empty vacuums
@item -empty
Produce a particularly empty vacuum. This is the default.
@end table
```

Here, we have a table of the options that *vacuum* supposedly supports. The command @table @samp begins a two-column table (which ends up looking more like a tagged list), where each item is emphasized using the @samp command. @samp is similar to @code and @var, except that it's meant to be used for literal input, such as command-line options.

A normal Texinfo document would contain nodes for examples, information on reporting bugs, and much more, but for brevity we're going to wrap up this example with the final node, Concept Index. This is an index of concepts presented in the document and is produced automatically with the @printindex command:

```
@node Concept Index, , Invoking, Top
@unnumbered Concept Index

@printindex cp
```

Here, @printindex cp tells the formatter to include the concept index at this point. There are other types of indices as well, such as a function index, command index, and so forth. All are generated with variants on the @cindex and @printindex commands.

The final three lines of our Texinfo source are:

```
@shortcontents
@contents
@bye
```

This instructs the formatter to produce a "summary" table of contents (@shortcontents) and a full table of contents (@contents), and to end formatting (@bye). @shortcontents produces a brief table of contents that lists only chapters and appendices. In reality, only long manuals would require @shortcontents in addition to @contents.

Formatting Texinfo

To produce an Info file from the Texinfo source, use the *makeinfo* command. (This command, along with the other programs used to process Texinfo, are included in the Texinfo software distribution, which is sometimes bundled with Emacs.) The command:

```
eggplant$ makeinfo vacuum.texi
```

produces *vacuum.info* from *vacuum.texi*. *makeinfo* uses the output filename specified by the @setfilename in the source; you can change this using the *–o* option.

If the resulting Info file is large, *makeinfo* splits it into a series of files named *vacuum.info-1*, *vacuum.info-2*, and so on, where *vacuum.info* will be the top-level file that points to the various split files. As long as all the *vacuum.info* files are in the same directory, the Info reader should be able to find them.

You can also use the Emacs commands M-x makeinfo-region and M-x makeinfo-buffer to generate Info from the Texinfo source.

The Info file can now be viewed from within Emacs, using the C-h i command. Within the Emacs Info mode, you'll need to use the g command and specify the complete path to your Info file, as in:

```
Goto node: (/home/loomer/mdw/info/vacuum.info)Top
```

This is because Emacs usually looks for Info files only within its own Info directory (which may be */usr/local/emacs/info* on your system).

Another alternative is to use the Emacs-independent Info reader, *info*. The command:

```
eggplant$ info -f vacuum.info
```

invokes *info*, reading your new Info file.

If you wish to install the new Info page for all users on your system, you must add a link to it in the *dir* file in the Emacs *info* directory. The Texinfo documentation describes how to do this in detail.

To produce a printed document from the source, you need to have TEX installed on your system. The Texinfo software comes with a TEX macro file, *texinfo.tex*, which includes all the macros used by Texinfo for formatting. If installed correctly, *texinfo.tex* should be in the *inputs* directory on your system. If not, you can copy *texinfo.tex* to the directory where your Texinfo files reside.

First, process the Texinfo file using:

```
eggplant$ tex vacuum.texi
```

This produces a slew of files in your directory, some of which pertain to processing and to the index. The *texindex* command (which is included in the Texinfo package) reformats the index into something the display systems can use. The next command to issue is therefore:

```
eggplant$ texindex vacuum.??
```

Using the ?? wildcard runs *texindex* on all files in the directory with two-letter extensions; these are the files produced by Texinfo for generating the index.

Finally, you need to reformat the Texinfo file using TEX, which clears up cross-references and includes the index:

```
eggplant$ tex vacuum.texi
```

This should leave you with *vacuum.dvi*, a device-independent file you can now view with *xdvi* or convert into something printable. See the section "TEX and LATEX" earlier in the chapter for a discussion of how to print *.dvi* files.

As usual, there's much more to learn about this system. Texinfo has a complete set of Info pages of its own, which should be available in your Info reader. Or, now that you know the basics, you could format the Texinfo documentation sources yourself using TEX. The *.texi* sources for the Texinfo documentation are found in the Texinfo source distribution.

Graphics

Many people are fascinated by computer graphics. Computers are being used to create photorealistic images of surreal scenes or fractally generated images of mountain ridges with lakes and valleys; to change images by bending, polishing, and aging them; or to make any other manipulations.

Linux does not need to step shyly aside when it comes to graphics. It can do just about anything that other computing environments can do, and in some areas, such as dealing with many graphics files at the same time, it even excels. The X Window System, described in the next chapter, forms a very good base for bitmapped graphics. There is now also hardware support for 3D graphics conforming to the OpenGL standard.

However, working with graphics on Linux is sometimes different from what you might be used to on other operating systems; the Unix model of small, interoperating tools is still alive and well here, too. This philosophy is illustrated most clearly with the *ImageMagick* suite of graphics manipulation programs, which we will describe here. ImageMagick is a collection of tools that operate on graphics files and are started from the command line or from shell scripts. Imagine that you have 2,000 files of one file format that you want to reduce to 256 colors, slant, and convert to another file format. On Linux, this requires only a few lines in a shell script. Now imagine doing this on Windows: click the File menu, click the Open menu entry, select a file, select an operation, specify the parameters for the operation in a dialog, click OK, choose Save from the menu, select a filename, and then click OK. Now repeat for next 1999 files. Can you say RSI?*

Graphics can not only be drawn, but also programmed. Certain tools, such as the ray-tracer POVRAY presented in this chapter, enable you to specify the graphics to be generated by a suite of commands, often in a full-blown graphics programming language. While this is perhaps more difficult than drawing the desired graphics with a mouse, it is also infinitely more flexible once you have mastered how to use it.

Now, not everybody wants to work with graphics from the command line. Part of the appeal of working with computer graphics is the immediate feedback you get when working with graphics programs, and Linux can provide this, too. The GIMP, which we will be covering shortly, is a fascinating package for interactive image manipulation that is superior to a lot of commercial graphics manipulation software on other systems.

Many more graphics programs are available for Linux, including 3D modelers and video players. Scouring some Linux archives will reveal a wealth of good software. Most of these programs require the X Window System, which we'll show you how to install and configure in later chapters.

---

* Repetitive Strain Injury—a malady that comes from typing too much. The better known carpal tunnel syndrome is one form of RSI.

ImageMagick

ImageMagick is a suite of programs that convert and manipulate graphics files from the command line. It is also well suited for batch conversions—that is, converting many files at once. In addition, ImageMagick includes PerlMagick, a binding that lets you invoke the ImageMagick utilities from the Perl programming language. It comes with most Linux distributions; if yours does not have it, you can get it from *ftp://ftp.x.org/contrib/applications/ImageMagick*.

ImageMagick consists of a library and a number of utilities:

display

> *display* is a graphical frontend to many of the functions provided by ImageMagick. It is very useful if you want to experiment with the effects of a function before you go and batch-convert hundreds of images with these effects. *display* can load many different graphics file formats and display them on the X Window System. You can start *display* and pass it one or more filenames on the command line, or load a file from the menu provided. If you have started *display* and do not see a menu, click the image displayed with the left mouse button. *display* features a huge number of command-line switches. See the manual page for details.

import

> *import* is a small program that captures either one window or the whole server into a file; that is, it allows you to make screenshots. For example, to make a screenshot of your whole screen and save it as *myscreen.xpm* in the graphics file format XPM, you would execute:

> tigger$ **import -window root myscreen.xpm**

> When you hear the first beep, the screen capture begins, and when the second one sounds, capturing is finished and the image data is in the process of being saved to the file you specified.

> If you want to capture the contents of only one window, the easiest way is to start *import* without the *-window* option:

> tigger$ **import mywindow.xpm**

> The cursor then turns into a crossbar, which prompts you to click any window. This window's contents are then captured and saved to the specified file.

> Like all ImageMagick programs, *import* has many command-line options; check the *image*(1) manual page.

montage

> *montage* is a very useful little tool with a functionality rarely found elsewhere. It takes a number of images and puts them together as one large image in a tiled manner. There are lots of options for changing how the images are exactly tiled and put together.

In order to tile all your JPEG images in the current directory and create the image *all.jpg* out of it, you could call:

```
tigger$ montage *.jpg all.jpg
```

By default, there will be a label with the filename below each image. You can avoid this by entering:

```
tigger$ montage +frame *.jpg all.jpg
```

convert

In a way, *convert* is the heart of the ImageMagick suite. It can convert between an amazing number of graphics formats. For example, let's assume that you want to port a GUI program from Windows to Linux. You have a large number of toolbar icons in Windows BMP format and want to convert those to XPM. You could do this with:

```
for i in *.bmp
do
convert $i xpm:'basename $i .bmp'.xpm
done
```

convert will happily chug through all the images and convert them. If you want to do other things to the images, just add the necessary switches—e.g., -despeckle for removing speckles from the images.

mogrify

mogrify is like *convert*, but it overwrites the original images and is meant more for applying filter functions than for converting file formats (even though you can easily change the file format by using the switch -format).

identify

identify outputs information about the images passed on the command line. For example:

```
tigger$ identify tux.gif
tux.gif 257x303+0+0 DirectClass 10968b GIF 1s
```

This tells you, among other things, that *tux.gif* is a GIF file 257 pixels wide and 303 pixels high. If this is not enough information for you, try the *-verbose* switch!

combine

As its name indicates, *combine* combines several images into one. You can, for example, put color-separated images together or put a logo on top of a larger image.

xtp

Like the *ftp* program, *xtp* downloads files from a remote site or uploads them to a remote site. But unlike *ftp*, it does not need interactive input (in order to get this with *ftp*, you would have to edit its configuration file). You can productively combine *xtp* with the other tools from the ImageMagick suite to automatically manipulate images on remote servers.

To sum up, the programs from the ImageMagick suite are an extremely versatile means to manipulate graphics files. However, it takes some time to familiarize yourself with all the command-line options in order to know what is available.

The GIMP

The GIMP (which expands to either GNU Image Manipulation Program or General Image Manipulation Program and is often written with the definite article) specializes in image manipulation like the ImageMagick package described in the last section. But while ImageMagick's strength is batch processing, GIMP does everything via its GUI. The GIMP is often cited as one of the most impressive and successful products for Linux (and other Unix versions). People who use image manipulation programs professionally have said that while GIMP can feel a little bit awkward to use, it is functionally comparable to its commercial competitor from the Windows and Macintosh world, Adobe Photoshop. Some people even have called it "the free alternative to Photoshop."

GIMP draws its power from an amazing number of plug-ins that are available for it. Thus, in order to be able to use a newly written image manipulation filter or file format import filter, you only need to install the plug-in and restart GIMP, and you are ready to go.

In addition, GIMP uses a clever tiling mechanism that allows you to load arbitrarily large images into it; GIMP will keep in memory only the part that is currently being used or visible. And if these features are not enough, GIMP also has its own scripting language called *script-fu*, and can be scripted with Perl as well.

GIMP comes with most Linux distributions on the market today and can be run simply by entering the command *gimp* in a shell after starting X. If your distribution does not have GIMP, you can get the source code from *www.gimp.org*. If you plan to do more work with GIMP, you should check this web site anyway because it also contains the documentation and sample images that show off what you can do with it. A screenshot showing the toolbar, dialog boxes, and a work area is shown in Figure 9-5.

POVRAY

While ImageMagick and GIMP are mainly for manipulating existing images, POVRAY (the first three letters stand for Persistence Of Vision) is a program for automatically creating new images. It is a so-called ray-tracer; a program that computes a scene from some information about which objects should be in the scene, what their physical and optical properties are, where the light is coming from, and where the spectator is standing. You describe this to POVRAY in a programming language of its own.

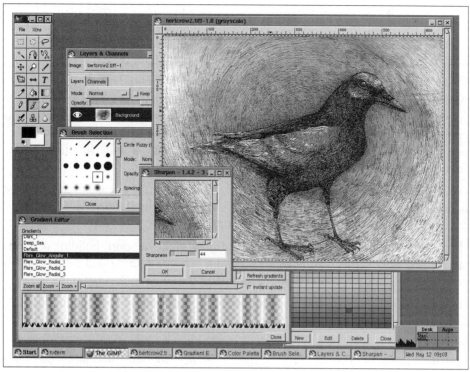

Figure 9-5. The Gimp

This brief description should already indicate that using POVRAY is not something you learn in one afternoon. If you are interested in this program, you can download it from *http://www.povray.org*, which is also the first source for all kinds of POVRAY resources like sample files, documentation, and so on. Since we cannot give you even a crash course into using POVRAY here, we'll refrain from attempting this futile task.

If you are interested in POVRAY, though, but find the task of describing your scenes in a programming language daunting, it might interest you to know that certain graphic modeling programs can be used with ray-tracers like POVRAY, so you do not have to create the 3D models completely by hand. One of these programs is Blender, about which you can find more information at *http://www.blender3d.com*.

Configuring and Using Linux Audio

This section covers the configuration of sound cards under Linux and other issues related to Linux sound support.

Sound has historically been one of the most challenging aspects of Linux, and one that did not receive as much attention from Linux distributions as it should have, perhaps because Linux was initially embraced by so many as a server operating system. On the desktop, users have come to take multimedia support and sound for granted. Once you're armed with a little knowledge, the good news is it's not too hard to get a sound card up and running, and in fact Linux is well suited to audio and other multimedia applications for a number of reasons.

We start off this section with a quick overview of digital audio concepts and terminology. Those familiar with the technology may wish to skip over this section. If you don't really care about how it all works or get lost in the first sentence of this section, don't worry, you can get sound on your system without understanding the difference between an MP3 and a WAV file.

We'll then look specifically at how sound is supported under Linux, what hardware is supported, the different device drivers available, and the different approaches to configuring sound taken by Linux distributions.

Next we'll step through the process of configuring sound support, building or locating the necessary kernel drivers and testing and debugging the sound devices. We'll provide some hints for troubleshooting and point out some common pitfalls.

Once you have sound support up and running, you'll want to run some multimedia applications. We'll take a quick look at the types of sound programs available for Linux.

Last, we'll round out this section with some references to more information on Linux audio that will help you get to the next level.

A word of advice: there are minor differences between Linux distributions. The Linux kernel and applications are also undergoing constant change and enhancement. We've made every effort to make the information in this chapter applicable to all Linux systems, and to point out areas where they are likely to differ, but for details you should consult the documentation for your distribution and consult fellow users.

A Whirlwind Tour of Digital Audio

In this section we will give a very quick overview of some concepts relevant to digital audio and sound cards.

Sound is produced when waves of varying pressure travel through a medium, usually air. It is inherently an *analog* phenomenon, meaning that the changes in air pressure can vary continuously over a range of values.

Modern computers are digital, meaning they operate on discrete values, essentially the binary ones and zeroes that are manipulated by the computer's CPU. In order for a computer to manipulate sound, it converts the analog sound information into digital format.

A hardware device called an analog-to-digital converter converts analog signals, such as the continuously varying electrical signals from a microphone, to digital format for manipulation by the computer. Similarly, a digital-to-analog converter converts digital values into analog form so that they can be sent to an analog output device such as a speaker. Sound cards typically contain several analog-to-digital and digital-to-analog converters.

The process of converting analog signals to digital form consists of taking measurements or *samples* of the values at regular periods of time, and storing these samples as numbers. The process of analog-to-digital conversion is not perfect, however, and introduces some loss or distortion. Two important factors that affect how accurately the analog signal is represented in digital form are the sample size and sampling rate.

The *sample size* is the range of values of numbers that are used to represent the digital samples, usually expressed in bits. For example, an 8-bit sample would convert the analog sound values into one of 2^8 or 256 discrete values. A 16-bit sample size would represent the sound using 2^{16} or 65,535 different values. A larger sample size allows the sound to be represented more accurately, reducing the sampling error that occurs when the analog signal is represented as discrete values. The tradeoff with using a larger sample size is that the samples require more storage (and the hardware is typically more complex and therefore expensive).

The *sample rate* is the speed at which the analog signals are periodically measured over time. It is properly expressed as samples per second, although sometimes informally but less accurately expressed in Hertz. A lower sample rate will lose more information about the original analog signal, while a higher sample rate will more accurately represent it. The sampling theorem states that to accurately represent an analog signal it must be sampled at least twice the rate of the highest frequency present in the original signal.

The range of human hearing is from approximately 20 to 20,000 Hertz under ideal situations. To accurately represent sound for human listening, then, a sample rate of twice 20,000 Hertz should be adequate. CD player technology uses 44,100 samples per second, which is in agreement with this simple calculation. Human speech has little frequency activity above 4,000 Hertz. Digital telephone systems typically use a sample rate of 8,000 samples per second, which is perfectly adequate for conveying speech. The tradeoff involved with using different sample rates is the additional storage requirement and more complex hardware needed as the sample rate increases.

Other issues that arise when storing sound in digital format are the number of channels and the sample encoding format. To support stereo sound, two channels are required. Some audio systems use four or more channels.

The samples themselves can be encoded in different formats. We've already mentioned sample size, with 8-bit and 16-bit samples being the most common. For a given sample size the samples might be encoded using signed or unsigned representation, and when the storage takes more than one byte, the ordering convention must be specified. These issues are important when transferring digital audio between programs or computers to ensure they agree on a common format. File formats, such as WAV, standardize how to represent sound information in a way that can be transferred between different computers and operating systems.

Often, sounds need to be combined or changed in volume. This is the process of *mixing*, and can be done in analog form (e.g., a volume control) or in digital form by the computer. Conceptually, you can mix two digital samples together simply by adding them, and you can change volume by multiplying the digital samples by a constant value.

Up to now we've discussed storing audio as digital samples. Other techniques are also commonly used. *FM synthesis* is an older technique that produces sound using hardware that manipulates different waveforms, such as sine and triangle waves. The hardware to do this is quite simple and was popular with the first generation of computer sound cards for generating music. Many sound cards still support FM synthesis for backward compatibility. Some newer cards use a technique called wavetable synthesis that improves on FM synthesis by generating the sounds using digital samples stored in the sound card itself.

MIDI stands for Musical Instrument Digital Interface. It is a standard protocol for allowing electronic musical instruments to communicate. Typical MIDI devices are music keyboards, synthesizers, and drum machines. MIDI works with events representing such things as a key on a music keyboard being pressed, rather than storing actual sound samples. MIDI events can be stored in a MIDI file, providing a way to represent a song in a very compact format. MIDI is most popular with professional musicians, although many consumer sound cards support the MIDI bus interface.

Earlier we mentioned CD audio, which uses a 16-bit sample size and a rate of 44,100 samples per second, with two channels (stereo). One hour of CD audio represents more than 600 MB of data. In order to make the storage of sound more manageable, various schemes for compressing audio have been devised. One approach is to simply compress the data using the same compression algorithms used for computer data. However, by taking into account the characteristics of human hearing, it is possible to compress audio more efficiently be removing components of the sound that are not audible. This is called lossy compression because information is lost during the compression process, but when properly implemented data size is reduced greatly, with little noticeable loss in audio quality. This is the approach that is used with MPEG-1 level 3 audio (MP3), which can achieve compression levels of 10:1 over the original digital audio. Another lossy compression algorithm that achieves similar results is Ogg Vorbis, which is popular with many Linux users because it avoids patent issues with MP3 encoding. Other compression algorithms are optimized for human speech, such as the GSM encoding used by some digital telephone systems. The algorithms used for encoding and decoding audio are sometimes referred to as *codecs*.

For applications in which sound is to be sent live via the Internet, sometimes broadcast to multiple users, sound files are not suitable. *Streaming media* is the term used to refer to systems that send audio, or other media, and play it back in real time.

Now that we've discussed digital audio concepts, let's look at the hardware used for audio. Sound cards follow a history similar to other peripheral cards for PCs. The first-generation cards used the ISA bus, and most aimed to be compatible with the SoundBlaster series from Creative Labs. With the introduction of the ISA Plug and Play (PnP) standard, many sound cards adopted this format, which simplified configuration by eliminating the need for hardware jumpers. Modern sound cards now typically use the PCI bus, either as separate peripheral cards or as on-board sound hardware that resides on the motherboard but is accessed through the PCI bus. Some USB sound devices are now available, the most popular being loudspeakers that can be controlled through the USB bus.

Some sound cards now support higher-end features such as surround sound using as many as six sound channels, and digital inputs and outputs that can connect to home theater systems. This is beyond the scope of this book, so we will not discuss such sound cards here. Much useful information on 3D sound can be found at *http://www.3dsoundsurge.com*. Information on the OpenAL 3D audio library can be found at *http://www.openal.org/home*.

Audio Under Linux

Now that we've covered the concepts and terminology of digital audio in general, it is time to look at some of the specifics of sound on Linux.

The lowest-level software component that talks directly to the sound hardware is the kernel. Early in the development of Linux (i.e., before the 1.0 kernel release), Hannu Savolainen implemented kernel-level sound drivers for a number of popular sound cards. Other developers also contributed to this code, adding new features and support for more cards. These drivers, part of the standard kernel release, are sometimes called OSS/Free, the free version of the Open Sound System.

Hannu later joined 4Front Technologies, a company that sells commercial sound drivers for Linux as well as a number of other Unix-compatible operating systems. These enhanced drivers are sold commercially as OSS/4Front.

In 1998 the Advanced Linux Sound Architecture, or ALSA project, was formed with the goal of writing new Linux sound drivers from scratch, and to address the issue that there was no active maintainer of the OSS sound drivers. With the benefit of hindsight and the requirements for newer sound card technology, the need was felt for a new design.

Some sound card manufacturers have also written Linux sound drivers for their cards, most notably the Creative Labs Sound Blaster Live! series.

The result is that there are as many as four different sets of kernel sound drivers from which to choose. This causes a dilemma when choosing which sound driver to use. Table 9-1 summarizes some of the advantages and disadvantages of the different drivers, in order to help you make a decision. Another consideration is that your particular Linux distribution will likely come with one driver and it will be more effort on your part to use a different one.

Table 9-1. Sound driver comparison

Driver	Advantages	Disadvantages
OSS/Free	Free	Not all sound cards supported
	Source code available	Most sound cards not auto detected
	Part of standard kernel	Does not support some newer cards
	Supports most sound cards	No single maintainer
OSS/4Front	Supports many sound cards	Payment required
	Auto-detection of most cards	Closed source
	Commercial support available	
	Compatible with OSS	
ALSA	Free	Not all sound cards supported
	Source code available	Not part of standard kernel
	Supports many sound cards	Not fully compatible with OSS
	Actively developed/supported	
	Clean design	
Commercial	May support cards with no other drivers	May be closed source
		May not be supported

In addition to the drivers mentioned in Table 9-1, kernel patches are sometimes available that address problems with specific sound cards.

The vast majority of sound cards are supported under Linux by one driver or another. The devices that are least likely to be supported are very new cards, which may not yet have had drivers developed for them, and some high-end professional sound cards, which are rarely used by consumers. You can find a reasonably up-to-date list of supported cards in the current Linux Sound HOWTO document, but often the best solution is to do some research on the Internet and experiment with drivers that seem likely to match your hardware.

Many sound applications use the kernel sound drivers directly, but this causes a problem: the kernel sound devices can be accessed by only one application at a time. In a graphical desktop environment, a user may want to simultaneously play an MP3 file, associate window manager actions with sounds, be alerted when there is new e-mail, etc. This requires sharing the sound devices between different applications. To address this, modern Linux desktop environments include a sound server that takes exclusive control of the sound devices and accepts requests from desktop applications to play sounds, mixing them together. They may also allow sound to be redirected to another computer, just as the X Window System allows the display to be on a different computer from where the program is running. The KDE desktop environment uses the *artsd* sound server and GNOME provides *esd*. As sound servers are a somewhat recent innovation, not all sound applications are written to support them yet.

This section will not cover software development issues, but for those who want to develop multimedia applications, a number of toolkits provide sound support more easily than the low-level kernel API. ALSA includes a sound library, and there are many sound toolkits, such as SDL (intended mainly for games) and OpenAL (for 3D audio). If you are a multimedia developer you should investigate these libraries to avoid reinventing work done by others.

Installation and Configuration

In this section we will discuss how to install and configure a sound card under Linux.

The amount of work you have to do depends on your Linux distribution. As Linux matures, some distributions are now providing automatic detection and configuration of sound cards. The days of manually setting card jumpers and resolving resource conflicts are becoming a thing of the past as sound cards become standardized on the PCI bus. If you are fortunate enough that your sound card is detected and working on your Linux distribution, the material in this section won't be particularly relevant because it has all been done for you automatically.

Some Linux distributions also provide a sound configuration utility such as *sndconfig* which will attempt to detect and configure your sound card, usually with some user intervention. You should consult the documentation for your system and run the supplied sound configuration tool, if any, and see if it works.

If you have an older ISA or ISA PnP card, or if your card is not properly detected, you will need to follow the manual procedure we outline here. These instructions also assume you are using the OSS/Free sound drivers. If you are using ALSA, the process is similar, but if you are using commercial drivers (OSS/4Front or a vendor-supplied driver), you should consult the document that comes with the drivers as the process may be considerably different.

The information here also assumes you are using Linux on an x86 architecture system. There is support for sound on other CPU architectures, but not all drivers are supported and there will likely be some differences in device names, etc.

Collecting hardware information

Presumably you already have a sound card installed on your system. If not, you should go ahead and install one. If you have verified that the card works with another operating system on your computer, that will assure you that any problem you encounter on Linux is caused by software at some level.

You should identify what type of card you have, including manufacturer and model. Determine if it is an ISA, ISA PnP, or PCI card. If the card has jumpers you should note the settings. If you know what resources (IRQ, I/O address, DMA channels) the card is currently using, note that information as well.

If you don't have all this information, don't worry. You should be able to get by without it; you just may need to do a little detective work later. On laptops or systems with on-board sound hardware, for example, you won't have the luxury of being able to look at a physical sound card.

Configuring ISA Plug and Play (optional)

Modern PCI bus sound cards do not need any configuration. The older ISA bus sound cards were configured by setting jumpers. ISA PnP cards are configured under Linux using the ISA Plug and Play utilities. If you aren't sure if you have an ISA PnP sound card, try running the command *pnpdump* and examining the output for anything that looks like a sound card. Output should include lines like the following for a typical sound card:

```
# Card 1: (serial identifier ba 10 03 be 24 25 00 8c 0e)
# Vendor Id CTL0025, Serial Number 379791851, checksum 0xBA.
# Version 1.0, Vendor version 1.0
# ANSI string -->Creative SB16 PnP<--
```

The general process for configuring ISA PnP devices is:

1. Save any existing */etc/isapnp.conf* file.
2. Generate a configuration file using the command *pnpdump >/etc/isapnp.conf*.
3. Edit the file, uncommenting the lines for the desired device settings.
4. Run the *isapnp* command to configure Plug and Play cards (usually on system startup).

Most modern Linux distributions take care of initializing ISA PnP cards. You may already have a suitable */etc/isapnp.conf* file, or it may just require some editing.

For more details on configuring ISA PnP cards, see the manpages for the *isapnp*, *pnpdump*, and *isapnp.conf* and read the ISA Plug and Play HOWTO from the Linux Documentation Project.

Configuring the kernel (optional)

You may want to compile a new kernel. If the kernel sound driver modules you need are not provided by the kernel you are currently running, you will need to do this. If you prefer to compile the drivers directly into the kernel rather than use loadable kernel modules, a new kernel will be required as well.

In the most common situation where you are running a kernel that was provided during installation of your Linux system, all sound drivers should be included as loadable modules and this step should not be necessary.

See "Building a New Kernel" in Chapter 7 for information on rebuilding your kernel.

Configuring kernel modules

In most cases the kernel sound drivers are loadable modules, which the kernel can dynamically load and unload. You need to ensure that the correct drivers are loaded. You do this using a configuration file, such as */etc/conf.modules*. A typical entry for a sound card might look like this:

```
alias sound sb
alias midi opl3
options opl3 io=0x388
options sb io=0x220 irq=5 dma=1 dma16=5 mpu_io=0x330
```

You need to enter the sound driver to use and the appropriate values for I/O address, IRQ, and DMA channels that you recorded earlier. The latter settings are needed only for ISA and ISA PnP cards because PCI cards can detect them automatically. In the preceding example, which is for a 16-bit SoundBlaster card, we had to specify the driver as sb in the first line, and specify the options for the driver in the last line.

Some systems use */etc/modules.conf* and/or multiple files under the */etc/modutils* directory, so you should consult the documentation for your Linux distribution for the details on configuring modules. On Debian systems, you can use the *modconf* utility for this task.

In practice, usually the only tricky part is determining which driver to use. The output of *pnpdump* for ISA PnP cards and *lspci* for PCI cards can help you identify the type of card you have. You can then reference this to documentation available either in the Sound HOWTO or in the kernel source, usually found on Linux systems in the */usr/src/linux/Documentation/sound* directory.

For example, a certain laptop system reports this sound hardware in the output of *lspci*:

```
00:05.0 Multimedia audio controller: Cirrus Logic CS 4614/22/24 [CrystalClear
SoundFusion Audio Accelerator] (rev 01)
```

For this system the appropriate sound driver is "cs46xx". Some experimentation may be required, and it is safe to try loading various kernel modules and see if they detect the sound card.

Testing the installation

The first step to verify the installation is to confirm that the kernel module is loaded. You can use the command *lsmod*; it should show that the appropriate module, among others, is loaded:

```
% /sbin/lsmod
```

```
Module             Size  Used by
parport_pc        21256  1 (autoclean)
lp                 6080  0 (autoclean)
parport           24512  1 (autoclean) [parport_pc lp]
3c574_cs           8324  1
serial            43520  0 (autoclean)
cs46xx            54472  4
soundcore          3492  3 [cs46xx]
ac97_codec         9568  0 [cs46xx]
rtc                5528  0 (autoclean)
```

Here the drivers of interest are *cs46xx*, *soundcore*, and *ac97_codec*. When the driver detected the card the kernel should have also logged a message that you can retrieve with the *dmesg* command. The output is likely to be long, so you can pipe it to a pager command, such as *less*:

```
PCI: Found IRQ 11 for device 00:05.0
PCI: Sharing IRQ 11 with 00:02.0
PCI: Sharing IRQ 11 with 01:00.0
Crystal 4280/46xx + AC97 Audio, version 1.28.32, 19:55:54 Dec 29 2001
cs46xx: Card found at 0xf4100000 and 0xf4000000, IRQ 11
cs46xx: Thinkpad 600X/A20/T20 (1014:0153) at 0xf4100000/0xf4000000, IRQ 11
ac97_codec: AC97 Audio codec, id: 0x4352:0x5914 (Cirrus Logic CS4297A rev B)
```

For ISA cards, the device file */dev/sndstat* shows information about the card. This won't work for PCI cards, however. Typical output should look something like this:

```
% cat /dev/sndstat
OSS/Free:3.8s2++-971130
Load type: Driver loaded as a module
Kernel: Linux curly 2.2.16 #4 Sat Aug 26 19:04:06 PDT 2000 i686
Config options: 0

Installed drivers:

Card config:

Audio devices:
0: Sound Blaster 16 (4.13) (DUPLEX)

Synth devices:
0: Yamaha OPL3

MIDI devices:
0: Sound Blaster 16

Timers:
0: System clock

Mixers:
0: Sound Blaster
```

If these look right you can now test your sound card. A simple check to do first is to run a mixer program and verify that the mixer device is detected and that you can

---

change the levels without seeing any errors. You'll have to see what mixer programs are available on your system. Some common ones are *aumix*, *xmix*, and *kmix*. Set all the levels to something reasonable.

Now try using a sound file player to play a sound file (e.g., a WAV file) and verify that you can hear it play. If you are running a desktop environment, such as KDE or GNOME, you should have a suitable media player; otherwise look for a command-line tool such as *play*.

If playback works you can then check recording. Connect a microphone to the sound card's mic input and run a recording program, such as *rec* or *vrec*. See whether you can record input to a WAV file and play it back. Check the mixer settings to ensure that you have selected the right input device and set the appropriate gain levels.

You can also test whether MIDI files play correctly. Some MIDI player programs require sound cards with an FM synthesizer, others do not. Some common MIDI players are *playmidi*, *kmid*, and *kmidi*. Testing of devices on the MIDI bus is beyond the scope of this book.

A good site for general information on MIDI and MIDI devices is *http://midistudio.com*. The official MIDI specifications are available from the MIDI Manufacturers Association. Their web site can be found at *http://www.midi.org*.

Troubleshooting and common problems

This section lists some common problems and possible solutions.

Kernel modules not loaded
> This could be caused by incorrect module configuration files. It will also occur if the kernel module loader (*kerneld* or *kmod*) is not running. Make sure the module is available for loading in the appropriate directory (typically something like */lib/modules/2.4.17/kernel/drivers/sound*).

Sound card not detected
> You are probably using the wrong kernel driver or the wrong settings for I/O address, IRQ, or DMA channel.

IRQ/DMA timeout or device conflicts
> You are using the wrong settings for I/O address, IRQ, and DMA, or you have a conflict with another card that is using the same settings.

No sound after rebooting
> If sound was working and then stopped when the system was rebooted, you probably have a problem with the module configuration files. This can also occur if the system *init* scripts are not configured to initialize PnP cards or to load the modules.

> If the drivers are loaded, it could be that the mixer settings are set too low to hear any audio.

Sound works only for root
> This probably indicates a permissions problem with the device files. Many systems allow only users who are members of the group "audio" to access the sound devices. Add the user(s) to this group or change the permissions on the audio devices using the *chmod.*

No sound is heard but there are no error messages
> If sound programs appear to be playing but nothing is heard, it is probably a problem with the mixer settings, or a problem with the connection of the speakers.

Unable to record audio
> This could indicate a problem with the mixer settings. You need to set the levels and select the input device. You might also have a bad microphone or are using the wrong input jack on the sound card.

Device busy error
> Either you likely have a device conflict, or another application is using the sound devices. This could be because you are running a sound server program, such as *esd* or *artsd.*

No sound when playing audio CD
> To play audio CDs you need a cable from the CD-ROM drive to your sound card. Make sure you have selected CD input using a mixer program. Try connecting headphones to the front panel jack of the CD-ROM drive. If you can hear audio, the problem is not with the drive itself. If you can't hear audio from the headphones, the problem is with the drive or CD player program.

Cannot play MIDI files
> Some MIDI applications work only with a sound card that has an FM synthesizer, and not all cards have this hardware (or the kernel driver for the sound card may not support it). Other MIDI applications use the standard audio device.

Linux Multimedia Applications

Once you have your sound card up and running under Linux you'll want to run some audio applications. So many are available for Linux that they can't possibly be listed here, so we will just describe some of the general categories of programs that are available. You can look for applications using the references listed here. We'll also go into a bit more detail about one of today's most popular audio applications, playing MP3 files.

- Mixer programs, for setting record and playback gain levels
- Media players, for file formats, such as WAV, MP3, and MIDI
- CD players, for playing audio CDs
- Recording tools, for generating sound files
- Effects and signal processing tools, for manipulating sound

- Speech tools, supporting speech recognition, and synthesis
- Games, which use audio to add realism
- Desktop environments, such as KDE and GNOME, which support multimedia

MP3 Players

MP3 (MPEG-1 Layer 3) is one of the most popular file formats for digital audio, and there are a number of MP3 player applications for Linux. If you are running a desktop environment, such as KDE or GNOME, you likely already have an MP3 player program. If so, it is recommended that you use this player since it should work correctly with the sound server used by these desktop environments.

These are some of the features you should look for when selecting an MP3 player application:

- Support for different sound drivers (e.g., OSS and ALSA) or sound servers (KDE and GNOME).
- An attractive user interface. Many MP3 players are "skinnable," meaning that you can download and install alternative user interfaces.
- Support for playlists, allowing you to define and save sequences of your favorite audio tracks.
- Various audio effects, such as a graphical equalizer, stereo expansion, reverb, voice removal, and visual effects for representing the audio in graphical form.
- Support for other file formats, such as audio CD, WAV, and video formats.

Xmms is one popular MP3 player, with a default user interface similar to Winamp. You can download it from *http://www.xmms.org*.

If you want to create your own MP3 files you will need an encoder program. There are also programs that allow you to extract tracks for audio CDs.

While you can perform MP3 encoding with open source tools, certain patent claims have made the legality of doing so in question. Ogg Vorbis is an alternative file format and encoder that claims to be free of patent issues. To use it, your player program needs to support Ogg Vorbis files because they are not directly compatible with MP3. However, many MP3 players like Xmms support Ogg Vorbis already; in other cases, there are direct equivalents (like *ogg123* for *mpg123*).

Installation of an MP3 player typically requires that you install the appropriate package (in RPM or *deb* format, depending on your Linux distribution). You may also choose to build it from source code. An MP3 player should install MIME types to associate it with MP3 and other supported file types so that you can launch it from applications in the same way as file managers, web browsers, and email clients.

References

Listed here are a few sources of information related to sound under Linux:

- The Linux Sound HOWTO, available from the Linux Documentation Project at *http://www.tlpd.org*
- The ALSA Project web site at *http://www.alsa-project.org*
- The 4Front Technologies web site at *http://www.opensound.com*
- The Sound and MIDI Software for Linux web site at *http://sound.condorow.net*
- The book *Linux Multimedia Guide*, published by O'Reilly
- The book *Linux Music and Sound*, published by No Starch Press

A number of mailing lists are related to sound and Linux. See the Sound HOWTO for details on how to join the lists.

Printing

The *lpr* command prints a document on Linux. You might not always invoke this command directly—you may just press a Print button on some glitzy drag-and-drop graphical interface—but ultimately, printing is handled by *lpr* and the other print-management utilities we'll describe here.

If you want to print a program listing, you might enter:

```
lpr myprogram.c
```

Input is also often piped to *lpr* from another command, as we will see later. *lpr* starts the printing process by storing the data temporarily to a directory called a print spool. Other parts of the print management system, which we showed you how to set up in the section "Managing Print Services" in Chapter 8, remove files from the print queue in the correct order, process the files for printing, and control the flow of data to the printer.

There is at least one print spool for each printer on the system.* By default, *lpr* looks for a printer named lp. But if you need to specify a printer of a different name, just include a –P option.

For example, to send your document to a printer named nene, enter:

```
lpr -Pnene myprogram.c
```

If you forget the name of a printer, you can look at the names of the spool directories under the */var/spool/lpd* directory or at the */etc/printcap* file entries to see all the names recognized for each printer. If you are using the *lprng* system (which many distributions do these days), you can also use *lpq -a* to see all installed printers.

---

* A printer that can be used in different modes of operation, such as for printing faxes as well as letters, may have a separate print spool for each purpose.

Note that as a user, you do not see whether a printer is connected directly to your computer or somewhere else on the network; all you see and need to know is the name of the printer queue. If you use a printer queue that points to a printer on another machine, the file to print will first be queued on your machine, then transmitted to the appropriate spool area of the machine connected to the printer, and finally be printed. "Managing Print Services" in Chapter 8 tells you more about setting up printer queues.

If you want to use a particular printer for most of your printing needs, you can also set it in the PRINTER environment variable. So, assuming that you are using the *bash* shell, you could make nene your personal default printer by putting this command in your *.bashrc* file:

```
export PRINTER=nene
```

The *-P* option in *lpr* overrides the PRINTER variable.

Once you know how to print a file, the next problem you might face is finding out what is happening if your file doesn't instantly print as you expect. You can find out the status of files in the print queue by using the *lpq* command. To find out the status of files sent to your default printer (the PRINTER environment variable applies to all the commands discussed in this section), enter:

```
$ lpq
nene is ready and printing
Rank    Owner      Job  Files                       Total Size
active lovelace   020  (standard input)             776708 bytes
1st    parcifal   024  (standard input)            2297842 bytes
1st    lark       023  (standard input)              10411 bytes
```

You see that the printer is running, but large jobs are queued ahead of yours (if you are *lark*). If you just can't wait, you might decide to remove the job from the print queue. You can use the job number of the printing task that *lpq* reported to remove the printing job:

```
$ lprm 23
023 dequeued
023 dequeued
```

The spooled print file identified as job 023 is discarded, along with an associated file that contains instructions for formatting the file.

You can narrow the *lpq* report by asking about a specific print job by task ID (rarely used), by printer, or by user ID. For example, to get a report that identifies spooled files sent to a printer named ada you would enter:

```
$ lpq ada
ada is ready and printing
Rank    Owner      Job  Files                       Total Size
active lovelace   788  standard input               16713 bytes
1st    lark       796  standard input               70750 bytes
```

If you are the root user, you can kill all pending printing tasks by entering the command:

```
lprm -
```

If you are not the root user, issuing that command kills only the printing tasks you own. This restriction also holds true if you specify a printer:

```
lprm ada
```

If you are root, the ada print queue is emptied. If you are a normal user, only the print files you own are removed from the specified print spool. The *lprm* utility reports on the tasks it kills.

The root user can kill all the print tasks issued by any user by specifying:

```
lprm username
```

If you issue *lprm* with no argument, it deletes the currently active print jobs that you own. This is equivalent to entering:

```
lprm yourusername
```

If you want to see whether a printer is down, you can use the *lpc* command:

```
/usr/sbin/lpc status ada
```

See the section "Controlling Printer Services with lpc" in Chapter 8 for details. The *lpc* utility is usually installed in the */sbin* or */usr/sbin* directory.

Now we'll discuss some more examples of common printing tasks and filters you can use.

To get a quick hardcopy printout of the printcap manual page, enter:

```
man printcap | col -b | lpr
```

The *man* command finds, formats, and outputs the printcap manual page in an enriched ASCII output that uses backspaces to overstrike and underline characters (in place of italics) for highlighting. The output is piped through *col*, a Unix text filter, where *-b* specifies stripping the "backspace" instructions embedded in the manpage, which results in simple text strings, still maintaining the layout of the formatted man page. The output of *col* is piped to *lpr*, which spools the text in a spool directory.

Suppose you want to print the fully enriched manpage with highlighting and all. You might use a command like this:

```
groff -man -Tps /usr/man/man5/printcap.5 | lpr
```

The *groff* command applies the man macros to the file specified, creating PostScript output (specified by *–Tps*); output is passed to *lpr*, which spools it, and *lpd* applies the default print-processing instructions from the */etc/printcap* file.

Another useful tool for printing pure-text files is the *pr* command, which formats them in a number of ways.

Most Linux installations use BSD-style print utilities developed for the Berkeley Software Distribution of Unix. If you find utilities named *lp*, *lpstat*, *cancel*, and *lpadmin*, your Linux host has a System V-based print system. You need to read the manual pages and perhaps other documentation for that package. Other printing systems could be installed on your system, such as the PLP package, but we document only the usual Linux BSD-based print-management utilities here. We also describe how to use some of the other commonly installed print support utilities for Linux, such as filters that prepare documents in special ways to print on your printers.

On Names of Printing Systems

The BSD-style print-management system is traditionally called "lp" after the line printers that were the standard print devices of the era in which the package was developed.[a] In the Linux community, the BSD print-management package is more commonly called "the lpr package." Of course, the *lpr* command is only one tool in the package. Finally, there is also the CUPS (Common Unix Printing System) package, which is much more modern and advanced than the other print-management packages, and will probably replace the older one over the course of the next two years. You can find more information about CUPS in "Managing Print Services" in Chapter 8.

---

[a] Don't be misled if you hear someone use the term "lp," which is a confusing misnomer. There is no *lp* utility in the BSD print-management package, but there is one in the later-developed System V print package. It is still possible that your BSD package allows you to use an *lp* command in order to print, though. Some systems use a shell script (filter) named *lp* to convert *lp* command options into *lpr* command options, and pass them on to *lpr*. This is solely for the convenience of users who are familiar with the System V *lp* command.

How the Printing System Processes a Queued File

Generally, after you have handed your document or file that you want printed over to the printing system, you can forget about it until the printed sheet comes out of the printer. But when things go wrong and the sheet does not appear, or if you are simply curious (like us!), you might want to know what goes on behind the scenes between the *lpr* command and the output tray of your printer. If you want, you can skip this section and come back here later.

Only the root user has the ability to access printers directly, without using the printing system. (That's not a wise thing to do, by the way.) Linux doesn't grant system users the ability to address various physical devices directly because crippling conflicts could result, and also because it's just too much work for them in which to bother. Instead, utilities call background system processes to schedule your printing among other tasks, convert source file data to print to a specific printer using its printer language and protocols, set print resolution and format the pages, and add (or know not to add) header and footer data and page numbering. Linux configures itself to handle its physical devices when it is booted, including setting up ports and protocols to handle printing.

The print-management system is controlled by *lpd*, the "line printer daemon," which has necessary privileges to access printers on behalf of the user. Once the print-management system is installed, *lpd* is started every time the Linux system is initialized (booted). The */etc/printcap* file provides the control information *lpd* needs to manage the files the user wants to print.

Here's what the print-management system is actually doing when it receives a printing command. When called, *lpr* checks whether a PRINTER environment variable is set. If so, *lpr* loads the print options stored there as instructions to process the print file it is receiving. Next, *lpr* applies any option parameters passed to it from the command line or by a program that preprocessed the file. Last, *lpr* sends the file to the spool directory for the printer that will be used, along with another temporary file that stores the processing specifications for *lpd* to apply. Then *lpr* notifies *lpd* that a print file has been spooled. If *lpr* receives an option it doesn't understand, it passes the option on to the print filter, which we'll discuss shortly.

When *lpd* finds a job in the print spool, it reads the processing specifications (which tell it how to pass the print file through filters and direct the output to a device) and completes the printing task, erasing the print file and processing file when the printer has received all of the processed print file.

All Unix printing systems process a file through at least one filter to prepare it for output. Appropriate filters are set up by the administrator and specified in the printcap file to meet your usual printing needs. An example could be a filter that converts plain text to PostScript if you have a printer that only understands PostScript. Print jobs enter the print-management system through the *lpr* command (directly on the command line or passed indirectly by some other command). The *lpr* command spools the print file in the correct print spool directory and stores the related processing instructions in an associated file in the same print spool.

When it is time to print the file, the *lpd* daemon reads any special processing directions for the print file, which may override default processing directions set in the */etc/printcap* file. When *lpd* passes the file to the correct filter for the selected printer, it also passes along any instructions on which it did not act. The filter then further processes the file itself according to the instructions, or calls yet other filters to perform the processing it could not. The file is then passed on to the printer by *lpd*. You can see that this hidden filter actually provides most of the print formatting control.

If you have special printing requirements, you need to learn the options to pass to the filter that control print formatting. The standard options are discussed in the *lpr* manual page. Additional filter options are documented in the filter package that is used. Later we discuss a couple of filters that are probably on your system. We can't possibly describe how to use all the filters and filter packages available to you for use with Linux. You should read the manual pages for the filters on your system to learn how to get the output you want.

A well-configured printcap file uses the printer's name to determine what kind of filtering to apply. For example, if your printer can automatically format and print an HTML (World Wide Web) document, you may be able to tell *lpr* to print to the html printer:

```
lpr -Phtml ~/homepage.html
```

This printer could actually be the same printer you use for PostScript, but by specifying a printer named html you cause *lpd* to use a different printcap definition that processes the file through an HTML filter into a graphics format the printer understands.

Since the system administrator controls the contents of */etc/printcap*, you are not at liberty to simply exchange one filtering process for another. You do have a lot of control on the command line and through environment variables that affect your typesetting tools, filter parameters, and printer selection. When necessary, you can filter files before submitting them to the print-management system. For example, if you receive email with an attached graphic that you cannot display or print, you might save the file to disk and then use one of the many graphics conversion utilities available for Linux to convert it (filter it) into a printable form, before passing the file to *lpr*.

Much depends on the cleverness of the filter. If an option is passed through *lpr* and the filter but is never interpreted, it may end up passed through to the printer, either before or after the actual print file. This may have no effect. In some cases, a printer configuration command is deliberately passed to the printer this way. More typically a passed option prints extra pages, probably with stray characters on them; usually this is harmless. If you observe such behavior, make sure you aren't causing the problem yourself with environment variables, badly formed commands, or unsupported options. If it wasn't your fault, the administrator should try to trace the problem to save paper and time.

Some filters automatically apply the PRINTER environment variable if you set it. You should know that the equivalent printer variable for a System V print system is LPDEST, and some print filters you acquire may expect or accept that variable. You may even work on a mixed network with accounts on different systems where one uses BSD print management and another uses System V. If you are a belt-and-suspenders kind of person, you can set both LPDEST and PRINTER in your shell initialization file.

Problems using a print filter may affect other users on a multiuser system. Report any difficulties to the print-system administrator.

nenscript and enscript

The *nenscript* utility, now often called *enscript*, is a flexible filter that provides good formatted output for PostScript printers, even from ASCII text files. It isn't a basic Linux utility, but it is included in a number of Linux distributions and can be retrieved from the usual Linux FTP sites. While you can invoke *nenscript* to send a prepared file to the printer, it usually is specified in the */etc/printcap* file as a pass-through filter that takes text from the standard input and sends it to the standard output.

Suppose you are printing out a C program and want line numbering and a printout on green-striped fanfold paper (not the same format you'd want when printing those graphics you downloaded from the Internet on your nifty PostScript printer). You need to have the program processed, and then insert the line numbers in front of the lines. The solution is to process the file through a filter such as the *nenscript* utility (if you have it installed). After doing its own processing, *nenscript* passes the file to *lpr* for spooling and printing to your trusty tractor-feed printer (named dino here):

```
nenscript -B -L66 -N -Pdino myprogram.c
```

The *nenscript* filter numbers each line of the file passed through it when you specify the *–N* option. The *–B* option suppresses the usual header information from being printed on each page, and the *–L66* option specifies formatting at 66 lines per page. The *nenscript* filter just passes the *–Pdino* option through to *lpr*, which interprets it and directs the output to dino's print spool directory for printing.

When called on the command line, *nenscript* automatically passes output to *lpr* unless you specify standard output by supplying the *–p* option. You don't need to pipe or redirect *nenscript* output to *lpr* explicitly.*

Suppose you are going to print a lot of program listings today. For convenience, you can set an environment variable for *nenscript* to specially process and print your listings each time:

```
export NENSCRIPT=" -B -L66 -N -Pdino"
```

Now, to print your listing correctly, all you need enter is:

```
nenscript myprogram.c
```

nenscript optionally sends output to a file, which is often useful for preparing PostScript files on Linux hosts that don't actually have a PostScript printer available. For example, to convert a text file to a PostScript file, formatted for two-column printing on the standard European A4 paper format in 6-point Courier font, you would type:

```
nenscript -2 -fCourier6 -TA4 -pdocument.ps document.txt
```

The *–2* option overrides the one-column default, and the *–fCourier6* option overrides the 7-point Courier default for two-column output. (The one-column default is Courier10; *nenscript* always uses Courier font when converting plain text into PostScript.) If *nenscript* was compiled using the US_VERSION variable, the default paper

---

* The *nenscript* utility could also be the default filter that the printcap file specifies for use with your printer. It won't hurt for the file to go through a properly designed filter more than once. A filter passes on a processing instruction only when it does not perform the processing itself. As a filter executes an instruction, it discards the processing option. You needn't worry that your file will end up with two sets of line numbers on the page.

format is 8.5x11 inches (if you're not using the US_VERSION environment variable, you can specify this size through –*TUS*). The –*p* option specifies that the output should be stored to *document.ps*, and the filename specified with no option is the input to *nenscript*. If no filename had been specified, *nenscript* would have taken standard input as the filename.

As another example, to print the *nenscript* manual page as basic text on a PostScript printer, enter:

```
man nenscript | col -b | nenscript
```

The *man* command retrieves the manual page and formats it for text display. The *col -b* command strips the backspace instructions for highlighting and underlining, leaving plain text that is piped to the *nenscript* filter. This turns the plain text into simple PostScript with some "pretty printing" that applies headers, footers, page numbering, and the like. Finally, the file is passed to *lpr*, which spools the file. The file passes once more through the filter specified in the printcap file, which could be a "dummy" filter that simply passes the text through. Or the filter could do additional things, such as attaching a formfeed character to the end of the print file.

If you specify the –*Z* option with *nenscript*, it attempts to detect PostScript files passed to it and passes them through unaltered.

If a PostScript file is passed to *nenscript* and is taken for a text file (probably because *nenscript* was not called with the -Z option), *nenscript* will encapsulate it and pass it through to print. This can result in the PostScript code being printed out literally. Even a small PostScript file can use up a lot of paper in this way.

Suppose the *lpd* daemon already applies *nenscript* to process files sent to the printer. The file should still process correctly if it does, but intervening with filtering could cause the second pass through *nenscript* to encapsulate the PostScript source. It would be safer to set the NENSCRIPT variable which specifies default processing options for *nenscript*. When the *nenscript* filter is applied by */etc/printcap* to a print file, the options set in your NENSCRIPT environment variable are used, but are overridden by explicit options passed through *lpr* from the command line or another utility.

Note that you could specify the default printer to use either in PRINTER or as a -*P* argument stored to NENSCRIPT. If you set NENSCRIPT to specify a printer to use, that printer will be used every time NENSCRIPT filters one of your files. We recommend that you set PRINTER rather than -*P* in NENSCRIPT so that you can change the printer specification and have it filtered appropriately.

CHAPTER 10

Installing the X Window System

We come now to the X Window System—one of the most powerful and important software packages available for Linux. If you've ever used X on a Unix system before, you're in luck; running X under Linux is almost no different from running it under Unix systems. And, if you've never had the occasion to use it before, never fear: salvation is at hand.

It's difficult to describe the X Window System in a nutshell. X is a complete windowing graphics interface for Unix systems. It provides a huge number of options to both the programmer and the user. For instance, at least half a dozen *window managers* are available for X, each one offering a different interface for manipulating windows. By customizing the attributes of the window manager, you have complete control over how windows are placed on the screen, the colors and borders used to decorate them, and so forth.

Even if you have not heard about the X Window System yet, you may already have heard about KDE and GNOME. These are so-called desktop environments that provide a user-friendly work environment for your daily Linux work. We'll cover these in great detail in the next chapter.

X was originally developed by Project Athena at MIT and Digital Equipment Corporation. The current version of X is Version 11 revision 6 (X11R6), which was first released in April 1994. Since the release of Version 11, X has virtually taken over as the de facto standard for Unix graphical environments.

Despite its commercial use, the X Window System remains distributable under a liberal license from the X Consortium. As such, a complete implementation of X is freely available for Linux systems. XFree86, an implementation of X originally for i386 Unix systems, is the version that Linux uses most often. Today, this version supports not only Intel-based systems, but also Alpha AXP, MicroSPARC, PowerPC, and other architectures. Further architectures will follow. XFree86 is based on X386-1.2, which was part of the official X11R5 sources, but is no longer maintained and is therefore outdated. The current versions now have very little in common with their ancestors. Support for innumerable graphics boards and many other operating systems (including Linux) has been added—and XFree86 implements the latest version, X11R6.3.

We should mention here that commercial X Window System servers are available for Linux that may have advantages over XFree86 (like support for certain video cards). Most people use XFree86 happily, though, so this should certainly be your first stop.

Linux distributions usually automatically install X. If you're lucky, you won't need this chapter at all. But a few users aren't lucky—the distribution doesn't recognize some graphics hardware, writes a file to the wrong location so that the X server can't start up, or has some other problem. One of the big advantages of this book is that we take you down to the depths of X configuration so that you can get it running no matter what your distribution does. You may not need to read this chapter, but if you do need it, you'll appreciate everything that's here.

One word of advice: if you plan to run your Linux machine as a server only, there is no need to install X on it (unless you want to use graphical administration tools). X requires system resources, and if your system never has a monitor attached to it, installing X is a waste of time and resources.

In this chapter, we will tell you how to install and configure the X Window System, and in the next chapter, we will explore how to use X.

X Concepts

X is based on a client-server model in which the X *server* is a program that runs on your system and handles all access to the graphics hardware. An X *client* is an applications program that communicates with the server, sending it requests, such as "draw a line" or "pay attention to keyboard input." The X server takes care of servicing these requests by drawing a line on the display or sending user input (via the keyboard, mouse, or whatever) to the client application. Examples of X clients are the now-famous image manipulation program *GIMP* and the many programs coming out of the aforementioned desktop environments KDE and GNOME—e.g., the KDE email program *kmail*.

It is important to note that X is a network-oriented graphics system. That is, X clients can run either locally (on the same system that the server is running) or remotely (on a system somewhere on a TCP/IP network). The X server listens to both local and remote network sockets for requests from clients. This feature is obviously quite powerful. If you have a connection to a TCP/IP network, you can log in to another system over the network and run an X application there, directing it to display on your local X server.

Further advantages of X are security (if the user so desires), the modular separation of functions, and the support for many different architectures. All this makes the X Window System technically superior by far to all other window systems.

The X Window System makes a distinction between application behavior and *window management*. Clients running under X are displayed within one or more *windows* on your screen. However, how windows are manipulated (placed on the display, resized, and so forth) and how they are decorated (the appearance of the window frames) are not controlled by the X server. Instead, such things are handled by another X client called a *window manager* that runs concurrently with the other X clients. Your choice of window manager will decide to some extent how X as a whole looks and feels. Most window managers are utterly flexible and configurable; the user can select the look of the window decoration, the focus policy, the meaning of the mouse buttons when the mouse is on the background part of the screen rather than on an application window, and many other things by editing the configuration files of the window manager. More modern systems even let you configure those aspects over a GUI.

In order to fully understand the concept of window managers, you need to know that the window manager does not affect what the client application does within the window. The window manager is only in charge of painting the window decoration—that is, the frame and the buttons that let you close, move, and resize windows.

There can be only one window manager on any X server. Theoretically, it is even possible to completely do away with window managers, but then you would not be able to move windows around the screen; put a hidden window on top; or minimize, maximize, or resize windows unless the programs themselves provide this functionality.

Let's shortly mention the desktop environments again. A desktop environment like KDE and GNOME is a collection of applications and tools with a common look-and-feel as well as many other common properties—e.g., the menus of the applications could all be set up according to the same concepts. Desktop environments on X always need a window manager, as described earlier. Some desktop environments provide their own window manager (such as *kwin* in the KDE desktop environment), while others do not have their own window manager. It is up to the user to install a window manager of his or her choice.

Hardware Requirements

As of XFree86 Version 4.2.0, released in January 2002, the video chipsets listed in this section are supported. The documentation included with your video adapter should specify the chipset used. If you are in the market for a new video card, or are buying a new machine that comes with a video card, have the vendor find out exactly what the video card's make, model, and chipset are. This may require the vendor to call technical support on your behalf; vendors usually will be happy to do this. Many PC hardware vendors will state that the video card is a "standard SVGA card" that "should work" on your system. Explain that your software (mention Linux and XFree86!) does not support all video chipsets and that you must have detailed information.

A good source for finding out whether your graphics board is supported and which X server it needs is *http://www.xfree86.org/cardlist.html*.

You can also determine your video card chipset by running the SuperProbe program included with the XFree86 distribution. This is covered in more detail later.

The following accelerated and nonaccelerated SVGA chipsets are supported (sorted by manufacturer):

3Dfx
> Voodoo Banshee, Voodoo Graphics, Voodoo2, Voodoo3, Voodoo4, Voodoo5

3Dlabs
> Permedia series, GLINT series

Alliance
> AT24, AT25, AT3D

ARK Logic
> ARK1000PV, ARK2000PV, ARK2000MT

ATI
> Most Mach32 chips, Mach64 and Rage chips (GX, CX, CT, ET, VT, VT3, GT, RageII+DVD), RagePro (GB, GD, GI, FP, GQ), VT4, Rage IIC (GV, GW, GZ), Rage LT Pro (LD, LB, LI, LP), Rage LT, Rage XL or XC (GL, GM, GN, GO, GR, GS), Rage Mobility (LM, LN, LR, LS), VGAWonder chipsets (18800, 18800-1, 28800-2, 28800-4, 28800-5, 28800-6), Rage 128

Chips and Technologies
> 65520, 65525, 65530, 65535, 65540, 65545, 65546, 65548, 65550, 65554, 65555, 68554, 69000, 64200, 64300

Cirrus Logic
> Alpine (5430, 5434, 5436, 5446, 5480, 7548), Laguna (5462, 5464, 5465)

Compaq/Digital
> DEC 21030 TGA 8-plane, 24-plane, 24-plane 3D chips

Cyrix
> Cyrix MediaGX

IBM
> Standard IBM VGA

Integrated Micro Solutions (IMS)
> IMS Twin Turbo 128, Twin Turbo 3D

Intel
> i740, i810, i815, i830

Matrox
> MGA2064W (Millenium I), MGA1064SG (Mystique), MGA2164W (Millenium II) PCI and AGP, G100, G200, G400, G450, G550

NeoMagic
> NM2070, NM2090, NM2093, NM2097, NM2160, NM2200, NM2230, NM2360, NM2380

NVIDIA
> Riva 128, 128ZX, TNT, TNT2 (Ultra, Vanta, M64), GeForce (DDR, 256), Quadro, GeForce2 (GTS, Ultra, MX), GeForce3, Quadro2

Number Nine
> Imagine 128, Ticket 2 Ride, Revolution 3D, Revolution IV

Rendition/Micro
> Verite 1000, 2100, 2200

S3
> 964 (revisions 0 and 1), 968, Trio32, Trio64, Trio64, Trio64V+, Trio64UV+, Aurora64V+, Trio64V2, and PLATO/PX (only models using the IBM RGB 524, Texas Instruments 3025, or an internal TrioDAC RAMDAC chip are supported); ViRGE, ViRGE/VX, ViRGE/DX, ViRGE/GX, ViRGE/GX2, ViRGE/MX, ViRGE/MX+, Trio3D, Trio3D/2X; Savage3D, Savage3D/MV, Savage4, Savage2000, SuperSavage

SGI
> Indy Newport (XL) cards

Silicon Integrated Systems (SIS)
> 300, 530, 540, 620, 630, 6326

Silicon Motion, Inc.
> Lynx, LynxE, Lynx3D, LynxEM, LynxEM+, Lynx3DM

Sun Microsystems
> BW2, CG3, CG6, CG14, FFB, LEO, TCX framebuffers

Trident Microsystems
> TVGA8900B, TVGA8900C, TVGA8900CL, TVGA9000, TVGA9000i, TVGA9100B, TVGA9200CXr, TVGA8900D, TGUI9440AGi, TGUI9660, TGUI9680, ProVidia 9682, ProVidia 9685, 3DImage975, 3DImage985, Blade3D, Cyber9320, Cyber9382, Cyber9385, Cyber9388, Cyber9397, Cyber9397/DVD, Cyber9520, Cyber9525/DVD, CyberBlade/Ai1, CyberBlade/i7, CyberBlade/i1, CyberBlade/DSTN/Ai1, CyberBlade/DSTN/i7, CyberBlade/DSTN/i1, CyberBlade/e4, CyberBladeXP, BladeXP

Tseng Labs
> ET4000AX, ET4000/W32, ET4000/W32i, ET4000/W32p, ET6000, ET6100

It should be noted that the XFree86 project recently switched to an entirely new driver architecture, which is much more flexible than the old one and will enable more timely support of new graphics hardware. However, this also means that not all the drivers that existed in previous versions have been ported to the new architecture yet. Thus, a fair number of (mostly older) graphics chips are supported by the previous version (3.3.6), but are not supported by the current version. If this is the case with your graphics hardware (the driver list at *http://xfree86.org* will tell you), you might want to consider installing the old version.

Video cards using these chipsets are normally supported on all bus types, including the PCI and AGP.

All these chipsets are supported in 256-color mode, some are supported in mono- and 16-color modes, and some are supported in higher color depths.

This list will undoubtedly expand as time passes. The release notes for the current version of XFree86 should contain the complete list of supported video chipsets. Please also always see the *README* file for your particular chipset.

Besides those chipsets, there is also support for the framebuffer device starting with the 2.2 kernel series via the fbdev driver. If your chipset is supported by the normal X server drivers, you should use those for better performance, but if it is not, you may still be able to run X by using the framebuffer. On some hardware, even the frame-buffer device provides accelerated graphics.

One problem faced by the XFree86 developers is that some video card manufacturers use nonstandard mechanisms for determining clock frequencies used to drive the card. Some of these manufacturers either don't release specifications describing how to program the card, or require developers to sign a nondisclosure statement to obtain the information. This would obviously restrict the free distribution of the XFree86 software, something that the XFree86 development team is not willing to do.

The suggested minimum setup for XFree86 under Linux is a '486 machine with at least 32 MB of RAM and a video card with a chipset listed earlier. You should check the documentation for XFree86 and verify that your particular card is supported before taking the plunge and purchasing expensive hardware. Benchmark rating comparisons for various video cards under XFree86 are posted to the Usenet news-groups *comp.windows.x.i386unix* and *comp.os.linux.misc* regularly.

As a side note, one author's (Kalle's) secondary personal Linux system is an AMD K6-2 with 128 MB of RAM and is equipped with a PCI Permedia II chipset card with 8 MB of DRAM. This setup is already a lot faster with respect to display speed than many workstations. XFree86 on a Linux system with an accelerated SVGA card will give you much greater performance than that found on commercial Unix worksta-tions (which often employ simple framebuffers for graphics and provide accelerated graphics hardware only as a high-priced add-on).

Your machine will need at least 16 MB of physical RAM and 32 MB of virtual RAM (for example, 16 MB physical and 16 MB swap). Remember that the more physical RAM you have, the less the system will swap to and from disk when memory is low. Because swapping is inherently slow (disks are very slow compared to memory), hav-ing 16 MB or more of RAM is necessary to run XFree86 comfortably. A system with 16 MB of physical RAM could run *much* more slowly (up to 10 times more slowly) than one with 32 MB or more.

Installing XFree86

You can find the Linux binary distribution of XFree86 on a number of FTP sites. On *ftp://ftp.xfree86.org*, you can find it in the directory */pub/XFree86/4.2.0/binaries*; there you will find systems for various architectures in subdirectories. (At the time of this writing, the current version is 4.2.0; newer versions are released periodically.)

It's quite likely you obtained XFree86 as part of a Linux distribution, in which case downloading the software separately is not necessary. If you are downloading XFree86 directly, see Tables 10.1 and 10.2, which list the files in the XFree86-4.2.0 distribution.

In order to find out the set of files you need to download, we highly advise that you download a small shell script called *Xinstall.sh* first and run it as follows:

```
sh Xinstall.sh -check
```

This will output the directory containing the set of binaries you need to download.

Table 10-1 lists the required files.

Table 10-1. Files required for installing XFree86

File	Description
Xinstall.sh	The installation program
extract	An unpacking utility
Xbin.tgz	X clients and utilities as well as the run-time libraries
Xlib.tgz	Datafiles needed at runtime
Xman.tgz	Manual pages
Xdoc.tgz	Documentation
Xfnts.tgz	The base font set
Xfenc.tgz	The base set of font encoding data
Xetc.tgz	Runtime configuration files
Xvar.tgz	Runtime data
Xxserv.tgz	The X server itself
Xmod.tgz	The various driver modules

There are also a number of optional files that you should download only if you need them, as shown in Table 10-2.

Table 10-2. Optional files for installing XFree86

File	Description
Xfsrv.tgz	The font server
Xnest.tgz	A nested X server

Table 10-2. Optional files for installing XFree86 (continued)

File	Description
Xprog.tgz	Header files for X programming, configuration files, and compile-time libraries
Xprt.tgz	The X Print server
Xvfb.tgz	An X server for the virtual framebuffer
Xf100.tgz	Fonts in 100 dpi resolution
Xfcyr.tgz	Cyrillic fonts
Xfscl.tgz	Scalable fonts
Xhtml.tgz	An HTML version of the documentation
Xps.tgz	A PostScript version of the documentation
Xjdoc.tgz	A Japanese version of the documentation

The XFree86 directory should contain *README* files and installation notes for the current version.

Obtain these files and save them in the directory */var/tmp* (you can use any other directory; just change the pathname accordingly in the following examples). Now run the installation script again, this time without the *–check* option:

```
sh Xinstall.sh
```

This will ask you a number of questions. Usually, you can just press the Enter key in order to accept the defaults. Particularly, when asked whether you want to create links for OpenGL, say yes. This will install a compatible version. OpenGL is a library for fast 3D graphics; applications that display 3D graphics often use it, other applications never do. If you plan to run any 3D graphics applications, you should enable this. The installer will also ask you whether you want a link to the *rstart* utility to be created. If you do not know what *rstart* is, you can safely say no here.

Once the script is done running, XFree86 is installed, and you can start configuring it. This is covered in the next section.

Configuring XFree86

Setting up XFree86 is not difficult in most cases. However, if you happen to be using hardware for which drivers are under development, or wish to obtain the best performance or resolution from an accelerated graphics card, configuring XFree86 can be somewhat time-consuming.

In this section, we describe how to create and edit the *XF86Config* file, which configures the XFree86 server. This file is located in */etc/X11/* in the current version of

XFree86, but in */etc/* in the previous versions. Also, the file format nas changed between Version 3 and Version 4; what we describe here applies to Version 4, the current version (to make things worse, some Red Hat versions call this file *XF86Config-4*). In many cases, it is best to start out with a "basic" XFree86 configuration—one that uses a low resolution. A good choice is 640x480, which should be supported on all video cards and monitor types. Once you have XFree86 working at a lower, standard resolution, you can tweak the configuration to exploit the capabilities of your video hardware. The idea is that you want to make sure XFree86 works at least minimally on your system and that something isn't wrong with your installation before attempting the sometimes difficult task of setting up XFree86 for real use. With current hardware, you should easily be able to get up to 1024x768 pixels.

But before you start to write an *XF86Config* file yourself, try one of the configuration programs that are available. In many cases, you can avoid going through the hassle that will be described on the next pages. Some programs that may help you are:

Distribution-specific configuration tools
> Some distributions also have their own configuration tools. For example, SuSE has *SaX2* and Red Hat has *Xconfigurator*. These tools are usually very convenient and should be your first try. But if these fail, it is good to know that you have other options at your disposal. Most installation programs start these programs automatically during the installation, but if you configure your X server after installation, you should be able to start them by invoking their name on the command line. When in doubt, consult the documentation of your distribution.

xf86cfg
> This graphical configuration program is, like *xf86config* described later, provided by the XFree86 team. It starts up a minimal X server (which is quite sure to run on just about any display hardware) and then lets you select your graphics board, your monitor type, your mouse type, and other options. At the end, it tries to start up a server as configured, and if you are satisfied, it offers to write the configuration file for you. We have found this program to be very useful and reliable in many cases.

The –configure option
> If you run
>
> ```
> XFree86 -configure
> ```
>
> as root the X server will try to probe as much information as possible about your hardware and write a suitable *XF86Config* file to */root/XF86Config.new* (i.e., it doesn't overwrite your old configuration file, if any). In order to try this configuration, you can run the X server manually with:
>
> ```
> XFree86 -xf86config /root/XF86Config.new
> ```
>
> which will use the freshly generated configuration file instead of the default one.

xf86config

> This is a text-based configuration program provided by the XFree86 team. It guides you through a set of questions and generates the *XF86Config* file based on your answers. It is not particularly user-friendly but has been reported to work when the other options have failed.

If one of these tools is able to configure your X server for you, you should use it and save yourself a lot of trouble. However, if all the tools fail or if you want to fine-tune your X server, you will have to know how to edit the *XF86Config* file yourself.

In addition to the information here, you should read the following documentation:

- The XFree86 documentation in */usr/X11R6/lib/X11/doc* (contained within the *Xdoc* package).
- The *README* file for your video chipset, if one exists, in the directory */usr/X11R6/lib/X11/doc*. These *README* files have names, such as *README.i740* and *README.cyrix*.
- The manual page for *XFree86*.
- The manual page for *XF86Config*.

The main configuration file you need to create is */etc/X11/XF86Config* (*/etc/XF86Config* in older versions). This file contains information on your mouse, video card parameters, and so on. The file *XF86Config.eg* is provided with the XFree86 distribution as an example. Copy this file to *XF86Config* and edit it as a starting point.

The *XF86Config* manual page explains the format of this file in detail. Read this manual page now if you have not done so already.

We are going to present a sample *XF86Config* file, piece by piece. This file may not look exactly like the sample file included in the XFree86 distribution, but the structure is the same. The *XF86Config* file format may change with each version of XFree86; this information is valid only for XFree86 Version 4.2.0.

Whatever you do, you should not simply copy the configuration file listed here to your own system and attempt to use it. Attempting to use a configuration file that doesn't correspond to your hardware could drive the monitor at a frequency that is too high for it; there have been reports of monitors (especially fixed-frequency monitors) being damaged or destroyed by using an incorrectly configured *XF86Config* file. The bottom line is this: make absolutely sure your *XF86Config* file corresponds to your hardware before you attempt to use it.

Now that we have written this warning, we would also like to mention that configuring XFree86 is much less dangerous than it used to be a few years ago, since the X server has become very good at detecting unsuitable configurations.

Each section of the *XF86Config* file is surrounded by the pair of lines `Section "section-name"`...`EndSection`. The first part of the *XF86Config* file is `Files`, which looks like this:

```
Section "Files"
    FontPath     "/usr/X11R6/lib/X11/fonts/misc:unscaled"
    FontPath     "/usr/X11R6/lib/X11/fonts/Type"
    RgbPath      "/usr/X11R6/lib/X11/rgb"
EndSection
```

There can be many more lines like these. The `RgbPath` line sets the path to the X11R6 RGB color database, and each `FontPath` line sets the path to a directory containing X11 fonts. In general, you shouldn't have to modify these lines; just be sure there is a `FontPath` entry for each font type you have installed (i.e., for each directory in */usr/X11R6/lib/X11/fonts*). If you add the string `:unscaled` to a `FontPath`, the fonts from this directory will not be scaled. This is often an improvement because fonts that are greatly scaled look ugly. In addition to `FontPath` and `RgbPath`, you can also add a `ModulePath` to this section, to point to a directory with dynamically loaded modules. Those modules are currently used for some special input devices, as well as the PEX and XIE extensions.

The next section is `ServerFlags`, which specifies several global flags for the server. This section is often empty or very small:

```
Section "ServerFlags"
  Option       "AllowMouseOpenFail"
EndSection
```

Here, we say that we want the X server to start up even if it cannot find the mouse. For more options, please see the *XF86Config(1)* manual page. Often, options will be autodetected at server startup, so they don't need to be listed here.

The next section is the `Module` section, with which you can dynamically load additional X server modules, such as support for special hardware or graphics libraries like PEX. Unless you want to use special modules (which are likely to have their own documentation), you can leave this section out entirely.

The next sections are `InputDevice`. You usually have at least two, one for the keyboard and one for the mouse. If you have other input devices, such as a graphics tablet, these will go into additional sections:

```
Section "InputDevice"
        Identifier  "Keyboard1"
        Driver      "Keyboard"
        Option          "AutoRepeat" "250 30"
        Option          "XkbRules" "xfree86"
        Option          "XkbModel" "pc105"
        Option          "XkbLayout" "us"
EndSection

Section "InputDevice"
```

```
        Driver      "mouse"
        Identifier  "Mouse[1]"
        Option      "Device" "/dev/mouse"
        Option      "Emulate3Buttons" "on"
        Option      "Emulate3Timeout" "50"
        Option      "InputFashion" "Mouse"
        Option      "Name" "Autodetection"
        Option      "Protocol" "ps/2"
        Option      "Vendor" "Sysp"
      EndSection
```

Again, other options are available as well. The keyboard configurations listed previously are for a U.S. keyboard; for other keyboards you will need to replace them with other lines suitable for your keyboard.

The mouse section tells the X server where the mouse is connected (*/dev/mouse* in this case, which is usually a link to the appropriate port, such as */dev/ttyS0*), what kind of mouse it is (the "Protocol" option) and some other operational details. It is important for the protocol to be right, but the aforementioned configuration programs should usually find out the protocol automatically. You can find the list of supported protocols in */usr/X11R6/lib/X11/doc/README.mouse*.

BusMouse should be used for the Logitech busmouse. Note that older Logitech mice that are not bus mice should use Logitech, but newer Logitech mice that are not bus mice use either the Microsoft or the Mouseman protocol. This is a case where the protocol doesn't necessarily have anything to do with the make of the mouse.

If you have a modern serial mouse, you could also try specifying Auto, which will try to autoselect a mouse driver.

It is easy to check whether you have selected the correct mouse driver once you have started up X; when you move your mouse, the mouse pointer on the screen should follow this movement. If it does this, your setup is very likely to be correct. If it doesn't, try another driver, and also check whether the device you specified is correct.

The next section of the *XF86Config* file is Device, which specifies parameters for your video card. If you have multiple video cards, there will also be multiple Device sections.

```
      Section "Device"
        BoardName   "SiS630 GUI Accelerator+3D"
        BusID       "1:0:0"
        Driver      "sis"
        Identifier  "Device[0]"
        Screen      0
        VendorName  "SiS"
      EndSection
```

The first entry here, BoardName, is simply a descriptive name that reminds you which graphics card you have configured here (important if you have more than one!). Similarly, VendorName is a free-form string that has purely descriptional purposes. Even the `Identifier` string can be picked freely, but needs to match the `Device` strings used in later sections of the configuration file. It is customary here to use the names `Device"0"`, `Device"1"`, and so on.

`BusID` identifies the actual graphics card in terms of the built-in hardware on the PCI bus. `PCI:1:0:0`, or the shorter `1:0:0`, is usually the right choice if you have only one choice. If you are unsure about what to put in here, run the X server as follows:

```
XFree86 -scanpci
```

and check the output carefully. At least one graphics card should be contained in the output (probably among other hardware not relevant here). For example, a line like:

```
(1:0:0) Matrox unknown card (0x19d8) using a Matrox MGA G400 AGP
```

tells you that you have a Matrox MGA G400 card with an AGP connector installed. The first digits in parentheses are the PCI bus ID, as described earlier.

The `Screen` section is mandatory on multihead graphics cards, which have more than one monitor output. For single-head graphics cards, always put in 0 here.

`Driver` is very important, as it determines the actual graphics driver to be loaded by the X server. A good way to find the right driver name is either to use the configuration programs described earlier or to run the X server like this:

```
XFree86 -probeonly
```

This will output information the X server has collected about your hardware, including the driver it thinks it should use.

There are lots of other options you can specify in this file, including the chipset, the RAMDAC, and other hardware properties, but the X server is very good at finding these out all by itself, so you usually don't have to do that. If you still want to, check out the driver-specific *README* file, which lists the options and their possible values for that driver.

The next section is `Monitor`, which specifies the characteristics of your monitor. As with other sections in the *XF86Config* file, there may be more than one `Monitor` section. This is useful if you have multiple monitors connected to a system, or use the same *XF86Config* file under multiple hardware configurations. In general, though, you will need only a single `Monitor` section:

```
Section "Monitor"
    Option       "CalcAlgorithm" "CheckDesktopGeometry"
    HorizSync    31-65
    Identifier   "Monitor[0]"
    ModelName    "1024X768@70HZ"
    VendorName   "--> LCD"
    VertRefresh  58-78
    UseModes     "Modes[0]"
EndSection
```

The `Identifier` line is used to give an arbitrary name to the `Monitor` entry. This can be any string; you will use it to refer to the `Monitor` entry later in the *XF86Config* file.

`HorizSync` specifies the valid horizontal sync frequencies for your monitor in kHz. If you have a multisync monitor, this can be a range of values (or several comma-separated ranges), as seen in the `Monitor` section. If you have a fixed-frequency monitor, this will be a list of discrete values, such as:

```
HorizSync    31.5, 35.2, 37.9, 35.5, 48.95
```

Your monitor manual should list these values in the technical specifications section. If you do not have this information, you should contact either the manufacturer or the vendor of your monitor to obtain it. There are other sources of information, as well; they are listed later.

You should be careful with those settings. While the settings `VertRefresh` and `HorizSync` (described next) help to make sure that your monitor will not be destroyed by wrong settings, you won't be very happy with your X setup if you get these values wrong. Unsteady pictures, flickering, or just plain snow can result.

`VertRefresh` specifies the valid vertical refresh rates (or vertical synchronization frequencies) for your monitor in Hz. Like `HorizSync`, this can be a range or a list of discrete values; your monitor manual should list them.

`HorizSync` and `VertRefresh` are used only to double-check that the monitor resolutions you specify are in valid ranges. This reduces the chance that you will damage your monitor by attempting to drive it at a frequency for which it wasn't designed.

You can use the `ModeLine` and `Mode` directive to specify resolution modes for your monitor. However, unlike earlier versions of XFree86, this is not strictly necessary any longer; the `Monitor` section shown earlier (which comes from a laptop) doesn't have one. Instead, this information is moved into the following section, `Modes`.

The `Modes` section, of which there should be one for every monitor you have configured, lists the various video modes that the X server should support. An example:

```
Section "Modes"
   Identifier    "Modes[0]"
   Modeline      "1024x768" 69.35 1024 1040 1216 1400 768 768 778 802
   Modeline      "1024x768" 79.55 1024 1040 1216 1400 768 768 778 802
   Modeline      "800x600" 42.43 800 816 928 1072 600 600 610 626
   Modeline      "800x600" 48.67 800 816 928 1072 600 600 610 626
EndSection
```

The `Identifier` line refers to a name specified in the `Monitor` section. The following `Modeline` lines each specify a video mode. The format of `Modeline` is:

```
Modeline name dot-clock horiz-values vert-values
```

name is an arbitrary string, which you will use to refer to the resolution mode later in the file. *dot-clock* is the driving clock frequency or *dot clock* associated with the resolution mode. A dot clock is usually specified in MHz and is the rate at which the video card must send pixels to the monitor at this resolution. *horiz-values* and *vert-values* are four numbers each; they specify when the electron gun of the monitor should fire and when the horizontal and vertical sync pulses fire during a sweep across the screen.

How can you determine the Modeline values for your monitor? That's difficult, especially since a lot of the documentation files that used to be shipped with XFree86 are no longer included, probably because they became outdated and haven't been updated yet. Your best bet is probably to use one of the configuration file generators mentioned in the previous section to get a set of start values and then tweaking these until you reach a satisfactory setting. For example, if while running XFree86 the image on the monitor shifts slightly or seems to flicker, tweak the values little by little to try to fix the image. Exactly what you need to adjust is difficult to say because it depends a lot on your actual graphics hardware, but with some experimenting, you usually get good results. Also, be sure to check the knobs and controls on the monitor itself! In many cases it is necessary to change the horizontal or vertical size of the display after starting up XFree86 in order for the image to be centered and of the appropriate size. Another option is to use the program *xvidtune* (see the manual page for how to use it), which can help you to get all the numbers for the modeline, lets you try your changes, and even allows you to undo them if you did something wrong.

Also, XFree86 has the so-called VESA monitor timings built in, so you might get along without a Modes section altogether. The VESA timings are standard values for the Modeline that work on most display hardware, at the expense of not using the individual hardware to its fullest potential.

Note that the *name* argument to Modeline (in this case "640x480") is an arbitrary string; the convention is to name the mode after the resolution, but *name* can be anything that describes the mode to you.

For each Modeline used, the server checks that the specifications for the mode fall within the range of values specified with HorizSync and VertRefresh. If they do not, the server will complain when you attempt to start up X (more on this later).

You shouldn't insert monitor timing values or Modeline values for monitors other than the model you own. If you attempt to drive the monitor at a frequency for which it was not designed, you can damage or even destroy it.

The next section is Screen, which specifies the monitor/video card combination to use for a particular server:

```
Section "Screen"
  DefaultDepth 16
  SubSection "Display"
    Depth      15
    Modes      "800x600"
  EndSubSection
```

```
    SubSection "Display"
      Depth     16
      Modes     "1024x768"
    EndSubSection
    SubSection "Display"
      Depth     24
      Modes     "800x600"
    EndSubSection
    SubSection "Display"
      Depth     32
      Modes     "800x600"
    EndSubSection
    SubSection "Display"
      Depth     8
      Modes     "800x600"
    EndSubSection
    Device      "Device[0]"
    Identifier  "Screen[0]"
    Monitor     "Monitor[0]"
  EndSection
  EndSection
```

This section ties together device, screen, and monitor definitions and lists the color depths to use with the video modes.

Finally, the section ServerLayout wraps things up by defining one actual configuration that consists of one or more Screen sections and one or more InputDevice sections. If you have a so-called multihead system (a system with more than one graphics board and one monitor attached to each, or one of those fancy multihead graphics boards to which you can connect multiple monitors), this section also specifies their relative layout. Here is an example:

```
  Section "ServerLayout"
    Identifier   "Layout[all]"
    InputDevice  "Keyboard[0]" "CoreKeyboard"
    InputDevice  "Mouse[1]" "CorePointer"
    Option       "Clone" "off"
    Option       "Xinerama" "off"
    Screen       "Screen[0]"
  EndSection
```

There are also other sections, but these are entirely optional and not needed in order to get your X server up and running.

Running XFree86

With your *XF86Config* file configured, you're ready to fire up the X server and give it a spin. First, be sure that */usr/X11R6/bin* is on your path.

The command to start up XFree86 is:

```
  startx
```

This is a frontend to *xinit* (in case you're used to using *xinit* on other Unix systems). You can still use *xinit*, which gives you precise control about what exactly is started but requires you to start all necessary programs manually.

This command starts the X server and runs the commands found in the file *.xinitrc* in your home directory. *.xinitrc* is just a shell script containing X clients to run. If this file does not exist, the system default */usr/X11R6/lib/X11/xinit/xinitrc* will be used.

You can change the initial display when starting up the X Window System by providing a different *.xinitrc* in your home directory. The next chapter tells you what you can put in this file.

If you are new to the X Window System environment, we strongly suggest picking up a book such as *The X Window System User's Guide* by Valerie Quercia and Tim O'Reilly (O'Reilly).

Running into Trouble

Often, something will not be quite right when you initially fire up the X server. This is almost always caused by a problem in your *XF86Config* file. Usually, the monitor timing values are off or the video card dot clocks are set incorrectly. If your display seems to roll, or the edges are fuzzy, this is a clear indication that the monitor timing values or dot clocks are wrong. Also be sure you are correctly specifying your video card chipset, as well as other options for the Device section of *XF86Config*. As of XFree86 Version 4, there is only one server binary, which loads the module needed for the graphics card in question. The module that loads depends on your Device settings.

If all else fails, try to start X "bare"; that is, use a command, such as:

```
X > /tmp/x.out 2>&1
```

You can then kill the X server (using the Ctrl-Alt-Backspace key combination) and examine the contents of */tmp/x.out*. The X server reports any warnings or errors—for example, if your video card doesn't have a dot clock corresponding to a mode supported by your monitor. This output can be very helpful in diagnosing all kinds of problems. Examine it closely if your X server does not start up at all, does not provide the resolutions you wanted, or shows a flaky, snowy, or otherwise insufficient picture. Even if everything works to your satisfaction, you might want to check this file for interesting information that the X server has found out about your hardware. The lines starting with (**) contain data that you provided yourself in the configuration file, while lines starting with (- -) contain data that the X server has found out itself.

Remember that you can use Ctrl-Alt with the plus or minus keys on the numeric keypad to switch between the video modes listed on the Modes line of the Screen section of *XF86Config*. If the highest-resolution mode doesn't look right, try switching to lower resolutions. This lets you know, at least, that the configurations for those lower resolutions in your X configuration are working correctly.

Also, check the vertical and horizontal size/hold knobs on your monitor. In many cases it is necessary to adjust these when starting up X. For example, if the display seems to be shifted slightly to one side, you can usually correct this using the monitor controls.

The Usenet newsgroup *comp.windows.x.i386unix* is devoted to discussions about XFree86. It might be a good idea to watch that newsgroup for postings relating to your video configuration; you might run across someone with the same problems as your own. If this fails, please contact your Linux distributor; their support staff should be able to help you as well.

CHAPTER 11
Customizing
Your X Environment

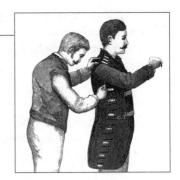

X is now running. But that's only half the story. In the last chapter, you learned how to set up the X Window System so that it recognizes your graphics board and your monitor. While this is clearly necessary, it is of course not the whole story. In this chapter, we will explain the other half: customizing your X environment. Why is customization important? When working in the X Window System, you might want to change your work environment from time to time because your work habits have changed, because new and better environments are available, or simply because the old one has become boring to you. Some of these environments are quite sophisticated. For example, they let you start up a program with all the options you want at the press of a key or the click of a mouse, they let you drag file icons onto a printer to have text printed, and they can do lots of other things that make you more productive in your daily work.

In this chapter, we'll first talk about some very basic aspects of X customization and then introduce you to the two most prominent desktop environments on Linux: KDE and GNOME. For readers who want to dig deeper or need a type of application that is provided with neither KDE nor GNOME, we'll then look at a general means of configuring (older) X applications, the X resources, as well as some general X applications that run independent of any desktop environment.

Until recently, the problem with using X on Unix systems in general and Linux in particular was that nothing was integrated. You would use a window manager and a number of X applications, but they would all look and behave differently, and operate in a manner that was not integrated. For example, drag-and-drop—ubiquitous on Windows or the Macintosh—was hardly heard of on Linux, and if it was, it was difficult to find two applications that could interact together with drag-and-drop.

A relatively new category of software, the so-called desktop environment, has accepted the challenge to produce a state-of-the-art Unix GUI and tries to provide an integrated, consistent desktop where all programs have the same look-and-feel, behave the same, and even provide the same menus in all applications (to the extent where this is possible).

Currently, two main desktop environments are available for Linux: the K Desktop Environment (KDE) and GNOME. KDE is a little bit older and much more advanced with respect to functionality and stability. It aims at making people coming from other computing environments feel at home, as well as providing long-term Unix users a more productive and friendly work environment. GNOME, on the other hand, has put a lot of work into the visual aspects of a desktop environment with colorful icons and the like, but it is less stable than KDE, and the individual programs are less integrated. KDE is the default environment with most distributions, but almost all of them ship both. If yours doesn't, this could mean that the distribution vendor is trying to decide over your head what to use. We will cover both KDE and GNOME here.

In Version 8.0 of Red Hat Linux, the appearance for both KDE and GNOME has been set to a custom Red Hat theme that makes them much more similar to each other. The goal is to provide a single, consistent look and feel for the software, regardless of whether they choose KDE or GNOME. That similarity is intended to make Red Hat Linux easier to support and to provide it with an identifiable appearance, regardless of the destop framework used. In some cases, it may even be difficult to tell whether you're running GNOME or KDE. If you don't like the new appearance, it's easy enough to change the settings back. Very little aside from the settings is different from the software as shipped by the GNOME and KDE projects themselves.

Basics of X Customization

Before running X applications, it's a good idea to learn the rudiments of X customization so that you're not forced to live with the (often unappealing) default configuration used on many systems. Note that the next few sections do not usually apply to the aforementioned desktop environments, which have more user-friendly, GUI-based ways to configure applications and the environment. It's still good to know the old-fashioned way of configuring things because you are likely to come across applications that still follow this scheme.

xinit

You run X with the *startx* command. This in turn is a frontend for *xinit*, the program responsible for starting the X server and running various X clients that you specify. *xinit* (via *startx*) executes the shell script *.xinitrc* in your home directory. This script merely contains commands that you wish to run when starting X, such as *xterm*, *xclock*, and so on. If you don't have a *.xinitrc* file, the system default */usr/lib/X11/xinit/xinitrc* is used instead.

 When using KDE, you will often have only one single command in your *.xinitrc* file: *startkde*. This is a shell script shipped with KDE that starts all necessary services. Your distributor might add other stuff to *.xinitrc*, though.

Here, we'll present a sample *.xinitrc* file for a bare-bones X system without any desktop environment and explain what it does. You could use this as your own, very bare-bones *.xinitrc* or copy the system default *xinitrc* as a starting point:

```
1  #!/bin/sh
2  # Sample .xinitrc shell script
3
4  # Start xterms
5  xterm -geometry 80x40+10+100 -fg black -bg white &
6  xterm -geometry -20+10 -fn 7x13bold -fg darkslategray -bg white &
7  xterm -geometry -20-30 -fn 7x13bold -fg black -bg white &
8
9  # Other useful X clients
10 oclock -geometry 70x70+5+5 &
11 xload -geometry 85x60+85+5 &
12 xbiff -geometry +200+5 &
13 xsetroot -solid darkslateblue &
14
15 # Start the window manager
16 exec fvwm2
```

 A number of programs are started here; obviously, this will work only if you have installed them. If you go with the default installation of your distribution, chances are that either the desktop environment KDE or GNOME will be installed and these older programs will not be available. They should be on the distribution media, though, waiting to be installed. While you cannot have more than one window manager running at the same time, you can have as many of them installed as you like.

This should be quite straightforward, even if you're not familiar with X. The first two lines simply identify the shell script. Lines 5–7 start up three *xterm* clients (recall that *xterm* is a terminal-emulator client). Other clients are started on lines 10–13, and on line 16 the window manager, *fvwm*, is started.

Running *startx* with this particular *.xinitrc* in place gives you something that looks like Figure 11-1.*

Let's look at this in more detail. On line 5, we see that *xterm* is started with several options, *–geometry*, *–fg*, and *–bg*. Most X clients support these standard options, among others.

The *–geometry* option allows you to specify the size and position of the window on the display. The geometry specification has the format:

```
xsizexysize+xoffset+yoffset
```

---

* All right, so it's not a work of art, but we needed something simple that would work correctly on most displays!

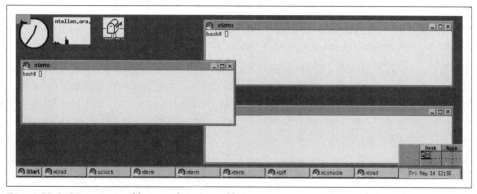

Figure 11-1. Screen created by sample .xinitrc file

In this case, the option *–geometry 80x40+10+100* puts the window at the location (10,100) on the screen (where (0,0) is the top-left corner), making it 80 characters wide by 40 characters high. Note that *xterm* measures the size of the window in *characters*, not pixels. The actual size of the window in pixels is determined by the font that is used.

The *–fg* and *–bg* arguments allow you to specify the foreground (text) and background colors for the *xterm* window, respectively. The colors used here are a rather boring black and white, but this should work on color and monochrome displays alike. Under X, colors are usually specified by name, although you can provide your own RGB values if you prefer. The list of color names (and corresponding RGB values) is given in the file */usr/lib/X11/rgb.txt*. Running *xcolors* will display these colors, along with their names.

Line 6 runs another *xterm*, although the arguments are slightly different:

```
xterm -geometry -20+10 -fn 7x13bold -fg darkslategray -bg white &
```

First of all, the geometry specification is just –20+10. Without size parameters, *xterm* will use the default, which is usually 80x25. Also, we see that the *xoffset* is prefixed with a -, instead of a +. This places the window 20 pixels from the *right* edge of the screen. Likewise, a geometry specification of –20-30 (as used on line 7) means to place the window 20 pixels from the right edge of the screen and 30 pixels from the bottom. In this way, the placement of windows is less dependent on the particular resolution you're using.

The *–fn* option on lines 6 and 7 specifies that the font used by *xterm* should be 7x13bold. Using the command *xlsfonts* displays a complete list of fonts on your system; the X client *xfontsel* allows you to select fonts interactively—more about fonts later.

On line 10 we start an *oclock* client, which is a simple analog clock. Line 11 starts *xload*, which displays a graph of the system *load average* (number of running processes) that changes with time. Line 12 starts *xbiff*, which just lets you know when mail is waiting to be read. Finally, on line 13 we do away with the bland gray X background and replace it with a flashy darkslateblue. (Fear not; there is more fun to be had with X decor than this example shows.)

You'll notice that each X client started on lines 6–13 is executed in the background (the ampersand on the end of each line forces this). If you forget to put each client in the background, *xinit* executes the first *xterm*, waits for it to exit (usually after you log out), executes the next *xterm*, and so on. The ampersands cause each client to start up concurrently.

What about line 16? Here, we start *fvwm* (Version 2), a window manager used on many Linux systems. As mentioned before, the window manager is responsible for decorating the windows, allowing you to place them with the mouse, and so forth. However, it is started with the command:

```
exec fvwm2
```

This causes the *fvwm2* process to replace the *xinit* process. This way, once you kill *fvwm*,* the X server shuts down. This is equivalent to, but more succinct than, using the Ctrl-Alt-Backspace key combination. Whether you are returned to the command line after the X server has shut down or are presented with a new graphical login depends on your system configuration.

In general, you should put an ampersand after each X client started from *.xinitrc*, and *exec* the window manager at the end of the file. Of course, there are other ways of doing this, but many users employ this technique.

The *fvwm2* window manager was the default window manager on most Linux systems for a very long time. It is still around, but has mostly been superseded by either the very advanced *kwin* window manager shipped with KDE or one of the more modern freestanding window managers, such as *blackbox* or *sawfish*.

If you read the manual pages for *xterm* and the other X clients, you'll see many more command-line options than those described here. As we said, virtually everything about X is configurable. *fvwm* (Version 2) uses a configuration file of its own, *.fvwm2rc*, described in its manual page. (If you have no *.fvwm2rc* file, the system default */usr/lib/X11/fvwm2/system.fvwmrc* is used instead.) More modern window managers still use configuration files, but usually provide you with user-friendly, GUI-based configuration programs that let you make your settings and then save them to the configuration file in the correct format. The manual pages, as well as books on using X, such as the *X Window System User's Guide* (O'Reilly), provide more information on configuring individual clients.

---

* If you have experimented with *fvwm*, you'll notice that pressing the first mouse button while the cursor is on the background causes a menu to pop up. Selecting the Quit fvwm option from this menu causes *fvwm* to exit.

The K Desktop Environment

The K Desktop Environment (KDE) is an open source software project that aims at providing a consistent, user-friendly, contemporary desktop for Unix, and hence, Linux systems. Since its inception in October 1996, it has made great progress. This is partly due to the choice of a very high-quality GUI toolkit, Qt, as well as the consequent choice of using C++ and its object-oriented features for the implementation.

It should be noted up front that KDE is *not* a window manager like *fvwm*, but a whole desktop system that can be used with any window manager. However, it also comes with its own window manager called *kwin*, which will give the best results and is therefore what we will cover here.

The current development version of KDE, as well as the upcoming KDE office suite (see *http://koffice.kde.org*), is based heavily on KParts, a component technology which, among other things, enables the embedding of office components, such as embedding the PDF viewer into the web browser for seemless viewing of downloaded PDF files, and so on.

KDE is in continuing development, but every few months the KDE team puts out a so-called official release that is considered very stable and suitable for end users. These releases are made available in both source and binary packages in various formats, often specifically adapted for the most common Linux distributions. If you don't mind fiddling around with KDE and can stand an occasional bug, you can also live on the bleeding edge and download daily snapshots of KDE, but this is not for the faint-hearted. At the time of this writing, the current stable release is 3.0.2, with 3.0.3 just looming around the corner.

General Features

We have already hinted a couple of times that configuring window managers and X applications for a long time meant learning the varying syntax of configuration files and editing those files, something that long-term Linux users take for granted but that often rebuffs new users. One of the goals of the KDE team is therefore to make everything in KDE configurable by GUI dialogs. You can still edit configuration files, if you prefer, but you don't need to, and even the most experienced users usually admit that in order to do simple things, such as change the background color of the desktop, it's faster to click a few buttons than to read the manual page, find the syntax for specifying the background color, open the configuration file, edit it, and restart the window manager.

Besides easy configuration, KDE sports a few other features that were previously unheard of on Linux. For example, it integrates Internet access fully into the desktop. It comes with a file manager that doubles as a web browser (or the other way around), and browsing files on some FTP sites is just the same as browsing your local hard disk. You can drag and drop icons that represent Internet locations to your desktop and thus easily find them again later. KDE integrates search engines and other Internet resources into your desktop and even lets you define your own favorite search engines and Internet links with ease. In addition, almost all KDE application are able to open and save files in remote locations.

Drag-and-drop, commonplace on Windows or the Macintosh, is also widely used in KDE. For example, to open a file in the text editor, you just grab its icon in the file manager window and drop it onto the editor window. This works no matter where the file is located; if it is on a remote server, KDE automatically downloads the file for you before opening it in the text editor or whichever application you choose to open it with. The same goes for multimedia files. Just by clicking an icon for an MP3 file on a remote server, you can download it in the background and play it locally.

While manual pages are designed well to give programmers instant access to terse information about system libraries, they are not really very well suited for end-user documentation. KDE therefore uses standard HTML files and comes with a fast help viewer, the KDE Help Center. The viewer also knows how to display manual page and Info files so that you can access all the documentation on your system from one application. In addition, most KDE applications support context-sensitive help.

For the past few releases, the X Window System has supported a feature called *session management*. When you leave your X environment, log off, or reboot, an application that understands session management will reappear at the same positions and in the same configuration. Unfortunately, this very user-friendly feature was rarely supported by X applications. KDE uses it extensively. KDE provides a session manager that handles session management, and all KDE applications are written to behave properly with that feature.

KDE contains a window manager, *kwin*, and an excellent one at that, but that is only one part of KDE. Some of the others are the file manager, the web browser, the panel, a pager, the control center for configuring your desktop, and many, many more. If you want to, you can even run KDE with another window manager, but you might lose some of the integration features. Also, KDE comes with tons of applications, from a full office productivity suite to PostScript and PDF viewers to multimedia software to games.

You might be thinking, "Well, this all sounds very nice, but I have a couple of normal X applications that I want to run." In this case, you will be delighted to hear that you can continue to do that. Yes, you can run all X applications on a KDE desktop, and KDE even provides some means of integrating them as far as possible into the overall desktop. For example, if you desire, KDE can try to reconfigure your other X applications to use the same colors as the overall desktop so that you get a nice consistent environment. Of course, non-KDE applications will not support some of KDE's advanced features like drag-and-drop or session management, but you can continue to use the programs you have grown accustomed to until someone releases KDE applications that address the same needs (or perhaps KDE versions of your favorite programs themselves).

Installing KDE

Most Linux distributions come with KDE nowadays, but if yours doesn't, or you want to use a newer version of KDE, you can download it from the Internet. *http://www.kde.org* is your one-stop shop for everything KDE-related, including documentation, screenshots, and download locations. *ftp://ftp.kde.org* is the KDE project's FTP site, but it is often overloaded, so you might be better off trying a mirror instead.

KDE consists of a number of packages. These include:

kdesupport

> This package contains third-party libraries that are not part of KDE itself but that are used by KDE. It is recommended that you install this package to make sure that you have the correct versions of all the libraries installed.

aRts

> *aRts* is short for "real-time sequencer" and forms the base of most of the multimedia capabilities of KDE.

kdelibs

> The KDE libraries. They contain the basic application frame, a number of GUI widgets, the configuration system, the HTML display system, and many other things. Without this package, nothing in KDE will run.

kdebase

> In this package, you will find the basic KDE applications that make a desktop a KDE desktop, including the file manager/web browser, the window manager, and the panel. You definitely need this package if you want to use KDE.

kdegames

> A number of games, including card games, action games, and strategy games. Everybody will probably want to install these, but only to get acquainted with the system, of course.

kdegraphics

> A number of graphics-related programs such as a *dvi* viewer, a PostScript viewer, and an icon editor.

kdeutils

> Some productivity tools, such as text editors, a calculator, printer managers, and an address-book program.

kdemultimedia

> As the name implies, this package contains multimedia programs, including a CD player, a MIDI player and—of all things—a Karaoke player.

kdenetwork

> Here, you will find programs for use with the Internet, including a mail reader, a news reader, and some network management tools.

kdeadmin

This package contains some programs for the system administrator, including a user manager, a runlevel editor, and a backup program.

kdepim

The notable tool in this package is *korganizer,* a full-featured personal information manager that even supports synchronization with Palm Pilots.

kdeedu

As the name implies, this package contains a set of educational programs, ranging from vocabulary trainers to programs teaching you the movements of the planets and stars.

koffice

KOffice is no less than a complete feature-rich office productivity suite. It may have a few rough edges here and there, but many people use it already for their daily work.

The release cycle of KOffice is today decoupled from KDE's release cycle. At the time of this writing, the current version is 1.1.2. You can read all about KOffice at *http://koffice.kde.org.*

In addition to the packages mentioned here, which are officially provided by the KDE team, literally hundreds of other KDE programs are available. See *http://www.kde.org/applications.html* for a list of applications that are currently available.

Once you have selected which packages to install, you can go on and actually install them. How you do that depends on which Linux distribution you use and whether you install a binary package or compile KDE yourself from the source code. If your distribution contains KDE, you will also be able to install KDE during your system installation.

Once the software is loaded onto your hard disk, there are only a few steps left to take. First, you have to make sure that the directory containing the KDE applications is in your PATH environment variable. The default location of the executable KDE programs is */opt/kde3/bin,* but if you have chosen to install KDE to another location, you will have to insert your path here.* You can add this directory to your PATH variable by issuing:

```
export PATH=/opt/kde3/bin:$PATH
```

To make this permanent, add this line to either the *.bashrc* configuration file in your home directory, or the system-wide configuration file, */etc/profile.*

Next, do the same with the directory containing the KDE libraries (by default */opt/kde3/lib*) and the environment variable LD_LIBRARY_PATH:

```
export LD_LIBRARY_PATH=/opt/kde3/lib:$LD_LIBRARY_PATH
```

* Some distributions might put the KDE programs elsewhere, such as in */usr/bin.*

Now you are almost done, but you still need to tell X that you want to run the KDE desktop when X starts. This is done in the file *.xinitrc* in your home directory. Make a backup copy first. Then remove everything in this file and insert the single line:

```
exec startkde
```

startkde is a shell script provided with KDE that simply starts up the KDE window manager *kwin* and a number of system services. Distributions will usually install a somewhat more complex *.xinitrc* file that may even start non-KDE applications and services.

Using KDE

Using KDE is quite easy. Most things are very intuitive, so you can often simply guess what to do. We will, however, give you some hints for what you can do with KDE here, to encourage you to explore your KDE desktop further.

The KDE panel and the K menu

When you start KDE for the first time, it looks like Figure 11-2. Along the lower border of the screen, you see the so-called *panel*. The panel serves several purposes, including fast access to installed applications. Along the upper border, you can see the *taskbar*. This bar shows all open windows and can be used to quickly access any window currently on the desktop. In addition, KDE opens a configuration program that lets you configure the initial settings when started for the first time.

KDE provides a number of workspaces that are accessible via the buttons in the middle of the panel, labeled One to Eight by default. Try clicking those buttons. You can see that windows that you have opened are visible only while you are on workspace One, while the panel and the taskbar are always visible. Now go to workspace Two and start a terminal window by clicking the terminal icon on the panel. When the panel appears, change workspaces again. You will see that the terminal window is visible only while you are on workspace Two, but its label is visible on the taskbar that appears in all workspaces. When you are on any other workspace, click the terminal label in the taskbar. This will immediately bring you back to the workspace where your terminal is shown.

To try another nifty feature, push the small button that looks like a pushpin in the titlebar of the terminal window. Now change workspaces again. You will see that the terminal window is now visible on every workspace—it has been "pinned down" to the background of the desktop, so to speak.

If you grow tired of seeing the terminal window on every workspace, simply click the pin again, and if you want to get rid of the window as a whole, click the button with the little x on it in the upper-right corner.

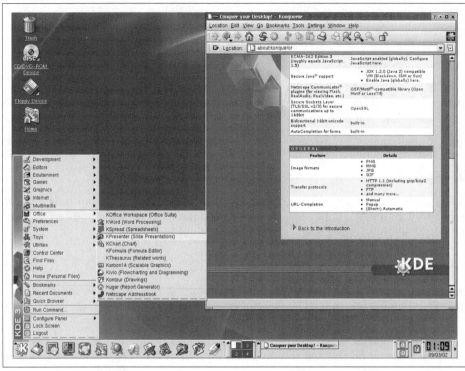

Figure 11-2. The KDE desktop at startup

There are lots of things that you can do with windows in KDE, but we'll switch now to a short exploration of the so-called *K menu*. You open the K menu by clicking the icon with the gear-and-K symbol to the far left of the panel. Besides some options for configuring the K menu and the panel itself, you will find all installed KDE applications here, grouped into submenus. To start one of those applications, select the menu entry.

We have promised that you can run old X applications on your KDE desktop. You can do that either by opening a terminal window and typing the application name on the command line, or by pressing Ctrl-F2 and entering the application name in the small command line that appears in the middle of the screen. But, with a little more work, you can also integrate non-KDE applications into the K menu and the panel, which then displays icons that you can click to run the associated programs

Depending on how you have installed KDE, it may well be that there is already a submenu of non-KDE programs in your K menu that contains a number of non-KDE applications. If you don't have this, run the application *KAppfinder*, which you can find in the System submenu. This searches your system for a number of applications that it has in its database and integrates each one into the KDE desktop by generating a so-called *.desktop* file for it. If the program that you want to integrate into KDE is not included in the *Appfinder*'s database, you will have to write such a *.desktop* file yourself. But as always in KDE, there are dialogs for doing this where you just have to fill in the required information. See the KDE documentation at *http://www.kde. org/documentation/index.html*.

By default, the panel already contains a number of icons to start the most often-used programs, but you can easily add your own. To do this, open the K menu again, and click the submenus Configure Panel → Add → Button. A copy of the whole K menu pops up. Find the application whose icon you want to add to the panel and select it, just as if you wanted to start it. KDE will then add the icon for this application to the panel. You can even add full submenus to the panel by selecting the first menu entry in a submenu in the Add/Button tree. The icon will then have a small black arrow in it, which indicates that clicking the icon opens a menu instead of starting an application.

There is only limited space on the panel, so you might need to remove some icons of programs that you do not often use. Just click with the right mouse button on the icon and select Remove. This does not remove the program, just its icon. In general, you can get at a lot of functionality in KDE by clicking the right mouse button!

The KDE Control Center

Next, we will show you how to configure your KDE desktop to your tastes. As promised, we will not edit any configuration files to do this.

Configuration is done in the KDE Control Center, which you can start from the K menu. All the configuration options are grouped at different levels. When you start up the control center, you will see the top-level groups. By clicking the plus signs, you can open a group to see the entries in this group.

Configuring the background. As an example, we will now change the background color to something else. To do this, open the Look & Feel group and choose Background. The configuration window for configuring the background will appear (see Figure 11-3).

You can select a single-colored background, a two-colored background with a number of gradients where one color is slowly morphed into another, a wallpaper (predefined or an image of your own choice), or a bleeding effect that combines various choices. To select colors, click either the Color 1 or the Color 2 color button; a color selection dialog pops up where you can select a color to your taste. When you close the color selection dialog, the new color is displayed in the monitor in the upper-right corner of the configuration window. When you configure KDE, you often see such monitors that allow you to preview your choice. However, you also have the option to see what your choice looks like when in full use. Simply click the Apply button at the lower border of the configuration window, and your change is automatically applied. There is no need to restart the desktop.

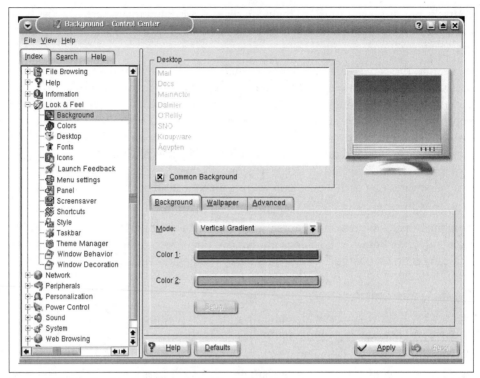

Figure 11-3. Configuring the background of the KDE desktop

If you'd rather have a monocolored background, select Flat from the Mode combo box. You will see that the color button for the Color 2 is grayed out then. Select the color you want with the Color 1 button.

On the Wallpaper tab, you can select a background image as your wallpaper. KDE ships with a large number of wallpapers, but you can also select your own pictures (such as a digitized photo of your family). You can even configure multiple wallpapers that appear in succession at intervals you define. Finally, on the Advanced tab, you can select different blendings. These are difficult to describe, so your best bet is to try them and watch the small monitor to see what effect you get.

You can do more things with the background, but we'll leave it at that for now and look at something else: configuring styles and colors of the windows.

Configuring window styles and colors. With normal window managers, you can configure the color of the window decorations, but not of the window contents. KDE is different. Since KDE is an integrated desktop, color and other settings apply both to the window decorations painted by the window manager and to the window contents painted by the applications. We'll now set off to configure a little bit of the appearance.

In the control center, open the Look & Feel group, and choose Colors. You'll see a preview window and a selection list where you can pick a color scheme. KDE does not work by configuring individual colors, but by defining so-called color schemes. This is because it does not make sense to change only one color; all colors must fit together to achieve a pleasing and eye-friendly look.

While KDE lets you create your own color schemes, doing so is a task that requires some knowledge about color psychology and human vision. We therefore suggest that you pick one of the predefined color schemes. Check in the preview monitor whether you like what you see. Now comes the fun part: click the Apply button and watch how all running applications flicker a bit and suddenly change colors—without you having to restart them. While Windows users tend to take this for granted, it was never seen on Unix before KDE.

The same feature applies to other settings. For example, open the Look & Feel group and choose Style. Here, you can select among a large number of so-called styles. The styles determine how the user interface elements are drawn—e.g., as in Windows (style Qt Windows), as in Motif (style Qt Motif), as in RISC OS (style RISC OS), or even something original as the "Light" styles. You can change this setting by clicking Apply and watch your running applications change their style. The same goes, by the way, for the fonts that you can select on the Font page.

Internationalization. There are many more things to configure in KDE, but we cannot go through all the options here. Otherwise there would not be much space left for other topics in this book. But there's one more thing that we'd like to show you. You will especially like this if English is not your native language or if you frequently converse in another language.

Go to the Country & Language page in the Personalization group (see Figure 11-4). Here, you can select the country settings and the language in which your KDE desktop and the KDE applications should be running. Currently, KDE lets you choose from more than 80 country settings and languages. Note that you need to have a language module installed in order to be able to select a particular language. You can either download those from the KDE FTP server (as explained earlier) or install them from your distribution media.

You might be wondering why you can select more than one language. The reason is that the KDE programs are translated by volunteers, and not all the applications are translated at the same time. Thus, a particular application might not be available in the language that you have chosen as your first language (the topmost one in the Language list). In this case, the next language is chosen automatically for that application, and if no translation is available for this application in that language either, the next language is chosen, and so on. If all else fails, English is chosen, which always exists.

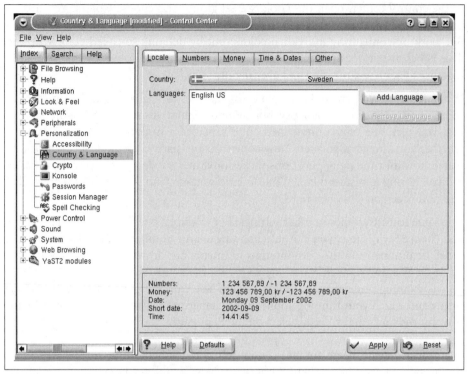

Figure 11-4. Configuring the language of the KDE desktop

There is much more to say about using the KDE desktop, but we'll let you explore it yourself. Besides the obvious and intuitive features, there are also some that are not so obvious but very useful nevertheless, so be sure to check the documentation at *http://www.kde.org/documentation/index.html*.

KDE Applications

Thousands of programs are available for KDE. They range from basic utilities (such as *konsole*, the terminal emulator, and *OClock*, the clock) to editors to programming aids to games to multimedia applications. The most we can provide here is a tiny slice of the software available for KDE. In this section, we'll present those applications that all KDE users should know how to use. These aren't necessarily the most exciting programs out there, but they should certainly be part of your toolbox. Also remember that if there really is no KDE program for a task you have to solve, you can always resort to one of the classic X applications, if available. These will not look as nice and integrate as well, but will still work on a KDE desktop.

Also, don't forget that there are many, many more KDE applications than the few we can list here. You will make the acquaintance of some of them, like KWord, the word processor, and KMail, the mail user agent, elsewhere in this book. But others, like the Personal Information Manager KOrganizer, haven't found space in this book, so you should search through your favorite Linux archive for more exciting KDE programs; there are hundreds of them to discover.

konsole: Your Home Base

Let's start our exploration of X applications with the workhorse that you might be spending a lot of your time within the terminal. This is simply a window that contains a Unix shell. It displays a prompt, accepts commands, and scrolls like a terminal.

 Traditionally, *xterm* was the classic Unix terminal emulator. It has been superseded by *konsole* in the KDE desktop environment.

Perhaps you are struck by the irony of buying a high-resolution color monitor, installing several megabytes of graphics software, and then being confronted by an emulation of an old VT100 terminal. But Linux is simply not a point-and-click operating system. There are plenty of nice graphical applications, but a lot of the time you'll want to manipulate text, and a command-line interface still offers the most powerful tools for doing that.

So let's take look at a *konsole* window. Figure 11-5 shows one containing a few commands.

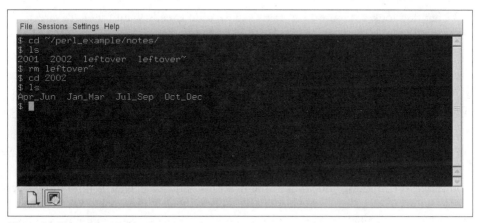

Figure 11-5. konsole window

Starting up konsole

You can start *konsole* in one of several ways, as all KDE programs:

- Start it from the panel, if you have a *konsole* icon there. This will be the default setup with most distributions.
- Select it from the K menu, where *konsole* can be found in Utilities/System/Konsole.
- Type Alt-F2, then in the small command window that opens, type "konsole."
- If you already have a *konsole* open, you can also type "konsole" there in order to get another one.

When you open a *konsole* window, a "Tip of the Day" window will open that gives you useful hints about using *konsole*. You can turn this off, but we suggest keeping it on for a while, as you will learn many useful things this way. You can also read through all the tips by clicking the Next button in that window repeatedly. Many KDE applications have such a Tip of the Day.

konsole allows you to run several sessions in one *konsole* window. You can simply open a new session by selecting a session type from the Session menu or by clicking the New toolbar button. The toolbar or the View menu lets you then switch between sessions. If you don't see any toolbar, select Settings/Show Toolbar from the menu to make it visible.

Cutting and pasting selections

Actually, *konsole* offers a good deal more than a VT100 terminal. One of its features is a powerful cut-and-paste capability.

Take another look at Figure 11-5. Let's say we didn't really want the *notes* directory; we wanted to look at *~/perl/_example/for_web_site* instead.

First, we'll choose the part of the *cd* command that interests us. Put the mouse just to the left of the c in cd. Press the left mouse button, and drag the mouse until it highlights the slash following example. The result is shown in Figure 11-6.

When the highlighted area covers just the right number of characters, click the middle button. *konsole* pastes in what you've selected on the next command line. See the result in Figure 11-7. Now you can type in the remainder of the directory name *for_website* and press the Enter key to execute the command.

You can select anything you want in the window—output as well as input. To select whole words instead of characters, double-click the left mouse button. To select whole lines, triple-click it. You can select multiple lines too. Selecting multiple lines is not useful when you're entering commands but is convenient if you're using the *vi* editor and want to cut and paste a lot of text between windows.

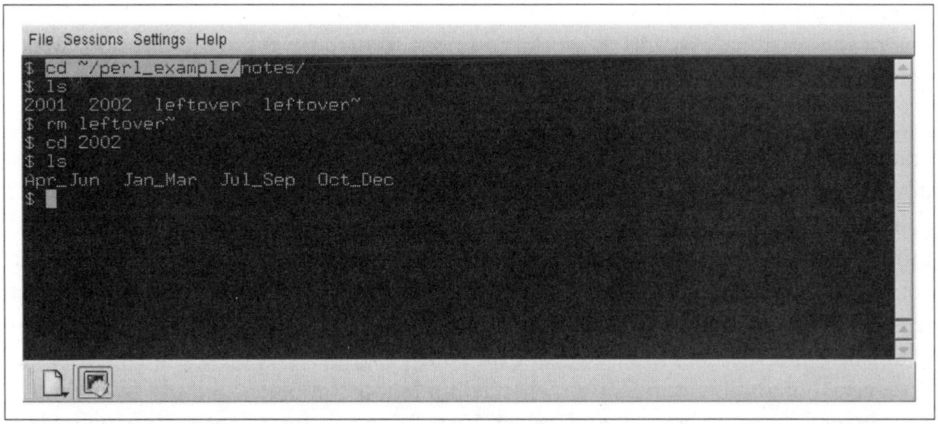

Figure 11-6. Selected text in konsole

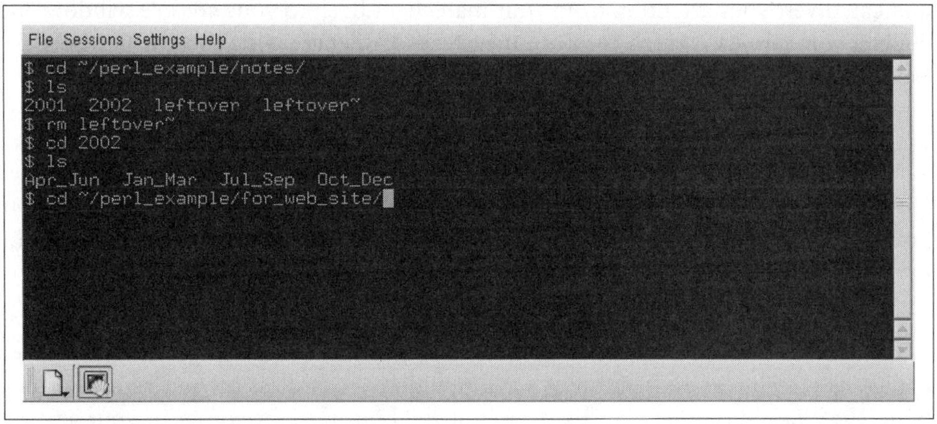

Figure 11-7. konsole window after text is pasted

Be careful: if a long line wraps around, you will end up with a newline in the selection even though you didn't press the Enter key when you entered the line.

Note that if you are more used to drag-and-drop style copying of text, *konsole* supports that as well.

More konsole tricks

There are lots of things you can configure in *konsole*. You can select fonts, color schemes, whether the scrollbar should be shown to the left, to the right, or not at all, and so on. The most often-used settings are available in the Settings menu, and if you can't find what you are looking for, go to Settings/Configure Konsole. There you can select the line spacing, whether the cursor should blink, and so on.

A particularly useful feature in *konsole* is the ability to watch for output or silence in one of the sessions. For this to work, you need to turn on the write daemon, which you do in the aforementioned configuration dialog on the Write Daemon page.

What is the *konsole* watcher good for? Imagine that you are working on a large program that takes a long time to compile. Non-programmers can imagine that you download a large file in a terminal window with *wget* or that you are computing a complex POVRAY image. While the compilation is running, you want to do something else (why do you have a multitasking operating system, after all?) and start composing an email message to a friend in your KDE mail client. Normally, you would have to check the console window every so often to see whether compilation is finished and then continue to work on your program. With the watcher, you can get a visual or audible notification when compilation completes. Simply switch to the session you want to watch and select View/Monitor for Silence. You will get a notification as soon as your compiler doesn't output any more messages for a while and can divert your attention from your mail client back to your *konsole* window. Of course, you can also watch for output instead of silence, which might be useful in long-running network operations that don't show any progress indicators.

Clocks

How can your screen be complete if it is unadorned by a little clock that tells you how much time you are wasting on customizing the screen's appearance? You can have a clock just the way you want it, square or round, analog or digital, big or small. You can even make it chime.

KDE contains a number of clocks, but usually you will want to run the small panel applet, as screen real estate is always at a premium, regardless of your screen resolution. The clock should appear by default at the bottom-right corner of your screen, in the confines of the panel (this is called a *panel applet*, or a small application that runs within the panel). If your distribution hasn't set up things this way, you can also right-click anywhere on the panel background and select Panel → Add → Applet → Clock from the menu, which will make the clock appear on the panel. If you'd rather have it somewhere else on the panel, you can right-click the small striped handle to the left of the clock, select Move from the context menu that appears, and move the clock with the mouse to the desired position. Other panel objects will automatically make room for the clock.

The panel clock applet has a number of different modes that you can select by right-clicking the clock itself and selecting Type as well as the desired mode from the context menu. There is a plain, a digital, an analog, and, most noteworthy, a fuzzy clock. The fuzzy clock is for everybody who doesn't like being pushed around by his clock. For example, if you run the fuzzy clock, it will show *Middle of the week*. If that is a bit too fuzzy for you, you can select Preferences/Fuzzy Clock from the clock's context menu and select the degree of fuzziness here. For example, I am typing this at 9:53 A.M. on a Thursday, and the four degrees of fuzziness are *Five to ten*, *Ten o'* *clock*, *Almost noon*, and the aforementioned *Middle of the week*.

The clock applet also lets you configure the date and time format to be used, as well as set the system clock (you need root permissions to do that; if you are logged in as a normal user, a dialog will pop up and ask you for the root password).

Finally, if you'd rather have a real big, traditional clock on the screen, you find a KDE version of the classic "OClock" in the K menu at Utilities/OClock.

KGhostview: Displaying PostScript

Adobe PostScript, as a standard in its own right, has become one of the most popular formats for exchanging documents in the computer world. Many academics distribute papers in PostScript format. The Linux Documentation Project offers its manuals in PostScript form, among others. This format is useful for people who lack the time to format input, or who have sufficient network bandwidth for transferring the enormous files. When you create documents of your own using *groff* or TEX, you'll want to view them on a screen before you use up precious paper resources by printing them.

KGhostview, a KDE application, offers a pleasant environment for viewing PostScript on the X Window System that, besides PostScript files, can also view files in Adobe's PDF. KGhostview is really mostly a more convenient frontend to an older application, Ghostview, so you can also get the functionality described here with Ghostview. The user experience is much better with KGhostview, however, so that's what we'll be describing here.

Using KGhostview is very simple; invoke it with the name of the file to be displayed, for instance:

```
eggplant$ kghostview article.ps
```

or simply click the icon of any PostScript or PDF file anywhere in KDE.

Since we are only concerned with viewing existing files here, we do not need to concern ourselves much with the benefits of PostScript and PDF. Both can be considered standards to the extent that many programs write them (and a few can read them), but both have been defined by one company, Adobe Systems. PDF is a bit more portable and self-contained, as it can even contain the fonts necessary to display the document. Also, PDF is better known on Microsoft Windows and the Macintosh, so you are more likely to come across PDF files than PostScript files on the Internet. And finally, while PostScript is really meant for printing, PDF has some features for interactive viewing, such as page icons, hyperlinks, and the like.

KGhostview is not a perfect PDF viewer, even though it is sufficient for most documents. If you have problems with a particular document, you may want to try either Adobe's own Acrobat Reader (which is not free software, but can be downloaded at no cost from *www.adobe.com*), or *xpdf*, which is probably included with your distribution.

The Ghostview window is huge; it can easily take up most of your screen. The first page of the document is displayed with scrollbars, if necessary. There is a menu bar and a toolbar, as in most KDE programs, as well as a page scroller and a page list on the left side of the window.

Like most X applications, KGhostview offers both menu options and keys (accelerators) for common functions. Thus, to view the next page, you can pull down the View menu and choose the Next Page option. Or you can just press the PgDn key (or the Space key, if you don't have a PgDn key, such as on a laptop).*

To go back to the previous page, choose Previous Page from the View menu. To go to any page you want, press the left mouse button on its number in the Page Number column. To exit, choose Quit from the File menu, or just press Ctrl-q.

Documents from different countries often use different page sizes. The Ghostview default is the standard U.S. letter size (but it can be overridden by comments in the PostScript file, and this is often done by PostScript tools set up on Linux distributions that are configured for European customs). You can select a different size from the Paper Size submenu in the View menu.

Ghostview lets you enlarge or reduce the size of the page, a useful feature for checking the details of your formatting work. (But be warned that fonts on the screen are different from the fonts on a printer, and therefore the exact layout of characters in Ghostview will not be the same as that in the hard copy.) To zoom in on a small part of the page, press Ctrl-+; to zoom out, use Ctrl--. You can also use the toolbar buttons or the Zoom In/Zoom Out menu entries in the View menu.

You can also adjust the window size to exactly fit the document's page width by selecting Fit To Page Width from the View menu.

To print a page, choose Print from the File menu or press Ctrl-P anywhere in the window. The standard KDE printer dialog will appear that lets you—among other things—choose the printer to use.

You can also print only the current page or a range of pages; just specify your selection in the printer dialog. This can also be combined with the PageMarks feature. The PageMarks menu lets you mark and unmark individual or groups of pages. Marked pages are displayed with a little red flag in the page list. If you have marked pages and select the printing functionality, the dialog will pop up with the marked pages already filled in as the selection of pages to print. Of course, you can override this setting before finally sending the document to the printer.

---

* There is a subtle difference between the Space key and the PgDn key: the PgDn key will always take you to the next page, while the Space key will first take you to the bottom of the current page if the window is too small to display the whole page on the screen at once. A second press of the Space key will then take you to the next page.

Reading Documentation with Konqueror

Konqueror is not only a high-class web browser and file manager, but it also serves as a documentation reader. KDE's documentation comes in HTML format anyway, but Konqueror is capable of displaying other documentation formats like info and manpages. For example, in order to show the manpage for the *ls* command, just open a mini command-line window by pressing Alt-F2 and typing in that window:

```
man:ls
```

KDE will recognize that you want to read the manpage of the *ls* command, open a Konqueror window, and display the manpage. The result is also much more nicely formatted than how the original man command (or its X11 replacement *xman*) would do it.

This works similarly for Info pages. For example, the documentation of the GNU C Compiler *gcc* comes in info format. Just type:

```
info:gcc
```

either in a mini command-line or in the Konqueror URL entry line, and the requested Info page will pop up (assuming it is installed, of course). If you have cursed at the really user-unfriendly command-line *info* program and weren't too happy with programs like *xinfo* either, this feature may be a boon for you.

But Konqueror doesn't stop here when it comes to getting information. Want to use a search engine on the Internet? To find pages about Tux (the Linux mascot) on, let's say, the AltaVista search engine, simply type the following in a mini command-line or the Konqueror URL entry line:

```
av:tux
```

and a Konqueror window with (at the time of this writing) 1,319,135 search results pops up. This works with many other search engines as well. See Table 11-1 for some of the most popular search engines together with their prefixes.

Table 11-1. Popular search engines and their prefixes

Search Engine	Prefix
AltaVista	`av:`
Lycos	`ly:`
SourceForge	`sf:`
Excite	`ex:`
Google	`gg:`

If your favorite search engine is not configured (which is quite unlikely, actually), you can configure it yourself by opening a Konqueror window and selecting Settings, Configure Konqueror, and then Enhanced Browsing. The Enable Web Shortcuts section on that configuration page contains all the preconfigured search engines and even lets you add your own.

The GNOME Desktop Environment

The GNOME desktop environment was conceived in 1999 as an alternative to KDE, with its roots in the GPL and LGPL. Like KDE, GNOME had the goal of providing modern, easy-to-use applications that work with each other and with existing X applications.

We're going to give you a tour of GNOME the way it commonly looks, but you should be aware that it's a general-purpose framework with really unlimited flexibility. For example, we show the current window manager, Sawfish, but you can install a different window manager with a completely different behavior and appearance. The GNOME libraries, as well as the X libraries, underlie all the components, and have appeared in command-line and even server-based applications as well as the graphical desktop. In addition, the GNOME project has developed some powerful applications in typical areas of office work, such as spreadsheets and address books. Any X application can run under GNOME (although it has to be written with the GNOME framework to use the most powerful desktop features, such as the virtual filesystem and themes). In particular, a lot of KDE applications work very nicely on GNOME, and vice versa.

Of course, for our purposes, the interesting parts are the core desktop and its associated applications. In the next sections, we'll go over the GNOME look and feel, talk a little bit about the customization options it offers to you, and then give a quick tour of major applications, such as Evolution and Gnumeric. But first, you'll want to make sure you have the software and that it's up to date.

Installing and Updating GNOME

Most Linux distributions include GNOME, but if you haven't installed it yourself, or if you want a newer version, you can visit *http://gnome.org* for source and *http://ximian.com* for convenient binaries. Ximian offers a preassembled distribution of the desktop for the most common Linux distributions. To install it, do the following:

1. Open a terminal window
2. Use the su command to become root
3. Run the command: `lynx -source http://go-gnome.com |sh`

The command downloads a graphical installation program, shown in Figure 11-8. Follow the on-screen instructions, and in a few minutes you'll have everything installed. The installer will ask you to log out, and when you log back in, a wizard will guide you through the process of setting some preferences for your new desktop.

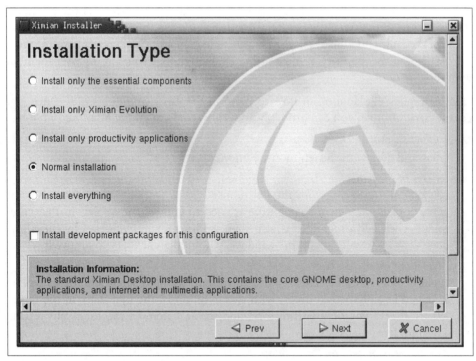

Figure 11-8. Installing GNOME

Updates are also easy in GNOME: the Red Carpet utility (red-carpet at the command line, or click System, and then Get Software from the GNOME menu panel) checks for updates to your entire system, including GNOME, and offers to install them for you. Software is divided into neat channels—one for your distribution, another for the GNOME desktop, another for additional software like the Opera web browser or the CodeWeavers WINE tools. When you subscribe to a channel, Red Carpet will check for updates to the software that's on your system from that channel. You can also add or remove software in each channel by choosing the Update, Install, or Remove buttons along the upper-right corner of the channel windows.

Core Desktop Interface

The GNOME desktop is designed to be familiar to anyone who has used a computer before. Although you can change the settings in almost any way, a typical installation will have a desktop with icons on it and a panel along the top and bottom. The panels are among the most important GNOME tools because they are so versatile and they allow a wide range of interactions with your system. Panels can exist along one edge of your screen, like the Windows control panel; along a portion of it, like the Macintosh Control Strip; in an arbitrary position on the screen, like the NeXT dock; or in a combination of styles. They can contain menus, buttons, and small applications or applets, such as clocks, window lists, network and system monitors, and even tiny games.

A few features differ slightly from other graphical interfaces, such as the ability to have multiple virtual workspaces (familiar to *fvwm* users, but not many others) and some of the bells and whistles in the Nautilus file manager. We'll cover some of them in passing, but the majority of them are small enough that you can discover them on your own.

Here is a quick explanation of how to perform the most common tasks. Once you get the hang of these, you can probably guess how to do anything else.

Move items around on the desktop
> Click and drag with the left mouse button.

Move items in the panel
> Clicking and dragging with the left mouse button works for launchers, but for some applets, the left mouse button is used to control the applet. In that case, middle-click and drag. This is also the case for moving windows by their borders—left-click will expand the window, but middle-click lets you move it.

Organize items on the desktop
> Right-click the desktop background and select Clean Up by Name. Items will be arranged in alphabetical order, with two exceptions: the first item, in the upper left, is always your home directory, and the last item in the list is always the Trash folder.

Open or activate an item on the desktop
> Double-click it. If you double-click a folder icon, it will open the folder in the Nautilus file management tool. If you double-click a spreadsheet document, the Gnumeric spreadsheet will start and open the document.

Open or activate an item in the panel
> Click once with the left button.

Get a list of options or set preferences for any object
> Click with the right mouse button to get a menu of available options for any object. For example, you can change the desktop background by right-clicking it and choosing Change Desktop Background. More general preferences are available in the GNOME Control Center, which you can access by choosing System → Settings or Applications → Desktop Preferences, or by typing gnome-control-center at the command line.

Paste text into any text area
> First, highlight the text you want to paste. Then, middle-click (if you have only two mouse buttons, use both at once to emulate the middle button) in the area where you want the text to go.

The panel

The preset configuration for many systems has a thin panel along the top and bottom of the screen. The top panel has a set of menus along the upper left, and a few buttons and a clock at the right. The bottom panel contains the window list applet, which should feel familiar to users of Microsoft Windows.

To create a new panel, click any blank space in an existing panel, and choose Panel → Create New Panel, then select the type of panel you would like. To change a panel's properties, such as its size and color, right-click it and choose Properties (the menu panel at the top of the screen has no available properties; it is preconfigured for one position and size). Experiment with different kinds of panels and with different sizes to see which ones you like best. If you use a smaller screen, like a laptop screen, you will want to choose a smaller panel size than if you have plenty of screen real estate to use.

To add application launcher buttons to your panels, you can drag them from menus, or right-click the panel and choose Panel → Add to Panel → Launcher. Then, enter the name of the application you want to run, and choose an icon. You may also choose a description of the launcher that will display as a tool tip when you hover the mouse over the icon in your panel. If you want to launch the application from a terminal, check the "Run in Terminal" box.

For more information on the panel, right-click any empty spot in the panel and select Panel → Panel Manual.

Panel applets are small applications that run inside the panel. You can add them to the panel from the Add to Panel menu or just run them by clicking Applications → Applets. Panel applets come in a bewildering variety of flavors, from games to utilities. Some of the most common are:

CPU Load
>   A graph that displays the load on your system resources for the past few seconds.

Workspace Switcher
>   In most installations, this applet will already be running when you log in, and is typically set to four workspaces. Each workspace is the equivalent of a new screenful of desktop space, and you can have as many as you like. The workspace switcher displays all the virtual workspaces you have created, and displays each window on the desktop as a tiny box. You can use the left mouse button to drag a window from one workspace to another. Right-click and select the Properties menu item to change the number or arrangement of workspaces.

Window List
>   Like the workspace applet, the Window List is included in most default configurations. It displays the windows that you have open so that you can switch easily among them, even when they are minimized. If you have multiple windows for a single application, they will be grouped under a single entry. To turn this feature off, or to set other options for the applet, right-click the Window List' and select Properties.

Battery Charge Monitor

The Battery Charge Monitor displays the remaining battery life for laptop systems. Options include display as a chart, as a percentage, or by estimated usage time remaining.

SlashApp

Displays headlines from Slashdot or the GNOME News web site in your panel.

Eyes

The Eyes applet consists of a pair of eyeballs that follow your mouse around. It may not be useful, but it's certainly amusing.

Nautilus: your desktop and file manager

Nautilus is the name of the GNOME desktop and file manager. It controls the display of your background image and the files on your desktop, allows you to interact with files without using a terminal, and keeps track of your trash for you. In other words, it's the GNOME equivalent of Windows Explorer, the Macintosh Finder, and KDE's Konqueror.

In most cases, Nautilus will be running when you log in. If it isn't (you'll know: your desktop will not have any icons on it), you can start it from a terminal window by typing nautilus. If you decide you *don't* want to run Nautilus at all, you can remove it from your session with the Session Properties tool in the Control Center.

Like those other applications, Nautilus lets you drag items from one place to another. You can also copy files using Ctrl-C, cut with Ctrl-X, and paste with Ctrl-V.

The quickest way to get started with Nautilus is to double-click the home icon in the upper-left corner of your desktop, labeled as your home. This will open your home directory.

Normally, the files on your desktop are stored in *~/.gnome-desktop*. However, if you prefer to have your home directory be displayed on the desktop, select Preferences, Edit Preferences, and under the Windows and Desktop category check the "Use your home folder as your desktop" checkbox.

Nautilus looks a good deal like a web browser, and in fact it can be used as one. At the top is a toolbar with buttons that you can use to navigate through your directory structure: back, forward, up, refresh, and home. The location bar, like in a web browser, describes the location of the file or directory you're looking at in this window. If your username is jdoe and you click your Home icon, you'll see /home/jdoe in the location bar.

The left side of the Nautilus window appears to be blank. However, if you look on the lower-left side, you'll notice tabs for Notes, Tree, Help, History, and News, as follows:

- The Notes tool is a virtual pad of paper where you can jot down any quick reminders you like.

- The Tree displays the directory tree for your system—click one of the triangles next to a directory and it will spin down, showing you the contents. You can use this tool to navigate your directory structure or to move items around quickly.

- The Help tab offers up an index of several help systems—help pages for GNOME and KDE applications, plus the more traditional man- and Info pages that come with command-line Linux applications.

- The History tab will help you trace your steps backward. Not sure where you left that file? You can find out here.

- The News tab displays headlines that it pulls from various web sites. You can choose your news sources and the frequency with which they update in the Preferences dialog box.

Click a tab and it will expand to fill the sidebar.

Nautilus has some additional fun features that you won't find in other applications, as in:

- Instead of a generic image icon for graphics files, Nautilus uses scaled-down thumbnails of the image itself. This makes it easy to organize directories full of images, such as those pulled from a digital camera.

- If you hover your mouse over a music file, the file will begin to play.

- For text files, the plain document icon is decorated by the actual text contents of the file. That way, you can remember how the file starts without having to open it, even if you didn't give it the most descriptive name.

- You can stretch icons by right-clicking them and choosing Stretch Icon. If you stretch a text icon enough, you can see the entire contents of the file, and use it as a desktop notepad.

- Drag any image file onto the background of the left-hand sidebar, and the image will be used as the sidebar background for that directory.

- For most directories, you can choose to view their contents as a list, or as a group of icons. However, some files have a wider range of options. For example, in a directory full of audio files, you can choose View, and then View as Music, and play the sound files in any order—Nautilus even shows you the artist, title, and playtime for individual files. The same is true of HTML files: Nautilus can display them as their source text or as fully rendered web pages.

All in all, Nautilus is a versatile tool that you can learn to use just by poking around a little. For additional help, just choose Help, and then Nautilus User Manual from any Nautilus window.

GNOME Applications

Now that you've got a feel for the desktop and how to get around it, let's take a look at some of the applications that are built to go with it. Note that these applications aren't restricted to the GNOME desktop, and they aren't the only applications you can run on the GNOME desktop—they're just built from the same materials and work particularly well together.

Ximian Evolution: Mail, Calendar, and Contacts

Ximian Evolution is what's known as a groupware suite; it combines email with a calendar and an address book so that communication and scheduling tasks all fall into one convenient package. We haven't got room to go into depth with all three, but a complete manual is included in the Help menu and is available online at *http://support.ximian.com*.

You can start Evolution by selecting Evolution from your Applications menu, or by typing evolution at the command line. A screen like the one in Figure 11-9 should come up.

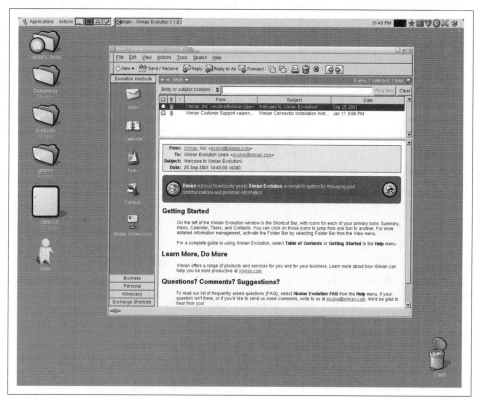

Figure 11-9. Evolution on the GNOME desktop

The first time you run Evolution, you'll be asked to create an email account by entering information about yourself and your email access. You can copy this information from your existing mail program, or ask your system administrator or ISP.

Evolution works with standard mail server protocols and can be used in almost any network environment. It lets you leave your mail on the server (the IMAP protocol), download mail to your local system (the POP protocol), or use mail spools on your local system, if you're running your own mail server. Ximian also sells a proprietary extension to Evolution called Ximian Connector, which connects to Microsoft Exchange 2000 servers for more extensive collaboration features.

Once you've created an account, you will be presented with the main Evolution window in its Summary view. The Evolution summary provides you with exactly that: weather, news, a list of upcoming tasks and appointments, and the number of new mail messages in your mail folders.

On the left side of the Evolution window is a shortcut bar, with a list of several important shortcuts. Click the buttons there to move to your Inbox, Contacts, or Calendar. For a different view of the available resources, select View, and then Folder Bar. The folder bar gives you a view that is more like a list of directories, and is especially useful if you have created a large number of folders.

The following sections describe Evolution's three major features.

Evolution mail

To start using Evolution mail, click the Inbox button, or select any mail folder in the folder bar. The mail view is divided into two portions: in the top half, a list of messages, and in the bottom half, the display of your selected message. You can change the proportions by dragging the gray bar between them.

In general, the mail features are fairly simple: click the Send and Receive button to check for new mail and send mail you've queued for later delivery, and the New Message button to compose a new message.

What distinguishes Evolution from other mail programs are the speed of its searches, the power and simplicity of its filters, and its unique vFolders, a sort of combination of searches and filters.

The search bar is located at the top of the message list. To search your mail, go to any mail folder, select a portion of the message to search (just the message body, the sender, the entire message, and so forth), enter a word into the text box, and press Enter. Evolution pre-indexes your mail, so the results are returned to you faster than with other tools.

Filters add an action to the end of a search: every time you get mail, Evolution will perform a search that you specify on the new messages, and then take actions based on those results. The most common uses of filters are to automatically file messages based on the senders, and to delete messages that are flagged as spam.

To create a filter, go to any mail view and open your list of filters by selecting Tools, and then Filters. Then, do the following:

1. Click the Add button to add a filter.
2. In the top half of the dialog, select a set of criteria you'll use to pick messages for the filter. For example, if you select Sender Contains in the first drop-down item, and enter gnome.org in the text box that appears next to it, your filter will act on mail that comes to you from all *gnome.org* email addresses.
3. In the bottom half of the window, select one or more actions for your messages. For example, if you select Move to Folder, you'll be offered a button labeled Click to Select Folder. Click that, select a destination folder, and your filter will file all mail from *gnome.org* addresses in your GNOME email folder.
4. Click OK in the filter creation box, and OK in the filter list. You're done.

If you find that you need more flexibility than filters offer you, you can use vFolders. A vFolder, or virtual folder, is essentially a complex saved search that looks like a folder. That also means that although an email message can exist only in a single standard folder, you can find it in several vFolders.

When you create a vFolder, you select criteria just like you would for a filter, but instead of choosing what to do with them, you specify where you want to look for these messages. Once you've created a vFolder, it appears in a list of vFolders at the bottom of your folder tree. Then, every time you open it, it searches your mail folders for messages that match the criteria you chose when you created it. So if you create your filters to file mail depending on its sender, you can create a vFolder that holds mail with a given subject, no matter who sent it.

Evolution calendar

The Evolution calendar allows you great flexibility in creating and viewing your schedule. To get started, click the Calendar button in the shortcut bar, or select the Calendar folder in the folder bar. You'll be presented with an empty work-week spread out before you, devoid of appointments.

To show less time, or more, you can select a range of days from the calendar in the upper right, or click one of the prebuilt ranges of days in the toolbar: today, one day, five days, a week, or a month.

Once you've got a feel for how to page through your datebook, you'll want to start scheduling events. To create one, click the New Appointment button. Enter a summary of the event, choose a time, and (optionally) enter a longer description.

At the lower right, you can select from a list of categories for this event. Events with categories, recurrences, or reminders are displayed with small icons in the calendar view: an alarm clock for reminders, arrows moving in a circle for recurrences, a birthday cake for birthdays, and so forth.

You can also schedule reminders and recurrences. For example, if you have an important meeting next week, you can schedule a reminder to pop up 15 minutes beforehand so that you have time to prepare. Just click the Reminder tab and choose a time and type of reminder, then click Add to add it to the list. Recurrences are similar: click the Recurrence tab, and choose how often you'd like to repeat the event. Is it just this Thursday and next Tuesday? Is it every Wednesday from now until Christmas? Is it a holiday that happens every year? Choose the recurrence rules, click Save and Close, and you've added the event to your calendar.

All that's left is to coordinate this event with other people. Select Actions, and then Forward as iCalendar to create an email message that has the event attached to it. When the recipient receives the message, he can click a single button to add the event to his calendar and send a note to you letting you know whether he'll attend.

Evolution contacts

The Evolution contact manager, or address book, is perhaps the least glamorous tool in the suite. However, it is interwoven with the email tools quite thoroughly. You can create contact cards by clicking the New Contact button in the contacts view, but you can also create a card by right-clicking any email address in an email someone has sent you.

If you're looking at your address book for someone's email address, you can right-click his card and have the option to send him a message, or to send his card to someone else, with just two clicks.

To have a look at the contact manager, click the Contacts button in the shortcut bar, or select any contact folder from the folder bar. You'll see a simple list of cards. If you prefer to have your contacts arranged as a phone list, select View, Current View, and then Phone List. You can also choose to display the list by organization rather than just by name.

Gnumeric Spreadsheet

If you work in an office and use spreadsheets, the odds are that you need to share those spreadsheets with Microsoft Excel users. It's also quite probable that you have used Excel and that it is the spreadsheet application with which you are most comfortable.

Those realities don't pose an obstacle to using Linux in your office, though, because Gnumeric is designed to be familiar to and comfortable for Excel users. In fact, unsuspecting observers have confused the two on more than one occasion.

Gnumeric can import and export Excel files easily, and its options and data processing are quite comparable.

The boxes in the body of the worksheet display the results of formulas or numbers, and the formula field at the top of the window displays the actual formula that calculated your result.

For example, most spreadsheet users are familiar with the procedure to add a column of numbers: click the mouse in any of the fields, and enter a number in the formula field at the top of the window. Press Return to move down to the next one, and enter a new number. Once you have a few, go to an empty cell and press the Sum button, labeled with the Greek letter sigma, to calculate the sum. Then, enter the range of cells you want to add, or just select them with the mouse.

Gnumeric comes with an extensive manual, which you can read by selecting Help, and then Gnumeric Manual.

gPhoto, the Digital Camera Tool

gPhoto, the GNOME digital camera tool, lets you copy pictures from a digital camera onto your hard drive, organize them, and turn them into prebuilt web page galleries.

gPhoto does take some setting up, and the process will vary depending on the camera you are using. The first time you run gPhoto, it will ask you what model of camera you are using, and what port to use to access it. If you have run gPhoto before and want to set that information now, select Configure, Select Port, and then Camera Model.

Some systems may identify your camera automatically, and you will be able to use */dev/camera* for your port name. Some may even have */mnt/camera* set up as a standard directory, and you will be able to point gPhoto there as though it were a directory (do this by selecting File, Open, and then Directory).

Otherwise, you're in for just a little bit of tinkering. If you're using a serial cable (the kind of cable with visible pins on the end), you have probably plugged your camera into */dev/ttyS0* or */dev/ttyS1*. If you have a USB cable, you have probably plugged the camera into */dev/usb*. For FireWire (also known as iLink or IEEE-1394), it may be */dev/sga0* or */dev/sga1*.

If none of these works, make sure that you have read and write permissions on the camera device—you can do this with Nautilus or with the *chmod* command at the command line. You may also try mounting the camera device as though it were a hard disk (do so according to your operating system's instructions). Some cameras will require this; others will not.

Once you have the setup complete, you're ready to go. To download a "thumbnail index" of all the images on your camera, press Ctrl+I or Camera, Download Index, and then Thumbnails. From there, you can decide which ones to keep and which to throw away. Select as many as you like (or choose Select, and then All to select them all), then press Ctrl+G or choose Camera, Download Selected, Images, and then Save to Disk to save them to a location on your hard disk.

To put your photos into a web gallery, start by selecting the items you want to include from the index. Then choose File, Export, and then HTML Gallery, or press Ctrl-M. You'll be prompted to choose a style for your pages, and a location to save the results. Make sure you choose a new and empty directory, and not your home directory, or you'll end up with a small web site scattered about your home directory.

gPhoto also lets you rotate, scale, and adjust the colors for individual images. However, it is not a dedicated image processing program—it's better to use the GIMP for serious editing tasks. For information about how to use the image alteration tools, or on other gPhoto features, select Help, and then User's Manual, or press Ctrl-H.

A significant set of changes is planned for gPhoto during the 2002-2003 development schedule. With gPhoto2, you will be able to install the "GnoCam" tool as well as gPhoto, use the GNOME Control Center to manage camera connections, and handle your camera's contents using the image thumbnail views of Nautilus. gPhoto2 promises to simplify the process of connecting to your camera and to let you use other graphical interfaces, depending on your choice of desktop environment. Visit *http://gphoto.sourceforge.net* for details.

Abiword Word Processor

Open the Abiword word processor by typing *abiword* from a terminal, or by selecting Abiword from your Applications menu. Abiword, like Gnumeric, is designed to be familiar to people who have used other, similar applications in the past. If you've used another word processor, you can probably guess that the *b* button in the toolbar makes your text bold, and that the *diskette* icon saves your files.

To use Abiword, you may need to install fonts or adjust your font path. To learn how, visit *http://abisource.com*.

Additional Applications and Resources

There are dozens, if not hundreds, of other GNOME applications, from software development tools to games to flow-charting and diagramming tools. The best ways to explore them are to visit the *http://gnome.org* web site and browse the software map, or to try installing a few from the *Red Carpet* GNOME channel.

If you get stuck, there are several places to turn for help. In addition to the Nautilus help system and the *gnome.org* web site, try looking for help in chat systems. Developers can be found on `irc.gnome.org` in #gnome, so if you have software development questions, go there. For help with using an application, visit *http://support.ximian. com*, join the mailing lists at *http://lists.gnome.org*, or try the user-supported help chat system built into Ximian applications by selecting Help, and then Help Chat.

Premium commercial support of GNOME and GNOME applications is also available from *support.ximian.com* for both individuals and corporations.

Other X Applications

In this section, we will cover some material about X applications that are neither KDE nor GNOME applications. As should be clear by now, you can run these in any of the desktop environments without problems, even though they might not be as integrated.

We'll particularly spend some time with one aspect of older X applications: X resources, a very powerful, but also confusing and difficult-to-learn way of customizing X applications.

Before we tackle the X resources, one more hint: many programs described elsewhere in this book are X applications as well and are run in an X environment (whether it is KDE, GNOME, or something else), just like the programs described here. And there are literally tens of thousands more out there on the Net—yours to discover!

The X Resource Database

If you aren't running a desktop or if you have to deal with applications that aren't well integrated into your desktop, you will be asked to deal directly with X resources; they are mentioned in virtually every manual page. X resources provide a more flexible and powerful way to configure X clients than using command-line options, such as *–geometry* and *–fg*. They allow you to specify defaults for entire classes of clients; for example, we could set the default font for all invocations of *xterm* to 7x13bold, instead of specifying it on each command line.

Recently, X resources have fallen out of favor with X developers. While they are really very flexible, they are not particularly easy to work with and feel more like a relic of ancient times. A growing number of programs are therefore customized not by X resources but instead via convenient configuration dialog boxes. However, it still pays to know about X resources because you will meet them for a long time to come.

Using X resources requires two steps. First, you create a file containing your X resource defaults. Typically, this file is called *.Xdefaults* and lives in your home directory. Then, you need to use *xrdb* to load the X resources into the server, which makes them available for use. In general, you run *xrdb* from your *.xinitrc* before starting any clients.

As a simple example, let's take the various command-line options used by the clients in the earlier sample *.xinitrc* and specify them as X resources instead. Afterward, we'll show you what kinds of changes need to be made to *.xinitrc* to make use of the resources.

First, a few words about resources and how they work. Each X application is part of a certain *application class*. For example, *xterm* is a member of the XTerm class. *xclock* and *oclock* are both members of the Clock class. Setting resources for the Clock class affects all applications that are part of that class; because *xclock* (a square analog clock) and *oclock* (an oval analog clock) are similar, they belong to the same class and share the same resources. Most applications are members of their own exclusive class; *xload* is the only member of the XLoad class. However, if another *xload*-like application were to be written, it might be part of the XLoad class as well. Placing X clients into application classes allows you to set resources for all applications in that class. (The manual page for each X client specifies the application class to which the client belongs)

Standard X clients employ resources such as foreground, background, geometry, and font. Also, many X clients have specific resources of their own; for example, *xterm* defines the resource logFile, which allows you to specify a file in which to log the terminal session. Again, the manual pages for X clients specify which resources are available.

Moreover, resources themselves are arranged into a hierarchy of classes. For instance, the background resource is a member of the Background class. Resource classes allow many separate resources to be members of the same class, for which you can set resource values for the class as a whole. For example, the background resource usually determines the primary background color of a window. However, if an application window has several panels or regions, you may wish to set the background for each panel separately. There might be resources such as background1, background2, and so on, for each panel, but they would all be members of the Background resource class. Setting the resource value for the Background class sets the value for all resources in that class.

In general, you won't need to concern yourself with the differences between resource classes and the resources within that class. In most cases, it's easier to set resource values for an entire class (such as Background) instead of individual resources in that class.

Now, let's look at how resource values are set in the X resource database. A complete resource specification is of the form:[*]

```
(ApplicationClass|applicationName)*(ResourceClass|resourceName) : value
```

---

[*] Actually, resource specifications have a more complex syntax than this, and the rules used to determine resource and value bindings are somewhat involved. For simplification, we are presenting a reasonable model for application resource settings—and we direct curious readers to a good book on using X, such as the *X Window System User's Guide*.

The vertical bar means "choose one or the other." Let's say you want to set the background color of an *xterm* window. The *complete* resource specification might be:

```
xterm*background: darkslategray
```

However, this sets only a particular background resource (not all the resources that might be in the Background class) and only for the *xterm* client when it is invoked as *xterm* (more on this later). Therefore, we might want to use resource classes instead:

```
XTerm*Background: darkslategray
```

This resource specification will apply to *all xterm* clients, and all Background-class resources used by *xterm*.

Now, let's look at translating the options given in the earlier *.xinitrc* file into application resources. Create a file in your home directory, called *.Xdefaults*. For the previous sample *.xinitrc*, it should contain:

```
 1  Clock*Geometry:          70x70+5+5
 2  XLoad*Geometry:          85x50+85+5
 3  XBiff*Geometry:            +200+5
 4
 5  ! Defaults for all xterm clients
 6  XTerm*Foreground:        white
 7  XTerm*Background:        black
 8
 9  ! Specific xterms
10  xterm-1*Geometry:        80x40+10+110
11
12  xterm-2*Geometry:        -20+10
13  xterm-2*Font:            7x13bold
14  xterm-2*Background:      darkslategray
15
16  xterm-3*Geometry:        80x25-20-30
17  xterm-3*Font:            7x13bold
```

Lines 1–3 set the Geometry resource class for the Clock, XLoad, and XBiff application classes. On lines 6–7, we set the Foreground and Background resource classes for the XTerm class as whole. All *xterm* clients will use these values for Foreground and Background by default.

On lines 10–17, we set resources specific to each invocation of *xterm*. This is necessary because not all the *xterms* are alike; they each have different geometry specifications, for example. In this case, we have named the individual *xterm* invocations xterm-1, xterm-2, and xterm-3. As you can see, we set the Geometry resource for each on lines 10, 12, and 16. Also, we set the Font class for xterm-2 and xterm-3. And we set the Background class to darkslategray for xterm-2.

X resource binding rules work so that certain bindings have precedence over others. In this case, setting a resource for a specific invocation of *xterm* (as in xterm-2*Background on line 14) has precedence over the resource setting for the XTerm class as a whole (XTerm*Background on line 7). In general, bindings for an application or resource class have *lower* precedence than bindings for particular instances of that class. In this way, you can set defaults for the class as a whole but override those defaults for particular instances of the class.

Now, let's look at the changes required to *.xinitrc* to use the X resources defined here. First, we need to add an *xrdb* command, which loads the application resources into the server. And, we can get rid of the various command-line options that the resources have replaced, as in:

```
#!/bin/sh
# Sample .xinitrc shell script

# Load resources
xrdb -load $HOME/.Xdefaults

# Start xterms
xterm -name "xterm-1" &
xterm -name "xterm-2" &
xterm -name "xterm-3" &

# Other useful X clients
oclock &
xload &
xbiff &
xsetroot -solid darkslateblue &

# Start the window manager
exec fvwm2
```

As you see, the *–name* argument given to the three instances of *xterm* lets us specify the application name that *xterm* uses for locating X resources. Most X clients don't support a *–name* argument; the name used is usually the one with which it was invoked. However, because many users run several *xterm*s at once, it is helpful to distinguish between them when setting resources.

Now, you should be able to modify your X environment to some degree. Of course, knowing how to configure X depends partly on being familiar with the many X clients out there, as well as the window manager (and how to configure it).

Emacs and Other Editors

The X features in Emacs are getting spiffier and spiffier. They include pull-down menus, different typefaces for different parts of your window, and a complete integration of cut-and-paste functions with the X environment.

 Most distributions nowadays also carry XEmacs, a version of Emacs that integrates even better into the X Window System and has a much nicer and more user-friendly appearance. You might want to try it out. Most of the concepts here apply to XEmacs, too.

Let's start by defining some nice colors for different parts of the Emacs window. Try this command:

```
eggplant$ emacs  -bg ivory  -fg slateblue  -ms orangered  -cr brown
```

You're setting the background color, foreground color, mouse color, and cursor color, respectively. The cursor is the little rectangle that appears in the window, representing what's called "point" in Emacs—the place where you type in text. We'll return to colors soon.

When you start Emacs, the menu bar on top and the scrollbar on the right side of the window stand out. See Figure 11-10.

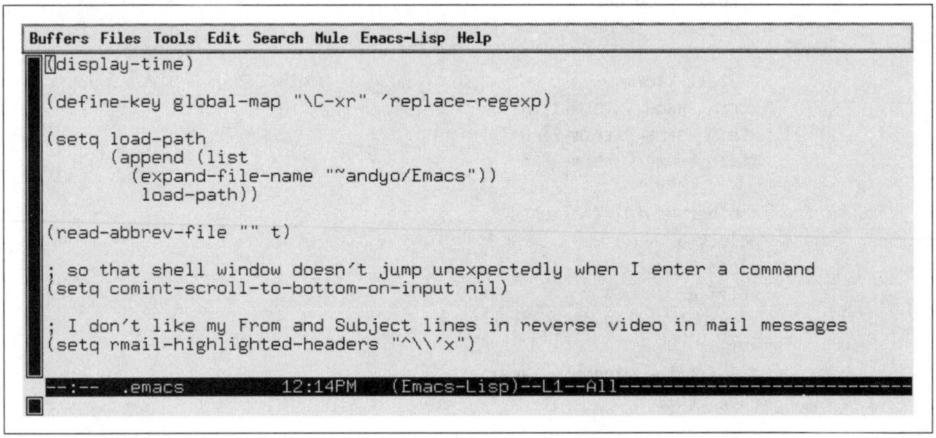

```
Buffers Files Tools Edit Search Mule Emacs-Lisp Help
(display-time)

(define-key global-map "\C-xr" 'replace-regexp)

(setq load-path
      (append (list
          (expand-file-name "~andyo/Emacs"))
          load-path))

(read-abbrev-file "" t)

; so that shell window doesn't jump unexpectedly when I enter a command
(setq comint-scroll-to-bottom-on-input nil)

; I don't like my From and Subject lines in reverse video in mail messages
(setq rmail-highlighted-headers "^\\'x")

--:--  .emacs           12:14PM   (Emacs-Lisp)--L1--All-------------------------
```

Figure 11-10. Emacs window

The scrollbar works just like the *xterm* scrollbar. The menu bar offers a lot of common functions. Some editing modes, such as C and TEX, have their own pull-down menus. The menus are not documented, so you will just have to experiment and try to figure out which Emacs functions to which they correspond.

When you want to use a function that doesn't have a simple key sequence—or you've forgotten the sequence—the menus come in handy. For instance, if you rarely use a regular expression search (a quite powerful feature, well worth studying), the easiest way to invoke it is to pull down the Edit menu and choose Regexp Search.

Another useful menu item is Choose Next Paste on the Edit menu. This offers something you can't get any other way: a list of all the pieces of text you've cut recently. In other words, it shows you the kill ring. You can choose the text you want to paste in next, and the next time you press C-y, it's put into your buffer.

If you get tired of the scrollbar and the menu, put the following LISP code in your .*emacs* file to make them go away:

```
(if (getenv "DISPLAY")
(progn (menu-bar-mode -1)
(scroll-bar-mode -1))
)
```

The mouse is the next X feature with interesting possibilities. You can cut and paste text much the same way as in *xterm*. And you can do this between windows; if you see some output in an *xterm* you'd like to put in a file, you can copy it from the *xterm* and paste it into your Emacs buffer. Moreover, any text you cut the normal way (such as through C-w) goes into the same selection as text you cut with the mouse. So you can cut a few words from your Emacs buffer and paste them into an *xterm*.

The right mouse button works a little unusually. If you select text with the left mouse button, you can click once on the right mouse button to copy it. A second click on the right mouse button removes it. To paste it back, press the middle mouse button. The text goes just before the character the mouse is currently on. Make a mistake? That's all right; the undo command reverses it just as for any other Emacs function. (Choose Undo from the Edit menu or just press the C-_ key.)

If you really love mouse work, you can define the buttons to execute any functions you want, just as with keys. Try putting the following command in your *.emacs* file. When you hold down the Shift key and press the left mouse button, a buffer for composing a mail message appears:

```
(define-key global-map [S-mouse-1] 'mail)
```

We don't recommend you redefine the existing mouse functions, but the Shift, Control, and Meta keys offer plenty of unused possibilities. Combine S-, C-, and M- any way you want in your definitions:

```
(define-key global-map [S-C-mouse-1] 'mail)
```

Now let's play around a bit with windows. Emacs has had windows of its own for decades, of course, long before the X Window System existed. So an Emacs window is not the same as an X window. What X considers a window, Emacs calls a *frame*.

How would you like to edit in two frames at once? Press C-x 5 2, and another frame appears. The new frame is simply another view onto the same editing session. You can edit different buffers in the two frames, but anything you do in one frame is reflected to the corresponding buffer in the other. When you exit Emacs by pressing C-x C-c, both frames disappear; if you want to close just one frame, press C-x 5 0.

To end our exploration of Emacs on the X Window System, we'll look at the exciting things you can do with colors. You can change these during an Emacs session, which makes it easy to play around with different possibilities. Press M-x, then type set-background-color and press the Enter key. At the prompt, type ivory or whatever other color you've chosen. (Remember, Emacs uses the convention M-x where we use Meta-x or Alt-x in the rest of the book.)

Be careful to make the foreground and background different enough so that you can see the text! In addition to set-background-color, Emacs offers set-foreground-color, set-cursor-color, and set-mouse-color.

Before finishing up this section, we would also like to mention that if Emacs or XEmacs is a bit too much for you, you will be delighted to know that KDE comes with a variety of text editors that range from quite simple to quite sophisticated. None of these is as big or powerful as (X)Emacs, but any of these may do the trick.

The three KDE text editors are called (sorted from least to greatest sophistication) *KEdit*, *KWrite*, and *Kate*, where the latter stands for KDE Advanced Text Editor. *Kate* can be used as a full-blown programmer's editor with syntax coloring, multiple files opened at the same time, etc. *KEdit* is similar in feature richness (or poverty) to the *Notepad* editor on Windows systems, and *KWrite* is somewhere in-between. You will find all three of them in the K menu, under the submenu Editors.

## CHAPTER 12

Windows Compatibility and Samba

Linux is a remarkably effective operating system, which in many cases can completely replace MS-DOS/Windows. However, there are always those of us who want to continue to use other operating systems as well as Linux, or at least to exchange files directly with them. Linux satisfies such yearnings with internal enhancements that allow it to access foreign filesystems and act on their files. It can mount DOS/Windows partitions on the system's hard disk, or access files and printers shared by Windows servers on the network. Linux can also run DOS and Windows applications, using compatibility utilities that allow it to invoke MS-DOS or Windows.

We use the terms MS-DOS and Windows somewhat generically in this chapter to refer to any of the DOS-based operating systems coming from Microsoft or those compatible with them. These include MS-DOS, PC-DOS, and DR-DOS/Novell DOS (all with or without Windows 3.x running on top of them), as well as the various Windows versions themselves, no matter whether they build upon a separate DOS installation, such as Windows 3.x, or whether they have a DOS kernel built in, such as Windows 95/98/ME. Windows NT/2000/XP are different, and some of the things described here will not work with them, or will work differently.

One of the most common reasons for needing to run Windows is that it often has better support for new hardware products. If you have installed Windows because you need to use a piece of hardware that is supported by Windows, but for which there is no Linux driver, do not despair. Although you may have to wait a while for it, most mainstream hardware devices that are supported by Windows will eventually be supported by Linux, too. For example, Linux drivers for USB devices used to be rare and flaky, but now many common USB devices work just fine on Linux. You can get updated information about which USB devices work on Linux at *http://www.linux-usb.org*.

You may also need to run Windows in order to use "standard" applications, such as Photoshop or Microsoft Office. In both of these cases, there are free, Open Source applications (namely, The Gimp, KOffice and OpenOffice) that can match or even outdo their proprietary, closed-source equivalents. However, it is still sometimes necessary to run Windows to obtain access to software products that have no Linux equivalent, or for which the Linux counterpart is not fully compatible.

There are essentially four ways in which Linux and Windows can cooperate:

- Sharing CDs and floppy disks ("sneakernet")
- Sharing a computer by being installed on separate partitions
- Sharing data over a network
- Running concurrently on the same computer using an emulator or virtual machine

When Windows and Linux are running on separate hardware, and the systems are not networked, a floppy disk or CD (either CD-R or CD-RW) can be written on one system and read on the other. Both Windows and Linux have the capability to read and write CDs in industry standard, ISO9660 format. The cdrecord program, which runs on Linux and other Unix flavors, can create CDs using Microsoft's Joliet extensions to the ISO9660 standard, making Windows feel right at home with the disc format.

Although floppy disks hold much less data than CDs, they can be useful when just a few small files need to be transferred. Data can be shared between Linux and Windows on MS-DOS formatted floppy disks using the MTools utilities described later in this chapter.

A more cost-effective approach is to install both Windows and Linux on the same computer, each in their own disk partitions. At boot time, the user is given the choice of which operating system to run. The section "Booting the System" in Chapter 5, tells you how to configure a multiboot system.

MTools can be used to access files on the Windows partition while running Linux, but a much more convenient method is to mount the Windows partition directly onto the Linux file system. Then Windows files can be accessed similarly to regular Unix files.

For networked computers, the most outstanding tool for getting Linux and Windows to cooperate is Samba, an Open Source software suite that lets you access Unix files and printers from Windows. Linux servers running Samba can—depending on the circumstances—serve Windows computers even faster than Windows servers can! In addition, Samba has proven to be very stable and reliable.

The Samba package also includes programs that work with the *smbfs* filesystem supported by Linux, which allows directories shared by Windows to be mounted onto the Linux file system. We'll discuss the *smbfs* filesystem and Samba in enough depth to help you mount shared directories and get a basic, functional server running.

Finally, there are methods that can be used to directly run Windows applications under Linux, or even run Windows itself. Wine is an Open Source project with the goal of directly supporting Windows applications, without needing to install Windows. Another approach is used by the commercial VMware application, which is able to concurrently run a number of installations of Windows, Linux, FreeBSD or some other operating systems. When running Windows under VMware, data is shared with the Linux host using the Samba tools.

You should be a little skeptical of some claims of compatibility. You might find, for example, that you need twice the disk storage in order to support two operating systems and their associated files and applications programs, plus file conversion and graphic-format conversion tools, and so on. You may find that hardware tuned for one OS won't be tuned for the other, or that even when you've installed and correctly configured all the necessary software, small unresolvable compatibility issues remain.

Sharing Disks with MTools

The MTools package is a collection of commands that let you manipulate files and directories on one or more MS-DOS disks. The commands work similarly to commonly-used MS-DOS commands, although there are significant differences that take a little getting used to.

The file */etc/mtools.conf* is used to conjure MTools, and you will probably find it already set up to identify your primary and secondary floppy disks as the MS-DOS A: and B: drives:

```
drive a: file="/dev/fd0" exclusive 1.44m mformat_only
drive b: file="/dev/fd1" exclusive 1.44m mformat_only
```

If you have a DOS partition on your hard drive, you can access it as C: using a line in *mtools.conf*, such as:

```
drive c: file="/dev/hda1"
```

When adding this line, use the filename corresponding to your MS-DOS partition instead of /dev/hda1. Be very careful to use the correct partition of your disk. If you make a mistake, you could very easily destroy an entire Linux partition, or other valuable data.

Occasionally, you will encounter a floppy disk that is not MS-DOS formatted. To use the floppy, you will first need to low-level format it using the *fdformat* command, which is not part of MTools. Then, you can use the MTools *mformat* command to put a FAT and directory structure on the floppy:

```
$ fdformat /dev/fd0
Double-sided, 80 tracks, 18 sec/track. Total capacity 1440 kB.
Formatting ... done
Verifying ... done
$ mformat a:
```

The *mdir* command, used for listing the contents of an MS-DOS directory, will now show:

```
$ mdir a:
 Volume in drive A has no label
 Volume Serial Number is 4077-6090
Directory for A:/

No files
                     1 457 664 bytes free
```

The disk is now ready to have files copied to it with the *mcopy* command:

```
$ mcopy /etc/hosts a:
$ mdir
 Volume in drive A has no label
 Volume Serial Number is 4077-6090
Directory for A:/

hosts                948 10-02-2002  19:28  hosts
         1 file                 948 bytes
                     1 456 640 bytes free
```

The file on the floppy can be read by any MS-DOS or Windows system. The above examples give you a basic idea of how the MTools utilities work. The *mcopy* command is typical in that it can accept either MS-DOS or Linux filenames as arguments, and performs the copy operation accordingly. Some other useful MTools commands are *mmd*, to create a directory, and *mcd*, to change directories. When you use *mcd* to change your working directory on an MS-DOS disk, the MTools utilities keep track of the working directory, to simulate the normal MS-DOS behavior. For example, consider the following command sequence:

```
$ mmd a:dir1
$ mcd a:dir1
$ copy c:file1 a:
$ mdir a:
 Volume in drive A has no label
 Volume Serial Number is 4077-6090
Directory for A:/dir1

 .              <DIR>     10-02-2002  19:42
 ..             <DIR>     10-02-2002  19:42
file1    TXT      948 10-02-2002  19:50  file1.txt
         3 files                 948 bytes
                     1 454 080 bytes free
```

The result is that *file1.txt* on the C: drive is copied to the *dir1* directory on the A: drive, and the *mdir* command shows the contents of *A:\dir1*. If you are not used to using the MS-DOS/Windows command shells, be careful of this, because it is different from standard Unix behavior.

Notice in the above directory listing that the directory name is printed as `A:/dir1`, using a forward slash instead of a backslash. This is your clue that when using MTools utilities, you must use a slash do specify directory paths, such as:

```
$ mdel c:/dir1/dir2/readme.txt
```

Also, the MTools commands use a dash instead of a slash to specify options. For example, to print a concise listing of the A: drive, we can use the following command:

```
$ mdir -b a:
A:/hosts
A:/dir1/
A:/file1
```

What follows is a quick description of each MTools command. You can learn more about them by reading the manual pages for *mtools*(1), and for each of the individual commands.

mattrib

Changes attributes of an MS-DOS file, which is assumed to be in the current MS-DOS working directory.

mbadblocks

Tests a disk, and writes entries in the disk's file allocation table (FAT) to mark bad blocks.

mcd

Changes the MS-DOS working directory.

mcopy

Copies files.

mdel

Deletes a file.

mdeltree

Deletes an MS-DOS directory and its contents, including any subdirectories.

mdir

Lists the contents of an MS-DOS directory. Defaults to the current MS-DOS working directory.

mdu

Reports on the amount of space on the disk used by each file on the MS-DOS disk, similarly to the Unix *du* command.

mformat

Creates an empty MS-DOS FAT filesystem on a disk. The disk must already have been low-level MS-DOS formatted (as with the *fdformat* command).

minfo

    Prints low-level information about an MS-DOS disk.

mkmanifest

    Creates a file containing a table of MS-DOS to Unix filename translations for the files on an MS-DOS disk. Useful when a number of Unix files are copied to an MS-DOS disk, and they need to be copied back later and given their original filenames on the Unix system.

mlabel

    Writes a disk volume label to an MS-DOS disk.

mmd

    Creates a directory on an MS-DOS disk.

mmount

    Mounts an MS-DOS disk onto the Linux file system. The disk must be low-level MS-DOS formatted, and contain an MS-DOS filesystem. In order for this to work, the */etc/fstab* file must have an entry similar to:

```
/dev/fd0      /mnt/floppy      auto    noauto,owner    0 0
```

    Using the above entry, the command `mmount a:` will mount the filesystem on the floppy on the directory */mnt/floppy*, which can then be accessed directly by Linux. Use the Linux *umount* command to unmount the disk.

mmove

    Moves or renames a file or directory on an MS-DOS disk.

mrd

    Removes one or more directories from an MS-DOS disk. The directory must be empty. To delete an MS-DOS directory and its contents, use the *mdeltree* command.

mren

    Renames a file or directory on an MS-DOS disk.

mtype

    Displays the contents of a file, which can be either on an MS-DOS disk or the local Linux system.

Sharing Partitions

As we showed you in the previous section, it is possible to use the MTools utilities to access a DOS-formatted hard disk partition, and you can even mount a DOS-formatted disk onto the Linux file system with *mmount*. These methods can be used on a dual-boot system containing a MS-DOS partition, but there's a better way.

As we've explained in section "Mounting Filesystems" in Chapter 6, partitions on local hard disks are accessed by mounting them onto a directory in the Linux file system. In order to be able to read and write to a specific filesystem, the Linux kernel needs to have support for it.

Linux has filesystem drivers that can read and write files on the traditional FAT filesystem and the newer VFAT filesystem, which was introduced with Windows 95 and supports long filenames. It also can read (and with some caveats) write to the NTFS filesystem of Windows NT/2000/XP.

In the section "Building a New Kernel" in Chapter 7, you learned how to build your own kernel. In order to be able to access DOS (used by MS-DOS and Windows 3.x) and VFAT (used by Windows 95/98/ME) partitions, you need to enable DOS FAT fs support in the File systems section during kernel configuration. After you say yes to that option, you can choose MSDOS fs support and VFAT (Windows-95) fs support. The first lets you mount FAT partitions and the second lets you mount FAT32 partitions.

If you want to access files on a Windows NT partition that carries an NTFS filesystem, you need another driver. Activate the option NTFS filesystem support during the kernel configuration. This lets you mount NTFS partitions by specifying the file system type ntfs. Note, however, that the current NTFS driver supports just read-only access. There is a version of this driver available that supports writing as well, but at the time of this writing, it was still under development, and not guaranteed to work reliably when writing to the NTFS partition. Read the documentation carefully before installing and using it!

While Linux is running, you can mount a Windows partition like any other type of partition. For example, if the third partition on your first IDE hard disk contains your Windows 98 installation, you can make the files in it accessible with the following command, which must be executed as root:

```
# mount -t vfat /dev/hda3 /mnt/windows98
```

The /dev/hda3 argument specifies the disk drive corresponding to the Windows 98 disk, while the /mnt/windows98 argument can be changed to any directory you've created for the purpose of accessing the files. But how do you know that you need—in this case—/dev/hda3? If you're familiar with the naming conventions for Linux filesystems, you'll know that hda3 is the third partition on the hard disk that is the master on the primary IDE port. You'll find life easier if you write down the partitions while you are creating them with fdisk, but if you neglected to do that, you can run fdisk again to view the partition table.

The filesystem drivers support a number of options that can be specified with the −o option of the mount command. The mount(8) manual page documents the options that can be used, with sections that explain options specific to the fat and ntfs filesystem types. The section for fat applies to both the msdos and vfat filesystems, and there are two options listed there that are of special interest.

The check option determines whether the kernel should accept filenames that are not permissible on MS-DOS and what it should do with them. This applies only to creating and renaming files. You can specify three values for check: relaxed lets you do just about everything with the filename. If it doesn't fit into the 8.3 convention of MS-DOS files, the filename will be truncated accordingly. normal, the default, will also truncate the filenames as needed, and also removes special characters like * and ? that are not allowed in MS-DOS filenames. Finally, strict forbids both long filenames and the special characters. In order to make Linux more restrictive with respect to filenames on the partition mounted above, the *mount* command could be used as follows:

```
# mount -o check=strict -t msdos /dev/sda5 /mnt/dos
```

This option is used with *msdos* filesystems only; the restrictions on filename length do not apply to *vfat* filesystems.

The *conv* option can be useful, but not as commonly as you might at first think. Windows and Unix systems have different conventions for how a line ending is marked in text files. Windows uses both a carriage return and a linefeed character, while Unix only uses a linefeed. While this does not make the files completely illegible on the other system, it can still be a bother. To tell the kernel to perform the conversion between Windows and Unix text file styles automatically, pass the *mount* command the option *conv*, which has three possible values: binary, the default, does not perform any conversion; text converts every file; and auto tries to guess whether the file in question is a text file or a binary file. Auto does this by looking at the filename extension. If this extension is included in the list of "known binary extensions," it is not converted, otherwise it will be converted.

It is not generally advisable to use *text*, because this will invariable damage any binary files, including graphics files and files written by word processors, spreadsheets, and other programs. Likewise, *auto* can be dangerous, because the extension-based detection mechanism is not very sophisticated. So we suggest you don't use the *conv* option, unless you are sure the partition contains only text files. Stick with *binary* (the default) and convert your files manually on an as-needed basis. See the section "File Translation Utilities" later in this chapter for directions on how to do this.

As with other filesystem types, you can mount MS-DOS and NTFS filesystems automatically at system bootup by placing an entry in your */etc/fstab* file. For example, the following line in */etc/fstab* mounts a Windows 98 partition onto */win*:

```
/dev/hda1    /win   vfat   defaults,umask=002,uid=500,gid=500    0  0
```

When accessing any of the *msdos*, *vfat* or *ntfs* filesystems from Linux, the system must somehow assign Unix permissions and ownerships to the files. By default, ownerships and permissions are determined using the UID and GID, and umasking of the calling process. This works acceptably well when using the *mount* command from the shell, but when run from the boot scripts, it will assign file ownerships to root, which may not be desired. In the above example, we use the *umask* option to specify the file and directory creation mask the system will use when creating files and directories in the filesystem. The *uid* option specifies the owner (as a numeric UID, rather than a text name), and the *gid* option specifies the group (as a numeric GID). All files in the filesystem will appear on the Linux system as having this owner and group. Since dual-boot systems are generally used as workstations by a single user, you will probably want to set the *uid* and *gid* options to the UID and GID of that user's account.

Mounting Windows Shares

When you have Linux and Windows running on separate computers that are networked, you can share files between the two. The built-in networking support in Windows uses Microsoft's Server Message Block (SMB) protocol, which is also known as Common Internet File System (CIFS) protocol. Linux has support for SMB protocol by way of Samba and the Linux *smbfs* filesystem.

In this section, we cover sharing in one direction: how to access files on Windows systems from Linux. The next section will show you how to do the reverse, to make selected files on your Linux system available to Windows clients.

The utilities *smbmount* and *smbmnt* from the Samba distribution work along with the smbfs filesystem drivers to handle the communication between Linux and Windows, and mount the directory shared by the Windows system onto the Linux file system. In some ways, it is similar to mounting Windows partitions, which we covered in the previous section, and in other ways similar to mounting an NFS filesystem.

This is all done without adding any additional software to Windows, because your Linux system will be accessing the Windows system the same way other Windows systems would. However, it's important that you run only TCP/IP protocol on Windows, and not NetBEUI or Novell (IPX/SPX) protocols. Although it is possible for things to work if NetBEUI and/or IPX/SPX are in use, it is much better to avoid them if possible. There can be name resolution conflicts and other similar problems when more than TCP/IP is in use.

TCP/IP protocol on your Windows system should be configured properly, with an IP address and netmask. Also, the workgroup (or domain) and computer name of the system should be set. A simple test is to try pinging the Windows system from Linux, using its computer name (hostname), in a matter, such as:

```
$ ping maya
PING maya.metran.cx (172.16.1.6) from 172.16.1.3 : 56(84) bytes of data.
64 bytes from maya.metran.cx (172.16.1.6): icmp_seq=2 ttl=128 time=362 usec
64 bytes from maya.metran.cx (172.16.1.6): icmp_seq=3 ttl=128 time=368 usec

--- maya.metran.cx ping statistics ---
2 packets transmitted, 2 packets received, 0% packet loss
round-trip min/avg/max/mdev = 0.344/0.376/0.432/0.038 ms
```

This shows that Linux is able to contact maya, the Windows server, and that name resolution and basic TCP/IP communication are working.

For now, we will assume that a TCP/IP connection can be established between your Linux and Windows computers, and that there is a directory on the Windows system that is being shared. Detailed instructions on how to configure networking and file sharing on Windows 95/98/Me and Windows NT/2000/XP can be found in *Using Samba* by Robert Eckstein and David Collier-Brown (O'Reilly).

On the Linux side, the following three steps are required:

1. Compile support for the *smbfs* filesystem into your kernel.
2. Install the Samba utility programs *smbmount* and *smbmnt*, and create at least a minimal Samba configuration file.
3. Mount the shared directory with the *mount* or *smbmount* command.

Your Linux distribution may come with *smbfs* and Samba already installed, but in case it doesn't, let's go through the above steps one at a time. The first one is easy: In the filesystems/Network File Systems section during kernel configuration, select SMB file system support (to mount WfW shares etc.). Compile and install your kernel, or install and load the module.

Next, you will need to install the *smbmount* and *smbmnt* utilities from Samba package. You can install Samba according directions in the next section, or if you already have Samba installed on a Linux system, you can simply copy the commands from there. You also may want to copy over some of the other Samba utilities, such as *smbclient* and *testparm*.

The *smbmount* program is meant to be run from the command line, or by *mount* when used with the *-t smbfs* option. Either way, *smbmount* calls *smbmnt*, which performs the actual mounting operation. While the shared directory is mounted, the *smbmount* process continues to run, and if you do a *ps ax* listing, you will see one *smbmount* process for each mounted share.

The *smbmount* program reads the Samba configuration file, although it doesn't need to gather much information from it. In fact, you may be able to get by with a configuration file that is completely empty! The important thing is to make sure the configuration file exists in the correct location, or you will get error messages. To find the location of the configuration file, run the *testparm* program. (If you copied the two utilities from another Linux system, run *testparm* on that system.) The first line of output identifies the location of the configuration file, as in this example:

```
$ testparm
Load smb config files from /usr/local/samba/lib/smb.conf
... deleted ...
```

You will learn more about writing the configuration file in the next section, but for our purposes here, it suffices to have the following content:

```
[global]
    workgroup = NAME
```

Simply replace *NAME* with the name of your workgroup, as it is configured on the Windows systems on your network.

The last thing to do is to mount the shared directory. Using *smbmount* can be quite easy. The command synopsis is:

```
smbmount share_name mount_point options
```

where *mount_point* specifies a directory just as in the *mount* command. *servicename* follows the Windows Universal Naming Convention (UNC) format, except that it replaces the backslashes with slashes. For example, if you want to mount a SMB share from the computer called maya that is exported under the name *mydocs* onto the directory */windocs*, you could use the following command:

```
# smbmount //maya/mydocs/ /windocs
```

If a username and/or password is needed to access the share, *smbmount* will prompt you for them. Now let's consider a more complex example of an *smbmount* command:

```
# smbmount //maya/d /maya-d/ \
-o credentials=/etc/samba/pw,uid=jay,gid=jay,fmask=600,dmask=700
```

In this example, we are using the -o option to specify options for mounting the share. Reading from left to right through the option string, we first specify a credentials file, which contains the username and password needed to access the share. This avoids having to enter them at an interactive prompt each time. The format of the credentials file is very simple:

```
username=USERNAME
password=PASSWORD
```

where *USERNAME* and *PASSWORD* are replaced by the username and password needed for authentication with the Windows workgroup server or domain. The *uid* and *gid* options specify the owner and group to apply to the files in the share, just as we did when mounting a MS-DOS partition in the previous section. The difference is that here, we are allowed to use either the username and group names or the numeric UID and GID. The *fmask* and *dmask* options allow permission masks to be logically ANDed with whatever permissions are allowed by the system serving the share. For further explanation of these options and how to use them, see the *smbmount*(8) manual page.

One problem with *smbmount* is that when the attempt to mount a shared directory fails, it does not really tell you what went wrong. To diagnose the problem, try accessing the share with *smbclient*, which also comes from the Samba package. *smbclient* lets you list the contents of a shared directory and copy files to and from it, and has the advantage of providing a little more detailed error messages. See the manual page for *smbclient*(1) for further details.

Once you have succeeded in mounting a shared directory using *smbmount*, you may want to add an entry in your */etc/fstab* file to have the share mounted automatically during system boot. It is a simple matter to reuse the arguments from the above *smbmount* command to create an */etc/fstab* entry such as the following:

```
//maya/d  /maya-d  smbfs/
credentials=/etc/samba/pw,uid=jay,gid=jay,fmask=600,dmask=700 0 0
```

Using Samba to Serve SMB Shares

Now that you can mount shared Windows directories on your Linux system, we will discuss networking in the other direction—serving files stored on Linux to Windows clients on the network. This also is done using Samba.

Samba can be used in many ways, and is very scalable. You might want to use it just to make files on your Linux system available to a single Windows client (such as when running Windows in a virtual machine environment on a Linux laptop). Or, you can use Samba to implement a reliable and high-performance file and print server for a network containing thousands of Windows clients.

A warning before you plunge into the wonderful world of Samba: the SMB protocol is quite complex, and because Samba has to deal with all those complexities, it provides a huge number of configuration options. In this section, we will show you a simple Samba setup, using as many of the default settings as we can. If you are really serious about supporting a large number of users that use multiple versions of Windows, or using more than Samba's most basic features, you are well advised to read the Samba documentation thoroughly and perhaps even read a good book about Samba, such as O'Reilly's *Using Samba*.

Setting up Samba involves the following steps:

1. Compiling and installing Samba, if it is not already present on your system.

2. Writing the Samba configuration file *smb.conf* and checking it for correctness.

3. Starting the two Samba daemons *smbd* and *nmbd*.

If you successfully set up your Samba server, it and the directories you share will appear in the browse lists of the Windows clients on your local network—normally accessed by clicking on the Network Neighborhood or My Network Places icon on the Windows desktop. The users on the Windows client systems will be able to read and write files according to your security settings just as they do on their local systems or a Windows server. The Samba server will appear to them as another Windows system on the network, and act almost identically.

Installing Samba

There are two ways in which Samba may be installed on a Linux system:

- From a binary package, such as Red Hat's RPM (also used with SuSE and some other distributions), or Debian's .deb package formats
- By compiling the Samba source distribution

Most Linux distributions include Samba, allowing you to install it simply by choosing an option when installing Linux. If Samba wasn't installed along with the operating system, it's usually a fairly simple matter to install the package later. Either way, the files in the Samba package will usually be installed as follows:

- Daemons in */usr/sbin*
- Command-line utilities in */usr/bin*
- Configuration files in */etc/samba*
- Log files in */var/log/samba*

There are some variations on this. For example, in older releases, you may find log files in */var/log*, and the Samba configuration file in */etc*.

If your distribution doesn't have Samba, you can download the source code, and compile and install it yourself. In this case, all of the files that are part of Samba are installed into subdirectories of */usr/local/samba*.

Either way, you can take a quick look in the directories just mentioned to see if Samba already exists on your system, and if so, how it was installed.

 If you are not the only system administrator of your Linux system, be careful. Another administrator might have used a source code release to upgrade an earlier version that was installed from a binary package, or vice-versa. In this case, you will find files in both locations, and it may take you a while to determine which installation is active.

If you need to install Samba, you can either use one of the packages created for your distribution, or install from source. Installing a binary release may be convenient, but Samba binary packages available from Linux distributors are usually significantly behind the most recent developments. Even if your Linux system already has Samba installed and running, you might want to upgrade to the latest stable source code release.

To install from source, go to the Samba web site at *http://www.samba.org*, and click on one of the links for a download site nearest you. This will take you to one of the mirror sites for FTP downloads. The most recent stable source release is contained in the file *samba-latest.tar.gz*. After downloading this file, unpack it and then read the file *docs/htmldocs/UNIX_INSTALL.html* from the distribution. This file will give you detailed instructions on how to compile and install Samba. Briefly, you will use the following commands:

```
$ tar xvfz samba-latest.tar.gz
$ cd samba-VERSION
```

```
$ su
Password:
# ./configure
# make
# make install
```

Make sure to become superuser before running the *configure* script. Samba is a bit more demanding in this regard than most other Open Source packages you may have installed. After running the above commands, Samba files can be found in the following locations:

- Executables in */usr/local/samba/bin*
- Configuration file in */usr/local/samba/lib*
- Log files in */usr/local/samba/log*
- smbpasswd file in */usr/local/samba/private*
- Manual pages in */usr/local/samba/man*

You will need to add the */usr/local/samba/bin* directory to your PATH environment variable to be able to run the Samba utility commands without providing a full path. Also, you will need to add the following two lines to your */etc/man.config* file to get the *man* command to find the Samba manual pages:

```
MANPATH /usr/local/samba/man
MANPATH_MAP /usr/local/samba/bin /usr/local/samba/man
```

Configuring Samba

The next step is to create a Samba configuration file for your system. Many of the programs in the Samba distribution read the configuration file, and although some of them can get by with minimal information from it (even an empty file), the daemons used for file sharing require that the configuration file be specified in full.

The name and location of the Samba configuration file depends on how Samba was compiled and installed. An easy way to find it is to use the *testparm* command, as we showed you in the section on mounting shared directories earlier in this chapter. Usually, the file is called *smb.conf*, and we'll use that name for it from now on.

The format of the *smb.conf* file is like that of the *.ini* files used by Windows 3.x: there are entries of the type:

```
key = value
```

When working with Samba, you will almost always see the keys referred to as *parameters* or *options*. Parameters are put into sections, which are introduced by labels made of the name of the section in square brackets. This section name goes by itself on a line, like this:

```
[section-name]
```

Each directory or printer you share is called a *share* or *service* in Windows networking terminology. You can specify each service individually using a separate section name, but we'll show you some ways to simplify the configuration file and support many services using just a few sections. One special section called [global] contains parameters that apply as defaults to all services, and parameters that apply to the server in general. While Samba understands literally hundreds of parameters, it is very likely that you will need to use only a few of them, because most have reasonable defaults. If you are curious which parameters are available, or you are looking for a specific parameter, read the manual page for *smb.conf*(5). But for now, let's get started with the following *smb.conf* file:

```
[global]
        workgroup = METRAN
        encrypt passwords = yes
        wins support = yes
        local master = yes

[homes]
        browsable = no
        read only = no
        map archive = no

[printers]
        printable = yes
        printing = BSD
        path = /var/tmp

[data]
        path = /export/data
        read only = no
        map archive = no
```

Although this is a very simple configuration, you may find it satisfactory for most purposes. We'll now explain each section in the file in order of appearance, so you can understand what's going on, and make the changes necessary for it to fit your own system. The parts you most likely need to change are emphasized in boldface.

In the [global] section, we are setting parameters that configure Samba on the particular host system. The workgroup parameter defines the workgroup to which the server belongs. You will need to replace METRAN with the name of your workgroup. If your Windows systems already have a workgroup defined, use that workgroup. Or if not, create a new workgroup name here and configure your Windows systems to belong to it. Use a workgroup name other than the Windows default of WORKGROUP, to avoid conflicts with misconfigured or unconfigured systems.

For our server's computer name (also called NetBIOS name), we are taking advantage of Samba's default behavior of using the system's hostname. That is, if the system's fully-qualified domain name is *dolphin.example.com*, it will be seen from Windows as *dolphin*. Make sure your system's hostname is set appropriately.

The encrypt passwords parameter tells Samba to expect clients to send passwords in "encrypted" form, rather than plaintext. This is necessary in order for Samba to work with Windows 98, Windows NT Service Pack 3, and later versions. If you are using Samba version 3.0 or later, this line is optional, because newer versions of Samba default to using encrypted passwords.

The wins support parameter tells Samba to function as a WINS server, for resolving computer names into IP addresses. This is optional, but helps to keep your network running efficiently.

The local master parameter is also optional. It enables Samba to function as the master browser on the subnet, keeping the master list of computers acting as SMB servers, and their shared resources. Usually, it is best to let Samba accept this role, rather than let it go to a Windows system.

The rest of the sections in our example *smb.conf* are all optional, and define the resources Samba offers to the network.

The [homes] share tells Samba to automatically share home directories. When clients connect to the Samba server, Samba looks up the username of the client in the Linux */etc/passwd* file, to see if the user has an account on the system. If the account exists, and has a home directory, the home directory is offered to the client as a shared directory. The username will be used as the name of the share (which appears as a folder on a Windows client). For example, if a user diane, who has an account on the Samba host, connects to the Samba server, she will see that it offers her home directory on the Linux system as a shared folder named *diane*.

The parameters in the [homes] section define how the home directories will be shared. It is necessary to set browsable = no to keep a shared folder named *homes* from appearing in the browse list. By default, Samba offers shared folders with read-only permissions. Setting read only = no causes the folder and its contents to be offered read/write to the client. Setting permissions like this in a share definition does not change any permissions on the files in the Linux filesystem, but rather acts to apply additional restrictions. A file that has read-only permissions on the server will not become writable from across the network as a result of read only being set to no. Similarly, if a file has read/write permissions on the Linux system, Samba's default of sharing the file read-only applies only to access by Samba's network clients.

Samba has the sometimes difficult job of making a Unix filesystem appear like a Windows filesystem to Windows clients. One of the differences between Windows and Unix filesystems is that Windows uses the archive attribute to tell backup software whether a file has been modified since the previous backup. If the backup software is performing an incremental backup, it backs up only files that have their archive bit set. On Unix, this information is usually inferred from the file's modification timestamp, and there is no direct analog to the archive attribute. Samba mimics the archive attribute using the Unix file's execute bit for owner. This allows

Windows backup software to function correctly when used on Samba shares, but has the unfortunate side-effect of making data files look like executables on your Linux system. We set the map archive parameter to no because we expect that you are more interested in having things work right on your Linux system than being able to perform backups using Windows applications.

The [printers] section tells Samba to make printers connected to the Linux system available to network clients. Each section in *smb.conf*, including this one, that defines a shared printer must have the parameter printable = yes. In order for a printer to be made available, it must have an entry in the Linux system's */etc/printcap* file. As explained in "Managing Print Services" in Chapter 8, the *printcap* file lists all the printers on your system and how they are accessed. The printer will be visible to users on network clients with the name it is listed by in the *printcap* file.

If you have already configured a printer for use, it may not work properly when shared over the network. Usually, when configuring a printer on Linux, the print queue is associated with a printer driver that translates data it receives from applications into codes that make sense to the specific printer in use. However, Windows clients have their own printer drivers, and expect the printer on the remote system to accept raw data files that are intended to be used directly by the printer, without any kind of intermediate processing. The solution is to add an additional print queue for your printer (or create one, if you don't already have the printer configured) that passes data directly to the printer. This is sometimes called "raw mode".

The first time the printer is accessed from each Windows client, you will need to install the Windows printer driver on that client. The procedure is the same as when setting up a printer attached directly to the client system. When a document is printed on a Windows client, it is processed by the printer driver, and then sent to Samba. Samba simply adds the file to the printer's print queue, and the Linux system's printing system handles the rest. Historically, most Linux distributions have used BSD-style printing systems, and so we have set printing = BSD to notify Samba that the BSD system is in use. Samba then acts accordingly, issuing the appropriate commands that tell the printing system what to do. More recently, some Linux distributions have used the LPRng printing system or CUPS. If your distribution uses LPRng, set printing = LPRNG. If it uses CUPS, then set printing = CUPS, and also set printcap name = CUPS.

We have set the path parameter to */var/tmp* to tell Samba where to temporarily put the binary files it receives from the network client, before they are added to the print system's queue. You may use another directory if you like. The directory must be made world-writable, to allow all clients to access the printer.

The [data] share in our example shows how to share a directory. You can follow this example to add as many shared directories as you want, by using a different section name and value for path for each share. The section name is used as the name of the share, which will show up on Windows clients as a folder with that name. As in previous sections, we have used read only = no to allow read/write access to the share, and map archive = no to prevent files from having their execute bits set. The path parameter tells Samba what directory on the Linux system is to be shared. You can share any directory, but make sure it exists and has permissions that correspond to its intended use. For our [data] share, the directory */export/data* has read, write and execute permissions set for all of user, group and other, since it is intended as a general-purpose shared directory for everyone to use.

After you are done creating your *smb.conf* file, run the *testparm* program, which checks your *smb.conf* for errors and inconsistencies. If your *smb.conf* file is correct, *testparm* should report satisfactory messages, as follows:

```
$ testparm
Load smb config files from /usr/local/samba/lib/smb.conf
Processing section "[homes]"
Processing section "[printers]"
Processing section "[data]"
Loaded services file OK.
Press enter to see a dump of your service definitions
```

If you have made any major errors creating the *smb.conf* file, you will get error messages mixed in with the output shown. You don't need to see the dump of service definitions at this point, so just type CTRL-C to exit *testparm*.

Adding users

Network clients must be authenticated by Samba before they can access shares. The configuration we are using in this example uses Samba's "user-level" security, in which client users are required to provide a username and password that must match those of an account on the Linux host system. The first step in adding a new Samba user is to make sure that the user has a Linux account, and if you have a [homes] share in your *smb.conf*, that the account has an existing home directory.

In addition, Samba keeps its own password file, which it uses to validate the encrypted passwords that are received from clients. For each Samba user, you must run the *smbpasswd* command to add a Samba account for that user:

```
# smbpasswd -a username
New SMB password:
Retype new SMB password:
```

Make sure that the username and password you give to *smbpasswd* are both be the same as those of the user's Linux account. We suggest you start off by adding your own account, which you can use a bit later to test your installation.

Starting the Samba daemons

The Samba distribution includes two daemon programs, *smbd* and *nmbd*, that must both be running in order for Samba to function. Starting the daemons is simple:

```
# smbd
# nmbd
```

Assuming your *smb.conf* file is error-free, it is rare for the daemons to fail to run. Still, you might want to run a *ps ax* command and check that they are in the list of active processes. If not, take a look at the Samba log files, *log.smbd* and *log.nmbd*, for error messages. To stop the daemons, you can use the *killall* command to send them the SIGTERM signal:

```
# killall -TERM smbd nmbd
```

Once you feel confident that your configuration is correct, you will probably want the Samba daemons to start up during system boot, along with other system daemons. If you are using a binary release of Samba, there is probably a script provided in the */etc/init.d* directory that will start and stop Samba. For example, on Red Hat and SuSE Linux, Samba can be started with the following command:

```
# /etc/init.d/smb start
```

The *smb* script can also be used to stop or restart Samba, by replacing the start argument with *stop or restart*. The name and location of the script may be different on other distributions. On Debian 3.0, the script is named *samba*, and on older versions of Red Hat, it is located in */etc/rc.d/init.d*.

If you installed from a source code distribution, you will have to write and install your own script that can perform the start and stop functions. (Or maybe you can copy the script from a Samba binary package for your distribution.) When started from a script, *smbd* and *nmbd* must be started with the *-D* option, so that they will detach themselves and run as daemons.

After you have tested the script and you are sure it works, create the appropriate symbolic links in your */etc/rcN.d* directories to start Samba in the runlevel you normally run in, and stop Samba when changing to other runlevels.

Now that you have Samba installed, configured, and running, try using the *smbclient* command to access one of the shared directories:

```
$ smbclient //localhost/data
added interface ip=172.16.1.3 bcast=172.16.1.255 nmask=255.255.255.0
Password:
Domain=[METRAN] OS=[Unix] Server=[Samba 2.2.5]
smb: \>
```

At the smb: \> prompt, you can enter any *smbclient* command. Try the *ls* command, to list the contents of the directory. Then try the *help* command, which will show you all of the commands that are available. The *smbclient* program works very much like *ftp*, so if you are used to *ftp*, you will feel right at home. Now exit *smbclient* (using the *quit* or *exit* command), and try some variations. First, use your server's hostname instead of localhost, to check that name resolution is functioning properly. Then try accessing your home directory by using your username instead of data.

And now for the really fun part: go to a Windows system, and log on using your Samba account username and password. (On Windows NT/2000/XP, you will need to add a new user account, using the Samba account's username and password.) Double-click on the Network Neighborhood or My Network Places icon on the desktop. Browse through the network to find your workgroup, and double-click on its icon. You should see an icon for your Samba server in the window that opens. By double-clicking on that icon, you will open a window that shows your home directory, printer, and *data* shares. Now you can drag and drop files to and from your home directory and data shares, and after installing a printer driver for the shared printer and send Windows print jobs to your Linux printer!

We have only touched the surface of what Samba can do, but this should already give you an impression why Samba—despite not being developed just for Linux—is one of the software packages that have made Linux famous.

File Translation Utilities

One of the most prominent problems when it comes to sharing files between Linux and Windows is that the two systems have different conventions for the line endings in text files. Luckily, there are a few ways to solve this problem:

- If you access files on a mounted partition on the same machine, let the kernel convert the files automatically, as described in the section "Sharing Partitions" earlier in this chapter. Use this with care!

- When creating or modifying files on Linux, common editors like Emacs and *vi* can handle the conversion automatically for you.

- There are a number of tools that convert files from one line-ending convention to the other. Some of these tools can also handle other conversion tasks as well.

- Use your favorite programming language to write your own conversion utility.

If all you are interested in is converting newline characters, writing programs to perform the conversions is surprisingly simple. To convert from DOS format to Unix format, replace every occurrence of CRLF (\r\f or \r\n) in the file to a newline (\n). To go the other way, convert every newline to a CRLF. For example, we will show you two Perl programs that do the job. The first, which we call *d2u*, converts from DOS format to Unix format:

```
#!/usr/bin/perl
while (<STDIN>) { s/\r$//; print }
```

And the following program (which we call *u2d*) converts from Unix format to DOS format:

```
#!/usr/bin/perl
while (<STDIN>) { s/$/\r/; print }
```

Both commands read the input file from the standard input, and write the output file to standard output. You can easily modify our examples to accept the input and output file names on the command line. If you are too lazy to write the utilities yourself, you can see if your Linux installation contains the programs *dos2unix* and *unix2dos*, which work similarly to our simple *d2u* and *u2d* utilities, and also accept filenames on the command line. Another similar pair of utilities is *fromdos* and *todos*. If you cannot find any of these, then try the *flip* command, which is able to translate in both directions.

If you find these simple utilities underpowered, you may want to try *recode*, a program that can convert just about any text-file standard to any other.

The most simple way to use *recode* is to specify both the old and the new character sets (encodings of text file conventions) and the file to convert. *recode* will overwrite the old file with the converted one; it will have the same file name. For example, in order to convert a text file from Windows to Unix, you would enter:

```
recode ibmpc:latin1 textfile
```

textfile is then replaced by the converted version. You can probably guess that to convert the same file back to Windows conventions, you would use:

```
recode latin1:ibmpc textfile
```

In addition to `ibmpc` (as used on Windows) and `latin1` (as used on Unix), there are other possibilities available, such as `latex` for the LaTeX style of encoding diacritics (see Chapter 9) and `texte` for encoding French email messages. You can get the full list by issuing:

```
recode -l
```

If you do not like *recode*'s habit of overwriting your old file with the new one, you can make use of the fact that *recode* can also read from standard input and write to standard output. To convert *dostextfile* to *unixtextfile* without deleting *dostextfile*, you could do:

```
recode ibmpc:latin1 < dostextfile > unixtextfile
```

Other document formats

With the tools just described, you can handle text files quite comfortably, but this is only the beginning. For example, pixel graphics on Windows are usually saved as *bmp* files. Fortunately, there are a number of tools available that can convert *bmp* files to graphics file formats, such as *png* or *xpm* that are more common on Unix. Among these are the Gimp, which is probably included with your distribution.

Things are less easy when it comes to other file formats like those saved by office productivity programs. While the various incarnations of the *doc* file format used by Microsoft Word have become a de facto lingua franca for word processor files on

Windows, it was until recently almost impossible to read those files on Linux. Fortunately, a number of software packages have appeared that can read (and sometimes even write) *.doc* files. Among them are the office productivity suite KOffice, the freely available OpenOffice, and the commercial StarOffice 6.0, a close relative to OpenOffice. Be aware, though, that these conversions will never be perfect; it is very likely that you will have to manually edit the files afterwards. Even on Windows, conversions can never be 100% correct; if you try importing a Microsoft Word file into WordPerfect (or vice versa), you will see what we mean.

In general, the more common a file format is on Windows, the more likely it is that Linux developers will provide a means to read or even write it. Another approach might be to switch to open file formats, such as Rich Text Format (RTF) or Extensible Markup Language (XML), when creating documents on Windows. In the age of the Internet, where information is supposed to float freely, closed, undocumented file formats are an anachronism.

Running MS-DOS and Windows Applications on Linux

When you are running Windows mainly for its ability to support a specific peripheral or hardware device, the best approach is usually to set up a dual-boot system or run Windows on a separate computer, to allow it direct access to hardware resources. But when your objective is to run Windows software, the ideal solution would be to have the applications run happily on Linux, without requiring you to reboot into Windows or move to another computer.

A number of attempts have been made by different groups of developers, both Open Source and commercial, to achieve this goal. The simplest is Dosemu (*http://www.dosemu.org*), which emulates PC hardware well enough for MS-DOS (or compatible system such as PC-DOS or DR-DOS) to run. It is still necessary to install DOS in the emulator, but since DOS is actually running inside the emulator, good application compatibility is assured. To a limited extent, it is even possible to run Windows 3.1.

Wine (*http://www.winehq.com*) is a more ambitious project, with the goal of reimplementing Microsoft's Win32 API, to allow Windows applications to run directly on Linux without the overhead of an emulator. This means you don't have to have a copy of Windows to run Windows applications. However, while the Wine development team has made amazing progress, considering the difficulty of their task, the number of applications that will run under Wine is very limited.

Another Open Source project is Bochs (*http://bochs.sf.net*), which emulates PC hardware well enough for it to run Windows and other operating systems. However, since every 386 instruction is emulated in software, performance is reduced to a small percent of what it would be if the operating system were running directly on the same hardware.

The plex86 project (*http://savannah.nongnu.org/projects/plex86*) takes yet another approach, and implements a virtualized environment in which Windows or other operating systems (and their applications) can run. Software running in the virtual machine runs at full speed, except for when it attempts to access the hardware. It is very much like Dosemu, except the implementation is much more robust, and not limited to running just DOS.

At the time this book was written, all of the projects discussed so far in this section were fairly immature, and significantly limited. To put it bluntly, the sayings, "Your mileage may vary," and, "You get what you pay for," go a long way here.

You may have better luck with a commercial product, such as VMware (*http://www. vmware.com*) or Win4Lin (*http://www.win4lin.com*). Both of these work by implementing a virtual machine environment (in the same manner as plex86), so you will need to install a copy of Windows before you can run Windows applications. The good news is that with VMware, at least, the degree of compatibility is very high. VMware supports versions of DOS/Windows ranging from MS-DOS to .NET, including every version in between. You can even install some of the more popular Linux distributions, to run more than one copy of Linux on the same computer. To varying extents, other operating systems, including FreeBSD, Netware and Solaris, can also be run. Although there is some overhead involved, modern multi-gigahertz CPUs are able yield acceptable performance levels for most common applications, such as office automation software.

Win4Lin is a more recent release than VMware. At the time of this writing, it ran Windows and applications faster than VMware, but was able to support only Windows 95/98/ME, and not Windows NT/2000/XP. As with other projects described in this section, we suggest keeping up to date with the product's development, and check once in a while to see if it is mature enough to meet your needs.

CHAPTER 13
Programming Languages

There's much more to Linux than simply using the system. One of the benefits of free software is that you can modify it to suit your needs. This applies equally to the many free applications available for Linux and to the Linux kernel itself.

Linux supports an advanced programming interface, using GNU compilers and tools, such as the *gcc* compiler, the *gdb* debugger, and so on. A number of other programming languages, including Perl, Python, and LISP, are also supported. Whatever your programming needs, Linux is a great choice for developing Unix applications. Because the complete source code for the libraries and Linux kernel is provided, programmers who need to delve into the system internals are able to do so.*

Linux is an ideal platform for developing software to run under the X Window System. The Linux X distribution, as described in Chapter 10, is a complete implementation with everything you need to develop and support X applications. Programming for X is portable across applications, so the X-specific portions of your application should compile cleanly on other Unix systems.

In this chapter, we'll explore the Linux programming environment and give you a five-cent tour of the many facilities it provides. Half of the trick to Unix programming is knowing what tools are available and how to use them effectively. Often the most useful features of these tools are not obvious to new users.

Since C programming has been the basis of most large projects (even though it is nowadays being replaced more and more by C++) and is the language common to most modern programmers—not only on Unix, but on many other systems as well—we'll start out telling you what tools are available for that. The first few sections of the chapter assume you are already a C programmer.

---

* On a variety of Unix systems, the authors have repeatedly found available documentation to be insufficient. With Linux, you can explore the very source code for the kernel, libraries, and system utilities. Having access to source code is more important than most programmers think.

But several other tools are emerging as important resources, especially for system administration. We'll examine one in this chapter: Perl. Perl is a scripting language like the Unix shells, taking care of grunt work like memory allocation, so you can concentrate on your task. But Perl offers a degree of sophistication that makes it more powerful than shell scripts and, therefore, appropriate for many programming tasks.

Lots of programmers are excited about trying out Java™, the new language from Sun Microsystems. While most people associate Java with interactive programs (applets) on web pages, it is actually a general-purpose language with many potential Internet uses. In a later section, we'll explore what Java offers above and beyond older programming languages, and how to get started.

Programming with gcc

The C programming language is by far the most often used in Unix software development. Perhaps this is because the Unix system was originally developed in C; it is the native tongue of Unix. Unix C compilers have traditionally defined the interface standards for other languages and tools, such as linkers, debuggers, and so on. Conventions set forth by the original C compilers have remained fairly consistent across the Unix programming board.

The GNU C compiler, *gcc*, is one of the most versatile and advanced compilers around. Unlike other C compilers (such as those shipped with the original AT&T or BSD distributions, or those available from various third-party vendors), *gcc* supports all the modern C standards currently in use—such as the ANSI C standard—as well as many extensions specific to *gcc*. Happily, however, *gcc* provides features to make it compatible with older C compilers and older styles of C programming. There is even a tool called *protoize* that can help you write function prototypes for old-style C programs.

gcc is also a C++ compiler. For those who prefer the more modern object-oriented environment, C++ is supported with all the bells and whistles—including most of the C++ introduced when the C++ standard was released, such as method templates. Complete C++ class libraries are provided as well, such as the Standard Template Library (STL).

For those with a taste for the particularly esoteric, *gcc* also supports Objective-C, an object-oriented C spinoff that never gained much popularity but may see a second spring due to its usage in Mac OS X. And there is *gcj*, which compiles Java code to machine code. But the fun doesn't stop there, as we'll see.

In this section, we're going to cover the use of *gcc* to compile and link programs under Linux. We assume you are familiar with programming in C/C++, but we don't assume you're accustomed to the Unix programming environment. That's what we'll introduce here.

The latest *gcc* version at the time of this writing is Version 3.0.4. However, the 3.0 series has proven to be still quite unstable, which is why Version 2.95.3 is still considered the official standard version. We suggest sticking with that one unless you know exactly what you are doing.

Quick Overview

Before imparting all the gritty details of *gcc*, we're going to present a simple example and walk through the steps of compiling a C program on a Unix system.

Let's say you have the following bit of code, an encore of the much-overused "Hello, World!" program (not that it bears repeating):

```
#include <stdio.h>
int main( ) {
  (void)printf("Hello, World!\n");
  return 0; /* Just to be nice */
}
```

Several steps are required to compile this program into a living, breathing executable. You can accomplish most of these steps through a single *gcc* command, but we've left the specifics for later in the chapter.

First, the *gcc* compiler must generate an *object file* from this *source code*. The object file is essentially the machine-code equivalent of the C source. It contains code to set up the *main()* calling stack, a call to the *printf()* function, and code to return the value of 0.

The next step is to *link* the object file to produce an executable. As you might guess, this is done by the *linker*. The job of the linker is to take object files, merge them with code from libraries, and spit out an executable. The object code from the previous source does not make a complete executable. First and foremost, the code for *printf()* must be linked in. Also, various initialization routines, invisible to the mortal programmer, must be appended to the executable.

Where does the code for *printf()* come from? Answer: the libraries. It is impossible to talk for long about *gcc* without mentioning them. A library is essentially a collection of many object files, including an index. When searching for the code for *printf()*, the linker looks at the index for each library it's been told to link against. It finds the object file containing the *printf()* function and extracts that object file (the entire object file, which may contain much more than just the *printf()* function) and links it to the executable.

In reality, things are more complicated than this. Linux supports two kinds of libraries: *static* and *shared*. What we have described in this example are static libraries: libraries where the actual code for called subroutines is appended to the executable. However, the code for subroutines such as *printf()* can be quite lengthy. Because many programs use common subroutines from the libraries, it doesn't make sense for each executable to contain its own copy of the library code. That's where shared libraries come in.[*]

With shared libraries, all the common subroutine code is contained in a single library "image file" on disk. When a program is linked with a shared library, *stub code* is appended to the executable, instead of actual subroutine code. This stub code tells the program loader where to find the library code on disk, in the image file, at runtime. Therefore, when our friendly "Hello, World!" program is executed, the program loader notices that the program has been linked against a shared library. It then finds the shared library image and loads code for library routines, such as *printf()*, along with the code for the program itself. The stub code tells the loader where to find the code for *printf()* in the image file.

Even this is an oversimplification of what's really going on. Linux shared libraries use *jump tables* that allow the libraries to be upgraded and their contents to be jumbled around, without requiring the executables using these libraries to be relinked. The stub code in the executable actually looks up another reference in the library itself—in the jump table. In this way, the library contents and the corresponding jump tables can be changed, but the executable stub code can remain the same.

Shared libraries also have another advantage: their upgradability. When someone fixes a bug in *printf()* (or worse, a security hole), you only need to upgrade the one library. You don't have to relink every single program on your system.

But don't allow yourself to be befuddled by all this abstract information. In time, we'll approach a real-life example and show you how to compile, link, and debug your programs. It's actually very simple; the *gcc* compiler takes are of most of the details for you. However, it helps to understand what's going on behind the scenes.

gcc Features

gcc has more features than we could possibly enumerate here. The *gcc* manual page and Info document give an eyeful of interesting information about this compiler. Later in this section, we'll give you a comprehensive overview of the most useful *gcc* features to get you started. This in hand, you should be able to figure out for yourself how to get the many other facilities to work to your advantage.

For starters, *gcc* supports the "standard" C syntax currently in use, specified for the most part by the ANSI C standard. The most important feature of this standard is function prototyping. That is, when defining a function *foo()*, which returns an int and takes two arguments, a (of type char *) and b (of type double), the function may be defined like this:

```
int foo(char *a, double b) {
  /* your code here... */
}
```

---

* It should be noted that some very knowledgeable programmers consider shared libraries harmful, for reasons too involved to be explained here. They say that we shouldn't need to bother in a time when most computers ship with 20GB hard disks and at least 128 MB of memory preinstalled.

This is in contrast to the older, nonprototype function definition syntax, which looks like this:

```
int foo(a, b)
char *a;
double b;
{
   /* your code here... */
}
```

and which is also supported by *gcc*. Of course, ANSI C defines many other conventions, but this is the one most obvious to the new programmer. Anyone familiar with C programming style in modern books, such as the second edition of Kernighan and Ritchie's *The C Programming Language* (Prentice Hall), can program using *gcc* with no problem.

The *gcc* compiler boasts quite an impressive optimizer. Whereas most C compilers allow you to use the single switch *-0* to specify optimization, *gcc* supports multiple levels of optimization. At the highest level, *gcc* pulls tricks out of its sleeve, such as allowing code and static data to be shared. That is, if you have a static string in your program such as Hello, World!, and the ASCII encoding of that string happens to coincide with a sequence of instruction code in your program, *gcc* allows the string data and the corresponding code to share the same storage. How clever is that!

Of course, *gcc* allows you to compile debugging information into object files, which aids a debugger (and hence, the programmer) in tracing through the program. The compiler inserts markers in the object file, allowing the debugger to locate specific lines, variables, and functions in the compiled program. Therefore, when using a debugger such as *gdb* (which we'll talk about later in the chapter), you can step through the compiled program and view the original source text simultaneously.

Among the other tricks *gcc* offers is the ability to generate assembly code with the flick of a switch (literally). Instead of telling *gcc* to compile your source to machine code, you can ask it to stop at the assembly-language level, which is much easier for humans to comprehend. This happens to be a nice way to learn the intricacies of protected-mode assembly programming under Linux: write some C code, have *gcc* translate it into assembly language for you, and study that.

gcc includes its own assembler (which can be used independently of *gcc* and is called *gas*), just in case you're wondering how this assembly-language code might get assembled. In fact, you can include inline assembly code in your C source, in case you need to invoke some particularly nasty magic but don't want to write exclusively in assembly.

Basic gcc Usage

By now, you must be itching to know how to invoke all these wonderful features. It is important, especially to novice Unix and C programmers, to know how to use *gcc* effectively. Using a command-line compiler such as *gcc* is quite different from, say, using a development system such as Visual Studio or C++ Builder under Windows.* Even though the language syntax is similar, the methods used to compile and link programs are not at all the same.

Let's return to our innocent-looking "Hello, World!" example. How would you go about compiling and linking this program?

The first step, of course, is to enter the source code. You accomplish this with a text editor, such as Emacs or *vi*. The would-be programmer should enter the source code and save it in a file named something like *hello.c*. (As with most C compilers, *gcc* is picky about the filename extension; that is, how it can distinguish C source from assembly source from object files, and so on. You should use the *.c* extension for standard C source.)

To compile and link the program to the executable *hello*, the programmer would use the command:

```
papaya$ gcc -o hello hello.c
```

and (barring any errors), in one fell swoop, *gcc* compiles the source into an object file, links against the appropriate libraries, and spits out the executable *hello*, ready to run. In fact, the wary programmer might want to test it:

```
papaya$ ./hello
Hello, World!
papaya$
```

As friendly as can be expected.

Obviously, quite a few things took place behind the scenes when executing this single *gcc* command. First of all, *gcc* had to compile your source file, *hello.c*, into an object file, *hello.o*. Next, it had to link *hello.o* against the standard libraries and produce an executable.

By default, *gcc* assumes that you want not only to compile the source files you specify, but also to have them linked together (with each other and with the standard libraries) to produce an executable. First, *gcc* compiles any source files into object files. Next, it automatically invokes the linker to glue all the object files and libraries into an executable. (That's right, the linker is a separate program, called *ld*, not part of *gcc* itself—although it can be said that *gcc* and *ld* are close friends.) *gcc* also knows about the "standard" libraries used by most programs and tells *ld* to link against them. You can, of course, override these defaults in various ways.

You can pass multiple filenames in one *gcc* command, but on large projects you'll find it more natural to compile a few files at a time and keep the *.o* object files

---

* A number of IDEs are available for Linux now. These include both commercial ones like Kylix, the Linux version of Delphi, and open source ones like KDevelop, which we will mention in the next chapter.

around. If you want only to compile a source file into an object file and forego the linking process, use the *–c* switch with *gcc*, as in:

```
papaya$ gcc -c hello.c
```

This produces the object file *hello.o* and nothing else.

By default, the linker produces an executable named, of all things, *a.out*. This is just a bit of left-over gunk from early implementations of Unix, and nothing to write home about. By using the *–o* switch with *gcc*, you can force the resulting executable to be named something different, in this case, *hello*.

Using Multiple Source Files

The next step on your path to *gcc* enlightenment is to understand how to compile programs using multiple source files. Let's say you have a program consisting of two source files, *foo.c* and *bar.c*. Naturally, you would use one or more header files (such as *foo.h*) containing function declarations shared between the two programs. In this way, code in *foo.c* knows about functions in *bar.c*, and vice versa.

To compile these two source files and link them together (along with the libraries, of course) to produce the executable *baz*, you'd use the command:

```
papaya$ gcc -o baz foo.c bar.c
```

This is roughly equivalent to the three commands:

```
papaya$ gcc -c foo.c
papaya$ gcc -c bar.c
papaya$ gcc -o baz foo.o bar.o
```

gcc acts as a nice frontend to the linker and other "hidden" utilities invoked during compilation.

Of course, compiling a program using multiple source files in one command can be time-consuming. If you had, say, five or more source files in your program, the *gcc* command in the previous example would recompile each source file in turn before linking the executable. This can be a large waste of time, especially if you only made modifications to a single source file since last compilation. There would be no reason to recompile the other source files, as their up-to-date object files are still intact.

The answer to this problem is to use a project manager such as *make*. We'll talk about *make* later in the chapter, in the section "Makefiles."

Optimizing

Telling *gcc* to optimize your code as it compiles is a simple matter; just use the *–O* switch on the *gcc* command line:

```
papaya$ gcc -O -o fishsticks fishsticks.c
```

As we mentioned not long ago, *gcc* supports different levels of optimization. Using –*O2* instead of –*O* will turn on several "expensive" optimizations that may cause compilation to run more slowly but will (hopefully) greatly enhance performance of your code.

You may notice in your dealings with Linux that a number of programs are compiled using the switch –*O6* (the Linux kernel being a good example). The current version of *gcc* does not support optimization up to –*O6*, so this defaults to (presently) the equivalent of –*O2*. However, –*O6* is sometimes used for compatibility with future versions of *gcc* to ensure that the greatest level of optimization is used.

Enabling Debugging Code

The –*g* switch to *gcc* turns on debugging code in your compiled object files. That is, extra information is added to the object file, as well as the resulting executable, allowing the program to be traced with a debugger such as *gdb*. The downside to using debugging code is that it greatly increases the size of the resulting object files. It's usually best to use –*g* only while developing and testing your programs and to leave it out for the "final" compilation.

Happily, debug-enabled code is not incompatible with code optimization. This means that you can safely use the command:

```
papaya$ gcc -O -g -o mumble mumble.c
```

However, certain optimizations enabled by –*O* or –*O2* may cause the program to appear to behave erratically while under the guise of a debugger. It is usually best to use either –*O* or –*g*, not both.

More Fun with Libraries

Before we leave the realm of *gcc*, a few words on linking and libraries are in order. For one thing, it's easy for you to create your own libraries. If you have a set of routines you use often, you may wish to group them into a set of source files, compile each source file into an object file, and then create a library from the object files. This saves you from having to compile these routines individually for each program in which you use them.

Let's say you have a set of source files containing oft-used routines, such as:

```
float square(float x) {
  /* Code for square()... */
}

int factorial(int x, int n) {
  /* Code for factorial()... */
}
```

and so on (of course, the *gcc* standard libraries provide analogs to these common routines, so don't be misled by our choice of example). Furthermore, let's say that the code for *square()* is in the file *square.c* and that the code for *factorial()* is in *factorial.c*. Simple enough, right?

To produce a library containing these routines, all you do is compile each source file, as so:

```
papaya$ gcc -c square.c factorial.c
```

which leaves you with *square.o* and *factorial.o*. Next, create a library from the object files. As it turns out, a library is just an archive file created using *ar* (a close counterpart to *tar*). Let's call our library *libstuff.a* and create it this way:

```
papaya$ ar r libstuff.a square.o factorial.o
```

When updating a library such as this, you may need to delete the old *libstuff.a*, if it exists. The last step is to generate an index for the library, which enables the linker to find routines within the library. To do this, use the *ranlib* command, as so:

```
papaya$ ranlib libstuff.a
```

This command adds information to the library itself; no separate index file is created. You could also combine the two steps of running *ar* and *ranlib* by using the *s* command to *ar*:

```
papaya$ ar rs libstuff.a square.o factorial.o
```

Now you have *libstuff.a*, a static library containing your routines. Before you can link programs against it, you'll need to create a header file describing the contents of the library. For example, we could create *libstuff.h* with the contents:

```
/* libstuff.h: routines in libstuff.a */
extern float square(float);
extern int factorial(int, int);
```

Every source file that uses routines from *libstuff.a* should contain an #include "libstuff.h" line, as you would do with standard header files.

Now that we have our library and header file, how do we compile programs to use them? First of all, we need to put the library and header file someplace where the compiler can find them. Many users place personal libraries in the directory *lib* in their home directory, and personal include files under *include*. Assuming we have done so, we can compile the mythical program *wibble.c* using the command:

```
papaya$ gcc -I../include -L../lib -o wibble wibble.c -lstuff
```

The *–I* option tells *gcc* to add the directory *../include* to the *include path* it uses to search for include files. *–L* is similar, in that it tells *gcc* to add the directory *../lib* to the *library path*.

The last argument on the command line is *–lstuff*, which tells the linker to link against the library *libstuff.a* (wherever it may be along the library path). The *lib* at the beginning of the filename is assumed for libraries.

Any time you wish to link against libraries other than the standard ones, you should use the *–l* switch on the *gcc* command line. For example, if you wish to use math routines (specified in *math.h*), you should add *–lm* to the end of the *gcc* command, which links against *libm*. Note, however, that the *order* of *–l* options is significant. For example, if our *libstuff* library used routines found in *libm*, you must include *–lm* after *–lstuff* on the command line:

```
papaya$ gcc -Iinclude -Llib -o wibble wibble.c -lstuff -lm
```

This forces the linker to link *libm* after *libstuff*, allowing those unresolved references in *libstuff* to be taken care of.

Where does *gcc* look for libraries? By default, libraries are searched for in a number of locations, the most important of which is */usr/lib*. If you take a glance at the contents of */usr/lib*, you'll notice it contains many library files—some of which have filenames ending in *.a*, others ending in *.so.version*. The *.a* files are static libraries, as is the case with our *libstuff.a*. The *.so* files are shared libraries, which contain code to be linked at runtime, as well as the stub code required for the runtime linker (*ld.so*) to locate the shared library.

At runtime, the program loader looks for shared library images in several places, including */lib*. If you look at */lib*, you'll see files such as *libc.so.6*. This is the image file containing the code for the *libc* shared library (one of the standard libraries, which most programs are linked against).

By default, the linker attempts to link against shared libraries. However, static libraries are used in several caese—e.g., when there are no shared libraries with the specified name anywhere in the library search path. You can also specify that static libraries should be linked by using the *–static* switch with *gcc*.

Creating shared libraries

Now that you know how to create and use static libraries, it's very easy to take the step to shared libraries. Shared libraries have a number of advantages. They reduce memory consumption if used by more than one process, and they reduce the size of the executable. Furthermore, they make developing easier: when you use shared libraries and change some things in a library, you do not need to recompile and relink your application each time. You need to recompile only if you make incompatible changes, such as adding arguments to a call or changing the size of a struct.

Before you start doing all your development work with shared libraries, though, be warned that debugging with them is slightly more difficult than with static libraries because the debugger usually used on Linux, *gdb*, has some problems with shared libraries.

Code that goes into a shared library needs to be *position-independent*. This is just a convention for object code that makes it possible to use the code in shared libraries.

You make *gcc* emit position-independent code by passing it one of the command-line switches *–fpic* or *–fPIC*. The former is preferred, unless the modules have grown so large that the relocatable code table is simply too small, in which case the compiler will emit an error message and you have to use *–fPIC*. To repeat our example from the last section:

```
papaya$ gcc -c -fpic square.c factorial.c
```

This being done, it is just a simple step to generate a shared library:[*]

```
papaya$ gcc -shared -o libstuff.so square.o factorial.o
```

Note the compiler switch *–shared*. There is no indexing step as with static libraries.

Using our newly created shared library is even simpler. The shared library doesn't require any change to the compile command:

```
papaya$ gcc -I../include -L../lib -o wibble wibble.c -lstuff -lm
```

You might wonder what the linker does if a shared library *libstuff.so* and a static library *libstuff.a* are available. In this case, the linker always picks the shared library. To make it use the static one, you will have to name it explicitly on the command line:

```
papaya$ gcc -I../include -L../lib -o wibble wibble.c libstuff.a -lm
```

Another very useful tool for working with shared libraries is *ldd*. It tells you which shared libraries an executable program uses. Here's an example:

```
papaya$ ldd wibble
        libstuff.so => libstuff.so (0x400af000)
        libm.so.5 => /lib/libm.so.5 (0x400ba000)
        libc.so.5 => /lib/libc.so.5 (0x400c3000)
```

The three fields in each line are the name of the library, the full path to the instance of the library that is used, and where in the virtual address space the library is mapped to.

If *ldd* outputs not found for a certain library, you are in trouble and won't be able to run the program in question. You will have to search for a copy of that library. Perhaps it is a library shipped with your distribution that you opted not to install, or it is already on your hard disk, but the loader (the part of the system that loads every executable program) cannot find it.

In the latter situation, try locating the libraries yourself and find out whether they're in a nonstandard directory. By default, the loader looks only in */lib* and */usr/lib*. If you have libraries in another directory, create an environment variable LD_LIBRARY_PATH and add the directories separated by colons. If you believe that everything is set

---

[*] In the ancient days of Linux, creating a shared library was a daunting task of which even wizards were afraid. The advent of the ELF object-file format a few years ago has reduced this task to picking the right compiler switch. Things sure have improved!

up correctly, and the library in question still cannot be found, run the command *ldconfig* as root, which refreshes the linker system cache.

Using C++

If you prefer object-oriented programming, *gcc* provides complete support for C++ as well as Objective-C. There are only a few considerations you need to be aware of when doing C++ programming with *gcc*.

First of all, C++ source filenames should end in the extension *.cpp* (most often used), *.C*, or *.cc*. This distinguishes them from regular C source filenames, which end in *.c*.

Second, you should use the *g++* shell script in lieu of *gcc* when compiling C++ code. *g++* is simply a shell script that invokes *gcc* with a number of additional arguments, specifying a link against the C++ standard libraries, for example. *g++* takes the same arguments and options as *gcc*.

If you do not use *g++*, you'll need to be sure to link against the C++ libraries in order to use any of the basic C++ classes, such as the cout and cin I/O objects. Also be sure you have actually installed the C++ libraries and include files. Some distributions contain only the standard C libraries. *gcc* will be able to compile your C++ programs fine, but without the C++ libraries, you'll end up with linker errors whenever you attempt to use standard objects.

Makefiles

Sometime during your life with Linux you will probably have to deal with *make*, even if you don't plan to do any programming. It's possible you'll want to patch and rebuild the kernel, and that involves running *make*. If you're lucky, you won't have to muck with the makefiles—but we've tried to direct this book toward unlucky people as well. So in this section, we'll explain enough of the subtle syntax of *make* so that you're not intimidated by a makefile.

For some of our examples, we'll draw on the current makefile for the Linux kernel. It exploits a lot of extensions in the powerful GNU version of *make*, so we'll describe some of those as well as the standard *make* features. A good introduction to *make* is provided in *Managing Projects with make* by Andrew Oram and Steve Talbott (O'Reilly). GNU extensions are well documented by the GNU *make* manual.

Most users see *make* as a way to build object files and libraries from sources and to build executables from object files. More conceptually, *make* is a general-purpose program that builds *targets* from *dependencies*. The target can be a program executable, a PostScript document, or whatever. The prerequisites can be C code, a TeX text file, and so on.

While you can write simple shell scripts to execute *gcc* commands that build an executable program, *make* is special in that it knows which targets need to be rebuilt and which don't. An object file needs to be recompiled only if its corresponding source has changed.

For example, say you have a program that consists of three C source files. If you were to build the executable using the command:

```
papaya$ gcc -o foo foo.c bar.c baz.c
```

each time you changed any of the source files, all three would be recompiled and relinked into the executable. If you changed only one source file, this is a real waste of time (especially if the program in question is much larger than a handful of sources). What you really want to do is recompile only the one source file that changed into an object file and relink all the object files in the program to form the executable. *make* can automate this process for you.

What make Does

The basic goal of *make* is to let you build a file in small steps. If a lot of source files make up the final executable, you can change one and rebuild the executable without having to recompile everything. In order to give you this flexibility, *make* records what files you need to do your build.

Here's a trivial makefile. Call it *makefile* or *Makefile* and keep it in the same directory as the source files:

```
edimh: main.o edit.o
        gcc -o edimh main.o edit.o

main.o: main.c
        gcc -c main.c

edit.o: edit.c
        gcc -c edit.c
```

This file builds a program named *edimh* from two source files named *main.c* and *edit.c*. You aren't restricted to C programming in a makefile; the commands could be anything.

Three entries appear in the file. Each contains a *dependency line* that shows how a file is built. Thus the first line says that *edimh* (the name before the colon) is built from the two object files *main.o* and *edit.o* (the names after the colon). This line tells *make* that it should execute the following *gcc* line whenever one of those object files changes. The lines containing commands have to begin with tabs (not spaces).

The command:

```
papaya$ make edimh
```

executes the *gcc* line if there isn't currently any file named *edimh*. However, the *gcc* line also executes if *edimh* exists, but one of the object files is newer. Here, *edimh* is called a *target*. The files after the colon are called either *dependencies* or *prerequisites*.

The next two entries perform the same service for the object files. *main.o* is built if it doesn't exist or if the associated source file *main.c* is newer. *edit.o* is built from *edit.c*.

How does *make* know if a file is new? It looks at the timestamp, which the filesystem associates with every file. You can see timestamps by issuing the *ls –l* command. Since the timestamp is accurate to one second, it reliably tells *make* whether you've edited a source file since the latest compilation or have compiled an object file since the executable was last built.

Let's try out the makefile and see what it does:

```
papaya$ make edimh
gcc -c main.c
gcc -c edit.c
gcc -o edimh main.o edit.o
```

If we edit *main.c* and reissue the command, it rebuilds only the necessary files, saving us some time:

```
papaya$ make edimh
gcc -c main.c
gcc -o edimh main.o edit.o
```

It doesn't matter what order the three entries are within the makefile. *make* figures out which files depend on which and executes all the commands in the right order. Putting the entry for *edimh* first is convenient because that becomes the file built by default. In other words, typing make is the same as typing make edimh.

Here's a more extensive makefile. See if you can figure out what it does:

```
install: all
        mv edimh /usr/local
        mv readimh /usr/local

all: edimh readimh

readimh: read.o edit.o
        gcc -o readimh main.o read.o

edimh: main.o edit.o
        gcc -o edimh main.o edit.o

main.o: main.c
        gcc -c main.c

edit.o: edit.c
        gcc -c edit.c

read.o: read.c
        gcc -c read.c
```

First we see the target install. This is never going to generate a file; it's called a *phony target* because it exists just so that you can execute the commands listed under it. But before `install` runs, `all` has to run because `install` depends on `all`. (Remember, the order of the entries in the file doesn't matter.)

So *make* turns to the `all` target. There are no commands under it (this is perfectly legal), but it depends on `edimh` and `readimh`. These are real files; each is an executable program. So *make* keeps tracing back through the list of dependencies until it arrives at the *.c* files, which don't depend on anything else. Then it painstakingly rebuilds each target.

Here is a sample run (you may need root privilege to install the files in the */usr/local* directory):

```
papaya$ make install
gcc -c main.c
gcc -c edit.c
gcc -o edimh main.o edit.o
gcc -c read.c
gcc -o readimh main.o read.o
mv edimh /usr/local
mv readimh /usr/local
```

This run of *make* does a complete build and install. First it builds the files needed to create *edimh*. Then it builds the additional object file it needs to create *readimh*. With those two executables created, the `all` target is satisfied. Now *make* can go on to build the `install` target, which means moving the two executables to their final home.

Many makefiles, including the ones that build Linux, contain a variety of phony targets to do routine activities. For instance, the makefile for the Linux kernel includes commands to remove temporary files:

```
clean:  archclean
        rm -f kernel/ksyms.lst
        rm -f core `find . -name '*.[oas]' -print`
        .
        .
        .
```

and to create a list of object files and the header files they depend on (this is a complicated but important task; if a header file changes, you want to make sure the files that refer to it are recompiled):

```
depend dep:
        touch tools/version.h
        for i in init/*.c;do echo -n "init/";$(CPP) -M $$i;done > .tmpdep
        .
        .
        .
```

Some of these shell commands get pretty complicated; we'll look at makefile commands later in this chapter, in the section "Multiple Commands."

Some Syntax Rules

The hardest thing about maintaining makefiles, at least if you're new to them, is getting the syntax right. OK, let's be straight about it, *make* syntax is really stupid. If you use spaces where you're supposed to use tabs or vice versa, your makefile blows up. And the error messages are really confusing.

Always put a tab—not spaces—at the beginning of a command. And don't use a tab before any other line.

You can place a hash sign (#) anywhere on a line to start a comment. Everything after the hash sign is ignored.

If you put a backslash at the end of a line, it continues on the next line. That works for long commands and other types of makefile lines, too.

Now let's look at some of the powerful features of *make*, which form a kind of programming language of their own.

Macros

When people use a filename or other string more than once in a makefile, they tend to assign it to a macro. That's simply a string that *make* expands to another string. For instance, you could change the beginning of our trivial makefile to read:

```
OBJECTS = main.o edit.o

edimh: $(OBJECTS)
        gcc -o edimh $(OBJECTS)
```

When *make* runs, it simply plugs in main.o edit.o wherever you specify $(OBJECTS). If you have to add another object file to the project, just specify it on the first line of the file. The dependency line and command will then be updated correspondingly.

Don't forget the parentheses when you refer to $(OBJECTS). Macros may resemble shell variables like $HOME and $PATH, but they're not the same.

One macro can be defined in terms of another macro, so you could say something like:

```
ROOT = /usr/local
HEADERS = $(ROOT)/include
SOURCES = $(ROOT)/src
```

In this case, HEADERS evaluates to the directory */usr/local/include* and SOURCES to */usr/local/src*. If you are installing this package on your system and don't want it to be in */usr/local*, just choose another name and change the line that defines ROOT.

By the way, you don't have to use uppercase names for macros, but that's a universal convention.

An extension in GNU *make* allows you to add to the definition of a macro. This uses a := string in place of an equals sign:

```
DRIVERS = drivers/block/block.a

ifdef CONFIG_SCSI
DRIVERS := $(DRIVERS) drivers/scsi/scsi.a
endif
```

The first line is a normal macro definition, setting the DRIVERS macro to the filename drivers/block/block.a. The next definition adds the filename drivers/scsi/scsi.a. But it takes effect only if the macro CONFIG_SCSI is defined. The full definition in that case becomes:

```
drivers/block/block.a drivers/scsi/scsi.a
```

So how do you define CONFIG_SCSI? You could put it in the makefile, assigning any string you want:

```
CONFIG_SCSI = yes
```

But you'll probably find it easier to define it on the *make* command line. Here's how to do it:

```
papaya$ make CONFIG_SCSI=yes target_name
```

One subtlety of using macros is that you can leave them undefined. If no one defines them, a null string is substituted (that is, you end up with nothing where the macro is supposed to be). But this also gives you the option of defining the macro as an environment variable. For instance, if you don't define CONFIG_SCSI in the makefile, you could put this in your *.bashrc* file, for use with the *bash* shell:

```
export CONFIG_SCSI=yes
```

Or put this in *.cshrc* if you use *csh* or *tcsh*:

```
setenv CONFIG_SCSI yes
```

All your builds will then have CONFIG_SCSI defined.

Suffix Rules and Pattern Rules

For something as routine as building an object file from a source file, you don't want to specify every single dependency in your makefile. And you don't have to. Unix compilers enforce a simple standard (compile a file ending in the suffix *.c* to create a file ending in the suffix *.o*), and *make* provides a feature called suffix rules to cover all such files.

Here's a simple suffix rule to compile a C source file, which you could put in your makefile:

```
.c.o:
        gcc -c $(CFLAGS) $<
```

The .c.o: line means "use a .c dependency to build a .o file." CFLAGS is a macro into which you can plug any compiler options you want: –g for debugging, for instance, or –O for optimization. The string $< is a cryptic way of saying "the dependency." So the name of your .c file is plugged in when *make* executes this command.

Here's a sample run using this suffix rule. The command line passes both the –g option and the –O option:

```
papaya$ make CFLAGS="-O -g" edit.o
gcc -c -O -g edit.c
```

You actually don't have to specify this suffix rule in your makefile because something very similar is already built into *make*. It even uses CFLAGS, so you can determine the options used for compiling just by setting that variable. The makefile used to build the Linux kernel currently contains the following definition, a whole slew of *gcc* options:

```
CFLAGS = -Wall -Wstrict-prototypes -O2 -fomit-frame-pointer -pipe
```

While we're discussing compiler flags, one set is seen so often that it's worth a special mention. This is the –D option, which is used to define symbols in the source code. Since all kinds of commonly used symbols appear in #ifdefs, you may need to pass lots of such options to your makefile, such as –DDEBUG or –DBSD. If you do this on the *make* command line, be sure to put quotation marks or apostrophes around the whole set. This is because you want the shell to pass the set to your makefile as one argument:

```
papaya$ make CFLAGS="-DDEBUG -DBSD" …
```

GNU *make* offers something called *pattern rules*, which are even better than suffix rules. A pattern rule uses a percent sign to mean "any string." So C source files would be compiled using a rule, as in the following:

```
%.o: %.c
        gcc -c -o $@ $(CFLAGS) $<
```

Here the output file %.o comes first, and the dependency %.c comes after a colon. In short, a pattern rule is just like a regular dependency line, but it contains percent signs instead of exact filenames.

We see the $< string to refer to the dependency, but we also see $@, which refers to the output file. So the name of the .o file is plugged in there. Both of these are built-in macros; *make* defines them every time it executes an entry.

Another common built-in macro is $*, which refers to the name of the dependency stripped of the suffix. So if the dependency is *edit.c*, the string $*.s would evaluate to *edit.s* (an assembly-language source file).

Here's something useful you can do with a pattern rule that you can't do with a suffix rule: you add the string _dbg to the name of the output file so that later you can tell that you compiled it with debugging information:

```
%_dbg.o: %.c
        gcc -c -g -o $@ $(CFLAGS) $<

DEBUG_OBJECTS = main_dbg.o edit_dbg.o

edimh_dbg: $(DEBUG_OBJECTS)
        gcc -o $@ $(DEBUG_OBJECTS)
```

Now you can build all your objects in two different ways: one with debugging information and one without. They'll have different filenames, so you can keep them in one directory:

```
papaya$ make edimh_dbg
gcc -c -g -o main_dbg.o main.c
gcc -c -g -o edit_dbg.o  edit.c
gcc -o edimh_dbg  main_dbg.o edit_dbg.o
```

Multiple Commands

Any shell commands can be executed in a makefile. But things can get kind of complicated because *make* executes each command in a separate shell. So this would not work:

```
target:
        cd obj
        HOST_DIR=/home/e
        mv *.o $HOST_DIR
```

Neither the *cd* command nor the definition of the variable HOST_DIR has any effect on subsequent commands. You have to string everything together into one command. The shell uses a semicolon as a separator between commands, so you can combine them all on one line, as in:

```
target:
        cd obj ; HOST_DIR=/home/e ; mv *.o $$HOST_DIR
```

One more change: to define and use a shell variable within the command, you have to double the dollar sign. This lets *make* know that you mean it to be a shell variable, not a macro.

You may find the file easier to read if you break the semicolon-separated commands onto multiple lines, using backslashes so that *make* considers them to be on one line:

```
target:
        cd obj ; \
        HOST_DIR=/home/e ; \
        mv *.o $$HOST_DIR
```

Sometimes makefiles contain their own *make* commands; this is called recursive *make*. It looks like this:

```
linuxsubdirs: dummy
        set -e; for i in $(SUBDIRS); do $(MAKE) -C $$i; done
```

The macro $(MAKE) invokes *make*. There are a few reasons for nesting makes. One reason, which applies to this example, is to perform builds in multiple directories (each of these other directories has to contain its own makefile). Another reason is to define macros on the command line, so you can do builds with a variety of macro definitions.

GNU *make* offers another powerful interface to the shell as an extension. You can issue a shell command and assign its output to a macro. A couple of examples can be found in the Linux kernel makefile, but we'll just show a simple example here:

```
HOST_NAME = $(shell uname -n)
```

This assigns the name of your network node—the output of the *uname −n* command—to the macro HOST_NAME.

make offers a couple of conventions you may occasionally want to use. One is to put an at sign before a command, which keeps *make* from echoing the command when it's executed:

```
@if [ -x /bin/dnsdomainname ]; then \
    echo #define LINUX_COMPILE_DOMAIN \"`dnsdomainname`\"; \
else \
    echo #define LINUX_COMPILE_DOMAIN \"`domainname`\"; \
fi >> tools/version.h
```

Another convention is to put a hyphen before a command, which tells *make* to keep going even if the command fails. This may be useful if you want to continue after an *mv* or *cp* command fails:

```
- mv edimh /usr/local
- mv readimh /usr/local
```

Including Other makefiles

Large projects tend to break parts of their makefiles into separate files. This makes it easy for different makefiles in different directories to share things, particularly macro definitions. The line:

```
include filename
```

reads in the contents of *filename*. You can see this in the Linux kernel makefile, for instance:

```
include .depend
```

If you look in the file *.depend*, you'll find a bunch of makefile entries: these lines declare that object files depend on particular header files. (By the way, *.depend* might not exist yet; it has to be created by another entry in the makefile.)

Sometimes include lines refer to macros instead of filenames, as in:

```
include ${INC_FILE}
```

In this case, *INC_FILE* must be defined either as an environment variable or as a macro. Doing things this way gives you more control over which file is used.

Interpreting make Messages

The error messages from *make* can be quite cryptic, so we'd like to give you some help in interpreting them. The following explanations cover the most common messages.

*** *No targets specified and no makefile found. Stop.*
> This usually means that there is no makefile in the directory you are trying to compile. By default, *make* tries to find the file *GNUmakefile* first; then, if this has failed, *Makefile*, and finally *makefile*. If none of these exists, you will get this error message. If for some reason you want to use a makefile with a different name (or in another directory), you can specify the makefile to use with the *–f* command-line option.

make: *** *No rule to make target 'blah.c', needed by 'blah.o'. Stop.*
> This means that *make* cannot find a dependency it needs (in this case *blah.c*) in order to build a target (in this case *blah.o*). As mentioned, *make* first looks for a dependency among the targets in the makefile, and if there is no suitable target, for a file with the name of the dependency. If this does not exist either, you will get this error message. This typically means that your sources are incomplete or that there is a typo in the makefile.

*** *missing separator (did you mean TAB instead of 8 spaces?). Stop.*
> The current versions of *make* are friendly enough to ask you whether you have made a very common mistake: not prepending a command with a TAB. If you use older versions of *make*, *missing separator* is all you get. In this case, check whether you really have a TAB in front of all commands, and not before anything else.

Autoconf, Automake, and Other Makefile Tools

Writing makefiles for a larger project usually is a boring and time-consuming task, especially if the programs are expected to be compiled on multiple platforms. From the GNU project come two tools called *Autoconf* and *Automake* that have a steep learning curve but, once mastered, greatly simplify the task of creating portable makefiles. In addition, *libtool* helps a lot to create shared libraries in a portable manner. You can probably find these tools on your distribution CD, or you can download them from *ftp://ftp.gnu.org/gnu/*.

From a user's point of view, using *Autoconf* involves running a program *configure*, which should have been shipped in the source package you are trying to build. This program analyzes your system and configures the makefiles of the package to be suitable for your system and setup. A good thing to try before running the *configure* script for real is to issue the command:

```
owl$ ./configure --help
```

This shows all command-line switches that the *configure* program understands. Many packages allow different setups—e.g., different modules to be compiled in—and you can select these with *configure* options.

From a programmer's point of view, you don't write makefiles, but rather files called *makefile.in*. These can contain place holders that will be replaced with actual values when the user runs the *configure* program, generating the makefiles that *make* then runs. In addition, you need to write a file called *configure.in* that describes your project and what to check for on the target system. The *Autoconf* tool then generates the *configure* program from this *configure.in* file. Writing the *configure.in* file is unfortunately way too involved to be described here, but the *Autoconf* package contains documentation to get you started.

Writing the *makefile.in* files is still a cumbersome and lengthy task, but even this can be mostly automated by using the *Automake* package. Using this package, you do not write the *makefile.in* files, but rather the *makefile.am* files, which have a much simpler syntax and are much less verbose. By running the *automake* tool, these *makefile.am* files are converted to the *makefile.in*, which you include when you distribute your source code and which are later converted into the *makefiles* themselves when the package is configured for the user's system. How to write *makefile.am* files is beyond the scope of this book as well. Again, please check the documentation of the package to get started.

These days, most open-source packages use the *libtool/automake/autoconf* combo for generating the makefiles, but this does not mean that this rather complicated and involved method is the only one available. Other makefile-generating tools exist as well, such as the *imake* tool used to configure the X Window System. Another tool that is not as powerful as the *Autoconf* suite (even though it still lets you do most things you would want to do when it comes to makefile generation) but extremely easy to use (it can even generate its own description files for you from scratch) is the *qmake* tool that ships together with the C++ GUI library Qt (downloadable from *http://www.trolltech.com*).

Shell Programming

In the section "Shells" in Chapter 4, we discussed the various shells available for Linux, but shells can also be powerful and consummately flexible programming tools. The differences come through most clearly when it comes to writing shell scripts. The Bourne shell and C shell command languages are slightly different, but the distinction is not obvious with most normal interactive use. In fact, many of the distinctions arise only when you attempt to use bizarre, little-known features of either shell, such as word substitution or some of the more oblique parameter expansion functions.

The most notable difference between Bourne and C shells is the form of the various flow-control structures, including if ...then and while loops. In the Bourne shell, an if ...then takes the form:

```
if list
then
    commands
elif list
then
    commands
else
    commands
fi
```

where *list* is just a sequence of commands to be used as the conditional expression for the if and elif (short for "else if") commands. The conditional is considered to be true if the exit status of the *list* is zero (unlike Boolean expressions in C, in shell terminology an exit status of zero indicates successful completion). The *commands* enclosed in the conditionals are simply commands to execute if the appropriate *list* is true. The then after each *list* must be on a new line to distinguish it from the *list* itself; alternately, you can terminate the *list* with a ;. The same holds true for the *commands*.

An example is:

```
if [ "$PS1" ]; then
    PS1="\h:\w% "
fi
```

This sequence checks to see whether the shell is a login shell (that is, whether the prompt variable PS1 is set), and if so, it resets the prompt to \h:\w%, which is a prompt expansion standing for the hostname followed by the current working directory. For example:

```
loomer:/home/loomer/mdw%
```

The [...] conditional appearing after the if is a *bash* built-in command, shorthand for *test*. The *test* command and its abbreviated equivalent provide a convenient mechanism for testing values of shell variables, string equivalence, and so forth. Instead of using [...], you could call any set of commands after the if, as long as the last command's exit value indicates the value of the conditional.

Under *tcsh*, an if ...then compound statement looks like the following:

```
if (expression) then
  commands
else if (expression) then
  commands
else
  commands
endif
```

The difference here is that the *expression* after the if is an arithmetic or logical expression evaluated internally by *tcsh*, while with *bash* the conditional expression is a command, and the expression returns true or false based on the command's exit status. Within *bash*, using *test* or [...] is similar to an arithmetic expression as used in *tcsh*.

With *tcsh*, however, if you wish to run external commands within the *expression*, you must enclose the command in braces: {*command*}.

The equivalent of the previous *bash* sequence in *tcsh* is:

```
if ($?prompt) then
  set prompt="%m:%/%% "
endif
```

where *tcsh*'s own prompt special characters have been used. As you can see, *tcsh* boasts a command syntax similar to the C language, and expressions are arithmetically and logically oriented. In *bash*, however, almost everything is an actual command, and expressions are evaluated in terms of exit status values. There are analogous features in either shell, but the approach is slightly different.

A similar change exists with the while loop. In *bash*, this takes the form:

```
while list
do
  commands
done
```

You can negate the effect by replacing the word while with until. Again, *list* is just a command sequence to be executed, and the exit status determines the result (zero for success and nonzero for failure). Under *tcsh* the loop looks like this:

```
while (expression)
  commands
end
```

where *expression* is a logical expression to be evaluated within *tcsh*.

This example should be enough to get a head start on understanding the overall differences of shell scripts under *bash* and *tcsh*. We encourage you to read the *bash*(1) and *tcsh*(1) manual pages (although they serve more as a reference than a tutorial) and Info pages, if you have them available. Various books and tutorials on using these two shells are available as well; in fact, any book on shell programming will do, and you can interpolate the advanced features of *bash* and *tcsh* into the standard Bourne and C shells using the manual pages. *Learning the bash Shell* by Cameron Newham and Bill Rosenblatt and *Using csh and tcsh* by Paul DuBois (both from O'Reilly) are also good investments.

Using Perl

Perl may well be the best thing to happen to the Unix programming environment in years; it is worth the price of admission to Linux alone.* Perl is a text- and file-manipulation language, originally intended to scan large amounts of text, process it, and produce nicely formatted reports from that data. However, as Perl has matured, it has developed into an all-purpose scripting language capable of doing everything from managing processes to communicating via TCP/IP over a network. Perl is free software originally developed by Larry Wall, the Unix guru who brought us the *rn* newsreader and various popular tools, such as *patch*. Today it is maintained by Larry and a group of volunteers.

Perl's main strength is that it incorporates the most widely used features of other powerful languages, such as C, *sed*, *awk*, and various shells, into a single interpreted script language. In the past, performing a complicated job required juggling these various languages into complex arrangements, often entailing *sed* scripts piping into *awk* scripts piping into shell scripts and eventually piping into a C program. Perl gets rid of the common Unix philosophy of using many small tools to handle small parts of one large problem. Instead, Perl does it all, and it provides many different ways of doing the same thing. In fact, this chapter was written by an artificial intelligence program developed in Perl. (Just kidding, Larry.)

Perl provides a nice programming interface to many features that were sometimes difficult to use in other languages. For example, a common task of many Unix system administration scripts is to scan a large amount of text, cut fields out of each line of text based on a pattern (usually represented as a *regular expression*), and produce a report based on the data. Let's say we want to process the output of the Unix *last* command, which displays a record of login times for all users on the system, as so:

```
mdw       ttypf   loomer.vpizza.co Sun Jan 16 15:30 - 15:54  (00:23)
larry     ttyp1   muadib.oit.unc.e Sun Jan 16 15:11 - 15:12  (00:00)
johnsonm  ttyp4   mallard.vpizza.c Sun Jan 16 14:34 - 14:37  (00:03)
jem       ttyq2   mallard.vpizza.c Sun Jan 16 13:55 - 13:59  (00:03)
linus     FTP     kruuna.helsinki. Sun Jan 16 13:51 - 13:51  (00:00)
linus     FTP     kruuna.helsinki. Sun Jan 16 13:47 - 13:47  (00:00)
```

---

* Truth be told, Perl also exists now on other systems, such as Windows. But it is not even remotely as well-known and ubiquitous there as it is on Linux.

If we want to count up the total login time for each user (given in parentheses in the last field), we could write a *sed* script to splice the time values from the input, an *awk* script to sort the data for each user and add up the times, and another *awk* script to produce a report based on the accumulated data. Or, we could write a somewhat complex C program to do the entire task—complex because, as any C programmer knows, text processing functions within C are somewhat limited.

However, you can easily accomplish this task with a simple Perl script. The facilities of I/O, regular-expression pattern matching, sorting by associative arrays, and number crunching are all easily accessed from a Perl program with little overhead. Perl programs are generally short and to the point, without a lot of technical mumbo jumbo getting in the way of what you want your program to actually *do*.

Using Perl under Linux is really no different than on other Unix systems. Several good books on Perl already exist, including the O'Reilly books *Programming Perl*, by Larry Wall, Randal L. Schwartz, and Tom Christiansen; *Learning Perl*, by Randal L. Schwartz and Tom Christiansen; *Advanced Perl Programming* by Sriram Srinivasan; and *Perl Cookbook* by Tom Christiansen and Nathan Torkington. Nevertheless, we think Perl is such a great tool that it deserves something in the way of an introduction. After all, Perl is free software, as is Linux; they go hand in hand.

A Sample Program

What we really like about Perl is that it lets you immediately jump to the task at hand; you don't have to write extensive code to set up data structures, open files or pipes, allocate space for data, and so on. All these features are taken care of for you in a very friendly way.

The example of login times, just discussed, serves to introduce many of the basic features of Perl. First, we'll give the entire script (complete with comments) and then a description of how it works. This script reads the output of the *last* command (see the previous example) and prints an entry for each user on the system, describing the total login time and number of logins for each. (Line numbers are printed to the left of each line for reference):

```
1     #!/usr/bin/perl
2
3     while (<STDIN>) {    # While we have input...
4         # Find lines and save username, login time
5         if (/^(\S*)\s*.*\((.*):(.*)\)$/) {
6             # Increment total hours, minutes, and logins
7             $hours{$1} += $2;
8             $minutes{$1} += $3;
9             $logins{$1}++;
10        }
11    }
12
13    # For each user in the array...
```

```
14      foreach $user (sort(keys %hours)) {
15          # Calculate hours from total minutes
16          $hours{$user} += int($minutes{$user} / 60);
17          $minutes{$user} %= 60;
18          # Print the information for this user
19          print "User $user, total login time ";
20          # Perl has printf, too
21          printf "%02d:%02d, ", $hours{$user}, $minutes{$user};
22          print "total logins $logins{$user}.\n";
23      }
```

Line 1 tells the loader that this script should be executed through Perl, not as a shell script. Line 3 is the beginning of the program. It is the head of a simple while loop, which C and shell programmers will be familiar with: the code within the braces from lines 4–10 should be executed while a certain expression is true. However, the conditional expression <STDIN> looks funny. Actually, this expression reads a single line from the standard input (represented in Perl through the name STDIN) and makes the line available to the program. This expression returns a true value whenever there is input.

Perl reads input one line at a time (unless you tell it to do otherwise). It also reads by default from standard input, again, unless you tell it to do otherwise. Therefore, this while loop will continuously read lines from standard input, until there are no lines left to be read.

The evil-looking mess on line 5 is just an if statement. As with most programming languages, the code within the braces (on lines 7–9) will be executed if the expression that follows the if is true. But what is the expression between the parentheses? Those readers familiar with Unix tools, such as *grep* and *sed,* will peg this immediately as a *regular expression*: a cryptic but useful way to represent a pattern to be matched in the input text. Regular expressions are usually found between delimiting slashes (/.../).

This particular regular expression matches lines of the form:

```
mdw      ttypf   loomer.vpizza.co Sun Jan 16 15:30 - 15:54  (00:23)
```

This expression also "remembers" the username (mdw) and the total login time for this entry (00:23). You needn't worry about the expression itself; building regular expressions is a complex subject. For now, all you need to know is that this if statement finds lines of the form given in the example, and splices out the username and login time for processing. The username is assigned to the variable $1, the hours to the variable $2, and the minutes to $3. (Variables in Perl begin with the $ character, but unlike the shell, the $ must be used when assigning to the variable as well.) This assignment is done by the regular expression match itself (anything enclosed in parentheses in a regular expression is saved for later use to one of the variables $1 through $9).

Lines 6–9 actually process these three pieces of information. And they do it in an interesting way: through the use of an *associative array*. Whereas a normal array is indexed with a number as a subscript, an associative array is indexed by an arbitrary string. This lends itself to many powerful applications; it allows you to associate one set of data with another set of data gathered on the fly. In our short program, the keys are the usernames, gathered from the output of *last*. We maintain three associative arrays, all indexed by username: hours, which records the total number of hours the user logged in; minutes, which records the number of minutes; and logins, which records the total number of logins.

As an example, referencing the variable $hours{'mdw'} returns the total number of hours that the user mdw was logged in. Similarly, if the username mdw is stored in the variable $1, referencing $hours{$1} produces the same effect.

In lines 6–9, we increment the values of these arrays according to the data on the present line of input. For example, given the input line:

```
jem      ttyq2     mallard.vpizza.c Sun Jan 16 13:55 - 13:59 (00:03)
```

line 7 increments the value of the hours array, indexed with $1 (the username, jem), by the number of hours that jem was logged in (stored in the variable $2). The Perl increment operator += is equivalent to the corresponding C operator. Line 8 increments the value of minutes for the appropriate user similarly. Line 9 increments the value of the logins array by one, using the ++ operator.

Associative arrays are one of the most useful features of Perl. They allow you to build up complex databases while parsing text. It would be nearly impossible to use a standard array for this same task. We would first have to count the number of users in the input stream and then allocate an array of the appropriate size, assigning a position in the array to each user (through the use of a hash function or some other indexing scheme). An associative array, however, allows you to index data directly using strings and without regard for the size of the array in question. (Of course, performance issues always arise when attempting to use large arrays, but for most applications this isn't a problem.)

Let's move on. Line 14 uses the Perl foreach statement, which you may be used to if you write shell scripts. (The foreach loop actually breaks down into a for loop, much like that found in C.) Here, in each iteration of the loop, the variable $user is assigned the next value in the list given by the expression sort(keys %hours). %hours simply refers to the entire associative array hours that we have constructed. The function keys returns a list of all the keys used to index the array, which is in this case a list of usernames. Finally, the sort function sorts the list returned by keys. Therefore, we are looping over a sorted list of usernames, assigning each username in turn to the variable $user.

Lines 16 and 17 simply correct for situations where the number of minutes is greater than 60; it determines the total number of hours contained in the minutes entry for this user and increments hours accordingly. The int function returns the integral portion of its argument. (Yes, Perl handles floating-point numbers as well; that's why use of int is necessary.)

Finally, lines 19–22 print the total login time and number of logins for each user. The simple print function just prints its arguments, like the *awk* function of the same name. Note that variable evaluation can be done within a print statement, as on lines 19 and 22. However, if you want to do some fancy text formatting, you need to use the printf function (which is just like its C equivalent). In this case, we wish to set the minimum output length of the hours and minutes values for this user to 2 characters wide, and to left-pad the output with zeroes. To do this, we use the printf command on line 21.

If this script is saved in the file logintime, we can execute it as follows:

```
papaya$ last | logintime
User johnsonm, total login time 01:07, total logins 11.
User kibo, total login time 00:42, total logins 3.
User linus, total login time 98:50, total logins 208.
User mdw, total login time 153:03, total logins 290.
papaya$
```

Of course, this example doesn't serve well as a Perl tutorial, but it should give you some idea of what it can do. We encourage you to read one of the excellent Perl books out there to learn more.

More Features

The previous example introduced the most commonly used Perl features by demonstrating a living, breathing program. There is much more where that came from—in the way of both well-known and not-so-well-known features.

As we mentioned, Perl provides a report-generation mechanism beyond the standard print and printf functions. Using this feature, the programmer defines a report "format" that describes how each page of the report will look. For example, we could have included the following format definition in our example:

```
format STDOUT_TOP =
User            Total login time    Total logins
-------------   --------------------  -------------------
.
format STDOUT =
@<<<<<<<<<<<<< @<<<<<<<<             @####
$user,          $thetime,            $logins{$user}
.
```

The STDOUT_TOP definition describes the header of the report, which will be printed at the top of each page of output. The STDOUT format describes the look of each line of output. Each field is described beginning with the @ character; @<<<< specifies a left-justified text field, and @#### specifies a numeric field. The line below the field definitions gives the names of the variables to use in printing the fields. Here, we have used the variable $thetime to store the formatted time string.

To use this report for the output, we replace lines 19–22 in the original script with the following:

```
$thetime = sprintf("%02d:%02d", $hours{$user}, $minutes{$user});
write;
```

The first line uses the sprintf function to format the time string and save it in the variable $thetime; the second line is a write command that tells Perl to go off and use the given report format to print a line of output.

Using this report format, we'll get something looking like this:

```
User            Total login time    Total logins
--------------  --------------------  --------------------
johnsonm        01:07                     11
kibo            00:42                      3
linus           98:50                    208
mdw             153:03                   290
```

Using other report formats we can achieve different (and better-looking) results.

Perl comes with a huge number of modules that you can plug in to your programs for quick access to very powerful features. A popular online archive called CPAN (for Comprehensive Perl Archive Network) contains even more modules: net modules that let you send mail and carry on with other networking tasks, modules for dumping data and debugging, modules for manipulating dates and times, modules for math functions—the list could go on for pages.

If you hear of an interesting module, check first to see whether it's already loaded on your system. You can look at the directories where modules are located (probably under /usr/lib/perl5) or just try loading in the module and see if it works. Thus, the command:

```
$ perl -MCGI -e 1
Can't locate CGI in @INC...
```

gives you the sad news that the *CGI.pm* module is not on your system. *CGI.pm* is popular enough to be included in the standard Perl distribution, and you can install it from there, but for many modules you will have to go to CPAN (and some don't make it into CPAN either). CPAN, which is maintained by Jarkko Hietaniemi and Andreas König, resides on dozens of mirror sites around the world because so many people want to download its modules. The easiest way to get onto CPAN is to visit *http://www.perl.com/CPAN-local/*.

The following program—which we wanted to keep short, and therefore neglected to find a useful task to perform—shows two modules, one that manipulates dates and times in a sophisticated manner and another that sends mail. The disadvantage of using such powerful features is that a huge amount of code is loaded from them, making the runtime size of the program quite large:

```perl
#! /usr/local/bin/perl

# We will illustrate Date and Mail modules
use Date::Manip;
use Mail::Mailer;

# Illustration of Date::Manip module
if ( Date_IsWorkDay( "today", 1) ) {

    # Today is a workday
    $date = ParseDate( "today" );

}
else {

    # Today is not a workday, so choose next workday
    $date=DateCalc( "today" , "+ 1 business day" );

}

# Convert date from compact string to readable string like "April  8"
$printable_date = UnixDate( $date , "%B %e" );

# Illustration of Mail::Mailer module
my ($to) = "the_person\@you_want_to.mail_to";
my ($from) = "owner_of_script\@system.name";

$mail = Mail::Mailer->new;

$mail->open(
        {
            From => $from,
            To => $to,
            Subject => "Automated reminder",
        }
        );

print $mail <<"MAIL_BODY";
If you are at work on or after
$printable_date,
you will get this mail.
MAIL_BODY

$mail->close;

# The mail has been sent! (Assuming there were no errors.)
```

The reason packages are so easy to use is that Perl added object-oriented features in version 5. The Date module used in the previous example is not object-oriented, but the Mail module is. The $mail variable in the example is a Mailer object, and it makes mailing messages straightforward through methods like new, open, and close.

To do some major task like parsing HTML, just read in the proper CGI package and issue a new command to create the proper object—all the functions you need for parsing HTML will then be available.

If you want to give a graphical interface to your Perl script, you can use the Tk module, which originally was developed for use with the Tcl language, the Gtk module, which uses the newer GIMP Toolkit (GTK), or the Qt module, which uses the Qt toolkit that also forms the base of the KDE. The book *Learning Perl/Tk* by Nancy Walsh (O'Reilly) shows you how to do graphics with the Perl/Tk module.

Another abstruse feature of Perl is its ability to (more or less) directly access several Unix system calls, including interprocess communications. For example, Perl provides the functions msgctl, msgget, msgsnd, and msgrcv from System V IPC. Perl also supports the BSD socket implementation, allowing communications via TCP/IP directly from a Perl program. No longer is C the exclusive language of networking daemons and clients. A Perl program loaded with IPC features can be very powerful indeed—especially considering that many client-server implementations call for advanced text processing features such as those provided by Perl. It is generally easier to parse protocol commands transmitted between client and server from a Perl script, rather than write a complex C program to do the work.

As an example, take the well-known SMTP daemon, which handles the sending and receiving of electronic mail. The SMTP protocol uses internal commands such as recv from and mail to to enable the client to communicate with the server. Either the client or the server, or both, can be written in Perl, and can have full access to Perl's text- and file-manipulation features as well as the vital socket communication functions.

Perl is a fixture of CGI programming—that is, writing small programs that run on a web server and help web pages become more interactive.

Pros and Cons

One of the features of (some might say "problems with") Perl is the ability to abbreviate—and obfuscate—code considerably. In the first script, we have used several common shortcuts. For example, input into the Perl script is read into the variable $_. However, most operations act on the variable $_ by default, so it's usually not necessary to reference $_ by name.

Perl also gives you several ways of doing the same thing, which can, of course, be either a blessing or a curse depending on how you look at it. In *Programming Perl*, Larry Wall gives the following example of a short program that simply prints its standard input. All the following statements do the same thing:

```
while ($_ = <STDIN>) { print; }
while (<STDIN>) { print; }
for (;<STDIN>;) { print; }
print while $_ = <STDIN>;
print while <STDIN>;
```

The programmer can use the syntax most appropriate for the situation at hand.

Perl is popular, and not just because it is useful. Because Perl provides much in the way of eccentricity, it gives hackers something to play with, so to speak. Perl programmers are constantly outdoing each other with trickier bits of code. Perl lends itself to interesting kludges, neat hacks, and both very good and very bad programming. Unix programmers see it as a challenging medium to work with—because Perl is relatively new, not all the possibilities have been exploited. Even if you find Perl too baroque for your taste, there is still something to be said for its artistry. The ability to call oneself a "Perl hacker" is a point of pride within the Unix community.

Java

Java is a network-aware, object-oriented language developed by Sun Microsystems. Java has been causing a lot of excitement in the computing community as it strives to provide a secure language for running applets downloaded from the World Wide Web. The idea is simple: allow web browsers to download Java applets, which run on the client's machine. The popular Netscape web browser (discussed in Chapter 1) as well as its open source variant Mozilla, the GNOME variant Galeon, and the KDE web browser Konqueror include support for Java. Furthermore, the Java Developer's Kit and other tools have been ported to Linux. But Java is suitable not only for those applets. Recently, it has been used more and more as a general-purpose programming language that offers fewer obstacles for beginners and that—because of its built-in networking libraries—is often used for programming client/server applications. A number of schools also choose it nowadays for programming courses.

The Promise of Java, or Why You Might Want to Use Java

All this may not sound too exciting to you. There are lots of object-oriented programming languages, after all, and with Netscape plug-ins you can download executable programs from web servers and execute them on your local machine.

But Java is more than just an object-oriented programming language. One of its most exciting aspects is *platform independence*. That means you can write and compile your Java program and then deploy it on almost every machine, whether it is a lowly '386 running Linux, a powerful Pentium II running the latest bloatware from Microsoft, or an IBM mainframe. Sun Microsystems calls this "Write Once, Run Anywhere." Unfortunately, real life is not as simple as design goals. There are tiny but frustrating differences that make a program work on one platform and fail on another. With the advent of the new GUI library Swing in Java 2, a large step has been made to remedy this.

This neat feature of compiling code once and then being able to run it on another machine is made possible by the JVM. The Java compiler does not generate object code for a particular CPU and operating system like *gcc* does, it generates code for the JVM. This machine does not exist anywhere in hardware (yet), but is instead a specification. This specification says which so-called opcodes the machine understands and what the machine does when it encounters them in the object file. The program is distributed in binary form containing so-called *byte codes* that follow the JVM specification.

Now all you need is a program that implements the JVM on your particular computer and operating system. These are available nowadays for just about any platform—no vendor can dare not provide a JVM for its hardware or operating system. Such programs are also called *Java interpreters* because they interpret the opcodes compiled for the JVM and translate them into code for the native machine.

This distinction, which makes Java both a compiled and an interpreted language, makes it possible for you to write and compile your Java program and distribute it to someone else, and no matter what hardware and operating system she has, she will be able to run your program as long as a Java interpreter is available for it.

Alas, Java's platform independence comes at a price. Because the object code is not object code of any currently existing hardware, it must pass through an extra layer of processing, meaning that programs written in Java typically run 10 to 20 times slower than comparable programs written in, for example, C. While this does not matter for some cases, in other cases it is simply unacceptable. so-called *just-in-time compilers* are available that first translate the object code for the JVM into native object code and then run this object code. When the same object code is run a second time, the precompiled native code can be used without any interpretation and thus runs faster. But the speed that can be achieved with this is still inferior to that of C programs. Sun Microsystems is working on a technology that is said to provide an execution speed "comparable to C programs," but whether this promise can be fulfilled remains to be seen—the company has been working on it for some time now.

Java also distinguishes between *applications* and *applets*. Applications are standalone programs that are run from the command line or your local desktop and behave like ordinary programs. Applets, on the other hand, are programs (usually smaller) that run inside your web browser. (To run these programs, the browser needs a Java interpreter inside.) When you browse a web site that contains a Java applet, the web server sends you the object code of the applet, and your browser executes it for you. You can use this for anything from simple animations to complete online banking systems.*

When reading about the Java applets, you might have thought, "And what happens if the applet contains mischievous code that spies my hard disk or even maybe deletes or corrupts files?" Of course, this would be possible if the Java designers had

---

* One of us does all his financial business with his bank via a Java applet that his bank provides when browsing a special area of its web server.

not designed a multistep countermeasure against such attacks: all Java applets run in a so-called sandbox, which allows them access only to certain resources. For example, Java applets can output text on your monitor, but they can't read data from your local filesystem or even write to it unless you explicitly allow them. While this sandbox paradigm reduces the usefulness of applets, it increases the security of your data. With recent Java releases, you can determine how much security you need and thus have additional flexibility. It should be mentioned that there have been reports of serious security breaches in the use of Java in browsers, although at least all known ones are found and fixed in current web browsers.

If you decide that Java is something for you, we recommend that you get a copy of *Thinking in Java* by Bruce Eckel (Prentice Hall). It covers most of the things you need to know in the Java world and also teaches you general programming principles. Other Java titles that are well worth looking into include *Learning Java* by Pat Niemeyer and Jonathan Knudsen (O'Reilly) and *Core Java* by Cay Horstmann and Gary Cornell (Prentice Hall).

Getting Java for Linux

Fortunately, there is a Linux port of the so-called JDK, the Java Developers Kit provided by Sun Microsystems for Solaris and Windows which serves as a reference implementation of Java. In the past, there was usually a gap between the appearance of a new JDK version for Solaris and Windows and the availability of the JDK for Linux. Luckily, this is no longer the case.

The "official" Java implementation JDK contains a compiler, an interpreter, and several related tools. Other kits are also available for Linux, often in the form of open source software. We'll cover the JDK here, though, because that's the standard. There are other Linux implementations, including a very good one from IBM, as well; you might even have them on your distribution CDs.

One more note: most distributions already contain the JDK for Linux, so it might be easier for you to simply install a prepackaged one. However, the JDK is moving fast, and you might want to install a newer version than the one your distribution contains.

Your one-stop shop for Java software for Linux is *http://www.blackdown.org*. Here, you will find documentation, news about the Linux ports, and links to the places where you can download a copy of the JDK for your machine.

After unpacking and installing the JDK according to the instructions, you have several new programs at your disposal. *javac* is the Java compiler, *java* is the interpreter, and *appletviewer* is a small GUI program that lets you run applets without using a full-blown web browser, and so on.

A Working Example of Java

The following program is a complete Java program that can run as a standalone application as well as an applet. It is a small painting program that lets you scribble on a virtual canvas. It also utilizes some GUI elements like a push button and an option menu.

The part of Java that lets you use GUI elements like windows and menus is called the *Abstract Window Toolkit* (AWT). It, too, helps fulfill Java's promise of "Write once, run anywhere." Even though different operating systems, Linux, Windows, and the Macintosh, have completely different windowing systems, you need to write your user interface code only once. The AWT then maps the platform-independent widgets to a native GUI library. Thus, your program will have the native look of the respective windowing systems, depending on the system on which you run it.

The AWT has a number of drawbacks, such as the different look that the programs have on each platform (some people consider this an advantage, though, because the program looks like a native application), the sluggish speed, and the numerous bugs. The newer Swing toolkit which was introduced into Java with version 2 remedies many of these drawbacks, such as the different looks (by providing pluggable look-and-feel styles), and supports many more user-interface components, such as tables and tree controls, but is even slower.

Enough talk now. Here is the code for the little scribbling program:

```java
import java.applet.*;
import java.awt.*;
import java.awt.event.*;
/** An applet that can also run as a standalone application */
public class StandaloneScribble extends Applet {
  /**
   * The main( ) method.  If this program is invoked as an application,
   * this method will create the necessary window, add the applet to it,

   * and call init( ), below.  Note that Frame uses a PanelLayout by
   * default.
   */
  public static void main(String[ ] args) {
    Frame f = new Frame( );                           // Create a window
    Applet a = new StandaloneScribble( );             // Create the applet panel
    f.add(a, "Center");                               // Add applet to window
    a.init( );                                        // Initialize the applet
    f.setSize(400, 400);                              // Set the size of the
                                                      // window
    f.show( );                                        // Make the window visible
    f.addWindowListener(new WindowAdapter( ) {        // Handle window close
                                                      // requests
```

```
        public void windowClosing(WindowEvent e) { System.exit(0); }
      });
    }
    /**
     * The init( ) method.  If the program is invoked as an applet, the
     * browser allocates screen space for it and calls this method to set
     * things up.
     */
    public void init( ) {
      // Define, instantiate, and register a MouseListener object.
      this.addMouseListener(new MouseAdapter( ) {
        public void mousePressed(MouseEvent e) {
          lastx = e.getX( );
          lasty = e.getY( );
        }
      });
      // Define, instantiate, and register a MouseMotionListener object.
      this.addMouseMotionListener(new MouseMotionAdapter( ) {
        public void mouseDragged(MouseEvent e) {
          Graphics g = getGraphics( );
          int x = e.getX( ), y = e.getY( );
          g.setColor(Color.black);
          g.drawLine(lastx, lasty, x, y);
          lastx = x; lasty = y;
        }
      });
      // Create a clear button.
      Button b = new Button("Clear");
      // Define, instantiate, and register a listener to handle button
      // presses.
      b.addActionListener(new ActionListener( ) {
        public void actionPerformed(ActionEvent e) {  // clear the scribble
          Graphics g = getGraphics( );
          g.setColor(getBackground( ));
          g.fillRect(0, 0, getSize( ).width, getSize( ).height);
        }
      });

      // And add the button to the applet.
      this.add(b);
    }
    protected int lastx, lasty;  // Coordinates of last mouse click.
  }
```

Save this code in a file named *StandaloneScribble.java*. The name is important; it must be the same as the name of the class implemented in the file with *.java* attached. To compile this code, issue the following command:

```
$tigger javac StandaloneScribble.java
```

This can take a while. The Java compiler is not particularly fast, mainly because it is written in Java itself.* When it is done, it will have created a file *StandaloneScribble.class* together with some more *.class* files which we won't talk about here.

Now you can run this program from the command line. Simply issue the command:

```
$tigger java StandaloneScribble
```

If you have installed the JDK correctly, you should get a window in which to scribble. Note that the argument passed to the Java command was *StandaloneScribble* without the *.class* extension. This is because, technically, the interpreter is not executing the file, but the class.

You can also run this program in a web browser or in the *appletviewer* from the JDK. For this, you need a bit of HTML code. The following should be enough:

```
<APPLET code="StandaloneScribble.class" width=150 height=100>
</APPLET>
```

Save this code to a file and open it with either a web browser like Netscape Navigator or the *appletviewer*, and you'll see the program in the browser window.

To finish this section, let's go through some of the most interesting lines of the program: in the first three lines, Java classes that come from the JDK are imported. This is roughly comparable to including header files in a C program, although there is no linking step in Java. When the program is run, the Java interpreter needs to be able to find the imported classes. It does this by looking in the directories relative to the interpreter binary itself as well as those mentioned in the environment variable CLASSPATH that you might have set up (not necessary to run this sample program).

The first large block contains the main( ) method. When the program is run as a standalone application, this method is called by the interpreter to start the execution of the program. In this method, a window is set up which is then used for screen output.

Most of the remaining code is the method init( ). It is called either from main( ) when run standalone or directly from the web browser when run as an applet. In the latter case, main( ) is not executed.

Other Languages

Many other popular (and not-so-popular) languages are available for Linux. For the most part, however, these work identically on Linux as on other Unix systems, so there's not much in the way of news there. There are also so many of them that we

---

* Other, faster, Java compilers are available. For example, Jikes is a blazing-fast (at least compared to *javac*) Java compiler that you can download from *http://www.alphaworks.ibm.com*.

can't cover them in much detail here. We do want to let you know what's out there, however, and explain some of the differences between the various languages and compilers.

Python has gained a lot of attention lately because it is a powerful mixture of different programming paradigms and styles. For example, it is one of the very few interpreted object-oriented programming languages (Perl being another example, but only relatively late in its existence). Python fans say it is especially easy to learn. Python was written and designed almost entirely by Guido van Rossum, who chose the name because he wrote the interpreter while watching reruns of the British TV show *Monty Python's Flying Circus*. The language is introduced in *Learning Python* by Mark Lutz and David Ascher and covered in detail in *Programming Python* by Mark Lutz (both published by O'Reilly).

As nice and useful as Perl is, it has one disadvantage—or at least many people think so—namely, that you can write the same code in many different ways. This has given Perl the reputation that it's easy to write code in Perl, but hard to read it. (The point is that another programmer might do things differently from you, and you are therefore not used to reading this style.)

This means that Perl might not be the right choice for developing code that later must be maintained for years to come.

If you normally develop software in C, C++, or Java, and from time to time you want to do some scripting, you might find that Perl's syntax is too different from what you are normally used to—e.g., you need to type a dollar in front of a variable:

```
foreach $user ...
```

Before we look into a bit more detail at what Python is, let us suggest that whether you choose to program in Perl or Python is largely a matter of "religion," just as it is a matter of "religion" whether you use Emacs or *vi*, or whether you use KDE or GNOME. Perl and Python both fill the gap between real languages like C/C++/Java and scripting languages like the language built into *bash* or *tcsh*.

In contrast to Perl, Python was designed from the beginning to be a real programming language, with many of the constructs inspired from C. This does undoubtedly mean that Python programs are easier to read than Perl ones, even though they might come out slightly longer.

Python is an object-oriented language, but you do not need to program in an object-oriented fashion if you do not want to. This makes it possible for you to start your scripting without worrying about object orientation, and as you go along and your script gets longer and more complicated, you can easily convert it to use objects.

Python scripts are interpreted, which means that you do not need to wait for a long compilation process to take place. Python programs are internally byte-compiled on the fly, which ensures that they still run at an acceptable speed. In normal daily use, you don't really notice all this, except for the fact that when you write a *.py* file, Python will create a *.pyc* file.

Python has lists, tuples, strings, and associative arrays (or in Python lingo, *dictionaries*) built into the syntax of the language, which makes working with these types very easy.

Python comes with an extensive library, similar in power to what we saw previously for Perl. See *http://www.python.org/doc/current/lib/lib.html* for a complete library reference.

Let's complete this short introduction to Python by looking at a small Python script. This will hopefully give you an idea of the level of abstraction Python works on. The script does the same as the earlier Perl script. Your first impression of the script might very well be that it is way longer than the Perl script. Remember that we are forcing Python to "compete" here in the area where Perl is most powerful. To compensate, we find that this script is more straightforward to read.

Also notice the indentation. While indentation is optional in most other languages and just makes the code more readable, it is required in Python and is one of its characterizing features.

```
1    #!/usr/bin/python
2
3    import sys, re, string
4
5    minutes = {}
6    count = {}
7    line = sys.stdin.readline()
8    while line:
9      match = re.match( "^(\S*)\s*.*\(([0-9]+):([0-9]+)\)\s*$", line )
10     if match:
11       user = match.group(1)
12       time = string.atoi(match.group(2))*60 + string.atoi(match.group(3))
13       if not count.has_key( user ):
14         minutes[ user ] = 0
15         count[ user ]   = 0
16       minutes[ user ] += time
17       count[user] += 1
18     line = sys.stdin.readline()
19
20   for user in count.keys():
21     hour = `minutes[user]/60`
22     min = minutes[user] % 60
23     if min < 10:
24       minute = "0" + `min`
25     else:
26       minute = `min`
27     print "User " + user + ", total login time " + \
28           hour + ":" + minute + \
29           ", total logins " + `count[user]`
```

The script should be self-explanatory, with a few exceptions. On line 3 we import the libraries we want to use. Having imported string, for instance, we may use it as in line 12, where we use the method *atoi* from the library string.

On lines 5 and 6 we initialize two dictionaries. In contrast to Perl, we need to initialize them before we can assign values to them. Line 7 reads a line from standard input. When no more lines can be read, the *readline* method returns None, which is the equivalent to a null pointer.

Line 9 matches the line read from stdin against a regular expression, and returns a match object as a result of matching. This object contains a method for accessing the subparts of the match. Line 21 converts the result of the division minutes[user]/60 to a string. This is done using two back quotes.

You can read all about Python at *http://www.python.org* or in *Learning Python* by Mark Lutz and David Ascher and in *Programming Python* by Mark Lutz, both from O'Reilly.

Another recent development in the area of scripting languages, the Ruby language was developed in Japan and has gained an impressive following there. It is an object-oriented scripting language that goes (if possible) even further than Python in its use of objects.

Tcl (Tool Command Language) is a language that was meant as a glue for connecting programs together, but it has become most famous for its included, easy-to-use windowing toolkit, Tk.

LISP is an interpreted language used in many applications, ranging from artificial intelligence to statistics. It is used primarily in computer science because it defines a clean, logical interface for working with algorithms. (It also uses a lot of parentheses, something of which computer scientists are always fond.) It is a functional programming language and is very generalized. Many operations are defined in terms of recursion instead of linear loops. Expressions are hierarchical, and data is represented by lists of items.

Several LISP interpreters are available for Linux. Emacs LISP is a fairly complete implementation in itself. It has many features that allow it to interact directly with Emacs—input and output through Emacs buffers, for example—but it may be used for non-Emacs–related applications as well.

Also available is CLISP, a Common LISP implementation by Bruno Haible of Karlsruhe University and Michael Stoll of Munich University. It includes an interpreter, a compiler, and a subset of CLOS (Common LISP Object System, an object-oriented extension to LISP). CLX, a Common LISP interface to the X Window System, is also available, and it runs under CLISP. CLX allows you to write X-based applications in LISP. Austin Kyoto Common LISP, another LISP implementation, is available and compatible with CLX as well.

SWI-Prolog, a complete Prolog implementation by Jan Wielemaker of the University of Amsterdam, is also available. Prolog is a logic-based language, allowing you to make logical assertions, define heuristics for validating those assertions, and make decisions based on them. It is a useful language for AI applications.

Also available are several Scheme interpreters, including MIT Scheme, a complete Scheme interpreter conforming to the R^4 standard. Scheme is a dialect of LISP that offers a cleaner, more general programming model. It is a good LISP dialect for computer science applications and for studying algorithms.

At least two implementations of Ada are available—AdaEd, an Ada interpreter, and GNAT, the GNU Ada Translator. GNAT is actually a full-fledged optimizing Ada compiler. It is to Ada what *gcc* is to C and C++.

Along the same vein, two other popular language translators exist for Linux—*p2c*, a Pascal-to-C translator, and *f2c*, a FORTRAN-to-C translator. If you're concerned that these translators won't function as well as bona fide compilers, don't be. Both *p2c* and *f2c* have proven to be robust and useful for heavy Pascal and FORTRAN use.

f2c is Fortran-77–compliant, and a number of tools are available for it as well. *ftnchek* is a FORTRAN checker, similar to *lint*. Both the LAPACK numerical methods library and the *mpfun* multiprecision FORTRAN library have been ported to Linux using *f2c*. *toolpack* is a collection of FORTRAN tools that includes such items as a source-code pretty printer, a precision converter, and a portability checker.

Among the miscellaneous other languages available for Linux are interpreters for APL, Rexx, Forth, ML, and Eiffel, as well as a Simula-to-C translator. The GNU versions of the compiler tools *lex* and *yacc* (renamed to *flex* and *bison*, respectively), which are used for many software packages, have also been ported to Linux. *lex* and *yacc* are invaluable for creating any kind of parser or translator, most commonly used when writing compilers.

CHAPTER 14

Tools for Programmers

Many judge a computer system by the tools it offers its programmers. Unix systems have won the contest by many people's standards, having developed a very rich set over the years. Leading the parade is the GNU debugger, *gdb*. In this chapter, we take a close look at this invaluable utility, and at a number of other auxiliary tools C programmers will find useful.

Even if you are not a programmer, you should consider using the Revision Control System (RCS). It provides one of the most reassuring protections a computer user could ask for—backups for everything you do to a file. If you delete a file by accident, or decide that everything you did for the past week was a mistake and should be ripped out, RCS can recover any version you want. If you are working on a larger project that involves either a large number of developers or a large number of directories (or both), Concurrent Versioning System (CVS) might be more suitable for you. It was originally based on RCS, but was rewritten from the ground up and provides many additional features. Currently, another rewrite from the ground up is taking place; that new tool will be called *Subversion*. It remains to be seen, however, whether it will replace CVS. Finally, the Linux kernel itself uses yet another versioning system, called BitKeeper.

Debugging with gdb

Are you one of those programmers who scoff at the very idea of using a debugger to trace through code? Is it your philosophy that if the code is too complex for even the programmer to understand, the programmer deserves no mercy when it comes to bugs? Do you step through your code, mentally, using a magnifying glass and a toothpick? More often than not, are bugs usually caused by a single-character omission, such as using the = operator when you mean +=?

Then perhaps you should meet *gdb*—the GNU debugger. Whether or not you know it, *gdb* is your friend. It can locate obscure and difficult-to-find bugs that result in core dumps, memory leaks, and erratic behavior (both for the program and the programmer). Sometimes even the most harmless-looking glitches in your code can cause everything to go haywire, and without the aid of a debugger like *gdb*, finding these problems can be nearly impossible—especially for programs longer than a few hundred lines. In this section, we'll introduce you to the most useful features of *gdb* by way of examples. There's a book on *gdb*, too—the Free Software Foundation's *Debugging with GDB* by Richard M. Stallman, Roland Pesch, Stan Shebs, *et al.*

gdb is capable of either debugging programs as they run, or examining the cause for a program crash with a core dump. Programs debugged at runtime with *gdb* can either be executed from within *gdb* itself or can be run separately; that is, *gdb* can attach itself to an already running process to examine it. First, we'll discuss how to debug programs running within *gdb* and then move on to attaching to running processes and examining core dumps.

Tracing a Program

Our first example is a program called *trymh* that detects edges in a grayscale image. *trymh* takes as input an image file, does some calculations on the data, and spits out another image file. Unfortunately, it crashes whenever it is invoked, as so:

```
papaya$ trymh < image00.pgm > image00.pbm
Segmentation fault (core dumped)
```

Now, using *gdb* we could analyze the resulting core file, but for this example, we'll show how to trace the program as it runs.[*]

Before we use *gdb* to trace through the executable *trymh*, we need to ensure that the executable has been compiled with debugging code (see the section "Programming Languages and Utilities" in Chapter 1). To do so, we should compile *trymh* using the *–g* switch with *gcc*.

Note that enabling optimization (*–O*) with debug code (*–g*) is legal but discouraged. The problem is that *gcc* is too smart for its own good. For example, if you have two identical lines of code in two different places in a function, *gdb* may unexpectedly jump to the second occurrence of the line, instead of the first, as expected. This is because *gcc* combined the two lines into a single line of machine code used in both instances.

Some of the automatic optimizations performed by *gcc* can be confusing when using a debugger. To turn off *all* optimization (even optimizations performed without specifying *–O*), use the *–O0* (that's *dash-oh-zero*) option with *gcc*.

Now we can fire up *gdb* to see what the problem might be:

```
papaya$ gdb trymh
```

---

[*] The sample programs in this section are not programs you're likely to run into anywhere; they were thrown together by the authors for the purpose of demonstration.

```
GNU gdb 20010316
Copyright 2001 Free Software Foundation, Inc.
GDB is free software, covered by the GNU General Public License, and you are
welcome to change it and/or distribute copies of it under certain conditions.
Type "show copying" to see the conditions.
There is absolutely no warranty for GDB.  Type "show warranty" for details.
This GDB was configured as "i386-suse-linux".
(gdb)
```

Now *gdb* is waiting for a command. (The command *help* displays information on the available commands.) The first thing we want to do is start running the program so that we can observe its behavior. However, if we immediately use the *run* command, the program simply executes until it exits or crashes.

First, we need to set a *breakpoint* somewhere in the program. A breakpoint is just a location in the program where *gdb* should stop and allow us to control execution of the program. For the sake of simplicity, let's set a breakpoint on the first line of actual code so that the program stops just as it begins to execute. The *list* command displays several lines of code (an amount that is variable) at a time:

```
(gdb) list
12        main( ) {
13
14          FloatImage inimage;
15          FloatImage outimage;
16          BinaryImage binimage;
17          int i,j;
18
19          inimage = (FloatImage)imLoadF(IMAGE_FLOAT,stdin);
20          outimage = laplacian_float(inimage);
21
(gdb) break 19
Breakpoint 1 at 0x289c: file trymh.c, line 19.
(gdb)
```

A breakpoint is now set at line 19 in the current source file. You can set many breakpoints in the program; breakpoints may be conditional (that is, triggered only when a certain expression is true), unconditional, delayed, temporarily disabled, and so on. You may set breakpoints on a particular line of code, a particular function, or a set of functions, and in a slew of other ways. You may also set a *watchpoint*, using the *watch* command, which is similar to a breakpoint but is triggered whenever a certain event takes place—not necessarily at a specific line of code within the program. We'll talk more about breakpoints and watchpoints later in the chapter.

Next, we use the *run* command to start running the program. *run* takes as arguments the same arguments you'd give *trymh* on the command line; this can include shell wildcards and input/output redirection, as the command is passed to */bin/sh* for execution:

```
(gdb) run < image00.pgm > image00.pfm
Starting program: /amd/dusk/d/mdw/vis/src/trymh < image00.pgm > image00.pfm

Breakpoint 1, main () at trymh.c:19
19              inimage = (FloatImage)imLoadF(IMAGE_FLOAT,stdin);
(gdb)
```

As expected, the breakpoint is reached immediately at the first line of code. We can now take over.

The most useful program-stepping commands are *next* and *step*. Both commands execute the next line of code in the program, except that *step* descends into any function calls in the program, and *next* steps directly to the next line of code in the same function. *next* quietly executes any function calls that it steps over but does not descend in their code for us to examine.

imLoadF is a function that loads an image from a disk file. We know this function is not at fault (you'll have to trust us on that one), so we wish to step over it using the *next* command:

```
(gdb) next
20              outimage = laplacian_float(inimage);
(gdb)
```

Here, we are interested in tracing into the suspicious-looking *laplacian_float* function, so we use the *step* command:

```
(gdb) step
laplacian_float (fim=0x0) at laplacian.c:21
21              i = 20.0;
(gdb)
```

Let's use the *list* command to get some idea of where we are:

```
(gdb) list
16              FloatImage laplacian_float(FloatImage fim) {
17
18                  FloatImage mask;
19                  float i;
20
21                  i = 20.0;
22                  mask=(FloatImage)imNew(IMAGE_FLOAT,3,3);
23                  imRef(mask,0,0) = imRef(mask,2,0) = imRef(mask,0,2) = 1.0;
24                  imRef(mask,2,2) = 1.0; imRef(mask,1,0) = imRef(mask,0,1) = i/5;
25                  imRef(mask,2,1) = imRef(mask,1,2) = i/5; imRef(mask,1,1) = -i;
(gdb) list
26
27                  return convolveFloatWithFloat(fim,mask);
28              }
(gdb)
```

As you can see, using *list* multiple times just displays more of the code. Because we don't want to *step* manually through this code, and we're not interested in the *imNew* function on line 22, let's continue execution until line 27. For this, we use the *until* command:

```
(gdb) until 27
laplacian_float (fim=0x0) at laplacian.c:27
27          return convolveFloatWithFloat(fim,mask);
(gdb)
```

Before we step into the *convolveFloatWithFloat* function, let's be sure the two parameters, fim and mask, are valid. The *print* command examines the value of a variable:

```
(gdb) print mask
$1 = (struct {...} *) 0xe838
(gdb) print fim

$2 = (struct {...} *) 0x0
(gdb)
```

mask looks fine, but fim, the input image, is null. Obviously, *laplacian_float* was passed a null pointer instead of a valid image. If you have been paying close attention, you noticed this as we entered *laplacian_float* earlier.

Instead of stepping deeper into the program (as it's apparent that something has already gone wrong), let's continue execution until the current function returns. The *finish* command accomplishes this:

```
(gdb) finish
Run till exit from #0  laplacian_float (fim=0x0) at laplacian.c:27
0x28c0 in main () at trymh.c:20
20       outimage = laplacian_float(inimage);
Value returned is $3 = (struct {...} *) 0x0
(gdb)
```

Now we're back in *main*. To determine the source of the problem, let's examine the values of some variables:

```
(gdb) list
15       FloatImage outimage;
16       BinaryImage binimage;
17       int i,j;
18
19       inimage = (FloatImage)imLoadF(IMAGE_FLOAT,stdin);
20       outimage = laplacian_float(inimage);
21
22       binimage = marr_hildreth(outimage);
23       if  (binimage == NULL) {
24          fprintf(stderr,"trymh: binimage returned NULL\n");
(gdb) print inimage
$6 = (struct {...} *) 0x0
(gdb)
```

The variable inimage, containing the input image returned from *imLoadF*, is null. Passing a null pointer into the image manipulation routines certainly would cause a core dump in this case. However, we know *imLoadF* to be tried and true because it's in a well-tested library, so what's the problem?

As it turns out, our library function *imLoadF* returns NULL on failure—if the input format is bad, for example. Because we never checked the return value of *imLoadF* before passing it along to *laplacian_float*, the program goes haywire when inimage is assigned NULL. To correct the problem, we simply insert code to cause the program to exit with an error message if *imLoadF* returns a null pointer.

To quit *gdb*, just use the command *quit*. Unless the program has finished execution, *gdb* will complain that the program is still running:

```
(gdb) quit
The program is running.  Quit anyway (and kill it)? (y or n) y
papaya$
```

In the following sections we examine some specific features provided by the debugger, given the general picture just presented.

Examining a Core File

Do you hate it when a program crashes and spites you again by leaving a 10MB core file in your working directory, wasting much-needed space? Don't be so quick to delete that core file; it can be very helpful. A core file is just a dump of the memory image of a process at the time of the crash. You can use the core file with *gdb* to examine the state of your program (such as the values of variables and data) and determine the cause for failure.

The core file is written to disk by the operating system whenever certain failures occur. The most frequent reason for a crash and the subsequent core dump is a memory violation—that is, trying to read or write memory to which your program does not have access. For example, attempting to write data using a null pointer can cause a *segmentation fault*, which is essentially a fancy way of saying, "you screwed up." Segmentation faults are a common error and occur when you try to access (read from or write to) a memory address that does not belong to your process's address space. This includes the address 0, as often happens with uninitialized pointers. Segmentation faults are often caused by trying to access an array item outside the declared size of the array, and are commonly a result of an off-by-one error. They can also be caused by a failure to allocate memory for a data structure.

Other errors that result in core files are so-called "bus errors" and "floating-point exceptions." Bus errors result from using incorrectly aligned data and are therefore rare on the Intel architecture, which does not pose the strong alignment conditions that other architectures do, such as SPARC. Floating-point exceptions point to a severe problem in a floating-point calculation like an overflow, but the most usual case is a division by zero.

However, not all such memory errors will cause immediate crashes. For example, you may overwrite memory in some way, but the program continues to run, not knowing the difference between actual data and instructions or garbage. Subtle memory violations can cause programs to behave erratically. One of the authors once witnessed a bug that caused the program to jump randomly around, but without tracing it with *gdb*, it still appeared to work normally. The only evidence of a bug was that the program returned output that meant, roughly, that two and two did not add up to four. Sure enough, the bug was an attempt to write one too many characters into a block of allocated memory. That single-byte error caused hours of grief.

You can prevent these kinds of memory problems (even the best programmers make these mistakes!) using the Valgrind package, a set of memory-management routines that replaces the commonly used *malloc()* and *free()* functions as well as their C++ counterparts, the operators *new* and *delete*. We'll talk about Valgrind in the section "Using Valgrind."

However, if your program does cause a memory fault, it will crash and dump core. Under Linux, core files are named, appropriately, *core*. The core file appears in the current working directory of the running process, which is usually the working directory of the shell that started the program, but on occasion, programs may change their own working directory.

Some shells provide facilities for controlling whether core files are written. Under *bash*, for example, the default behavior is not to write core files. In order to enable core file output, you should use the command:

```
ulimit -c unlimited
```

probably in your *.bashrc* initialization file. You can specify a maximum size for core files other than `unlimited`, but truncated core files may not be of use when debugging applications.

Also, in order for a core file to be useful, the program must be compiled with debugging code enabled, as described in the previous section. Most binaries on your system will not contain debugging code, so the core file will be of limited value.

Our example for using *gdb* with a core file is yet another mythical program called *cross*. Like *trymh* in the previous section, *cross* takes an image file as input, does some calculations on it, and outputs another image file. However, when running *cross*, we get a segmentation fault:

```
papaya$ cross < image30.pfm > image30.pbm
Segmentation fault (core dumped)
papaya$
```

To invoke *gdb* for use with a core file, you must specify not only the core filename, but also the name of the executable that goes along with that core file. This is because the core file does not contain all the information necessary for debugging:

```
papaya$ gdb cross core
GDB is free software and you are welcome to distribute copies of it
```

```
     under certain conditions; type "show copying" to see the conditions.
     There is absolutely no warranty for GDB; type "show warranty" for details.
     GDB 4.8, Copyright 1993 Free Software Foundation, Inc...
     Core was generated by `cross'.
     Program terminated with signal 11, Segmentation fault.
     #0  0x2494 in crossings (image=0xc7c8) at cross.c:31
     31              if ((image[i][j] >= 0) &&
     (gdb)
```

gdb tells us that the core file was created when the program terminated with signal 11. A *signal* is a kind of message that is sent to a running program from the kernel, the user, or the program itself. Signals are generally used to terminate a program (and possibly cause it to dump core). For example, when you type the interrupt character, a signal is sent to the running program, which will probably kill the program.

In this case, signal 11 was sent to the running *cross* process by the kernel when *cross* attempted to read or write to memory to which it did not have access. This signal caused *cross* to die and dump core. *gdb* says that the illegal memory reference occurred on line 31 of the source file *cross.c*:

```
(gdb) list
26              xmax = imGetWidth(image)-1;
27              ymax = imGetHeight(image)-1;
28
29              for (j=1; j<xmax; j++) {
30                for (i=1; i<ymax; i++) {
31                  if ((image[i][j] >= 0) &&
32                      (image[i-1][j-1] < 0) ||
33                      (image[i-1][j] < 0) ||
34                      (image[i-1][j+1] < 0) ||
35                      (image[i][j-1] < 0) ||
(gdb)
```

Here, we see several things. First of all, there is a loop across the two index variables i and j, presumably in order to do calculations on the input image. Line 31 is an attempt to reference data from image[i][j], a two-dimensional array. When a program dumps core while attempting to access data from an array, it's usually a sign that one of the indices is out of bounds. Let's check them:

```
(gdb) print i
$1 = 1
(gdb) print j
$2 = 1194
(gdb) print xmax
$3 = 1551
(gdb) print ymax
$4 = 1194
(gdb)
```

Here we see the problem. The program was attempting to reference element image[1][1194], however, the array extends only to image[1550][1193] (remember that arrays in C are indexed from 0 to *max-1*). In other words, we attempted to read the 1195th row of an image that has only 1194 rows.

If we look at lines 29 and 30, we see the problem: the values xmax and ymax are reversed. The variable j should range from 1 to ymax (because it is the row index of the array), and i should range from 1 to xmax. Fixing the two for loops on lines 29 and 30 corrects the problem.

Let's say that your program is crashing within a function that is called from many different locations, and you want to determine where the function was invoked from and what situation led up to the crash. The *backtrace* command displays the *call stack* of the program at the time of failure. If you are like the author of this section and are too lazy to type backtrace all the time, you will be delighted to hear that you can also use the shortcut *bt*.

The call stack is the list of functions that led up to the current one. For example, if the program starts in function *main*, which calls function *foo*, which calls *bamf*, the call stack looks like this:

```
(gdb) backtrace
#0  0x1384 in bamf () at goop.c:31
#1  0x4280 in foo () at goop.c:48
#2  0x218 in main () at goop.c:116
(gdb)
```

As each function is called, it pushes certain data onto the stack, such as saved registers, function arguments, local variables, and so forth. Each function has a certain amount of space allocated on the stack for its use. The chunk of memory on the stack for a particular function is called a *stack frame*, and the call stack is the ordered list of stack frames.

In the following example, we are looking at a core file for an X-based animation program. Using *backtrace* gives us:

```
(gdb) backtrace
#0  0x602b4982 in _end ()
#1  0xbffff934 in _end ()
#2  0x13c6 in stream_drawimage (wgt=0x38330000, sn=4)\
at stream_display.c:94
#3  0x1497 in stream_refresh_all () at stream_display.c:116
#4  0x49c in control_update_all () at control_init.c:73
#5  0x224 in play_timeout (Cannot access memory at address 0x602b7676.
(gdb)
```

This is a list of stack frames for the process. The most recently called function is frame 0, which is the "function" _end in this case. Here, we see that *play_timeout* called *control_update_all*, which called *stream_refresh_all*, and so on. Somehow, the program jumped to *_end* where it crashed.

However, *_end* is not a function; it is simply a label that specifies the end of the process data segment. When a program branches to an address such as *_end*, which is not a real function, it is a sign that something must have caused the process to go haywire, corrupting the call stack. (This is known in hacker jargon as "jumping to hyperspace.") In fact, the error "Cannot access memory at address 0x602b7676" is another indication that something bizarre has occurred.

We can see, however, that the last "real" function called was *stream_drawimage*, and we might guess that it is the source of the problem. To examine the state of *stream_drawimage*, we need to select its stack frame (frame number 2), using the *frame* command:

```
(gdb) frame 2
#2  0x13c6 in stream_drawimage (wgt=0x38330000, sn=4)\
at stream_display.c:94
94          XCopyArea(mydisplay,streams[sn].frames[currentframe],\
XtWindow(wgt),
(gdb) list
91
92          printf("CopyArea frame %d, sn %d, wid %d\n",currentframe,sn,wgt);
93
94          XCopyArea(mydisplay,streams[sn].frames[currentframe],\
XtWindow(wgt),
95                    picGC,0,0,streams[sn].width,streams[sn].height,0,0);
(gdb)
```

Well, not knowing anything else about the program at hand, we can't see anything wrong here, unless the variable sn (being used as an index into the array streams) is out of range. From the output of *frame*, we see that *stream_drawimage* was called with an sn parameter of 4. (Function parameters are displayed in the output of *backtrace*, as well as whenever we change frames.)

Let's move up another frame, to *stream_refresh_all*, to see how *stream_display* was called. To do this, we use the *up* command, which selects the stack frame above the current one:

```
(gdb) up
#3  0x1497 in stream_refresh_all () at stream_display.c:116
116           stream_drawimage(streams[i].drawbox,i);
(gdb) list
113     void stream_refresh_all(void) {
114        int i;
115        for (i=0; i<=numstreams; i++) {
116           stream_drawimage(streams[i].drawbox,i);
117
(gdb) print i
$2 = 4
(gdb) print numstreams
$3 = 4
(gdb)
```

Here, we see that the index variable i is looping from 0 to numstreams, and indeed i here is 4, the second parameter to *stream_drawimage*. However, numstreams is also 4. What's going on?

The for loop on line 115 looks funny; it should read:

```
for (i=0; i<numstreams; i++) {
```

The error is in the use of the <= comparison operator. The streams array is indexed from 0 to numstreams-1, not from 0 to numstreams. This simple off-by-one error caused the program to go berserk.

As you can see, using *gdb* with a core dump allows you to browse through the image of a crashed program to find bugs. Never again will you delete those pesky core files, right?

Debugging a Running Program

gdb can also debug a program that is already running, allowing you to interrupt it, examine it, and then return the process to its regularly scheduled execution. This is very similar to running a program from within *gdb*, and there are only a few new commands to learn.

The *attach* command attaches *gdb* to a running process. In order to use *attach* you must also have access to the executable that corresponds to the process.

For example, if you have started the program *pgmseq* with process ID 254, you can start up *gdb* with:

```
papaya$ gdb pgmseq
```

and once inside *gdb*, use the command:

```
(gdb) attach 254
Attaching program `/home/loomer/mdw/pgmseq/pgmseq', pid 254
__select (nd=4, in=0xbffff96c, out=0xbffff94c, ex=0xbffff92c, tv=0x0)
    at __select.c:22
__select.c:22: No such file or directory.
(gdb)
```

The No such file or directory error is given because *gdb* can't locate the source file for *__select*. This is often the case with system calls and library functions, and it's nothing to worry about.

You can also start *gdb* with the command:

```
papaya$ gdb pgmseq 254
```

Once *gdb* attaches to the running process, it temporarily suspends the program and lets you take over, issuing *gdb* commands. Or you can set a breakpoint or watchpoint (with the *break* and *watch* commands) and use *continue* to cause the program to continue execution until the breakpoint is triggered.

The *detach* command detaches *gdb* from the running process. You can then use *attach* again, on another process, if necessary. If you find a bug, you can *detach* the current process, make changes to the source, recompile, and use the *file* command to load the new executable into *gdb*. You can then start the new version of the program and use the *attach* command to debug it. All without leaving *gdb*!

In fact, *gdb* allows you to debug three programs concurrently: one running directly under *gdb*, one tracing with a core file, and one running as an independent process. The *target* command allows you to select which one you wish to debug.

Changing and Examining Data

To examine the values of variables in your program, you can use the *print*, *x*, and *ptype* commands. The *print* command is the most commonly used data inspection command; it takes as an argument an expression in the source language (usually C or C++) and returns its value. For example:

```
(gdb) print mydisplay
$10 = (struct _XDisplay *) 0x9c800
(gdb)
```

This displays the value of the variable mydisplay, as well as an indication of its type. Because this variable is a pointer, you can examine its contents by dereferencing the pointer, as you would in C:

```
(gdb) print *mydisplay
$11 = {ext_data = 0x0, free_funcs = 0x99c20, fd = 5, lock = 0,
   proto_major_version = 11, proto_minor_version = 0,
   vendor = 0x9dff0 "XFree86", resource_base = 41943040,
   ...
   error_vec = 0x0, cms = {defaultCCCs = 0xa3d80 "",\
clientCmaps = 0x991a0 "'",
      perVisualIntensityMaps = 0x0}, conn_checker = 0, im_filters = 0x0}
(gdb)
```

mydisplay is an extensive structure used by X programs; we have abbreviated the output for your reading enjoyment.

print can print the value of just about any expression, including C function calls (which it executes on the fly, within the context of the running program):

```
(gdb) print getpid( )
$11 = 138
(gdb)
```

Of course, not all functions may be called in this manner. Only those functions that have been linked to the running program may be called. If a function has not been linked to the program and you attempt to call it, *gdb* will complain that there is no such symbol in the current context.

More complicated expressions may be used as arguments to *print* as well, including assignments to variables. For example:

```
(gdb) print mydisplay->vendor = "Linux"
$19 = 0x9de70 "Linux"
(gdb)
```

assigns to the vendor member of the mydisplay structure the value "Linux" instead of "XFree86" (a useless modification, but interesting nonetheless). In this way, you can interactively change data in a running program to correct errant behavior or test uncommon situations.

Note that after each *print* command, the value displayed is assigned to one of the *gdb* convenience registers, which are *gdb* internal variables that may be handy for you to use. For example, to recall the value of mydisplay in the previous example, we need to merely print the value of $10:

```
(gdb) print $10
$21 = (struct _XDisplay *) 0x9c800
(gdb)
```

You may also use expressions, such as typecasts, with the *print* command. Almost anything goes.

The *ptype* command gives you detailed (and often long-winded) information about a variable's type or the definition of a struct or typedef. To get a full definition for the struct _XDisplay used by the mydisplay variable, we use:

```
(gdb) ptype mydisplay
type = struct _XDisplay {
    struct _XExtData *ext_data;
    struct _XFreeFuncs *free_funcs;
    int fd;
    int lock;
    int proto_major_version;
    ...
    struct _XIMFilter *im_filters;
} *
(gdb)
```

If you're interested in examining memory on a more fundamental level, beyond the petty confines of defined types, you can use the *x* command. *x* takes a memory address as an argument. If you give it a variable, it uses the *value* of that variable as the address.

x also takes a count and a type specification as an optional argument. The count is the number of objects of the given type to display. For example, x/100x 0x4200 displays 100 bytes of data, represented in hexadecimal format, at the address 0x4200. Use *help x* to get a description of the various output formats.

To examine the value of mydisplay->vendor, we can use:

```
(gdb) x mydisplay->vendor
0x9de70 <_end+35376>:    76 'L'
(gdb) x/6c mydisplay->vendor
0x9de70 <_end+35376>:    76 'L'  105 'i' 110 'n' 117 'u' 120 'x' 0 '\000'
(gdb) x/s mydisplay->vendor
0x9de70 <_end+35376>:    "Linux"
(gdb)
```

The first field of each line gives the absolute address of the data. The second represents the address as some symbol (in this case, _end) plus an offset in bytes. The remaining fields give the actual value of memory at that address, first in decimal, then as an ASCII character. As described earlier you can force *x* to print the data in other formats.

Getting Information

The *info* command provides information about the status of the program being debugged. There are many subcommands under *info*; use *help info* to see them all. For example, *info program* displays the execution status of the program:

```
(gdb) info program
Using the running image of child process 138.
Program stopped at 0x9e.
It stopped at breakpoint 1.
(gdb)
```

Another useful command is *info locals*, which displays the names and values of all local variables in the current function:

```
(gdb) info locals
inimage = (struct {...} *) 0x2000
outimage = (struct {...} *) 0x8000
(gdb)
```

This is a rather cursory description of the variables. The *print* or *x* commands describe them further.

Similarly, *info variables* displays a list of all known variables in the program, ordered by source file. Note that many of the variables displayed will be from sources outside of your actual program—for example, the names of variables used within the library code. The values for these variables are not displayed because the list is culled more or less directly from the executable's symbol table. Only those local variables in the current stack frame and global (static) variables are actually accessible from *gdb*. *info address* gives you information about exactly where a certain variable is stored. For example:

```
(gdb) info address inimage
Symbol "inimage" is a local variable at frame offset -20.
(gdb)
```

By frame offset, *gdb* means that *inimage* is stored 20 bytes below the top of the stack frame.

You can get information on the current frame using the *info frame* command, as so:

```
(gdb) info frame
Stack level 0, frame at 0xbffffaa8:
 eip = 0x9e in main (main.c:44); saved eip 0x34
 source language c.
 Arglist at 0xbffffaa8, args: argc=1, argv=0xbffffabc
 Locals at 0xbffffaa8, Previous frame's sp is 0x0

 Saved registers:
  ebx at 0xbffffaa0, ebp at 0xbffffaa8, esi at 0xbffffaa4, eip at\
0xbffffaac
(gdb)
```

This kind of information is useful if you're debugging at the assembly-language level with the *disass*, *nexti*, and *stepi* commands (see the section "Instruction-level debugging").

Miscellaneous Features

We have barely scratched the surface of what *gdb* can do. It is an amazing program with a lot of power; we have introduced you only to the most commonly used commands. In this section, we'll look at other features of *gdb* and then send you on your way.

If you're interested in learning more about *gdb*, we encourage you to read the *gdb* manual page and the Free Software Foundation manual. The manual is also available as an online Info file. (Info files may be read under Emacs, or using the *info* reader; see the section "Tutorial and Online Help" in Chapter 9 for details.)

Breakpoints and watchpoints

As promised, we're going to demonstrate further use of breakpoints and watchpoints. Breakpoints are set with the *break* command; similarly, watchpoints are set with the *watch* command. The only difference between the two is that breakpoints must break at a particular location in the program—on a certain line of code, for example—and watchpoints may be triggered whenever a certain expression is true, regardless of location within the program. Though powerful, watchpoints can be horribly inefficient; any time the state of the program changes, all watchpoints must be reevaluated.

When a breakpoint or watchpoint is triggered, *gdb* suspends the program and returns control to you. Breakpoints and watchpoints allow you to run the program (using the *run* and *continue* commands) and stop only in certain situations, thus saving you the trouble of using many *next* and *step* commands to walk through the program manually.

There are many ways to set a breakpoint in the program. You can specify a line number, as in *break 20*. Or, you can specify a particular function, as in *break stream_unload*. You can also specify a line number in another source file, as in *break foo.c:38*. Use *help break* to see the complete syntax.

Breakpoints may be conditional; that is, the breakpoint triggers only when a certain expression is true. For example, using the command:

```
break 184 if (status == 0)
```

sets a conditional breakpoint at line 184 in the current source file, which triggers only when the variable status is zero. The variable status must be either a global variable or a local variable in the current stack frame. The expression may be any valid expression in the source language that *gdb* understands, identical to the expressions used by the *print* command. You can change the breakpoint condition (if it is conditional) using the *condition* command.

Using the command *info break* gives you a list of all breakpoints and watchpoints and their status. This allows you to delete or disable breakpoints, using the commands *clear*, *delete*, or *disable*. A disabled breakpoint is merely inactive, until you reenable it (with the *enable* command). A breakpoint that has been deleted, on the other hand, is gone from the list of breakpoints for good. You can also specify that a breakpoint be enabled once; meaning that once it is triggered, it will be disabled again.

To set a watchpoint, use the *watch* command, as in:

```
watch (numticks < 1024 && incoming != clear)
```

Watchpoint conditions may be any valid source expression, as with conditional breakpoints.

Instruction-level debugging

gdb is capable of debugging on the processor-instruction level, allowing you to watch the innards of your program with great scrutiny. However, understanding what you see requires not only knowledge of the processor architecture and assembly language, but also some gist of how the operating system sets up process address space. For example, it helps to understand the conventions used for setting up stack frames, calling functions, passing parameters and return values, and so on. Any book on protected-mode 80386/80486 programming can fill you in on these details. But be warned: protected-mode programming on this processor is quite different from real-mode programming (as is used in the MS-DOS world). Be sure that you're reading about native *protected-mode* '386 programming, or else you might subject yourself to terminal confusion.

The primary *gdb* commands used for instruction-level debugging are *nexti*, *stepi*, and *disass*. *nexti* is equivalent to *next*, except that it steps to the next instruction, not the next source line. Similarly, *stepi* is the instruction-level analog of *step*.

The *disass* command displays a disassembly of an address range that you supply. This address range may be specified by literal address or function name. For example, to display a disassembly of the function *play_timeout*, use the command:

```
(gdb) disass play_timeout
Dump of assembler code for function play_timeout:
to 0x2ac:
0x21c <play_timeout>:         pushl  %ebp
0x21d <play_timeout+1>:       movl   %esp,%ebp
0x21f <play_timeout+3>:       call   0x494 <control_update_all>
0x224 <play_timeout+8>:       movl   0x952f4,%eax
0x229 <play_timeout+13>:      decl   %eax
0x22a <play_timeout+14>:      cmpl   %eax,0x9530c
0x230 <play_timeout+20>:      jne    0x24c <play_timeout+48>
```

```
0x232 <play_timeout+22>:        jmp     0x29c <play_timeout+128>
0x234 <play_timeout+24>:        nop
0x235 <play_timeout+25>:        nop
...

0x2a8 <play_timeout+140>:       addb    %al,(%eax)
0x2aa <play_timeout+142>:       addb    %al,(%eax)
(gdb)
```

This is equivalent to using the command *disass 0x21c* (where 0x21c is the literal address of the beginning of *play_timeout*).

You can specify an optional second argument to *disass*, which will be used as the address where disassembly should stop. Using *disass 0x21c 0x232* will display only the first seven lines of the assembly listing in the previous example (the instruction starting with 0x232 itself will not be displayed).

If you use *nexti* and *stepi* often, you may wish to use the command:

```
display/i $pc
```

This causes the current instruction to be displayed after every *nexti* or *stepi* command. *display* specifies variables to watch or commands to execute after every stepping command. $pc is a *gdb* internal register that corresponds to the processor's program counter, pointing to the current instruction.

Using Emacs with gdb

Emacs (described in the section "The Emacs Editor" in Chapter 9) provides a debugging mode that lets you run *gdb*—or another debugger—within the integrated program-tracing environment provided by Emacs. This so-called "Grand Unified Debugger" library is very powerful and allows you to debug and edit your programs entirely within Emacs.

To start *gdb* under Emacs, use the Emacs command M-x gdb and give the name of the executable to debug as the argument. A buffer will be created for *gdb*, which is similar to using *gdb* alone. You can then use *core-file* to load a core file or *attach* to attach to a running process, if you wish.

Whenever you step to a new frame (when you first trigger a breakpoint), *gdb* opens a separate window that displays the source corresponding to the current stack frame. You may use this buffer to edit the source text just as you normally would with Emacs, but the current source line is highlighted with an arrow (the characters =>). This allows you to watch the source in one window and execute *gdb* commands in the other.

Within the debugging window, you can use several special key sequences. They are fairly long, though, so it's not clear that you'll find them more convenient than just entering *gdb* commands directly. Some of the more common commands include:

C-x C-a C-s
    The equivalent of a *gdb step* command, updating the source window appropriately

---

`C-x C-a C-i`
> The equivalent of a *stepi* command

`C-x C-a C-n`
> The equivalent of a *next* command

`C-x C-a C-r`
> The equivalent of a *continue* command

`C-x C-a <`
> The equivalent of an *up* command

`C-x C-a >`
> The equivalent of a *down* command

If you do enter commands in the traditional manner, you can use M-p to move backward to previously issued commands and M-n to move forward. You can also move around in the buffer using Emacs commands for searching, cursor movement, and so on. All in all, using *gdb* within Emacs is more convenient than using it from the shell.

In addition, you may edit the source text in the *gdb* source buffer; the prefix arrow will not be present in the source when it is saved.

Emacs is very easy to customize, and you can write many extensions to this *gdb* interface yourself. You can define Emacs keys for other commonly used *gdb* commands or change the behavior of the source window. (For example, you can highlight all breakpoints in some fashion or provide keys to disable or clear breakpoints.)

Programming Tools

Along with languages and compilers, there is a plethora of programming tools out there, including libraries, interface builders, debuggers, and other utilities to aid the programming process. In this section, we'll talk about some of the most interesting bells and whistles of these tools to let you know what's available.

Debuggers

Several interactive debuggers are available for Linux. The de facto standard debugger is *gdb*, which we just covered in detail.

In addition to *gdb*, there are several other debuggers, each with features very similar to *gdb*. *xxgdb* is a version of *gdb* with an X Window System interface similar to that found on the *xdbx* debugger on other Unix systems. There are several panes in the *xxgdb* debugger's window. One pane looks like the regular *gdb* text interface, allowing you to input commands manually to interact with the system. Another pane automatically displays the current source file along with a marker displaying the current line. You can use the source pane to set and select breakpoints, browse the source, and so on, while typing commands directly to *gdb*. The *xxgdb* window also contains several buttons that provide quick access to frequently used commands, such as *step*, *next*, and so on. Given the buttons, you can use the mouse in conjunction with the keyboard to debug your program within an easy-to-use X interface.

Two other graphical frontends for *gdb* deserve mention. DDD, the Data Display Debugger, has the same features as *xxgdb* but with a nicer, Motif user interface. In addition, it can display structures and classes in a graphical manner, which is especially useful if you want to explore the data structures of an unknown program. *kdbg* comes from the KDE project and—in addition to the features that *xxgdb* provides—is fully integrated into the KDE desktop.

Profiling and Performance Tools

There are several utilities out there that allow you to monitor and rate the performance of your program. These tools help you locate bottlenecks in your code—places where performance is lacking. These tools also give you a rundown on the call structure of your program, indicating what functions are called, from where, and how often (in other words, everything you ever wanted to know about your program, but were afraid to ask).

gprof is a profiling utility that gives you a detailed listing of the running statistics for your program, including how often each function was called, from where, the total amount of time that each function required, and so forth.

In order to use *gprof* with a program, you must compile the program using the *–pg* option with *gcc*. This adds profiling information to the object file and links the executable with standard libraries that have profiling information enabled.

Having compiled the program to profile with *–pg*, simply run it. If it exits normally, the file *gmon.out* will be written to the working directory of the program. This file contains profiling information for that run and can be used with *gprof* to display a table of statistics.

As an example, let's take a program called *getstat*, which gathers statistics about an image file. After compiling *getstat* with *–pg*, and run it:

```
papaya$ getstat image11.pgm > stats.dat
papaya$ ls -l gmon.out
-rw-------   1 mdw      mdw          54448 Feb  5 17:00 gmon.out
papaya$
```

Indeed, the profiling information was written to *gmon.out*.

To examine the profiling data, we run *gprof* and give it the name of the executable and the profiling file *gmon.out*:

```
papaya$ gprof getstat gmon.out
```

If you do not specify the name of the profiling file, *gprof* assumes the name *gmon.out*. It also assumes the executable name *a.out* if you do not specify that, either.

gprof output is rather verbose, so you may want to redirect it to a file or pipe it through a pager. It comes in two parts. The first part is the "flat profile," which gives a one-line entry for each function, listing the percentage of time spent in that function, the time (in seconds) used to execute that function, the number of calls to the function, and other information. For example:

```
Each sample counts as 0.01 seconds.
  %   cumulative   self              self     total
 time   seconds   seconds    calls  ms/call  ms/call  name
45.11     27.49     27.49       41   670.51   903.13  GetComponent
16.25     37.40      9.91                              mcount
10.72     43.93      6.54  1811863     0.00     0.00  Push
10.33     50.23      6.30  1811863     0.00     0.00  Pop
 5.87     53.81      3.58       40    89.50   247.06  stackstats
 4.92     56.81      3.00  1811863     0.00     0.00  TrimNeighbors
```

If any of the fields are blank in the output, *gprof* was unable to determine any further information about that function. This is usually caused by parts of the code that were not compiled with the *–pg* option; for example, if you call routines in nonstandard libraries that haven't been compiled with *–pg*, *gprof* won't be able to gather much information about those routines. In the previous output, the function *mcount* probably hasn't been compiled with profiling enabled.

As we can see, 45.11% of the total running time was spent in the function *GetComponent*—which amounts to 27.49 seconds. But is this because *GetComponent* is horribly inefficient or because *GetComponent* itself called many other slow functions? The functions *Push* and *Pop* were called many times during execution: could they be the culprits?[*]

The second part of the *gprof* report can help us here. It gives a detailed "call graph" describing which functions called other functions and how many times they were called. For example:

```
index % time    self  children    called     name
                                             <spontaneous>
[1]     92.7    0.00    47.30                 start [1]
                0.01    47.29     1/1             main [2]
                0.00     0.00     1/2             on_exit [53]
                0.00     0.00     1/1             exit [172]
```

The first column of the call graph is the index: a unique number given to every function, allowing you to find other functions in the graph. Here, the first function, *start*, is called implicitly when the program begins. *start* required 92.7% of the total running time (47.30 seconds), including its children, but required very little time to run itself. This is because *start* is the parent of all other functions in the program, including *main*; it makes sense that *start* plus its children require that percentage of time.

---

[*] Always a possibility where this author's code is concerned!

The call graph normally displays the children as well as the parents of each function in the graph. Here, we can see that *start* called the functions *main*, *on_exit*, and *exit* (listed below the line for *start*). However, there are no parents (normally listed above *start*); instead, we see the ominous word <spontaneous>. This means that *gprof* was unable to determine the parent function of *start*; more than likely because *start* was not called from within the program itself but kicked off by the operating system.

Skipping down to the entry for *GetComponent*, or function-under-suspect, we see the following:

```
index % time    self  children    called     name
                0.67    0.23       1/41           GetFirstComponent [12]
               26.82    9.30      40/41           GetNextComponent [5]
[4]     72.6   27.49    9.54        41        GetComponent [4]
                6.54    0.00 1811863/1811863     Push [7]
                3.00    0.00 1811863/1811863     TrimNeighbors [9]
                0.00    0.00       1/1           InitStack [54]
```

The parent functions of *GetComponent* were *GetFirstComponent* and *GetNextComponent*, and its children were *Push*, *TrimNeighbors*, and *InitStack*. As we can see, *GetComponent* was called 41 times—one time from *GetFirstComponent* and 40 times from *GetNextComponent*. The *gprof* output contains notes that describe the report in more detail.

GetComponent itself requires more than 27.49 seconds to run; only 9.54 seconds are spent executing the children of *GetComponent* (including the many calls to *Push* and *TrimNeighbors*!). So it looks as though *GetComponent* and possibly its parent *GetNextComponent* need some tuning; the oft-called *Push* function is not the sole cause of the problem.

gprof also keeps track of recursive calls and "cycles" of called functions and indicates the amount of time required for each call. Of course, using *gprof* effectively requires that all code to be profiled is compiled with the –*pg* option. It also requires a knowledge of the program you're attempting to profile; *gprof* can tell you only so much about what's going on. It's up to the programmer to optimize inefficient code.

One last note about *gprof*: running it on a program that calls only a few functions—and runs very quickly—may not give you meaningful results. The units used for timing execution are usually rather coarse—maybe one one-hundredth of a second—and if many functions in your program run more quickly than that, *gprof* will be unable to distinguish between their respective running times (rounding them to the nearest hundredth of a second). In order to get good profiling information, you may need to run your program under unusual circumstances—for example, giving it an unusually large data set to churn on, as in the previous example.

If *gprof* is more than you need, *calls* is a program that displays a tree of all function calls in your C source code. This can be useful to either generate an index of all called functions or produce a high-level hierarchical report of the structure of a program.

Use of *calls* is simple: you tell it the names of the source files to map out, and a function-call tree is displayed. For example:

```
papaya$ calls scan.c
  1    level1 [scan.c]
  2        getid [scan.c]
  3            getc
  4            eatwhite [scan.c]
  5                getc
  6                ungetc
  7            strcmp
  8        eatwhite [see line 4]
  9        balance [scan.c]
 10            eatwhite [see line 4]
```

By default, *calls* lists only one instance of each called function at each level of the tree (so that if *printf* is called five times in a given function, it is listed only once). The *–a* switch prints all instances. *calls* has several other options as well; using *calls –h* gives you a summary.

Using strace

strace is a tool that displays the system calls being executed by a running program.[*] This can be extremely useful for real-time monitoring of a program's activity, although it does take some knowledge of programming at the system-call level. For example, when the library routine *printf* is used within a program, *strace* displays information only about the underlying *write* system call when it is executed. Also, *strace* can be quite verbose: many system calls are executed within a program that the programmer may not be aware of. However, *strace* is a good way to quickly determine the cause of a program crash or other strange failure.

Take the "Hello, World!" program given earlier in the chapter. Running *strace* on the executable *hello* gives us:

```
papaya$ strace hello
execve("./hello", ["hello"], [/* 49 vars */]) = 0
mmap(0, 4096, PROT_READ|PROT_WRITE, MAP_PRIVATE|MAP_ANONYMOUS,\
  -1, 0) = 0x40007000
mprotect(0x40000000, 20881, PROT_READ|PROT_WRITE|PROT_EXEC) = 0
mprotect(0x8048000, 4922, PROT_READ|PROT_WRITE|PROT_EXEC) = 0
stat("/etc/ld.so.cache", {st_mode=S_IFREG|0644, st_size=18612,\
  ...}) = 0
open("/etc/ld.so.cache", O_RDONLY)      = 3
mmap(0, 18612, PROT_READ, MAP_SHARED, 3, 0) = 0x40008000
close(3)                                = 0
stat("/etc/ld.so.preload", 0xbffff52c)  = -1 ENOENT (No such\
```

---

[*] You may also find the *ltrace* package useful. It's a library call tracer that tracks all library calls, not just calls to the kernel. Several distributions already include it; users of other distributions can download the latest version of the source at *ftp://ftp.debian.org/debian/dists/unstable/main/source/utils/*.

```
 file or directory)
open("/usr/local/KDE/lib/libc.so.5", O_RDONLY) = -1 ENOENT (No\
 such file or directory)
open("/usr/local/qt/lib/libc.so.5", O_RDONLY) = -1 ENOENT (No\
 such file or directory)
open("/lib/libc.so.5", O_RDONLY)        = 3
read(3, "\177ELF\1\1\1\0\0\0\0\0\0\0\0\0\3"..., 4096) = 4096
mmap(0, 770048, PROT_NONE, MAP_PRIVATE|MAP_ANONYMOUS, -1, 0) = \
0x4000d000
mmap(0x4000d000, 538959, PROT_READ|PROT_EXEC, MAP_PRIVATE|MAP_\
FIXED, 3, 0) = 0x4000d000
mmap(0x40091000, 21564, PROT_READ|PROT_WRITE, MAP_PRIVATE|MAP_\
FIXED, 3, 0x83000) = 0x40091000
mmap(0x40097000, 204584, PROT_READ|PROT_WRITE, MAP_PRIVATE|MAP_\
FIXED|MAP_ANONYMOUS, -1, 0) = 0x40097000
close(3)                                = 0
mprotect(0x4000d000, 538959, PROT_READ|PROT_WRITE|PROT_EXEC) = 0
munmap(0x40008000, 18612)               = 0
mprotect(0x8048000, 4922, PROT_READ|PROT_EXEC) = 0
mprotect(0x4000d000, 538959, PROT_READ|PROT_EXEC) = 0
mprotect(0x40000000, 20881, PROT_READ|PROT_EXEC) = 0
personality(PER_LINUX)                  = 0
geteuid()                               = 501
getuid()                                = 501
getgid()                                = 100
getegid()                               = 100
fstat(1, {st_mode=S_IFCHR|0666, st_rdev=makedev(3, 10), ...}) = 0
mmap(0, 4096, PROT_READ|PROT_WRITE, MAP_PRIVATE|MAP_ANONYMOUS,\
 -1, 0) = 0x40008000
ioctl(1, TCGETS, {B9600 opost isig icanon echo ...}) = 0
write(1, "Hello World!\n", 13Hello World!
)               = 13
_exit(0)                                = ?
papaya$
```

This may be much more than you expected to see from a simple program. Let's walk through it, briefly, to explain what's going on.

The first call *execve* starts the program. All the *mmap*, *mprotect*, and *munmap* calls come from the kernel's memory management and are not really interesting here. In the three consecutive *open* calls, the loader is looking for the C library and finds it on the third try. The library header is then read and the library mapped into memory. After a few more memory-management operations and the calls to *geteuid, getuid, getgid,* and *getegid*, which retrieve the rights of the process, there is a call to *ioctl*. The *ioctl* is the result of a *tcgetattr* library call, which the program uses to retrieve the terminal attributes before attempting to write to the terminal. Finally, the *write* call prints our friendly message to the terminal and *exit* ends the program.

The calls to *munmap* (which unmaps a memory-mapped portion of a file) and *brk* (which allocates memory on the heap) set up the memory image of the running process. The *ioctl* call is the result of a *tcgetattr* library call, which retrieves the terminal attributes before attempting to write to it. Finally, the *write* call prints our friendly message to the terminal, and *exit* ends the program.

strace sends its output to standard error, so you can redirect it to a file separate from the actual output of the program (usually sent to standard output). As you can see, *strace* tells you not only the names of the system calls, but also their parameters (expressed as well-known constant names, if possible, instead of just numerics) and return values.

Using Valgrind

Valgrind is a replacement for the various memory-allocation routines, such as *malloc*, *realloc*, and *free*, used by C programs, but it also supports C++ programs. It provides smarter memory-allocation procedures and code to detect illegal memory accesses and common faults, such as attempting to free a block of memory more than once. Valgrind displays detailed error messages if your program attempts any kind of hazardous memory access, helping you to catch segmentation faults in your program before they happen. It can also detect memory leaks—for example, places in the code where new memory is *malloc*'d without being *free*'d after use.

Valgrind is not just a replacement for *malloc* and friends. It also inserts code into your program to verify all memory reads and writes. It is very robust and therefore considerably slower than the regular *malloc* routines. Valgrind is meant to be used during program development and testing; once all potential memory-corrupting bugs have been fixed, you can run your program without it.

For example, take the following program, which allocates some memory and attempts to do various nasty things with it:

```
#include <malloc.h>
int main( ) {
  char *thememory, ch;

  thememory=(char *)malloc(10*sizeof(char));

  ch=thememory[1];      /* Attempt to read uninitialized memory */
  thememory[12]=' ';    /* Attempt to write after the block */
  ch=thememory[-2];     /* Attempt to read before the block */
}
```

To find these errors, we simply compile the program for debugging and run it by prepending the *valgrind* command to the command line:

```
owl$ gcc -g -o nasty nasty.c
owl$ valgrind nasty
==18037== valgrind-20020319, a memory error detector for x86 GNU/Linux.
==18037== Copyright (C) 2000-2002, and GNU GPL'd, by Julian Seward.
==18037== For more details, rerun with: -v
==18037==
```

```
==18037== Invalid write of size 1
==18037==    at 0x8048487: main (nasty.c:8)
==18037==    by 0x402D67EE: __libc_start_main (in /lib/libc.so.6)
==18037==    by 0x8048381: __libc_start_main@@GLIBC_2.0 (in /home/kalle/tmp/nasty)
==18037==    by <bogus frame pointer> ???
==18037==    Address 0x41B2A030 is 2 bytes after a block of size 10 alloc'd
==18037==    at 0x40065CFB: malloc (vg_clientmalloc.c:618)
==18037==    by 0x8048470: main (nasty.c:5)
==18037==    by 0x402D67EE: __libc_start_main (in /lib/libc.so.6)
==18037==    by 0x8048381: __libc_start_main@@GLIBC_2.0 (in /home/kalle/tmp/nasty)
==18037==
==18037== Invalid read of size 1
==18037==    at 0x804848D: main (nasty.c:9)
==18037==    by 0x402D67EE: __libc_start_main (in /lib/libc.so.6)
==18037==    by 0x8048381: __libc_start_main@@GLIBC_2.0 (in /home/kalle/tmp/nasty)
==18037==    by <bogus frame pointer> ???
==18037==    Address 0x41B2A022 is 2 bytes before a block of size 10 alloc'd
==18037==    at 0x40065CFB: malloc (vg_clientmalloc.c:618)
==18037==    by 0x8048470: main (nasty.c:5)
==18037==    by 0x402D67EE: __libc_start_main (in /lib/libc.so.6)
==18037==    by 0x8048381: __libc_start_main@@GLIBC_2.0 (in /home/kalle/tmp/nasty)
==18037==
==18037== ERROR SUMMARY: 2 errors from 2 contexts (suppressed: 0 from 0)
==18037== malloc/free: in use at exit: 10 bytes in 1 blocks.
==18037== malloc/free: 1 allocs, 0 frees, 10 bytes allocated.
==18037== For a detailed leak analysis,  rerun with: --leak-check=yes
==18037== For counts of detected errors, rerun with: -v
```

The figure at the start of each line indicates the process ID; if your process spawns other processes, even those will be run under Valgrind's control.

For each memory violation, Valgrind reports an error and gives us information on what happened. The actual Valgrind error messages include information on where the program is executing as well as where the memory block was allocated. You can coax even more information out of Valgrind if you wish, and, along with a debugger such as *gdb*, you can pinpoint problems easily.

You may ask why the reading operation in line 7, where an initialized piece of memory is read has not led Valgrind to emit an error message. This is because Valgrind won't complain if you pass around initialized memory, but it still keeps track of it. As soon as you use the value (e.g., by passing it to an operating system function or by manipulating it), you receive the expected error message.

Valgrind also provides a garbage collector and detector you can call from within your program. In brief, the garbage detector informs you of any memory leaks: places where a function *malloc*'d a block of memory but forgot to *free* it before returning. The garbage collector routine walks through the heap and cleans up the results of these leaks. Here is an example of the output:

```
owl$ valgrind --leak-check=yes --show-reachable=yes nasty
...
```

```
==18081== ERROR SUMMARY: 2 errors from 2 contexts (suppressed: 0 from 0)
==18081== malloc/free: in use at exit: 10 bytes in 1 blocks.
==18081== malloc/free: 1 allocs, 0 frees, 10 bytes allocated.
==18081== For counts of detected errors, rerun with: -v
==18081== searching for pointers to 1 not-freed blocks.
==18081== checked 4029376 bytes.
==18081==
==18081== definitely lost: 0 bytes in 0 blocks.
==18081== possibly lost:   0 bytes in 0 blocks.
==18081== still reachable: 10 bytes in 1 blocks.
==18081==
==18081== 10 bytes in 1 blocks are still reachable in loss record 1 of 1
==18081==    at 0x40065CFB: malloc (vg_clientmalloc.c:618)
==18081==    by 0x8048470: main (nasty.c:5)
==18081==    by 0x402D67EE: __libc_start_main (in /lib/libc.so.6)
==18081==    by 0x8048381: __libc_start_main@@GLIBC_2.0 (in /home/kalle/tmp/nasty)
==18081==
==18081== LEAK SUMMARY:
==18081==    possibly lost:   0 bytes in 0 blocks.
==18081==    definitely lost: 0 bytes in 0 blocks.
==18081==    still reachable: 10 bytes in 1 blocks.
==18081==
```

Interface Building Tools

A number of applications and libraries let you easily generate a user interface for your applications under the X Window System. If you do not want to bother with the complexity of the X programming interface, using one of these simple interface-building tools may be the answer for you. There are also tools for producing a text-based interface for programs that don't require X.

The classic X programming model has attempted to be as general as possible, providing only the bare minimum of interface restrictions and assumptions. This generality allows programmers to build their own interface from scratch, as the core X libraries don't make any assumptions about the interface in advance. The X Toolkit Intrinsics (Xt) provides a rudimentary set of interface widgets (such as simple buttons, scrollbars, and the like), as well as a general interface for writing your own widgets if necessary. Unfortunately this can require a great deal of work for programmers who would rather use a set of premade interface routines. A number of Xt widget sets and programming libraries are available for Linux, all of which make the user interface easier to program.

In addition, the commercial Motif library and widget set is available from several vendors for an inexpensive single-user license fee. Also available is the XView library and widget interface, which is another alternative to using Xt for building interfaces under X. XView and Motif are two sets of X-based programming libraries that in some ways are easier to program than the X Toolkit Intrinsics. Many applications are available that utilize Motif and XView, such as XVhelp (a system for generating interactive hypertext help for your program). Binaries statically linked with Motif may be distributed freely and used by people who don't own Motif.

Before you start developing with XView or Motif, a word of caution is in order. XView, which was once a commercial product of Sun Microsystems, has been dropped by the developers and is no longer maintained. Also, while some people like the look, the programs written with XView look very nonstandard. Motif, on the other hand, is still being actively developed (albeit rather slowly), but it also has some problems. First, programming with Motif can be frustrating. It is difficult, error-prone, and cumbersome since the Motif API was not designed according to modern GUI API design principles. Also, Motif programs tend to run very slowly. For these reasons, you might want to consider one of the following:

Xaw3D
> A modified version of the standard Athena widget set which provides a 3D, Motif-like look and feel

Qt
> A C++ GUI toolkit written by the Norwegian company Troll Tech

GTK
> A C GUI toolkit that was originally written for the image manipulation program GIMP

Many people complain that the Athena widgets are too plain in appearance. Xaw3D is completely compatible with the standard Athena set and can even replace the Athena libraries on your system, giving all programs that use Athena widgets a modern look. Xaw3D also provides a few widgets not found in the Athena set, such as a layout widget with a TeX-like interface for specifying the position of child widgets.

Qt is an excellent package for GUI development in C++ that sports an ingenious mechanism for connecting user interaction with program code, a very fast drawing engine, and a comprehensive but easy-to-use API. Qt is considered by many as the successor to Motif and the de facto GUI programming standard because it is the foundation of the desktop (see "The K Desktop Environment" in Chapter 11), which is the most prominent desktop on today's Linux systems.

Qt is a commercial product, but it is also released under the GPL, meaning that you can use it for free if you write software for Unix (and hence Linux) that is licensed under the GPL as well. In addition, (commercial) Windows and Mac OS X versions of Qt are also available, which makes it possible to develop for Linux, Windows, and Mac OS X at the same time and create an application for another platform by simply recompiling. Imagine being able to develop on your favorite Linux operating system and still being able to target the larger Windows market! One of the authors, Kalle, uses Qt to write both free software (the KDE just mentioned) and commercial software (often cross-platform products that are developed for Linux, Windows, and MacOS X). Qt is being very actively developed; for more information, see *Programming with Qt* by Kalle Dalheimer (O'Reilly). Another exciting recent addition to Qt is that it can run on embedded systems, without the need for an X server. And which operating system would it support on embedded systems if not Embedded Linux!

Expect to see many small devices with graphical screens that run Embedded Linux and Qt/Embedded in the near future.

Qt also comes with a GUI builder called Qt Designer that greatly facilitates the creation of GUI applications. It is included in the GPL version of Qt as well, so if you download Qt (or simply install it from your distribution CDs), you have the Designer right away.

For those who do not like to program in C++, GTK might be a good choice (or you simply use the Python bindings for Qt!). GTK programs usually offer response times that are just as good as those of Qt programs, but the toolkit is not as complete. Documentation is especially lacking. For C-based projects, though, GTK is good alternative if you do not need to be able to recompile your code on Windows. Recently, a Windows port has been developed, but it is not ready for prime time yet.

Many programmers are finding that building a user interface, even with a complete set of widgets and routines in C, requires much overhead and can be quite difficult. This is a question of flexibility versus ease of programming: the easier the interface is to build, the less control the programmer has over it. Many programmers are finding that prebuilt widgets are adequate enough for their needs, so the loss in flexibility is not a problem.

One of the problems with interface generation and X programming is that it is difficult to generalize the most widely used elements of a user interface into a simple programming model. For example, many programs use features such as buttons, dialog boxes, pull-down menus, and so forth, but almost every program uses these widgets in a different context. In simplifying the creation of a graphical interface, generators tend to make assumptions about what you'll want. For example, it is simple enough to specify that a button, when pressed, should execute a certain procedure within your program, but what if you want the button to execute some specialized behavior the programming interface does not allow for? For example, what if you wanted the button to have a different effect when pressed with mouse button 2 instead of mouse button 1? If the interface-building system does not allow for this degree of generality, it is not of much use to programmers who need a powerful, customized interface.

The Tcl/Tk combo, consisting of the scripting language Tcl and the graphical toolkit Tk, has won some popularity, partly because it is so simple to use and provides a good amount of flexibility. Because Tcl and Tk routines can be called from interpreted "scripts" as well as internally from a C program, it is not difficult to tie the interface features provided by this language and toolkit to functionality in the program. Using Tcl and Tk is, on the whole, less demanding than learning to program Xlib and Xt (along with the myriad of widget sets) directly. It should be noted, though, that the larger a project gets, the more likely it is that you will want to use a language like C++ that is more suited toward large-scale development. For several reasons, larger projects tend to become very unwieldy with Tcl: the use of an interpreted language slows the execution of the program, Tcl/Tk design is hard to scale up to large projects, and important reliability features like compile- and link-time type checking are missing. The scaling problem is improved by the use of namespaces (a way to keep names in different parts of the program from clashing) and an object-oriented extension called [incr Tcl].

Tcl and Tk allow you to generate an X-based interface complete with windows, buttons, menus, scrollbars, and the like, around your existing program. You may access the interface from a Tcl script (as described in the section "Other Languages" in Chapter 13) or from within a C program.

If you require a nice text-based interface for a program, several options are available. The GNU *getline* library is a set of routines that provide advanced command-line editing, prompting, command history, and other features used by many programs. As an example, both *bash* and *gdb* use the *getline* library to read user input. *getline* provides the Emacs and *vi*-like command-line editing features found in *bash* and similar programs. (The use of command-line editing within *bash* is described in the section "Typing Shortcuts" in Chapter 4.)

Another option is to write a set of Emacs interface routines for your program. An example of this is the *gdb* Emacs interface, which sets up multiple windows, special key sequences, and so on, within Emacs. The interface is discussed in the earlier section "Using Emacs with gdb." (No changes were required to *gdb* code in order to implement this: look at the Emacs library file *gdb.el* for hints on how this was accomplished.) Emacs allows you to start up a subprogram within a text buffer and provides many routines for parsing and processing text within that buffer. For example, within the Emacs *gdb* interface, the *gdb* source listing output is captured by Emacs and turned into a command that displays the current line of code in another window. Routines written in Emacs LISP process the *gdb* output and take certain actions based on it.

The advantage to using Emacs to interact with text-based programs is that Emacs is a powerful and customizable user interface within itself. The user can easily redefine keys and commands to fit her needs; you don't need to provide these customization features yourself. As long as the text interface of the program is straightforward enough to interact with Emacs, customization is not difficult to accomplish. In addition, many users prefer to do virtually everything within Emacs—from reading electronic mail and news, to compiling and debugging programs. Giving your program an Emacs frontend allows it to be used more easily by people with this mindset. It also allows your program to interact with other programs running under Emacs—for example, you can easily cut and paste between different Emacs text buffers. You can even write entire programs using Emacs LISP, if you wish.

Revision Control Tools—RCS

Revision Control System (RCS) has been ported to Linux. This is a set of programs that allow you to maintain a "library" of files that records a history of revisions, allows source-file locking (in case several people are working on the same project), and automatically keeps track of source-file version numbers. RCS is typically used with program source-code files, but is general enough to be applicable to any type of file where multiple revisions must be maintained.

Why bother with revision control? Many large projects require some kind of revision control in order to keep track of many tiny complex changes to the system. For example, attempting to maintain a program with a thousand source files and a team of several dozen programmers would be nearly impossible without using something like RCS. With RCS, you can ensure that only one person may modify a given source file at any one time, and all changes are checked in along with a log message detailing the change.

RCS is based on the concept of an *RCS file*, a file which acts as a "library" where source files are "checked in" and "checked out." Let's say that you have a source file *importrtf.c* that you want to maintain with RCS. The RCS filename would be *importrtf.c,v* by default. The RCS file contains a history of revisions to the file, allowing you to extract any previous checked-in version of the file. Each revision is tagged with a log message that you provide.

When you check in a file with RCS, revisions are added to the RCS file, and the original file is deleted by default. In order to access the original file, you must check it out from the RCS file. When you're editing a file, you generally don't want someone else to be able to edit it at the same time. Therefore, RCS places a lock on the file when you check it out for editing. Only you, the person who checked out this locked file, can modify it (this is accomplished through file permissions). Once you're done making changes to the source, you check it back in, which allows anyone working on the project to check it back out again for further work. Checking out a file as unlocked does not subject it to these restrictions; generally, files are checked out as locked only when they are to be edited but are checked out as unlocked just for reading (for example, to use the source file in a program build).

RCS automatically keeps track of all previous revisions in the RCS file and assigns incremental version numbers to each new revision that you check in. You can also specify a version number of your own when checking in a file with RCS; this allows you to start a new "revision branch" so that multiple projects can stem from different revisions of the same file. This is a good way to share code between projects but also to assure that changes made to one branch won't be reflected in others.

Here's an example. Take the source file *importrtf.c*, which contains our friendly program:

```
#include <stdio.h>

int main(void) {
  printf("Hello, world!");
}
```

The first step is to check it into RCS with the *ci* command:

```
papaya$ ci importrtf.c
importrtf.c,v  <--  importrtf.c
enter description, terminated with single '.' or end of file:
NOTE: This is NOT the log message!
>> Hello world source code
>> .
initial revision: 1.1
done
papaya$
```

The RCS file *importrtf.c,v* is created, and *importrtf.c* is removed.

In order to work on the source file again, use the *co* command to check it out. For example:

```
papaya$ co -l importrtf.c
importrtf.c,v  -->  importrtf.c
revision 1.1 (locked)
done
papaya$
```

will check out *importrtf.c* (from *importrtf.c,v*) and lock it. Locking the file allows you to edit it, and to check it back in. If you only need to check the file out in order to read it (for example, to issue a *make*), you can leave the *–l* switch off of the *co* command to check it out unlocked. You can't check in a file unless it is locked first (or if it has never been checked in before, as in the example).

Now, you can make some changes to the source and check it back in when done. In many cases, you'll want to keep the file checked out and use *ci* to merely record your most recent revisions in the RCS file and bump the version number. For this, you can use the *–l* switch with *ci*, as so:

```
papaya$ ci -l importrtf.c
importrtf.c,v  <--  importrtf.c
new revision: 1.2; previous revision: 1.1
enter log message, terminated with single '.' or end of file:
>> Changed printf call
>> .
done
papaya$
```

This automatically checks out the file, locked, after checking it in. This is a useful way to keep track of revisions even if you're the only one working on a project.

If you use RCS often, you may not like all those unsightly *importrtf.c,v* RCS files cluttering up your directory. If you create the subdirectory *RCS* within your project directory, *ci* and *co* will place the RCS files there, out of the way from the rest of the source.

In addition, RCS keeps track of all previous revisions of your file. For instance, if you make a change to your program that causes it to break in some way and you want to revert to the previous version to "undo" your changes and retrace your steps, you can specify a particular version number to check out with *co*. For example:

```
papaya$ co -l1.1 importrtf.c
importrtf.c,v  -->  importrtf.c
revision 1.1 (locked)
writable importrtf.c exists; remove it? [ny](n): y
done
papaya$
```

checks out version 1.1 of the file *importrtf.c*. You can use the program *rlog* to print the revision history of a particular file; this displays your revision log entries (entered with *ci*) along with other information such as the date, the user who checked in the revision, and so forth.

RCS automatically updates embedded "keyword strings" in your source file at check-out time. For example, if you have the string:

```
/* $Header: /work/linux/running4/RCS/ch14,v 1.1 2002/09/20 20:51:50 sierra Exp sierra
$ */
```

in the source file, *co* will replace it with an informative line about the revision date, version number, and so forth, as in:

```
/* $Header: /work/linux/hitch/programming/tools/RCS/rcs.tex
      1.2 1994/12/04 15:19:31 mdw Exp mdw $ */
```

(We broke this line to fit on the page, but it is supposed to be all on one line.)

Other keywords exist as well, such as $Author: jhawks $, $Date: 2002/09/24 15:30:14 $, and $Log: ch14,v $

Many programmers place a static string within each source file to identify the version of the program after it has been compiled. For example, within each source file in your program, you can place the line:

```
static char rcsid[ ] = "\@(#)$Header: /work/linux/running4/RCS/ch14,v 1.3 2002/09/24
15:30:14 andrews Exp ssherman $;
```

co replaces the keyword $Header: /work/linux/running4/RCS/ch14,v 1.3 2002/09/24 15:30:14 andrews Exp ssherman $ with a string of the form given here. This static string survives in the executable, and the *what* command displays these strings in a given binary. For example, after compiling *importrtf.c* into the executable *importrtf*, we can use the command:

```
papaya$ what importrtf
importrtf:
        $Header: /work/linux/hitch/programming/tools/RCS/rcs.tex
                1.2 1994/12/04 15:19:31 mdw Exp mdw $
papaya$
```

what picks out strings beginning with the characters @(#) in a file and displays them. If you have a program that has been compiled from many source files and libraries, and you don't know how up-to-date each component is, you can use *what* to display a version string for each source file used to compile the binary.

RCS has several other programs in its suite, including *rcs*, used for maintaining RCS files. Among other things, *rcs* can give other users permission to check out sources from an RCS file. See the manual pages for *ci*(1), *co*(1), and *rcs*(1) for more information.

Revision Control Tools—CVS

CVS, the *Concurrent Versioning System*, is more complex than RCS and thus perhaps a little bit oversized for one-person projects. But whenever more than one or two programmers are working on a project or the source code is distributed over several directories, CVS is the better choice. CVS uses the RCS file format for saving changes, but employs a management structure of its own.

By default, CVS works with full directory trees. That is, each CVS command you issue affects the current directory and all the subdirectories it contains, including their subdirectories and so on. You can switch off this recursive traversal with a command-line option, or you can specify a single file for the command to operate on.

CVS has formalized the sandbox concept that is used in many software development shops. In this concept, a so-called *repository* contains the "official" sources that are known to compile and work (at least partly). No developer is ever allowed to directly edit files in this repository. Instead, he checks out a local directory tree, the so-called *sandbox*. Here, he can edit the sources to his heart's delight, make changes, add or remove files, and do all sorts of things that developers usually do (no, not playing Quake or eating marshmallows). When he has made sure that his changes compile and work, he transmits them to the repository again and thus makes them available for the other developers.

When you as a developer have checked out a local directory tree, all the files are writable. You can make any necessary changes to the files in your personal workspace. When you have finished local testing and feel sure enough of your work to share the changes with the rest of the programming team, you write any changed files back into the central repository by issuing a CVS *commit* command. CVS then checks whether another developer has checked in changes since you checked out your directory tree. If this is the case, CVS does not let you check in your changes, but asks you first to take the changes of the other developers over to your local tree. During this update operation, CVS uses a sophisticated algorithm to reconcile ("merge") your changes with those of the other developers. In cases in which this is not automatically possible, CVS informs you that there were conflicts and asks you to resolve them. The file in question is marked up with special characters so that you can see where the conflict has occurred and decide which version should be used. Note that CVS makes sure conflicts can occur only in local developers' trees. There is always a consistent version in the repository.

Setting up a CVS repository

If you are working in a larger project, it is likely that someone else has already set up all the necessary machinery to use CVS. But if you are your project's administrator or you just want to tinker around with CVS on your local machine, you will have to set up a repository yourself.

First, set your environment variable CVSROOT to a directory where you want your CVS repository to be. CVS can keep as many projects as you like in a repository and makes sure they do not interfere with each other. Thus, you have to pick a directory only once to store all projects maintained by CVS, and you won't need to change it when you switch projects. Instead of using the variable CVSROOT, you can always use the command-line switch -d with all CVS commands, but since this is cumbersome to type all the time, we will assume that you have set CVSROOT.

Once the directory exists for a repository, you can create the repository with the following command (assuming that CVS is installed on your machine):

```
$tigger cvs init
```

There are several different ways to create a project tree in the CVS repository. If you already have a directory tree, but it is not yet managed by RCS, you can simply import it into the repository by calling:

```
$tigger cvs import directory manufacturer tag
```

where *directory* is the name of the top-level directory of the project, *manufacturer* is the name of the author of the code (you can use whatever you like here), and *tag* is a so-called release tag that can be chosen at will. For example:

```
$tigger cvs import dataimport acmeinc initial
... lots of output ...
```

If you want to start a completely new project, you can simply create the directory tree with *mkdir* calls and then import this empty tree as shown in the previous example.

If you want to import a project that is already managed by RCS, things get a little bit more difficult because you cannot use *cvs import*. In this case, you have to create the needed directories directly in the repository and then copy all RCS files (all files that end in *,v*) into those directories. Do not use RCS subdirectories here!

Every repository contains a file named *CVSROOT/modules* that lists the names of the projects in the repository. It is a good idea to edit the *modules* file of the repository to add the new module. You can check out, edit, and check in this file like every other file. Thus, in order to add your module to the list, do the following (we will cover the various commands soon):

```
$tigger cvs checkout CVSROOT/modules
$tigger cd CVSROOT
```

```
$tigger emacs modules
... or any other editor of your choice, see below for what to enter ...
$tigger cvs commit modules
$tigger cd ..
$tigger cvs release -d CVSROOT
```

If you are not doing anything fancy, the format of the *modules* file is very easy: each line starts with the name of module, followed by a space or tab and the path within the repository. If you want to do more with the *modules* file, check the CVS documentation at *http://www.loria.fr/~molli/cvs-index.html*. There is also a short but very comprehensive book about CVS, the *CVS Pocket Reference* by Gregor N. Purdy (O'Reilly).

Working with CVS

In the following section, we will assume that either you or your system administrator has set up a module called dataimport. You can now check out a local tree of this module with the following command:

```
$tigger cvs checkout dataimport
```

If no module is defined for the project you want to work on, you need to know the path within the repository. For example, something like the following could be needed:

```
$tigger cvs checkout clients/acmeinc/dataimport
```

Whichever version of the *checkout* command you use, CVS will create a directory called *dataimport* under your current working directory and check out all files and directories from the repository that belong to this module. All files are writable, and you can start editing them right away.

After you have made some changes, you can write back the changed files into the repository with one command:

```
$tigger cvs commit
```

Of course, you can also check in single files:

```
$tigger cvs commit importrtf.c
```

Whatever you do, CVS will ask you—as RCS does—for a comment to include with your changes. But CVS goes a step beyond RCS in convenience. Instead of the rudimentary prompt from RCS, you get a full-screen editor to work in. You can choose this editor by setting the environment variable CVSEDITOR; if this is not set, CVS looks in EDITOR, and if this is not defined either, CVS invokes *vi*. If you check in a whole project, CVS will use the comment you entered for each directory in which there have been changes, but will start a new editor for each directory that contains changes so that you can optionally change the comment.

As already mentioned, it is not necessary to set *CVSROOT* correctly for checking in files, because when checking out the tree, CVS has created a directory *CVS* in each

---

work directory. This directory contains all the information that CVS needs for its work, including where to find the repository.

While you have been working on your files, a co-worker might have checked in some of the files that you are currently working on. In this case, CVS will not let you check in your files but asks you to first update your local tree. Do this with the command:

```
$tigger cvs update
M importrtf.c
A exportrtf.c
? importrtf
U importword.c
```

(You can specify a single file here as well.) You should carefully examine the output of this command: CVS outputs the names of all the files it handles, each preceded by a single key letter. This letter tells you what has happened during the update operation. The most important letters are shown in Table 14-1.

Table 14-1. Key letters for files under CVS

Letter	Explanation
P	The file has been updated. The P is shown if the file has been added to the repository in the meantime or if it has been changed, but you have not made any changes to this file yourself.
U	You have changed this file in the meantime, but nobody else has.
M	You have changed this file in the meantime, and somebody else has checked in a newer version. All the changes have been merged successfully.
C	You have changed this file in the meantime, and somebody else has checked in a newer version. During the merge attempt, conflicts have arisen.
?	CVS has no information about this file—that is, this file is not under CVS's control.

The C is the most important of the letters in Table 14-1. It signifies that CVS was not able to merge all changes and needs your help. Load those files into your editor and look for the string <<<<<<<. After this string, the name of the file is shown again, followed by your version, ending with a line containing =======. Then comes the version of the code from the repository, ending with a line containing >>>>>>>. You now have to find out—probably by communicating with your co-worker—which version is better or whether it is possible to merge the two versions by hand. Change the file accordingly and remove the CVS markings <<<<<<<, =======, and >>>>>>>. Save the file and once again commit it.

If you decide that you want to stop working on a project for a time, you should check whether you have really committed all changes. To do this, change to the directory above the root directory of your project and issue the command:

```
$tigger cvs release dataimport
```

CVS then checks whether you have written back all changes into the repository and warns you if necessary. A useful option is *−d*, which deletes the local tree if all changes have been committed.

CVS over the Internet

CVS is also very useful where distributed development teams[*] are concerned because it provides several possibilities to access a repository on another machine.

Today, both free (like SourceForge) and commercial services are available that run a CVS server for you so that you can start a distributed software development project without having to have a server that is up 24/7.

If you can log into the machine holding the repository with *rsh*, you can use remote CVS to access the repository. To check out a module, do the following:

```
cvs -d :ext:user@domain.com:/path/to/repository checkout dataimport
```

If you cannot or do not want to use *rsh* for security reasons, you can also use the secure shell *ssh*. You can tell CVS that you want to use *ssh* by setting the environment variable CVS_RSH to *ssh*.

Authentication and access to the repository can also be done via a client/server protocol. Remote access requires a CVS server running on the machine with the repository; see the CVS documentation for how to do this. If the server is set up, you can log in to it with:

```
cvs -d :pserver:user@domain.com:path/to/repository login
CVS password:
```

As shown, the CVS server will ask you for your CVS password, which the administrator of the CVS server has assigned to you. This login procedure is necessary only once for every repository. When you check out a module, you need to specify the machine with the server, your username on that machine, and the remote path to the repository; as with local repositories, this information is saved in your local tree. Since the password is saved with minimal encryption in the file *.cvspass* in your home directory, there is a potential security risk here. The CVS documentation tells you more about this.

When you use CVS over the Internet and check out or update largish modules, you might also want to use the *–z* option, which expects an additional integer parameter for the degree of compression, ranging from 1 to 9, and transmits the data in compressed form.

Patching Files

Let's say you're trying to maintain a program that is updated periodically, but the program contains many source files, and releasing a complete source distribution with every update is not feasible. The best way to incrementally update source files is with *patch*, a program by Larry Wall, author of Perl.

---

[*] The use of CVS has burgeoned along with the number of free software projects developed over the Internet by people on different continents.

patch is a program that makes context-dependent changes in a file in order to update that file from one version to the next. This way, when your program changes, you simply release a patch file against the source, which the user applies with *patch* to get the newest version. For example, Linus Torvalds usually releases new Linux kernel versions in the form of patch files as well as complete source distributions.

A nice feature of *patch* is that it applies updates in context; that is, if you have made changes to the source yourself, but still wish to get the changes in the patch file update, *patch* usually can figure out the right location in your changed file to which to apply the change. This way, your versions of the original source files don't need to correspond exactly to those against which the patch file was made.

In order to make a patch file, the program *diff* is used, which produces "context diffs" between two files. For example, take our overused "Hello World" source code, given here:

```
/* hello.c version 1.0 by Norbert Ebersol */
#include <stdio.h>

int main( ) {
  printf("Hello, World!");
  exit(0);
}
```

Let's say you were to update this source, as in the following:

```
/* hello.c version 2.0 */
/* (c)1994 Norbert Ebersol */
#include <stdio.h>

int main( ) {
  printf("Hello, Mother Earth!\n");
  return 0;
}
```

If you want to produce a patch file to update the original *hello.c* to the newest version, use *diff* with the *–c* option:

```
papaya$ diff -c hello.c.old hello.c > hello.patch
```

This produces the patch file *hello.patch* that describes how to convert the original *hello.c* (here, saved in the file *hello.c.old*) to the new version. You can distribute this patch file to anyone who has the original version of "Hello, World," and they can use *patch* to update it.

Using *patch* is quite simple; in most cases, you simply run it with the patch file as input:*

```
papaya$ patch < hello.patch
Hmm...  Looks like a new-style context diff to me...
```

---

* The output shown here is from the last version that Larry Wall has released, Version 2.1. If you have a newer version of patch, you will need the —*verbose* flag to get the same output.

```
The text leading up to this was:
--------------------------
|*** hello.c.old        Sun Feb  6 15:30:52 1994
|--- hello.c    Sun Feb  6 15:32:21 1994
--------------------------
Patching file hello.c using Plan A...
Hunk #1 succeeded at 1.
done
papaya$
```

patch warns you if it appears as though the patch has already been applied. If we tried to apply the patch file again, *patch* would ask us if we wanted to assume that *–R* was enabled—which reverses the patch. This is a good way to back out patches you didn't intend to apply. *patch* also saves the original version of each file that it updates in a backup file, usually named *filename~* (the filename with a tilde appended).

In many cases, you'll want to update not only a single source file, but also an entire directory tree of sources. *patch* allows many files to be updated from a single diff. Let's say you have two directory trees, *hello.old* and *hello*, which contain the sources for the old and new versions of a program, respectively. To make a patch file for the entire tree, use the *–r* switch with *diff*:

> papaya$ **diff –cr hello.old hello > hello.patch**

Now, let's move to the system where the software needs to be updated. Assuming that the original source is contained in the directory *hello*, you can apply the patch with:

> papaya$ **patch –p0 < hello.patch**

The *–p0* switch tells *patch* to preserve the pathnames of files to be updated (so that it knows to look in the *hello* directory for the source). If you have the source to be patched saved in a directory named differently from that given in the patch file, you may need to use the *–p* option without a number. See the *patch*(1) manual page for details about this.

Indenting Code

If you're terrible at indenting code and find the idea of an editor that automatically indents code for you on the fly a bit annoying, you can use the *indent* program to pretty-print your code after you're done writing it. *indent* is a smart C-code formatter, featuring many options that allow you to specify just what kind of indentation style you wish to use.

Take this terribly formatted source:

```
double fact (double n) { if (n==1) return 1;
else return (n*fact(n-1)); }
int main () {
printf("Factorial 5 is %f.\n",fact(5));
printf("Factorial 10 is %f.\n",fact(10)); exit (0); }
```

Running *indent* on this source produces the relatively beautiful code:

```
#include <math.h>

double
fact (double n)
{
  if (n == 1)
    return 1;
  else
    return (n * fact (n - 1));
}
void
main ()
{

  printf ("Factorial 5 is %f.\n", fact (5));
  printf ("Factorial 10 is %f.\n", fact (10));
  exit (0);
}
```

Not only are lines indented well, but also whitespace is added around operators and function parameters to make them more readable. There are many ways to specify how the output of *indent* will look; if you're not fond of this particular indentation style, *indent* can accommodate you.

indent can also produce *troff* code from a source file, suitable for printing or for inclusion in a technical document. This code will have such nice features as italicized comments, boldfaced keywords, and so on. Using a command such as:

```
papaya$ indent -troff importrtf.c | groff -mindent
```

produces *troff* code and formats it with *groff*.

Finally, *indent* can be used as a simple debugging tool. If you have put a } in the wrong place, running your program through *indent* will show you what the computer thinks the block structure is.

Integrated Development Environments

While software development on Unix (and hence Linux) systems is traditionally command-line–based, developers on other platforms are used to so-called Integrated Development Environments (IDEs) that integrate an editor, a compiler, a debugger, and possibly other development tools in the same application. Developers coming from these environments are often dumbfounded when confronted with the Linux command line and asked to type in the *gcc* command.[*]

---

[*] We can't understand why it can be more difficult to type in a *gcc* command than to select a menu item from a menu, but then again, this might be due to our socialization.

In order to cater to these migrating developers, but also because Linux developers are increasingly demanding more comfort, IDEs have been developed for Linux as well. There are few of them out there, but only one of them, *KDevelop*, has seen wide-spread use.

KDevelop is a part of the KDE project, but can also be run independently of the KDE desktop. It keeps track of all files belonging to your project, generates makefiles for you, lets you parse C++ classes, and includes an integrated debugger and an application wizard that gets you started developing your application. KDevelop was originally developed in order to facilitate the development of KDE applications, but can also be used to develop all kinds of other software, like traditional command-line programs and even GNOME applications.

KDevelop is way too big and feature-rich for us to introduce it here to you, but we want to at least whet your appetite with a screenshot (see Figure 14-1) and point you to *http://www.kdevelop.org* for downloads and all information, including complete documentation.

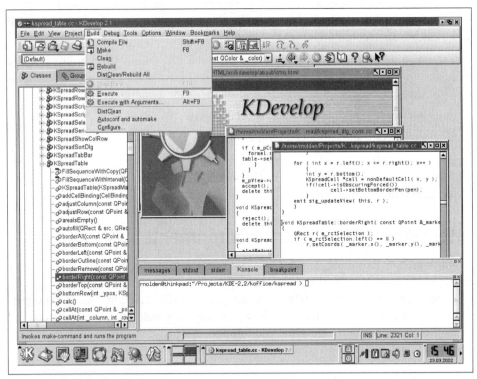

Figure 14-1. The KDevelop IDE

Emacs and XEmacs, by the way, make for a very fine IDE that integrates many additional tools such as *gdb*, as shown earlier in this chapter.

## CHAPTER 15

TCP/IP and PPP

So, you've staked out your homestead on the Linux frontier, and installed and configured your system. What's next? Eventually you'll want to communicate with other systems—Linux and otherwise—and the Pony Express isn't going to suffice.

Fortunately, Linux supports a number of methods for data communication and networking. This includes serial communications, TCP/IP, and UUCP. In this chapter and the next, we will discuss how to configure your system to communicate with the world.

The *Linux Network Administrator's Guide*, available from the Linux Documentation Project and also published by O'Reilly & Associates, is a complete guide to configuring TCP/IP and UUCP networking under Linux. For a detailed account of the information presented here, we refer you to that book.

Networking with TCP/IP

Linux supports a full implementation of the Transmission Control Protocol/Internet Protocol (TCP/IP) networking protocols. TCP/IP has become the most successful mechanism for networking computers worldwide. With Linux and an Ethernet card, you can network your machine to a local area network (LAN) or (with the proper network connections) to the Internet—the worldwide TCP/IP network.

Hooking up a small LAN of Unix machines is easy. It simply requires an Ethernet controller in each machine and the appropriate Ethernet cables and other hardware. Or if your business or university provides access to the Internet, you can easily add your Linux machine to this network.

Linux TCP/IP support has had its ups and downs. After all, implementing an entire protocol stack from scratch isn't something that one does for fun on a weekend. On the other hand, the Linux TCP/IP code has benefited greatly from the hoard of beta testers and developers to have crossed its path, and as time has progressed many bugs and configuration problems have fallen in their wake.

The current implementation of TCP/IP and related protocols for Linux is called NET-4. This has no relationship to the so-called NET-2 release of BSD Unix; instead, in this context, NET-4 means the fourth implementation of TCP/IP for Linux. Before NET-4 came (no surprise here) NET-3, NET-2, and NET-1, the last having been phased out around kernel Version 0.99.pl10. NET-4 supports nearly all the features you'd expect from a Unix TCP/IP implementation and a wide range of networking hardware.

Linux NET-4 also supports Serial Line Internet Protocol (SLIP) and Point-to-Point Protocol (PPP). SLIP and PPP allow you to have dial-up Internet access using a modem. If your business or university provides SLIP or PPP access, you can dial in to the SLIP or PPP server and put your machine on the Internet over the phone line. Alternatively, if your Linux machine also has Ethernet access to the Internet, you can configure it as a SLIP or PPP server.

In the following sections, we won't mention SLIP anymore because nowadays most people use PPP. If you want to run SLIP on your machine, you can find all the information you'll need in the *Linux Network Administrator's Guide* by Olaf Kirch and Terry Dawson (O'Reilly).

Besides the *Linux Network Administrator's Guide*, the Linux NET-4 HOWTO contains more or less complete information on configuring TCP/IP and PPP for Linux. The Linux Ethernet HOWTO is a related document that describes configuration of various Ethernet card drivers for Linux.

Also of interest is *TCP/IP Network Administration* by Craig Hunt (O'Reilly). It contains complete information on using and configuring TCP/IP on Unix systems. If you plan to set up a network of Linux machines or do any serious TCP/IP hacking, you should have the background in network administration presented by that book.

If you really want to get serious about setting up and operating networks, you will probably also want to read *DNS and BIND* by Cricket Liu and Paul Albitz (O'Reilly). This book tells you all there is to know about name servers in a refreshingly funny manner.

TCP/IP Concepts

In order to fully appreciate (and utilize) the power of TCP/IP, you should be familiar with its underlying principles. TCP/IP is a suite of *protocols* (the magic buzzword for this chapter) that define how machines should communicate with each other via a network, as well as internally to other layers of the protocol suite. For the theoretical background of the Internet protocols, the best sources of information are the first volume of Douglas Comer's *Internetworking with TCP/IP* (Prentice Hall) and the first volume of W. Richard Stevens' *TCP/IP Illustrated* (Addison-Wesley).

TCP/IP was originally developed for use on the Advanced Research Projects Agency network, ARPAnet, which was funded to support military and computer-science research. Therefore, you may hear TCP/IP being referred to as the "DARPA Internet Protocols." Since that first Internet, many other TCP/IP networks have come into use, such as the National Science Foundation's NSFNET, as well as thousands of other local and regional networks around the world. All these networks are interconnected into a single conglomerate known as the Internet.

On a TCP/IP network, each machine is assigned an *IP address*, which is a 32-bit number uniquely identifying the machine. You need to know a little about IP addresses to structure your network and assign addresses to hosts. The IP address is usually represented as a dotted quad: four numbers in decimal notation, separated by dots. As an example, the IP address 0x80114b14 (in hexadecimal format) can be written as 128.17.75.20.

Two special cases should be mentioned here, dynamic IP addresses and masqueraded IP addresses. Both have been invented to overcome the current shortage of IP addresses (which will not be of concern any longer once everybody has adopted the new IPv6 standard that prescribes six bytes for the IP addresses—enough for every amoeba in the universe to have an IP address).

Dynamic IP addresses are often used with dial-up accounts: when you dial into your ISP's service, you are being assigned an IP number out of a pool that the ISP has allocated for this service. The next time you log in, you might get a different IP number. The idea behind this is that only a small number of the customers of an ISP are logged in at the same time, so a smaller number of IP addresses are needed. Still, as long as your computer is connected to the Internet, it has a unique IP address that no other computer is using at that time.

Masquerading allows several computers to share an IP address. All machines in a masqueraded network use so-called private IP numbers, numbers out of a range that is allocated for internal purposes and that can never serve as real addresses out there on the Internet. Any number of networks can use the same private IP numbers, as they are never visible outside of the LAN. One machine, the "masquerading server," will map these private IP numbers to one public IP number (either dynamic or static), and ensure through an ingenious mapping mechanism that incoming packets are routed to the right machine.

The IP address is divided into two parts: the network address and the host address. The network address consists of the higher-order bits of the address and the host address of the remaining bits. (In general, each *host* is a separate machine on the network.) The size of these two fields depends upon the type of network in question. For example, on a Class B network (for which the first byte of the IP address is between 128 and 191), the first two bytes of the address identify the network, and the remaining two bytes identify the host (see Figure 15-1). For the example address just given, the network address is 128.17, and the host address is 75.20. To put this another way, the machine with IP address 128.17.75.20 is host number 75.20 on the network 128.17.

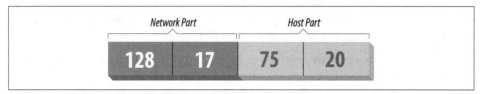

Figure 15-1. IP address

In addition, the host portion of the IP address may be subdivided to allow for a *subnetwork address*. Subnetworking allows large networks to be divided into smaller subnets, each of which may be maintained independently. For example, an organization may allocate a single Class B network, which provides two bytes of host information, up to 65,534 hosts on the network. The organization may then wish to dole out the responsibility of maintaining portions of the network so that each subnetwork is handled by a different department. Using subnetworking, the organization can specify, for example, that the first byte of the host address (that is, the third byte of the overall IP address) is the subnet address, and the second byte is the host address for that subnetwork (see Figure 15-2). In this case, the IP address 128.17.75. 20 identifies host number 20 on subnetwork 75 of network 128.17.*

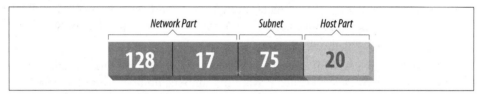

Figure 15-2. IP address with subnet

Processes (on either the same or different machines) that wish to communicate via TCP/IP generally specify the destination machine's IP address as well as a *port address*. The destination IP address is used, of course, to route data from one machine to the destination machine. The port address is a 16-bit number that specifies a particular service or application on the destination machine that should receive the data. Port numbers can be thought of as office numbers at a large office building: the entire building has a single IP address, but each business has a separate office there.

Here's a real-life example of how IP addresses and port numbers are used. The *ssh* program allows a user on one machine to start a login session on another, while

---

* Why not 65,536 instead? For reasons to be discussed later, a host address of 0 or 255 is invalid.

encrypting all the data traffic between the two so that nobody can intercept the communication. On the remote machine, the *ssh* "daemon," *sshd*, is listening to a specific port for incoming connections (in this case, the port number is 22).*

The user executing *ssh* specifies the address of the machine to log in to, and the *ssh* program attempts to open a connection to port 22 on the remote machine. If it is successful, *ssh* and *sshd* are able to communicate with each other to provide the remote login for the user in question.

Note that the *ssh* client on the local machine has a port address of its own. This port address is allocated to the client dynamically when it begins execution. This is because the remote *sshd* doesn't need to know the port number of the incoming *ssh* client beforehand. When the client initiates the connection, part of the information it sends to *sshd* is its port number. *sshd* can be thought of as a business with a well-known mailing address. Any customers who wish to correspond with the *sshd* running on a particular machine need to know not only the IP address of the machine to talk to (the address of the *sshd* office building), but also the port number where *sshd* can be found (the particular office within the building). The address and port number of the *ssh* client are included as part of the "return address" on the envelope containing the letter.

The TCP/IP family contains a number of protocols. Transmission Control Protocol (TCP) is responsible for providing reliable, connection-oriented communications between two processes, which may be running on different machines on the network. User Datagram Protocol (UDP) is similar to TCP except that it provides connectionless, unreliable service. Processes that use UDP must implement their own acknowledgment and synchronization routines if necessary.

TCP and UDP transmit and receive data in units known as *packets*. Each packet contains a chunk of information to send to another machine, as well as a header specifying the destination and source port addresses.

Internet Protocol (IP) sits beneath TCP and UDP in the protocol hierarchy. It is responsible for transmitting and routing TCP or UDP packets via the network. In order to do so, IP wraps each TCP or UDP packet within another packet (known as an IP *datagram*), which includes a header with routing and destination information. The IP datagram header includes the IP address of the source and destination machines.

Note that IP doesn't know anything about port addresses; those are the responsibility of TCP and UDP. Similarly, TCP and UDP don't deal with IP addresses, which (as the name implies) are only IP's concern. As you can see, the mail metaphor with return addresses and envelopes is quite accurate: each packet can be thought of as a

---

* On many systems, *sshd* is not always listening to port 22; the Internet services daemon *inetd* is listening on its behalf. For now, let's sweep that detail under the carpet.

letter contained within an envelope. TCP and UDP wrap the letter in an envelope with the source and destination port numbers (office numbers) written on it.

IP acts as the mail room for the office building sending the letter. IP receives the envelope and wraps it in yet another envelope, with the IP address (office building address) of both the destination and the source affixed. The post office (which we haven't discussed quite yet) delivers the letter to the appropriate office building. There, the mail room unwraps the outer envelope and hands it to TCP/UDP, which delivers the letter to the appropriate office based on the port number (written on the inner envelope). Each envelope has a return address that IP and TCP/UDP use to reply to the letter.

In order to make the specification of machines on the Internet more humane, network hosts are often given a name as well as an IP address. The Domain Name System (DNS) takes care of translating hostnames to IP addresses, and vice versa, as well as handles the distribution of the name-to-IP address database across the entire Internet. Using hostnames also allows the IP address associated with a machine to change (e.g., if the machine is moved to a different network), without having to worry that others won't be able to "find" the machine once the address changes. The DNS record for the machine is simply updated with the new IP address, and all references to the machine, by name, will continue to work.

DNS is an enormous, worldwide distributed database. Each organization maintains a piece of the database, listing the machines in the organization. If you find yourself in the position of maintaining the list for your organization, you can get help from the *Linux Network Administrator's Guide* or *TCP/IP Network Administration*, both from O'Reilly. If those aren't enough, you can really get the full scoop from the book *DNS and BIND* (O'Reilly).

For the purposes of most administration, all you need to know is that a daemon called *named* (pronounced "name-dee") has to run on your system. This daemon is your window onto DNS.

Now, we might ask ourselves how a packet gets from one machine (office building) to another. This is the actual job of IP, as well as a number of other protocols that aid IP in its task. Besides managing IP datagrams on each host (as the mail room), IP is also responsible for routing packets between hosts.

Before we can discuss how routing works, we must explain the model upon which TCP/IP networks are built. A network is just a set of machines that are connected through some physical network medium—such as Ethernet or serial lines. In TCP/IP terms, each network has its own methods for handling routing and packet transfer internally.

Networks are connected to each other via *gateways* (also known as *routers*). A gateway is a host that has direct connections to two or more networks; the gateway can then exchange information between the networks and route packets from one network to another. For instance, a gateway might be a workstation with more than one Ethernet interface. Each interface is connected to a different network, and the operating system uses this connectivity to allow the machine to act as a gateway.

In order to make our discussion more concrete, let's introduce an imaginary network, made up of the machines *eggplant*, *papaya*, *apricot*, and *zucchini*. Figure 15-3 depicts the configuration of these machines on the network.

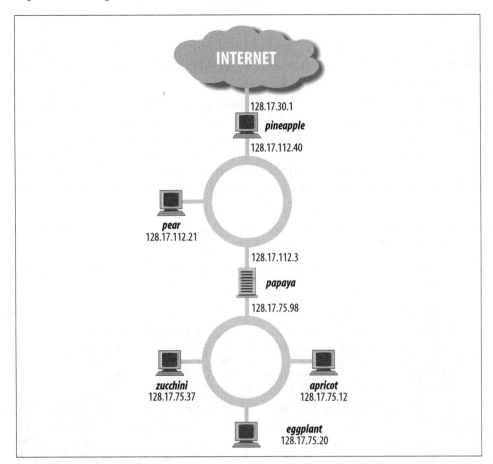

Figure 15-3. Network with two gateways

Note that *papaya* is connected to another network as well, which includes the machines *pineapple* and *pear*. These machines have the respective IP addresses:

Hostname	IP address
eggplant	128.17.75.20
apricot	128.17.75.12
zucchini	128.17.75.37
papaya	128.17.75.98, 128.17.112.3
pear	128.17.112.21
pineapple	128.17.112.40, 128.17.30.1

As you can see, *papaya* has two IP addresses—one on the 128.17.75 subnetwork and another on the 128.17.112 subnetwork. *pineapple* has two IP addresses as well—one on 128.17.112 and another on 128.17.30.

IP uses the network portion of the IP address to determine how to route packets between machines. In order to do this, each machine on the network has a *routing table*, which contains a list of networks and the gateway machine for that network. To route a packet to a particular machine, IP looks at the network portion of the destination address. If there is an entry for that network in the routing table, IP routes the packet through the appropriate gateway. Otherwise, IP routes the packet through the "default" gateway given in the routing table.

Routing tables can contain entries for specific machines as well as for networks. In addition, each machine has a routing table entry for itself.

Let's examine the routing table for *eggplant*. Using the command *netstat –rn*, we see the following:

```
eggplant:$ netstat -rn
Kernel IP routing table
Destination    Gateway       Genmask         Flags  MSS  Window irtt Iface
128.17.75.0    128.17.75.20  255.255.255.0   UN     1500 0         0 eth0
default        128.17.75.98  0.0.0.0         UGN    1500 0         0 eth0
127.0.0.1      127.0.0.1     255.0.0.0       UH     3584 0         0 lo
128.17.75.20   127.0.0.1     255.255.255.0   UH     3584 0         0 lo
```

The first column displays the destination networks (and hosts) that the routing table includes. The first entry is for the network 128.17.75 (note that the host address is 0 for network entries), which is the network that *eggplant* lives on. Any packets sent to this network should be routed through 128.17.75.20, which is the IP address of *eggplant*. In general, a machine's route to its own network is through itself.

The Flags column of the routing table gives information on the destination address for this entry; U specifies that the route is "up," N that the destination is a network, and so on. The MSS field shows how many bytes are transferred at a time over the respective connection, Window indicates how many frames may be sent ahead before a confirmation must be made, irtt gives statistics on the use of this route, and Iface lists the network device used for the route. On Linux systems, Ethernet interfaces are named *eth0*, *eth1*, and so on. *lo* is the loopback device, which we'll discuss shortly.

The second entry in the routing table is the default route, which applies to all packets destined for networks or hosts for which there is no entry in the table. In this case, the default route is through *papaya*, which can be considered the door to the outside world. Every machine on the 128.17.75 subnet must go through *papaya* to talk to machines on any other network.

The third entry in the table is for the address 127.0.0.1, which is the *loopback* address. This address is used when a machine wants to make a TCP/IP connection to itself. It uses the *lo* device as its interface, which prevents loopback connections from using the Ethernet (via the *eth0* interface). In this way, network bandwidth is not wasted when a machine wishes to talk to itself.

The last entry in the routing table is for the IP address 128.17.75.20, which is the *eggplant* host's own address. As we can see, it uses 127.0.0.1 as its gateway. This way, any time *eggplant* makes a TCP/IP connection to itself, the loopback address is used as the gateway, and the *lo* network device is used.

Let's say that *eggplant* wants to send a packet to *zucchini*. The IP datagram contains a source address of 128.17.75.20 and a destination address of 128.17.75.37. IP determines that the network portion of the destination address is 128.17.75 and uses the routing table entry for 128.17.75.0 accordingly. The packet is sent directly to the network, which *zucchini* receives and is able to process.

What happens if *eggplant* wants to send packets to a machine not on the local network, such as *pear*? The destination address is 128.17.112.21. IP attempts to find a route for the 128.17.112 network in the routing tables, but none exists, so it selects the default route through *papaya*. *papaya* receives the packet and looks up the destination address in its own routing tables. The routing table for *papaya* might look like this:

```
Destination    Gateway        Genmask        Flags MSS  Window irtt Iface
128.17.75.0    128.17.75.98   255.255.255.0  UN    1500 0      0    eth0
128.17.112.0   128.17.112.3   255.255.255.0  UN    1500 0      0    eth1
default        128.17.112.40  0.0.0.0        UGN   1500 0      0    eth1
127.0.0.1      127.0.0.1      255.0.0.0      UH    3584 0      0    lo
128.17.75.98   127.0.0.1      255.255.255.0  UH    3584 0      0    lo
```

As you can see, *papaya* is connected to the 128.17.75 network through its *eth0* device and to 128.17.112 through *eth1*. The default route is through *pineapple*, which is a gateway to the Wild Blue Yonder (as far as *papaya* is concerned).

Once *papaya* receives a packet destined for *pear*, it sees that the destination address is on the network 128.17.112 and routes that packet to the network using the second entry in the routing table.

Similarly, if *eggplant* wants to send packets to machines outside the local organization, it would route packets through *papaya* (its gateway). *papaya* would, in turn, route outgoing packets through *pineapple*, and so forth. Packets are handed from one gateway to the next until they reach the intended destination network. This is the basic structure upon which the Internet is based: a seemingly infinite chain of networks, interconnected via gateways.

Hardware Requirements

You can use Linux TCP/IP without any networking hardware; configuring "loopback" mode allows you to talk to yourself. This is necessary for some applications and games that use the loopback network device.

However, if you want to use Linux with an Ethernet TCP/IP network, you'll need an Ethernet adapter card. Many Ethernet adapters are supported by Linux for the ISA, EISA, and PCI buses, as well as pocket and PCMCIA adapters. In Chapter 1, we provided a partial list of supported Ethernet cards; see the Linux Ethernet HOWTO for a complete discussion of Linux Ethernet hardware compatibility.

Over the last few years, support has been added for non-Ethernet high-speed networking like HIPPI. This topic is beyond the scope of this book, but if you are interested, you can get some information from the directory *Documentation/networking* in your kernel sources.

If you have an ADSL connection and use an ADSL router, this looks to Linux just like a normal Ethernet connection. As such, you need neither specific hardware (except an Ethernet card, of course) nor special drivers besides the Ethernet card driver itself. If you want to connect your Linux box directly to your ADSL modem, you still don't need to have any particular hardware or driver, but you do need to run a protocol called PPPoE (PPP over Ethernet); more about this later.

Linux also supports SLIP and PPP, which allow you to use a modem to access the Internet over a phone line. In this case, you'll need a modem compatible with your SLIP or PPP server; for example, many servers require a 56kbps V.90 modem (most also support K56flex). In this book, we describe the configuration of PPP because it is what most Internet service providers offer. If you want to use the older SLIP, please see the *Linux Network Administrator's Guide* (O'Reilly).

Finally, there is PLIP, which let's you connect two computers directly via parallel ports, requiring a special cable between the two.

Configuring TCP/IP with Ethernet

In this section, we discuss how to configure an Ethernet TCP/IP connection on a Linux system. Presumably this system will be part of a local network of machines that are already running TCP/IP; in this case, your gateway, name server, and so forth are already configured and available.

The following information applies primarily to Ethernet connections. If you're planning to use PPP, read this section to understand the concepts, and follow the PPP-specific instructions in the section "Dial-up PPP" later in this chapter.

On the other hand, you may wish to set up an entire LAN of Linux machines (or a mix of Linux machines and other systems). In this case, you'll have to take care of a number of other issues not discussed here. This includes setting up a name server for yourself, as well as a gateway machine if your network is to be connected to other networks. If your network is to be connected to the Internet, you'll also have to obtain IP addresses and related information from your access provider.

In short, the method described here should work for many Linux systems configured for an existing LAN—but certainly not all. For further details, we direct you to a book on TCP/IP network administration, such as those mentioned at the beginning of this chapter.

First of all, we assume that your Linux system has the necessary TCP/IP software installed. This includes basic clients such as *ssh* and FTP, system-administration commands such as *ifconfig* and *route* (usually found in */etc* or */sbin*), and networking configuration files (such as */etc/hosts*). The other Linux-related networking documents described earlier explain how to go about installing the Linux networking software if you do not have it already.

We also assume that your kernel has been configured and compiled with TCP/IP support enabled. See the section "Building a New Kernel" in Chapter 7 for information on compiling your kernel. To enable networking, you must answer yes to the appropriate questions during the *make config* or *make menuconfig* step, rebuild the kernel, and boot from it.

Once this has been done, you must modify a number of configuration files used by NET-4. For the most part this is a simple procedure. Unfortunately, however, there is wide disagreement between Linux distributions as to where the various TCP/IP configuration files and support programs should go. Much of the time, they can be found in */etc*, but in other cases they may be found in */usr/etc*, */usr/etc/inet*, or other bizarre locations. In the worst case, you'll have to use the *find* command to locate the files on your system. Also note that not all distributions keep the NET-4 configuration files and software in the same location; they may be spread across several directories.

Here we cover how to set up and configure networking on a Linux box manually. This should help you get some insight into what goes on behind the scenes and enable you to help yourself if something goes wrong with automatic setup tools provided by your distribution. It can be a good idea, though, to first try setting up your network with the configuration programs that your distribution provides; many of these are quite advanced these days and detect many of the necessary settings automatically.

This section also assumes use of one Ethernet device on the system. These instructions should be fairly easy to extrapolate if your system has more than one network connection (and hence acts as a gateway).

Here, we also discuss configuration for loopback-only systems (systems with no Ethernet or PPP connection). If you have no network access, you may wish to configure your system for loopback-only TCP/IP so that you can use applications that require it.

Your network configuration

Before you can configure TCP/IP, you need to determine the following information about your network setup. In most cases, your local network administrator or network access provider can provide you with this information:

Your IP address
> This is the unique machine address in dotted-decimal format. An example is 128.17.75.98. Your network administrators will provide you with this number.
>
> If you're configuring loopback mode (i.e., no PPP, no Ethernet card, just TCP/IP connections to your own machine), your IP address is 127.0.0.1.

Your subnetwork mask
> This is a dotted quad, similar to the IP address, which determines which portion of the IP address specifies the subnetwork number and which portion specifies the host on that subnet.
>
> The subnetwork mask is a pattern of bits, which, when bitwise-ANDed with an IP address on your network, will tell you which subnet that address belongs to. For example, your subnet mask might be 255.255.255.0. If your IP address is 128.17.75.20, the subnetwork portion of your address is 128.17.75.
>
> We distinguish here between "network address" and "subnetwork address." Remember that for Class B addresses, the first two bytes (here, 128.17) specify the network, while the second two bytes specify the host. With a subnet mask of 255.255.255.0, however, 128.17.75 is considered the entire subnet address (e.g., subnetwork 75 of network 128.17), and 20 the host address.
>
> Your network administrators choose the subnet mask and therefore can provide you with this information.
>
> This applies as well to the loopback device. Since the loopback address is always 127.0.0.1, the netmask for this device is always 255.0.0.0.

Your subnetwork address
> This is the subnet portion of your IP address as determined by the subnet mask. For example, if your subnet mask is 255.255.255.0 and your IP address 128.17.75.20, your subnet address is 128.17.75.0.
>
> Loopback-only systems don't have a subnet address.

Your broadcast address

This address is used to broadcast packets to every machine on your subnet. In general, this is equal to your subnet address (see previous item) with 255 replaced as the host address. For subnet address 128.17.75.0, the broadcast address is 128.17.75.255. Similarly, for subnet address 128.17.0.0, the broadcast address is 128.17.255.255.

Note that some systems use the subnetwork address as the broadcast address. If you have any doubt, check with your network administrators.

Loopback-only systems do not have a broadcast address.

The IP address of your gateway

This is the address of the machine that acts as the default route to the outside world. In fact, you may have more than one gateway address—for example, if your network is connected directly to several other networks. However, only one of these will act as the *default* route. (Recall the example in the previous section, where the 128.17.112.0 network is connected to both 128.17.75.0 through *papaya* and the outside world through *pineapple*.)

Your network administrators will provide you with the IP addresses of any gateways on your network, as well as the networks they connect to. Later, you will use this information with the *route* command to include entries in the routing table for each gateway.

Loopback-only systems do not have a gateway address. The same is true for isolated networks.

The IP address of your name server

This is the address of the machine that handles hostname-to-address translations for your machine. Your network administrators will provide you with this information.

You may wish to run your own name server (by configuring and running *named*). However, unless you absolutely must run your own name server (for example, if no other name server is available on your local network), we suggest using the name-server address provided by your network administrators. At any rate, most books on TCP/IP configuration include information on running *named*.

Naturally, loopback-only systems have no name-server address.

The networking rc files

rc files are systemwide resource configuration scripts executed at boot time by *init*. They run basic system daemons (such as *sendmail*, *crond*, and so on) and are used to configure network parameters. *rc* files are usually found in the directory */etc/init.d*.

Note that there are *many* ways to carry out the network configuration described here. Every Linux distribution uses a slightly different mechanism to help automate the process. What we describe here is a generic method that allows you to create two *rc* files that will run the appropriate commands to get your machine talking to the network. Most distributions have their own scripts that accomplish more or less the same thing. If in doubt, first attempt to configure networking as suggested by the documentation for your distribution and, as a last resort, use the methods described here. (As an example, the Red Hat distribution uses the script */etc/rc.d/init.d/network*, which obtains network information from files in */etc/sysconfig*. The *control-panel* system administration program provided with Red Hat configures networking automatically without editing any of these files. The SuSE distribution, on the other hand, distributes the configuration over several files, such as */sbin/init.d/network* and */sbin/init.d/route*, among others, and lets you configure most networking aspects via the tool *yast2*.)

Here, we're going to describe the *rc* files used to configure TCP/IP in some of the better known distributions:

Red Hat
> Networking is scattered among files for each *init* level that includes networking. For instance, the */etc/rc.d/rc1.d* directory controls a level 1 (single-user) boot, so it doesn't have any networking commands, but the */etc/rc.d/rc3.d* controlling a level 3 boot has files specifically to start networking.

SuSE
> All the startup files for all system services, including networking, are grouped together in the */sbin/init.d* directory. They are quite generic and get their actual values from the systemwide configuration file */etc/rc.config*. The most important files here are */sbin/init.d/network*, which starts and halts network interfaces, */sbin/init.d/route*, which configures routing, and */sbin/init.d/ serial*, which configures serial ports. If you have ISDN hardware, the files */sbin/init.d/i4l* and */sbin/init.d/i4l_hardware* are applicable, too. Note that in general, you do not need to (and should not) edit those files; edit */etc/rc.config* instead.

Debian
> The network configuration (Ethernet cards, IP addresses, and routing) is set up in the file */etc/init.d/network*. The base networking daemons (*portmap* and *inetd*) are initialized by the start-stop script */etc/init.d/netbase*.

We'll use two files here for illustrative purposes, */etc/rc.d/rc.inet1* and */etc/rc.d/rc.inet2*. The former will set up the hardware and the basic networking, while the latter will configure the networking services. Many distributions follow such a separation, even though the files might have other names.

init uses the file */etc/inittab* to determine what processes to run at boot time. In order to run the files */etc/rc.d/rc.inet1* and */etc/rc.d/rc.inet2* from *init*, */etc/inittab* might include entries, such as:

```
n1:34:wait:/etc/rc.d/rc.inet1
n2:34:wait:/etc/rc.d/rc.inet2
```

The *inittab* file is described in the section "init, inittab, and rc Files" in Chapter 5. The first field gives a unique two-character identifier for each entry. The second field lists the runlevels in which the scripts are run; on this system, we initialize networking in runlevels 3 and 4. The word wait in the third field tells *init* to wait until the script has finished execution before continuing. The last field gives the name of the script to run.

While you are first setting up your network configuration, you may wish to run *rc.inet1* and *rc.inet2* by hand (as *root*) in order to debug any problems. Later you can include entries for them in another *rc* file or in */etc/inittab*.

As mentioned earlier, *rc.inet1* configures the basic network interface. This includes your IP and network address and the routing table information for your system. Two programs are used to configure these parameters: *ifconfig* and *route*. Both of these are usually found in */sbin*.

ifconfig is used for configuring the network device interface with certain parameters, such as the IP address, subnetwork mask, broadcast address, and the like. *route* is used to create and modify entries in the routing table.

For most configurations, an *rc.inet1* file similar to the following should work. You will, of course, have to edit this for your own system. Do not use the sample IP and network addresses listed here; they may correspond to an actual machine on the Internet:

```
#!/bin/sh
# This is /etc/rc.d/rc.inet1 - Configure the TCP/IP interfaces

# First, configure the loopback device

HOSTNAME=`hostname`

/sbin/ifconfig lo 127.0.0.1    # uses default netmask 255.0.0.0
/sbin/route add 127.0.0.1      # a route to point to the loopback device

# Next, configure the Ethernet device. If you're only using loopback or
# SLIP, comment out the rest of these lines.

# Edit for your setup.
IPADDR="128.17.75.20"       # REPLACE with your IP address
NETMASK="255.255.255.0"     # REPLACE with your subnet mask
NETWORK="128.17.75.0"       # REPLACE with your network address
BROADCAST="128.17.75.255"   # REPLACE with your broadcast address
GATEWAY="128.17.75.98"      # REPLACE with your default gateway address

# Configure the eth0 device to use information above.
/sbin/ifconfig eth0 ${IPADDR} netmask ${NETMASK} broadcast ${BROADCAST}

# Add a route for our own network.
/sbin/route add ${NETWORK}
```

```
# Add a route to the default gateway.
/sbin/route add default gw ${GATEWAY} metric 1

# End of Ethernet Configuration
```

As you can see, the format of the *ifconfig* command is:

```
ifconfig interface device options…
```

For example:

```
ifconfig lo 127.0.0.1
```

assigns the *lo* (loopback) device the IP address 127.0.0.1, and:

```
ifconfig eth0 127.17.75.20
```

assigns the *eth0* (first Ethernet) device the address 127.17.75.20.

In addition to specifying the address, Ethernet devices usually require that the subnetwork mask be set with the *netmask* option and the broadcast address be set with *broadcast*.

The format of the *route* command, as used here, is:

```
route add [ -net | -host ] destination [ gw gateway ]
[ metric metric ] options
```

where *destination* is the destination address for this route (or the keyword default), *gateway* is the IP address of the gateway for this route, and *metric* is the metric number for the route (discussed later).

We use *route* to add entries to the routing table. You should add a route for the loopback device (as seen earlier), for your local network, and for your default gateway. For example, if our default gateway is 128.17.75.98, we would use the command:

```
route add default gw 128.17.75.98
```

route takes several options. Using *–net* or *–host* before *destination* will tell *route* that the destination is a network or specific host, respectively. (In most cases, routes point to networks, but in some situations you may have an independent machine that requires its own route. You would use *–host* for such a routing table entry.)

The *metric* option specifies a *metric value* for this route. Metric values are used when there is more than one route to a specific location, and the system must make a decision about which to use. Routes with lower metric values are preferred. In this case, we set the metric value for our default route to 1, which forces that route to be preferred over all others.

How could there possibly be more than one route to a particular location? First of all, you may use multiple *route* commands in *rc.inet1* for a particular destination—if you have more than one gateway to a particular network, for example. However, your routing tables may dynamically acquire additional entries in them if you run *routed* (discussed later). If you run *routed*, other systems may broadcast routing information to machines on the network, causing extra routing table entries to be created on your machine. By setting the `metric` value for your default route to 1, you ensure that any new routing table entries will not supersede the preference of your default gateway.

You should read the manual pages for *ifconfig* and *route*, which describe the syntax of these commands in detail. There may be other options to *ifconfig* and *route* that are pertinent to your configuration.

Let's move on. *rc.inet2* is used to run various daemons used by the TCP/IP suite. These are not necessary in order for your system to talk to the network, and are therefore relegated to a separate *rc* file. In most cases you should attempt to configure *rc.inet1*, and ensure that your system is able to send and receive packets from the network, before bothering to configure *rc.inet2*.

Among the daemons executed by *rc.inet2* are *inetd*, *syslogd*, and *routed*. The version of *rc.inet2* on your system may currently start a number of other servers, but we suggest commenting these out while you are debugging your network configuration.

The most important of these servers is *inetd*, which acts as the "operator" for other system daemons. It sits in the background and listens to certain network ports for incoming connections. When a connection is made, *inetd* spawns off a copy of the appropriate daemon for that port. For example, when an incoming FTP connection is made, *inetd* forks *in.ftpd*, which handles the FTP connection from there. This is simpler and more efficient than running individual copies of each daemon. This way, network daemons are executed on demand.

syslogd is the system logging daemon; it accumulates log messages from various applications and stores them into log files based on the configuration information in */etc/syslogd.conf*.

routed is a server used to maintain dynamic routing information. When your system attempts to send packets to another network, it may require additional routing table entries in order to do so. *routed* takes care of manipulating the routing table without the need for user intervention.

Here is a sample *rc.inet2* that starts up *syslogd*, *inetd*, and *routed*:

```
#! /bin/sh
# Sample /etc/rc.d/rc.inet2

# Start syslogd
if [ -f /usr/sbin/syslogd ]
then
/usr/sbin/syslogd
fi

# Start inetd
if [ -f /usr/sbin/inetd ]
```

```
then
/usr/sbin/inetd
fi

# Start routed
if [ -f /usr/sbin/routed ]
then
/usr/sbin/routed -q
fi
```

Among the various additional servers you may want to start in *rc.inet2* is *named*. *named* is a name server; it is responsible for translating (local) IP addresses to names, and vice versa. If you don't have a name server elsewhere on the network, or if you want to provide local machine names to other machines in your domain, it may be necessary to run *named*. *named* configuration is somewhat complex and requires planning; we refer interested readers to *DNS and BIND* (O'Reilly).

/etc/hosts

/etc/hosts contains a list of IP addresses and the hostnames they correspond to. In general, */etc/hosts* contains entries for your local machine and perhaps other "important" machines (such as your name server or gateway). Your local name server provides address-to-name mappings for other machines on the network transparently.

For example, if your machine is *eggplant.veggie.com* with the IP address 128.17.75. 20, your */etc/hosts* would look like this:

```
127.0.0.1              localhost
128.17.75.20           eggplant.veggie.com eggplant
```

If you're just using loopback, the only line in the */etc/hosts* file should be for the address 127.0.0.1.

/etc/networks

The */etc/networks* file lists the names and addresses of your own and other networks. It is used by the *route* command and allows you to specify a network by name instead of by address.

Every network you wish to add a route to using the *route* command (generally called from *rc.inet1*) should have an entry in */etc/networks* for convenience; otherwise, you will have to specify the network's IP address instead of the name.

As an example:

```
default        0.0.0.0        # default route    - mandatory
loopnet        127.0.0.0      # loopback network - mandatory
veggie-net     128.17.75.0    # Modify for your own network address
```

Now, instead of using the command:

```
route add 128.17.75.20
```

we can use:

```
route add veggie-net
```

/etc/host.conf

The *⁄etc⁄host.conf* file specifies how your system resolves hostnames. It should contain the two lines:

```
order hosts,bind
multi on
```

These lines tell the resolver libraries to first check the *⁄etc⁄hosts* file and then ask the name server (if one is present) for any names it must look up. The `multi` entry allows you to have multiple IP addresses for a given machine name in *⁄etc⁄hosts*.

On systems that use *glibc2* (which applies to most recent distributions), *⁄etc⁄nsswitch. conf* is used instead of *⁄etc⁄host.conf*. In this case, this file should contain the lines `hosts: files dns` and `networks: files dns`.

/etc/resolv.conf

This file configures the name resolver, specifying the address of your name server (if any) and domains that you want to search by default if a specified hostname is not a fully specified hostname. For example, if this file contains the line:

```
search vpizza.com vpasta.com
```

using the hostname *blurb* will try to resolve the names *blurb.vpizza.com* and *blurb. vpasta.com* (in this order). This is convenient because it saves you typing in the full names of often-used domains. On the other hand, the more domains you specify here, the longer the DNS lookup will take.

For example, the machine *eggplant.veggie.com* with a name server at address 128.17. 75.55 would have the following lines in *⁄etc⁄resolv.conf*:

```
domain     veggie.com
nameserver 128.17.75.55
```

You can specify more than one name server; each must have a `nameserver` line of its own in *resolv.conf*.

Setting your hostname

You should set your system hostname with the *hostname* command. This is usually executed from *⁄etc⁄rc.d⁄rc.sysinit* (*⁄sbin⁄init.d⁄boot* on SuSE systems); simply search your system *rc* files to determine where it is invoked. For example, if your (full) hostname is *eggplant.veggie.com*, edit the appropriate *rc* file to execute the command *⁄bin⁄ hostname eggplant.veggie.com*. Note that the *hostname* executable may be found in a directory other than *⁄bin* on your system.

Trying out your network

Once you have the various networking configuration files modified for your system, you should be able to reboot (using a TCP/IP-enabled kernel) and attempt to use the network.

When first booting the system, you may wish to disable execution of *rc.inet1* and *rc.inet2* and run them by hand once the system is up. This allows you to catch any error messages, modify the scripts, and retry. Once you have things working, you can enable the scripts from */etc/inittab*.

One good way of testing network connectivity is to simply *ssh* to another host. You should first try to connect to another host on your local network, and if this works, attempt to connect to hosts on other networks. The former will test your connection to the local subnet; the latter, your connection to the rest of the world through your gateway.

You may be able to connect to remote machines via the gateway if connecting to machines on the subnet fails. This is a sign that there is a problem with your subnetwork mask or the routing table entry for the local network.

When attempting to connect to other machines, you should first try to connect using only the IP address of the remote host. If this seems to work, but connecting via the hostname does not, there may be a problem with your name server configuration (e.g., */etc/resolv.conf* and */etc/host.conf*) or with your route to the name server.

The most common source of network trouble is an ill-configured routing table. You can use the command:

```
netstat -rn
```

to display the routing table; in the previous section, we described the format of the routing tables as displayed by this command. The *netstat*(8) manual page provides additional insight as well. Using *netstat* without the –n option forces it to display host and network entries by name instead of by address.

To debug your routing tables, you can either edit *rc.inet1* and reboot, or use the *route* command by hand to add or delete entries. The manual page for *route*(8) describes the full syntax of this command. Note that simply editing *rc.inet1* and re-executing it will not clear out old entries in the routing table; you must either reboot or use *route del* to delete the entries.

If absolutely nothing seems to work, there may be a problem with your Ethernet device configuration. First, be sure that your Ethernet card was detected at the appropriate address and/or IRQ at boot time. The kernel boot messages will give you this information; if you are using *syslogd*, kernel boot-time messages are also saved in a file, such as */var/log/messages*.

A good way to determine whether it was really the Ethernet card that created the trouble is to use the command *ifconfig interface_name*, as in:

```
ifconfig eth0
```

This will output statistics about the interface. If it has received or sent any packets, it must have been recognized by the kernel, and there cannot be a general hardware problem. If your card is not listed when issuing:

```
ifconfig
```

it wasn't even recognized by the kernel.

If detection of your Ethernet card is faulty, you may have to modify kernel parameters to fix it. The Linux Ethernet HOWTO includes much information on debugging Ethernet card configurations. In many cases, the fix is as simple as specifying the appropriate IRQ and port address at the LILO boot prompt. For example, booting via LILO with the command:

```
lilo: linux ether=9,0x300,0,1,eth0
```

will select IRQ 9, base address 0x300, and the external transceiver (the fourth value of 1) for the *eth0* device. To use the internal transceiver (if your card supports both types), change the fourth value of the ether option to 0.

Also, don't overlook the possibility that your Ethernet card is damaged or incorrectly connected to your machine or the network. A bad Ethernet card or cable can cause no end of trouble, including intermittent network failures, system crashes, and so forth. When you're at the end of your rope, consider replacing the Ethernet card and/or cable to determine if this is the source of the problem.[*]

If your Ethernet card is detected, but the system is still having problems talking to the network, the device configuration with *ifconfig* may be to blame. Be sure you have specified the appropriate IP address, broadcast address, and subnet mask for your machine. Invoking *ifconfig* with no arguments displays information on your Ethernet device configuration.

Dial-up PPP

In order to communicate over TCP/IP using a modem (such as through a dial-up account to an Internet service provider) or through some other serial device (such as a "null modem" serial cable between two machines), Linux provides the Point-to-Point Protocol software suite, commonly known as PPP. PPP is a protocol that takes packets sent over a network (such as TCP/IP) and converts them to a format that can be easily sent over a modem or serial wire. Chances are, if you have an Internet

---

[*] One of the authors once spent three hours trying to determine why the kernel wouldn't recognize an Ethernet card at boot time. As it turned out, the 16-bit card was plugged into an 8-bit slot—mea culpa.

account with an ISP, the ISP's server uses PPP to communicate with dial-up accounts. By configuring PPP under Linux, you can directly connect to your ISP account in this way.

SLIP is an earlier protocol that has the same basic features as PPP. However, it lacks certain important qualities, such as the ability to negotiate IP addresses and packet sizes. These days SLIP has more or less been supplanted entirely by PPP; however, some older ISPs may still use SLIP rather than PPP. If this is the case for you, we refer you to other sources of information, such as the *Linux Network Administrator's Guide* (O'Reilly).

In this section, we will cover configuration of a PPP *client*—that is, a system that will connect to an ISP (or other PPP server) in order to communicate with the Internet. Setting up a Linux machine as a PPP server is also possible but is somewhat more involved; this is covered in the *Linux Network Administrator's Guide* (O'Reilly).

Basic PPP Configuration for Modems

In the U.S. and many parts of the world, people use traditional dial-up modems to send digital data over telephone lines. So we'll cover configuration for modems first. Then we'll show how to configure PPP for the faster and more convenient type of line called Integrated Services Digital Network (ISDN), which is especially popular in Europe and is available but not very well marketed in most of the U.S.

Requirements

Most Linux systems come preinstalled with all the software needed to run PPP. Essentially, you need a kernel compiled with PPP support and the *pppd* daemon and related tools, including the *chat* program.

Most Linux distributions include PPP support in the preconfigured kernel or as a kernel module that is loaded on demand. However, it may be necessary to compile kernel PPP support yourself; this is a simple matter of enabling the PPP options during the kernel configuration process and rebuilding the kernel. PPP is usually compiled as a separate module, so it is sufficient to recompile only the kernel modules if this is the case. See "Building the Kernel" in Chapter 7 for information on compiling the kernel and modules.

The *pppd* and *chat* utilities are user-level applications that control the use of PPP on your system; they are included with nearly every Linux distribution. On Red Hat systems, these utilities are installed in */usr/sbin* and are found in the *ppp* RPM package.

Also required for PPP usage is a modem that is compatible with both Linux and the type of modems used by your ISP's server. Most 14.4, 28.8, 56K, and other standard modem types fit into this category; very few modem types are not supported by Linux, and it would be unusual for an ISP to use anything so esoteric as to require you to buy something else.

One type of modem to watch out for is the so-called "Winmodem." This was originally a product sold by US Robotics but has now been produced in several varieties by other vendors. Winmodems use the host CPU to convert digital signals into analog signals so that they can be sent over the phone line, unlike regular modems which have a special chip to perform this function. The problem with Winmodems is that, as of this writing, the programming details for these devices are proprietary, meaning that it is very difficult to write Linux drivers for this class of devices. Some work has been done on Winmodem drivers, but your mileage using them may vary a lot. Unless you are ready to do some serious tinkering and maybe even driver hacking, Winmodems are best avoided on Linux. (Besides, some people scoff at the idea of wasting precious CPU cycles to generate modem signals, a job best left to specialized hardware. One perceived advantage of these so-called "software modems," on the other hand, is that upgrading their functionality is simply a matter of upgrading the operating system driver that controls them, rather than buying new hardware.)

Serial device names

Under Windows 95/98/ME and MS-DOS, modems and other serial devices are named COM1 (for the first serial device), COM2 (for the second), and so forth, up to COM4. (Most systems support up to four serial devices, although multiport cards are available that can increase this number.) Under Linux, these same devices are referred to as /dev/ttyS0, /dev/ttyS1, on up to /dev/ttyS3.* On most systems, at installation time a symbolic link called /dev/modem will be created. This link points to the serial device on which the modem can be found, as shown in the following listing:

```
% ls -l /dev/modem
lrwxrwxrwx   1 root      root      10 May  4 12:41 /dev/modem -> /dev/ttyS0
```

If this link is incorrect for your system (say, because you know that your modem is not on /dev/ttyS0 but on /dev/ttyS2), you can easily fix it as root by entering:

```
# ln -sf /dev/ttyS2 /dev/modem
```

Setting up PPP

Several steps are involved in PPP configuration. The first is to write a so-called "chat script," which performs the "handshaking" necessary to set up a PPP connection between your machine and the ISP. During this handshaking phase, various pieces of information might be exchanged, such as your ISP username and password. The second step is to write a script that fires up the *pppd* daemon; running this script causes the modem to dial the ISP and start up PPP. The final step is to configure your system's /etc/resolv.conf file so that it knows where to find a domain name server. We'll go through each step in turn.

---

* Older versions of Linux also used special "callout" devices, called /dev/cua0 through /dev/cua3. These are obsolete as of Linux kernel Version 2.2.

Before you start, you need to know the following pieces of information:

- The ISP dial-in account phone number
- Your ISP username and password
- The IP address of the ISP's domain name server

Your ISP should have told you this information when you established the account.

In addition, you might need to know the following:

- The IP address of the ISP's server
- The IP address of your system (if not dynamically assigned by the ISP)
- The subnet mask you should use

These last three items can usually be determined automatically during the PPP connection setup; however, occasionally this negotiation does not work properly. It can't hurt to have this information in case you need it.

Writing a chat script

chat is a program that can perform simple handshaking between a PPP client and server during connection setup, such as exchange usernames and passwords. *chat* is also responsible for causing your modem to dial the ISP's phone number and other simple tasks.

chat is automatically invoked by *pppd* when started (this is discussed later). All you need to do is write a simple shell script that invokes *chat* to handle the negotiation. A simple chat script is shown in the following example. Edit the file */etc/ppp/my-chat-script* (as *root*) and place in it the following lines:

```
#!/bin/sh
# my-chat-script: a program for dialing up your ISP
exec chat -v            \
'' ATZ                  \
OK ATDT555-1212         \
CONNECT ''              \
ogin: mdw               \
assword: my-password
```

Specifying `ogin` and `assword` without the initial letters allows the prompts to be either `Login` or `login`, and `Password` or `password`.

Be sure that the file *my-chat-script* is executable; the command `chmod 755 /etc/ppp/my-chat-script` will accomplish this.

Note that each line ending in a backslash should not have any characters *after* the backslash; the backslash forces line-wrapping in the shell script.

The third line of this script runs *chat* with the options on the following lines. Each line contains two whitespace-delimited fields: an "expect" string and a "send" string. The idea is that the chat script will respond with the send string when it receives the expect string from the modem connection. For example, the last line of the script informs chat to respond with my-password when the prompt assword is given by the ISP's server.

The first line of the handshaking script instructs *chat* to send ATZ to the modem, which should cause the modem to reset itself. (Specifying an expect string as " means that nothing is expected before ATZ is sent.) The second line waits for the modem to respond with OK, after which the number is dialed using the string ATDT555-1212. (If you use pulse dialing rather than tone dialing change this to ATDP555-1212. The phone number, of course, should be that of the remote system's modem line.)

When the modem responds with CONNECT, a newline is sent (indicated by " as the send string). After this, *chat* waits for the prompt ogin: before sending the username and assword: before sending the password.

The various send strings starting with AT in the previous example are simply Hayes-modem–standard modem control strings. The manual that came with your modem should explain their usage; this is not specific to Linux or any other operating system. As one example, using a comma in a phone number indicates that the modem should pause before sending the following digits; one might use ATDT9,,,555-1212 if a special digit (9 in this case) must be dialed to reach an outside line.

Note that this is a very simple *chat* script that doesn't deal with timeouts, errors, or any other extraordinary cases that might arise while you're attempting to dial into the ISP. See the *chat* manual pages for information on how to spruce up your script to deal with these cases. Also, note that you need to know in advance what prompts the ISP's server will use (we assumed login and password). There are several ways of finding out this information; possibly, the ISP has told you this information in advance, or supplied a handshaking script for another system such as Windows 95 (which uses a mechanism very similar to *chat*). Otherwise, you can dial into the ISP server "by hand," using a simple terminal emulator, such as *minicom* or *seyon*. The manpages for those commands can help you do this.

Starting up pppd

Now, we're ready to configure the *pppd* daemon to initiate the PPP connection using the *chat* script we just wrote. Generally, you do this by writing another shell script that invokes *pppd* with a set of options.

The format of the *pppd* command is:

```
pppd device-name baudrate options
```

Table 15-1 shows the options supported by *pppd*. You almost certainly won't need all of them.

Table 15-1. Common pppd options

Option	Effect
lock	Locks the serial device to restrict access to *pppd*.
crtscts	Uses hardware flow control.
noipdefault	Doesn't try to determine the local IP address from the hostname. The IP is assigned by the remote system.
user *username*	Specifies the hostname or username for PAP or CHAP identification.
netmask *mask*	Specifies the netmask for the connection.
defaultroute	Adds a default route to the local system's routing table, using the remote IP address as the gateway.
connect *command*	Uses the given *command* to initiate the connection. *pppd* assumes this script is in */etc/ppp*. If not, specify the full path of the script.
local_IP_address:*remote_IP_address*	Specifies the local and/or remote IP addresses. Either or both of these could be 0.0.0.0 to indicate that the address should be assigned by the remote system.
debug	Logs connection information through the syslog daemon.

It is common to invoke the *pppd* command from a shell script. Edit the file */etc/ppp/ppp-on* and add the following lines:

```
#!/bin/sh
# the ppp-on script

exec /usr/sbin/pppd /dev/modem 38400 lock crtscts noipdefault \
defaultroute 0.0.0.0:0.0.0.0 connect my-chat-script
```

As with the *my-chat-script* file in the earlier example, be sure this is executable and watch out for extra characters after a backslash at the end of a line.

With this script in place, it should be possible to connect to the ISP using the command:

```
% /etc/ppp/ppp-on
```

You need not be *root* to execute this command. Upon running this script, you should hear your modem dialing, and if all goes well, after a minute PPP should be happily connected. The *ifconfig* command should report an entry for ppp0 if PPP is up and running:

```
# ifconfig
lo        Link encap:Local Loopback
inet addr:127.0.0.1  Bcast:127.255.255.255  Mask:255.0.0.0
UP BROADCAST LOOPBACK RUNNING  MTU:3584  Metric:1
RX packets:0 errors:0 dropped:0 overruns:0 frame:0
TX packets:0 errors:0 dropped:0 overruns:0 carrier:0
collisions:0
```

```
ppp0      Link encap:Point-to-Point Protocol
inet addr:207.25.97.248  P-t-P:207.25.97.154  Mask:255.255.255.0
UP POINTOPOINT RUNNING  MTU:1500  Metric:1
RX packets:1862 errors:0 dropped:0 overruns:0 frame:0
TX packets:1288 errors:0 dropped:0 overruns:0 carrier:0
collisions:0
Memory:73038-73c04
```

Here, we can see that PPP is up, the local IP address is 207.25.97.248, and the remote server IP address is 207.25.97.154.

If you wish to be notified when the PPP connection is established (the *ppp-on* script returns immediately), add the following line to */etc/ppp/ip-up*:

```
/usr/bin/wall "PPP is up!"
```

/etc/ppp/ip-up is executed when PPP establishes an IP connection, so you can use this script to trigger the *wall* command when the connection is complete.

Another simple shell script can be used to kill the PPP session. Edit the file */etc/ppp/ ppp-off* as follows:

```
#!/bin/sh
# A simple ppp-off script

kill `cat /var/run/ppp0.pid`
```

Running */etc/ppp/ppp-off* now kills the PPP daemon and shuts down the modem connection.

Configuring DNS

By itself, use of *pppd* along with *chat* only establishes a PPP connection and assigns you an IP address; in order to use domain names, you need to configure the system to be aware of the domain name server provided by your ISP. You do this by editing */etc/resolv.conf*. The manpage for *resolver* describes this file in detail. However, for most purposes it suffices to simply include lines of two forms: one that specifies the list of domains to search whenever a domain name is used, and another that specifies the address of a DNS server.

A sample */etc/resolv.conf* file might look like this:

```
# Sample /etc/resolv.conf
search cs.nowhere.edu nowhere.edu
nameserver 207.25.97.8
nameserver 204.148.41.1
```

The first line indicates that every time a domain name is used (such as *orange* or *papaya*), it should be searched for in the list of specified domains. In this case, resolver software would first expand a name like *papaya* to *papaya.cs.nowhere.edu* and try to find a system by that name, then expand it to *papaya.nowhere.edu* if necessary and try again.

The lines beginning with nameserver specify the IP address of domain name servers (which should be provided by your ISP) that your system contacts to resolve domain names. If you specify more than one nameserver line, the given DNS servers will be contacted in order, until one returns a match; in this way, one DNS server is treated as a primary and the others as backups.

Troubleshooting PPP configuration

The PPP configuration described here is meant to be very simple and will certainly not cover all cases; the best sources for additional information are the manpages for *pppd* and *chat* as well as the Linux PPP HOWTO and related documents.

Happily, both *chat* and *pppd* log messages on their progress, as well as any errors, using the standard *syslog* daemon facility. By editing */etc/syslog.conf*, you can cause these messages to be captured to a file. To do this, add the following lines:

```
# Save messages from chat
local2.*                                /var/log/chat-log

# Save messages from pppd
daemon.*                                /var/log/pppd-log
```

This will cause messages from *chat* to be logged to */var/log/chat-log* and messages from *pppd* to be logged to */var/log/pppd-log*.

Note that these log messages will contain private information, such as ISP usernames and passwords! It is important that you leave this logging enabled only while you are debugging your PPP configuration; after things are working, remove these two log files and remove the lines from */etc/syslog.conf*.

chat will also log certain errors to */etc/ppp/connect-errors*, which is not controlled through the *syslog* daemon. (It should be safe to leave this log in place, however.)

PAP and CHAP

Some ISPs may require you to use a special authentication protocol, such as PAP (Password Authentication Protocol) or CHAP (Challenge Handshake Authentication Protocol). These protocols rely on some form of "shared secret" known to both the client and the server; in most cases, this is just your ISP account password.

If PAP or CHAP are required by your ISP, they are configured by adding information to the files */etc/ppp/pap-secrets* and */etc/ppp/chap-secrets*, respectively. Each file has four fields separated by spaces or tabs. Here is an example of a *pap-secrets* file:

```
# Secrets for authentication using PAP
# client        server              secret              IP or Domain
mdw             *                   my-password
```

The first field is your system's name as expected by the remote system, usually your ISP username. The second field specifies the ISP's server name; an asterisk allows this entry to match all ISP servers to which you might connect. The third field specifies the shared secret provided by your ISP; as stated earlier, this is usually your ISP password. The fourth field is primarily used by PPP servers to limit the IP addresses to which users dialing in have access. These addresses can be specified as either IP addresses or domain names. For most PPP client configurations, however, this field is not required.

The *chap-secrets* file has the same four fields, but you need to include an entry other than * for the service provider's system; this is a secret the ISP shares with you when you establish the account.

If PAP or CHAP is being used, it's not necessary for the *chat* script to include handshaking information after CONNECT is received; *pppd* will take care of the rest. Therefore, you can edit */etc/ppp/my-chat-script* to contain only the lines:

```
#!/bin/sh
# my-chat-script: a program for dialing up your ISP
exec chat -v              \
'' ATZ                    \
OK ATDT555-1212           \
CONNECT ''
```

You will also need to add the user option to the *pppd* command line in */etc/ppp/ppp-on*, as so:

```
#!/bin/sh
# the ppp-on script

exec /usr/sbin/pppd /dev/modem 38400 lock crtscts noipdefault \
user mdw defaultroute 0.0.0.0:0.0.0.0 connect my-chat-script
```

PPP over ISDN

ISDN has offered convenient, high-speed data communications—at a price—for many years; it is particularly popular in Europe where rates and marketing have been more favorable to its use than in the U.S. ISDN, which integrates data and regular voice transmission over a single line, offers both a faster connection setup and much better throughput than traditional modems.

ISDN lines can transfer 64 kbits/second. And unlike analog lines, they can achieve this speed all the time because their transmission does not depend on the vagaries of analog transmission with interference by various kinds of noise. A newer protocol called ADSL (Asymmetric Digital Subscriber Line) is upping the ante for fast data access over phone lines, but ISDN still has a bigger market right now.

In this section, we describe how to configure dial-up access to your Internet provider over an ISDN line. We'll cover only the most common style of connection, synchronous PPP, not the special mode called *Raw IP* over ISDN. Furthermore, this section discusses just internal ISDN boards, which require a kind of setup that's different from the dial-up access covered in the previous section. To set up external ISDN devices, or the so-called ISDN modems (a term that is an oxymoron because there is no modulation and demodulation), you can use commands similar to those in the previous section because these devices present themselves to the computer and the operating system like a normal modem that offers some additional commands, faster connection setup, and higher throughput.

If you want to have more information beyond what we present here, the source for all ISDN-related information for Linux is *http://www.isdn4linux.de* (despite this domain being registered in Germany, all the information here is in English).

In a way, setting up ISDN connections is much easier than setting up analog connections because many of the problems (bad lines, long connection setup times, and so on) simply cannot occur with digital lines. Once you dial the number, the connection is set up within milliseconds. But this can lead to problems. Since the connections are set up and shut down so fast, a misconfigured system that dials out again and again can cost you a fortune. This is even more problematic because with internal ISDN cards, you hear no clicking and whistling as you do with modems, and there are no lights that inform you that a connection has been made. You can check the status of your ISDN line with some simple programs, though.

Follow these two steps to set up dial-up PPP over ISDN:

1. Configure your ISDN hardware.
2. Configure and start the PPP daemon and change the routing table to use your ISDN line.

We will cover those steps in the next sections.

Configuring Your ISDN Hardware

The first step involves making your ISDN board accessible to the kernel. As with any other hardware board, you need a device driver that must be configured with the correct parameters for your board.

Linux supports a large number of ISDN hardware boards. We cannot cover every single board here, but the procedure is more or less the same for each one. Reading the documentation for your specific card in the directory *Documentation/isdn* in the Linux kernel sources will help you a lot if your board is not covered here.

We will concentrate here on boards that use the so-called *HiSax* driver. This device driver works with almost all cards that use the Siemens HSCX chipset (and thus with most passive cards available on the market today). That includes, for instance, the USR Sportster internal TA and the well-known Teles, ELSA, and Fritz boards. Other boards are similarly configured. Even some active cards are supported by Linux, including the well-known AVM B1 and the IBM Active 2000 ISDN card.

The first thing you need to do is configure the kernel so that it includes ISDN support. We advise you to compile everything ISDN-related as modules, especially while you are experimenting with setting it up. You will need the following modules:

- ISDN support.
- Support for synchronous PPP.
- One device driver module for your hardware. If you pick the HiSax driver, you will also have to specify which specific brand of ISDN card you have and which ISDN protocol you want to use. The latter is almost certainly EURO/DSS1 in Europe—unless you live in Germany and have had your ISDN for a long time, in which case it might be 1TR6—and US NI1 in the U.S. If you live elsewhere, or when in doubt, ask your phone company.

Compile and install the modules as described in Chapter 7. Now you are ready to configure your ISDN hardware. Some distributions like SuSE make setting up ISDN lines very easy and comfortable. We cover the hard way here in case your distribution is not so user-friendly, the automatic configuration does not work, or you simply want to know what is going on behind the scenes.

Now you need to load the device driver module using *modprobe*. This will automatically load the other modules as well. All the device driver modules accept a number of module parameters; the hisax module accepts, among others, the following:

id=*boardid*
> Sets an identifier for the ISDN board. You can pick any name you like here, but you cannot have the same identifier for more than one board in your system.

type=*boardtype*
> Specifies the exact board brand and type. For example, a value of 16 for *boardtype* selects the support for the USR Sportster internal TA. See *Documentation/isdn/README.hisax* in the kernel sources for the full list of board types.

protocol=*protocoltype*
> Selects an ISDN subprotocol. Valid values for *protocoltype* are 1 for the old German 1TR6 protocol, 2 for the common EDSS1 (so-called Euro ISDN), and 3 for leased lines.

irq=*irqno*
> Specifies the interrupt line to use. Not all boards need this.

io=*addr*
> Specifies the I/O address to use. Not all boards need this. Some boards need two I/O addresses. In this case, the parameters to use are io0 and io1.

For example, the following command loads the HiSax driver for use with a Teles 16.3 board, Euro ISDN, IO address 0x280, and IRQ line 10 (a very common case):

```
tigger # modprobe hisax type=3 protocol=2 io=0x280 irq=10
```

Please see *Documentation/isdn/README.HiSax* or the equivalent file for your hardware for more information.

This module is not much of a talker; if there is no output from the *modprobe* command, it is likely that everything went well. You might also want to check your system log at */var/log/messages*. You should see a few lines starting with HiSax: (or the name of the driver you are using), ending with:

```
HiSax: module installed
```

If the module did not load, you will also most likely find the answer in */var/log/messages*. The most common problem is that the IRQ or I/O address was wrong or that you selected the wrong card type. If all else fails, and you have Windows installed on the same machine, boot up Windows and check what it reports for the IRQ and I/O address lines.

You should do one more check before you jump to the next section, and this check involves calling yourself. This can work because, with ISDN, you always have two phone lines at your disposal. Thus one line will be used for the outgoing "phone call" and the other line will be used for the incoming one.

In order to have the ISDN subsystem report what is going on with your phone lines, you will need to configure it to be more verbose than it is by default. You do this by means of three utility programs that are all part of the isdn4k-utils package that you can find at your friendly Linux FTP server around the corner.

The isdn4k-utils contain, among other things, the three utilities *hisaxctrl* for configuring the device driver, *isdnctrl* for configuring the higher levels of the ISDN subsystem, and *isdnlog*, a very useful tool that logs everything happening on your ISDN lines. While you can use *hisactrl* and *isdnctrl* without any configuration, you will need to provide a small configuration file for *isdnlog*. For now, we will content ourselves with a quick solution, but once your ISDN connection is up and running, you will want to configure *isdnlog* to see where your money is going. So for now, copy one of the sample configuration files contained in the *isdnlog* package to */etc/isdn/isdn.conf*. You will need to edit at least the following lines:

COUNTRYCODE=
> Add your phone country code here—for example, 1 for the U.S. and Canada, 44 for the United Kingdom, 46 for Sweden, and so on.

AREAPREFIX=
> If the area codes in your country are prefixed by a fixed digit, put this in here. The prefix is 0 for most European countries, 9 for Finland, and nothing for the U.S., Denmark, and Norway.

AREACODE=
> Put your area code in here. If you have specified an AREAPREFIX in the last step, don't repeat that here. For example, Stockholm, Sweden, has the area code 08. You put 0 into AREAPREFIX and 8 into AREACODE.

Once you have set this up, execute the following commands to make your ISDN system more verbose:

```
tigger # /sbin/hisaxctrl boardid 1 4
tigger # /sbin/isdnctrl verbose 3
tigger # /sbin/lsdnlog /dev/isdnctrl0 &
```

If you need to use a driver other than HiSax, you might need to use a different command. For example, for the PCBit driver, the command *pcbitctl* is available in the isdn4k-utils package.

Now you can go ahead and phone yourself. You should try all your MSNs (multiple subscriber numbers, which are your ISDN phone numbers) to see that the board can detect all of them. During or after each call, check */var/log/messages*. You should see lines like the following:

```
Mar 16 18:34:22 tigger kernel: isdn_net: call from 4107123455,1,0 -> 123456
Mar 16 18:34:33 tigger kernel: isdn_net: Service-Indicator not 7, ignored
```

This shows that the kernel has detected voice call (the service indicator is 0) from the phone number 123455 in the area with the area code (0)4107 to the MSN 123456.

Note how the number called is specified because you will need this information later. The number is sent with the area code in some phone networks, but without the area code in others. Anyway, congratulations if you have come this far. Your ISDN hardware is now correctly configured.

Setting Up Synchronous PPP

Setting up the PPP daemon again involves several substeps. On Linux, the ISDN board is treated like a network interface that you have to configure with special commands. In addition, you need to specify the username and password that your ISP has assigned you. When everything is configured, you start up the *ipppd* daemon, which lurks in the background until a connection request is made.

First, let's configure the "network interface." This involves a number of commands that most system administrators simply put into a script that they store in a file, such as */sbin/pppon*. Here is a sample file that you can modify to your needs:

```
/sbin/isdnctrl addif ippp0
/sbin/isdnctrl addphone ippp0 out 0123456789
/sbin/isdnctrl dialmax ippp0 2
/sbin/isdnctrl eaz ippp0 123456
/sbin/isdnctrl huptimeout ippp0 100
/sbin/isdnctrl l2_prot ippp0 hdlc
/sbin/isdnctrl l3_prot ippp0 trans
/sbin/isdnctrl encap ippp0 syncppp
/sbin/ifconfig ippp0 1.1.1.1 pointopoint 123.45.67.89 metric 1
```

Let's go through these commands one by one:

`isdnctrl addif ippp0`
> Tells the kernel that a new ISDN interface with the name `ippp0` will be used. Always use names starting with `ippp`.

`isdnctrl addphone ippp0 out 0123456789`
> Tells the ISDN interface which phone number to use. This is the phone number that you use to dial up your provider. If you have used analog dial-up so far, check with your provider because the phone number for ISDN access could be different.

`isdnctrl dialmax ippp0 2`
> Specifies how many times the kernel should dial if the connection could not be established, before giving up.

`isdnctrl eaz ippp0 123456`
> Specifies one of your own MSNs here. This is very important—without this, not much will work. In case your provider verifies your access via your phone number, make sure you specify here the MSN that you have registered with your provider.

`isdnctrl huptimeout ippp0 100`
> Specifies the number of seconds that the line can be idle before the kernel closes the connection (specified by the last number in this command). This is optional, but can save you a lot of money if you do not have a flat phone rate. Thus, if you forget to shut down the connection yourself, the kernel will do that for you.

`isdnctrl l2_prot ippp0 hdlc`
> Specifies the layer 2 protocol to use. Possible values here are `hdlc`, `x75i`, `x75ui`, and `x75bui`. Most providers use `hdlc`. When in doubt, ask your provider.

`isdnctrl l3_prot ippp0 trans`
> Specifies the layer 3 protocol to use (the 1 in the option is the letter L). Currently, only `trans` is available.

`isdnctrl encap ippp0 syncppp`
> Specifies the encapsulation to use. A number of values are possible here, but if you want to use synchronous PPP (or your provider demands that), you have to specify `syncppp` here. Another not-so-uncommon value is `rawip`. But since this provides only very weak authentication facilities, few providers still use it, even though it gives slightly better throughput because it requires less overhead.

`ifconfig ippp0 1.1.1.1 pointopoint 123.45.67.89 metric 1`
> Creates the new network interface. If your IP address is not assigned dynamically (as is the case with most dial-up connections), you need to specify your IP address instead of the 1.1.1.1 here. Also, you need to change the 123.45.67.89 to the IP address of your provider's dial-up server.

If you want, you can also reverse the setup by creating a script that shuts down the interfaces, etc. For example, it would use the `isdnctrl delif` command. But such a script is not strictly necessary, unless you want to disable all dialing at runtime.

Phew! But we are not finished yet. Next, you need to configure the *ipppd* daemon, which you do in the file */etc/ppp/ioptions*. You can also have a configuration file specific to each *ipppd* daemon, but that is necessary only if you want to be able to use different ISDN connections—that is, if you have multiple dial-up accounts.

The following is an *ioptions* file that is generic enough to work with most providers. It does not give maximum throughput but is quite stable. If you want to optimize it, ask your provider about the possible settings and read the manual page for *ipppd*(8):

```
debug
/dev/ipppo
user yourusername
name yourusername
mru 1500
mtu 1500
ipcp-accept-local
ipcp-accept-remote
noipdefault
-vj -vjccomp -ac -pc -bsdcomp
defaultroute
```

You have to change only two things here: change yourusername in the third and fourth lines to the username that your provider has assigned you for connecting to his system. We won't go through all the options here; see the manual page when in doubt.

ISDN access requires the same security as an analog modem. See the section "PAP and CHAP" earlier in this chapter for directions on setting up your *pap-secrets* or *chap-secrets* file as required by your service provider.

Now we have got our things together and can start having fun! First run the *ipppd* daemon:

```
tigger # /sbin/ipppd pidfile /var/run/ipppd.ipppo.pid file /etc/ppp/ioptions &
```

The *ipppd* daemon will now wait for connection requests. Since we have not configured it yet to automatically make a connection, we have to manually trigger the connection. You do this with the following command:

```
tigger # isdnctrl dial ipppo
```

You should now check */var/log/messages*. There should be lots of messages that start with ipppd. The last of those messages should contain the words local IP address and remote IP address together with the IP addresses. Once you find those messages, you are done. Because we have used the defaultroute option previously, the kernel has set up the default route to use the ISDN connection, and you should now be able to access the wide, wide world of the Internet. Start by pinging your provider's IP address. Once you are done and want to shut down the connection, enter:

```
tigger # isdnctrl hangup ippp0
```

And If It Does Not Work?

If you have no connection even though your hardware was successfully recognized and you have set up everything as described here, */var/log/messages* is again your friend. It is very likely that you will find the cause of the error there, even though it might be buried a bit.

The most common error is specifying the password or the username incorrectly. You know that you have a problem with the authentication if you see a line, such as:

```
PAP authentication failed
```

or:

- CHAP authentication failed

in the log file. Check your *chap-secrets* or *pap-secrets* very carefully. Your provider might also be able to see from her log files where exactly the authentication went wrong.

Of course, your provider might not support synchronous PPP as described here, even though most providers do nowadays. If this is the case, ask your provider for exact settings.

If it still does not work, ask your provider. A good ISP has a phone support line and can help you connect your Linux box. If your provider tells you that he "only supports Windows," it's time to switch. Many Linux-friendly providers are out there. Often the support staff is using Linux and can help you even though the provider's official policy is not to support Linux.

If for some reason you are stuck with an uncooperative provider, try finding other customers of this provider that also use Linux. Setting up your connection in nonstandard cases means fiddling with the options and parameters of the ISDN subsystem in the kernel and the *ipppd* daemon, and if somebody else has already found out what to do, you don't have to.

Where to Go from Here?

Once your ISDN connection works and you can access the Internet, you might want to set up some conveniences or other customizations. Here are some suggestions:

- Make *ipppd* dial your remote site automatically. You can do this can by setting the default route to the *ippp0* device like this:

```
/sbin/route add default netmask 0.0.0.0 ippp0
```

Now, whenever the kernel needs to send an IP packet to an IP address for which it has no specific route configured, it will trigger the *ipppd* daemon to build a connection. Use this only if you have also specified the huptimeout option of the ISDN subsystem, otherwise you could pay a fortune to your telephone company (unless you have a flat rate).

Since some programs try to build up Internet connections from time to time (Netscape is one of those candidates), setting this up can be dangerous for your wallet. If you use this, make sure to check the state of the connection often (as described later in this section).

- Try tools that monitor your ISDN connection. The isdn4k-utils package contains a number of those tools, including the command-line tools *imon* and *imontty* and X-based tools.

- Configure *isdnlog* to log exactly what you need, and use *isdnrep* to get detailed reports about the usage of your ISDN line. This works not only for calls to and from computer systems, but also for calls to other ISDN-enabled devices like phones and fax machines. There is only one caveat: your ISDN board cannot capture outgoing phone numbers for connections being set up by other devices. Most telephone companies provide a service, though, that echoes this phone number back to you and thus lets the ISDN subsystem pick it up. This service is often available for free or for a nominal fee. Ask your telephone company.

- For the truly adventurous: experiment with Multilink-PPP. As you know, with ISDN you have at least two lines. If you need extra-high capacity, why not use both? That's what Multilink-PPP does. In order to use this, you need to turn on the Support generic MP option during kernel configuration, and read the files *Documentation/isdn/README.syncppp* and *Documentation/isdn/syncppp.FAQ* in the kernel sources for hints on how to do this. Of course, your provider has to support this, too.

ADSL

The 64-KBit-per-second rate that ISDN supports is nice, but if you want to access multimedia files via the Internet or simply are using the Internet a lot, you may want even more bandwidth. Without drawing additional cables to your house or office, ADSL (Asynchronous Digital Subscriber Line) is a convenient alternative that gives you eight times the bandwidth of standard dial-up access and is run via your ordinary telephone line. A drawback with ADSL is that it only works within a distance of about 3-4 kilometers (2-3 miles) around the next switching station, which makes this service unavailable in rural areas. Note that there are other technologies with similar-sounding names, such as SDSL. While these are fundamentally different on the wire level, setting them up on your Linux box should be no different from ADSL.

ADSL is not dial-up access; once you have logged into your account, you are always connected. Some providers cut your connection after a while (often after 24 hours), upon which you have to log in again in order to regain access.

As we have already mentioned, there are no such things as ADSL cards or ADSL drivers. As far as hardware is concerned, an ADSL connection is just a normal Ethernet connection, using the same cables.

How you connect your Linux box to your ADSL line depends a lot on your ISP. With some ISPs, you rent the necessary equipment, such as an ADSL modem and an ADSL router, as part of your subscription. With others, you have to purchase the necessary hardware yourself, either on the free market or from the ISP. Your ISP can give you all the information you need.

There are two ways to use ADSL, either connecting directly to an ADSL modem or with an intervening ADSL router. If you have an ADSL router (either with a built-in ADSL modem, or in addition to one), you plug your Ethernet cable in there and are ready for action. If you want to connect your Linux box directly to your ADSL modem, you still connect the computer and the modem with an Ethernet cable, but you need to run a special protocol, called PPPoE (PPP over Ethernet), on it. This protocol is handled by a special daemon called *pppoed*. How this is set up depends on your distribution and should be documented there. Some distributions also let you set up PPPoE from their respective configuration programs.

Finally, we should mention that a small number of weirdo ADSL modems are not connected with an Ethernet, but rather USB cable. This is technically a bad idea, so you should avoid these modems if possible, but if you are stuck with one, you can find more information, including a driver that runs PPPoE on a USB connection (that would be PPP over Ethernet over USB, then!) at *http://www.prout.be/ECI/*.

Whichever way you use ADSL (with or without an ADSL router), you need to set up the correct IP address. This can either be static (in which case you should find it in the information you have received from your ISP), or dynamic and assigned via DHCP (Dynamic Host Communication Protocol), in which case you can request a dynamic IP address with the following command:

```
dhclient eth0
```

Of course, if the Ethernet card you use has another name, you need to replace the eth0 with the correct name. Instead of *dhclient*, you can also use the utility *pump*. There is also a DHCP daemon called *dhcpcd* that runs in the background and assigns a dynamic IP address whenever necessary.

Finally, many ISPs require that you activate your line from time to time. How you do this depends on your ISP, but often the activation requires nothing more than browsing to a certain web site and entering the credentials there that your ISP has assigned to you. As mentioned before, you may have to repeat this step from time to time.

NFS and NIS Configuration

Once you have TCP/IP enabled on your system, you may wish to configure your system to use the Network File System (NFS) or Network Information Service (NIS). NFS allows your system to share files directly with a network of machines. File access across NFS is transparent; you simply access the files as if they were stored on your local disk. In system administration terms, one system mounts another's filesystem on a local directory, just as a local filesystem can be mounted. NFS also allows you to export filesystems, allowing other systems on the network to mount your disks directly.

NIS (formerly known as the Yellow Pages, or YP, service) is a system that allows your host to obtain information automatically on user accounts, groups, filesystem mount points, and other system databases from servers on the network. For example, let's say you have a large collection of machines that should have the same user accounts and groups (information usually found in */etc/passwd* and */etc/group*). Users should be able to log into any of these machines and access their files directly (say, by mounting their home filesystem from a central location using NFS). Obviously, maintaining user accounts across many machines would be problematic; in order to add a new user, you would need to log into each machine and create the user account on each. When you use NIS, however, the system automatically consults centrally maintained databases across the network for such information, in addition to local files such as */etc/passwd*. NIS+ is an enhanced NIS service that is coming into use at some sites.

If your Linux system is to interact with other systems on a LAN, it's quite possible that NFS and NIS are in wide use on your LAN. In this section, we'll show you how to configure your system as an NFS and NIS client; that is, to mount remote filesystems and to participate in an existing NIS domain. It is possible to configure your system as an NFS and NIS server, but many subtle issues are involved in configuring any Unix or Linux system as an NFS/NIS server. Instead of providing a dangerously incomplete account of server configuration here, we refer you to O'Reilly & Associate's *Managing NFS and NIS* by Hal Stern. If you are already familiar with NFS/NIS configuration on other Unix systems, Linux is really no different; the manual pages and Linux HOWTO documents provide all the specifics.

Configuring NFS

Configuring your system to mount remote filesystems over NFS is a breeze. Assuming that you have TCP/IP configured and hostname lookup works correctly, you can simply add a line to your */etc/fstab* file such as the following:

```
# device          directory          type    options
allison:/usr          /fsys/allison/usr   NFS     defaults
```

As with regular filesystem mounts, be sure to create the mount-point directory (in this case, /fsys/allison/usr) first. The line in the /etc/fstab example allows your system to mount the directory /usr from the machine allison on the network.

Before the example NFS mount will work, however, the system administrator for the NFS server (here, allison) must configure the system to export the given directory (here, /usr) to your system. On most Unix systems, this is simply a matter of editing a file, such as /etc/exports, or running a simple command. Exporting a directory makes it available for other systems to mount it using NFS. It is not necessary for the exported directory to be the root of a filesystem itself; that is, you can export /usr even if /usr does not have its own separate filesystem.

In exporting a directory, the administrator may choose to make the directory available for read-only access. In this case you will not be able to write to the filesystem when mounted on your system. You should set the options field of the/etc/fstab line in the previous example to ro instead of defaults.

A few words of warning about NFS. First of all, NFS is not very happy when the servers for remote filesystems go down or the network connection fails. When the NFS server is unreachable for any reason, your system prints warning messages to the console (or system logs) periodically. If this is a problem, you can attempt to unmount any remote filesystems from the affected servers.

Another detail to watch out for when mounting NFS filesystems is the owner (UIDs) and group IDs (GIDs) of the files on the remote filesystem. In order to access your own files via NFS, the user and group ID for your own account must match those on the NFS server. One easy way to check this is with an ls -l listing: if the UID or GID does not match any local user, ls displays the UID/GID of files as numbers; otherwise, the user or group name is printed.

If IDs do not match, you have a few ways to remedy this problem. One is to simply change the UID of your user account (and the GID of your primary group) to match those on the NFS server (say, by editing your local /etc/passwd). This approach requires you to chown and chgrp all your local files after making the change. Another solution is to create a separate account with matching UID/GID. However, the best approach may be to use NIS to manage your user and group databases. With this solution, you do not create your user and group accounts locally; instead, they are provided to you by an NIS server. More on this later.

Another NFS caveat is the restriction of root permissions on NFS-mounted filesystems. Unless the NFS server explicitly grants your system root access on NFS-mounted filesystems, you will not have total access to files when logged in as root on your local system. The reason for this is security: allowing unlimited root access to files on a remote-mounted NFS filesystem opens itself up to abuse, especially when the NFS server and the NFS client are maintained or owned by different people. For this reason, you will not have omnipotent power to access or modify remote-mounted files when logged in as root on your local system.

Finally, you should be aware that NFS provides absolutely no encryption. If you mount your filesystems over the Internet, the transferred files can be interfered and even tampered with at any time (some people joke that NFS is short for "No File Security"). On the other hand, NFS mounts beyond your local network are probably too slow anyway, unless you are on a really big pipe.

Configuring NIS

NIS is a complex system, simply because it is so flexible. NIS is a general-purpose network database system, allowing your machine to transparently access information on user accounts, groups, filesystems, and so forth, from databases stored across the network. One goal of NIS is to ease network management. Allowing user account information (such as that stored in */etc/passwd*), for example, to be maintained on a single server makes it easy for many machines to share the same user accounts. In the previous section on NFS, we showed how user and group IDs on the NFS server and client should match in order to effectively access your files remotely. Using NIS allows your UID and GID to be defined from a remote site, not locally.

If your machine is connected at a site where NIS is used, chances are you can add your machine as an NIS client, thus allowing it to obtain user, group, and other databases directly from the network. To some extent this makes it unnecessary to create local user accounts or groups at all; apart from the locally defined users such as *root*, *bin*, and so forth, all other users will be created from the NIS server. If you couple the use of NIS with mounting user home directories from an NFS server, it's also unnecessary to set aside local storage for users. NIS can greatly lessen the amount of work you need to do as a system administrator.

In an NIS configuration, there may be NIS *servers*, *slaves*, and *clients*. As you can guess, servers are the systems where NIS databases originate and are maintained. NIS slaves are systems to which the server copies its databases. The slaves can provide the information to other systems, but changes to the databases must be made from the server. NIS clients are those systems that request database information from servers or slaves. Slaves are simply used as a way to ease the load on the NIS server; otherwise, all NIS requests would have to be serviced by a single machine.

To completely understand how NIS works and to maintain an NIS server is enough material for a whole book (again, see *Managing NFS and NIS*). However, when reading about NIS you are likely to come across various terms. NIS was originally named YP. This usage has been discontinued as Yellow Pages is trademarked in the United Kingdom (it's the phone book, after all).

There are at least two implementations of NIS for Linux: the "traditional" NIS implementation and a separate implementation known as "NYS" (standing for NIS+, YP, and Switch). The NIS client code for the "traditional" implementation is contained within the standard C library and is already installed on most Linux systems. (This is necessary to allow programs such as *login* to transparently access NIS databases as well as local system files.) The NYS client code is contained within the Network Services Library, *libnsl*. Linux systems using NYS should have compiled programs such as *login* against this library. On the other hand, the *glibc2* standard C library which most distributions use these days comes with support for NIS+. Different Linux distributions use different versions of the NIS or NYS client code, and some use a mixture of the two. To be safe, we'll describe how to configure a system for both traditional NIS and NYS implementations, meaning that no matter which is installed on your system, it should be able to act as a client. To make matters even more complex, there is also the PAM (Pluggable Authentication Modules) system that some distributions employ. In this case, programs like *login* are linked against the PAM library, which in turn loads a PAM library module that implements the authentication system in use on the system, or in turns delegates the task to other libraries.

We do assume here that you have installed and started all the necessary NIS daemon processes (such as *ypbind*) used by traditional NIS to talk to the NIS server. If your Linux system does not appear to have any NIS support, consult documents such as the Linux NIS HOWTO to configure it from scratch. Nearly all current Linux distributions come prepackaged with NIS client (and server) support, and all that's required of you is to edit a few configuration files.

The first step is to set the NIS domain in which your system will be operating. Your network administrators can provide this information to you. Note that the NIS domain name is not necessarily identical to the DNS domain name, which can be set with the *hostname* command. For example, if the full hostname of your system is *loomer.vpizza.com*, your DNS domain name is *vpizza.com*. However, your NIS domain name could be entirely different—for example, *vpizzas*. The NIS domain name is selected by the NIS server administrators and is not related to the DNS domain name described earlier.

Setting the domain name is usually a matter of running the *domainname* command at boot time, perhaps in one of your system *rc* files (such as */etc/rc.d/rc.inet1* described earlier). You should first check that *domainname* is not being executed in one of the existing *rc* files. The command takes the format:

```
domainname domain-name
```

for example, domainname vpizzas. The command is usually found in */sbin/domainname* and may have a slightly different name, such as *domainname-yp*.

A slightly different method sets the domain name under NYS. You should create (or edit) the file */etc/yp.conf*. This file should contain two lines: one specifying the name of your NIS domain and another specifying the hostname of the NIS server. As an example:

```
domain vpizzas
ypserver allison.vpizza.com
```

sets the NIS domain name to *vpizzas* and specifies that *allison.vpizza.com* should be used as the NIS server. If no ypserver line is included in this file, the system broadcasts a message on the network at boot time to determine the name of the NIS server. Your network administrators can provide you with the hostname of your preferred NIS server.

Once these two steps are complete, your system should be able to transparently access NIS databases. One way to test this is to query the system for a password database entry from the NIS server. The *ypwhich* queries specific NIS databases, for example:

```
ypwhich username passwd
```

If this returns the line from the NIS *passwd* database for the given user, you have successfully queried the NIS database. (One way to verify that the information returned is correct is to run this same command on another system in your NIS domain whose NIS configuration is known to be working.) The NIS *passwd* database is not identical to the */etc/passwd* file on your system, although it is in the same format. The Linux HOWTO documents contain additional information on troubleshooting your NIS configuration.

CHAPTER 16

The World Wide Web and Electronic Mail

The previous chapter put you on a network. It may have been hard work, but the result was quite an accomplishment: your system is now part of a community. If you are connected to the Internet, the next step is to get access to all the riches this medium offers. People generally agree that the most useful applications on the Internet are the World Wide Web and electronic mail; they are the subjects of this chapter.

The World Wide Web

Most certainly, everybody who has even the slightest connection with computers has used the World Wide Web by now. Like word processors or spreadsheets some centuries ago, the Web is what gets many people to use computers at all in the first place. We'll cover here some of the tools you can use to access the Web on Linux.

Linux was from the beginning intimately connected to the Internet in general and the Web in particular. For example, the Linux Documentation Project (LDP) provides various Linux-related documents via the Web. The LDP home page, located at *http:// www.tldp.org*, contains links to a number of other Linux-related pages around the world. The LDP home page is shown in Figure 16-1.

Linux web browsers usually can display information from several types of servers, not just HTTP servers sending clients HTML pages. For example, when accessing a document via HTTP, you are likely to see a page such as that displayed in Figure 16-1—with embedded pictures, links to other pages, and so on. When accessing a document via FTP, you might see a directory listing of the FTP server, as seen in Figure 16-2. Clicking a link in the FTP document either retrieves the selected file or displays the contents of another directory.

The way to refer to a document or other resource on the Web, of course, is through its *Uniform Resource Locator*, or URL. A URL is simply a pathname uniquely identifying a web document, including the machine it resides on, the filename of the

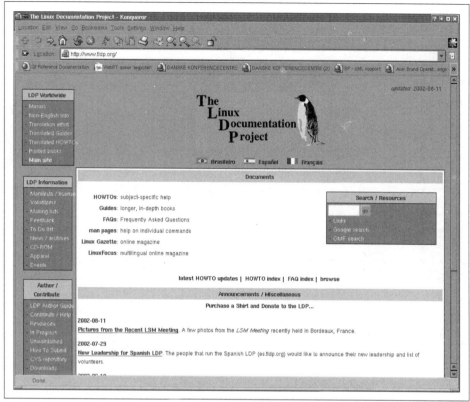

Figure 16-1. LDP home page on the World Wide Web

document, and the protocol used to access it (FTP, HTTP, etc.). For example, the Linux Gazette, an online Linux periodical on the LDP web site, has the URL:

http://www.tldp.org/LDP/LG/current/index.html

Let's break this down. The first part of the URL, *http:*, identifies the protocol used for the document, which in this case is HTTP. The second part of the URL, *//www.tldp.org*, identifies the machine where the document is provided. The final portion of the URL, *LDP/LG/current/index.html*, is the logical pathname to the document on *www.tldp.org*. This is similar to a Unix pathname, in that it identifies the file *index.html* in the directory *LDP/LG/current*. Therefore, to access the current issue of the Linux Gazette, you'd fire up a browser, telling it to access *http://www.tldp/LDP/LG/current/index.html*. What could be easier?

Actually, the conventions of web servers do make it easier. If you specify a directory as the last element of the path, the server understands that you want the file *index.html* in that directory. So you can reach the current Linux Gazette issue with a URL as short as:

http://www.tldp.org/LDP/LG/current/

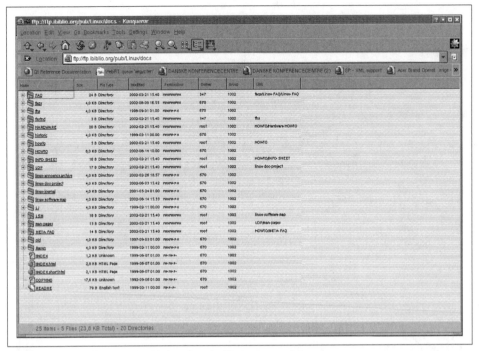

Figure 16-2. FTP directory as displayed in the Konqueror web browser

To access a file via anonymous FTP, we can use a URL, such as:

ftp://ftp.ibiblio.org/pub/linux/docs/INFO-SHEET/

This URL retrieves the introductory Linux information on *ftp.ibiblio.org*. Using this URL with your browser is identical to using *ftp* to fetch the file by hand.

The best way to understand the Web is to explore it. In the following section we'll explain how to get started with some of the available browsers. Later in the chapter, we'll cover how to configure your own machine as a web server for providing documents to the rest of the Web.

Of course, in order to access the Web, you'll need a machine with direct Internet access (via either Ethernet or PPP). In the following sections, we assume that you have already configured TCP/IP on your system and that you can successfully use clients, such as *ssh* and *ftp*.

Using Konqueror and Other Web Browsers

Konqueror is one of the most popular browsers for Linux. It features JavaScript and Java support, can run Netscape plug-ins (which allow you to add functions such as viewing Flash presentations), and is well integrated into the KDE desktop described in "The K Desktop Environment" in Chapter 11. Actually, when you install KDE, Konqueror will be installed as an integral part of the system. In the section on KDE, we have already described how to use Konqueror to read local information files. Now we are going to use it to browse the web.

Most things in Konqueror are quite obvious, but if you want to read more about it, you can use Konqueror to check out *http://www.konqueror.org.*

Here, we assume that you're using a networked Linux machine running X and that you have Konqueror installed. As stated before, your machine must be configured to use TCP/IP, and you should be able to use clients, such as *ssh* and *ftp.*

Starting Konqueror is simple. Run the command:

```
eggplant$ konqueror url
```

where *url* is the complete web address, or URL, for the document you wish to view. If you don't specify a URL, Konqueror will display a splash screen as shown in Figure 16-3.

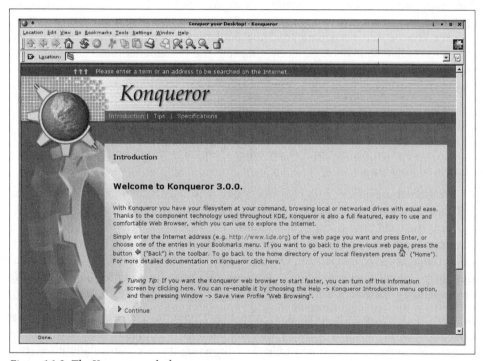

Figure 16-3. The Konqueror splash screen

If you run Konqueror from within KDE, you can simply type Alt-F2 to open the so-called *minicli* window, and type the URL. This will start up Konqueror and point it directly to the URL you have specified.

We assume that you have already used a web browser to browse the Web on some computer system, so we won't go into the very basics here; we'll just point out a few Linux-specific things.

Keep in mind that retrieving documents on the Web can be slow at times. This depends on the speed of the network connection from your site to the server, as well as the traffic on the network at the time. In some cases, web sites may be so loaded that they simply refuse connections; if this is the case, Konqueror displays an appropriate error message. At the bottom edge of the Konqueror window, a status report is displayed, and while a transfer is taking place, the KDE gear logo in the upper-right corner of the window animates. Clicking the logo takes you back to the Konqueror home page.

As you traverse links within Netscape Navigator, each document is saved in the *window history*, which can be recalled using the Go menu. Pressing the Back button (the one that shows an arrow pointing to the left) in the top toolbar of the Konqueror window moves you back through the window history to previously visited documents. Similarly, the Forward button moves you forward through the history.

You can also bookmark frequently visited web sites (or URLs) to Konqueror's "bookmarks." Whenever you are viewing a document that you might want to return to later, choose Add Bookmark from the Bookmarks menu, or simply press Ctrl-B. You can display your bookmarks by choosing the Bookmarks menu. Selecting any item in this menu retrieves the corresponding document from the Web. Finally, you can also display your bookmarks permanently in a separate subwindow to the left of the main browser window by selecting Window → Show Navigation Panel, and clicking the first of the selection buttons here (the one that looks like a real bookmark). You can also use the navigation panel for navigating your home directory, your hardware, your session history, and many other things. Just try it, and you will discover many useful features.

As mentioned previously, you can access new URLs by running *konqueror* with the URL as the argument. However, you can also simply type the URL in the location bar near the top of the Konqueror window. The location bar has autocompletion: if you start typing an address that you have visited before, Konqueror will automatically display it for your selection. Once you are done entering the URL (with or without help from autocompletion), you simply press the Enter key, and the corresponding document is retrieved.

Konqueror is a powerful application with many options. You can customize Konqueror's behavior in many ways by selecting Settings → Configure Konqueror.... The sections Konqueror Browser and Enhanced Browsing provide particularly interesting settings. In the section Cookies, you can configure whether you want to accept cookies domain by domain and even check the cookies already stored on your computer. Compare this to browsers that hide the cookies deep in some hidden directory and make it hard for you to view them (or even impossible without the use of extra programs!).

Finally, one particular feature deserves mention. Web browsers register themselves with the server using the so-called "User Agent" string, which is a piece of text that can contain anything, but usually contains the name and version of the web browser, and the name and version of the host operating system. Some notably stupid web-masters serve different web pages (or none at all!) when the web browser is not Internet Explorer because they think that Internet Explorer is the only web browser capable of displaying their web site.* But by going to the User Agent section, you can fool the web server into believing that you are using a different browser, one that the web server is not too snobbish to serve documents to. Simply click New, select the domain name that you want to access, and either type a User Agent string of your own, or select one of the predefined ones.

Konqueror is not the only browser that reads web documents. Another browser available for Linux is Mozilla, the open source version of Netscape Navigator, the browser that made the Web popular to many in the first place. If your distribution does not contain Mozilla already, you can get it from *http://www.mozilla.org*. Mozilla's features are quite similar to Konqueror's, and whatever you do with one you should be able to do with the other. One thing Mozilla sports, but Konqueror doesn't, is the possibility of keeping several web pages in different "tab pages" within the main browser window. In order to view different web pages at the same time in Konqueror, you have to open several Konqueror windows (a mode that Mozilla supports as well).

Yet another versatile browser is Lynx. It is a text-based browser, so you miss the pictures on a web site. But this makes it fast, and you may find it convenient. You can also use it without the X Window System. Furthermore, when you want to save a page as plain text, Lynx often provides a better format than other browsers. And finally, for those who never want to leave Emacs, there is Emacs/W3, a fully featured web browser you can use within Emacs or XEmacs.

Configuring Your Own Web Server

Now that you've seen what the Web provides, you're ready to set up your own gas station on the information superhighway. Running your own web server is easy. It consists of two tasks: configuring the *httpd* daemon and writing documents to provide on the server.

httpd is the daemon that services HTTP requests on your machine. Any document accessed with an *http* URL is retrieved using *httpd*. Likewise, *ftp* URLs are accessed using *ftpd*, *gopher* URLs using *gopherd*, and so on. There is no single web daemon; each URL type uses a separate daemon to request information from the server.

Several HTTP servers are available. The one discussed here is the Apache *httpd* server, which is easy to configure and very flexible. In this section, we'll discuss how

---

* A web site that can be browsed with only one browser or that calls itself "optimized for browser X" should make you virtually run away, wringing your hands in wrath over such incompetence on the part of the web-master.

to install and configure the basic aspects of this version of *httpd*. Later in the chapter, we talk about how to write your own documents in HyperText Markup Language (HTML, the markup language used by web pages) as well as more advanced aspects of server configuration, such as providing interactive forms.

All Linux versions should carry Apache today as their default *httpd* server. However, if you have selected a "minimal" or "desktop" install, it might not have been installed during the installation procedure, and you might have to install it manually afterward. Or you may want to have a newer version than the one that your distribution carries (at the time of this writing, 2.0.40 is the current stable version); in this case you can download both sources and binaries from *http://www.apache.org* and build it yourself. The *apache.org* web site contains complete documentation for the software.

Apache—The Definitive Guide by Ben Laurie and Peter Laurie (O'Reilly) covers everything about Apache, including sophisticated configuration issues.

Where the various files of an Apache installation go depends on your distribution or the package you installed, but the following is a common setup. You should locate the various pieces in your system before continuing:

/usr/sbin/httpd
> The binary executable, which is the server itself. On Debian, this is */usr/sbin/apache* instead.

/etc/httpd
> Contains the configuration files for *httpd*, most notably *httpd.conf*. We discuss how to modify these files later. On Debian systems, this is */etc/apache* instead of */etc/httpd*.

/usr/local/httpd
> Contains the HTML scripts to be served up to the site's clients. This directory and those below it, the *web space*, are accessible to anyone on the Web and therefore pose a severe security risk if used for anything other than public data.

/var/log/httpd
> Holds log files stored by the server.

Our task now is to modify the configuration files in the configuration subdirectory. You should notice at least the following four files in this directory: *access.conf-dist*, *httpd.conf-dist*, *mime.types*, and *srm.conf-dist*. Copy the files with names ending in *-dist* and modify them for your own system. For example, *access.conf-dist* is copied to *access.conf* and edited.

The latest version of Apache pretty much configures itself, but in case things go wrong, we'll tell you here how to do it manually so that you can fix things yourself.

At *http://www.apache.org*, you will find complete documentation on how to configure *httpd*. Here, we'll present sample configuration files that correspond to an actual running *httpd*.

httpd.conf

The file *httpd.conf* is the main server-configuration file. First, copy *httpd.conf-dist* to *httpd.conf* and edit it. We'll only cover some of the more important options here; the file *httpd.conf-dist* is vastly commented.

The ServerType directive is used to specify how the server will run—either as a standalone daemon (as seen here) or from *inetd*. For various reasons, it's usually best to run *httpd* in standalone mode. Otherwise, *inetd* must spawn a new instance of *httpd* for each incoming connection.

One tricky item here is the port number specification. You may wish to run *httpd* as a user other than *root* (that is, you may not have *root* access on the machine in question and wish to run *httpd* as yourself). In this case, you must use a port numbered 1024 or above. For example, if we specify:

```
Port 2112
```

we may run *httpd* as a regular user. In this case, HTTP URLs to this machine must be specified as:

http://www.ecoveggie.org:2112/...

If no port number is given in the URL (as is the usual case), port 80 is assumed.

With:

```
DocumentRoot "/usr/local/httpd/htdocs"
```

we specify the DocumentRoot directive, where documents to be provided via HTTP are stored. These documents are written in HTML.

For example, if someone were to access the URL:

http://www.ecoveggie.org/fruits.html

the actual file accessed would be */usr/local/httpd/htdocs/fruits.html*.

The UserDir directive specifies a directory each user may create in his home directory for storing public HTML files. For example, if we were to use the URL:

http://www.ecoveggie.org/~mdw/linux-info.html

the actual file accessed would be *~mdw/public_html/linux-info.html*.

The following lines enable the indexing features of *httpd*.

```
# If a URL is received with a directory but no filename, retrieve this
# file as the index (if it exists).
DirectoryIndex index.html

# Turn on 'fancy' directory indexes
IndexOptions FancyIndexing
```

In this case, if a browser attempts to access a directory URL, the file *index.html* in that directory is returned, if it exists. Otherwise, *httpd* generates a "fancy" index with icons representing various file types. Figure 16-2 shows an example of such an index.

Icons are assigned using the AddIcon directive, as seen here:

```
# Set up various icons for use with fancy indexes, by filename
# E.g., we use DocumentRoot/icons/movie.xbm for files ending
#    in .mpg and .qt
AddIcon /icons/movie.xbm .mpg
AddIcon /icons/back.xbm ..
AddIcon /icons/menu.xbm ^^DIRECTORY^^
AddIcon /icons/blank.xbm ^^BLANKICON^^
DefaultIcon /icons/unknown.xbm
```

The icon filenames (such as *icons/movie.xbm*) are relative to DocumentRoot by default. (There are other ways to specify pathnames to documents and icons—for example, by using aliases. This is discussed later.) There is also an AddIconByType directive, which lets you specify an icon for a document based on the document's MIME type, and an AddIconByEncoding directive, which lets you specify an icon for a document based on the document's encoding (i.e., whether and how it is compressed).

You can also specify an icon to be used when none of the above matches. This is done with the DefaultIcon directive.

The optional ReadmeName and HeaderName directives specify the names of files to be included in the index generated by *httpd*:

```
ReadmeName README
HeaderName HEADER
```

Here, if the file *README.html* exists in the current directory, it will be appended to the index. The file *README* will be appended if *README.html* does not exist. Likewise, *HEADER.html* or *HEADER* will be included at the top of the index generated by *httpd*. You can use these files to describe the contents of a particular directory when an index is requested by the browser:

```
# Local access filename.
AccessFileName .htaccess

# Default MIME type for documents.
DefaultType text/plain
```

The AccessFileName directive specifies the name of the *local access file* for each directory. (This is described later, along with the discussion about the *access.conf* file.) The DefaultType directive specifies the MIME type for documents not listed in *mime. types*.

The following lines specify directories for useful files.

```
# Set location of icons.
Alias /icons/ /usr/local/html/icons/

# Set location of CGI binaries.
ScriptAlias /cgi-bin/ /usr/local/httpd/cgi-bin/
```

The `Alias` directive specifies a pathname alias for any of the documents listed in *srm.conf* or accessed by a URL. Earlier, we used the `AddIcon` directive to set icon names using pathnames such as *icons/movie.xbm*. Here, we specify that the pathname */icons/* should be translated to */usr/local/html/icons/*. Therefore, the various icon files should be stored in the latter directory. You can use `Alias` to set aliases for other pathnames as well.

The `ScriptAlias` directive is similar in nature, but it sets the actual location of CGI scripts on the system. Here, we wish to store scripts in the directory */usr/local/httpd/cgi-bin/*. Anytime a URL is used with a leading directory component of */cgi-bin/*, it is translated into the actual directory name. More information on CGI and scripts is included in the book *CGI Programming with Perl* by Scott Guelich, Shishir Gundavaram, and Gunther Birznieks (O'Reilly).

`<Directory>` entries specify the options and attributes for a particular directory, as in:

```
# Set options for the cgi-bin script directory.
<Directory /usr/local/html/cgi-bin>
Options Indexes FollowSymLinks
</Directory>
```

Here, we specify that the CGI script directory should have the access options `Indexes` and `FollowSymLinks`. A number of access options are available. These include:

FollowSymLinks
: Symbolic links in this directory should be followed to retrieve the documents to which they point.

ExecCGI
: Allow the execution of CGI scripts from this directory.

Indexes
: Allow indexes to be generated from this directory.

None
: Disable all options for this directory.

All
: Enable all options for this directory.

There are other options as well; see the *httpd* documentation for details.

Next, we enable several options and other attributes for */usr/local/httpd/htdocs*, the directory containing our HTML documents:

```
<Directory /usr/local/httpd/htdocs>

Options Indexes FollowSymLinks

# Allow the local access file, .htaccess, to override any attributes
```

```
# listed here.
AllowOverride All

# Access restrictions for documents in this directory.
<Limit GET>
order allow,deny
allow from all
</Limit>

</Directory>
```

Here, we turn on the `Indexes` and `FollowSymLinks` options for this directory. The `AllowOverride` option allows the local access file (named *.htaccess*) in each directory that contains documents to override any of the attributes given here. The *.htaccess* file has the same format as the global *access.conf* but applies only to the directory in which it is located. This way, we can specify attributes for particular directories by including a *.htaccess* file in those directories instead of listing the attributes in the global file.

The primary use for local access files is to allow individual users to set the access permissions for personal HTML directories (such as *~/public_html*) without having to ask the system administrator to modify the global access file. Security issues are associated with this, however. For example, a user might enable access permissions in her own directory such that any browser can run expensive server-side CGI scripts. If you disable the `AllowOverride` feature, users cannot get around the access attributes specified in the global *access.conf*. This can be done by using:

```
AllowOverride None
```

which effectively disables local *.htaccess* files.

The `<Limit GET>` field is used to specify access rules for browsers attempting to retrieve documents from this server. In this case, we specify `order allow,deny`, which means that `allow` rules should be evaluated before deny rules. We then instate the rule `allow from all`, which simply means any host may retrieve documents from the server. If you wish to deny access from a particular machine or domain, you could add the line:

```
deny from .nuts.com biffnet.biffs-house.us
```

The first entry denies access from all sites in the *nuts.com* domain. The second denies access from the site *biffnet.biffs-house.us*.

srm.conf and access.conf

These files should be kept empty. In earlier Apache versions, *srm.conf* stood for Server Resource Map and listed facilities provided by the server, while *access.conf* controlled access to Apache files. All the resources originally placed in those files are now listed in the main *httpd.conf* file.

Starting httpd

Now you're ready to run *httpd*, allowing your machine to service HTTP URLs. As mentioned previously, you can run *httpd* from *inetd* or as a standalone server. Here, we describe how to run *httpd* in standalone mode.

All that's required to start *httpd* is to run the command:

```
httpd -f configuration-file
```

where *configuration-file* is the pathname of *httpd.conf*. For example:

```
/usr/sbin/httpd -f /etc/httpd/httpd.conf
```

starts up *httpd*, with configuration files found in */etc/httpd*.

Watch the *httpd* error logs (the location of which is given in *httpd.conf*) for any errors that might occur when trying to start up the server or when accessing documents. Remember you must run *httpd* as *root* if it is to use a port numbered 1023 or less. Once you have *httpd* working to your satisfaction, you can start it automatically at boot time by including the appropriate *httpd* command line in one of your system *rc* files, such as */etc/init.d/boot.local*.

Some releases of Apache also provide a utility called *apachectl* that controls the starting, stopping, reloading, and so on of the *httpd* process. Particularly, calling:

```
apachectl configtest
```

is a good way of checking whether the configuration file is actually correct before starting the server. Finally, we should mention that you can also start, restart, and stop Apache by using */etc/init.d/apache* plus one of the parameters start, restart, or stop.

Of course, in order to request documents via HTTP from your browser, you'll need to write them, something that we cannot cover in this book. Two good sources for HTML information are the O'Reilly books *HTML & XML—The Definitive Guide* by Chuck Musciano and Bill Kennedy and *HTML Pocket Reference* by Jennifer Niederst. A special kind of web page, that which is filled with data from a database, is also covered in Chapter 18 of this book.

Electronic Mail

Electronic mail (email) is one of the most desirable features of a computer system. You can send and receive email on your Linux system locally between users on the host and between hosts on a network. You have to set up three classes of software to provide email service. These are the *mail user agent* or mailer, the *mail transport agent* (MTA), and the *transport protocol*.

The mailer provides the user interface for displaying mail, writing new messages, and filing messages. Linux offers you many choices for mailers. They are always being improved, and a particular mailer may provide certain features, such as the ability to serve as a newsreader or to serve as a web browser. Mailers tend to differ in terms of their MIME support. (MIME stands for Multimedia Internet Mail Extensions. It is really not multimedia-specific, but more a general standard for describing the contents of email messages.) Some do it better than others. It's difficult to give a recommendation here, though, since all mailers are continually moving toward better MIME support.

The mailer relies on the MTA to route mail from one user to another, whether locally or across systems. The MTA in turn uses a transport protocol, usually either Unix-to-Unix Copy (UUCP) or Simple Mail Transport Protocol (SMTP), to provide the medium for mail transfer.

There are a number of possible scenarios when using email on a Linux system, and depending on those scenarios, you will have to install a different set of software packages. However, no matter which option you choose, you will always need a mailer.

The first scenario applies to dial-up access to the Internet via an Internet Service Provider (ISP). In this scenario, there is often only one user on the Linux machine, although this is not a requirement. The ISP accepts your mail from the Internet and stores it for you on its hard disks. You can then retrieve the mail whenever you want by using the common POP3 (Post Office Protocol) protocol or the newer IMAP protocol. Outgoing mail in this scenario is almost exclusively sent via the SMTP protocol, which is universally used to transport mail over the Internet.

In the easiest case, you use your mailer both to retrieve the mail via POP3 or IMAP and to send it back via SMTP. When you do this, you do not even need to set up an MTA because the mailer handles everything. This is not terribly flexible, but if all you want is to access your mail easily, this might be an option for you. Mailers that support this include KMail from KDE and Mozilla's built-in mail program (both described later).

If you want more flexibility (which comes at the price of more configuration and maintenance work), you can install an MTA such as Postfix, described in the next section. You will need a program that transports the mail from your provider's POP3 or IMAP server. This program fetches your mail when you ask it to and passes the messages on to the MTA running on your system, which then distributes the mail to the recipients' mail folders. One program that does exactly that is fetchmail, which we will cover later in this chapter. Outgoing mail is again sent via SMTP, but with an MTA running on your machine, you can choose not to send the outgoing messages directly to your provider's SMTP server, but rather to your own server, which is provided by the MTA. The MTA then forwards the mail to your provider, which in turn sends it to the recipients. With this setup, you can instruct your MTA to send outgoing mail at certain intervals only so that you do not always have to make a dial-up connection.

The third scenario is meant for machines that have a permanent connection to the Internet, either because they are in a network that has a gateway with a permanent connection, or because they are using a leased line to your Internet provider. In this case, you might want to receive mail messages as soon as they arrive at your provider and not have them stored there. This also requires setting up an MTA. Incoming mail will be directed to your SMTP server (i.e., your MTA). Your provider will have to set things up accordingly for this to work.

Of course, there are many more scenarios for using mail, and mixtures between the three mentioned are possible as well. If you are going to set up a mail service for a whole network, you will most certainly want to read the *Linux Network Administrator's Guide* (O'Reilly) as well as a book about your MTA.

You have a number of software choices for setting up email on a Linux host. We can't describe all the available email solutions, but we do describe some packages that are often used and quite suitable for their respective tasks. We document what we think are the most popular Linux solutions at this time: the mailers KMail and Mozilla, the Postfix mail transport agent, and the fetchmail implementation of the POP3 and IMAP protocols. These are relatively simple to configure but provide all the features most users need. In addition, with these tools, you can cover all the scenarios described earlier.

The Postfix MTA

Several MTAs are available for Linux. Historically, the most common MTA on Unix has been Sendmail, which has been around for a long time. It is generally considered somewhat more difficult to use than the alternatives, but it is thoroughly documented in the book *sendmail* by Bryan Costales with Eric Allman (O'Reilly).

Postfix is a newer MTA, developed by security guru Wietse Venema as a replacement for Sendmail. It's designed to be compatible with Sendmail but to provide a higher level of security and be easier to configure.

Postfix is a highly flexible and secure piece of software that contains multiple layers of protection against would-be attackers. Postfix was also written with performance in mind, and employs techniques to limit slower activities such as creating new processes and accessing the filesystem. It is one of the easier email packages to configure and administer because it uses straightforward configuration files and simple lookup tables for address rewriting. It is remarkable in that it is simple to use as a basic MTA, yet still able to handle much more complicated environments.

Many Linux distributions have Postfix built-in, so you may already have it installed on your system. If not, you can find prebuilt packages or compile it yourself from the source code. The Postfix home page (*http://www.postfix.org/*) contains links to download both the source code ("Download") and packages for different Linux distributions ("Packages and Ports").

Postfix has two different release tracks: official and experimental. The experimental releases contain all the latest patches and new features, although these might change before they are included in the official release. Don't be put off by the term "experimental"; these releases are very stable and have been tested thoroughly. If you are looking for a feature that is available only in the experimental release, you should feel more than comfortable using it. Read the release notes for both tracks to know what the current differences are.

A word about DNS

Before setting up Postfix, you should understand that if your system is going to receive mail from others across the Internet, the DNS for your domain has to be configured correctly. DNS is discussed in Chapter 15.

Let's assume for this discussion that you are configuring a host called *halo* in the domain *example.org*, and that you have a user account *michael* on your system. Regardless of how you want to receive mail, your host *halo.example.org* must have a DNS A record that maps its hostname to its IP address.

In this example your email address is going to be either *michael@halo.example.org* or *michael@example.org*. If you want to use the first form, configuring the DNS A record is enough for messages to reach you.

If your system is going to receive all mail for *example.org* (*michael@example.org*), the domain should have a DNS MX record pointing to your host *halo.example.org*. If you are configuring the DNS for your domain yourself, make sure you read the documentation to understand how it works; otherwise, speak to your DNS administrator or ISP about routing mail to your system.

Postfix frequently uses DNS in its normal operation, and it uses the underlying Linux libraries to perform its DNS queries. Make sure your system is configured correctly to perform DNS lookups (see "Configuring DNS" in Chapter 15). Postfix usually has to find an MX record to make its deliveries. Don't assume that if Postfix reports a DNS problem with an address, and you find that the domain resolves correctly, that email delivery should succeed. If Postfix reports a problem, you can be almost certain there is a problem.

Installing Postfix

Although prepackaged distributions are available, you may want to build the package yourself if you want to use any of the add-on libraries or functions that are not included in your distribution. You might also want to get the latest version to obtain a new feature that has not yet been included in your distribution.

Before you install Postfix, be aware that it includes the three commands */usr/bin/newaliases*, */usr/bin/mailq*, and */usr/sbin/sendmail* that are normally used by Sendmail. Postfix provides replacements that work with the Postfix system rather than with Sendmail. You should rename your existing Sendmail commands so that the Postfix installation doesn't overwrite them in case you ever want to use the original Sendmail binaries again:

```
# mv /usr/bin/newaliases /usr/bin/newaliases.orig
# mv /usr/bin/mailq /usr/bin/mailq.orig
# mv /usr/sbin/sendmail /usr/sbin/sendmail.orig
```

Postfix uses Unix database files to store its alias and lookup table information. You must, therefore, have the db3 libraries installed on your system before building Postfix. These libraries are contained within the db3-devel RPM package or the Debian libdb3 package. If you are not using a package manager, you can obtain them directly from Sleepycat Software (*http://www.sleepycat.com/*). If you are using RPM, execute the following command to see if the necessary libraries have been installed on your system:

```
# rpm -qa | grep db3-devel
db3-devel-3.2.9-5
```

You should see a line similar to the second line in the preceding command that displays the db3-devel package with a version number. If *rpm* returns nothing, you must install the libraries before installing Postfix.

On Debian, you can use *dpkg* to see if the libraries are installed.

```
# dpkg -l libdb3
```

If you download a prepackaged Postfix, use your package manager (described in Chapter 7) to install it. If you download the source *postfix-1.1.11.tar.gz*, move that file to a suitable directory (such as your home directory) to unpack it. The numbers in the name of the file represent the version of this release. Your file may have different numbers depending on the current release when you download it.

Follow this basic procedure to build Postfix. Note that you'll have to be the *root* user to create the user and group and to install the package.

1. Rename your Sendmail binaries as described earlier.
2. Create a user account called *postfix* and a group called *postdrop*. See "Managing User Accounts" in Chapter 5 for information on setting up accounts and groups.
3. Run *gunzip* on the compressed file to produce a file named *postfix-1.1.11.tar*.
4. Execute:

    ```
    tar -xvf postfix-1.1.11.tar
    ```

    to unpack the source into a directory called *postfix-1.1.11*.
5. Move to the directory created when you unpacked the file. You'll find a file called *INSTALL* with detailed instructions about building your Postfix system. In most cases, building Postfix should be as simple as typing make in the directory.
6. If your build completes without any errors, type make install to install Postfix on your system. You should be able to accept all the defaults when prompted by the installation script.

After installation, you will have Postfix files in the following directories:

/usr/libexec/postfix

This directory contains the various Postfix daemons. Postfix uses a split architecture in which several discrete programs handle separate tasks. The *master* daemon is started first. It deals with starting other programs as they are needed. For the most part, you don't need to worry about any of the programs here. Stopping and starting Postfix is handled with the *postfix* command found in the */usr/ sbin* directory.

/etc/postfix

Typically this directory contains dozens of Postfix configuration files, but only *master.cf* and *main.cf* and a few lookup tables are used by Postfix. The rest of the files are examples that document the various parameters used for configuration.

The *master.cf* file controls the various Postfix processes. It includes a line for each component of Postfix. The layout of the file is described by comments in the file itself. Usually, you shouldn't have to make any changes to run a simple Postfix installation.

The *main.cf* file is the global SMTP configuration file. It includes a list of parameters set to one or more values using the format:

```
parameter = value
```

Comments are marked with a hash mark (#) at the beginning of the line. You cannot put comments on the same line as parameters. Commented lines can begin with whitespace (spaces or tabs), but they must appear on lines by themselves.

Multiple values for parameters can be separated by either commas or whitespace (including newlines), but if you want to have more than one line for a parameter, start the second and subsequent lines with whitespace. Values can refer to other parameters by preceding the parameter name with a dollar sign ($).

Here's an example of an entry that includes comments, multiple lines, and a parameter reference:

```
# Here are all the systems I accept mail from.
mynetworks = $myhostname
192.168.75.0/24
10.110.12.15
```

/usr/sbin

All the Postfix commands are located in */usr/sbin* and have names starting with post. There are commands to create index files, manage the mail queue and otherwise administer your Postfix system. The *postfix* command, which is used to stop and start Postfix (described later), is found here.

/var/spool/postfix

The Postfix queue manager is an important component of the Postfix system that accepts incoming email messages and arranges with other Postfix components to deliver them. It maintains its files under the */var/spool/postfix* directory.

The queues it maintains are shown next. Postfix provides several tools to manage the queues, such as *postcat*, *postsuper*, and *mailq*, but you might also use the usual Linux commands, such as *find* and *cat* to inspect your queue.

/var/spool/postfix/incoming

All incoming messages, whether from over the network or sent locally.

/var/spool/postfix/active

Messages that the queue manager is delivering or preparing to deliver.

/var/spool/postfix/deferred

Messages that could not be delivered immediately. Postfix will attempt to deliver them again.

/var/spool/postfix/corrupt

Messages that are completely unreadable or otherwise damaged and not deliverable. They are stored here for you to look at if necessary to figure out the problem. This queue is rarely used.

/usr/local/man

Postfix installs documentation in the form of manpages on your system. The documentation includes information on command-line utilities, daemons, and configuration files.

As mentioned earlier, Postfix also installs replacements for */usr/bin/newaliases*, */usr/bin/mailq*, and */usr/sbin/sendmail*.

Postfix configuration

Before you start Postfix for the first time, you have to make sure that the aliases table is formatted correctly and that a few of the critical configuration parameters are set correctly for your system.

Historically Sendmail has used the file */etc/aliases* to map one local username to another. Postfix continues the tradition. The */etc/aliases* file is a plain-text file that is used as input to create an indexed database file for faster lookups of aliases on your system. There are at least two important aliases on your system that must be set in your */etc/aliases* file. If you have been running Sendmail on your system, these aliases are probably already set correctly, but make sure your file has entries for root and postmaster pointing to a real account that receives mail on your system. Once you have verified the aliases, execute the command *newaliases* to rebuild the index file in the correct format for Postfix.

The */etc/postfix/main.cf* file contains many parameters, but there are just a few important ones that you should verify before starting Postfix; we'll explain these in this section. If you installed Postfix from a prepackaged distribution, these parameters might already be set correctly. It's also possible that the Postfix defaults work for your system, but edit your */etc/postfix/main.cf* file to make sure.

myhostname

This is the fully qualified hostname for your system. By default, Postfix uses the name returned by the gethostname function. If this value is not fully qualified, and you have not set this parameter, Postfix will not start. You can check it by executing the command *hostname*. It's probably a good idea to specify your fully qualified hostname here explicitly:

```
myhostname = halo.example.org
```

mydomain

Specifies the domain name for this system. This value is then used as the default in other places. If you do not set it explicitly, Postfix uses the domain portion of myhostname. If you have set myhostname as shown previously and *example.org* is correct for your system, you do not have to set this parameter.

mydestination

Specifies a list of domain names for which this system should accept mail. In other words, you should set the value of this parameter to the domain portions of email addresses for which you want to receive mail. By default, Postfix uses the value specified in myhostname. If you are setting up your system to accept mail for your entire domain, specify the domain name itself. You can use the variables $myhostname and $mydomain as the value for this parameter:

```
mydestination = $myhostname $mydomain
```

myorigin

This parameter is used to append a domain name to messages sent locally that do not already include one. For example, if a user on your system sends a message with only the local username in the From: address, Postfix appends this value to the local name. By default, Postfix uses myhostname, but if your system is handling mail for the entire domain, you might want to specify $mydomain instead:

```
myorigin = $mydomain
```

Some Linux distributions that already include Postfix configure it to use *procmail* by default. *procmail* is a separate mail delivery agent (MDA) that can filter and sort mail as it makes deliveries to individual users on your system. If you need the features it provides, you should study the *procmail* documentation carefully to understand how it interacts with Postfix. For many systems, which don't filter mail for users at the MTA level, *procmail* is an unnecessary additional layer of complexity because Postfix can also make local deliveries and provide some of the same functions. Your distribution might be configured to use *procmail* in either the mailbox_command or mailbox_transport parameters. If you want Postfix to handle local deliveries directly, you can safely comment out either of these parameters in your */etc/postfix/main.cf* file.

Starting Postfix

Once you have verified the important configuration parameters described earlier and rebuilt your aliases index file, you are ready to start Postfix. As the superuser, execute:

```
postfix start
```

You can stop Postfix by executing:

```
postfix stop
```

Whenever you make changes to either of Postfix's configuration files, you must reload the running Postfix image by executing:

```
postfix reload
```

Once you have Postfix running, all the users on your system should be able to send and receive email messages.

Any of your applications that depend on Sendmail should still work, and you can use the *sendmail* command as you always did. You can pipe messages to it from within scripts and execute sendmail -q to flush the queue. The native Postfix equivalent for flushing the queue is postfix flush. Options to Sendmail that deal with it running as a daemon and setting queue delays do not work because those functions are not handled by the *sendmail* command in Postfix. All the Postfix options are set in its two configuration files. Many parameters deal with the Postfix queue. You can find them in the manpage for *qmgr*(8).

Postfix logging

After starting or reloading Postfix, you should check the log to see if Postfix reports any problems. (Most Linux distributions use */var/log/maillog*, but you can also check the file */etc/syslog.conf* to be sure.) You can see Postfix's most recent messages by running the command *tail /var/log/maillog*. Since Postfix is a long-running process, it's a good idea to check the log periodically even if you haven't been restarting it. You can execute the following to see if Postfix has reported anything interesting while running:

```
egrep '(reject|warning|error|fatal|panic):' /var/log/maillog
```

In general, Postfix keeps you informed of what is going on with your system by logging lots of good information to *syslogd*. On Linux *syslogd* uses synchronous writes by default, which means that after every write to the log file, there is also a sync to force everything in memory to be written to the disk. Therefore, the performance of Postfix (and other processes) can suffer. You can change this default by preceding the name of the log file with a hyphen in */etc/syslog.conf*. Your entry in *syslog.conf* for mail logging should look like the following:

```
mail.*                  -/var/log/maillog
```

Be sure to have *syslogd* reread its configuration file after you make any changes. You can execute killall -HUP syslogd to reinitialize it.

Running Postfix on system startup

Because of Postfix's compatibility with Sendmail, if you have your system configured to start Sendmail at system initialization, more than likely Postfix will start correctly when your system boots. However, system shutdown will probably not work correctly. Most Linux distributions shut down Sendmail by locating a process called *sendmail* and then killing that process. The Postfix processes, while in many ways compatible with Sendmail, do not run under the name *sendmail*, so this shutdown fails.

If you would like your system to shut down cleanly, you should create your own *rc* script for Postfix, as described in Chapter 5. The commands you need to include in your script to start and stop Postfix are exactly the same as those you execute on the command line, *postfix start* and *postfix stop*. Here's an example of a basic script to get you started. You may want to review other *rc* scripts on your system to see if you should add more system checks or follow other conventions and then make your adjustments to this example:

```
#!/bin/sh
PATH=""
RETVAL=0

if [ ! -f /usr/sbin/postfix ] ; then
    echo "Unable to locate Postfix"
    exit 1
fi
if [ ! -f /etc/postfix/main.cf ] ; then
    echo "Unable to locate Postfix configuration"
    exit 1
fi

case "$1" in
    start)
        echo -n "Starting Postfix: "
        /usr/sbin/postfix start > /dev/null 2>1
        RETVAL=$?
        echo
        ;;

    stop)
        echo -n "Stopping Postfix: "
        /usr/sbin/postfix stop > /dev/null 2>1
        RETVAL=$?
        echo
        ;;

    restart)
        echo -n "Restarting Postfix: "
        /usr/bin/postfix reload > /dev/null 2>1
        RETVAL=$?
        echo
        ;;

    *)
        echo "Usage: $0 {start|stop|restart}"
        RETVAL=1
```

```
      esac
      exit $RETVAL
```

Place this script in */etc/rc.d/init.d* or */etc/init.d*, depending on your Linux distribution. Then make the appropriate symlinks in each of the *rcN.d* directories for each runlevel in which Postfix should start (see "init, inittab, and rc Files" in Chapter 5). For example, if you want to have Postfix start at runlevels 3 and 5 and stop at runlevels 0 and 6, create symlinks like those that follow for RedHat. For Debian the *rcN.d* directories are directly below */etc*:

```
# cd /etc/rc.d/rc3.d
# ln -s ../init.d/postfix S97postfix
# cd /etc/rc.d/rc5.d
# ln -s ../init.d/postfix S97postfix
# cd /etc/rc.d/rc0.d
# ln -s ../init.d/postfix K97postfix
# cd /etc/rc.d/rc6.d
# ln -s ../init.d/postfix K97postfix
```

If you create a Postfix *rc* script, you should configure your system not to start Sendmail at startup.

Postfix relay control

The default installation allows any system on the same subnet as yours to relay mail through your mail server. If you want to override the default, you can set the parameter mynetworks to be a list of hosts or networks that you trust to relay mail through your system. You can specify a list of IP addresses or network/netmask patterns, and any connecting SMTP client that matches will be allowed to relay mail. You can list network or IP addresses that reside anywhere. So, for example, if you want to be able to relay mail through your home Postfix system from your work machine, you can specify the IP address of your machine at work in your home Postfix configuration.

Here's an example that allows mail from the local subnet (192.168.75.0/28) and a single host located elsewhere:

```
mynetworks = 192.168.75.0/28 10.150.134.15
```

If you want to allow relaying for mobile users that do not have static IP addresses, you have to use some kind of SMTP authentication mechanism. Postfix can work with SASL Authentication (which requires that Postfix be compiled with additional libraries, and that users' client software be specially configured) and pop-before-smtp (which requires a POP server running on the same system to first authenticate users).

It is important not to open relay access to anyone except users you trust. In the early days of the Internet, open relays were commonplace. Unfortunately the current prevalence of spam has precluded that kind of freedom. If your MTA is not protected, you leave yourself and other Internet systems vulnerable to abuse. Spammers constantly scan for open relays, and if you place one on the network, it is only a matter of time before it will be found. Fortunately, the default Postfix installation behaves correctly. However, if you make lots of changes to your Postfix configuration (especially in setting up antispam controls, ironically), you may inadvertently open yourself up to relay abusers.

If you want your own Postfix installation to relay mail through another MTA, specify the IP address of the relay server using the relayhost parameter. Postfix normally figures out where to deliver messages on its own, based on the destination address. However, if your system is behind a firewall, for example, you may want Postfix to hand off all messages to another mail server to make the actual delivery. When you specify a relay server, Postfix normally performs a DNS query to obtain the mail exchanger (MX) address for that system. You can override this DNS lookup by putting the hostname in square brackets:

```
relayhost = [mail.example.org]
```

Additional configurations

The configuration described here creates a simple Postfix installation to send and receive messages for users on your system. But Postfix is an extremely flexible MTA with many more configuration options, such as hosting multiple virtual domains, maintaining mailing lists, blocking spam, and virus scanning. The manpages, HTML files, and sample configuration files that come with Postfix contain a lot of information to guide you in the more advanced configurations.

Getting the Mail to Your Computer with Fetchmail

If your provider stores your mail for you until you fetch it, and you do not want to use your mailer to download the mail, you need a program that retrieves the mail from your provider's computer. There are a lot of programs for doing this; we will discuss *fetchmail* here briefly because it is both robust and flexible and can handle both POP3 and IMAP.

You can get *fetchmail* from your friendly Linux archive; chances are that your distribution carries it, too. In case you download a source distribution of *fetchmail*, unpack, build, and install it according to the installation instructions. At the time of this writing, the current version is 5.9.13.

You can control *fetchmail*'s behavior via both command-line options and a configuration file. It is a good idea to first try to fetch your mail by passing the necessary information on the command line, and when this works, to write the configuration file.

As an example, let's assume that my provider is running the POP3 protocol, that my username there is joeuser, and that my password is secret. The hostname of the machine where the POP3 server is running is *mail.isp.com*. I can then retrieve my mail with the following command:

```
fetchmail --protocol POP3 --username joeuser mail.isp.com
```

fetchmail then asks me for my password and, after I specify it correctly, retrieves the mail waiting for me and passes it on to my MTA for further delivery. This assumes that a SMTP server is running on port 25 of my machine, but this should be the case if I have set up my MTA correctly.

While you are experimenting with *fetchmail*, it might be a good idea to also specify the option *--keep*. This prevents *fetchmail* from deleting the messages from your POP3 account. Normally, all messages are deleted from your provider's hard disk once they are safely stored on your own machine. This is a good thing because most providers limit the amount of mail you can store on their machines before retrieving them, and if you don't delete the messages after fetching them, you might reach this limit quite quickly. On the other hand, while testing, it is a good idea to be on the safe side and use *--keep* so as not to lose any mail.

With the aforementioned options to *fetchmail*, you should be able to get your mail in most cases. For example, if your provider uses the newer IMAP protocol, simply specify IMAP in the command line instead of POP3. If your provider has some unusual setup, you might need one of the other options that the *fetchmail*(1) manual page tells you about.

Once you are satisfied with the download process, you can write a *fetchmail* configuration file in order not to have to enter all the options each time you use the command. This configuration file is called *.fetchmailrc* and should reside in your home directory. Once you are done editing it, make sure it has the permission value 0600 so that nobody except yourself can read it because this file might contain your password:

```
chmod 0600 ~/.fetchmailrc
```

The full syntax of the configuration file is detailed in the *fetchmail* manpage, but in general you need only very simple lines that start with poll. To specify the same data as on the command line in the previous example, but this time include the password, put the following line into your configuration file:

```
poll mail.isp.com protocol pop3 username joeuser password secret
```

Now you can run *fetchmail* without any parameters. Since *fetchmail* already knows about your password from the configuration file, it will not prompt you for it this time. If you want to play it safe while testing, add the word keep to the poll line.

Using *fetchmail* with a configuration file has one additional advantage: you can fetch mail from as many mailboxes as you want. Just add more poll lines to your *.fetchmailrc*, and *fetchmail* happily retrieves your mail from one server after the other.

When and how you run *fetchmail* depends on your connection to the Internet. If you have a permanent connection or a cheap, flat rate, you might want to have *fetchmail* invoked by *cron* at a suitable interval (like once an hour). However, if your Internet connection is nonpermanent (dial-up) and costly, you might want to choose to run *fetchmail* by hand whenever you actually want to fetch and read your mail so as to minimize your Internet connection time. Finally, if you are using PPP for dialing in to your Internet service provider, you might want to invoke *fetchmail* from the *ip-up* script, which is invoked as soon as an Internet connection is made. With this setup, when you browse a web page and your computer dials up your provider, your mail is fetched automatically.

Other Email Administrative Issues

In this section we describe tasks, services, and some additional utilities involved in managing your electronic mail system.

You should normally use only one Internet host to get all your mail. It is possible to use a more complex arrangement, but this is frowned upon because of the possibility of setting up loops—virtual Sargasso Seas of lost network information. Loops can route mail in circles, passing over and over through the same machines until they "time out" by exceeding the limit on the number of machines they can pass through.

Registering an address

If you want to get your mail directly from the Internet, you need to register an Internet domain name for your system. Please see the earlier section "A word about DNS" for more information about this.

Mail system maintenance

You should set up a *cron* task to occasionally check the mail queue (usually */var/spool/mqueue*) and force an attempt to deliver mail that wasn't previously delivered for some reason. Mail can be queued because a host is temporarily unreachable, or a filesystem is full, or for myriad other little reasons. *cron* is discussed in the section "Scheduling Jobs Using cron" in Chapter 8.

The mail administrator also should occasionally check the mail queue and make sure no messages are "stuck" there:

```
$ mailq
```

This command generates a report on any mail in the queue. The actual name and syntax of the command may vary depending on the MTA chosen.

Using KMail

KMail is a very user-friendly, feature-rich mailer that comes with KDE and integrates mail smoothly with other utilities. For example, if an email message you receive contains a link to a web page, you can click this link in the message, and the KDE web browser Konqueror will pop up and display the web page. Or, if the email contains an MP3 file as an attachment, you can click it to play the file with one of KDE's MP3 players. Figure 16-4 shows a screenshot of KMail at work.

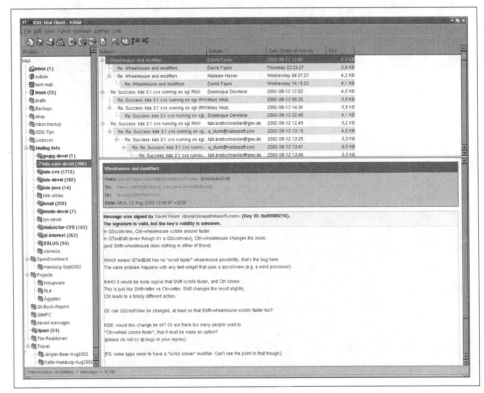

Figure 16-4. KMail mailer

KMail has a lot of features and settings, but we'll only cover those that get you started quickly and leave it to you to explore KMail further. As you can see in Figure 16-4, the KMail window is divided by default into three parts. On the left, you see a tree of your folders (at first startup, you will have only the default folders, of course). The upper part of the right side shows a listing of messages in the currently selected folder, and the lower part of the right side shows the currently selected message. You can change how the space is distributed between these parts by dragging the separator lines between them. The latest KMail versions even have a fourth part that lets you drill further into the structure of an individual message by displaying the MIME parts the message is composed of. However, this display is turned off by default, as most people do not need it.

Before you can use KMail, you have to set up some information in it. Select Configure KMail from the Settings menu and then open the configuration group Identity by clicking its icon. You can create a number of different identities here; for example, you may want to use different return addresses when emailing as an employee of your company or as a private person. For starters, it is sufficient to fill in the fields Name and Email Address on the General tab (see Figure 16-5).

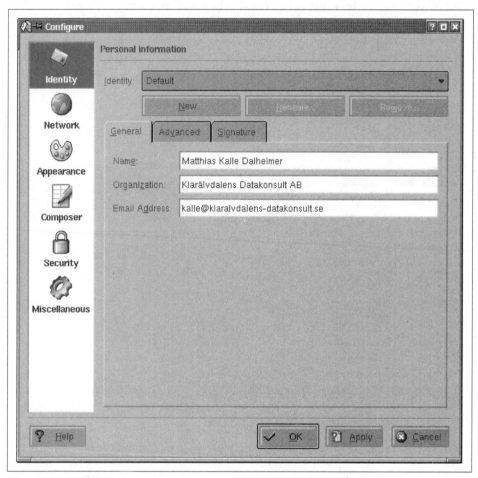

Figure 16-5. KMail identity configuration

Next, go to the Network configuration group. Here, you need to create at least one account for outgoing mail and one for incoming mail.

Let's start with the outgoing mail that you will find on the Sending tab (see Figure 16-6). Click the Add... button. You will be asked whether you want to use SMTP or talk to a *sendmail* installation directly. In almost all cases, if you have an MTA installed locally, you will want to select SMTP. Then, on the General tab of the SMTP transport configuration, give the transport a name (which you can choose arbitrarily because it exists only for you to recognize the settings later and will not be used in any network communication). In any case, you need to enter the hostname of the port. The port is almost always 25; the hostname should be given to you by your provider. If you have a local MTA installed and want to use it, simply enter localhost. If your mail server requires authentication (check with your provider if you are unsure), check the appropriate checkbox and fill in the login name and password.

Figure 16-6. KMail identity for outgoing mail

This should be enough to let you send outgoing email, but we recommend that you take a few additional steps to make this as secure as possible. KMail makes this easy for you by autodetecting the security settings of the SMTP server you are using. Go to the Security tab and click the button labelled "Check what the server supports." KMail will check the connection to the server and use the settings with the highest supported security. Alas, many providers run their mail servers without any security at all.

Now let's continue by configuring the receiving end. Close all subdialogs until you are back at the Network configuration group, and select the Receiving tab. Here you can set up a number of accounts to be queried. This can be useful if you have more than one provider that stores email for you. Click the Add... button and select the type of mail server. If you run your own MTA locally, you need to select Local Mailbox. Usually, you can then accept the defaults on the next page (but change the name to something more appropriate than "Default").

If you retrieve your messages directly from your provider's server, you need to select either POP3 or IMAP, depending on what your provider supports. In the dialog that appears again enter a name of your own choice, then specify your login name, your password, the name of the host that stores your email, and the port (usually 110 for POP3 and 143 for IMAP). All this information should be given to you by your provider or system administrator. You can leave all other options as they are for now, and experiment later with them.

Close all dialogs with the OK button. You should now be ready to retrieve your email. To do so, select File → Check Mail from the menu. This will retrieve all messages from all incoming mailboxes that you have specified. If it does not work or you get any error messages, check all the values you entered on the various configuration pages again and compare them to the information given to you by your provider or system administrator. The most typical error is a typo in the hostname, username, or password.

In order to send a message, press Ctrl-N or select Message → New Message. A composer window opens where you can type in the recipient's address, the subject, and the actual message body. If you have configured more than one identity, you can also select the one to be used for this message. When you are done composing your message, press Ctrl-N. Depending on how you have configured your outgoing mail transport, the message will either be put into the output folder and wait there for further handling (this is the default) or be transmitted directly. If you want to override your setting for a particular email, just select Message → Queue or Message → Send Now from the menu bar of the composer window.

Messages put into the output folder are by default not sent automatically (you can, however, configure KMail to always send messages in the outbox when it checks for incoming messages). To send all messages in your outbox, select File → Send Queued from the menu bar of the main KMail menu.

If you have problems sending your messages, again please check the settings you have made for typos. Also, in order to prevent the relaying of unsolicited commercial email (so-called spam) via their servers, some providers require that you check your mailbox on the server (providing your username and password as you go) in order to identify yourself, before you can send any email via that server. After you have checked your incoming email, you have a certain period of time (often 15 minutes) to send your outgoing email.

You should now know enough about how to use KMail in order to continue exploring the mailer on your own. One of the first things you may want to do (especially if you have a large number of messages to handle everyday!) is to create folders by selecting Folder → Create and then set up filters by selecting Settings → Configure Filters. This lets you redirect messages with certain characteristics (e.g., certain senders or subjects) to predefined folders. For example, you may want to gate all messages from a mailing list to a folder dedicated to that purpose.

Using Mozilla Mail & News

Mozilla Mail & News is the mail client that comes with the Mozilla web browser if you install more than the minimal installation (which only contains the browser and the composer itself). Chances are that your distribution already carries Mozilla, but if it doesn't, or you'd rather have a newer version, you can download that from *http://www.mozilla.org*.

The concepts for setting up and using Mozilla Mail are quite similar to those for KMail, so we will cover only the differences here. In order to open the mail client, start Mozilla and select Windows → Mail and Newsgroups from the menu. If you are starting the mailer for the first time, a wizard will pop up that lets you configure your email. Check Email account on the first page and your identity information on the second page (Mozilla's account handling is slightly less flexible than KMail's because it ties identities to accounts, while you can change identities at will with KMail).

On the third page, select whether you get your incoming mail via POP or IMAP (it's not possible to retrieve your email locally with Mozilla Mail & News, a big drawback), and specify the incoming and outgoing server name (specify localhost both times if you are running your own MTA). Complete the remaining information on the next pages, and you are ready to run Mozilla Mail & News. The screen layout is by default exactly the same as that of KMail.

As when using KMail, one of the first things you probably want to set up when using Mozilla Mail & News is additional folders and filters that sort your incoming messages into these folders. You can create new folders by right-clicking the folder list and selecting New Folder... in the context menu that appears. You can configure the filter rules by selecting Tools → Message Filters....

This concludes our discussion of using email on Linux. As you can see, many options, from simple to sophisticated, are available to help you administer and digest the daily flood of email messages.

CHAPTER 17

Basic Security

In this chapter we'll discuss basic Linux system security. Security is unfortunately a topic of ever-growing importance, especially with the increasing use of permanently network-connected systems that are vulnerable to remote attacks even while unattended.

Most system security is common-sense good practice. Many of the best techniques are the simplest, yet frequently ignored practices; we'll cover those first. We'll then move on to some of the less obvious practices, and we'll conclude with a short discussion on the complex subject of network security. We'll also include some firewall recipes to protect simple installations against network attack.

A Perspective on System Security

It's sometimes difficult keeping a balanced perspective on system security. The media tends to sensationalize stories relating to security breaches, especially when they involve well-known companies or institutions. On the other hand, managing security can be a technically challenging and time-consuming task. Many Internet users take the view that their system holds no valuable data, so security isn't much of an issue. Others spend large amounts of effort nailing down their systems to protect against unauthorized use. No matter where you sit in this spectrum you should be aware that there is always a risk that you will become the target of a security attack. There are a whole host of reasons as to why someone might be interested in breaching your system security. The value of the data on your system is only one of them; we discuss some others later in the chapter. You must make your own judgment as to how much effort you will expend, though we recommend you err on the side of caution.

Traditional system security focused on systems that were accessible through either a connected hard-wired terminal or the system console. In this realm the greatest risks typically came from within the organization owning the system, and the best form of defense was physical security, in which system consoles, terminals, and hosts were in locked rooms. Even when computer systems started to become net-work-connected, access was still very limited. The networks in use were often expensive to gain access to, or were closed networks that did not allow connections to hosts from just anywhere.

The popularity of the Internet has given rise to a new wave of network-based security concerns. An Internet-connected computer is open to potential abuse from tens of millions of hosts around the world. With improved accessibility comes an increase in the number of antisocial individuals intent upon causing nuisance. On the Internet, a number of forms of antisocial behavior are of interest to the system administrator. Those that we'll address in this chapter are:

Denial of service (DoS)
> This kind of attack degrades or disrupts a service on the system.

Intrusion
> This kind of attack accesses the system by guessing passwords or compromising some service. Once an intruder has access to a system he may then vandalize or steal data, or use the target system to launch attacks on some other host.

Snooping
> This kind of attack involves intercepting the data of another user and listening for passwords or other sensitive information. Sometimes this form of attack involves modification of data, too. Snooping usually involves eavesdropping on network connections, but can also be performed by compromising a system to intercept library or system calls that carry sensitive information (e.g., passwords).

Viruses, worms, and Trojan Horses
> These attacks each rely on compelling users of your system to execute programs supplied by the attacker. The programs could have been received in an email message, or from a web site, or even from within some other apparently harmless program retrieved from somewhere on the Internet and installed locally.

A DoS attack commonly involves generating an abnormally large number of requests to a service provided by a system. This rush of activity may cause the host system to exhaust its memory, processing power, or network bandwidth. As a result, further requests to the system are refused, or the system's performance degrades to an unusable point. For this attack to work, an attacker must either exploit a poorly designed service, or be able to generate a number of requests far exceeding the capacity of the service.

A more insidious form of DoS attack is the distributed denial of service (DDoS). In this form of attack, a large number of computers are caused to generate requests against a service. This increases the damage of a DoS attack in two ways: by overwhelming the target with a huge volume of traffic, and by hiding the perpetrator behind thousands of unwitting participants. Using a large number of hosts from which to launch an attack also makes DDoS attacks particularly difficult to control and remedy once they've occurred. Even people who have no concerns about the state of their own data should protect themselves against this form of attack so as to minimize the risk of becoming an unwitting accomplice in a DDoS attack against someone else.

The second form of attack, sometimes known as *cracking*,* is the one that most people associate with security. Companies and institutions often store sensitive data on network-accessible computer systems. A common example of concern to the average Internet user is the storage of credit-card details by web sites. Where there is money involved there is incentive for dishonest individuals to gain access and steal or misuse this kind of sensitive data.

Sometimes the methods that are used to gain unauthorized access or disrupt service are very ingenious, if not unethical. Designing an intrusion mechanism often requires a strong knowledge of the target system to uncover an exploit. Often, once an intrusion mechanism has been discovered, it is packaged in the form of a so-called *rootkit*, a set of programs or scripts that anyone possessing only basic knowledge can use to exploit a security hole. The vast majority of intrusion attacks are launched by "script kiddies" that make use of these prepackaged intrusion kits without any real knowledge of the systems they are attacking. The good news is that it is usually straightforward for a system administrator to protect a system from these well-known attacks; we discuss various ways to secure your system in this chapter.

Initial Steps in Setting Up a Secure System

There are some very basic things you can do to protect a Linux system from the most basic security risks. Of course, depending on your configuration, the ways in which you will be using your system, and so forth, they might be more involved than the simple setup described here. In this section we briefly cover the basic mechanisms to secure a Linux system from the most common attacks—this is the basic approach one of the authors takes whenever installing a new machine.

Shutting Down Unwanted Network Daemons

The first step in securing a Linux machine is to shut down or disable all network daemons and services that you don't need. Basically, any network port that the system is listening for connections on is a risk, since there might be a security exploit against

---

The terms *cracking* and *hacking* are often confused in popular usage. While *cracking* involves immoral or illegal behavior (such as compromising the security of a system), *hacking* is a generic word meaning to program, tinker with, or have an intense interest in something. The popular media often uses the term *hacking* to refer to *cracking*; the Linux community is trying to reassociate *hacking* with positive connotations.

the daemon using that port. The fast way to find out what ports are open is to use *netstat -an*, as shown next (we've truncated some of the lines, however):

```
# netstat -an
Active Internet connections (servers and established)
Proto Recv-Q Send-Q Local Address           Foreign Address         State
tcp        0      0 0.0.0.0:7120            0.0.0.0:*               LISTEN
tcp        0      0 0.0.0.0:6000            0.0.0.0:*               LISTEN
tcp        0      0 0.0.0.0:22              0.0.0.0:*               LISTEN
```

Here we see that this system is listening for connections on ports 7120, 6000, and 22. Looking at */etc/services*, or using the *-p* to *netstat*, can often reveal what daemons are associated with these ports. In this case it's the X font server, the X Window System server, and the *ssh* daemon.

If you see a lot of other open ports—for things like *telnetd*, *sendmail*, and so forth ask yourself whether you really need these daemons to be running. From time to time, security exploits are announced for various daemons, and unless you are very good at keeping track of these security updates, your system might be vulnerable to attack. Also, *telnetd*, *ftpd*, and *rshd* all involve sending clear-text passwords across the Internet for authentication; a much better solution is to use *sshd*, which encrypts data over connections and uses a stronger authentication mechanism. Even if you never use *telnetd*, it's not a good idea to leave it running on your system in case someone finds a way to break into it.

Shutting down services is usually a matter of editing the appropriate configuration files for your distribution and rebooting the system (to be sure they're good and dead). On Red Hat systems, for example, many daemons are started by scripts in the */etc/rc.d/init.d* directory; renaming or removing these scripts can prevent the appropriate daemons from starting up. Other daemons are launched by *inetd* or *xinetd* in response to incoming network connections; modifying the configuration of these systems can limit the set of daemons running on your system.

If you absolutely need a service running on your machine (such as the X server!), find ways of preventing connections to that service from unwanted hosts. For example, it might be safest to allow *ssh* connections only from certain trusted hosts, such as from machines in your local network. In the case of the X server and X font server, which run on many desktop Linux machines, there is usually no reason to allow connections to those daemons from anything but the local host itself. Filtering connections to these daemons can be performed by TCP wrappers or IP filtering, which are described later in this chapter.

Top 10 Things You Should Never Do

We've made the claim that security is mostly common sense, so what is this common sense? In this section we summarize the most common security mistakes. (There aren't actually 10 items in this list, but there are enough to merit the use of the common "top 10" phrase.) Consistently avoiding them all is harder work than it might first seem.

Never use simple or easily guessed passwords

Never use a password that's the same as (or closely related to) your user ID, name, date of birth, the name of your company, or the name of your dog. If you're an amateur radio operator don't use your callsign; if you love cars don't use the make/model or registration number of your car—you get the idea. Always ensure that your passwords are not simple words that can be found in a dictionary. The best passwords are nonsense strings. One good practice is to use a password based on a simple rule and a phrase that you can remember. For example, you might choose a rule like: the last letter of each word in the phrase "Mary had a little lamb, its fleece was white as snow," hence the password would become ydaebsesesw, certainly not something that will be easily guessed, but a password that will be easily remembered. Another common technique is to use numbers and punctuation characters in the password; indeed some *passwd* programs insist upon this. A combination of the two techniques is even better.

Don't use the root account unless you have to

One of the reasons that many common desktop operating systems (such as Windows) are so vulnerable to attack through email "viruses" and the like is the lack of a comprehensive privilege system. In such systems, any user has permission to access any file, execute any program, or reconfigure the system in any way. Because of this it's easy to coerce a user to execute a program that can do real damage to the system. In contrast, the Linux security model limits a wide range of privileged tasks, such as installing new software or modifying configuration files, to the *root* user. Do not succumb to the temptation to use the *root* account for everything! In doing so you are throwing away one of the more powerful defenses against virus and "Trojan Horse" attacks (not to mention accidental *rm -rf* * commands!). Always use a normal user account, and use the *su* or *sudo* commands to temporarily obtain *root* access when you need to undertake privileged tasks. There is an additional benefit in this limited use of the *root* account: logging. The *su* and *sudo* commands write messages to the system log file when they're invoked, mentioning the ID of the user performing the *su* or *sudo*, as well as the date and time that the command was invoked. This is very helpful for keeping track of when *root* privileges are being used, and by whom.

Don't share your passwords

Don't tell anybody your passwords, ever. This also means you shouldn't write your passwords on little sticky notes attached to your monitor, or into the diary you keep in the top drawer. If you want to allow someone temporary access to your system, create an account for them to use. This allows you some convenience in monitoring what they do, and you can easily clean up afterward. If you really must trust someone with your *root* account, use the *sudo* command, which allows you to give users *root* access without revealing the root password.

Don't blindly trust binaries that have been given to you

While it is very convenient to retrieve and install binary copies of programs on your system, you should always question how much you trust the binary before running it. If you're installing software packages that you've retrieved directly from the official sites of your distribution, or a significant development site, you can be fairly confident the software is safe. If you're getting them from an unofficial mirror site, you need to consider how much you trust the administrators of the site. It is possible that someone is distributing a modified form of the software with back doors that would allow someone to gain access to your machine. While this is a rather paranoid approach, it is nevertheless one that many Linux distribution organizations are embracing. For example, the Debian organization is developing a means of validating a software package to confirm that it hasn't been modified. Other distributions are sure to adopt similar techniques to protect the integrity of their own packaged software.

If you do want to install and execute a program that has been given to you in binary form, there are some things you can do to help minimize risk. Unfortunately, none of these techniques is easy if you're new to the Linux environment. First, always run untrusted programs as a non-*root* user unless the program specifically requires *root* privileges to operate. This will contain any damage the program might do, affecting only files and directories owned by that user. If you want to get some idea of what the program might do before you execute it, you can run the *strings* over the binaries. This will show you all the hard-coded strings that appear in the code. You should look for any references to important files or directories, such as */etc/passwd*, */bin/login*, etc. If you see a reference to an important file, you should ask yourself whether that is in keeping with the purpose of the program in question. If not, beware. If you're more technically inclined, you might also consider first running the program and watching what it is doing using a program like *strace* or *ltrace*, which display the system and library calls that the program is making. Look for references to unusual file system or network activity in the traces.

Don't ignore your log files

Your system log files are your friend, and they can tell you a lot about what is happening on your system. You can find information about when network connections have been made to your system, who has been using the *root* account, and failed login attempts. You should check your log files periodically and get to know what is normal, and more usefully what is abnormal. If you see something unusual, investigate.

Don't let your system get too far out of date

It's important to keep the software on your system fairly current. That Linux kernel 1.2 system you have running in the corner that's been reliably serving your printers for years might be a great subject at cocktail parties, but it's probably a security incident waiting to happen. Keeping the software on your system up-to-date helps ensure that all bug and security fixes are applied. Most Linux distributions provide a set of packages that are security fixes only, so you don't have to worry about issues, such as configuration file and feature changes in order to keep your system secure. You should at least keep track of these updates.

Don't forget about physical security

Most security breaches are performed by people inside the organization running the target system. The most comprehensive software security configuration in the world means nothing if someone can walk up to your machine and boot a floppy containing exploit code. If your machine uses a BIOS or system PROM that allows the device boot order to be configured, set it so that the floppy and CD-ROM drives boot after the hard drive. If your BIOS provides support for password protection of its configuration, use it. If you can padlock the machine case closed, consider doing so. If you can keep the machine in a physically secure area such as a locked room, that's even better.

TCP Wrapper Configuration

We explained earlier that connecting your system to a network significantly increases the risk of attack. With the common-sense considerations out of the way, it's time to look more closely at basic network security. Here we'll discuss a simple yet effective method of reducing the risk of unwanted network access, using a tool called *TCP wrappers*. This mechanism "wraps" an existing service (such as the mail server), screening the network connections that are made to it and refusing connections from unauthorized sites. This is a simple way of adding access control to services that weren't originally designed for it, and is most commonly used in conjunction with the *inetd* or *xinetd* daemons.

TCP wrappers are somewhat equivalent to the security guards, or "bouncers," that you might find protecting the entrance to large parties or nightclubs. When you approach a venue you first encounter the security guard, who may ask you your name and address. The guard then consults a guest list, and if you're approved, the guard moves aside and allows you entry to the party.

When a network connection is made to a service protected by TCP wrappers, the wrapper is the first thing encountered. The wrapper checks the source of the network connection using the source hostname or address and consults a list that describes who is allowed access. If the source matches an entry on the list, the wrapper moves out of the way and allows the network connection access to the actual daemon program.

There are two ways to use TCP wrappers, depending on your Linux distribution and configuration. If you are using the *inetd* daemon for managing services (check to see if the file */etc/inetd.conf* exists), TCP wrappers are implemented using a special daemon called *tcpd*. If you are using the *xinetd* daemon instead (check for the directory */etc/xinetd.d*), *xinetd* is usually configured to use TCP wrappers directly. We'll describe each case in the following sections.

Using TCP Wrappers with inetd

If your system uses the *inetd* daemon to launch network services, it may be necessary to edit your */etc/inetd.conf* file to use TCP wrappers. Let's use the finger daemon, *in.fingerd*, as an example. The basic idea is that instead of running the actual *in.fingerd* daemon, *inetd* launches the *tcpd* daemon instead. *tcpd* performs the TCP wrapper operation and then runs *in.fingerd* in its place if the connection is accepted.

Configuring TCP wrappers requires a very simple change to */etc/inetd.conf*. For the finger daemon, you might have an entry in this file, such as:

```
# /etc/in.fingerd finger daemon
finger    stream tcp nowait  root /usr/sbin/in.fingerd  in.fingerd
```

To protect the finger daemon using *tcpd*, simply modify the */etc/inetd.conf* entry, as so:

```
# /etc/in.fingerd finger daemon
finger    stream tcp nowait  root /usr/sbin/tcpd /usr/sbin/in.fingerd
```

Here we've caused the *tcpd* command to be executed instead of the actual *in.fingerd* command. The full pathname of the finger daemon is passed to *tcpd* as an argument, and *tcpd* uses this argument to launch the real daemon after it has confirmed that access should be allowed.

You'll need to make this change for each daemon program you wish to protect. On most Linux systems you may find that *tcpd* is already configured, so these changes won't be necessary.

Using TCP Wrappers with xinetd

xinetd is a replacement for *inetd* that some distributions (such as Red Hat) are adopting. In most cases, *xinetd* has built-in support for TCP wrappers, so all you'll need to do is modify the TCP wrapper configuration files (*/etc/hosts.allow* and */etc/hosts.deny*) as described in the next section. If you are installing *xinetd* yourself, be sure to compile support for TCP wrappers; this is described in the *xinetd* documentation.

/etc/hosts.allow and /etc/hosts.deny

TCP wrappers use two configuration files, */etc/hosts.allow* and */etc/hosts.deny*. These files are used to specify the access rules for each network daemon protected with TCP wrappers. The files are described in detail in the *hosts_access* manual page, but we'll cover the mechanics here because common cases are fairly simple.

When a TCP wrapper is invoked, it obtains the IP address of the connecting host and attempts to find its hostname using a reverse DNS lookup. Next, it consults the */etc/hosts.allow* file to see if this host is specifically allowed access to the requested service. If a match is found, access is allowed and the actual network daemon is invoked. If no match is found in the */etc/hosts.allow* file, */etc/hosts.deny* is consulted to see if this host has been specifically denied access. If a match is found here, the connection is closed. If no match is found in either file, access is granted. This simple technique is powerful enough to cover most access requirements.

The syntax of *hosts.allow* and *hosts.deny* is fairly simple. Each file contains a set of rules. Each rule is generally on one line but may be split across multiple lines using a backslash at the end of the line. Each rule has the general form:

```
daemon_list : client_list : shell_command
```

The daemon_list is a comma-separated list of daemons to which the rule applies. The daemons are specified using their command basename; that is, the name of the actual executable daemon program that is executed to fulfill the requested service. The client_list is a comma-separated list of hostnames or IP addresses for which the rule will match. We'll demonstrate this later using an example. The shell_command is optional, and specifies a command that will be executed when the rule matches. This can be used, for example, to log incoming connections.

daemon_list and client_list may contain patterns that allow you to match a number of daemons or hosts without having to explicitly name each one. In addition, you can use a number of predefined tokens to make rules simpler to read and build. The patterns are quite sophisticated, so we don't cover them in detail here; instead we refer you to the *hosts_access* manual page.

Let's start with a simple *hosts.deny* file that looks like this:

```
# /etc/hosts.deny
ALL: ALL
```

The first line is a comment. The next line is a rule that is interpreted as follows: "Deny access requests to ALL services from ALL hosts." If our */etc/hosts.allow* is empty, this rule will have the effect of denying access to everything from all hosts on the Internet—including the local host! To get around this problem, we can make a simple change to the file:

```
# /etc/hosts.deny
ALL: ALL EXCEPT localhost
```

This is nearly always a safe rule to have in place, as it's a secure default. Remember that the */etc/hosts.allow* rules are consulted *before /etc/hosts.deny*, so by adding rules to *hosts.allow* we can override this default setting in *hosts.deny*. For example, imagine that we want to allow every host on the Internet to access the finger daemon. To do this we add a rule to */etc/hosts.allow* that looks like the following:

```
# /etc/hosts.allow
in.fingerd: ALL
```

A more common use of TCP wrappers is to restrict the set of hosts that can access a service. Hosts can be specified using IP address, hostname, or some pattern based on the address or hostname (e.g., to specify a group of hosts). For example, consider making the finger daemon available only to a small set of trusted hosts. In this case our *hosts.allow* file would be modified as follows:

```
# /etc/hosts.allow
in.fingerd: spaghetti.vpasta.com, .vpizza.com, 192.168.1.
```

In this example we've chosen to allow FTP requests from the host named *spaghetti.vpasta.com*, as well as from any host in the *vpizza.com* domain, and from any system with an IP address beginning with the pattern 192.168.1.

The host and IP address matching rules in *hosts.allow* and *hosts.deny* are important to understand, and the presence and location of the period characters are critical. A pattern beginning with a period is assumed to be the name of a domain to which requesting systems must belong. A pattern ending with a period is assumed to specify an IP address pattern. There are other ways of specifying groups of hosts, including NIS netgroups and explicit IP address netmasks. Full details on the configuration syntax of these patterns is available in the *hosts_access* manual page.

Firewalls: Filtering IP Packets

While TCP wrappers can be used to restrict the set of hosts that can establish connections to certain services on a machine, in many cases it is desirable to exert finer-grained control over the packets that can enter (or leave!) a given system. It's also the case that TCP wrappers only work with services configured using *inetd* or *xinetd*; some services (such as *sshd* on some systems) are "standalone" and provide their own access control features. Still other services don't implement any access control themselves, so it's necessary to provide another level of protection if we wish to control the connections made to these services.

Today it is commonplace for Internet users to protect themselves against the threat of network-based attacks using a technique called *IP filtering*. IP filtering involves having the kernel inspect each network packet that is transmitted or received and deciding whether to allow it to pass, to throw it away, or to modify it in some way before allowing it through. IP filtering is often called "firewalling," because by carefully filtering packets entering or leaving a machine you are building a "firewall" between the system and the rest of the Internet. IP filtering won't protect you against virus and Trojan Horse attacks or application defects, but it can protect you against many forms of network-based attacks, such as certain types of DoS attacks and IP spoofing (packets that are marked as coming from a system they don't really come from). IP filtering also provides an additional layer of access control that prevents unwanted users from trying to gain access to your system.

To make IP filtering work, we need to know which packets to allow and which to deny. Usually, the decision to filter a packet is based on the packet headers, which contain information such as the source and destination IP addresses, the protocol type (TCP, UDP, and so on), and the source and destination port numbers (which identify the particular service for which the packet is destined). Different network services use different protocols and port numbers; for example, most web servers receive requests on TCP port 80. If we wanted to filter out all incoming HTTP traffic from our system, we'd set up an IP filter that rejects all TCP packets destined for port 80.

Sometimes inspecting just the header of a packet is not sufficient to accomplish a particular filtering task, so we need to inspect and interpret the actual data carried within the packet. This technique is sometimes called "stateful inspection" because a packet is considered in the context of an ongoing network connection rather than in isolation. For example, we might want to allow users inside our network to use FTP servers outside our network. FTP is a complex protocol that uses one TCP connection to send commands to the server, but another to transfer the actual data. Unfortunately the FTP specification does not mandate a particular port number for data transfers, so the client and server must negotiate port numbers using the command session. Without stateful packet inspection, allowing FTP transfers would require allowing TCP connections to arbitrary ports. Stateful inspection solves this problem by interpreting the port number negotiation between the client and server, and automatically allowing TCP packets on the negotiated port to pass through.

IP filtering is implemented by the Linux kernel, which contains code to inspect each packet that is received and transmitted, applying filtering rules that determine the fate of the packet. The rules are configured using a user-space configuration tool that accepts arguments from the command line and translates them into filter specifications that are stored and used as rules by the kernel.

There are three generations of kernel-based IP filtering in Linux, and each has had its own configuration mechanism. The first generation was called *ipfw* (for "IP firewall"), and provided basic filtering capability but was somewhat inflexible and inefficient for complex configurations. *ipfw* is rarely used now. The second generation of IP filtering, called *IP chains*, improved greatly on *ipfw*, and is still in common use. The latest generation of filtering is called *netfilter/iptables*. *netfilter* is the kernel component and *iptables* is the user-space configuration tool; these terms are often used interchangeably. *netfilter* is not only much more flexible to configure, but is extensible as well. In the following sections we'll describe *netfilter* and some simple configurations as examples.

netfilter Basics

netfilter is implemented in Linux kernels 2.4.0 and newer. The primary tool for manipulating and displaying the filtering tables is called *iptables* and is included in all current Linux distributions. The *iptables* command allows configuration of a rich and complex set of firewall rules and hence has a large number of command-line options. We'll address the most common of these here. The *iptables* manpage offers a complete explanation.

Just to whet your appetite, take a look at a sneak preview of where we're heading:

```
iptables -A INPUT -m state --state NEW -m tcp -p tcp --dport 22 -j ACCEPT
```

This command installs an IP filtering rule that accepts new incoming connections to TCP port 22 (the *ssh* service) on our local system. It also uses an extension module called *state* to perform connection tracking. On the following pages we'll explain how all this works.

An important concept in *netfilter* is the notion of a *chain*, which consists of a list of rules that are applied to packets as they enter, leave, or traverse through the system. The kernel defines three chains by default, but the administrator can specify new chains of rules and link them to the predefined chains. The three predefined chains are:

INPUT

This chain applies to packets that are received and are destined for the local system.

OUTPUT

This chain applies to packets that are transmitted by the local system.

FORWARD

This chain applies whenever a packet will be routed from one network interface to another through this system. It is used whenever the system is acting as a packet router or gateway, and applies to packets that are neither originating from nor destined to this system.

Each rule in a chain provides a set of criteria that specify which packets match the rule, and an action that should be taken on packets that match. Actions that can be taken on a packet include *accepting* the packet (allowing it to be either received or transmitted), *dropping* the packet (simply refusing to receive or transmit it), or passing the packet onto another chain. (The latter is useful when building user-defined chains, which allow complex packet-filtering rules to be built up hierarchically.) A packet traverses each rule in the chain until it is accepted, dropped, or reaches the end of the chain; if it reaches the end, the default action of the chain determines the fate of the packet. The default action of a chain can be configured to either accept or drop all packets.

The Linux *netfilter* supports a number of other interesting things you can do in filtering rules. One of the key advantages of *netfilter* is that it is extensible. It is possible to develop extensions that enhance the way *netfilter* operates. Some examples of more sophisticated packet handling actions are:

Packet logging

You can create rules that do nothing more than log a description of the matching packet so that it can be captured for analysis later. This is very useful for detecting attacks and for testing a filtering configuration.

Stateful inspection

netfilter includes a set of helper modules that can perform stateful connection inspection, such as management of FTP connections, as described earlier.

Network Address Translation

Network Address Translation (NAT), also called *IP masquerading*, provides a means of rewriting the IP addresses and port numbers of packets as they pass through a chain. NAT is most commonly used to allow systems on a private network to use a connection to the Internet with a single IP address. NAT is a complex subject that we don't discuss at length, but a simple example is provided later in this chapter. You can learn more about NAT in the *NAT HOWTO* or the *Network Administrators Guide* (O'Reilly).

Packet and byte accounting

netfilter provides counters that allow you to measure how the network traffic handled each rule, and several IP accounting systems are based on these statistics. These counters are visible when you use *iptables* to list rulesets in verbose mode; we'll demonstrate this in Example 17-3.

Using the iptables command

The *iptables* command is used to make changes to the *netfilter* chains and rulesets. You can create new chains, delete chains, list the rules in a chain, flush chains (that is, remove all rules from a chain), and set the default action for a chain. *iptables* also allows you to insert, append, delete, and replace rules in a chain.

The *iptables* command has a large number of command-line arguments and options, but once you've used it a few times, the syntax becomes fairly obvious. In this section we are only going to cover the most common uses of *iptables*, so some arguments and options are left out of the following discussion. Specifically, we don't discuss user-defined chains here. Table 17-1 lists a summary of the *iptables* arguments that operate on chains, and Table 17-2 summarizes the *iptables* arguments that operate on individual rules.

Table 17-1. iptables operations on chains

Argument	Description
-L *chain*	List the rules in the specified chain or all chains.
-F *chain*	Flush (delete) the rules from the specified chain or all chains.
-Z *chain*	Zero the byte counters in the specified chain or all chains.
-P *chain action*	Set the default action on the specified chain to *action*.

Table 17-2. iptables operations on rules

Argument	Description
-A *chain rule-specification*	Append a rule to *chain*.
-D *chain rulenum*	Delete the rule with rule number *rulenum* from *chain*.
-R *chain rulenum rule-specification*	Replace rule number *rulenum* in *chain* with *rule-specification*.
-I *chain rulenum rule-specification*	Insert a rule into *chain* at slot number *rulenum* with specification *rule-specification*. If no *rulenum* is specified, "1" is assumed.

Each filtering rule includes parameters that describe which packets match the rule. The most common rule parameters are summarized in Table 17-3. Using an exclamation point (!) before a parameter inverts it. For example, the parameter -dport 80 means "match destination port 80," while the parameter -dport ! 80 means "match any destination port except 80."

Table 17-3. iptables rule parameters

Parameter	Matches
-p ! protocol	The packet protocol. Valid settings are tcp, udp, icmp, or all.
-s ! source/mask	Source address of the packet, specified as a hostname or IP address. mask specifies an optional netmask as either a literal netmask or a number of bits. For example, /255.255.255.0 gives the literal netmask, /24 gives the number of bits in the mask.
-d ! source/mask	Destination address of the packet. Uses the same syntax as the source address.
--sport ! port	The source port of the packet. Specifies as a literal port number or as a service name from /etc/services.
--dport ! port	The destination port of the packet. Uses the same syntax as the source address.
-i ! interface	The network interface on which the packet was received.
-o ! interface	The network address on which the packet will be sent.

A number of important options are used when building rulesets, summarized in Table 17-4.

Table 17-4. Other important iptables options

Option	Description
-v	Enable verbose output. Most useful when listing rules with -L.
-n	Display IP addresses in numeric form (i.e., avoid DNS lookup).
-m module	Load the iptables extension named module.

In addition to specifying matching parameters, each *netfilter* rule must specify some action to take for each packet matching the rule. Generally a rule specifies that a packet should be accepted or dropped, as described next. If no action is specified for a rule, the packet and byte counters for that rule will be incremented and the packet passed on to the next rule in the chain. This allows a rule to be used for accounting purposes only. To specify an action for a rule, use the syntax:

-j *target*

Here, *-j* stands for "jump," meaning that if a packet matches this rule, processing will jump to the action named by *target*. *target* can be one of:

ACCEPT
Allow this packet to be transmitted or received.

DROP
Drop the packet.

QUEUE

    Pass the packet to a userspace program for processing.

RETURN

    If used with a user-defined chain, causes the packet to be returned to the "calling" chain. If used with a built-in chain, causes the packet to jump to the end of the chain (where it is subject to the default action for that chain).

When using the *-j* option, `target` can also be the name of a user-specified chain, which allows the user to define a "subchain" of rules that will process this packet. As described earlier, the target RETURN is used to cause a packet to return from a user-defined chain back to the "calling" chain.

Developing IP Filtering Rulesets

Often the most difficult part of IP firewall implementation is deciding what you actually want it to do. Do you want to allow outgoing connections freely? Should you allow ICMP packets? What UDP services do you want? What kind of logging do you want to do?

One of the great challenges with building filtering rulesets is that most people aren't accustomed to thinking in terms of addresses, protocols, and port numbers. Instead, we more often think in terms of applications and end users. To build filtering rulesets, we must be able to translate our higher-level requirements into the low-level detail with which the filtering operates.

You can't get around the need to understand a bit of how the services that you are managing with IP filtering actually work. First and foremost, it is important to know whether a service uses TCP or UDP, and which port numbers it uses. The */etc/services* file can often provide a good deal of what you need to know. For example, searching for smtp in this file yields tcp/25, which indicates that the SMTP protocol uses TCP port 25. Likewise, searching for the DNS returns two entries, one for udp/53 and another for tcp/53; this means that the service uses port 53, but uses either the TCP or UDP protocols.

Some protocols, such as FTP, have two related but different entries in */etc/services*. As described earlier, FTP uses one port for the command session (tcp/21) and another for the data transfer sessions (tcp/20). Unfortunately, FTP clients and servers are free to use different ports for the data transfer session. Therefore, FTP has been somewhat of a nuisance for filtering rules. Fortunately, *netfilter* provides some assistance with a feature called *connection tracking*, along with a helper module that specifically understands the FTP service. Because of this it is necessary only to create a rule for the FTP command session, and *netfilter* will automatically track and allow the data transfer sessions for you. We demonstrate this later in Example 17-2.

If */etc/services* doesn't provide enough information, you may need to read the relevant RFC document that specifies the protocol used by the service. Usually you don't need to know much more about a service other than what protocols and ports it uses, which is generally easy to find in the RFC.

IP Filter Management and Script Files

Filtering rules are stored and used by the kernel in much the same way as routing entries: when the system reboots, IP filtering rules must be reconfigured. To ensure that a firewall configuration is reinstated when a reboot occurs, you should place the appropriate *iptables* commands in a script file that is automatically executed at system boot time. Bundled with the *iptables* software package come two programs called *iptables-save* and *iptables-restore* that respectively save the current *netfilter* configuration to a file and restore it from that file. These tools greatly simplify the task of managing firewall configuration.

Each Linux distribution takes a slightly different approach to managing firewall configuration:

Red Hat (versions 7.0 and later)
First configure your IP filtering rules using the appropriate *iptables* commands. Then, execute the following command:

```
/sbin/service iptables save
```

This causes the filtering rules to be saved to */etc/sysconfig/iptables*, which is automatically read at boot time.

Debian
Set up your *iptables* rules as follows:

1. Edit */etc/default/iptables* and set `enable_iptables_initd=true`.

2. Manually configure your *iptables* using *iptables* commands.

3. Invoke */etc/init.d/iptables save_active* to save the configuration.

At system boot time the saved configuration will be restored automatically.

SuSE Linux
For a simple, albeit not as flexible, configuration, run *yast2* and select the firewall configuration module Security&Users → Firewall. Otherwise:

1. Edit */etc/sysconfig/SuSEfirewall2*. This file is thoroughly documented.

2. If necessary, define custom filter rules in */etc/sysconfig/scripts/SuSEfirewall2-custom*. This requires deeper knowledge about how firewalls work on Linux.

3. Start the firewall by invoking */sbin/SuSEfirewall2 start*.

Sample netfilter Configurations

In this section we'll provide some simple but useful IP filtering configurations. The aim here is not to provide you with a set of solutions that you accept uncritically.

Instead, we'll introduce you to what a useful set of IP filtering rules looks like and provide you with a skeleton on which you could base your own configurations.

Simple IP filtering example

Here we'll demonstrate the basic use of IP filtering, which is similar to our use of TCP wrappers described earlier in the chapter. Here we want to screen out packets from all hosts on the Internet, except for packets destined for the finger daemon from a small set of hosts. While TCP wrappers can be used to perform the same function, IP filtering can be used to screen many different types of packets (for example, ICMP "ping" packets), and is often necessary to protect services that aren't managed by TCP wrappers.

Unlike TCP wrappers, *iptables* rules cannot use hostnames to identify the origin or destination of a packet; you must use IP addresses when specifying rules. This is a good idea, anyway, since reverse hostname lookup is not a completely secure way to identify a packet (it is possible to spoof DNS, making it appear as though some IP address has a different hostname). In Example 17-1 and Example 17-2, we use IP addresses instead of hostnames, which can be obtained using a tool such as *nslookup*.

Example 17-1. Simple ipchains example

```
# Load the connection tracking modules if they're not compiled into the
# kernel.
modprobe ip_conntrack
modprobe ip_conntrack_ftp

# Set default policy on the INPUT chain to DROP.
iptables -P INPUT DROP

# ACCEPT packets belonging to an existing connection.
# '-A INPUT' is used to append to the INPUT chain.
# '-m state' uses the stateful inspection module.
iptables -A INPUT -m state --state ESTABLISHED,RELATED -j ACCEPT

# ACCEPT all packets that have come from the loopback interface, that
# is, from the local host. '-i lo' identifies the loopback interface.
iptables -A INPUT -i lo -j ACCEPT

# ACCEPT new incoming connections, and packets belonging to existing
# connections, to port 22 (ssh).
iptables -A INPUT -m state --state NEW -m tcp -p tcp \
        --dport 22 -j ACCEPT

# ACCEPT new incoming FTP connections from 192.168.1/24.
iptables -A INPUT -m state --state NEW -m tcp -p tcp -s 192.168.1/24 \
        --dport 21 -j ACCEPT

# ACCEPT new incoming FTP connections from spaghetti.vpizza.com,
# which has IP address 10.21.2.4.
iptables -A INPUT -m state --state NEW -m tcp -p tcp -s 10.21.2.4 \
```

Example 17-1. Simple ipchains example (continued)

```
        --dport 21 -j ACCEPT

# ACCEPT new incoming FTP connections from *.vpizza.com.
# They have two networks: 172.18.1.0 and 172.25.3.0.
iptables -A INPUT -m state --state NEW -m tcp -p tcp -s 172.18.1/24 \
        --dport 21 -j ACCEPT
iptables -A INPUT -m state --state NEW -m tcp -p tcp -s 172.25.3/24 \
        --dport 21 -j ACCEPT
```

The ruleset specifically accepts all packets that belong to an existing connection. This is needed in the case of FTP, in which the client and server may negotiate an alternate port for the data transfer connection. The connection tracking module (specified with `-m state` in the rules) ensures that the data transfer connection can be accepted.

IP filtering to protect an entire network

The previous example demonstrated IP filtering on a single host. In this section, we deal with the case where a network of machines (such as all the machines in a home or small office) are connected to the Internet through a gateway machine. We can write *netfilter* rules to filter the traffic between the Internet and the internal network. In this case, we place rules on both the INPUT and FORWARD chains. Recall that INPUT is used to filter incoming packets destined for this host, while FORWARD is used for packets being forwarded by the gateway (i.e., packets destined for the internal network or the Internet). Here, we assume that the gateway machine uses the ppp0 interface to communicate with the Internet.

Example 17-2. Using netfilter to protect an IP network

```
# Load the connection tracking modules if they're not compiled into the
# kernel.
modprobe ip_conntrack
modprobe ip_conntrack_ftp

# Set default policy on INPUT and FORWARD chains to DROP.
iptables -P INPUT DROP
iptables -P FORWARD DROP

# ACCEPT all packets from the loopback interface.
iptables -A INPUT -i lo -j ACCEPT

# Create a new user-defined chain. This chain will contain rules
# relevant to both INPUT and FORWARD, so by grouping them together on
# a single chain we avoid stating the rules twice.
iptables -N allowfwdin

# ACCEPT packets belonging to an existing connection.
# Note that this rule (and subsequent rules) are placed
# on the user-defined chain.
```

Example 17-2. Using netfilter to protect an IP network (continued)

```
iptables -A allowfwdin -m state --state ESTABLISHED,RELATED -j ACCEPT

# ACCEPT new connection requests from machines on the internal network.
# This allows machines on the internal network to establish connections
# to the Internet, but not the other way around. Note the use of
# '-i ! ppp0' to specify packets coming from interfaces other than ppp0.
iptables -A allowfwdin -m state --state NEW -i ! ppp0 -j ACCEPT

# ACCEPT new incoming connections to port 22 (ssh).
iptables -A allowfwdin -m state --state NEW -m tcp -p tcp \
        --dport 22 -j ACCEPT

# ACCEPT new incoming FTP connections from 192.168.1/24.
iptables -A allowfwdin -m state --state NEW -m tcp -p tcp -s 192.168.1/24 \
        --dport 21 -j ACCEPT

# ACCEPT new incoming FTP connections from spaghetti.vpizza.com.
iptables -A allowfwdin -m state --state NEW -m tcp -p tcp -s 10.21.2.4 \
        --dport 21 -j ACCEPT

# ACCEPT new incoming FTP connections from *.vpizza.com.
iptables -A allowfwdin -m state --state NEW -m tcp -p tcp -s 172.18.1/24 \
        --dport 21 -j ACCEPT
iptables -A allowfwdin -m state --state NEW -m tcp -p tcp -s 172.25.3/24 \
        fs

# Any packets that have passed through the user-defined chain are now
# subject to the action LOG, which causes them to be logged.
# Use the 'limit' module to prevent logging blocked packets too
# rapidly.
iptables -A allowfwdin -m limit --limit 2/sec -j LOG

# Set default action on the user-defined chain to DROP.
iptables -A allowfwdin -j DROP

# Direct all packets received for INPUT or FORWARD to our user-defined chain.
iptables -A INPUT -j allowfwdin
iptables -A FORWARD -j allowfwdin

# Enable IP routing (required by all IP routers, regardless of the use
# of IP filtering).
echo 1 >/proc/sys/net/ipv4/ip_forward
```

To keep track of any attempts to breach security, we've added a rule that will log any packets that would be dropped. However, if a large number of bad packets were to arrive, this rule might fill up the disk with log entries, or slow down the gateway to a crawl (as it takes much longer to log packets than it does to forward or filter them). So, we use the `limit` module which controls the rate at which a rule action is taken. In the preceding example, we allowed an average rate of two bad packets per second to be logged. All other packets will pass through the rule and simply be dropped.

To view the rules that have been configured (see Example 17-3), use the *iptables* list option *-L*. Using the verbose mode (*-v*) displays more information than the basic output of the command.

Example 17-3. Listing iptables rulesets for Example 17-2

```
# iptables -L -v
Chain INPUT (policy DROP 0 packets, 0 bytes)
 pkts bytes target    prot opt in     out     source             destination
   16  1328 ACCEPT    all  --  lo     any     anywhere           anywhere
    0     0 allowfwdin all  --  any    any     anywhere           anywhere

Chain FORWARD (policy DROP 0 packets, 0 bytes)
 pkts bytes target    prot opt in     out     source             destination
    0     0 allowfwdin all  --  any    any     anywhere           anywhere

Chain OUTPUT (policy ACCEPT 9756 packets, 819K bytes)
 pkts bytes target    prot opt in     out     source             destination

Chain allowfwdin (2 references)
 pkts bytes target    prot opt in     out     source             destination
    0     0 ACCEPT    all  --  any    any     anywhere           anywhere  \
    state RELATED,ESTABLISHED
    0     0 ACCEPT    all  --  !ppp0  any     anywhere           anywhere  \
    state NEW
    0     0 ACCEPT    tcp  --  any    any     anywhere           anywhere  \
    state NEW tcp dpt:ssh
    0     0 ACCEPT    tcp  --  any    any     192.168.0.0/24     anywhere  \
    state NEW tcp dpt:ftp
    0     0 ACCEPT    tcp  --  any    any     10.21.2.4          anywhere  \
    state NEW tcp dpt:ftp
    0     0 ACCEPT    tcp  --  any    any     172.18.0.0/24      anywhere  \
    state NEW tcp dpt:ftp
    0     0 ACCEPT    tcp  --  any    any     172.25.0.0/24      anywhere  \
    state NEW tcp dpt:ftp
    0     0 LOG       all  --  any    any     anywhere           anywhere  \
    limit: avg 2/sec burst 5 LOG level warning
    0     0 DROP      all  --  any    any     anywhere           anywhere
```

IP masquerading example

netfilter rules can also be used to implement IP masquerading, a specific type of NAT that rewrites packets from an internal network to make them appear as though they are originating from a single IP address. This is often used in cases where one has a number of machines connected to a LAN, with a single Internet-connected machine with one IP address. This is a common situation in home networks where the ISP has allocated a single IP address; using IP masquerading, however, an entire network of machines can share the address. By having the gateway perform IP masquerading, packets from the internal LAN will appear as though they are originating from the gateway machine, and packets from the Internet will be forwarded back to the appropriate host on the internal LAN. You can accomplish all of this with a bit of clever packet rewriting using *netfilter*.

Configuring *netfilter* to support IP masquerading is much simpler than explaining how it works! More complete information about how IP masquerading and NAT are accomplished is provided in the *NAT HOWTO*. We'll show the most basic configuration in Example 17-4.

In this configuration we've assumed that we have a Linux system that will act as a gateway for an internal network. The gateway has a PPP connection to the Internet on interface ppp0, and a LAN connection to the internal network on interface eth0. This configuration allows outgoing connections from the internal network to the Internet, but will block incoming connections from the Internet to machines on the internal network except for the gateway. As it turns out, we don't need to provide explicit commands to achieve this, as it is the default behavior when using NAT in this fashion.

Example 17-4. Basic IP masquerade configuration

```
# Load the module supporting NAT, if not compiled into the kernel.
modprobe iptables_nat

# Masquerade any routed connections supported by the ppp0 device.
iptables -t nat -A POSTROUTING -p ppp0 -j MASQUERADE

# Enable IP routing.
echo 1 >/proc/sys/net/ipv4/ip_forward
```

There are some important details to note in this configuration. The NAT functionality is provided in a module of its own, which must be loaded unless it is built into your kernel. The NAT module uses a new chain called POSTROUTING that processes packets after the kernel performs routing operations on them (that is, decides whether the packets are destined for the Internet or for internal LAN machines). The MASQUERADE target does the hard work of the address translation and tracking.

Note that this configuration provides no filtering of outgoing connections. All hosts on the private network will be able to establish outgoing connections to any host and any port. The *packet filtering HOWTO* provides useful information about how to combine IP filtering with address translation.

## CHAPTER 18

LAMP

Just writing a couple of lines of HTML code is not enough for most web sites; dynamic content is what people want today. Well, web-site visitors don't usually want as much as web designers are eager give them, but the designers are in control, so dynamic content is what we are going to talk about in this chapter.

Linux is—you guessed it—an excellent platform for serving dynamic content. A bazillion web sites serving dynamic content are already running on Linux today; this is one of the foremost application areas where Linux excels.

Dynamic content can be achieved by two entirely different ways of programming: server-side programming and client-side programming. JavaScript and Java applets are the most common ways of getting interactive HTML pages with client-side programming.

But because of the limitations of JavaScript and Java, most people use server-side programs. You can use server-side programs in many different flavors with many different software packages, but one combination has become ubiquitous for implementing these techniques. This combination is so common nowadays that it even has received a phony acronym: LAMP, which is short for Linux-Apache-MySQL-PHP. We have been talking about the Apache web server already, and this whole book is about Linux, so what we have left to talk about here are the latter two packages—MySQL and PHP—as well as how the four go together.

In order to get a working LAMP installation, you will need to have Apache set up as described in "Configuring Your Own Web Server" in Chapter 16, as well as install MySQL and PHP. We will cover how to get the latter two running in this chapter.

Before we get into the technical details, however, we should review why you might want to bother setting up and learning how to use a LAMP system.

LAMP makes it easy to provide a large amount of content and navigate your web-site users through it easily.

Let's say you have a site with lots of JPEGs of photographs you've taken on numerous occasions. Visitors may want to view photographs along a number of different dimensions. That is, some visitors want to see photographs of historic buildings, whenever you took them. Others might want to see photographs taken on your latest trip, whenever that was.

To make navigation and retrieval easy, you start by inserting your JPEGs into a MySQL database, which provides a datatype specifically for binary large objects (BLOBs) such as JPEGs. You organize them any way you want (by subject matter, by trip, and so on) and store all this information in tables within the database.

Now you provide a form on your web site that visitors can fill out to indicate the dimension along which they want to view photographs. The form could be as simple as that shown in Figure 18-1.

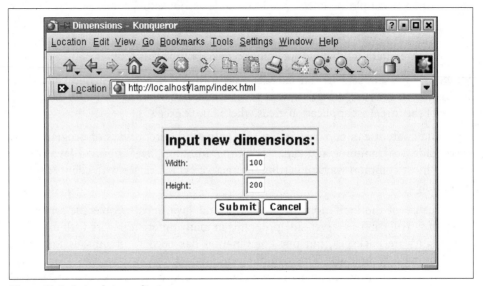

Figure 18-1. A simple input form

Your next page is a dynamic one, along the lines of that which we are describing in this chapter. A bit of PHP code retrieves the visitor's request and determines what is displayed in the page. This could look like Figure 18-2.

Where is the MySQL in all this? It's not immediately visible, but it plays a crucial role behind the scenes because it is queried by the PHP code. The combination of inline PHP code and a fast database makes the whole experience fairly pleasant for the visitor.

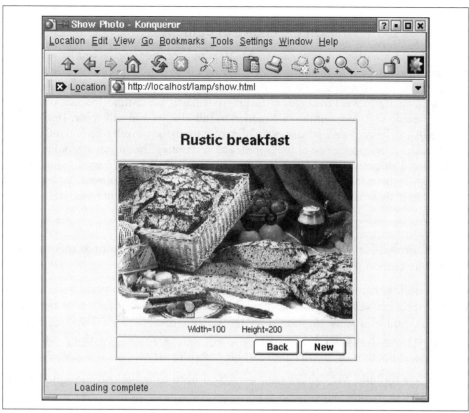

Figure 18-2. A dynamic web page generated by PHP

MySQL

MySQL is an open-source database that is very fast and comparatively easy to administer. If you need the most advanced database features like reduplication or distributed databases, or if you plan to store gigabytes of data, the big iron databases, such as Oracle might be a better choice, but for most intents and purposes, MySQL is an excellent database choice.

It is very likely that your distribution contains an installable MySQL system, but if you'd rather have the latest and greatest, you can go to *http://www.mysql.com/ downloads/* and download the package yourself. At the time of this writing, the latest stable version is 3.23.47. Please note that some MySQL users have reported database table corruptions with 2.2.14 kernels under heavy load, so if you plan to use

MySQL for real-life applications, you might want to upgrade your kernel to something more current.

A problem that can occur with MySQL versions compiled with gcc 2.96 is random crashes. This gcc version is not an official stable version, but at least one distributor (Red Hat) unfortunately shipped it as the default compiler. So if you experience strange crashes in the database server, and are using gcc 2.96, try using one of the precompiled binaries or install a more stable compiler version, such as 2.95.3.

If you want to build MySQL on your own, you need to download the source package, unpack it, and install with:

```
owl$ ./configure --prefix=/usr/local/mysql
owl$ make
owl# make install
```

Note that depending on your system, you might select a different installation path. You will also probably need to be *root* for the third step. You need to remember the installation path because you will need it for the PHP configuration later on.

For the next step, we recommend that you create a user and a group called *mysql* as described in "Creating Accounts" in Chapter 5. Change to this user with *su - mysql* and execute:

```
owl$ scripts/mysql_install_db
```

For security reasons, it might be a good idea to disable logins by the *mysql* user. You can simply do this as *root* by putting a star in the second (password) column in */etc/password* and/or */etc/shadow*.

After this step, you need to perform just one more command before returning from *root* to your normal user account. The following command starts the MySQL server:

```
owl# /usr/local/mysql/bin/safe_mysqld &
```

You might also want to add either the option *--log* or the option *--log-long-format* in order to get a log file about what is going on in the database server.

To check whether your server was started correctly, you can try (as normal user again) the following command (you need to change the path, of course, if you have installed MySQL in a different location):

```
owl$ /usr/local/mysql/bin/mysqladmin version
mysqladmin  Ver 8.19 Distrib 3.23.37, for suse-linux on i686
Copyright (C) 2000 MySQL AB & MySQL Finland AB & TCX DataKonsult AB
This software comes with ABSOLUTELY NO WARRANTY. This is free software,
and you are welcome to modify and redistribute it under the GPL license.

Server version          3.23.37-log
Protocol version    10
Connection              Localhost via UNIX socket
UNIX socket             /var/lib/mysql/mysql.sock
Uptime:                     43 days 11 hours 39 min 17 sec

Threads: 1  Questions: 142  Slow queries: 0  Opens: 160  Flush tables: 1  Open
tables: 13 Queries per second avg: 0.000
```

This should work without entering a password. We would like to point out, though, that it is not a good idea to have a database without a password because that increases the odds for a possible intruder to get at your potentially valuable data in the database. You might perhaps want to leave the database without a password for testing, but then you should make sure that you do not forget to set a password after you are done with your tests and retest to see whether everything works with the password in place. If you have created a password for the *root* database user (or if your distribution has done so for you; check your documentation in case of any problems), you must specify the *-p* option which makes *mysqladmin* ask you for your password.

We should add here that most distributions include a startup script for the MySQL server that you can use instead of starting the server manually (especially if you have installed MySQL from your installation media). Often, this script is in */etc/init.d/ mysql*.

With the database server started and working, we can start to define database users and create new databases. We would like to point out that a usable tutorial is included with the MySQL sources and you cancan find lots of documentation on *http://www.mysql.com*, so we will just cover the very basics here to get you started. If you really want to become a MySQL expert, we suggest you look into *Managing & Using MySQL* by Randy Jay Yarger, George Reese, and Tim King (O'Reilly).

There are two ways of communicating with the MySQL engine: you can either use a console-based database client, or write so-called SQL scripts and feed them to the database in order to execute many SQL commands at once. SQL stands for Structured Query Language and is the database language used with relational databases; we will cover its use later in this chapter. Both ways of executing SQL commands assume that you have the correct username/password combination.

An important thing you need to know about MySQL is that Linux user accounts are different from MySQL user accounts. In other words, MySQL has its own account management. Most people give their MySQL user accounts the same names as their Linux user accounts in order to avoid confusion, though.

By default, there is one MySQL account called *root* which has no password (talk about "security by default"...). This means that you can access the database server with the interactive command-line tool *mysql* as follows:

```
owl$ mysql -u root

Welcome to the MySQL monitor.  Commands end with ; or \g.
Your MySQL connection id is 13 to server version: 3.23.39.

Type 'help;' or '\h' for help. Type '\c' to clear the buffer.

mysql:
```

The *-u* option specifies the database user to use. If this does not work, maybe your MySQL installation has a password set for the *root* user. Try to find this password in the documentation and start the *mysql* program with:

```
owl$ mysql -u root -p
```

which will prompt you for the password.

Assuming that you have been able to log into the database server, let's try to issue a command:*

```
mysql> show databases;
+-------------+
| Database    |
+-------------+
| mysql       |
| test        |
+-------------+
2 rows in set (0.11 sec)
```

This tells you that two databases are managed by this database server. One is called *mysql* and contains MySQL's internal configuration information including the usernames, and the other one is called *test* and can be used by you for your experiments. It's also no problem at all to create additional databases; we'll show you how in a minute. As you can see, all SQL commands need to be terminated with a semicolon—probably in order to make the C programmers happy.

---

* This is not a real SQL command, but rather a MySQL administration command.

Now you should give the *root* account a password (in case it does not have one already). This is done with two SQL commands:

```
mysql> SET PASSWORD FOR root=PASSWORD('new_topsecret_passwd');
mysql> FLUSH PRIVILEGES;
```

Notice again the semicolon at the end of these commands; if you forget to type them before pressing the Enter key, MySQL will just stare at you, waiting for you to enter more.

By the way, SQL commands are case-insensitive; we have written them in uppercase here because that makes it a bit easier to see in an SQL script where the command keywords and the variable parameters are.

Also note the use of the *FLUSH PRIVILEGES* command. This is important because only after this command has been executed will MySQL update its user database.

Now we want to create a new user called *olof*, which has the same access rights as *root*, except that it cannot create new users. Apart from that, *olof* may use and manipulate all MySQL databases on this database server:

```
mysql> GRANT ALL PRIVILEGES ON *.* TO olof@localhost IDENTIFIED BY 'olof_passwd';
mysql> FLUSH PRIVILEGES;
```

The user *olof* can log into the database only from the local machine. This is a good idea since it leaves one less security issue to think about. We recommend that you only allow access from the local machine unless you have a very good reason not to do it this way. Even in the LAMP combo, local access is enough, because the web server process is running on the local machine, and this is the process that connects to the database, not the user's web browser process.

But if you really require access to the database over the network, you could use these commands instead:

```
mysql> GRANT ALL PRIVILEGES ON *.* TO username@"%"  IDENTIFIED BY 'user_passwd';
mysql> FLUSH PRIVILEGES;
```

If you think that having all access rights except creating new users is a bit too much, let's create another user that may execute the SELECT, INSERT, UPDATE, DELETE, and DROP operations, but only on the database called *test* (and only when connected from the local machine):

```
mysql> GRANT SELECT, INSERT, UPDATE, DELETE, DROP ON test.* TO gonzo@localhost
       IDENTIFIED BY 'gonzo_passwd';
mysql> FLUSH PRIVILEGES;
```

If you haven't worked with SQL databases before, these operations will probably not make much sense to you. Since you are going to need to use them anyway when setting up your LAMP system, we might just as well shortly describe them here:

SELECT

This is the most commonly used SQL command. It queries the database for data with certain properties—e.g., you could ask for all customers in a certain town. SELECT never changes anything in the database.

INSERT

This SQL command inserts new records into a database table. You use this (either interactively or, more likely, as part of a program) to insert a customer record into the customer table in your database, for example.

UPDATE

This SQL command changes existing records in a database. You could use this to, for example, increase the retail prices of all articles in the database by 15% (talk about inflation!).

DELETE

This SQL command deletes entire records from the database. Be careful with this command, as there is no way of restoring the data short of restoring from a (hopefully available!) backup tape.

There are even more SQL commands and corresponding privileges (like DROP, which lets you delete entire tables or even entire databases), but these are used less often than the "big four" listed here.

Now we want to create a new database which we can then fill with tables and data later. This is done with the SQL command CREATE DATABASE:

```
mysql> create database test_database;
Query OK; 1 row affected (0.03 sec)
```

The output from MySQL already indicates that everything went fine, but in order to be really sure, we can ask anew which databases the server manages:

```
mysql> show databases;
+------------------+
| Database         |
+------------------+
| mysql            |
| test             |
| test_database    |
+------------------+
6 rows in set (0.00 sec)
```

Now we want to define a table in our new database, but the first thing we need to do is tell the MySQL server that we actually want to use this database:

```
mysql> use test_database
Database changed
```

As you can see, we didn't use a semicolon at the end here, since this is again not an SQL command, but rather a control statement for the MySQL console client. It wouldn't hurt to add a semicolon here, too.

You define a table, which is ultimately where your data will be stored, by means of the SQL command CREATE TABLE. Here is an example:

```
mysql> CREATE TABLE comment_table(
    ->    id INT NOT NULL auto_increment,
    ->    comment TEXT,
    ->    PRIMARY KEY(id));
Query OK, 0 rows affected (0.10 sec)
```

Here we defined a table called comment_table with two columns—i.e., there are two data fields in each record. One is called id. This one serves as a unique identifier for each record that cannot occur twice in different records and is therefore marked as the *primary key*, which is just a fancy term in database-speak for "unique identifier." The other column is a variable of type TEXT which can store up to 65,535 characters.

Now we can check which tables we have within our database test_database:

```
mysql> show tables;
+-------------------------+
| Tables_in_test_database |
+-------------------------+
| comment_table           |
+-------------------------+
1 row in set (0.00 sec)
```

Now we know that everything is alright and can start to add data records to our table. This is done with the SQL command INSERT:

```
mysql> INSERT INTO comment_table VALUES ('0','comment');
Query OK, 1 row affected (0.06 sec)
```

Finally, we can check which data our table contains:

```
mysql> SELECT * FROM comment_table;
+----+---------+
| id | comment |
+----+---------+
|  1 | comment |
+----+---------+
1 row in set (0.01 sec)
```

Here we ask for all (*) columns in the table comment_table. But you might have noticed something odd here: we have asked MySQL to insert a 0 in the first column, but instead there is a 1 now. That's because we have defined this column to be of the type INT NOT NULL auto_increment, which means that the column value cannot be NULL and that MySQL will automatically choose the next available value. This is nice because we can insert new records into the table without having to ensure that we pick unique values for the first column:

```
mysql> INSERT INTO comment_table VALUES ('0','comment1');
Query OK, 1 row affected (0.00 sec)

mysql> SELECT * FROM comment_table;
+----+----------+
```

```
| id | comment  |
+----+----------+
|  1 | comment  |
|  2 | comment1 |
+----+----------+
2 rows in set (0.00 sec)
```

As you can see, we have specified 0 as the value for the first column again, but MySQL has automatically selected the next available valid value.

At this point, you know already enough about MySQL in order to experiment yourself or start reading another book about databases and dream about building the next hugely successful e-commerce web site.*

But instead of dreaming, you can also read on here and learn about SQL scripts.

You do not necessarily need to type in all commands at MySQL's own command-line prompt, you can also execute batch files with SQL commands by piping them to the *mysql* program. For example, if you save the following SQL code as *create_db.sql*:

```
DROP DATABASE IF EXISTS test_database;
CREATE DATABASE test_database;
USE test_database;
CREATE TABLE comment_table( id INT NOT NULL auto_increment,\
 comment TEXT,PRIMARY KEY(id));

INSERT INTO comment_table VALUES ('0','comment');
INSERT INTO comment_table VALUES ('0','comment1');
```

you can execute this script from the ordinary Linux command line with:

```
mysql -u root -p < create_db.sql
```

The line:

```
DROP DATABASE IF EXISTS test_database;
```

is of course pretty dangerous; you should use it only if you don't have important data in your database.

To tell the truth, it is not absolutely necessary (albeit strongly recommended) to create a new database for each project. In theory, you could lump all your data into the *test* database that is preinstalled with MySQL as long as you make sure the table names are all different. In practice, this would be a maintenance nightmare if you have more than a handful of tables.

PHP

In order to complete our combo of Linux, Apache, PHP, and MySQL, we still need the PHP language interpreter. PHP is a recursive acronym that expands to PHP:

---

* Or the first successful e-commerce web site, as some people would like to rectify.

Hypertext Preprocessor. It has been in development for several years now; the versions most commonly used are Version 3 and Version 4. We will use PHP4 for this chapter, as it was the most current stable version at the time of this writing.

Some Sample PHP

One of the nice things about PHP is that PHP code can be entered directly into HTML code. The web server will pass everything between <?php and ?> to the PHP module, which will interpret and execute the commands. Here is a very simple example for some PHP code in an HTML page; if you already have set up PHP, you could run this directly from your web server (if not, we'll tell you how to set up PHP below):

```
<html>
<body>
<?php
echo "Hi,";
?>
LAMP enthusiasts.
</body>
</html>
```

As you probably already have expected, your browser will output the following text:

```
Hi, LAMP enthusiasts.
```

This extremely simple example shows how Apache works together with the PHP interpreter: the code in <?php and ?> is passed to the PHP interpreter, which executes the echo command, which in turn outputs its parameters to the web browser. In addition to this, the line *LAMP enthusiasts* is simply added as ordinary HTML text (and since it doesn't have any markup, it doesn't look like HTML).

Of course, PHP can do much more. Like most programming languages, it can use variables and make decisions, as in the following script (we'll leave out the HTML framework here for brevity):

```
<?php
echo "Dear friends, today's date is: ";
echo date("F d, Y")."\n";
echo "<br>";
echo "We are in the ";

if ( date ("m") <= 6 ) {
        echo "first ";
        } else {
        echo "second ";
}
echo "half of the year ".date("Y");
?>
```

You have probably already guessed that this script bases its decision in the if statement depending on the current month. Notice that we have used an HTML tag (<br>)

in the PHP output; this is completely acceptable and a very common technique when using PHP. Your web browser will receive the following data (of course, with other dates, unless your computer clock goes wrong or you were trapped in a time warp):

```
Dear friends, today's date is: May 04, 2002
<br>We are in the first half of the year of 2002
```

The web browser will then break the line at the position of the <br> tab.

In order to modularize your code, PHP also supports functions, as do most other programming languages. These functions enable you to execute a piece of code in many different places without having to rewrite it over and over again.

PHP comes with very extensive function libraries, and you can download even more from the Net. In order to include a function library, you can use the include( ) and the require( ) statements, which differ only marginally.

If you want to program with PHP, you should familiarize yourself with the documentation of the function libraries that are shipped together with the PHP interpreter, since their use means you do not have to reinvent the wheel when performing common tasks.

Here is the definition of two simple functions—show_date, which outputs the current date in a hardcoded date format and appends a line break, and show_halfyear, which outputs first or second depending on the current month:

```php
<?php

function show_date( )}

echo  date("F d, Y")."\n <br>";
{

function show_semester( ) {
if (date ("m")<=6){
        echo "first ";
        } else {
        echo "second ";
}

?>
```

Let's call this script *functions.php* and rewrite our initial script using these functions:

```php
<?php

require(functions.php);
echo "Dear friends, the date today is: ";

show_date( );

echo "<br>";
```

```
echo "We are in the ";

show_semester();

echo "semester of ".date("Y");
?>
```

The require( ) statement tells the PHP interpreter to load our function script and make the functions contained therein available to the current script.

Of course, we have only scratched the surface of what PHP can do. If this has whetted your appetite, you might want to look into *Programming PHP* by Rasmus Lerdorf, the original author of PHP, and Kevin Tatroe (O'Reilly).

Until PHP3, PHP was an interpreted language, the code of which was kept in a buffer. Loops and other often-run pieces of code were parsed over and over again before executing the code. Of course, this led to somewhat suboptimal performance.

PHP4 is a complete rewrite and consists of the language core (called "Zend") and the function modules (which are very flexible and extensible). Unlike PHP3, PHP4 can be used in multithreaded environments, which also makes it possible to use PHP as a module in various web servers.

In addition to running PHP4 as a module, you can also run it as a CGI program started by the web server, at the expense of some additional overhead. When running PHP as a CGI program, each new page that contains PHP code requires starting a new instance of the PHP interpreter, which in turn requires creating a new process and loading the PHP interpreter into this process. When the interpreter is finished creating the page, its process ends, the memory is freed, all file handles are closed, and all database connections are shut down.

As a web server module, the PHP interpreter becomes part of the web server and is always loaded into memory. In addition, it can keep resources like database connections alive across different pages, which can bring huge performance benefits.

All big-ticket PHP sites use PHP as a module, mostly because of the better performance it affords.

PHP4 as an Apache Module

As we have already said, running the PHP interpreter as a web server module is best for getting good performance. Today, most distributions (including Slackware, Debian, SuSE, and RedHat) ship both Apache and the PHP4 module for Apache, so it is generally not necessary to build the PHP4 module yourself. It may be a good idea to do so anyway, however.

Because of its vast amount of functionality, the PHP4 module needs quite a number of additional libraries or modules. If you install the module from your installation CDs, the installation program will have automatically installed the necessary modules. However, the modules shipped with distributions are typically loaded with functionality to satisfy all needs and tastes. The result can be a system that's heavier and slower than it needs to be.

Thus, the advantage of building PHP4 by yourself is that you can decide which functionality you want to go into the module. Check the documentation to see which additional libraries you might need to install.

Since we firmly believe that you should know what goes on behind the scenes, even if you use the more comfortable ready-made solutions, we will give you some hints regarding how to work from scratch and how the pieces work together.

In order to load the PHP4 module into the Apache web server at runtime, you need to have the Apache module *mod_so*. You can check whether this module is presented by issuing:

```
owl$ httpd -l
Compiled-in modules:
        http_core.c
        mod_so.c
```

If this module is not available, please check whether you may have missed installing some of the additional Apache packages in your distribution. If you have built Apache from scratch, follow the documentation to get this module.

It is also possible to compile the PHP4 module directly into Apache, but this requires some very intertwined building of both Apache and PHP4 and does not really give you a big advantage, so we won't cover this here.

Now we need to build PHP and make a Dynamic Shared Object (DSO) out of it. Luckily, this is not as involved as it sounds. Download PHP4 from *http://www.php. net/download.php*. You will end up with a package called *php-4.1.1.tar.gz* (the actual version number may differ slightly). Unpack the *tar* file and configure PHP with:

```
owl ./configure \
                --with-mysql=/usr/lib/mysql\
                --with-ldap=yes\
                --with-gd=yes\
                --with-zlib=yes\
                --with-config-file-path=/etc/\
                --with-apxs=/usr/lib/apache/apxs\
                --enable-versioning\
                --enable-track-vars\
                --enable-thread-safety
```

You can read about numerous additional options in the extensive PHP documentation, but for starters, this will do. Note that you might need to replace some of the paths here with the actual locations on your system. After *configure* is finished, do a *make* and then a *make install* to install PHP (you may need to do the *make install* as *root*).

Next, edit the *httpd.conf* file, Apache's configuration file. If you have installed Apache from your installation CDs, chances are the following lines are already there and you just need to uncomment them. In any case, you should have the following lines in your *httpd.conf*:

```
LoadModule php4_module libexec/libphp4.so
AddModule mod_php4.c

AddType application/x-httpd-php .php
```

Now restart Apache:

```
owl$ apachectl restart
```

Once the server is restarted, you should test whether the PHP4 module can be loaded correctly. You can do this by writing a small PHP program, such as:

```
<?php
phpinfo();
?>
```

Save this file as *phpinfo.php* in the *htdocs* directory of your Apache installation (often */usr/local/httpd/htdocs*) and make it executable with *chmod*. Now you should be able to browse this file with your web browser by accessing *http://localhost/info.php*. If everything is OK, you should see the configuration of the PHP4 module.

The LAMP Server in Action

Now you have all the components for your LAMP server in place; it is time to run a few examples.

If you haven't done so already while following the last section, we suggest that you test your setup now with a very simple PHP file. Save the following PHP code into a file called *info.php*:

```
<?
phpinfo();
?>
```

Now place this file in the directory where your Apache web server is looking for its contents files. Often, this is */usr/local/httpd/htdocs*, and it may already contain the files that your distribution has installed for you during installation (at least if you have installed Apache from the installation media). If this doesn't work for you, you should look for the Apache configuration file *httpd.conf*. Often, this file is in the */etc/httpd/* directory, but if this is not the case on your system, you can search for it with:

```
locate httpd.conf
```

In this file, look for the line starting with DocumentRoot. You should find a directory listed here, and a subdirectory named *htdocs* should be under that directory; put the file *info.php* here. Now you can use any web browser to access the URL *http://localhost/info.php*. This will give you some information about the setup of your PHP module.

PHP comes with a number of built-in functions that manipulate and manage the data stored in MySQL (and other databases).

A relational database consists of a number of tables. If you have sufficient access rights, PHP can query and manipulate data in these tables. We can now write a few PHP scripts to use the database tables. We assume here that you have created the database test_database and the table comment_table, as well as the user *olof* as described earlier.

Use your favorite text editor and enter the following code, which creates a small HTML page that lets you add data to this table by means of an HTML form:

```
<html>
<?php
if ($comment){
$conn=mysql_connect("localhost","olof","secret" )
 or die("Could not connect to MySQL as olof");

mysql_select_db("test_database", $conn)
  or die("could not select the test_database");

 $string="INSERT INTO comment_table VALUES ('0','$comment')";
 mysql_query($string)
  or die(mysql_error());}
?>

<form action=<? echo $PHP_SELF ?> method="get">
 <input  type="text" name="comment" size="80"> <br>
<input type="submit">
</form>

</html>
```

You can execute this script by saving it as a file with the extension *.php*, copying it into the document directory of your web server, and accessing the script with your web browser. For example, if you have saved it as *edit.php*, you could access the URL *http://localhost/edit.php* to execute this script. The web server knows that it needs to run everything between <? and ?> through the PHP module. Thus, the PHP code can be directly embedded into an HTML page.

Now that we can enter comments into our database, we also want to review them. Thus, next up is a script to read from the database:

```
 <<
<html>
<?php
$conn=mysql_connect("localhost","olof","secret" )
 or die("Could not connect to MySQL as olof");
```

```
mysql_select_db("test_database", $conn)
  or die("could not select the test_database");

$string="SELECT * FROM comment_table";
$result= mysql_query($string)
  or die(mysql_error());

$numbers_cols= mysql_num_fields($result);

print "<b>query: $string</b>";
print "<table border =1>\n";
print "<tr>";
print "<td> ID</td>";
print "<td> Comment </td>";
print "</tr>";
while (list($id,$comment) = mysql_fetch_array($result)){
        print "<tr>";
        print "<td>$id</td>";
        print "<td>$comment</td>";
        print "</tr>";}
print "</table>";


?>
</html>
```

As you can see, we are using the HTML tags for laying out tables in order to display the contents of the database, which is a very natural and obvious thing to do.

It was our intention to keep these examples as simple as possible so as not to overload you with too much information at the same time. If you want to dive deeper into the wonderful world of LAMP, we recommend that you read a good book like *Web Database Applications with PHP & MySQL* by Hugh E. Williams and David Lane (O'Reilly) or *MySQL/PHP Database Applications* by Jay Greenspan and Brad Burger (John Wiley & Sons).

Sources of Linux Information

This appendix lists various online sources of Linux information. While all these documents are available electronically on the Internet, many are also available in printed form.

Linux distributions often include some of this documentation in the distribution itself and make them available on the runtime system. As mentioned in the text, documentation on a Linux system can be found in a number of places, including Unix manual pages, GNU info pages, and HTML help documentation (such as that displayed by the KDE Help Center).

Most Linux distributions store documentation on individual programs, such as README files and release notes under the *rusr/share/doc* directory, and if you have the kernel source installed, the documentation included with the kernel will usually be found in the directory */usr/src/linux/Documentation*.

For information of a more interactive nature, the following sources are commonly used by Linux users:

Usenet newsgroups
> Most newsgroups relevant to Linux are under the *comp.os.linux* hierarchy, but many also are regional, distribution-specific, or dedicated to open source projects.

IRC
> Internet Relay Chat (IRC) is the traditional Unix chat system, and is often used for getting immediate answers to questions from other users.

Mailing Lists
> Most Linux and open source projects, from the kernel to KDE, use mailing lists as the primary means for project developers to communicate. Many Linux user groups have mailing lists that can provide a local perspective.

Linux Documentation Project

The primary source of free documentation on Linux is the Linux Documentation Project (LDP). The main LDP web site is *http://www.tldp.org*, but there are many mirror sites around the world, one of which may be closer to you or less busy.

The documentation in the Linux Documentation Project is organized into several types. The *Guides* are long, often book-length, manuals covering in detail such larger topics as networking,. The *HOWTOs* are medium-length documents covering specific tasks, such as configuring a sound card. For smaller tasks on specialized topics that don't justify a full HOWTO, there are *mini-HOWTOs*. Finally, there are a number of *FAQs* that answer frequently asked questions on Linux.

The LDP documents are provided in a number of different formats, including HTML, plain text, PDF, and PostScript. Many of the documents have also been translated into different languages by a team of volunteer translators.

The bibliography lists a number of the LDP documents in more detail.

FTP Sites

While your Linux distribution provides precompiled binary packages for many Linux applications, often you need to build them from source code because the software is not available in binary form, you need to look at the source code, or you simply prefer to build it yourself from source. Here are some popular sites for the main sources of software that runs on Linux.

Many of these sites are extremely popular and busy. It is highly recommended that you use a mirror site (another computer system that downloads the software from the primary site on a regular basis) that is closer to you. A mirror site is usually easier to connect to and runs faster.

As well as the FTP sites listed here, many of the web sites listed in this appendix also have corresponding FTP sites for downloads.

FTP site	Description
ftp://ftp.gnu.org	The main download site for the GNU Project
ftp://ftp.ibiblio.org	A large Linux archive site, formerly known as *metalab.unc.edu* and *sunsite.unc.edu*, one of the first Linux archive sites to be set up
ftp://ftp.x.org	Archive for X Window System software

World Wide Web Sites

This section lists just a few of the thousands of Linux web sites on the Internet, broken down into somewhat arbitrary categories. Due to the dynamic nature of the Web, some of these sites may no longer be active and many new ones will undoubtedly exist by the time you read this.

General Documentation

These sites offer on-line documentation, articles about Linux, or information geared to specific areas of Linux.

Web site	Description
http://www.andamooka.org	A web site with a number of free online books, some of which are Linux-related, such as *KDE 2.0 Development*
http://www.linas.org/linux	Linux Enterprise Computing site
http://www.linux-laptop.net	Linux on Laptops site
http://www.linuxfocus.org	*Linux Focus*, a free online magazine
http://www.linuxgazette.com	*Linux Gazette*, a monthly on-line magazine
http://www.linuxjournal.com	Web site for *Linux Journal* magazine
http://www.linuxmagazine.com	The web site for *Linux Magazine*
http://www.linuxnewbie.org	An information site for Linux beginners
http://www.tldp.org	Main site for the Linux Documentation Project

Open Source Projects

Listed here are web sites for some of the more popular open source and free software projects.

Web site	Description
http://koffice.kde.org	The KDE Office Suite project
http://www.abisource.com	The AbiWord word processor
http://www.alsa-project.org	Alternative Linux Sound Architecture (ALSA) sound driver project
http://www.apache.org	The Apache web server project
http://www.cups.org	The Common UNIX Printing System (CUPS)
http://www.dosemu.org	The Linux DOS Emulator project
http://www.gnome.org	The GNOME Desktop project
http://www.gnu.org	The GNU project
http://www.isdn4linux.de	ISDN4Linux, supporting ISDN on Linux

Web site	Description
http://www.kde.org	The K Desktop Environment (KDE)
http://www.kernel.org	The official Linux kernel site
http://www.linux-usb.org	The Linux USB project
http://www.mozilla.org	The Mozilla web browser project
http://www.mysql.com	The MySQL database
http://www.openoffice.org	The OpenOffice.org office suite project, the open source version of StarOffice
http://www.postfix.org	The Postfix mailer project
http://www.povray.org	The Persistence Of Vision ray tracer
http://www.winehq.com	The WINE project
http://www.xfree86.org	The XFree86 project

Programming Languages and Tools

These sites are related to popular Linux programming languages and to the hosting of Linux software projects.

Web site	Description
http://www.sourceforge.net	A site that hosts many Linux software projects, providing a place for documentation, a source code repository, bug tracking, and software building
http://savannah.gnu.org	GNU Savannah, a site offering features similar to SourceForge, but officially endorsed by the Free Software Foundation because all the hosting software is licensed under the GPL
http://www.blackdown.org	The home page of the Linux Java porting project
http://www.perl.com	Official site of the Perl programming language
http://www.php.net	Web site for the PHP programming language
http://www.python.org	Home page of the Python programming language
http://www.tcl.tk	One of the main web sites for the TCL/Tk programming language
http://sal.kachinatech.com	SAL, a site dedicated to Scientific Applications on Linux

News and Information Sites

These sites offer news of interest to Linux users.

Web site	Description
http://www.desktoplinux.com	A site dedicated to Linux on the desktop
http://www.linux.com	A general Linux information and news site (with a very desirable URL)
http://www.linuxdailynews.net	Linux Daily News web site
http://www.linuxtoday.com	Linux Today web site
http://www.lwn.net	Linux Weekly News web site

Web site	Description
http://linuxsecurity.com	News and general information on Linux security issues
http://www.newsforge.com	NewsForge web site
http://www.slashdot.org	The popular news and discussion site that bills itself as "News for Nerds. Stuff that Matters"
http://www.theregister.co.uk	The Register, a UK site for IT industry news with a pro-Linux slant
http://www.theregus.com	The US edition of The Register
http://www.varlinux.org	VarLinux news site, for Value Added Resellers (VARs)

Linux Software Directories and Download Sites

Listed here are some sites that maintain large searchable libraries of Linux software with links to download sites.

Web site	Description
http://www.freshmeat.net	A huge directory of Linux and open source software
http://www.icewalkers.com	Another large Linux software directory site
http://www.linuxapps.com	A large Linux software directory site
http://www.portalux.com	Linux Center, a portal with a catalog of applications and links to news and articles

Linux Distributions

Listed here is a long but by no means comprehensive list of some of the different Linux distributions available. These range from those backed by large companies, such as Red Hat, to small specialized distributions developed by individuals or small groups.

Web site	Description
http://www.archlinux.org	Arch Linux
http://www.asp-linux.com	ASyPLinux
http://www.bearops.com	BearOps Linux
http://www.beehive.nu	Beehive Linux
http://www.connectiva.com	Connectiva
http://www.crux.nu	CRUX Linux
http://www.debian.org	Debian GNU/Linux
http://www.elxlinux.com	ELX Linux
http://www.eridani.co.uk	Eridani Linux
http://www.icepack-linux.com	Icepack Linux
http://www.libranet.com	Libranet Linux
http://www.lindows.com	Lindows.com

Web site	Description
http://www.lycoris.com	Lycoris
http://www.linuxmandrake.com	Mandrake Linux
http://murix.sourceforge.net	Murix
http://www.ibiblio.org/peanut	Peanut Linux
http://www.probatus.com	Probatus
http://www.redhat.com	Red Hat Linux
http://www.rocklinux.org	ROCK Linux
http://www.rootlinux.org	ROOT Linux
http://www.sco.com	SCO Linux (formerly Caldera)
http://www.slackware.com	Slackware Linux
http://www.suse.com	SuSE Linux
http://www.turbolinux.com	Turbolinux
http://www.unitedlinux.com	United Linux
http://www.ibiblio.org/vectorlinux	Vector Linux
http://www.voodoolinux.com	Voodoo Linux
http://www.xandros.com	Xandros Desktop Linux
http://www.yellowdoglinux.com	Yellow Dog Linux

Commercial Linux Software Companies

Listed here are some companies that offer commercial software and services, other than Linux distributions, for the Linux platform.

Web site	Description
http://www.codeweavers.com	CodeWeavers, developer of CrossOver Office and CrossOver Plugin, products based on the software of the Wine project that offer the ability to run Windows applications on Linux.
http://www.oeone.com	OEone, developersof a Linux-based operating environment.
http://www.opensound.com	4Front Technologies, developer of enhanced kernel sound drivers for Linux and a number of other operating systems.
http://www.trolltech.com	TrollTech, developer of Qt, a cross-platform graphical toolkit. Qt is used as the basis for the KDE.
http://www.vistasource.com	VistaSource, formerly Applix, is the developer of the Applixware Office Suite.
http://www.vmware.com	VmWare sells virtual machine software that allows running one operating system on top of another, such as Windows on Linux, and vice versa.
http://www.ximian.com	Ximian develops and supports an enhanced version of the GNOME desktop environment.

Internet RFCs and Other Standards

These are a few of the many sites that host standards used by Linux and the Internet.

Web site	Description
http://www.faqs.org/rfcs	An archive site for Requests For Comments or RFCs, the technical documents that describe many of the protocols around which the Internet is built. It also includes many other standards documents and FAQs.
http://www.freestandards.org	The Free Standards Group, a nonprofit organization dedicated to accelerating the use and acceptance of open source technologies through the development, application, and promotion of standards.
http://www.linuxbase.org	The Linux Standard Base, a project of the Free Standards Group that develops and promotes a set of standards to increase compatibility among Linux distributions and enable software applications to run on any compliant Linux system.
http://www.w3c.org	The World Wide Web Consortium, an organization that develops specifications, guidelines, software, and tools for the World Wide Web.

Miscellaneous

Finally, here are some sites that defied categorization in any of the other sections.

Web site	Description
http://counter.li.org	The Linux Counter, a unique site that collects data in an attempt to estimate the total number of Linux users worldwide
http://www.li.org	Linux International, a non-profit organization that works toward the promotion of Linux and the Linux community
http://www.google.com	Perhaps the most popular search engine on the Web, powered by a server farm of several thousand Linux computers

Installing Linux on Digital/Compaq Alpha Systems

In 1992, Digital Equipment Corporation (later purchased by Compaq) introduced a 64-bit, superscaler, RISC-based architecture called the Alpha that won impressive reviews in the industry for speed. Linux is an attractive alternative to the traditional operating systems shipped with the Alpha, especially for the older Alpha hardware now being sold into the marketplace. But installation varies from system to system because the Alpha evolved rapidly and has been shipped over the years with a wide variety of hardware and firmware (startup programs stored in ROM). This appendix is an introduction to the main issues and tasks in installing Linux, but you will also need to read the documents for Linux installation and your hardware carefully, and show a somewhat adventurous willingness to experiment.

A discussion of Alpha systems would have to cover years of hardware evolution from the older style UDB system to the current DS and ES series systems, as well as standard OEM configurations. Because there are so many different BIOS configurations and boot options, it's impossible to give detailed installation instructions for every type of Alpha system. We hope this discussion will be a guide to help users who are new to the Alpha architecture understand what to do when installing a new system.

 This discussion does not cover VAX, MIPS, AMD, or Intel CPU-based systems or hardware that share peripheral and packaging technologies with Alpha-based systems. We will focus only on the installation of Linux on Alpha systems and components manufactured by Compaq or licensees of Alpha technology, such as Samsung Semiconductor, API NetWorks Inc., or Mitsubishi Semiconductor.

Alpha History and Status

In 1992, Digital Equipment Corporation, also known as DEC or Digital, introduced the Alpha with support for seven hardware platforms, three operating systems, multiple networking protocols, and multiple language compilers.

The Alpha constitutes the largest engineering project ever undertaken by Digital, involving more than 30 engineering groups spread across 10 countries. It was not the first RISC-based semiconductor that Digital produced, but it was the first that Digital decided to sell in the open market. Digital Semiconductor (DS) was created as an internal business group to manufacture, sell, and distribute Digital's semiconductors on the merchant market.

To keep up with demand and evolving semiconductor manufacturing technology, Digital outsourced manufacturing of the Alpha semiconductor, which included agreements with Samsung Electronics and Mitsubishi Electric to manufacturer current and future implementations of the Alpha semiconductors. In addition, the agreements granted Samsung and Mitsubishi licenses to market, sell, and distribute Alpha semiconductors worldwide and included joint development projects related to the Alpha semiconductor family.

The relatively small installed base of Alpha systems, and the fact that most existing systems are "development platforms" that allow tinkering and tuning supported by massive archives of hardware documentation, have encouraged continued development of Alpha chipsets. However, it also makes it hard for Linux developers to gather the wide range of systems under one simple installation procedure.

Compaq had its eyes set on having its own enterprise server architecture and operating system—an alternative to Microsoft and Intel. On January 26, 1998, Digital and the Compaq Computer Corporation announced a $9.6 billion-dollar merger where Digital became a wholly owned subsidiary of Compaq. DS came with the multibillion dollar package, and the name Digital was absorbed into Compaq.

Since the takeover Compaq has continued to develop the Alpha chip with the EV7 slated for introduction in 2002. Unfortunately Compaq has also announced that development will be stopped with EV7 and that future Compaq high end servers will utilize Intel's IA64 architecture instead of Alpha.

To summarize, Alpha architecture is a superscaler, open-industry standard, 64-bit, RISC-based architecture that is engineered by Compaq and manufactured in volume by Samsung and its subsidiaries.

The Linux Port and Distributions

The Alpha port of Linux did not happen overnight. It began as a rather humble patch to the Linux kernel. The first kernel patch was developed with funding and support from Digital. Even with all the patches to the kernel, most of the distributions' drivers and "userlands" were not 64-bit clean. (In other words, programs assuming a 64-bit word might fail because of hidden 32-bit calculations or declarations in underlying software.) The mainstream kernel itself was not 64-bit clean until the 2.1.x development kernels. When development work on the 2.1.x kernels began, the Alpha port was adopted directly into the Linux kernel source tree. At this stage, the Alpha port of the Linux kernel was supported directly by the mainstream kernel distributions.

During the development efforts of the 2.1.x kernel, the Linux kernel and its drivers were made 64-bit clean. Most of the unaligned traps in the kernel were corrected, and the userland became much more 64-bit aware. At this time, Red Hat Software, Inc., quickly saw that the server and workstation processor market was headed in the direction of 64-bit architectures and released a full Alpha port of their Linux distribution, Red Hat Linux 2.1. Other distributions followed, including Debian and SuSE. The distributions are described in the following list:

Debian

> The Debian Linux distribution is the "official" Free Software Foundation GNU/Linux distribution, providing one of the most extensive sets of software available. See *http://www.debian.org*.

Red Hat

> Red Hat Software, Inc. has for several years produced an Alpha port of their distribution. Recently, in order to become profitable, RedHat has concentrated on their core business and the Alpha port has fallen somewhat behind. Compaq has stepped in and is working with RedHat to keep the new versions coming, but it is not known how many times Compaq will commit to this. See *http://www.redhat.com*.

SuSE

> SuSE's Linux distributions are developed with attention to internationalization needs and graphics interface support. (SuSE is sensitive to European market needs.) SuSE also uses RPM to provide updates and has a full Alpha port. See *http://www.suse.com*.

Other distributions

> Several other smaller distributions also have Alpha ports. These include Rock-Linux (*http://www.rocklinux.org*(, Polish Linux Distribution (*http://www.pld.org.pl*), and Kondara (*http://www.kondara.org*).

Chipsets

There are five classes of Alpha CPU: the 21064, 21066, 21164, 21264 and the upcoming 21364. The 21064 and 21066 classes are both first-generation Alpha architectures, but the 21066 incorporates functions normally supplied on support chips into the CPU itself, creating special platform characteristics and requirements. The 21164 and 21264 classes represent second- and third-generation chip architectures, respectively. Various chip architectures have been coupled with different system buses and interfaces, which subdivide the CPU types into different families of Alpha computers ranging from desktop systems to supercomputing clusters.*

For purposes of installing Linux from a CD-ROM distribution, the subdivisions differ in the support that the Linux kernel provides for the features of the chips and in system assemblies and interfaces that use those features. If you cannot boot a kernel that appears to match your system, try a similar kernel from a related system or try a generic kernel. And, if that does not work, go to the AlphaLinux FTP site and try an earlier kernel or a later, developmental kernel. For the most part, however, your installation should be straightforward if you have selected the right image files to load and install Linux.

Sources of Information

Before you choose a Linux distribution, use the considerable resources about Linux and Alpha on the Internet. A wealth of detailed hardware information about Alpha chips and platforms designed to support it are available for downloading and printing, including technical manuals that would be expensive to purchase or completely unavailable through marketing channels. Be aware that much useful documentation may be supplied by a different vendor than the manufacturer of your CPU or system, and from other distribution resources as well.

You should probably have at least a hardware manual for your system, which will describe hardware configuration and the use of the firmware consoles for your system, as well as provide useful error codes and diagnostics if there are difficulties. There will be an appendix near the end of each of Digital's system or evaluation board manuals that lists related documents, some of which are also useful. The document numbers will identify the files that you want from the Alpha library archive.

There are web sites providing FAQ files and other useful information for some specific Alpha systems as well.

You should also have the installation documents and addenda for your CD-ROM installation and information regarding any bugs and fixes for the distribution you are installing. Where your documentation is incomplete or describes a generic Linux installation, rather than the specific Linux Alpha installation, you may want to use the following sequence as a guide for installation.

Following is a partial list of important Internet sources for Alpha hardware information and information about installing Linux on Alpha systems.

---

* We will not discuss embedded systems and display terminal uses of Alpha CPUs here.

AlphaLinux sites

The AlphaLinux Organization
The Official AlphaLinux web site is at *http://www.linuxalpha.org*.

The Compaq AlphaLinux web site
This site contains interesting information on the use of Linux on Alpha hardware. It's at *http://www.compaq.com/products/software/linux/index.html*.

AlphaLinux mailing lists

AXP-List from RedHat
Send email to the following address with subscribe in the subject line: *axp-list-request@redhat.com*.

Debian Alpha mailing list
Send email to the following address with subscribe in the body: *debian-alpha-request@lists.debian.org*.

AlphaLinux FTP sites

The official AlphaLinux FTP site
This site is located at *ftp://ftp.linuxalpha.org*.

The digital FTP site
This site is located at *ftp://gatekeeper.dec.com*.

Minimum Hardware

You can run Linux on Alpha systems using as little as 8 MB of RAM, but most installation programs, like the Red Hat installer, require a minimum of 32 MB. The minimum disk space for the installation is 170 MB. To run the full X Window System and a desktop comfortably and have adequate storage for applications, you need a minimum of 16 MB RAM and 500 MB of hard-disk storage.

Many users of more recent Linux distributions have found that 24 MB or 32 MB of RAM is required to complete the installation. While it should still require no more than 16 MB to run Linux on a properly configured Alpha system (with a kernel compiled to support just that system's features), you may need more memory to install some distributions. An alternative is to install an earlier, smaller kernel.

Installation takes a huge amount of RAM because of the combined memory requirements of the bootstrap loader, Milo (if used) and the loading Linux kernel image, not because of the memory requirements of the Linux kernel itself. If you cannot complete your initial installation, you can also try to use an earlier and smaller Milo to boot your Linux distribution or a Milo that has been stored in nonvolatile RAM. You can select compact applications to conserve memory and storage. For more information, see *http://www.linuxalpha.org*.

IDE/ATAPI Drive Support

Some Alpha systems, especially those intended for use as network servers, do not support IDE or ATAPI drives.* We recommend a fast SCSI drive as a basic system element, whether installed internally or attached externally. If your system has a free PCI slot, you can add a current PCIbus ATAPI/EIDE controller card supported by Linux in order to attach cheaper EIDE hard disks or fast CD-ROM drives. But you will most likely not be able to boot from this device because the SRM console will not have a driver for it.

Mice and Serial Ports

Problems are often reported during Linux installations in connecting a serial mouse to the system. Some Linux installation programs map device definitions to the serial ports incorrectly during kernel configuration. Most of these complaints involve auto-detection of a mouse installed on the first serial port. We recommend that you install a three-button PS/2-type mouse, if your system has a PS/2 hardware port, rather than a serial mouse. Moreover, do not put a modem on serial port 1, because Milo will echo its output to serial port 1 with strange results.

Preparations and General Procedure for Installation

There are many different Alpha systems, each requiring different installation methods. Because different Linux kernels are compiled to meet these variations in CPU and system designs, you should identify your Alpha hardware in case the generic kernel doesn't work properly. In the Linux kernel the different Alpha systems are mostly known by their engineering code name. Provided you know the official system name you can usually find the codename. On such resource for looking up these names is the system type table available at *http://www.linuxalpha.org/docs/systypes.txt*.

Before you install an operating system, you must know the machine's graphics options and audio components, system memory, CPU class, disk-drive interfaces and sizes, existing operating systems/filesystems (if any), and attached peripherals, especially any CD-ROM drive and floppy drives. Some Alpha systems require firmware configuration changes and even actual hardware changes to complete a Linux installation.

---

* Early Alpha systems provided 10 Mbps SCSI-2, and some of the latest Alpha system boards provide "fast and wide" 160 Mbps SCSI-3. The very earliest board (Jensen) provided an Adaptec 1740 ISA bus controller, but most SCSI controllers are from either the NCR (LSI Logic) or Adaptec family of controllers. These were considered high-performance controllers when adopted.

Potential Incompatibilities and Hardware Problems

Which Linux distribution you choose to install may depend on the hardware you have and any other operating systems that you run on it. After you gather your hardware information, you can determine which distribution best suits your needs. You can always build any source packages from other installations once you have a bootable system. Here are a few examples of hardware factors that dictate your choice of distribution or method of installation:

- Some Alpha systems require setting jumpers to load Linux and install it as a native, firmware-bootable operating system.

- If your system has no floppy disk drive, you may not be able to install the Linux distribution you want on your system, because of firmware constraints in supporting filesystems and devices on systems that do not have floppy disk devices. We recommend that you install or attach a floppy drive to your system. If your system's floppy drive simply "died," it's very inexpensive to replace.*

- If your Linux installation shares the computer with another operating system (installed on different hard-disk partitions or different hard disks), different versions of Linux offer different levels of filesystem and utility compatibility with co-resident operating systems. For example, if you want to run Tru64 Unix (Digital Unix, or DU) on your system as well as the Debian Linux Alpha distribution, their default disk filesystem, partitioning, and labeling would conflict. Likewise, if you apply BSD-style disk labeling from Linux, that partition will not be accepted as valid by DU. If you want to set up Linux co-resident with another operating system on an Alpha system, the safest way is to partition the disk from within that operating system and define the partition for Linux to be installed to.

- The Linux *fdisk* utility fails to label DOSFS filesystems so that SRM and other firmware utilities can access them. Therefore, as a general rule, format your MS-DOS diskettes for configuring your system using MS-DOS or Windows NT (or buy preformatted MS-DOS diskettes).

- The first time you install Linux on older machines (especially UDB/Multias), your installation may fail if your system's internal battery is not charged. Reports of motherboards shipped from a vendor with a dead battery are common. Some systems have a rechargeable battery that nevertheless will not recharge on a powered-up system if the battery is discharged when the system is turned on. For instance, the monitor will not work, and firmware changes that you need to complete a self-booting installation will not be saved.

---

* Even the extra-thin 3.5 inch floppy used in the older Multia and Alphabook 1 "systems" can be replaced with a standard laptop drive. On newer Alpha systems hardware, most hardware is interchangeable with standard OEM PC hardware.

Installation Choices

Once you have gathered your hardware data and selected your Linux distribution, choose your installation method. Alpha systems vary more than typical PC systems (having been engineered to be used as everything from basic display terminals to supercomputers), so you should evaluate your hardware and choose the booting method you will use with your Linux distribution. Otherwise, you may find that you cannot complete the installation as you expected, or that Linux will be difficult to boot without rebuilding the installation.

If you add a CD-ROM drive to your system to install Linux, check your hardware documentation and Linux package documentation to make sure that the CD-ROM will be recognized natively in the BIOS or that SRM will support that drive. Most standard SCSI CD-ROM and IDE drives connected to an onboard controller are recognized and supported by SRM. But IDE CD-ROMs attached to add-in PCI IDE controllers will most likely not be seen by SRM.

Although network installation of Linux (storing the files on one machine and downloading them over the network to the machine where you want Linux to run) is possible, major distributions have had persistent problems supporting this capability. We are not going to describe the technique. We assume you are installing Linux on a stand-alone Alpha system. You can configure it for network use later.

Configuring and setting booting behavior on some older Alpha systems requires changing jumper settings on the motherboard or changing system data stored in non-volatile RAM, or both. You may need to change jumper settings initially for installation and again afterward to configure the system.

Even a routine AlphaLinux installation procedure is more complex than a Linux installation on the usual Intel PC. While the Intel PC provides the system hardware interface in the onboard BIOS, Alpha systems require that the system bootstrap itself by defining and loading a firmware interface before loading the operating system. The various ways this is done are the subject of the following section.

Firmware options

Each Alpha contains at least one firmware program stored in system ROM or flash ROM that provides a configuration-program execution environment to set up hardware configurations, specify boot options, and perform other system maintenance tasks. This firmware is the usual starting point for installing Linux. Types of firmware include:

System Reference Maintenance (SRM)
> Available on systems set up for Tru64 Unix or Open VMS. The only exceptions are systems based around the UX motherboard, which have their own ARC BIOS firmware and the Digtal XL series, for which SRM was never released. SRM is the best environment for installing Linux, and the one we concentrate on

in this appendix. The SRM is described in an online manual at *http://ftp.digital. com/pub/Digital/info/semiconductor/literature/srmcons.pdf.*[*]

Alpha Reference Console (ARC)

> Available on older systems set up for Windows NT. It offers a simple, menu-driven console interface for managing the system's hardware.

AlphaBIOS

> A replacement for ARC that attempts to make OS installation on Alpha systems more uniform and automatic, such as OS installation on an Intel-architectured PC. It offers a graphical user interface.

Firmware programs are small and efficient. Alpha system ROMs typically include space to hold several of them, along with other essential programs, such as debugging and diagnostic tools (which should not be overwritten).

To load Linux, many Alpha installations in the past used Milo, mainly because the SRM console used to boot Tru64 Unix and OpenVMS was not easily available for many machines. The standard firmware was initially loaded by accessing a system console when the system was booted and instructing it to load Milo from a diskette. Then a current Milo miniloader image was loaded from diskette, and it in turn was told to load the Linux kernel from the CD-ROM or boot diskette.

By now, Compaq has made the SRM console available for almost all the Alpha machines (one exception being the XL series). Since SRM is much more readily available now, it is the preferred way of booting Linux. Milo is still available and still being updated for those that do not have this option. While you can get by using a slightly old Red Hat Milo for your hardware with the latest Red Hat Linux, the best solution is to change over to SRM console when it is available and supported by your hardware.

Once Linux is installed, many systems provide a flash-RAM management utility (FMU) to allow you to "blow" a Milo image into system nonvolatile RAM. Other such utilities may come with your purchase of a commercial OS release or a developer package. Some are distributed on an EPROM chip that you install. Because ARC and AlphaBIOS firmware provide a graphical interface environment, they take more space, and you will find at most one of them on a standard system.

Booting Linux can be made as automatic as booting MS-DOS or Windows. We do not recommend that you use an FMU, because booting from an SRM console is just as efficient. In this appendix, we focus on an SRM and *aboot* because they work on all significant Alpha platforms and offer the most consistent and predictable results. You will learn about other installation options as you review your resource materials.

---

[*] SRM console firmware for Multia, AlphaStation, AlphaServer, AlphaPC164, and AXPpcisystems is available at *ftp://gatekeeper.dec.com* or *http//ftp.digital.com/pub/DEC/Alpha/firmware.*

In many cases, it won't matter whether you have an old or a new version of your firmware. In fact, some users advise you not to update firmware unless you know you need to do so. In other words, you can upgrade firmware if Linux fails to install properly on your system. Indeed, some Linux installations require some systems to be "downgraded" to an earlier firmware version to succeed.

But generally, we recommend using the most recent version of your firmware to install Linux, especially if you use AlphaBIOS. Follow your hardware manual's directions for upgrading firmware. You can get firmware upgrades from *http://ftp.digital. com/pub/DEC/Alpha/firmware/*.

Features and limitations of SRM

The SRM console can load data from IDE/ATAPI, SCSI, or floppy drives, and can use a system's native SCSI drive controller to access a recognized SCSI device for booting. SRM can read a floppy drive. It can access MS-DOS–format filesystems (but not those created by Linux *fdisk*), BSD-labeled UFS filesystems (but not BSD-style filesystems labeled by Linux), and ISO9660 filesystems.

The SRM console allows you to boot the system by transferring control to the secondary bootstrap loader that it loads blindly. SRM knows little about disk partitions or filesystems and treats disk devices as block devices. It reads from the first 512-byte sector of the storage device. This sector should contain a sector address and offset from which SRM can begin reading the size of data block. SRM goes to that location and loads contiguous data into memory. The data should be an image file of the secondary loader that boots the system.

Alpha systems usually have two secondary loaders: the "raw" loader from the Linux kernel and the separate *aboot* utility. The *aboot* utility is more flexible than the raw loader and is installed by default with most distributions. However, you can also use the SRM console to load the Milo loader. Some machines do not currently have a MILO available (DS20), so, in those cases, using SRM and *aboot* is mandatory.

When you use SRM and *aboot* to boot Linux, the first partition of the disk should start at cylinder number 2. This leaves room at the beginning of the disk to install *aboot*. The SRM Howto at *http://www.linuxalpha.org/faq/srm.html* provides more information about SRM and *aboot*.

Features and limitations of ARC Firmware

This firmware is severely limited. It knows how to access files only in MS-DOS, HPFS, and ISO9660 filesystems. When accessing files in MS-DOS or ISO9660, the system recognizes only 8.3 filenames.

Features and limitations of AlphaBIOS Firmware

AlphaBIOS firmware is no longer in active development (the last version being 5.70). If your system has AlphaBIOS, install the latest AlphaBIOS firmware update before installing Linux. AlphaBIOS knows how to access files only in MS-DOS and ISO9660 filesystems. Like ARC, when accessing files, the system recognizes only 8.3 filenames.

Features and limitations of Milo Miniloader

The Milo miniloader does not know how to boot itself from disk. Before Milo can load Linux, Milo itself must be loaded either from system flash memory or from disk using an operating system loader (OSloader) developed for Alpha systems, such as Windows NT Alpha's boot manager. Linux distributions provide *linload.exe*.

When Milo is on disk, it is bootstrap-loaded by a ARC, AlphaBIOS, or SRM console after you use *linload.exe*. *linload.exe* knows MS-DOS (FAT) filesystems, but does not recognize HPFS or VMS filesystems. Milo is apparently limited to MS-DOS, ISO9660, and *ext2* filesystems when it has been loaded by *linload.exe*.

Milo can read *ext2* filesystems by default and can load operating system images in ISO9660 or MS-DOS (FAT) formats using a command-line option. Milo should be able to load compressed kernel image files made using *gzip*, if given the full filename (e.g., *vmlinux.gz*), but we have found that at least some Milo distributions cannot process such files, at least not when loaded from ISO9660 or MS-DOS filesystems. MILO is also available only for certain platforms. A chart listing these systems is available at *http://www.linuxalpha.org/docs/systypes.txt*. For more information, go to *http://www.linuxalpha.org/faq/milo.html*.

Installing Linux

Okay, you have collected your hardware manuals and selected the Linux distribution to install (one that meets your requirements based on the hardware you have). This section guides you through a high-level view of what you need to do in order to successfully install Linux.

General Procedure

A typical Linux CD-ROM installation generally proceeds as follows:

1. Collect system hardware information to select the correct installation files and procedures. Look at your system hardware manuals or system administration manuals. Get bug reports and review the patches to the current software distribution that you will use to install your package. Collect current software installation documentation if you believe the information provided by the vendor is obsolete or incomplete.

2. Consider the size of your hard-disk drives and decide how they are (or will be) partitioned for Linux. Chapter 3 offers basic considerations for allocating disk space and partitioning, although you must adjust the numbers for Alpha. The installation utilities that you choose will support one or another disk-partitioning method, but cannot be used for all partitioning requirements.

3. Determine how you want Linux to boot when the installation is complete. This may affect your choice of installation method.

4. Choose your Linux installation method based on your hardware and its firmware, your disk-partitioning requirements, and Linux's booting behavior. For almost all installations, we think that SRM is the best firmware utility for loading Linux.

5. If you're not booting from CD-ROM then create the correct data diskettes (kernel image, and ramdisk image) diskettes for your system.

6. Configure your system hardware as needed to support the installation of Linux.

7. If you use the usual Milo installation procedure, create the correct Milo image diskette for your system.

8. Power up the system and access its console. If you are using MILO, you will need to load your Linux loader (usually the LINLOAD.EXE program, which is then used to load Milo). If you have Windows NT installed on your system, you can use the NT OSloader to load Milo; otherwise you will use system firmware to load a bootstrap loader that will then be used to prepare the system to install Linux.

9. If using Milo, use Milo to boot the kernel, and run the CD-ROM installation program.

10. Perform any additional disk partitioning and formatting for your system booting requirements.

11. Load additional Linux utilities, applications, compilers, and programming languages or libraries. Recompiling a current, stable release of the Linux kernel tailored to your system requirements is highly recommended.

12. When you are happy with your Linux installation, set it up to autoboot or boot from a boot manager selection menu. For some older systems, this may also require setting jumpers. Most systems require changes in the firmware console.

Preparing Software for Installation

Check the web site of the company that provided your CD-ROM distribution for bug reports, patches, and later versions of the software version you are installing. Also check the AlphaLinux web site for independent verification of bug fixes and patches.

If you are not booting from a CD-ROM, make the boot diskettes that you need for the Linux installation (2 for booting from SRM, 3 for booting from AlphaBIOS or ARC via MILO). To determine what diskette you may need for booting, visit the chart located on the AlphaLinux web site at:

http://www.linuxalpha.org/docs/systypes.txt

You can make the diskettes on an IBM PC/MS-DOS system by invoking RAWRITE. EXE to create image file disks or using *dd* under Unix.

Preparing Hardware for Installation

The key issues you have to consider with Alpha hardware are disk-drive partitions and filesystems and supported video adapters. During disk configuration, we recommend that you use basic *fdisk* tools for reliability rather than a GUI-based utility.

Your hardware manual will assist you in any required troubleshooting, such as providing beep code definitions. The UDB, for example, has a diagnostic LED character array that flashes a number or letter if a necessary firmware program in nonvolatile RAM (NVRAM) or system ROM (SROM) error is detected on system boot.

 If your system has been idle for some time, make sure that the cooling fans are working. Overheating your system in the middle of firmware reconfiguration would be particularly annoying.

Setting Up the System Firmware to Start the Installation

Because we cannot possibly cover all BIOS configurations in this book, we give pointers in the following table on where to find detailed installation and configuration information for each type of firmware used with Milo.

Firmware	Location of information
ARC Console	*http://www.linuxalpha.org/faq/alphabios-howto.html*
AlphaBIOS	*http://www.linuxalpha.org/faq/alphabios-howto.html*
SRM	*http://www.linuxalpha.org/faq/srm.html*

Loading the Linux Boot Kernel

As we said earlier, there are two possible paths to follow in loading Linux on an Alpha system. We will cover the SRM path first, followed by the MILO path. We will not cover loading MILO from SRM.

When SRM console has finished initializing you should be presented with the following prompt (note that later systems prepend a P00 to this prompt):

```
>>
```

To see a list of devices that SRM recognizes, use the *show dev* command:

```
>> show dev
```

It's important to look through the list of devices that SRM recognizes to see if your boot device it visible, and to find out its name in SRM.

Now we are ready to load a Linux kernel and start the installation. The basic syntax used when booting from SRM is:

```
boot device -file file_name -flags "kernel flags"
```

The following directions show how to start the installation from the floppy drive.

1. Enter a command such as the following at the SRM prompt:

    ```
    >> boot dva0 -file vmlinux.gz -flags "root=/dev/fd0 load_ramdisk=1"
    ```

    In the above example we are assuming that the kernel is named *vmlinux.gz*, but this could differ based upon the distribution you are installing. It is important that the flags section be enclosed by double quotes. If they are not, the kernel will be passed only the first of the flags parameters.

2. When prompted, insert the root floppy disk that you created earlier and press the Enter key to continue.

3. Continue with the installation as directed by the distribution's software.

The following directions show how to start the installation from the CD-ROM drive.

1. Determine the CD-ROM device name using the *show dev* command described earlier. If your CD-ROM drive is SCSI, the name will start with *dk*. If it is IDE-based, the name will start with *dq*. For the sake of this discussion we'll assume the name to be *dka400*.

2. Start the CD-ROM installation using a command, such as the following:

    ```
    >> boot dka400 -file vmlinux.gz -fl "root=/dev/sr0"
    ```

    In the case of an IDE CD-ROM, you would also need to change the flags line to represent the Linux kernel's naming convention for IDE devices. Also note that many newer distributions set up a preconfigured boot selection in *aboot*. Consult your distribution's documentation for directions on using these boot selections.

3. Continue with the installation as directed by the distirution's software.

If you have chosen to boot the installation through MILO, you will see the Milo prompt after you have successfully configured your BIOS to load Milo:

```
MILO>
```

Because Milo is a microkernel, it has many options you may want to explore before bootstrapping the Linux kernel. To see Milo options, enter Milo's help command:

```
MILO> help
```

To see how Milo is configured up, what devices it knows, and the filesystems that it recognizes, enter the show command:

```
MILO> show
```

If everything looks fine, you can continue with the installation and load Linux from the prepared Linux kernel image.

Bootstrapping the kernel with Milo is very straightforward: one command.

1. To load the Linux kernel from the first disk drive, type the following:

    ```
    MILO> boot fd0:vmlinux.gz root=/dev/fd0 load_ramdisk=1
    ```

Note that this assumes you use the floppy image file that you prepared from a disk image file; Milo assumes an *ext2* partition by default and that *fd0* is the correct floppy drive. If you wanted to boot from an MS-DOS–formatted disk, such as the alternate disk previously prepared, you could enter:

```
MILO> boot fd0 -t msdos -fi vmlinux.gz load_ramdisk=1
```

2. Insert the ramdisk floppy when prompted.

3. Run your CD-ROM distribution's installation and configuration program.

4. After you finish installation, install Milo on a small disk partition on your machine to use for reconfiguring. If you want Milo to be able to load on booting, this partition must be a primary MS-DOS partition. You can create it using MS-DOS's or Window NT's *fdisk* command.

Tuning and Post-Installation Considerations

Linux should now boot and work adequately. However, we recommend several enhancements.

Kernel Tuning

Once you have completed the installation, compile your own kernel, because the kernel shipped with your distribution probably contains more device drivers than you need. You can find information on compiling a kernel at the AlphaLinux web site (*http://www.linuxalpha.org*), as well as in the kernel HOWTO (available from any Linux archive site).

Performance and Library Tuning

To increase the performance of AlphaLinux, you can replace the standard math libraries with the Compaq Portable Math Library (CPML). The CPML is identical in content to the Compaq Tru64 Unix *libm* and replaces the AlphaLinux *libm* directly. For more information on the CPML, visit:

> *http://www.unix.digital.com/linux/cpml.htm*

A good resource for AlphaLinux performance tuning is available at:

> *http://cyclone.ncsa.uiuc.edu/ PCA/PerformanceTuning.html*

Binary Emulation

AlphaLinux is mostly binary compatible with Tru64 Unix (Digital Unix or DU); however, not all the system calls have been implemented. To run Tru64 Unix binaries on AlphaLinux, you need some of the shared libraries from Tru64 Unix. These are now available with several Linux distributions or can be downloaded with Netscape Communicator from Compaq. A more detailed explanation on how to set this up can be found in the AlphaLinux FAQ at *http://www.linuxalpha.org/faq/FAQ.html*.

AlphaLinux can also execute i386 Linux binaries through a program called em86. Information on this is available in the AlphaLinux FAQ. Please note that patching the kernel is no longer necessary, although you must compile in support for i386 binaries when building the kernel.

Graphical Browser Considerations

Netscape has not ported the Netscape Communicator to AlphaLinux. But do not despair, because with binary emulation for x86 and Tru64 Unix, the x86 and Tru64 native binaries will run on AlphaLinux. Thanks to Download a Netscape RPM with the necessary Tru64 libraries from:

http://www.compaq.com/partners/netscape/downloads/register_nav4_Linux.html

The Mozilla browser is also an alternative. Information on Mozilla and other browser options can be found at *http://www.linuxalpha.org/software*. Precompiled RPMs can also be found at *http://ftp://ftp.mozilla.org/pub/mozilla/releases/*. Choose the directory that corresponds to the Mozilla release, then choose either the RedHat 6.x or 7.x directories and then the alpha directory.

Another option is the KDE file manager from the K desktop environment (*http://www.kde.org*).

Bibliography

This bibliography references a number of books on Linux and related topics. It is by no means exhaustive—well over 500 Linux-related books have been published.

Also listed here are some of the more useful references from the Linux Documentation Project, some of which are available in printed form and all available from the LDP web site, *http://www.tldp.org/guides.html*, and its mirrors.

Linux Documentation Project Guides

Cooper, Mendel. *Advanced Bash-Scripting Guide.*

Erlich, Shie. *Custom Linux: A Porting Guide—Porting LinuxPPC to a Custom SBC.*

Jobst, Jennifer. *Emacspeak User's Guide.*

Welsh et al, Matt. *Linux Installation and Getting Started.*

Komarinski, Mark F., Jorge Godoy, and David C. Merrill. *LDP Author Guide.*

Seifried, Kurt. *Linux Administrator's Security Guide.*

Drake, Joshua. *Linux Consultants Guide.*

Beekmans, Gerard. *Linux From Scratch.*

Aivazian, Tigran. *Linux Kernel 2.4 Internals.*

Burkett, B. Scott, Sven Goldt, John D. Harper, Sven van der Meer, and Matt Welsh. *Linux Programmer's Guide.*

Frampton, Steve. *Linux System Administration Made Easy.*

Greenfield, Larry. *Linux User's Guide.*

Mourani, Gerhard. Securing and Optimizing Linux Red Hat Edition—A Hands-on Guide. Barnson, Matthew P. *The Bugzilla Guide.*

Stutz, Michael. *The Linux Cookbook: Tips and Techniques for Everyday Use.*

Rusling, David A. *The Linux Kernel.*

Johnson, Michael K. *The Linux Kernel Hackers' Guide.*

Pomerantz, Ori. *The Linux Kernel Module Programming Guide.*

Kirch, Olaf. *The Linux Network Administrators' Guide.*

Wirzenius, Lars, Joanna Oja, and Stephen Stafford. *The Linux System Administrators' Guide.*

Linux Documentation Project FAQs

Merrill, David. *Linux Frequently Asked Questions with Answers.*

Zanella, Neil. *Brief Linux FAQ (BLFAQ).*

Sullivan, Andrew. *AfterStep FAQ.*

De Wit, Johan. *FTape FAQ.*

Kirsch, Mathew E. *Linux ATAPI FAQ.*

Walton, Sean. *Linux Threads FAQ.*

Leblanc, Gregory. *Linux-RAID FAQ.*

Wolff, R. E. *The Sig11 FAQ.*

Ridgway, Douglas. *Wine FAQ.*

Moen, Rick. *WordPerfect on Linux FAQ.*

Linux Documentation Project HOWTOs (Partial Listing)

Gonzato, Guido. *From DOS/Windows to Linux HOWTO.*

Tranter, Jeff. *Linux CD-ROM HOWTO.*

Langfeldt, Nicolai, and Jamie Norrish. *Linux DNS HOWTO.*

Grennan, Mark. *Linux Firewall and Proxy Server HOWTO.*

Pritchard, Steven. *Linux Hardware Compatibility HOWTO.*

Ward, Brian. *Linux Kernel HOWTO.*

Heuser, Werner. *Linux Laptop HOWTO.*

Lawyer, David S. *Linux Modem HOWTO.*

Barr, Tavis, Nicolai Langfeldt, Seth Vidal, and Tom McNeal. *Linux NFS HOWTO.*

Drake, Joshua. *Linux Networking HOWTO.*

Hinds, David. *Linux PCMCIA HOWTO.*

Taylor, Grant. *Linux Printing HOWTO.*

Wood, David. *Linux SMB HOWTO.*

Tumenbayar, Enkh. *Linux SMP HOWTO.*

Lawyer, Dave S. *Linux Serial HOWTO.*

Tranter, Jeff. *Linux Sound HOWTO.*

Arcomano, Roberto. *Linux Wireless HOWTO.*

Raymond, Eric S. *Linux XFree86 HOWTO.*

Raymond, Eric S. *Unix Hardware Buyer HOWTO.*

General Linux Books

Siever et al, Ellen. *Linux in A Nutshell: A Desktop Quick Reference.* O'Reilly & Associates.

LeBlanc, Dee-Ann, Melanie Hoag, and Evan Blomquist. *Linux for Dummies.* John Wiley & Sons.

Ricart, Manuel Alberto. *The Complete Idiot's Guide to Linux.* Alpha Books.

Ball, Bill, Stephen Smoogen, and Ryan K. Stephens. *Sams' Teach Yourself Linux in 24 Hours.* Sams.

Tranter, Jeff. *Linux Multimedia Guide.* O'Reilly & Associates.

Phillips, Dave. *Linux Music and Sound.* No Starch Press.

Negus, Christopher. *Red Hat Linux 7.3 Bible.* John Wiley & Sons.

Unix and Unix Shells

Todino-Gonguet, Grace, John Strang, and Jerry Peek. *Learning the Unix Operating System, 5th Edition.* O'Reilly & Associates.

Bach, Maurice. *Design of the Unix Operating System.* Prentice Hall.

Kernighan, Brian W, and Rob Pike. *The UNIX Programming Environment.* Prentice Hall.

Vahalia, Uresh. *UNIX Internals: The New Frontiers.* Prentice Hall.

Kochan, Stephen G., and Patrick H. Wood. *UNIX Shell Programming.* Sams.

Applications

Stallman, Richard M. *GNU Emacs Manual*. GNU Press.

Robbins, Arnold, and Linda Lamb. *Learning the vi Editor*. O'Reilly & Associates.

Rosenblatt, Bill, Eric S. Raymond, and Debra Cameron. *Learning Gnu Emacs*. O'Reilly & Associates.

Lampaport, Leslie. *LaTeX: A Document Preparation System*. Addison Wesley.

Reese, George, Randy Jay Yarger, Tim King, and Hugh E. Williams. *Managing and Using MySQL*. O'Reilly & Associates.

Greenspan, Jay, and Brad Bulger. *MySQL/PHP Database Applications*. John Wiley & Sons.

DuBois, Paul, and Michael Widenius. *MySQL*. New Riders.

Meadhra, Michael. *StarOffice for Linux For Dummies*. Hungry Minds.

Knuth, Donald E. *The TEXbook*. AddisonWesley.

Oualline, Steve. *Vi iMproved (VIM)*. New Riders.

Levine Young, Margaret, David C. Kay, David Guertin, and Kathy Warfel. *WordPerfect for Linux for Dummies*. Hungry Minds.

The Internet

Laurie, Peter, and Ben Laurie. *Apache: The Definitive Guide*. O'Reilly & Associates.

Aulds, Charles. *Linux Apache Web Server Administration*. Sybex.

Musciano, Chuck, and Bill Kennedy. *HTML & XHTML — The Definitive Guide*. O'Reilly & Associates.

Niederst, Jennifer. *HTML Pocket Reference*. O'Reilly & Associates.

Williams, Hugh E., and David Lane. *Web Database Applications with PHP & MySQL*. O'Reilly & Associates.

Networks and Communications

Albitz, Paul, and Cricket Liu. *DNS and BIND*. O'Reilly & Associates.

Comer, Douglas E, and David L. Stevens. *Internetworking with TCP/IP*. Prentice Hall.

Kirch, Olaf, and Terry Dawson. *Linux Network Administrator's Guide*. O'Reilly & Associates.

Stern, Hal, Mike Eisler, and Ricardo Labiaga. *Managing NFS and NIS.* O'Reilly & Associates.

Costales, Bryan, and Eric Allman. *Sendmail.* O'Reilly & Associates.

Stevens, W. Richard, and Gary R. Wright. *TCP/IP Illustrated.* Addison Wesley.

Hunt, Craig. *TCP/IP Network Administration.* O'Reilly & Associates.

Eckstein, Robert, and David Collier-Brown. *Using Samba.* O'Reilly & Associates.

Programming and Linux Internals

Stevens, W. Richard. *Advanced Programming in the UNIX Environment.* Addison Wesley.

Matthew, Neil, and Richard Stones. *Beginning Linux Programming.* Wrox Press.

Stallman, Richard M., Roland Pesch, and Stan Shebs. *Debugging with GDB.* GNU Press.

Keogh, Jim. *Linux Programming for Dummies.* John Wiley & Sons.

Niemeyer, Pat, and Jonathan Knudsen. *Learning Java.* O'Reilly & Associates.

Schwartz, Randal L., and Tom Phoenix. *Learning Perl.* O'Reilly & Associates.

Rubini, Alessandro, and Jonathan Corbet. *Linux Device Drivers.* O'Reilly & Associates.

Wall, Larry, Tom Christiansen, and Jon Orwant. *Programming Perl.* O'Reilly & Associates.

Loukides, Mike, and Andy Oram. *Programming with GNU Software.* O'Reilly & Associates.

Kernighan, Brian W., and Dennis M. Ritchie. *The C Programming Language.* Prentice Hall.

Eckel, Bruce. *Thinking in Java.* Prentice Hall.

Bovet, Daniel P., and Marco Cesati. *Understanding the Linux Kernel.* O'Reilly & Associates.

System Administration

Nemeth, Evi, Garth Snyder, and Trent R. Hein. *Linux Administration Handbook.* Prentice Hall.

Shah, Steve. *Linux Administration: A Beginner's Guide.* Osborne McGraw-Hill.

Collings, Terry, and Kurt Wall. *Red Hat Linux Networking and System Administration*. John Wiley & Sons.

Maginnis, Tobin. *Sair Linux and GNU Certification Level I, Installation and Configuration*. John Wiley & Sons.

Security

Hatch, Brian, James Lee, and George Kurtz. *Hacking Linux Exposed*. Osborne McGraw-Hill.

Silverman, Richard, and Daniel J. Barrett. *SSH, the Secure Shell: The Definitive Guide*. O'Reilly & Associates.

Bauer, Michael D. *Building Secure Servers with Linux*. O'Reilly & Associates.

Garfinkel, Simson, and Gene Spafford. *Practical UNIX & Internet Security, 2nd Edition*. O'Reilly & Associates.

Index

We'd like to hear your suggestions for improving our indexes. Send email to *index@oreilly.com*.

documents, format support, 423
domain name registering, 576
Domain Name Service (DNS), 514, 576
    configuring, 535
domainname command, 550
DOS compatibility, utilities for, 23
DOSEMU, 24
Dosemu (Windows emulation software), 424
dotted quad notation, 511
doublesided printing, 243
down command (lpc), 261
drag-and-drop (KDE), 368
du utility, 95
dynamic IP addresses, 511

E

e2fsck program, troubleshooting
    superblock, 271
echo command shell, 89
edit mode (vi), 275
editing
    command-line
        arrow keys and, 92
        word completion, 91
    etc/fstab file, 66
electronic mail
    adminstrative issues, 576
    Internet mail feed, 576
    mail queue, 576
Emacs
    advantages, 13
    customizing, 295–298
    launching, 285
    macros, 292
    programming, 293
    viewing files, 86
    yanking text, 290
Emacs editor, 284, 399
    customizing, 286
    as program interface, 496
    saving files, 287
emacs file, 295
emacs startup file, 107
email, 563
    Evoloution mail, 391
    fetchmail package, 574
    sending from Emacs, 293
    system maintenance, 233
embedded processor support, 10
emergency disk, 269

emergency troubleshooting, 268
Enhanced IDE/MFM/RLL drive support,
    enabling, 214
enscript utility, 341
enterprise applications
    suitability of Linux for, 7
error messages
    installation troubleshooting, 76–77
    make command, 446
    printer, 247
    saving, 94
errors
    kernel too big, 217
    mounting filesystems, 156
    symbols missing, 219
etc directory, 108
    backups and, 224
    etc/ld.so.cache, 188
    etc/ld.so.conf, 188
etc/fstab file editing, 66
etc/lilo.conf file, 124–126
etc/printcap file, 237, 244, 336
    troubleshooting printing, 265
etc/skel directory, 109
etc/syslog.conf file, 234
ether= boot option, 52
Ethernet cards, 518
    troubleshooting, 528, 529
Ethernet configuration, 518
Evolution calendar, 392
Evolution contact manager, 393
Evolution mail, 391
ex mode (vi), 279
executables, support for, 12
execute permission, 101
exrc startup file, 107
ext2fs compared to reiserfs, 152
ext2fs filesystem, 60
Eyes (GNOME), 388

F

f2c translator, 467
fax devices, support, 243
FBDev server, 349
fdisk
    LILO, removing, 128
    Linux partitions, creating, 55–59
    options, 56
fdisk utility, 44
features, overview, 10, 11

About the Authors

Matt Welsh is a computer scientist with research interests spanning many aspects of complex systems, including operating systems design, distributed systems, networking, and parallel computing. Matt is a longtime Linux advocate and developer and has fielded questions from thousands of Linux users over the years. He was the original coordinator of the Linux Documentation Project and author of the original *Linux Installation and Getting Started* guide. He completed his Ph.D at UC Berkeley and is currently a researcher at Intel Research Labs in Berkeley. He will be joining the faculty of the computer science department at Harvard University in July 2003.

Matthias Kalle Dalheimer is an independent author, translator, and software consultant in northern Germany. After studying computer science and general linguistics, he worked for Star Division, where he was responsible for porting the office suite StarOffice to Linux. Kalle mainly uses Linux for his development work and uses XEmacs 20.4 for most of his programming and writing tasks. In his spare time, he helps write the K Desktop Environment, a free desktop for Unix systems.

Terry Dawson is an amateur radio operator and longtime Linux enthusiast. He is the author of a number of network-related HOWTO documents for the Linux Documentation Project, coauthor of *Linux Network Administrator's Guide*, Second Edition (O'Reilly), and is an active participant in a number of other Linux projects. Terry has 15 years of professional experience in telecommunications and is currently engaged in network management research in the Telstra Research Laboratories.

Lar Kaufman is a documentation consultant living in Concord, Massachusetts. He began writing about Unix in 1983 and has since written on System V, BSD, Mach, OSF/1, and now Linux. His hobbies include interactive media as art/literature, homebuilt and antique aircraft (he's a licensed aircraft mechanic), and natural history. Formerly a BBS operator, in 1987 Lar founded the Fidonet echoes (newsgroups) Biosphere and BioNews. He is currently leading a project to establish a global biological conservation network, using a Linux host as the mail, news, and file server.

Colophon

Our look is the result of reader comments, our own experimentation, and feedback from distribution channels. Distinctive covers complement our distinctive approach to technical topics, breathing personality and life into potentially dry subjects.

The image on the cover of *Running Linux,* Fourth Edition is a rearing horse. A horse will often rear to avoid going forward—as a way to avoid either further work or a frightening object. Other factors may include poorly fitted tack or an overly aggressive rider. For some horses, rearing is a learned behavior. Often a very difficult vice to correct, rearing is not a very common problem with most reasonably trained horses, and it is not breed-specific or discipline-specific. Rearing is an unsettling, difficult move to ride, not to mention dangerous. When a horse rears, its rider must lean forward on the horse's neck, to avoid shifting weight and flipping the horse over backwards.

Sarah Sherman was the production editor and proofreader for *Running Linux*, Fourth Edition. Audrey Doyle was the copyeditor. Andrew Savikas and Genevieve d'Entremont provided production assistance. Emily Quill and Claire Cloutier provided quality control. Tom Dinse wrote the index.

Edie Freedman designed the cover of this book, based on a series design by herself and Hanna Dyer. The cover image is a 19th-century engraving from *Marvels of the New West*. Emma Colby produced the cover layout with QuarkXPress 4.1 using Adobe's ITC Garamond font.

David Futato designed the interior layout. The chapter opening images are from *Marvels of the New West: A Vivid Portrayal of the Stupendous Marvels in the Vast Wonderland West of the Missouri River*, by William Thayer (The Henry Bill Publishing Co., 1888). This book was converted to FrameMaker 5.5.6 with a format conversion tool created by Erik Ray, Jason McIntosh, Neil Walls, and Mike Sierra that uses Perl and XML technologies. The text font is Linotype Birka; the heading font is Adobe Myriad Condensed; and the code font is LucasFont's TheSans Mono Condensed. The illustrations that appear in the book were produced by Robert Romano and Jessamyn Read using Macromedia FreeHand 9 and Adobe Photoshop 6. The tip and warning icons were drawn by Christopher Bing. This colophon was written by Sarah Sherman.

Other Titles Available from O'Reilly

Linux

Linux in a Nutshell, 3rd Edition

*By Ellen Siever, Stephen Spainhour,
Jessica P. Hekman & Stephen Figgins
3rd Edition August 2000
800 pages, ISBN 0-596-00025-1*

Linux in a Nutshell covers the core
commands for common Linux distributions. This complete reference user,
programming, administration, and
networking commands with options also documents a
wide range of GNU tools. New material in the third edition includes common configuration tasks for the
GNOME and KDE desktops and the fvwm2 window
manager, the dpkg Debian package manager, expanded
coverage of the rpm Red Hat package manager, and
many new commands.

The Root of All Evil

*By Illiad
1st Edition August 2001
144 pages, ISBN 0-596-00193-2*

It's back to Columbia Internet, "the
friendliest, hardest-working, and most
neurotic little Internet Service
Provider in the world," for our third installment from
the hit online comic, *User Friendly*. The cast: hardcore
techies, self-absorbed sales staff, well-meaning execs,
and assorted almost-humans. The background: too little
office space, warring operating systems, and eternally
clueless customers.

The Linux Web Server CD Bookshelf

*By O'Reilly & Associates, Inc.
1st Edition September 2001
(Includes CD-ROM)
812 pages, ISBN 0-59600-208-4*

Six best selling O'Reilly Animal
Guides are now available on CD-
ROM, easily accessible and searchable
with your favorite web browser: *Run-
ning Linux*, 3rd Edition; *Linux in a Nutshell*, 3rd Edition; *Apache: The Definitive Guide*, 2nd Edition; *MySQL
& mSQL*; *Programming the Perl DBI*; and *CGI Programming with Perl*, 2nd Edition. As a bonus, you get the new
paperback version of *Linux in a Nutshell*.

Practical PostgreSQL

*By Command Prompt, Inc
1st Edition January 2002
636 pages, ISBN 1-56592-846-6*

Practical PostgreSQL is a fast-paced,
business-oriented guide to installing,
config-uring, and running PostgreSQL. Readers will find all the
basics here, such as how to create databases and objects,
such as tables, within those databases. Or they can go
straight to advanced topics like inheritance, replication,
user management, and backup and recovery. The book
also introduces the PL/pgSQL procedural language.
Finally, a complete PostgreSQL command reference
makes "looking it up" easy.

Learning Red Hat Linux, 2nd Edition

*By Bill McCarty
1st Edition January 2001
368 pages, ISBN 0-59600-071-5*

This second edition of *Learning Red
Hat Linux* is an excellent introduction
to one of the most popular distributions of Linux in the U.S. This is the
book for first-time Linux users who want to learn how
to install and configure Red Hat Linux on their personal computer, or convert an existing system over to Linux.

Peer-to-Peer: Harnessing the Power of Disruptive Technologies

*Edited by Andy Oram
1st Edition March 2001
448 pages, ISBN 0-596-00110-X*

This book presents the goals that
drive the developers of the best-
known peer-to-peer systems, the problems they've faced, and the technical
solutions they've found. The contributors are leading
developers of well-known peer-to-peer systems, such as
Gnutella, Freenet, Jabber, Popular Power, SETI@Home,
Red Rover, Publius, Free Haven, Groove Networks, and
Reputation Technologies. Topics include metadata, performance, trust, resource allocation, reputation, security,
and gateways between systems.

O'REILLY®

To order: *800-998-9938* • *order@oreilly.com* • *www.oreilly.com*
Online editions of most O'Reilly titles are available by subscription at *safari.oreilly.com*
Also available at most retail and online bookstores.

Linux

O'REILLY®

To order: 800-998-9938 • order@oreilly.com • www.oreilly.com
Online editions of most O'Reilly titles are available by subscription at safari.oreilly.com
Also available at most retail and online bookstores.

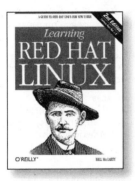

How to stay in touch with O'Reilly

1. Visit our award-winning web site

http://www.oreilly.com/

★ "Top 100 Sites on the Web"—PC Magazine
★ CIO Magazine's Web Business 50 Awards

Our web site contains a library of comprehensive product information (including book excerpts and tables of contents), downloadable software, background articles, interviews with technology leaders, links to relevant sites, book cover art, and more. File us in your bookmarks or favorites!

2. Join our email mailing lists

Sign up to get email announcements of new books and conferences, special offers, and O'Reilly Network technology newsletters at:

http://elists.oreilly.com

It's easy to customize your free elists subscription so you'll get exactly the O'Reilly news you want.

3. Get examples from our books

To find example files for a book, go to:

http://www.oreilly.com/catalog

select the book, and follow the "Examples" link.

4. Work with us

Check out our web site for current employment opportunities:

http://jobs.oreilly.com/

5. Register your book

Register your book at:

http://register.oreilly.com

6. Contact us

O'Reilly & Associates, Inc.
1005 Gravenstein Hwy North
Sebastopol, CA 95472 USA
TEL: 707-827-7000 or 800-998-9938
    (6am to 5pm PST)
FAX: 707-829-0104

order@oreilly.com
For answers to problems regarding your order or our products. To place a book order online visit:

http://www.oreilly.com/order_new/

catalog@oreilly.com
To request a copy of our latest catalog.

booktech@oreilly.com
For book content technical questions or corrections.

corporate@oreilly.com
For educational, library, government, and corporate sales.

proposals@oreilly.com
To submit new book proposals to our editors and product managers.

international@oreilly.com
For information about our international distributors or translation queries. For a list of our distributors outside of North America check out:

http://international.oreilly.com/distributors.html

adoption@oreilly.com
For information about academic use of O'Reilly books, visit:

http://academic.oreilly.com

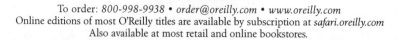